AMSTERDAM, BRUSSELS & BRUGES

KAREN TURNER

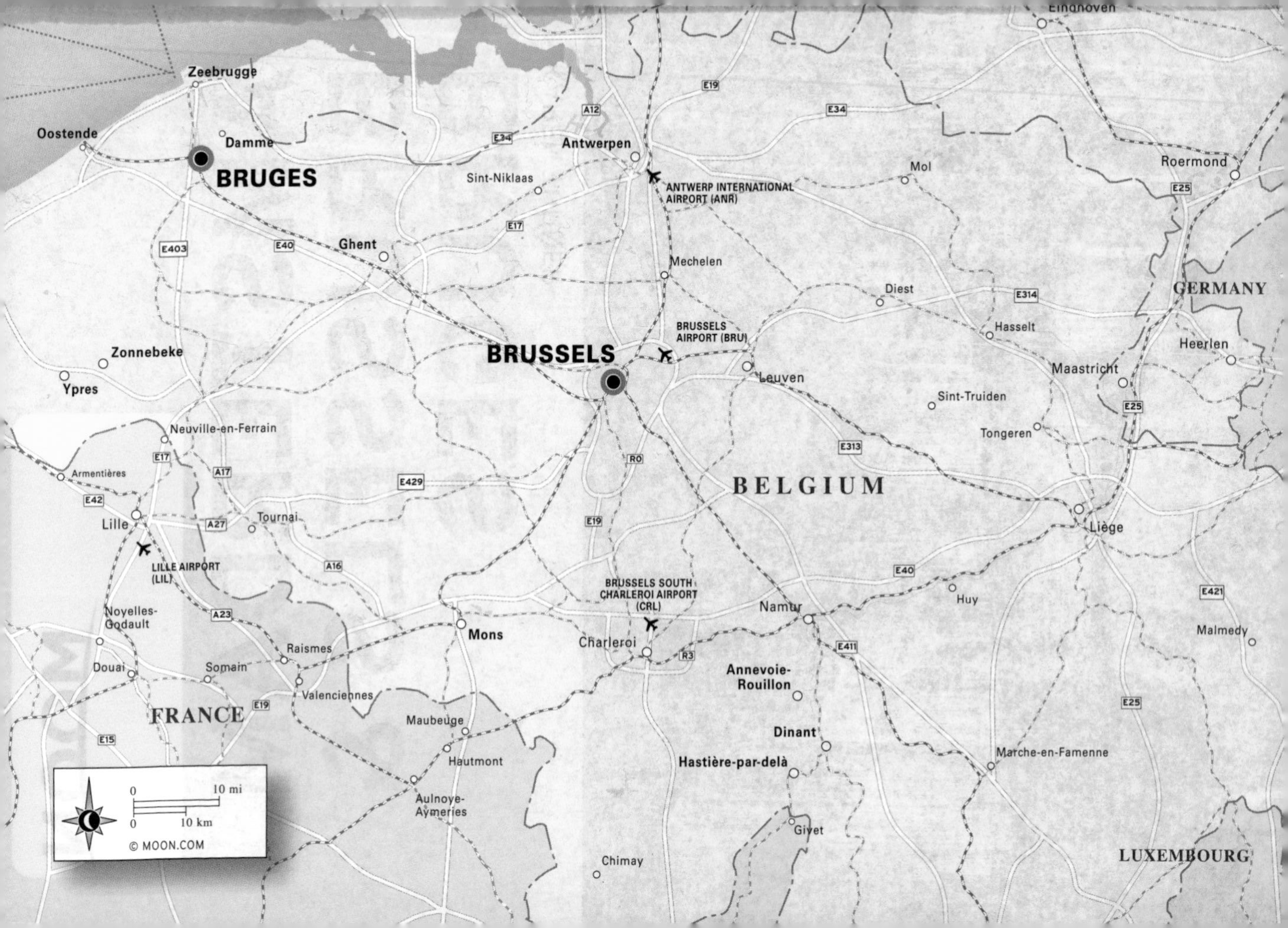
Zeebrugge
Oostende
Damme
BRUGES
Antwerpen
Sint-Niklaas
ANTWERP INTERNATIONAL AIRPORT (ANR)
Mol
Roermond
Ghent
Mechelen
Diest
GERMANY
Hasselt
Heerlen
BRUSSELS AIRPORT (BRU)
Zonnebeke
BRUSSELS
Ypres
Leuven
Maastricht
Sint-Truiden
Neuville-en-Ferrain
Tongeren
Armentières
BELGIUM
Lille
Tournai
Liège
LILLE AIRPORT (LIL)
BRUSSELS SOUTH CHARLEROI AIRPORT (CRL)
Huy
Noyelles-Godault
Namur
Malmedy
Mons
Raismes
Charleroi
Douai
Somain
Annevoie-Rouillon
Valenciennes
FRANCE
Maubeuge
Dinant
Hautmont
Hastière-par-delà
Marche-en-Famenne
Aulnoye-Aymeries
Givet
Chimay
LUXEMBOURG
E19
E34
A12
E25
E17
E403
E40
E314
E313
A17
E429
R0
E42
A27
E19
A16
E40
E421
A23
E411
R3
E19
E25
E15
0
10 mi
0
10 km
© MOON.COM

AMSTERDAM
NETHERLANDS
English Channel
IJsselmeer
Markermeer
Den Helder
Joure
Emmeloord
Alkmaar
Lelystad
Zwolle
Wijk aan Zee
Haarlem
Almere
Hillegom
AMSTERDAM AIRPORT SCHIPHOL (AMS)
Lisse
Apeldoorn
Leiden
Haarzuilens
Amersfoort
The Hague
Utrecht
Ede
Delft
Arnhem
Hoek van Holland
Rotterdam
Kinderdijk
Nijmegen
Dordrecht
Kranenburg
's-Hertogenbosch
Breda
Tilburg
E22
A9
A6
E232
E19
A27
E35
E30
A50
E311
E31
E25
A29
A59
A73
North Sea
Copenhagen
DNK
Dublin
IRL
UNITED KINGDOM
NETHERLANDS
Amsterdam
Berlin
The Hague
London
GERMANY
Bruges
Brussels
Liège
BELGIUM
English Cannel
CZE
Luxembourg
Paris
Bern
CHE
Vaduz
AUT
FRANCE
Bay of Biscay
ITA
0 200 mi
0 200 km
San Marino
Monaco
SPAIN

Contents

Although every effort was made to make sure the information in this book was accurate when going to press, research was impacted by the COVID-19 pandemic and things may have changed since the time of writing. Be sure to confirm specific details, like opening hours, closures, and travel guidelines and restrictions, when making your travel plans. For more detailed information, see page 352.

DISCOVER

Amsterdam, Brussels & Bruges

Many visitors already have a clear vision of the cities of Amsterdam, Brussels, and Bruges: envisioning picturesque canals, centuries-old buildings with grand facades, and quaint cobblestone streets. There's no doubt that if you're looking to step into a European fairy tale, the Netherlands and Belgium offer many breathtaking opportunities to do so. You can travel back in time simply by opening a door into a hidden courtyard, surveying a castle in the middle of a park, or sitting down at a cozy café for a beer made by monks who have perfected the recipe over generations.

But the highlights of this region go beyond the grandeur of Amsterdam's charming canal houses, Brussels's Grand Place, and the Belfry of Bruges. Its museums show off cultural and architectural contributions spanning from literature to art. In winter, the cities transform their centers into inviting Christmas markets. In summer, do like the locals do and pause for a cold drink at a café balcony.

If you're looking to satisfy your sweet tooth, you'll already have heard about Dutch markets serving up warm *stroopwafel* and Brussels's famous chocolatiers. Say *"Proost"* or *"Santé"* to seemingly endless beer menus. But recent immigration as well as the complicated legacy of colonialism have also resulted in a

Clockwise from top left: Amsterdam's Amstel River; National Tulip Day on Dam Square in Amsterdam; Pierre Marcolini macarons in Brussels; houses on a canal in Haarlem; *stroopwafel*; winter in Bruges.

surprisingly rich gastronomic landscape, from African to Indonesian. Dutch and Belgian restaurants reflect the diversity of their populations, with high-quality fusion and delicious international offerings.

The region's compactness and excellent public transportation make it easy to take a quick train ride through the countryside, past polders, livestock, windmills, and attractive towns for any number of scenic day trips. In the Netherlands, 30 minutes by train takes you from Amsterdam to towns with blooming tulip fields, picturesque windmills, and traditional cheese markets. In just an hour, traverse the cultural boundary between Flanders and Wallonia for old-world charm complete with French-influenced chateaux amid the dramatic rock formations of the Ardennes. The next day, you can sit along canals with locals in Ghent as you watch the sunset and see this lively student city let its hair down.

Although *gezelligheid* is not as famous as *hygge,* this Dutch term describing a warm, cozy experience encompasses much of local life here. You'll find lovely watering holes where locals are keen to chat in English, independent shops where you'll find the perfect souvenir, and modern cafés where you'll want to linger over your coffee. Don't be afraid to slow down to enjoy the quieter side of the Netherlands and Belgium, as it's where the real magic of this small region happens. *Welkom* and *Bienvenue* to Amsterdam, Bruges, and Brussels.

Clockwise from top left: canal in De Jordaan, Amsterdam; restaurants in the historic part of Brussels; spring in the Keukenhof gardens, Netherlands; *frites* in Brussels.

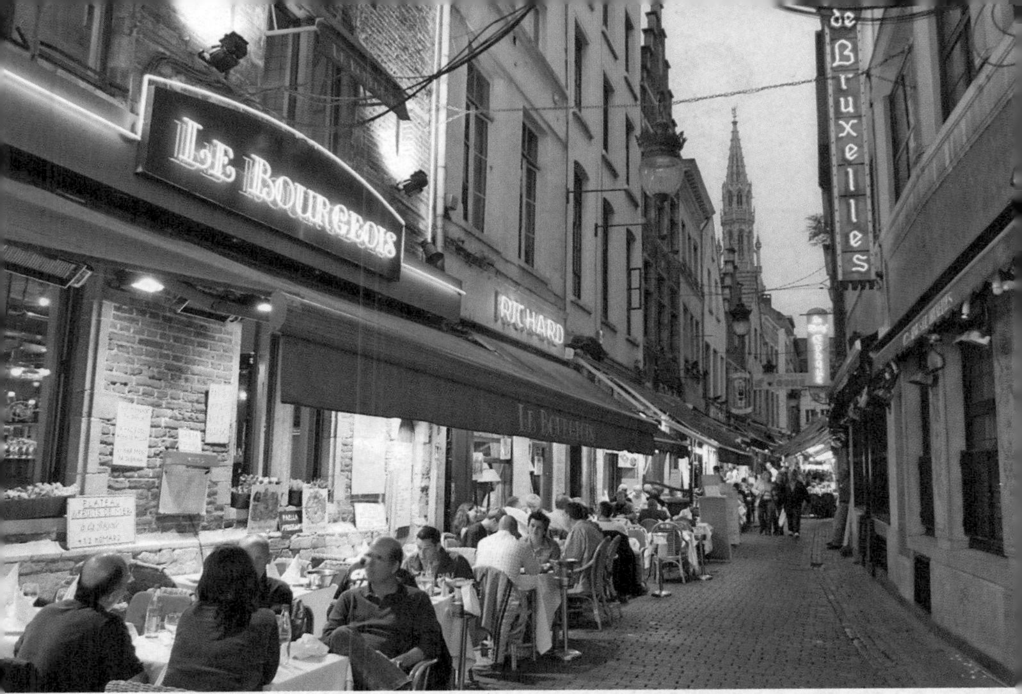

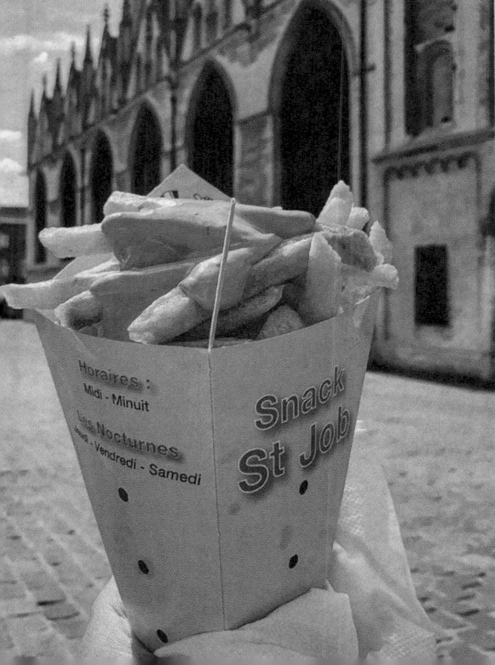

LE BOURGEOIS
RICHARD
de Bruxelles
Horaires :
Midi - Minuit
Les Nocturnes
Vendredi - Samedi
Snack
St Job

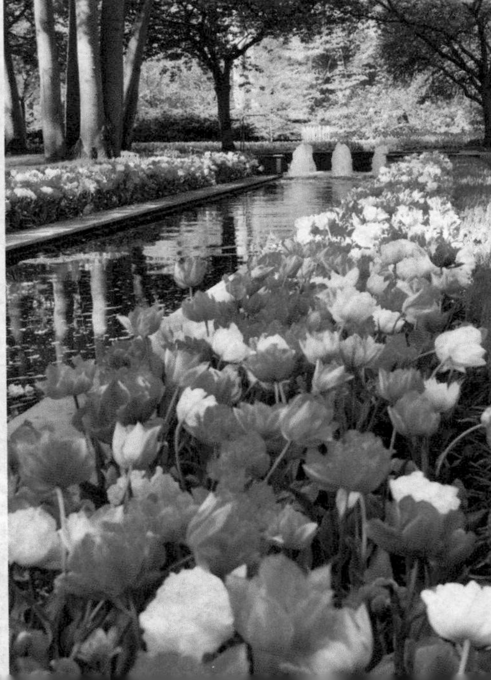

9 TOP EXPERIENCES

1 **Cycling in Amsterdam Noord,** flying past windmills, polders, and sheep away from the crowds (page 77).

2 Getting up close and personal with the region's World War history, from the **Anne Frank House** in Amsterdam (page 58) to the **cemeteries and memorials around Ypres** (page 321).

3 Strolling the unique two-story **canals of Utrecht,** as beautiful as Amsterdam's and half as crowded (page 151).

4 Finding the coziest bars, from Amsterdam's atmospheric **brown bars** (page 109) to warmly lit **Bruges cafés** (page 284).

5 Tasting **chocolate in Brussels** (page 218) and **Bruges** (page 276): You'll find it's famous for a reason.

6 Sipping the best of **Belgian beer,** from ales brewed in century-old monasteries to microbreweries continuing the tradition (page 32).

7 Searching for **art nouveau in Brussels,** the unlikely birthplace of this decorative, elegant architectural style (page 207).

8 Browsing **Bruges's markets,** especially the Wednesday market that takes place in the city's stunning Markt square (page 278).

9 Viewing the best of **Dutch and Flemish art,** from the old masters to the Ghent Altarpiece to Van Gogh (page 29).

Planning Your Trip

Where to Go

Amsterdam

Amsterdam is the crown jewel of the Netherlands, pulling in tourists with its world-class **museums** and scenic **canals.** Beyond the touristy center, Amsterdam thrives on cool **cafés,** multicultural eateries, and a wild **nightlife** scene with something for everyone. Although Amsterdam is small compared to many other European capitals, visitors are often surprised by the surrounding areas, which includes **scenic villages** out of a storybook and diverse neighborhoods filled with colorful markets.

Day Trips from Amsterdam

Holland conjures up magical images for many visitors, with good reason. In April, the fields surrounding **Lisse** burst into bloom with tulips and other flowers. See **Alkmaar's** historic cheese market in action and beautiful ceramics painted by artisans in **Delft. The Hague** often surprises visitors with its international charm and its many family-friendly attractions. **Rotterdam** wows with its modern architecture and cutting-edge cafés, while **Haarlem** and **Utrecht** mesmerize with countless streets of independent shops along quaint avenues.

Brussels

Many arrive in Brussels for the biggest hits, from **Manneken Pis** to **Grand Place,** but the city has even more to offer in terms of culture, a rich **chocolate-making** tradition, and history. Brussels's contributions to literature and architecture are on display via colorful street art and

traditional cheese market in Alkmaar

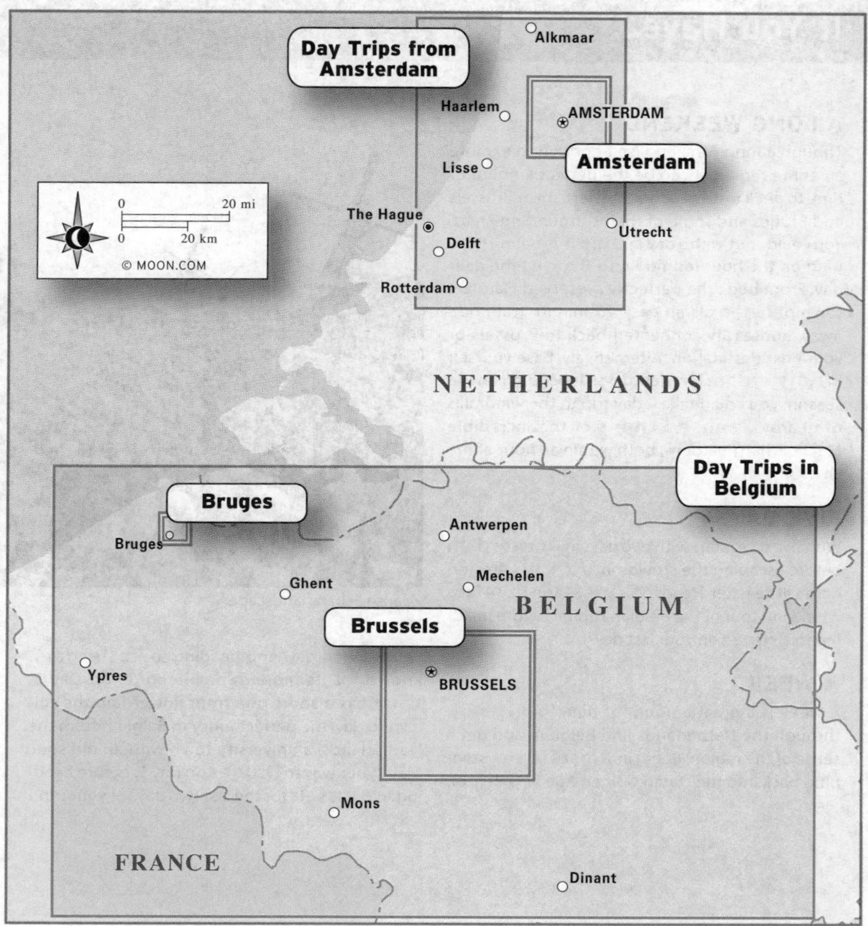

stately **art nouveau** buildings. Beyond the center, Brussels is diverse, from hip neighborhoods filled with stylish coffee shops in **Dansaert,** to Congolese restaurants close to the **European Parliament,** to the village-within-a-city of **Saint Gilles.** Take a stroll through Brussels's leafy **parks** for some quiet along with glimpses of stunning hidden chateaux.

Bruges

One of Belgium's calling cards certainly has to be Bruges's stunning **canals,** a siren call for visitors all around the world. Bruges is small enough that visitors can quickly cover the highlights, including the **Sint-Janshuismolen windmill, Markt,** and the **Belfry,** before tasting Belgium's world-class **beer** and **chocolate** at a cozy café with old-world charm. Many visitors quickly pass through Bruges, missing out on its charming neighborhoods filled with independent shops, enchanting hidden courtyards, and outstanding **museums** featuring Flemish Masters.

If You Have...

A LONG WEEKEND

Though a long weekend isn't enough to explore an entire region, it can be the perfect amount of time to get a taste of either Amsterdam or Brussels and Bruges and some of their surrounding areas. You could start with a day in **Brussels** before hopping on the hour-long train to **Bruges** the next day. From here, the perfectly preserved Flanders town of **Ghent** is an easy 40-minute train ride away, and easily connected back to Brussels or your next destination. Alternatively, base yourself in **Amsterdam** for a few days; depending on the season, you could take a day trip to the windmills of nearby **Zaanse Schans** or the incredible **Keukenhof** gardens, both within an hour of the city.

Zaanse Schans landscape

FIVE DAYS

With five days, start with two days in **Amsterdam** before escaping the crowds in **Utrecht,** Amsterdam's little sister. Head to **Brussels** on Day 4 for a whirlwind tour of the Belgian capital before heading to **Bruges** on your last day.

A WEEK

A week is a great amount of time to **city-hop** through the Netherlands and Belgium and get a sense of the region. Begin in **Amsterdam,** stepping back into the Dutch Golden Age in **Delft** on your second day, and heading to **Rotterdam,** known for its modern architecture, on Day 3. **Ghent** is a short ride from Rotterdam the following day, the perfect entry to Belgium from the Netherlands, a university town with an old soul. Make your way to **Bruges** on Day 5, before heading to **Brussels** for the last two days of your trip.

Day Trips in Belgium

Don't hesitate to take a train ride to Belgium's other charming towns and cities, where life goes slower. Culture and history enthusiasts will fall in love with the northern part of Belgium, known as Flanders, whose lesser-known cities of **Mechelen, Ghent,** and **Antwerpen** boast stunning belfries, impressive historic city centers, and high-quality beer. Pay your respects to the brave in **Ypres,** site of World War I's most infamous trenches, before tasting Belgium's most famous beer at a Trappist abbey. Nature lovers will fall in love with the picturesque **Dinant** in Wallonia, the southern part of Belgium, nestled in rolling hills. History geeks will flip over the Neolithic flint mines in **Mons.**

When to Go

High Season

April-August is high season in the Netherlands and Belgium, and in Europe more generally. April is when **King's Day** is celebrated in the Netherlands, making Amsterdam quite crowded, but most attractions tend to have **extended hours** during this time. Weather-wise, spring in the region tends toward **cold and rainy,** with temperatures ranging from 5-18°C (41-64°F), but it can be worth braving the often-wet days and crowds to see the **tulip fields** outside Amsterdam and **bluebells** outside Brussels.

The joke goes that **summer** in the Netherlands and Belgium is the shortest day of the year. Given that the average high temperature is 22°C (71°F) in July and August, any good weather needs to be savored, as it might drop back to 13°C (55°F) the following day. Layers are your friend.

Christmas markets usually begin **mid-December** in the Netherlands and Belgium, bringing crowds of both locals and tourists. Attractions also tend to extend their hours throughout the month, although expect closures linked to Sinterklaas (early December) as well as on Christmas itself. The temperature is generally a bit above freezing, between 2-7°C (35-44°F). In December, Amsterdam holds the **Amsterdam Light Festival,** which also draws significant crowds.

Shoulder Seasons

February-March and **September-November** are shoulder seasons. Most attractions are open, albeit on potentially **more limited hours.** These are quiet times to visit the region if you want to **avoid the crowds** and secure **better hotel rates.** In **fall,** the sight of **turning leaves** over the many canals in Amsterdam and Bruges is underrated. Brussels's parks are also beautiful during this time. For those who enjoy a little cold nip

Christmas tree in front of Grand Place in Brussels

in the air and a good excuse to step into a brown bar café, October is a great time, with temperatures generally around 10-15°C (50-60°F). That being said, though temperatures are relatively mild, the **rain** and **windchill** are often worst during these seasons.

Low Season

January, after the Christmas markets close, is generally low season in the region. In Bruges, many businesses linked to tourism are **closed,** including hotels. If they are open, many attractions will have **limited hours** during this period. Finding meals can also be very hard. It's the **coldest season** in the Netherlands and Belgium, with the average temperature dipping down to 2°C (36°F). **Snow is rare,** but seeing the canals of Amsterdam frozen over is a treat.

Know Before You Go

Getting There

Both **Amsterdam Schiphol Airport** and **Brussels International Airport** are easily accessible from overseas destinations, and well-connected to the rest of Europe.

FROM NORTH AMERICA

There are direct flights from North America to Amsterdam from cities including **New York, Atlanta,** and **Toronto,** taking around 8 hours and starting at $600 round-trip. Flights originating from the West Coast will likely require a stopover somewhere else in North America or another European hub, such as **Dublin, Lisbon,** or **London.** Direct flights to Brussels are slightly less frequent, from New York and **Montreal,** but can be found for around $500 round-trip and take about 7 hours.

FROM NEW ZEALAND, AUSTRALIA, AND SOUTH AFRICA

As they're farther afield, travel from New Zealand, Australia, and South Africa is more complicated, involving at least one **layover in Southeast Asia,** the **Middle East,** or elsewhere in **Europe.** Altogether, travel time from New Zealand and Australia clocks in at around 20 hours; deals can sometimes be found for $700, but tend to cost around $1,000 round-trip. From South Africa, usually **Johannesburg,** there are some direct flights, which take 11 hours and start at $750 round-trip. Flights with a change, in a city like **Zurich** or **Hamburg,** are cheaper, sometimes as little as $400 round-trip.

FROM ELSEWHERE IN EUROPE

If you're traveling from elsewhere in Europe (such as Southern Europe), you might be flying into Amsterdam Schiphol Airport or Brussels International Airport, or smaller airports within the region that service budget-friendly flights, including **Eindhoven Airport** and **Rotterdam The Hague Airport** in the Netherlands or **Brussels South Charleroi Airport** for Belgium. Note that these airports are often quite far from the nearest city center, sometimes negating the deals you might have gotten on your flight. From popular cities in Southern Europe (Rome, Venice, Barcelona), flights can be as cheap as €30 each way with budget airlines—without baggage of course.

From France, it is possible to take the **Thalys,** a high-speed train that travels from Paris to Brussels and Amsterdam in 1-3 hours (€29-100). Otherwise, the **German rail network** connects with both Belgium and the Netherlands 3-11 hours; from €50). **Overnight trains** will be increasing in quantity in the coming year as more travelers opt for eco-friendly travel.

From the UK, travelers have a few options including a direct high-speed train (the **Eurostar**) from London to Brussels (2.5 hours; from €60) or a direct high-speed train (4 hours; from €60) from London to Amsterdam. Many UK travelers,

What's New

- In 2021, Bruges opted to limit the number of cruise ships allowed into its nearby port of Zeebrugge on weekends, as well as the number of days ships are allowed to dock, to help cap the number of tourists for a better visitor experience.
- COVID-19 provided many museums with the opportunity to restore priceless works of art, from the Rembrandt's *The Night Watch,* housed in Amsterdam's Rijksmuseum, to the Ghent Altarpiece in St. Bavo's Cathedral.
- Another crowd control measure given extra priority after 2020's coronavirus pandemic, Amsterdam's Red Light District is rapidly changing due to new regulations on Airbnbs, limits on opening new touristic shops, and bans on drinking alcohol on the street. Although the neighborhood is still quite crowded, plans to decentralize by creating an out-of-town Erotic Center are in progress in 2021.

especially those outside London, opt to fly with some of the many airlines that connect the UK with the Netherlands, such as **Ryanair, KLM, Transavia,** and **easyJet** (from €20, €100 on average). A slower option is an **overnight boat** from Hull in the UK (€150 one-way without a car) to the port outside Bruges (Zeebrugge) and outside Rotterdam (Hoek van Holland) or Amsterdam. The shortest ferries begin at 6-plus hours, but the average time is closer to 13 hours.

Getting Around

The Netherlands and Belgium are part of one of the densest, most well-connected road and public transit networks in the world. In just three hours, you can drive from Amsterdam to Ypres, the westernmost city covered in this book, passing worthwhile destinations en route almost every 30 minutes.

Within cities, well-run **public transit networks** and **your own two feet** make it easy to get around. Cyclists will love the well-marked and connected **bike routes** throughout the Netherlands and Belgium, though cycling with the experienced bikers in city centers is a bit of a learning curve.

TRAIN

Both the Netherlands and Belgium have good public transit within and between major cities, making the train the best way to travel in the region. Trains run regularly between the Netherlands and Belgium, including several **high-speed trains** that connect Amsterdam/Rotterdam with Antwerp/Brussels, operated by **NS International** (www.nsinternational.com) or the **SNCB** (www.belgiantrain.be), so frequently that they often don't need to be booked in advance. Amsterdam to Brussels via the Thalys costs about €29-40 booked a few months in advance (closer to €100 shortly before departure) and takes about 2 hours. Bruges and Brussels are well-connected by a train that takes 1 hour 15 minutes (€14.30 per way per adult). To get to Bruges from Amsterdam, the fastest way is to take the Thalys to Brussels before transferring to a train to Bruges.

RENTAL CAR

Speedy trains in the region mean a car is not necessary, and is often even a liability due to **traffic** and **expensive, difficult parking.** That said, one can come in handy in some parts of Belgium, especially if you wish to explore the natural landscapes around **Dinant** and World War I battlefields around **Ypres.** Renting a car can provide flexibility for travelers and can also be economical for larger groups or people with mobility issues.

BUS

Despite how compact the region is, buses between cities are not as common as you might think, mostly because of the efficient train network. There are a few bus companies that operate between Amsterdam, Brussels, and Bruges, but the schedule tends to be fairly limited. Popular bus companies operating within Europe are **Eurolines** (www.eurolines.de) and **Flixbus**

Day Trips at a Glance

The cities of Amsterdam, Brussels, and Bruges are justifiable highlights of this region. But when it comes to the many easily accessible excursions from the cities covered in this book, it can be harder to choose. The following chart should help you decide which of the day trips to visit.

If You Like...	Destination	Getting There
	The Netherlands	
Uncrowded spaces, friendly locals, historic architecture	Under half an hour from Amsterdam, lovely **Haarlem** is the Dutch capital in miniature (page 136).	20-minute train ride from Amsterdam
Dutch cheese, local traditions	**Alkmaar** is a picturesque canal town with a historic cheese market (page 141).	35-minute train ride from Amsterdam
Cycling, gardens, tulips in bloom	Famed for the nearby Keukenhof gardens, **Lisse** is the place to fulfill your dream of cycling through fields of flowers (page 146).	1-hour train and bus transfer from Amsterdam
Beautiful canals, lesser known destinations	**Utrecht** boasts some of the most beautiful canals in Europe, without the crowds (page 151).	30-minute train ride from Amsterdam
Learning about politics and diplomacy, art, hitting the beach	Refined and home to important UN sites as well as the Netherlands' most famous beach, **the Hague** surprises (page 157).	1-hour train ride from Amsterdam
Traditional souvenirs, picturesque towns	Best known for its traditional Dutch pottery, Delftware, **Delft** is a pretty town made for strolling (page 168).	1-hour train ride from Amsterdam

(https://global.flixbus.com). Fares for the buses tend to be cheaper last-minute compared to the trains, but it's best to **be aware of the drop-off locations** as many bus companies stop outside the city center compared to more centrally located train stations.

Passports and Visas

Travelers from the **United States, Canada, Australia,** and **New Zealand** are able to enter the Netherlands and Belgium, in the Schengen Zone, without a visa for visits shorter than 90 days within a 180-day period. You will need a **passport** that is valid more than three months after your date of departure and with at least two blank pages. Entry into the Netherlands and Belgium from the **United Kingdom** may be different in the post-Brexit landscape, but it's likely to fall under this visa-free scheme.

South African travelers to the Netherlands and Belgium require a **Schengen visa** from the Dutch or Belgian consulates in South Africa.

If You Like...	Destination	Getting There
Modern architecture, hip art and design scenes	The Netherlands' modern side, **Rotterdam** is known for its state-of-the art architecture and (page 175).	1-hour train ride from Amsterdam, 1.5-hour train ride from Brussels
	Belgium	
Medieval townscapes, university towns	**Mechelen** is a beautiful medieval university town less than half an hour from Brussels (page 305).	30-minute train ride from Brussels
Trendy architecture and design, foodie tourism	**Antwerpen** is Belgium's lovely second city with a bit of everything, from history to food and design (page 310).	40-minute train ride from Brussels, 1-hour train ride from Amsterdam
Canals and castles, avoiding the crowds	Picturesque **Ghent** surprises with its lovely, uncrowded medieval center (page 315).	35-minute train ride from Brussels, 20-minute train ride from Bruges
World War I history, Belgian beer	**Ypres** is surrounded by World War I battle sites, as well as a Trappist monastery (page 320).	1.5-hour train and bus ride from Bruges, 2-hour train from Brussels, or rent a car
Quirky Belgian traditions, Neolithic history	**Mons** offers a bit of everything, from unique festivals to ancient archaeological sites (page 325).	1-hour train ride from Brussels
Outdoor recreation, scenic countryside	In **Dinant,** outdoorsy travelers can hike, see castles and cruise the Meuse River (page 330).	2-hour train ride (with transfer) from Brussels

What to Pack

Both the Netherlands and Belgium are prone to significant amounts of rain and wind, so bringing **waterproof layers** and **a good umbrella** is a good idea. Pack a **jacket** for chillier evenings. In the Netherlands and Belgium, formal attire is not expected in most public places, and **jeans** are worn by practically everyone. If you opt for a nicer dinner out at a sit-down restaurant, you might want to bring **one dressier outfit,** but there's no need for black-tie attire. Even for nightlife establishments, the dress code is much more informal than in other nearby countries.

Standard European plugs (230 V with plug type C) are used within the Netherlands and Belgium.

Advance Reservations and Tourist Passes

Between April and August, it's best to book your hotel at the same time as you book your flight, as many hotels sell out. Purchase advance tickets for

a tram in Amsterdam

popular museums in Amsterdam to avoid lines, especially the **Anne Frank House,** where you should check for tickets two months prior to your trip. Many popular restaurants and bars also require reservations made in advance. Call at least a week ahead to be sure. To mitigate the spread of COVID-19, reservations became obligatory at most museums, and even some bars and restaurants. It's possible these systems will stay in place even after the threat of COVID-19 recedes.

If you'll be spending a significant amount of time in Amsterdam, the **iAmsterdam pass** (www.iamsterdam.com) includes access to numerous museums and public transportation. You can choose the period that the card is active (e.g. 48 hours), and save significantly by visiting museums during that time. In Belgium, the **museumPASSmusées** (www.museumpassmusees.be) provides entry to 180 museums for just €60, but some of the best deals come from the Belgian train system, which adds museum entry to train transport via a program called **B-Excursion** (www.belgiantrain.be/en/leisure/b-excursions). Brussels and Bruges both also have their own individual tourist cards, the **Brussels Card** (https://visit.brussels/en/sites/brusselscard) and the **Discover Bruges card** (https://discoverbruges.com/en/discount-card/attractions-museums).

The Best of Amsterdam, Brussels & Bruges

The compactness of the Netherlands and Belgium means you can get a captivating glimpse into their cultures in a relatively short time. Most cities are only 1-2 hours away from each other, connected by an efficient train network, so it doesn't matter too much whether you fly into Brussels or Amsterdam. On this 10-day itinerary, you'll get a taste of the best of Amsterdam and Brussels, world-class cities known for their museums, impressive restaurant scenes, and lovely walkable neighborhoods. As the respective capitals of the Netherlands and Belgium, these cities provide easy access to the smaller towns, castles, windmills, and scenic landscapes nearby, and don't forget to spend a day or two strolling Bruges's stunning canals.

From big cities to smaller towns and landmarks of the larger area, this itinerary will give you a taste of what keeps travelers coming back to the Netherlands and Belgium. It's not the marijuana in Amsterdam or the beer in Belgium, but the laid-back and relaxed feeling of the region, perhaps best experienced by enjoying a coffee a centuries-old café. With that relaxed spirit in mind, if this itinerary seems too packed, don't be afraid to cut some of the day trips and side trips out of this itinerary, and enjoy Amsterdam, Brussels, and Bruges at a slower pace.

Amsterdam and Utrecht

DAY 1

On your first day, stroll through **Amsterdam Centrum** and the infamous **Red Light District** toward **Museumkwartier,** where you can take in the best of Amsterdam's world-class museums, like the **Rijksmuseum.** Wander through **Vondelpark,** Amsterdam's answer to Central Park, and have a light lunch at a park-side

Rijksmuseum

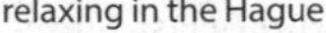

relaxing in the Hague

Belfry tower in Bruges

café or brewery, before heading to the **Albert Cuypmarkt** in **De Pijp** to try some **Surinamese food.** Head east until you find the **Amstel River** and enjoy a walk with views of the canal houses and the **Magere Brug,** before trying ***rijsttafel,*** an Indonesian-inspired feast that's a complicated (though delicious) legacy of Dutch colonialism.

DAY 2

Get off the beaten path in Amsterdam by taking a cycle in **Amsterdam Noord,** passing polders, **windmills,** and sheep before stopping at Noord's hipster **cafés** and **breweries** to experience the city's less traditional side. After a siesta, get a taste of Amsterdam's infamous **nightlife,** whether you like dancing the night away to **electronic music** or rubbing elbows with locals in a **historic bar** that looks like it hasn't changed in 100 years.

DAY 3

Escape the crowds of Amsterdam in Utrecht, Amsterdam's little sister. If you had a late night, Utrecht has the perfect remedy, with its many **foodie-centric cafes.** Climb the **Dom Tower** for views of medieval Utrecht from above before exploring its unique **two-story canals** up close, either on foot or by **kayak.** End the evening at a **canal-side restaurant** before heading back to your hotel in Amsterdam.

The Hague and Rotterdam

DAY 4

Pack your bags for the 1-hour train ride from Amsterdam to the Hague. As the seat of the Dutch parliament and the United Nations, the Hague's culture is cosmopolitan. Be sure to stop by the **Binnenhof,** home to the government of the Netherlands, and wander through the excellent **Mauritshuis** museum, which houses *Girl with a Pearl Earring.* Next, you'll hop on another train to Rotterdam, which you'll explore the following day.

DAY 5

Step into Manhattan on the Maas, or Rotterdam, the most striking city in the Netherlands, known for its modern architecture and lively food scene. After dropping off your bags, visit the **Cube**

Dutch and Flemish Art 101

Art lovers will have some difficult decisions to make when it comes to choosing which art museums to visit in the Netherlands and Belgium.

THE FLEMISH PRIMITIVES

Then one country, the region first became known for art during the medieval period, when artists known as the Flemish Primitives began creating portable wooden paneled paintings called triptychs. These painters were known for their realism and works that touched on religious themes. Notably, **Hieronymus Bosch** often depicted hell in his elaborate and sometimes twisted triptychs, including the well-known *The Last Judgment,* housed in the Groeninge Museum in Bruges. **Jan van Eyck** pioneered the style, creating realistic portraits and religious works including the famous *The Adoration of the Mystic Lamb,* known as the Ghent Altarpiece today. **Rogier van der Weyden's** work hangs in the Royal Museums of Fine Arts of Belgium, and **Hans Memling** is best known for his painting of the Shrine of St. Ursula in Sint-Janshospitaal in Bruges.

THE RENAISSANCE ERA

The 16th century brought the influence of the Italian Renaissance, with the best-known Flemish painters of the time including **Pieter Bruegel the Elder** (1525-1569) and his sons **Pieter Brueghel the Younger** and **Jan Brueghel.** Many of their works can be viewed at the Royal Museums of Fine Arts of Belgium in Brussels.

THE GOLDEN AGE

Perhaps the most famous period of Flemish painting is the Flemish Baroque period, or the Dutch "Golden Age," which lasted from the early 17th-18th centuries. The most famous Flemish artist from the period, **Peter Paul Rubens,** lived in Antwerp and served the Spanish royalty after learning from Caravaggio and other masters in Italy. He is best known for his biblical and historical paintings, many of which can be viewed at the Rijksmuseum in Amsterdam. At the same time, his counterparts in the Netherlands were producing fine art that veered into less religious territory, such as landscapes, portraits, and still lifes. Famous painters include **Johannes Vermeer** (best known for *Girl with a Pearl Earring*), **Frans Hals, Jan Steen,** and **Rembrandt van Rijn.** The Rijksmuseum in Amsterdam, Frans Hals Museum in Haarlem, and Mauritshuis in the Hague are the best places to view work by these artists.

IMPRESSIONISM AND BEYOND

Impressionism influenced many Dutch artists, but the most well-known is **Vincent Van Gogh,** who lived throughout Belgium and the Netherlands, famed worldwide for his portraits, still lifes, and landscapes. Many of his works are housed in the Van Gogh Museum in Amsterdam.

During the time of Van Gogh and following his death, surrealism and symbolism were rising in Belgium, perhaps most encapsulated by Brussels-based painter **René Magritte.** The Royal Museums of Fine Arts of Belgium in Brussels is the best place to view his dreamlike works, such as *The Return* and *The Empire of Light.*

WHERE TO SEE DUTCH AND FLEMISH ART

- **Rijksmuseum:** This is the premier spot in the Netherlands for viewing art from the Dutch Golden Age, from Rembrandt's *The Night Watch* to Vermeer's *The Milkmaid* (page 62).
- **Van Gogh Museum:** If you're crazy about Van Gogh, this museum in Amsterdam houses the largest collection of his work in the world (page 68).
- **Mauritshuis:** View *Girl with a Pearl Earring* by Vermeer and works from other Dutch Masters in the beautiful former home of a prince in the Hague (page 160).
- **Royal Museums of Fine Arts of Belgium:** Whether you prefer Flemish masters like Bruegel or modernist paintings by Magritte, there's something for everyone at this museum in Brussels (page 199).
- **Groeninge Museum:** Take in the Flemish Primitives from van Eyck to Memling at Bruges's most impressive art museum (page 257).

Houses, a fascinating example of urban housing from the 1970s, and leave the afternoon open to take the ferry to **Kinderdijk,** a charming village with dozens of windmills outside of Rotterdam. After you've returned, consider ending your evening with a meal at the trendy **Markthal,** a striking piece of architecture itself.

Brussels and Dinant

DAY 6

After checking out of your hotel in Rotterdam, hop on the high-speed train to Brussels, where you can take in the grand view of the city from **Grand Place** before making your way south to Sablon to sample the finest of **Brussels's chocolatiers.** On your sugar rush, head south to hunt for treasures at the **Marolles Flea Market.** Visit the **Horta Museum,** one of Brussels's art nouveau masterpieces, or stroll through the **Ixelles** neighborhood to spot more buildings in the iconic architectural style, before a classy dinner and a cocktail.

DAY 7

Spend the morning at the **Royal Museums of Fine Arts of Belgium** before heading south to have lunch at one of the Congolese restaurants in **Matonge.** Post-lunch, head to the **Parlamentarium** or the **House of European History** to learn about the history of the continent and the European Union. From here, take the tram or walk toward **Dansaert,** Brussels's hippest neighborhood, for dinner and a craft brew at **Brussels Beer Project.**

DAY 8

If you're tired of cityscapes, take the train southward to Dinant, a beautiful town in southern Belgium, or **Wallonia.** The town is situated underneath an epic fortress, the **Dinant Citadel,** that provides scenic views and insight into centuries of Belgian history. After the Citadel, take a **river cruise** along the **Meuse,** one of the most scenic landscapes of Belgium, passing chateaux and rolling hills. End the day trip with a **Trappist beer** produced near Dinant before heading back to Brussels.

Bruges

DAY 9

From Brussels, the train ride to Bruges takes just an hour. This beautiful city can be easily covered on foot in one day. From the train station, make a beeline for **Markt,** the glittering central square of Bruges, before climbing the **Belfry.** Get lunch along **Noordzandstraat,** possibly stopping at a **chocolate shop** or two, before visiting the **Groeninge Museum** to see the Flemish Primitives. Enjoy a beer at a **brown bar** before walking back along the canals. If you happen to spot a **hidden courtyard,** don't hesitate to peek inside.

DAY 10

On your second day in Bruges, take things easy with a leisurely **brunch** before discovering the some of the **quieter canals** outside Bruges's more touristy areas. Relive favorite **scenes from *In Bruges*,** including the jaw-dropping **Adornes Domain,** and browse for handmade lace at Bruges's dedicated **lace shops.** Enjoy the **windmills** of the **Bruges ramparts** before looping back to **Langestraat,** a quieter residential neighborhood known for boutique shopping, dinner, and drinks away from the center. From Bruges, it's an easy train ride back to Brussels for your return flight or to go on to your next destination.

Quintessential Netherlands

Canals. Windmills. Tulips. Cheese. If the picturesque image of a typical Dutch landscape is what you seek, you'll find it aplenty, all surprisingly close to the dense urban capital that is Amsterdam. The flower fields of the Dune and Bulb Region and the traditional cheese market in Alkmaar to the north are famous for a reason—and once you've seen them, it's easy to find a tucked-away café to chat with a local away from the tourist track. Best of all, it's easy to get everywhere on a day trip thanks to the Netherlands' capable public transit system; if you base yourself in Amsterdam, you can come back to your hotel and favorite brown bar each night.

Day 1: Amsterdam

Start your quintessential Amsterdam day by walking along the iconic canals west of Amsterdam Centrum in **Grachtengordel West and De Jordaan** before breakfast, then explore these neighborhoods' charming, busy **markets.** Visit the **Anne Frank House**—book your spot well in advance—to learn more about the tragic story of Anne and her family and get a fascinating glimpse into World War II history. Pick your favorite canal from your earlier wanderings and grab a **coffee,** the beverage of choice of Dutchies throughout the day, for a canal-side pick-me-up. Then, go for a scenic stroll through **Vondelpark** before stopping off at **Vondelpark3** for dinner.

Day 2: Alkmaar

Just 30 minutes north of Amsterdam by train, the beautiful city of Alkmaar is home to a sight that has changed little in hundreds of years: white-aproned cheese mongers running huge wheels of cheese to-and-fro at the town's famous **cheese market**—a touristy sight to be sure, but one that's bound to please cheese lovers and the lactose intolerant alike. Afterward, be sure to grab some cheese or maybe an **ice cream** for yourself at a local shop and enjoy Alkmaar's picturesque

windmills at Zaanse Schans

The Best of Belgian Beer

blonde beer at Brussels's Moeder Lambic

A visit to Belgium, where people have been brewing for more than 800 years, is the holy grail for many beer lovers. Once made in city breweries and monasteries regulated by the Catholic Church, beer has evolved into a thriving national tradition. Today, more than 1,500 types of beer are produced in Belgium, often divided between **abbey beers,** which refer to brews made using traditional brewing methods and recipes, and **Trappist beers,** which are still produced entirely by Trappist monks. Belgian beers tend to be heavier in alcohol than other European brews, so do pay attention to the ABV while you're imbibing.

BEER TYPES

Most bars have a solid selection of Belgian beers; ask your bartender for recommendations of local options that might be harder to find elsewhere. In order of decreasing ABV, here are some brews to look for:

- **Quadrupel** (9.1-14.2%): A heavy and rich Belgian beer style with often fruity undertones and a yeasty flavor. Try: Westvleteren 12.
- **Triple** (Tripel; 8-12%): A heavy yet smooth malty abbey-style beer first produced by Westmalle abbey in the 1930s. Try: Westmalle Tripel.
- **Double** (Dubbel; 6.3-7.6%): A malty abbey-style brown ale first produced by Westmalle, with a dark complexion. Try: Westmalle Dubbel, Affligem Dubbel.
- **Blonde** (4-5%, can be higher): A less bitter and smoother abbey-style pale ale with a yeasty taste and a golden color slightly closer to an IPA. Try: Brugse Zot Blonde, La Chouffe Blonde.
- **Saison** (4.5-6.5%): A light and easy-to-drink pale ale originating from Wallonia, perfect for warm weather. Try: Saison Dupont, Saison Du Meyboom.

churches and **canals** before heading back to your hotel (and the 21st century) in Amsterdam for the evening.

Day 3: Lisse

If you're lucky enough to be visiting the Netherlands in spring, usually mid-April, you can witness a sight many come from around the world to see: the **tulip fields** around the small town of Lisse, about an hour away from Amsterdam by train, in full bloom. Take a **cycle** down the narrow lanes to spot the best blooms. If you're not here during the right season, don't despair: The spectacular **Keukenhof gardens** are worth a visit any time in the summer. Grab a **beer** or a **Dutch pancake** at a nearby brewery or restaurant before hopping on the bus back to Amsterdam.

- **Witbier** (4-7%): A light unfiltered ale often spiced with herbs and a higher percentage of wheat. Try: Super 8 Blanche, Grimbergen Blanche.
- **Gueuze** (5-9%): A sour blend of lambics, with a significant amount of head, similar to Champagne, traditionally produced in the Brussels region. Try: Cantillon Lambic, Boon Oude Gueuze.
- **Flemish red ale** (5-6.02%): A sour ale produced in West Flanders with heavy fruit undertones brewed in oak barrels. Try: Rodenbach Flemish Red Ale, Duchesse de Bourgogne.
- **Flemish brown** (Oud Brown; 4-8%): A sour brown ale with a more malty taste. Try: Bourgogne des Flandres.
- **Kriek** (Fruit Beer; under 5%): A sour Belgian fruit beer brewed with cherries, sometimes with additional sugar, with roots in Brussels. Try: Cantillon Kriek Lambic, Timmermans Kriek Lambic, Mort Subite Kriek Lambic.
- **Framboise** (under 3%): A lambic beer produced with raspberries. Try: Cantillon Rose de Gambrinus.

BELGIUM'S BEST BREWERIES

- **Brussels Beer Project:** The future of Belgian beer is being brewed by Brussels Beer Project, a collaborative brewery housed in the trendy Dansaert neighborhood (page 230).
- **Brasserie Cantillon:** Sample a rare *gueuze* at the last brewery in Brussels still brewing lambics in a traditional manner (page 231).
- **Brouwerij de Halve Maan:** Bruges's best-known brewery has been brewing beer in the same location for more than 500 years (page 287).
- **Café Vlissinghe:** Sip beer at Bruges's oldest café, dating back to 1515 (page 288).
- **Brouwerij De Anker:** For a taste of Belgium's beer history, visitor-friendly Het Anker has been perfecting their beer for centuries (page 309).
- **Sint-Sixtus Brewery:** Considered by some the best beer in the world, Westvleteren 12 is brewed and sold to the public at this unassuming Trappist brewery in West Flanders outside of Ypres. It's worth the trek (page 324).
- **Maredsous Abbey:** Try Trappist beer at one of the most accessible and visitor-friendly Trappist breweries in Belgium (page 332).

Day 4: Zaanse Schans

Spend your last day in typically Dutch Zaanse Schans, a perfectly preserved village only 30 minutes from Amsterdam. Here you'll see the iconic **windmills** you've likely been craving since your arrival in the Netherlands, as well as quaint **museums** on Dutch history and a charming wooden shoe workshop. It may be touristy, but that doesn't mean you won't enjoy a beer at the local **brewery** before heading back to your lodging in Amsterdam after your day of exploring, feeling like a true city-hopper.

Architectural Highlights

The Netherlands and Belgium are rightfully famous for their beautiful 15th-, 16th-, and 17th-century architecture, but their contributions to more modern styles of building are a bit less well known. Base yourself in Brussels or Antwerpen, or spend a night in each city covered here, for this tour of unique Dutch and Belgian architecture from the 20th century and beyond.

Day 1: Brussels

Brussels is the birthplace of art nouveau, and architecture lovers' first stop should be the **Horta Museum,** the former home of the founder of the elaborate, decorative architectural movement. After exploring this perfectly preserved art nouveau masterpiece, stroll the chic streets of **Ixelles** to spot many more beautiful examples, and be sure to stop in **Matonge** for some Congolese food. Next, browse through one of Brussels's beautiful **covered arcades,** reminiscent of the galleries of nineteenth-century Paris, before taking a peek into the past at the 17th-century **Saint John the Baptist at the Béguinage** and grabbing some typical Brussels seafood snacks at lively **Noordzee.**

Day 2: Antwerpen

Just over halfway between Brussels and the Netherlands, Antwerpen surprises many visitors. You'll arrive in the stunning **Antwerpen Centraal** train station, a neo-Renaissance masterpiece in itself. After taking in the impressive **Grote Markt** and its centuries-old guild houses, the strikingly modern glass architecture of **MAS**—Museum aan de Stroom—might shock you. Visit the museum's terrace to get a view of the contrast between old and new, then grab a beer surrounded by religious paraphernalia in

shops and cafés in the Royal Galleries of Saint Hubert, Brussels

Antwerpen Centraal train station

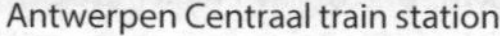

Rotterdam

Elfde Gebod, a café that once belonged to Antwerpen's cathedral.

Day 3: Rotterdam

An hour north of Antwerpen by train, Rotterdam is thoroughly modern city, from its famous tilted **Cube Houses** to the monumental stone-arch **Markthal.** After touring these architectural contributions from the last hundred years (and grabbing a snack at the market), step back into the 17th century in **Delftshaven,** a picturesque neighborhood built by the Pilgrims that survived bombing in World War II. You're a quick train ride from Amsterdam or Brussels here, well-positioned for your return flight or to head on to your next destination.

Amsterdam

Amsterdam's lush, tree-lined canals are on many a traveler's bucket list, but what Amsterdammers love about their city may surprise visitors who think of it as a weed-filled party hub. Amsterdam's reputation as a disruptor and intellectual hub has long lured visitors and transplants, who are impressed by the high quality of life and typically Dutch tolerance toward diversity and different lifestyles. Although it's hard to feel this emphasis on multiplicity in the Red Light District, you'll feel this buzzing energy as you shop in independent shops, dance to electronic music in one of the city's many nightlife venues, and talk to locals at its trendy coffee cafés.

Biking or walking along the grand yet well-preserved 17th- and 18th-century canal houses, it's easy to feel like you're stepping back in

Highlights

Look for ★ to find recommended sights, activities, dining, and lodging.

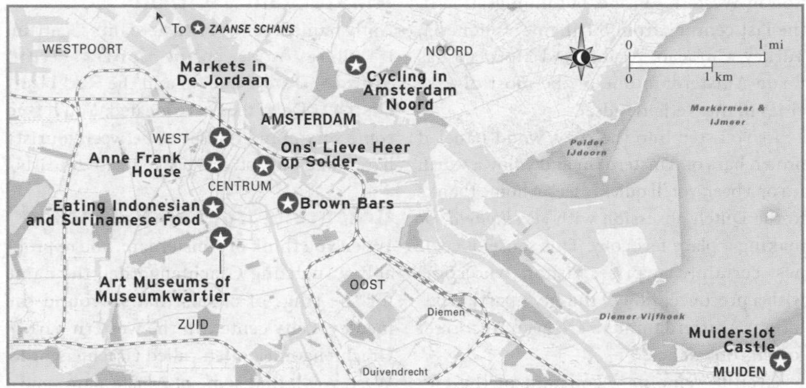

★ **Ons' Lieve Heer op Solder:** Climb the stairs into Amsterdam's biggest secret, a delightful museum tucked into the Red Light District (page 50).

★ **Anne Frank House:** Step behind the bookshelf for a glimpse into Anne Frank's short and tragic life in this former home turned museum, where Anne and her family stayed hidden for two years during World War II (page 58).

★ **Art Museums of Museumkwartier:** Amsterdam is spoiled for museums, from the Dutch masters in the Rijksmuseum to the wonderful Van Gogh Museum (page 62).

★ **Cycling in Amsterdam Noord:** Escape from the crowds and into the countryside on two wheels, just across the river from the city center (page 77).

★ **Markets in De Jordaan:** Pick up breakfast and maybe a souvenir at one of the many bustling markets in this charming neighborhood (page 97).

★ **Eating Indonesian and Surinamese Food:** Sample some of the tastiest food that the Netherlands has to offer, from savory *roti* to innovative Indonesian cuisine (page 98).

★ **Brown Bars:** Enjoy a drink in one of Amsterdam's typically cozy, dimly lit bars that has likely looked much the same for centuries (page 109).

★ **Muiderslot Castle:** Transport yourself to a fairy tale at a well-preserved medieval castle just outside Amsterdam (page 126).

★ **Zaanse Schans:** Take in a typically Dutch view of polders and windmills only 30 minutes from Amsterdam Centrum (page 127).

time to the world of Rembrandt and the Dutch masters; countless museums provide a peek into this history. While Amsterdam takes pride in its storied past, it is now beginning to confront its colonial legacy as part owner of Suriname and perpetuator of slavery there. In 2020, the Amsterdam City Council voted a proposal to formally apologize for its role in Suriname, and there is an increasing emphasis on the city's Black and minority history—which shouldn't be surprising, considering 45 percent of Amsterdam's population comes from a minority background. For many tourists, the multicultural society of Amsterdam can be a surprise, given Amsterdam's location in Western Europe, but immigration in the last century from Suriname, Indonesia, Turkey, Curaçao, Aruba, and Morocco has made Amsterdam one of the most diverse cities in the Netherlands.

As you step into the cozy, wood-paneled brown bars of Amsterdam and enjoy a warm tea or a beer, you'll quickly feel at home thanks to the Dutch obsession with *gezelligheid,* or making a place feel cozy. This sense of coziness certainly surprises visitors who come with a preconception of the city's party reputation; Amsterdammers are keen to correct for this imbalance.

Cycling remains a constant of the city throughout the year, even in winter and in rain. On these cold days, Amsterdammers bundle up in their winter clothes before tucking into brown bars for a warm conversation and a *glühwein* (mulled wine). On warmer days or simply any sunny day, locals jostle for a seat on the terraces to people-watch and take in the sun with picnics, bicycles, and parties on boats. Regardless of the day, you're likely to feel an immediate sense of warmth as you browse the local markets, greet the neighborhood cats guarding many of the businesses, and make conversation with shopkeepers. This is the *gezellig* side of Amsterdam that so many locals adore.

ORIENTATION

Many first-time visitors to Amsterdam stay within **Amsterdam Centrum,** with a brief visit for museums in the **Museumkwartier,** but the Gratchengordel's beautiful canals are less crowded than those in the center, and **De Jordaan** offers charming markets. Farther outside of the center, you'll find trendy, diverse neighborhoods, such as hip **De Pijp.**

Getting orientated in Amsterdam is easy due to the circle of canals that surround the city center, and big squares, such as Dam Square, that provide ample signage to major attractions.

Amsterdam Centrum

Aptly named, central Amsterdam's Centrum is where **Amsterdam Central Train Station, Dam Square,** and the **Red Light District** (De Wallen) are located. You'll find some very grand houses in between touristy bars—and busy streets packed with tourists.

Grachtengordel and Plantage

When you think of Amsterdam, you're probably visualizing Grachtengordel, the name for the rings of canals that surround the medieval city center. In the western part of Grachtengordel, often called Grachtengordel West, you'll find some of Amsterdam's most classic views, beautiful 17th-century canal houses, and the moving (and enduringly popular) **Anne Frank House.**

To the south, the part of the Grachtengordel between Amsterdam Centrum in the north and De Pijp to the south, often called Grachtengordel Zuid, is home to a lively club scene on **Leidseplein** and **Rembrandtplein** squares, as well as the picturesque **Hortus Botanicus** gardens in Plantage, farther east.

De Jordaan and Haarlemmerdijk

De Jordaan, a thin strip just west of Grachtengordel, is one of Amsterdam's most

Previous: a lively canal scene in Amsterdam; boats in front of the Amsterdam Central Train Station; Dappermarkt.

atmospheric neighborhoods, with its countless hidden courtyards, charming neighborhood bars, and busy weekly markets. Just north of Brouwersgracht canal, you'll find **Haarlemmerdijk/Haarlemmerstraat,** a charming shopping street packed with independent cafés, shops, and restaurants.

Amsterdam West

Farther west, Amsterdam West is relatively unknown to tourists. For a taste of a more local Amsterdam, explore sprawling **Westerpark** and its **Westergasfabriek,** former factories converted into shopping and dining. This area is home to a large percentage of the city's Turkish, Moroccan, and Surinamese population.

Museumkwartier and Oud Zuid

Tucked just south of Amsterdam West, Oud Zuid is known for being expensive—there's even a song about it. But that money has begot some of Amsterdam's best art museums and cultural institutions, from the **Rijksmuseum** to the **Royal Concertgebouw. Vondelpark,** the most iconic park in Amsterdam, also sits in the center of Oud Zuid.

De Pijp

Moving east of the Oud Zuid and south of Grachtengordel, De Pijp feels like a village within a city, a diverse neighborhood where Amsterdammers and visitors from all around the world shop in the always-busy **Albert Cuypmarkt** street market. De Pijp is also home to Amsterdam's trendiest cafés, shops, and bars popular with expats from other parts of Europe and Dutchies alike.

Amsterdam Oost

To the east, Amsterdam Oost is off the beaten path, with a lot to offer in terms of dining and shopping. Estates such as **Frankendael** were once on the outskirts of the city, where wealthy families would escape for nature and quiet; today the neighborhood's lively bar and restaurant scene and hip **Czaar Peterstraat** with its indie shops are great for escaping the busy Centrum. Amsterdam Oost has a high percentage of immigrant residents originally from Indonesia, Suriname, and Turkey, and many of the streets are named after islands in Indonesia. More than 100 languages are spoken in this diverse neighborhood.

Amsterdam canals

Amsterdam

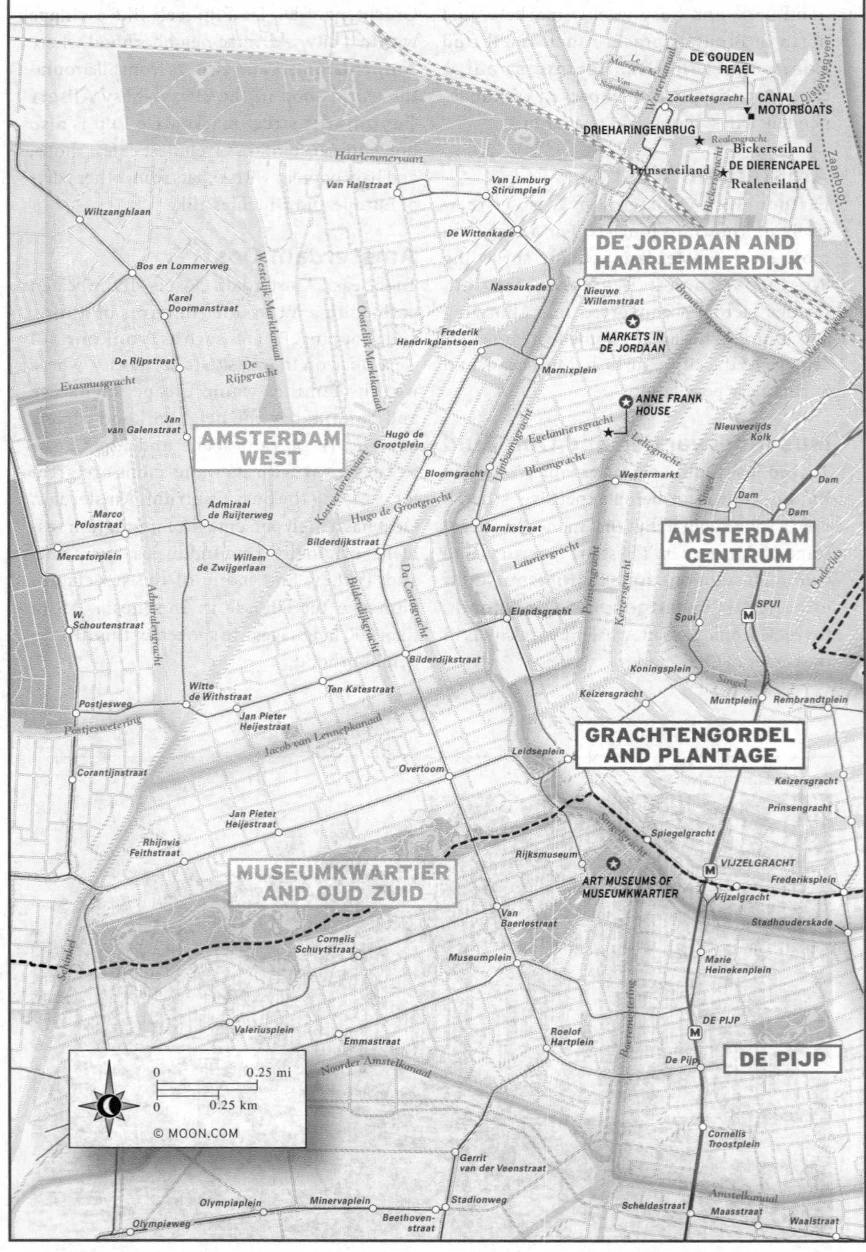
DE GOUDEN REAEL
CANAL MOTORBOATS
DRIEHARINGENBRUG
DE DIERENCAPEL
Bickerseiland
Prinseneiland
Realeneiland
Zoutkeetsgracht
Realengracht
Westerkanaal
Bickersgracht
Zaanboot
Haarlemmervaart
Van Hallstraat
Van Limburg Stirumplein
Wiltzanghlaan
De Wittenkade
DE JORDAAN AND HAARLEMMERDIJK
Bos en Lommerweg
Nassaukade
Nieuwe Willemstraat
Karel Doormanstraat
Westelijk Marktkanaal
Oostelijk Marktkanaal
Brouwersgracht
MARKETS IN DE JORDAAN
Frederik Hendrikplantsoen
De Rijpstraat
Marnixplein
De Rijpgracht
Erasmusgracht
ANNE FRANK HOUSE
Nieuwezijds Kolk
Jan van Galenstraat
AMSTERDAM WEST
Hugo de Grootplein
Egelantiersgracht
Leliegracht
Lijnbaansgracht
Bloemgracht
Westermarkt
Dam
Kostverlorenvaart
Hugo de Grootgracht
Singel
Admiraal de Ruijterweg
Marco Polostraat
Marnixstraat
AMSTERDAM CENTRUM
Mercatorplein
Bilderdijkstraat
Willem de Zwijgerlaan
Lauriergracht
Bilderdijkgracht
Da Costagracht
Admiralengracht
W. Schoutenstraat
Elandsgracht
Prinsengracht
Keizersgracht
Spui
SPUI
Bilderdijkstraat
Koningsplein
Witte de Withstraat
Ten Katestraat
Postjesweg
Jan Pieter Heijestraat
Keizersgracht
Muntplein
Rembrandtplein
Postjeswetering
Jacob van Lennepkanaal
Leidseplein
GRACHTENGORDEL AND PLANTAGE
Corantijnstraat
Overtoom
Keizersgracht
Prinsengracht
Jan Pieter Heijestraat
Singelgracht
Spiegelgracht
Rhijnvis Feithstraat
Rijksmuseum
VIJZELGRACHT
MUSEUMKWARTIER AND OUD ZUID
ART MUSEUMS OF MUSEUMKWARTIER
Frederiksplein
Vijzelgracht
Van Baerlestraat
Stadhouderskade
Cornelis Schuytstraat
Museumplein
Schinkel
Marie Heinekenplein
Boerenwetering
DE PIJP
Valeriusplein
Emmastraat
Roelof Hartplein
0
0.25 mi
0
0.25 km
© MOON.COM
Noorder Amstelkanaal
De Pijp
DE PIJP
Cornelis Troostplein
Gerrit van der Veenstraat
Olympiaplein
Minervaplein
Stadionweg
Scheldestraat
Amstelkanaal
Maasstraat
Waalstraat
Beethovenstraat
Olympiaweg

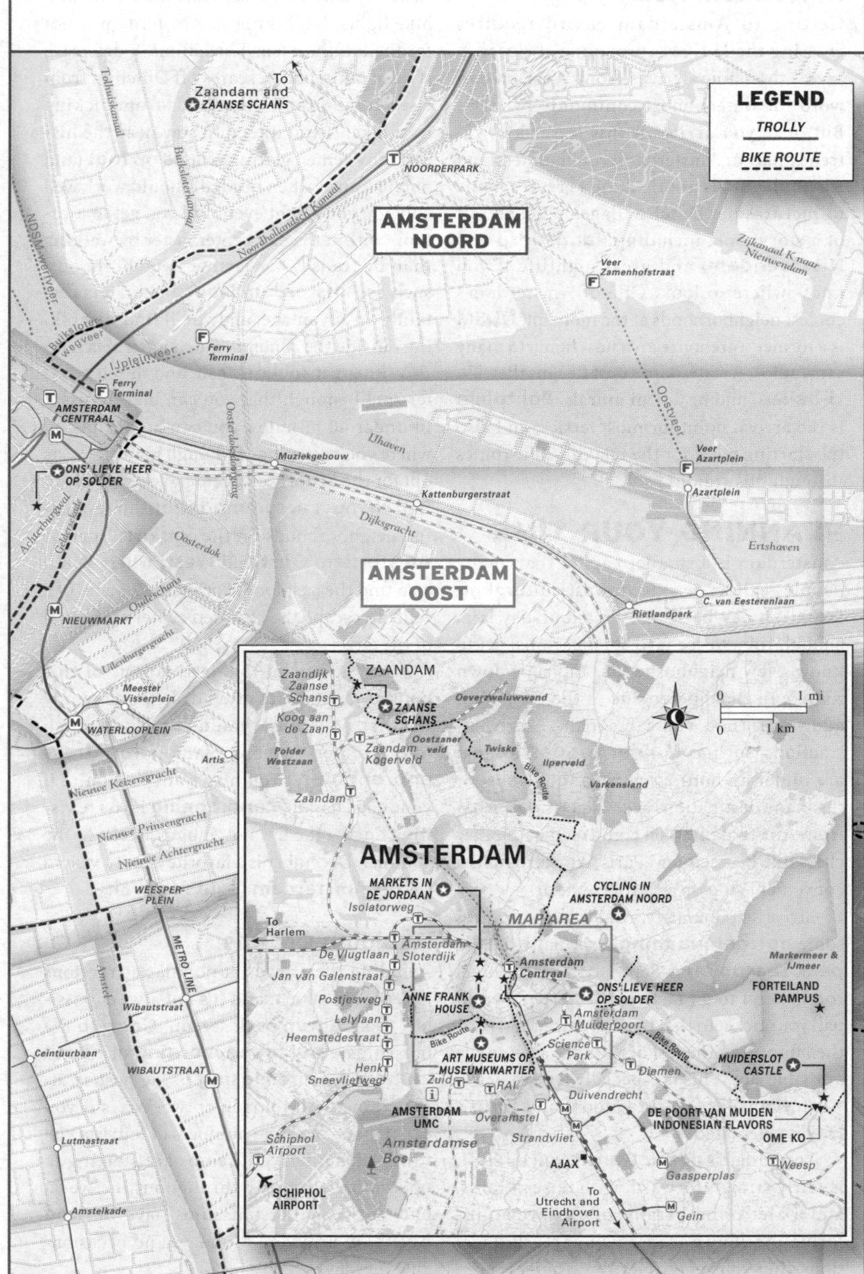
LEGEND
TROLLY
BIKE ROUTE
To Zaandam and ZAANSE SCHANS
NOORDERPARK
AMSTERDAM NOORD
Noordhollandsch Kanaal
Tolhuiskanaal
Buiksloterkanaal
NDSM-werfveer
Buiksloterwegveer
IJpleinveer
Ferry Terminal
Ferry Terminal
AMSTERDAM CENTRAAL
Veer Zamenhofstraat
Zijkanaal K naar Nieuwendam
Oostveer
Veer Azartplein
Azartplein
IJhaven
Muziekgebouw
Kattenburgerstraat
Dijksgracht
Oosterdok
Oosterdoksdoorgang
ONS' LIEVE HEER OP SOLDER
Achterburgwal
Geldersekade
AMSTERDAM OOST
Ertshaven
C. van Eesterenlaan
Rietlandpark
Oudeschans
NIEUWMARKT
Uilenburgergracht
Meester Visserplein
WATERLOOPLEIN
Artis
Nieuwe Keizersgracht
Nieuwe Prinsengracht
Nieuwe Achtergracht
WEESPERPLEIN
METRO LINE
Amstel
Wibautstraat
WIBAUTSTRAAT
Ceintuurbaan
Lutmastraat
Amstelkade
ZAANDAM
Zaandijk Zaanse Schans
ZAANSE SCHANS
Oeverzwaluwwand
Koog aan de Zaan
Zaandam Kogerveld
Oostzaner veld
Twiske
Ilperveld
Varkensland
Polder Westzaan
Bike Route
Zaandam
0 1 mi
0 1 km
AMSTERDAM
MARKETS IN DE JORDAAN
Isolatorweg
CYCLING IN AMSTERDAM NOORD
MAP AREA
To Harlem
Amsterdam Sloterdijk
De Vlugtlaan
Jan van Galenstraat
Amsterdam Centraal
Postjesweg
ANNE FRANK HOUSE
ONS' LIEVE HEER OP SOLDER
Amsterdam Muiderpoort
Markermeer & IJmeer
FORTEILAND PAMPUS
Lelylaan
Heemstedestraat
Bike Route
Science Park
Bike Route
ART MUSEUMS OF MUSEUMKWARTIER
Henk Sneevlietweg
Zuid
RAI
Diemen
MUIDERSLOT CASTLE
Duivendrecht
AMSTERDAM UMC
Overamstel
DE POORT VAN MUIDEN INDONESIAN FLAVORS
OME KO
Strandvliet
Schiphol Airport
Amsterdamse Bos
AJAX
Weesp
Gaasperplas
SCHIPHOL AIRPORT
To Utrecht and Eindhoven Airport
Gein

Amsterdam Noord

Getting to Amsterdam Noord requires crossing the **IJ river** (pronounced closer to "eye," the name derives from West Frisian word for water), most commonly by ferry. But once you arrive in this lesser-known, trendy part of Amsterdam, you'll understand why millennials are flocking here: It's home to picturesque Dutch villages plucked out of a storybook, including **Randsdorp** and **Nieuwendam,** and great nightlife if you know where to look. One of Amsterdam's coolest neighborhoods at the moment, **NDSM** is a former warehouse area now home to many art studios, Amsterdam's best flea market, **De IJ-hallen,** and beautiful murals. **Pontplein** is the arrival point for most ferries, and also the starting point for the relaxing bike routes through this region.

PLANNING YOUR TIME

Amsterdam is a smaller capital than many people realize; despite its vast cultural offerings, it can be seen over a four-day trip, enough time to see favorite museums, get to know a few neighborhoods, and slow down to take in the quieter side of the city. With additional time, you can explore nearby attractions, such as **Muiderslot Castle,** that are under an hour away by train or bus, or the many destinations accessible as **day trips** from Amsterdam. Well connected with other cities like Brussels and Paris, Amsterdam is a convenient stop on a European tour.

Given its popularity, Amsterdam requires some **upfront planning,** especially during **peak season** (Apr.-Sept.). Affordable hotel rooms tend to go fast, and it's often best to nab your ticket to that popular attraction first, then figure out the rest of your day around the available slot. This is especially true in April, when the **tulips** go into bloom and **King's Day** is celebrated.

Amsterdam's **public transit,** run by **GVB,** is fairly straightforward, with buses, trams, and a Metro line. Trams often have an information booth where you can ask questions after you get on. Getting around is even easier by **bike,** with separate bike lanes and bike lights, but biking in Amsterdam is not for the fainthearted. The hallmark defensive style of biking often scares off Dutchies from elsewhere in the Netherlands from picking up a bike. If you intend to stay near the historic city center, getting around **on foot** (and public transit when needed) should work well enough; you might even find you get to locations within the city center faster by walking than by transit. For farther neighborhoods, such as **Amsterdam Noord,** a bike is certainly an advantage, and you'll find that biking outside the center is much more relaxed.

With great public transit, and the city center small enough that you can bike across it in under 40 minutes, you can be flexible on where you're staying. Although many tourists opt for the historic city center, you're likely to find **cheaper accommodations** in residential neighborhoods on the outskirts, such as **Amsterdam Oost** and **West,** where you'll also find the best food. For many, it's a bit of a relief to escape the crowded center at the end of the day.

Like the rest of the destinations of this book, Amsterdam's often dreary and windy weather hopefully shouldn't put too much of a damper on your plans if you **dress appropriately.** You may want to inquire if your hotel has **air-conditioning** if you're visiting during the few hot, muggy weeks in the summer. December is a favorite time to visit to see the **Amsterdam Light Festival.**

Avoiding Crowds

Avoiding the crowds at popular attractions is certainly an art, and it's not always possible, especially in peak season. Going to the museums **early in the morning** or **about an hour before closing** is the best strategy, along with touring on weekdays if you can. Due to the large numbers of tourists visiting Amsterdam, museums are starting to open more regularly throughout the week, but many smaller museums have **limited hours,** typically on Mondays and occasionally Tuesdays.

Reservations and Advance Bookings

Advance bookings are generally smiled upon in Amsterdam, from **restaurants** to **museums.** Although not mandatory, in order to get the best seat at many cafés, it's generally recommended to make a reservation at least a few hours beforehand. After COVID-19, reservations have become even more normalized to limit crowds.

Reservations are important if you intend to visit popular museums such as the **Van Gogh Museum, Rijksmuseum,** and the **Anne Frank House** in peak season. Tickets should be reserved about two months ahead of your visit.

Sightseeing Passes

The main sightseeing pass in Amsterdam is the **iAmsterdam City Card** (www.iamsterdam.com; from 24-120 hours; €65-130), which is great for a short trip focused on museums. The pass includes entry to more than 70 museums and attractions along with public transit within Amsterdam, a canal cruise, and access to nearby attractions in Zaanse Schans, Haarlem, and Muiden. Most of the museums mentioned in this chapter are included with the iAmsterdam City Card, with the exclusion of the Anne Frank House.

The **Museumkaart** (www.museumkaart.nl; adults €64.90, children €32.45) used to be one of the best-value solutions for travelers visiting Amsterdam for a longer period, but under a recent change, visitors can only use the temporary pass five times within 30 days. It can still make some economic sense if you'll be visiting more expensive museums, but it might be simpler to buy admission out of pocket. Visitors can buy the pass at one of the participating institutions (including the Rijksmuseum).

The newest sightseeing pass is the **Holland Pass** (https://hollandpass.com; €45-80), a more flexible option for good planners. It includes credits that can be used to enter one more expensive attraction, such as Keukenhof outside the city or the Rijksmuseum, and one less expensive attraction. Check the cost of simply booking directly, which is sometimes cheaper, before buying the pass.

Itinerary Ideas

DAY 1: MARKETS AND NEIGHBORHOODS

This itinerary is best on a Saturday. About two months before your trip, book your place at the extremely popular **Anne Frank House** so you can add it to this day, which includes exploring some of Amsterdam's best street markets and shops. Be sure to take out some **cash** at an ATM for some of the market stands and shops, some of which may not take credit cards. It's a good idea to make a reservation for your Indonesian feast at **Tempo Doeloe** as well.

1 Start by strolling down Haarlemmerstraat, a few blocks from the canals of Grachtengordel West, and enjoy the independent businesses that make up the core of this busy shopping street. Grab a coffee and a sweet treat for breakfast from **Toki.**

2 Shop the **Noordermarkt,** open Saturdays and Monday mornings, for souvenirs, food stuffs, and just for fun. There are plenty of lovely cafés surrounding these streets where you can people-watch.

3 Head to the **Anne Frank House,** a 10-minute walk south across the Prinsengracht canal, in the early afternoon—since you've booked ahead, you won't have to wait in line!

4 Continue south for another 5 minutes to reach the **9 Streets,** which are full of atmospheric independent shops, concept stores, and cozy coffee cafés that you won't be able to

Itinerary Ideas

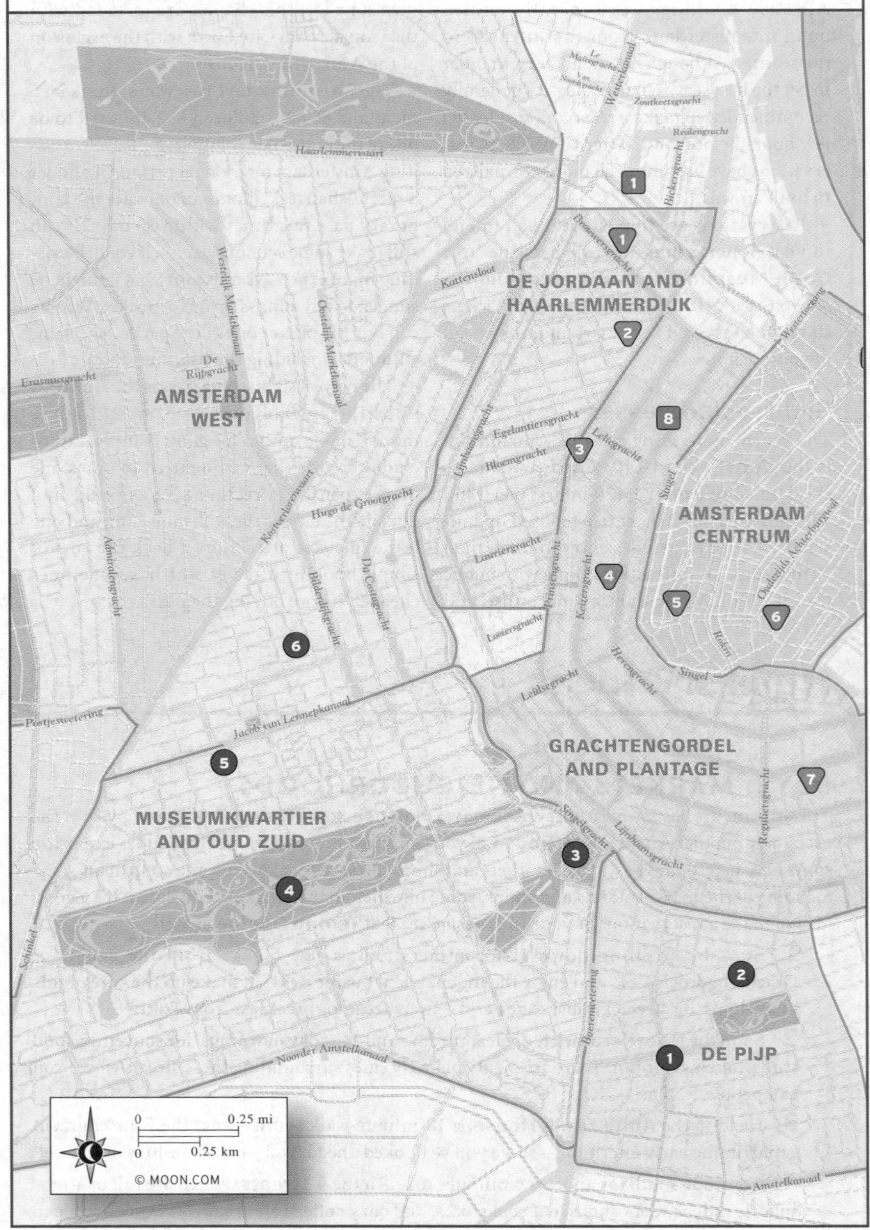

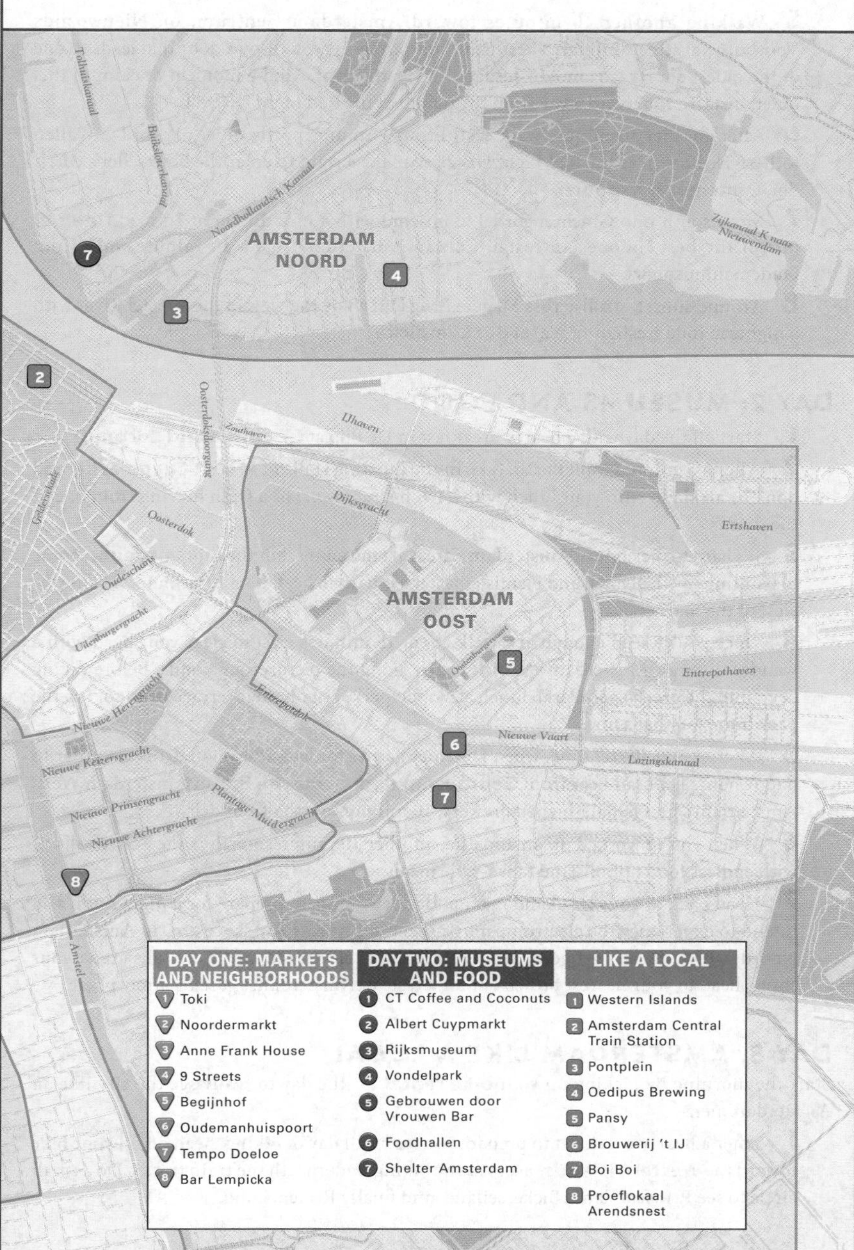
Tolhuiskanaal
Buiksloterkanaal
Noordhollandsch Kanaal
AMSTERDAM NOORD
Zijkanaal K naar Nieuwendam
Oosterdoksdoorgang
Zouthaven
IJhaven
Geldersekade
Oosterdok
Dijksgracht
Ertshaven
Oudeschans
Uilenburgergracht
AMSTERDAM OOST
Oostenburgervaart
Entrepothaven
Nieuwe Herengracht
Entrepotdok
Nieuwe Vaart
Lozingskanaal
Nieuwe Keizersgracht
Nieuwe Prinsengracht
Plantage Muidergracht
Nieuwe Achtergracht
Amstel
DAY ONE: MARKETS AND NEIGHBORHOODS
1 Toki
2 Noordermarkt
3 Anne Frank House
4 9 Streets
5 Begijnhof
6 Oudemanhuispoort
7 Tempo Doeloe
8 Bar Lempicka
DAY TWO: MUSEUMS AND FOOD
1 CT Coffee and Coconuts
2 Albert Cuypmarkt
3 Rijksmuseum
4 Vondelpark
5 Gebrouwen door Vrouwen Bar
6 Foodhallen
7 Shelter Amsterdam
LIKE A LOCAL
1 Western Islands
2 Amsterdam Central Train Station
3 Pontplein
4 Oedipus Brewing
5 Pansy
6 Brouwerij 't IJ
7 Boi Boi
8 Proeflokaal Arendsnest

resist popping into. Pause along Keizersgracht or Herengracht canals to enjoy the boats passing underneath the bridges, which are often decorated with flowers.

5 Walking another 10 minutes toward Amsterdam Centrum, on Nieuwezijds Voorburgwal street through a beautiful stone archway, you'll spy a door that leads to one of the oldest courtyards in Amsterdam, the **Begijnhof.** Find a moment of calm in this quiet, hisotirc courtyard away from the hubub of the Red Light District.

6 After another 10-minute walk east through an unexpectly quiet part of De Wallen (otherwise known as the Red Light District), make a right to enter the bookseller's corridor, **Oudemanhuispoort.**

7 Move south into Grachtengordel to unwind with a nice dinner at **Tempo Doeloe,** one of the best Indonesian restaurants in Amsterdam. It's a 10-minute walk from Oudemanhuispoort.

8 Around sunset, stroll across Magere Brug and enjoy the view of the Amstel River with a nightcap (or a fresh mint tea) at **Bar Lempicka.**

DAY 2: MUSEUMS AND FOOD

1 Start off the day with a hearty breakfast in De Pijp at **CT Coffee and Coconuts.**

2 After a 5-minute walk north, take in the bustling stalls of **Albert Cuypmarkt,** and don't be afraid to ruin your lunch with a fresh *stroopwafel* or a fresh herring from one of the stands.

3 It's hard to pick one of Amsterdam's great art museums, but the **Rijksmuseum,** home to paintings by the Dutch and Flemish masters, is hard to beat. It's a 10-minute walk northwest of the market.

4 Once you've seen enough art, walk about 15 minutes west to clear your head with a wander through Amsterdam's **Vondelpark** along the picturesque ponds. Before diving deep into the green space, grab lunch at Vondelpark3; sit on their terrace overlooking the park if the weather's fine.

5 After 4pm is *borrel* time, when Dutchies gather for late-afternoon drinks, similar to happy hour. Try craft beer from **Gebrouwen door Vrouwen Bar** in Amsterdam West, Amsterdam's first female-owned brewery, 10 minutes north of Vondelpark.

6 When you've worked up an appetite, another 10 minutes north is the **Foodhallen,** with endless food options and tapas-style meals.

7 Head back to your hotel and rest up for a few hours to prepare for a night out if you intend to experience the electronic music scene at **Shelter Amsterdam,** in Amsterdam Noord, which doesn't get going until midnight. If electronic music or clubs aren't your thing, head to your nearest brown bar for a taste of Amsterdam's *gezellig* atmosphere.

DAY 3: AMSTERDAM LIKE A LOCAL

Start the morning by picking up your **bike rental** for the day to really see the city like an Amsterdammer.

1 After a hearty breakfast to prepare you for a full day of biking, head off on your bike toward the **Western Islands,** accessed by biking underneath the train tracks. Do a small circle to see Prinseneiland, Bickerseiland, and finally Realeneiland.

2 Next, bike 10 minutes southeast on the dedicated bike path along the IJ river to **Amsterdam Central Train Station** to catch the ferry across the river to Amsterdam Noord.

3 Cycle through the bucolic former villages of Amsterdam Noord, starting in **Pontplein,** and enjoy the quiet polder landscape.

4 After you've completed the loop, stop off at **Oedipus Brewing** for a hard-earned beer.

5 Head back on the ferry to Amsterdam Central Train Station. Cycle 20 minutes east of the station and down Czaar Peterstraat to browse the shops on this street, such as **Pansy.**

6 A few minutes farther south, stop for a beer at Amsterdam institution **Brouwerij 't IJ,** in front of the picturesque De Gooyer windmill.

7 Another 5 minutes south by bike, head to a hearty Thai dinner at **Boi Boi.**

8 Return your bike before resting your weary legs either back at your hotel room or while sitting on a picturesque terrace along the Grachtengordel/Amstel, such as the one at **Proeflokaal Arendsnest,** where you can sample the local brews canal-side.

Sights

AMSTERDAM CENTRUM

Dam Square

Dam 1

Amsterdam's most iconic square has long been at the heart of daily life in Amsterdam. The name originates from a dam that once separated the medieval town of Amsterdam from the waters of the Amstel River. The square itself is largely modern besides a few landmarks on the square's western side, including the **Royal Palace** and the **New Church** (De Nieuwe Kerk; tel. 020 626 8168; www.nieuwekerk.nl; 10am-5pm daily; €10) with its neo-Gothic facade, now mostly known for its rotating exhibitions, including the annual World Press Photo competition.

Dam Square is an iconic place, largely used for large-scale events such as **National Tulip Day,** when the entire square is filled with tulips. Though it doesn't require too much of your time, it's a good point of reference for navigating the city.

ROYAL PALACE AMSTERDAM (Paleis Amsterdam)

Dam 1; tel. 020 522 6161; www.paleisamsterdam.nl; noon-5pm Fri., 10am-5pm Sat.-Sun.; adults €10, children free

It's hard to miss the massive neoclassical 17th-century palace in Dam Square. Built during the Dutch Golden Age as Amsterdam's town hall, its grandeur is muddled by the Netherlands' complicated history. The exterior is adorned with a representation of a woman, symbolizing Amsterdam, holding her hands out to receive the products of the Dutch empire, which of course at that time depended on the labor of enslaved people. Within this building, the Society of Suriname, a partner in the slave trade, met to discuss commerce with the city. The building was converted into a palace by King Louis Bonaparte during the short-lived Batavian Republic (1795-1806), when the Netherlands was more or less a client state of the French Empire.

The Royal family does not live in the palace today, but it's still used for official events. Technically at the disposal of the King and Queen, it is generally left open for the public to enjoy, with a free audio tour. Seventeen rooms are open to the public, including the impressive Citizens' Hall, with marble floors inspired by world maps and star charts. For more information on the palace's role in Dutch colonialism and slavery, go on the

Amsterdam Centrum

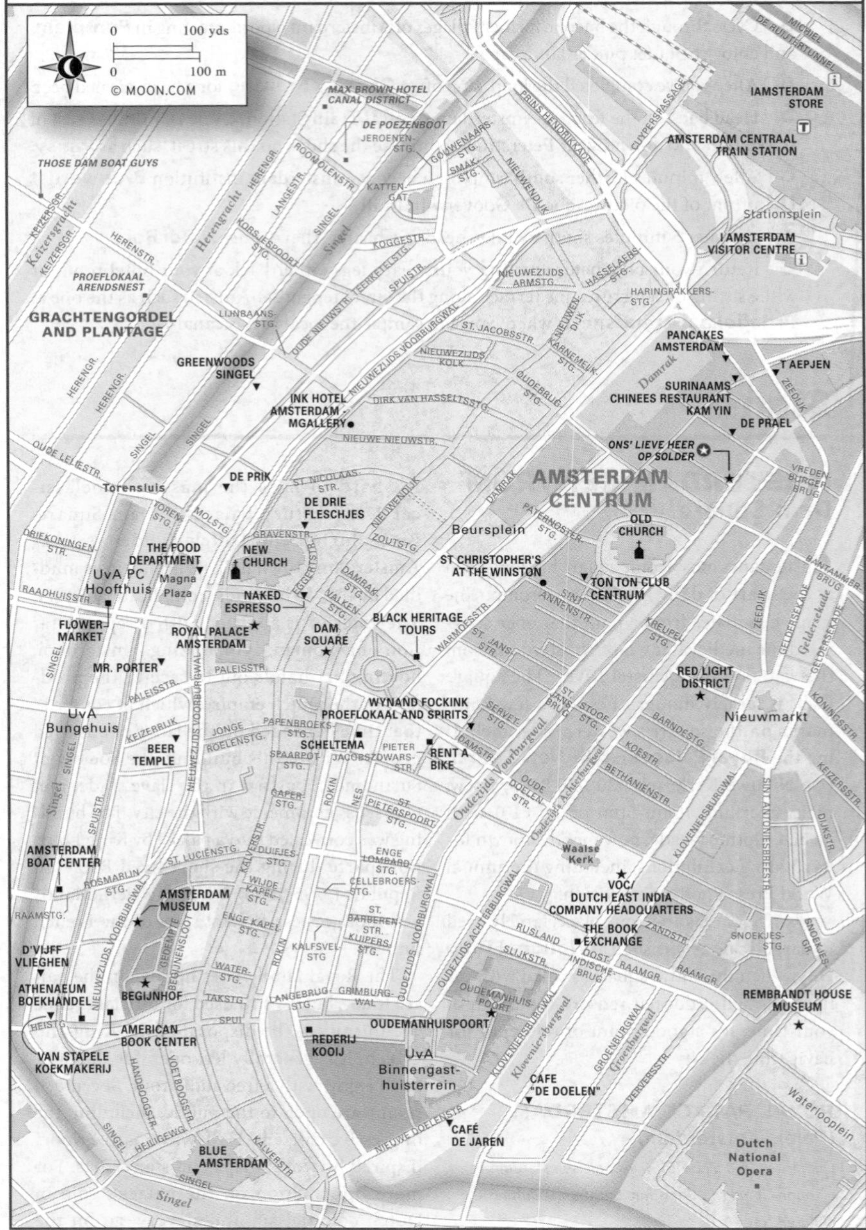

0 100 yds
0 100 m
© MOON.COM
MAX BROWN HOTEL CANAL DISTRICT
DE POEZENBOOT
THOSE DAM BOAT GUYS
PROEFLOKAAL ARENDSNEST
GRACHTENGORDEL AND PLANTAGE
GREENWOODS SINGEL
INK HOTEL AMSTERDAM - MGALLERY
DE PRIK
Torensluis
DE DRIE FLESCHJES
THE FOOD DEPARTMENT
NEW CHURCH
UvA PC Hoofthuis
Magna Plaza
NAKED ESPRESSO
FLOWER MARKET
ROYAL PALACE AMSTERDAM
DAM SQUARE
BLACK HERITAGE TOURS
MR. PORTER
UvA Bungehuis
BEER TEMPLE
SCHELTEMA
RENT A BIKE
WYNAND FOCKINK PROEFLOKAAL AND SPIRITS
AMSTERDAM BOAT CENTER
AMSTERDAM MUSEUM
D'VIJFF VLIEGHEN
ATHENAEUM BOEKHANDEL
BEGIJNHOF
AMERICAN BOOK CENTER
VAN STAPELE KOEKMAKERIJ
REDERIJ KOOIJ
UvA Binnengasthuisterrein
OUDEMANHUISPOORT
CAFÉ DE JAREN
BLUE AMSTERDAM
CAFE "DE DOELEN"
THE BOOK EXCHANGE
VOC/ DUTCH EAST INDIA COMPANY HEADQUARTERS
Waalse Kerk
REMBRANDT HOUSE MUSEUM
Dutch National Opera
Waterlooplein
Nieuwmarkt
RED LIGHT DISTRICT
ST CHRISTOPHER'S AT THE WINSTON
TON TON CLUB CENTRUM
OLD CHURCH
Beursplein
AMSTERDAM CENTRUM
ONS' LIEVE HEER OP SOLDER
DE PRAEL
SURINAAMS CHINEES RESTAURANT KAM YIN
T AEPJEN
PANCAKES AMSTERDAM
I AMSTERDAM VISITOR CENTRE
Stationsplein
AMSTERDAM CENTRAAL TRAIN STATION
IAMSTERDAM STORE
MICHIEL DE RUIJTERTUNNEL
Damrak
Singel
Herengracht
Keizersgracht
Geldersekade
Oudezijds Voorburgwal
Oudezijds Achterburgwal
Kloveniersburgwal
Groenburgwal

The Legacy of Dutch Colonialism

the former VOC Headquarters

As you wander among the beautiful canal houses, grand churches, and museums of Amsterdam, it's important to remember the role that slavery, and the Netherlands' history as a colonial powerhouse, played in all that wealth. Many of the products that brought riches to the Dutch colonial empire, such as spices, sugar, coffee, and tobacco, were produced through the labor of enslaved people, notably in Suriname and Curaçao.

For centuries, the coasts of Holland were important hubs of European trade, which expanded to the Mediterranean, Brazil, the Dutch Gold Coast of Africa, and the Indian Ocean in the 16th century. In 1602, the **Dutch East India Company (VOC,** or Vereenigde Oostindische Compagnie in Dutch) was founded to capitalize on booming trade with India, mostly in silks and textiles. The equally important **Dutch West India Company (GWC,** or Geoctroyeerde Westindische Compagnie) followed soon after in 1621. These chartered companies eventually grew into huge trade conglomerates that played a huge role in Dutch history. It wasn't until 1814 that slavery was banned in the Dutch colonies, and this change didn't come until 1864 in Suriname and the Dutch Antilles. There are traces of this history all over Amsterdam if you know where to look.

- The VOC was once headquartered at **Kloveniersburgwal 48** in De Wallen, which served as a warehouse, auction room, and administrative center. Though this building, part of the University of Amsterdam, is not open to the public, you can still stop by for a look and a solemn moment to think about the estimated 175,000 people who were directly traded by the VOC during the "Dutch Golden Age," not including the enslaved people transported from Africa to the Americas by Dutch ships.
- The Dutch West India Company was headquartered at **Herenmarkt 99,** now a wine bar and café in Grachtengordel West. Decisions crucial to Dutch colonies and outposts in Brazil, New York, the Antilles, Ghana, Benin, Guyana, and Suriname were made here.
- Walking around Amsterdam, it's hard to ignore the plaques often linked to products produced in the colonies, as well as depictions of Black servants—a good example is at **Oudezijds Voorburgwal 136.** Part of the global movement of goods that resulted from booming Dutch trade, Black people were moved to Amsterdam as well, where they served in a wide range of roles, from bookkeeping and household management to musicianship and horse grooms. Whether these Black people were truly servants, or enslaved and forced to perform this work, is a matter of historical debate. Having Black servants was considered a sign of prestige by Amsterdam's wealthy.

In the 21st century, Amsterdam is finally starting to come to terms with the complication of its colonial legacy, beyond glorifying the wealth imperial trade brought to the city. The first **National Slavery Monument** (Nationaal Slavernijmonument, Oosterpark 9; tel. 020 214 9640; www.ninsee.nl; open 24/7; free) was finally erected in 2002 in Oosterpark. Surinamese sculptor Erwin de Vries created the sculpture in three parts, one that looks back on slavery's dark history; the second breaking free from it through resistance, rebellion, and independence; and the last with an outstretched form representing the hope for a better future.

Black Heritage Tour (www.blackheritagetours.com/tours.html), which gives fuller history and context to the landmarks of Dam Square.

Red Light District

(De Wallen)

De Wallen is the neighborhood better known as the Red Light District, a 0.5-hectare (1.6-acre) area just east of Dam Square, between Rokin/Damrak streets and Kloveniersburgwal canal and running from Amsterdam Centraal in the north to Rokin canal in the south. This neighborhood of canals and skinny streets is best known today for its windows with sex workers, but it is also one of the oldest neighborhoods of Amsterdam.

In the 13th century, a dam was built where Dam Square stands today to block the Amstel River. The area was named for the walled canals intended to protect a growing city from flooding, a significant issue in Dutch history. With many attractions steeped in history, many visitors end up spending a significant time in the area even if they opt to avoid the Old Church, where most of the alleyways are filled with windows.

THE OLD CHURCH

(De Oude Kerk)

Oudekerksplein 23; tel. 020 625 8284; https://oudekerk.nl; 1pm-5pm Sat.-Wed., 1pm-5pm and 6pm-8pm Thurs.-Fri.; adults €15, students €5, children under 13 free

First erected in 1213, the Oude Kerk is one of Amsterdam's most iconic buildings, known for its location surrounded by the windows of De Wallen. Over the centuries, the church has been renovated, lengthened, and even converted from Catholic to Calvinist. Although some of the older altarpieces have been lost to time, there are still original paintings on the ceilings. The church is home to the graves of many notable stakeholders in the Dutch East India Company (VOC) and Dutch West India Company (GWC), as well as the grave of Jacob Matroos Beeldsnijder, a free Black man.

★ ONS' LIEVE HEER OP SOLDER

Oudezijds Voorburgwal 38; tel. 020 624 6604; www.opsolder.nl; adults €12.50, children €6, free with iAmsterdam card; 10am-6pm Mon.-Sat.

One of Amsterdam's best museums, and best-kept secrets, certainly has to be Ons' Lieve Heer op Solder (Our Lord in the Attic). This museum in the heart of the Red Light District made of three stunning Amsterdam canal houses, and its namesake, secret, two-story church hidden inside, can be easily missed. Ons' Lieve Heer Op Solder is a museum on the history of Amsterdam that beautifully summarizes the Dutch Golden Age (1581-1672). These houses are a perfectly preserved time capsule of life at the time, which makes it friendly to both children and adults.

Within the walls of the museum, you'll understand how people lived during this important period of Dutch hsitory, enjoy scenic canal views from the top stories, and learn about the darker side to the Protestant Reformation, when religious freedom was limited, so much so that Catholics had to attend mass in secret—hence the Our Lord in the Attic Church hidden within. The houses contain original architectural elements rarely seen today, such as an original 17th-century staircase. Don't miss the video in the kitchen for the amusing story of the ornate plates on display, or the chance to learn about the Miracle of Amsterdam (a fascinating tale of fire, miracles, and faith) in the modern building where you end your free audio tour.

The many narrow stairs make the museum inaccessible to visitors with disabilities; however, if you can manage it, it's certainly worth the steep climbs (that occasionally require a rope!) to get an intimate view of the history of Amsterdam.

Oudemanhuispoort

Oudemanhuispoort; 11:30am-5pm daily; free

After you walk through the small yet ornate gate of the Oudemanhuispoort, named for the elderly men's home that once stood

Red Light District Etiquette

Sex work has long been an important industry in the Red Light District, or De Wallen, so much so that married men were prohibited from entering the neighborhood during the medieval period. Under Napoleon, prostitution became legalized under the condition that sex workers had their health checked regularly. Today, sex work is legal in the Netherlands, and although there are other parts of Amsterdam with windows for sex workers, the narrow alleyways of De Wallen, including the narrowest street in Amsterdam, Trompettersteeg, have become quite famous throughout the world. But as a visitor, you have a responsibility to be respectful when visiting De Wallen.

Red Light District windows

TIPS FOR VISITING

- Put away your phone and camera. Beyond the fact that pickpockets often look for easy targets on the crowded streets, taking photos of the sex workers puts their identities at risk, as not all of their families know about their work.
- Abstain from knocking or gawking if you happen to pass a window; please respect that sex workers are people, too.
- Avoid yelling and keep your voice down. De Wallen is still a residential neighborhood, and residents have been very frustrated with the noise level that prevents them from sleeping at night.

For more information about De Wallen, check out the **Prostitution Information Center** (Enge Kerksteeg 3; https://pic-amsterdam.com; 2:30pm-5:30pm Wed.-Sat.), an educational center opened by sex workers to give visitors a different perspective on sex work.

DE WALLEN AND COVID-19

In this complicated neighborhood, the COVID-19 has allowed Amsterdam to hit pause on overtourism and think about ways to create a more sustainable future. One notable change is **banning tours** of the Red Light District, to stop normalizing looking at sex workers as entertainment. Similarly, **drinking in public spaces is banned** and a fine is given out for any alcohol containers. Amsterdam is further **clamping down on new businesses** that cater to tourists and **banning holiday apartments** within De Wallen.

here, you'll find yourself in a covered passage surrounded by stacks of secondhand books. Books have been sold in this passage since the 1750s; prior to the Holocaust, the booksellers were mostly Jewish.

Today, you can certainly find a steal if you're willing to dig through the piles of books in English, Dutch, and German. It's also a great spot to find bookish souvenirs, sheet music, and postcards. Bring cash; not all sellers accept cards.

Jewish Cultural Quarter

Nieuwe Amstelstraat 1; https://jck.nl; adults €17, youth 13-17 €13.50, children 6-12 €4.25

East of De Wallen, a number of museums dedicated to Judaism and Jewish history have joined forces as the Jewish Cultural Quarter, in order to educate visitors about the history of Dutch Jews as well as the Holocaust in the Netherlands. Although Anne Frank's story is famous, it's a lesser-known fact that, among Western European countries, the Netherlands

1
2
3
4

lost the highest percentage of its Jewish population during the Holocaust. These museums pay testament to the rich history of the Netherlands' Jewish community and the painful history of the Holocaust through objects, stories, and architecture. One ticket gets you into all the museums, which are housed in different buildings in the historic Jewish quarter.

NATIONAL HOLOCAUST MUSEUM AND HOLLANDSCHE SCHOUWBURG MONUMENT

Plantage Middenlaan 27; tel. 020 531 0380; https://jck.nl/nhm; 11am-5pm daily

The National Holocaust Museum is currently being renovated, together with the Hollandsche Schouwburg monument to the Holocaust, until 2022. This museum will tell the stories of those who died during the Holocaust—and those who survived to educate the next generation. The building was once a teaching college where the Dutch resistance would smuggle Jewish children to safety.

The Hollandsche Schouwburg is the National Holocaust Memorial and the only free museum in the Jewish Cultural Quarter. The facade of this grand building has been preserved, while the interior is an open courtyard where a theater once stood, used as a collection point for Dutch Jews in World War II prior to deportation. Today, the courtyard is a remembrance of those who perished in the Holocaust.

PORTUGUESE SYNAGOGUE

Mr. Visserplein 3; tel. 020 624 5351; www.esnoga.com; 10am-4pm/5pm Sun.-Thurs., 10am-2pm Fri. Nov.-Feb., 10am-4pm/5pm Sun.-Fri. Feb.-Oct.

This beautiful Sephardic synagogue, completed in 1675, is still active and regularly hosts evening services and concerts within its original wooden interior. Amsterdam once held one of the largest Jewish populations in Western Europe due to the Spanish Inquisition. Many Jews fleeing Spain were attracted by the Dutch tolerance, which resulted in a large number of Portuguese Jews immigrating to Amsterdam to escape persecution. The interior, lit by 1,000 candles, is full of beautiful silver religious objects and brass chandeliers. If you're a bibliophile, make a special appointment to see the **Ets Haim library,** the oldest functioning Jewish library in the world, a UNESCO World Heritage Site.

JEWISH HISTORICAL MUSEUM

Nieuwe Amstelstraat 1; tel. 020 531 0310; https://jck.nl/nl/locatie/joods-historisch-museum; 11am-5pm daily

Housed within several historic Ashkenazi synagogues, this museum focuses on Jewish culture, history, and art.

Rembrandt House Museum

Jodenbreestraat 4; tel. 020 520 0400; www.rembrandthuis.nl; 10am-6pm daily; €14

Dedicated to the life of Rembrandt van Rijn, the Dutch master who was born in Leiden and lived for 19 years in Amsterdam, this house, which dates back to 1607, is a reconstruction of what his studio and home might have been like. Rembrandt is known for his self-portraits as well as his sketches, which are on display here, but you'll need to go to other museums, such as the Rijksmuseum, to see his more famous works.

Begijnhof

Nieuwezijds Voorburgwal 373; tel. 020 622 1918; https://begijnhofkapelamsterdam.nl; 9am-5pm daily; free

Blink and you'll miss this ornate doorway that feels like something out of *Alice in Wonderland:* one moment, you're surrounded by people in the middle of Amsterdam, and the next, you're in a serene, historic oasis. The Begijnhof is one of the best-preserved courtyards in Amsterdam, dating back to the Middle Ages, home to the oldest wooden house in the city. It's not fully known when the Begijnhof in Amsterdam was first constructed, but it was certainly before 1346.

1: Dam Square **2:** Anne Frank House **3:** De Jordaan street **4:** Westerkerk

The name of the Begijnhof originates from its former residents, the Beguines, a group of Christians who wished to live a simple life dedicated to prayer and charity. Many of the women chose to live in communities surrounded by other Beguine women. Unlike a nunnery, Beguines had no set leadership, instead operating as a collective. The last Beguine died in Amsterdam in 1971.

Today, the Begijnhof is composed of 47 townhouses, with facades mostly from the 17th and 18th centuries. Though most of the townhouses are private residence, the courtyard is accessible to tourists, except for areas beyond gates that are designated for residences only. The courtyard also includes a hidden church, the **Begijnhof Chapel,** which is open to visitors. Please be respectful of the residents of the courtyard by being quiet, and avoid walking on the lawn.

Amsterdam Museum

Nieuwezijds Voorburgwal 359; tel. 020 523 1791; www.amsterdammuseum.nl; 10am-5pm daily; adults €15, children free

Set in a former convent turned orphanage, this museum tells the story of Amsterdam's founding through paintings, artifacts, and interactive items. Notably, it includes a replica of one of the first gay bars in the Netherlands, opened in 1927.

GRACHTENGORDEL AND PLANTAGE

Westerkerk

Prinsengracht 279; tel. 020 624 7766; www.westerkerk.nl; 10am-3pm Mon.-Fri.; free

As you stroll down the leafy Prinsengracht canal, the westernmost of Grachtengordel West's canals, you're likely to notice the soaring tower of the Westerkerk church. The largest Protestant church in the Netherlands, it's also one of the most impressive, with its many graves dedicated to famous Dutchmen and Dutchwomen (including Rembrandt, buried here in an unmarked grave).

Though Dutch Protestant churches tend to be more sparsely decorated than their Catholic counterparts, this church boasts white walls, golden chandeliers, and a large organ. Westerkerk's organ is certainly a highlight; you can catch **concerts** on Fridays at 1pm. Anne Frank famously described the sound of the 51 carillon bells, which you'll hear every 15 minutes, in her diary. (The carillon master plays a concert every Tuesday at noon.)

The **Westerkerk Tower** (Westertoren; 9am-8:30pm Mon.-Sat. Apr.-Sept., 9am-6pm

Begijnhof

Black Communities in Amsterdam, Past and Present

As a result of its former colonies, Black people have resided in the Netherlands since at least the 17th century, and today the country has a relatively large minority population, many of whom identify as Black. Although the role that Black people played in European history is frequently skipped over, there are traces of Black history all throughout Amsterdam if you know where to look.

Suriname exhibit in Nieuwe Kerk

FREE BLACK COMMUNITIES IN THE 17TH CENTURY

In the 17th century, there was a sizable Black community in the area surrounding **Jodenbreestraat,** now the old Jewish Quarter. The Black community here was made up of free sailors, soldiers, and servants, and records show that their origins spanned from other European countries to Africa to the West Indies. The Netherlands at the time had a very contradictory policy of banning slavery strictly within the Netherlands' land borders while turning a blind eye to it otherwise, which allowed an international Black community in Amsterdam to exist here and within the surrounding streets. This community was depicted by Rembrandt and the other Dutch masters in notable paintings, many of which can be seen in museums throughout the Netherlands.

SURINAMESE CULTURE

An important part of the Netherlands' multicultural society is its sizable Surinamese population, some of whom identify as Black. The bulk of Surinamese immigrants came after Surinamese independence in 1975; the following year, 40,000 people immigrated to the Netherlands from Suriname. Suriname's independence brought economic difficulty to a country so historically dependent on the Netherlands, forcing many Surinamese to make a choice between staying in their homeland and the promise of prosperity in bustling cities like Amsterdam. Surinamese people could only keep their Dutch nationality if they emigrated to the Netherlands within five years of independence.

Ketikoti (meaning "the chain is cut"; July 1) is a great day to learn more about Surinamese history, celebrating the day that slavery in Suriname was abolished in 1863. At first slavery was only abolished by name; enslaved people truly received their freedom after another 10 years of forced labor. Despite not yet being named a national holiday, Ketikoti has become an important day, full of festivals and cultural performances. Another way to get to know Surinamese culture in Amsterdam is trying **Surinamese food,** especially in restaurants owned by Black entrepreneurs.

LEARN MORE

Projects like **Mapping Slavery** (https://mappingslavery.nl) are striving to rediscover the often-forgotten history of Amsterdam. To learn more, you can also join a highly recommended tour operated by **Black Heritage Tours** (www.blackheritagetours.com).

Grachtengordel and Plantage

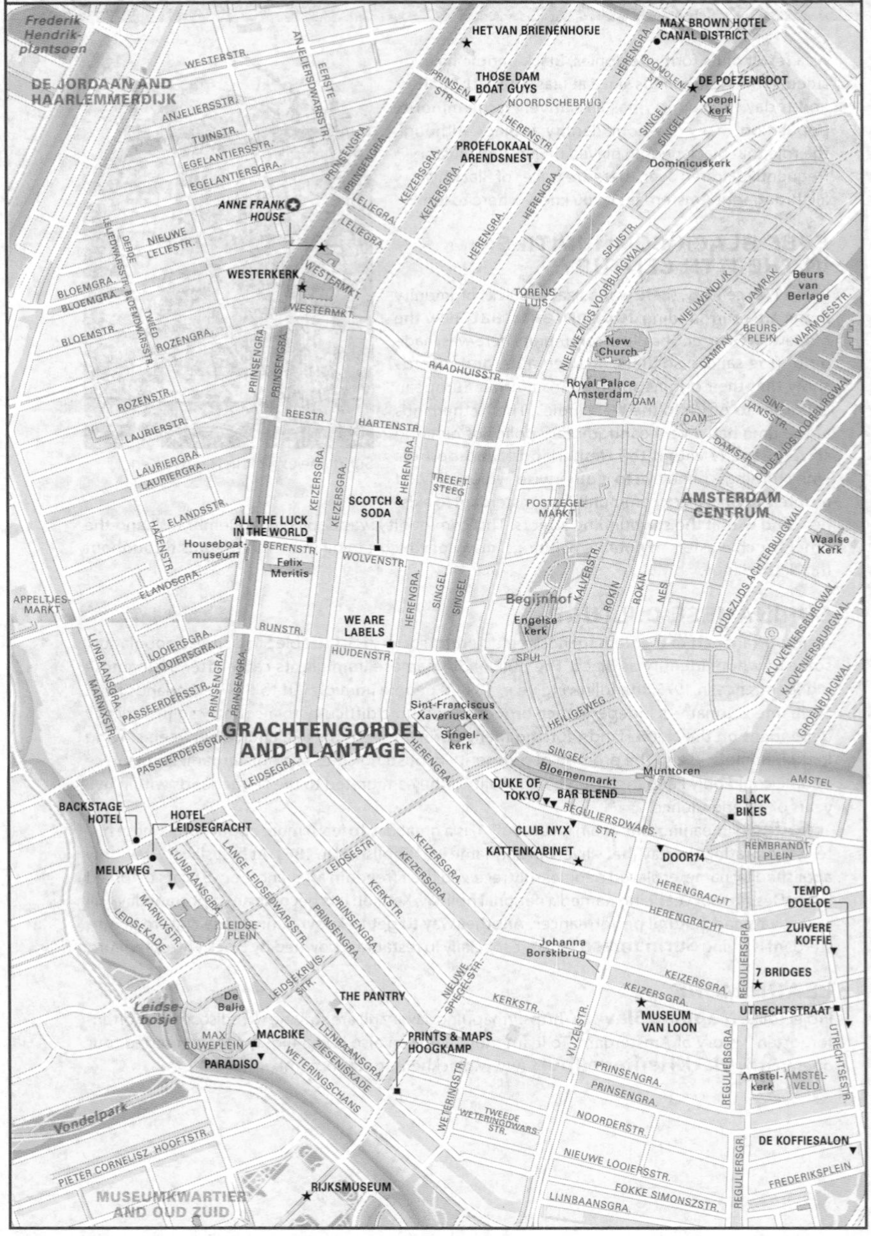
Frederik Hendrik-plantsoen
DE JORDAAN AND HAARLEMMERDIJK
HET VAN BRIENENHOFJE
MAX BROWN HOTEL CANAL DISTRICT
THOSE DAM BOAT GUYS
DE POEZENBOOT
Koepel-kerk
PROEFLOKAAL ARENDSNEST
Dominicuskerk
ANNE FRANK HOUSE
WESTERKERK
TORENSLUIS
Beurs van Berlage
BEURSPLEIN
New Church
Royal Palace Amsterdam
DAM
SCOTCH & SODA
ALL THE LUCK IN THE WORLD
Houseboat-museum
Felix Meritis
POSTZEGELMARKT
AMSTERDAM CENTRUM
Waalse Kerk
APPELTJESMARKT
Begijnhof
Engelse kerk
WE ARE LABELS
SPUI
Sint-Franciscus Xaveriuskerk
Singelkerk
GRACHTENGORDEL AND PLANTAGE
Bloemenmarkt
Munttoren
DUKE OF TOKYO
BAR BLEND
BLACK BIKES
BACKSTAGE HOTEL
HOTEL LEIDSEGRACHT
CLUB NYX
KATTENKABINET
DOOR74
REMBRANDTPLEIN
MELKWEG
TEMPO DOELOE
ZUIVERE KOFFIE
LEIDSEPLEIN
Johanna Borskibrug
7 BRIDGES
THE PANTRY
MUSEUM VAN LOON
UTRECHTSTRAAT
Leidsebosje
De Balie
MAX EUWEPLEIN
MACBIKE
PARADISO
PRINTS & MAPS HOOGKAMP
Amstelkerk
AMSTELVELD
Vondelpark
DE KOFFIESALON
RIJKSMUSEUM
MUSEUMKWARTIER AND OUD ZUID
WESTERSTR.
ANJELIERSSTR.
TUINSTR.
EGELANTIERSSTR.
EGELANTIERSGRA.
NIEUWE LELIESTR.
BLOEMGRA.
BLOEMSTR.
ROZENGRA.
ROZENSTR.
LAURIERSTR.
LAURIERGRA.
ELANDSSTR.
ELANDSGRA.
HAZENSTR.
LOOIERSGRA.
PASSEERDERSSTR.
PASSEERDERSGRA.
LIJNBAANSGRA.
MARNIXSTR.
LEIDSEKADE
LEIDSEGRA.
LANGE LEIDSEDWARSSTR.
LEIDSESTR.
KERKSTR.
KEIZERSGRA.
PRINSENGRA.
HERENGRA.
SINGEL
RAADHUISSTR.
REESTR.
HARTENSTR.
BERENSTR.
WOLVENSTR.
RUNSTR.
HUIDENSTR.
TREEFTSTEEG
KALVERSTR.
ROKIN
NES
HEILIGEWEG
REGULIERSDWARSSTR.
HERENGRACHT
REGULIERSGRA.
UTRECHTSESTR.
NIEUWE SPIEGELSTR.
VIJZELSTR.
WETERINGSTR.
TWEEDE WETERINGDWARSSTR.
NOORDERSTR.
NIEUWE LOOIERSSTR.
FOKKE SIMONSZSTR.
FREDERIKSPLEIN
WETERINGSCHANS
ZIESENISKADE
LEIDSEKRUISSTR.
PIETER CORNELISZ. HOOFTSTR.
SPUISTR.
NIEUWEZIJDS VOORBURGWAL
NIEUWENDIJK
DAMRAK
WARMOESSTR.
SINT JANSSTR.
DAMSTR.
OUDEZIJDS VOORBURGWAL
OUDEZIJDS ACHTERBURGWAL
KLOVENIERSBURGWAL
GROENBURGWAL
AMSTEL
NOORDSCHEBRUG
HERENSTR.
LELIEGRA.
WESTERMKT.
ROOMOLENSTR.
EERSTE ANJELIERSDWARSSTR.

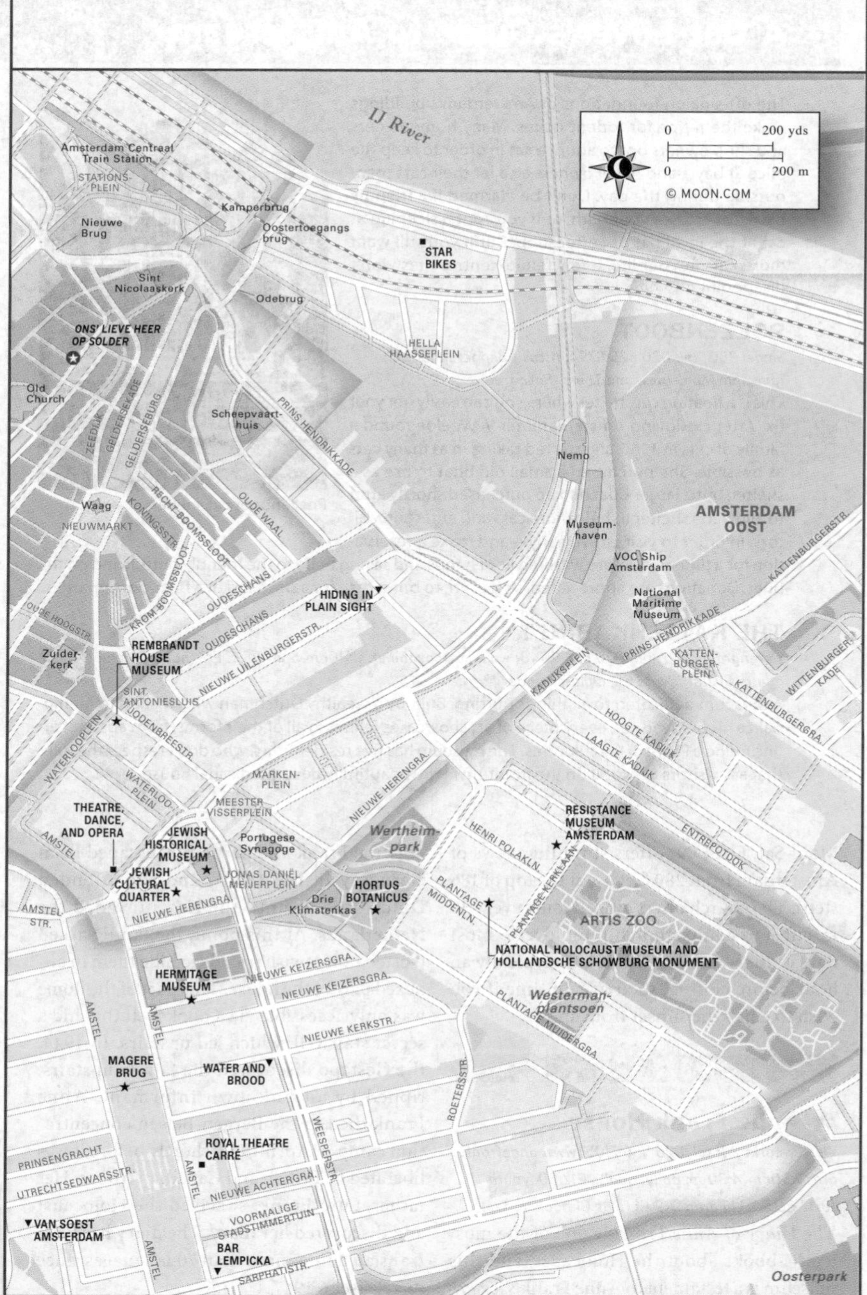
IJ River
0
200 yds
0
200 m
© MOON.COM
Amsterdam Centraal Train Station
STATIONSPLEIN
Kamperbrug
Nieuwe Brug
Oostertoegangsbrug
STAR BIKES
Sint Nicolaaskerk
Odebrug
ONS' LIEVE HEER OP SOLDER
HELLA HAASSEPLEIN
Old Church
Scheepvaarthuis
PRINS HENDRIKKADE
ZEEDIJK
GELDERSEKADE
GELDERSEBURG
Nemo
Waag
NIEUWMARKT
KONINGSSTR.
RECHT BOOMSSLOOT
OUDE WAAL
AMSTERDAM OOST
Museumhaven
VOC Ship Amsterdam
KATTENBURGERSTR.
OUDESCHANS
HIDING IN PLAIN SIGHT
National Maritime Museum
OUDE HOOGSTR.
KROM BOOMSSLOOT
NIEUWE UILENBURGERSTR.
Zuiderkerk
REMBRANDT HOUSE MUSEUM
KADIJKSPLEIN
KATTENBURGERPLEIN
WITTENBURGERKADE
SINT. ANTONIESLUIS
JODENBREESTR.
KATTENBURGERGRA.
HOOGTE KADIJK
LAAGTE KADIJK
WATERLOOPLEIN
MARKENPLEIN
NIEUWE HERENGRA.
MEESTER VISSERPLEIN
THEATRE, DANCE, AND OPERA
JEWISH HISTORICAL MUSEUM
Portugese Synagoge
Wertheimpark
RESISTANCE MUSEUM AMSTERDAM
HENRI POLAKLN.
ENTREPOTDOK
AMSTEL
JONAS DANIËL MEIJERPLEIN
JEWISH CULTURAL QUARTER
HORTUS BOTANICUS
Drie Klimatenkas
PLANTAGE MIDDENLN.
PLANTAGE KERKLAAN
ARTIS ZOO
AMSTEL STR.
NATIONAL HOLOCAUST MUSEUM AND HOLLANDSCHE SCHOWBURG MONUMENT
HERMITAGE MUSEUM
NIEUWE KEIZERSGRA.
Westermanplantsoen
PLANTAGE MUIDERGRA.
NIEUWE KERKSTR.
MAGERE BRUG
WATER AND BROOD
ROETERSSTR.
WEESPERSTR.
ROYAL THEATRE CARRÉ
PRINSENGRACHT
UTRECHTSEDWARSSTR.
NIEUWE ACHTERGRA.
VOORMALIGE STADSTIMMERTUIN
VAN SOEST AMSTERDAM
BAR LEMPICKA
SARPHATISTR.
Oosterpark

A Cat Lover's Guide to Amsterdam

The oft-sinking foundations of Amsterdam's buildings make them ripe for rodent issues. Many homeowners and shop owners opt to adopt a cat in order to keep the mice at bay—and many owners also let their cats roam outside during the day. Don't be alarmed if a friendly black cat crosses your path, or if you spot a sleeping at cat at the local bar or coffeeshop. But if you still want more cats in your life, a few feline-centric sites won't disappoint.

Poezenboot cat shelter

POEZENBOOT

Singel 38G; tel. 020 625 8794; https://depoezenboot.nl; 1pm-3pm Mon.-Tues. and Thurs.-Sat.; free

This is a floating cat shelter where you can easily get your fix. After cat-loving Amsterdammer V. Weelde found a family of cats in 1966, she started taking in as many cats as possible. She purchased a small old boat to use as a shelter, but a larger boat had be purchased shortly after to allow the shelter to help more cats and entertain visitors. In order to visit, arrive early—and make a reservation for a time slot before washing your hands and saying hello to the friendly fluffs living on the boat. Donations are appreciated, so be sure to bring cash for a postcard or a financial donation.

THE KATTENKABINET

Herengracht 497; tel. 020 626 9040; www.kattenkabinet.nl; 10am-5pm Tues.-Fri., noon-5pm Sat.-Sun.; adults €10, students €5, children under 12 free

A museum dedicated to all things purring. Built by a wealthy Dutchman who wished to memorialize his beloved cat, every piece of art showcases felines in all of their forms, from abstract art (including a Picasso) to sculptures. The museum has five resident cats, who don't respect the rules that ask visitors not to sit on the furniture in the beautifully decorated canal house.

Mon.-Sat. Oct.; €9) offers stunning views of Amsterdam from 280 feet up, at the top of 186 steps. The church offers guided tours every 30 minutes to adults and children over 6 most days of the week. The last tour is typically an hour before closing, so arrive on time if you wish to enjoy the sunset from above.

TOP EXPERIENCE

★ Anne Frank House

Westermarkt 20; tel. 020 556 7105; www.annefrank.org; 9:30am-4:30pm daily; adults €12.50, youth 10-17 €6.50, children 0-9 €1 (plus €1 booking fee)

The Diary of Anne Frank is one of the most iconic books about the Holocaust, and this museum is a testament to Anne Frank's legacy.

Anne Frank and her family escaped from Germany in the 1930s, and she attended Dutch schools until the Nazis invaded the Netherlands. At this point, the family asked trusted non-Jewish friends to hide them in annexed part of the house. This part of the home was only accessible via a bookshelf that hid a secret stairwell, which led upstairs. In 1944, the Gestapo discovered the family upstairs, tipped by an unknown informant. Anne Frank died in the Bergen-Belsen concentration camp in April 1945, shortly before it was liberated by British and Canadian troops. Her father, Otto Frank, survived the Holocaust and discovered her diary. The diary has been translated into more than 70 languages since its release in 1947.

The museum is well suited for those who know Anne's story intimately, as well as for those who aren't as knowledgeable, and it is quite an emotional journey. As you walk on your own through the original home and the adjoining house-turned-museum, you'll walk in Anne's shoes while also learning about the Holocaust as a whole. The secret annex has been recreated with replicas to give visitors an idea of what life was like for the family at the time. Despite the heavy subject matter covered by the museum, it does have some exhibitions suitable for children.

Entry is limited, as the space is quite confined, so be sure to make a reservation online 1-2 months ahead of your visit to Amsterdam. The line for the Anne Frank House is infamously long, especially during peak times, and the museum has tried to open up more slots in the morning and early afternoon for visitors to reserve ahead. Those who have disabilities or have difficulty with stairs will not be able to enter the secret annex. Photography is not allowed.

Hermitage Amsterdam

Niewe Keizesgracht 1, entrance on Amstel 51; 020 530 8755; www.hermitage.nl; 10am-5pm daily; €27.50 for entire museum

A branch of the Hermitage Museum of Saint Petersburg, Russia, this extraordinary, sizeable museum has two permanent exhibits, one on relations between Russia and the Netherlands, the other on the history of the museum building itself, known as the Amstelhof. This 17th-century, classically-styled building was opened as a retirement home for elderly women, opening to men in starting 1817 and operating until the 2000s. Dutch royalty and Russian president Dmitry Medvedev collaborated together in 2009 to open this unique institution focusing on the special relationship between the Russians and the Dutch, starting with Peter the Great in the 18th century, who built his capital, Saint Petersburg, using Dutch techniques for constructing on muddy, swampy land.

All objects in the museum come from the Russian Hermitage museum, ranging from works of art to historical artifacts. Temporary exhibitions have ranged from the history of Russain tsars to showcasing the Dutch masters.

Hortus Botanicus

Plantage Middenlaan 2a; tel. 020 625 9021; www.dehortus.nl; 10am-5pm daily; adults €9.75, students a children 5-14 €5.50

Amsterdam is largely a modern city with limited green space, so the Hortus Botanicus, one of the oldest botanical gardens in the world, comes as a bit of a surprise. This garden was founded in 1638 to give doctors and pharmacists working in the Netherlands access to medicinal plants. Much of the collection of over 6,000 plants is sourced from the former Dutch colonies, and propagations from the collection, such as oil palms and coffee plants, have been planted across the world.

The most stunning building is the 20th-century **Palm Greenhouse,** a perfect respite from a cold, rainy day. Be sure to take a relaxing stroll along its canopy walkway above all the plants—and enjoy the rare plants in its collection, including a ginkgo tree.

Magere Brug

open 24/7; free

Amsterdam's most famous bridge has to be the Magere Bridge. First built in the 1600s, the bridge has many Amsterdam urban legends built around it, including a tale about two sisters who wished to visit each other. However, the real story is likely that a skinny bridge across the Amstel Bridge made more fiscal sense than a stone one. The bridge has been rebuilt many times, and the current one dates back to 1969. It's pedestrian-only at this point, and crossing the bridge provides a dreamy glimpse of Amsterdam's skyline north of the Amstel River. It's a favorite among couples and of filmmakers (you may recognize it from the James Bond movie *Diamonds Are Forever*). It's still said that if you kiss someone on the bridge, or on a boat underneath it, you'll be in love forever. Thousands of lights illuminate the bridge at night, which makes it a great spot for an evening stroll.

Resistance Museum Amsterdam

(Verzetsmuseum Amsterdam)

Plantage Kerklaan 61; tel. 020 620 2535; www.verzetsmuseum.org; 10am-5pm Mon.-Fri., 11am-5pm Sat.-Sun.; adults €12, ages 7-17 €6.50, children under 7 free

The excellent Resistance Museum's goal is to educate visitors about World War II from a very specific angle: from the perspective of normal, everyday Dutchies reacting to Nazi occupation, which took place from May 1940-May 1945. Using archival photographs and artifacts, the Resistance Museum tells the story of how citizens of Amsterdam alternately struggled, resisted, and sometimes ignored or even abetted, the Nazis, teaching memorable lessons to modern visitors on how fascism takes hold. The well-planned, chronological exhibitions really put you in the shoes of Amsterdammers in the 1930s and 40s; there's also a separate section on the history of how former Dutch colonies in the East Indies fared during World War II.

Museum van Loon

Keizersgracht 672; tel. 020 624 5255; www.museumvanloon.nl; noon-7pm Wed.-Fri., 10am-5pm Sat.-Sun.; adults €10, children €5.50

One of Amsterdam's grandest canal houses, Museum van Loon is an impressive mansion from 1672 that still belongs to the Van Loon family. The grand interior decorations and paintings, which provide a glimpse into the grandeur of the Dutch Golden Age, are largely from that period. Be sure to enjoy the sculpted garden that leads to the original coach house, now a café. Sit and enjoy a moment in the garden and try to spot the neighbor's naughty cat, who likes to sneak into the garden.

DE JORDAAN AND HAARLEMMERDIJK

Windy, narrow streets can make relatively small and compact De Jordaan a bit hard to navigate. **Noorderkerk** (Noordermarkt 48) sits on the corner of **Noordermarkt** and is a sort of landmark for the neighborhood. First built in 1620, this simple church was one of the first churches built after the Protestant Reformation.

Houseboat Museum

Prinsengracht 296 K; tel. 020 427 0750; https://houseboatmuseum.nl; 11am-5pm Tues.-Sun. Mar.-Oct., 11am-5pm Fri.-Sat. Nov.-Feb.; adults €4.50, children €3.50

As you walk down the canals of Amsterdam, you're bound to spot at least one houseboat. Historically, living on a boat meant that you were poor and could not afford to live elsewhere in the city, but today, houseboats cost nearly as much as a standard apartment in Amsterdam. The Houseboat Museum gives you a small glimpse into a functioning houseboat that was once a skipper. The museum is small but worth a peek for curious minds.

AMSTERDAM WEST

Museum The Ship

(Het Schip)

Oostzaanstraat 45; tel. 020 686 8595; www.hetschip.nl; 11am-5pm Tues.-Sun.; adults €15, students €7.50, children 5-12 €5, children 0-4 free

Museum The Ship should be on your list if you're a lover of Amsterdam School architecture, invented in the early 20th century and typically featuring brick buildings with round elements, such as towers or spires, wrought iron details, and elaborate glass windows. There's an element of restraint in masterpiece Amsterdam School buildings such as the Museum The Ship, the movement's best-preserved example. Originally built as a self-contained neighborhood intended for working-class Amsterdammers in 1916, Eigen Haard (Own Hearth) was nicknamed "The Ship" for its distinctive shape and size. The interior includes a community hall, post office, and apartments intended for a comfortable life. The museum details the history of the movement as well as the history of social housing in the Netherlands. There are **tours**

De Jordaan and Haarlemmerdijk

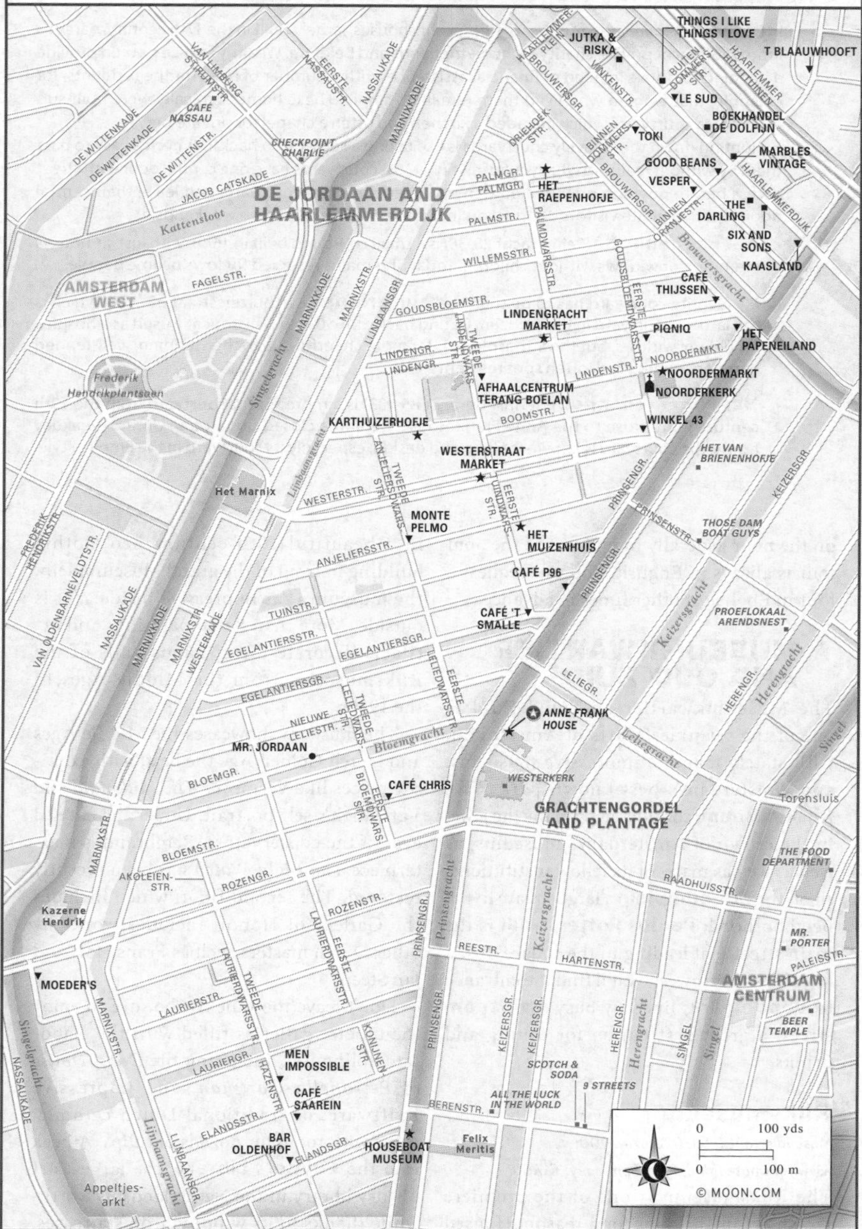

Hofjes of De Jordaan

In De Jordaan, there are a number of former almshouses, largely built in the 17th century, part of a long tradition of private charity in the Netherlands and Belgium. Wealthy families would provide a building for those in need of financial assistance, with a number of rules for the residents, for example, that women who lived there remained single. These homes typically were built surrounding a courtyard, which included a kitchen and often a chapel for private prayer.

Hunting down these lovely courtyards is like taking a secret step back in time; it's easy to pass them by without realizing what you're missing. Most courtyards have one central door with street access before opening up into a garden or shared common courtyard, and leave their central doors open to polite visitors during working hours (9am-5pm) and on weekends.

- **Het Raepenhofje** (Palmgracht 28-38) is a small courtyard built in 1648, with just six houses intended for widows without children. Today, it remains reserved for low-income people.
- My favorite courtyard has to be the **Karthuizerhofje** (Karthuizersstraat 89–171), which is the largest courtyard in the Jordaan. Dating back to 1650, it was historically used as a hospice for elderly widows, but the atmosphere is far more cheerful due to the stunning, well-tended gardens, where you'll often spot residents' cats.
- **Het van Brienenhofje** (Prinsengracht 85-133) is a more recent courtyard from the 19th century fairly close to the Anne Frank House. Behind a closed door, open during weekday hours, the courtyard is known for its grand design, especially its courtyard in the Empire style.

on the hour generally in Dutch, but the 3pm tour is always in English. You can request a tour in English at other times in advance.

★ MUSEUMKWARTIER AND OUD ZUID

The Museumkwartier and Oud Zuid is one of the swankiest parts of Amsterdam, with stately manors, impressive musuems, and Amsterdam's best-known park. **The Rijksmuseum,** considered by many the jewel in the crown of Amsterdam's museums, as well as well as many of its fellow institutions, sit on the **Museumplein** a large square in the neighborhood; **Paulus Potterstraat** is the main street that leading to the square. Just a few blocks northwest, you'll find the entrance to **Vondelpark,** lined by busy **Overtoom** street, a great destination for dining and drinks.

Rijksmuseum

Museumstraat 1; tel. 020 674 7000; www.rijksmuseum.nl; 9am-5pm daily; €17.50

The Rijksmuseum is one of the premiere Dutch art institutions for a reason. Housed in a beautiful 19th-century neo-Gothic building in front of the grand Museumplein, the museum is as impressive inside as it is outside. More than 8,000 paintings and artifacts decorate the spacious halls of the Rijksmuseum, from the Middle Ages to the 1950s.

The museum showcases the Middle Ages and Dutch Golden Age the best, with exquisite pieces like Vermeer's *The Milkmaid* and Van Gogh's self-portrait. Under the careful eyes of the conservators, Rembrandt's masterpiece *The Night Watch* has been recently restored. The second floor, which includes the Gallery of Honor, includes works by other Dutch masters such as Frans Hals and Jan Steen.

Don't leave too quickly; be sure to enjoy the quieter galleries filled with the elaborate dollhouses, including the *Dolls' House of Petronella Oortman,* and impressive Delftware, or traditional Dutch ceramic, vases with room for dozens of tulips. A peek into the **Cuypers Library,** the largest art history library in the Netherlands, is worthwhile thanks to its winding iron staircases,

Amsterdam West

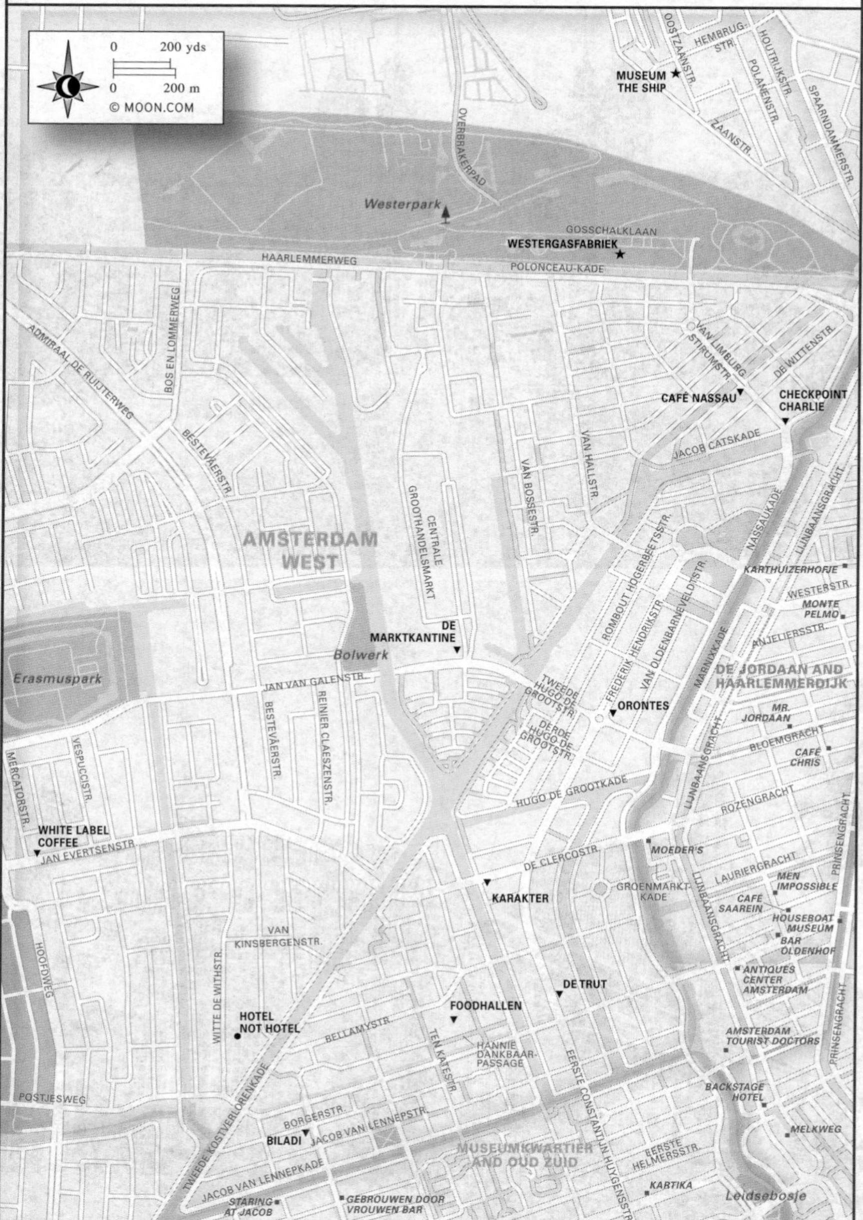

1

2

Western Islands

The Western Islands of Amsterdam (**Prinseneiland, Bickerseiland,** and **Realeneiland**) are undiscovered gems that many tourists and even Amsterdammers don't know about, as entering the islands requires passing underneath the train tracks that run toward Amsterdam Central Train Station.

Western Islands

HISTORY

After the Port of Amsterdam was created in 1615, these three human-made islands were created to help stabilize the loose peat at the bottom of the IJ river. Their proximity to the water brought many shipbuilders to the area; some of the houses on Zandhoek are still emblazoned with symbols of the shipping past. Many of the three-story 17th-century warehouses, once used to store goods for shops, have been converted into homes and artist studios.

SIGHTS AND ACTIVITIES

The charm of the Western Islands is in the quieter streets and the beautiful white 17th-century bridge, the **Drieharingenbrug,** that connects Prinseneiland with Realeneiland. There is also children's petting zoo along the canal with goats, rabbits, and sheep called **De Dierencapel** (Bickersgracht 207; www.dedierencapel.nl; 9am-5pm Tues.-Sun.; free, donation-based). It's hard to remember that the Western Islands are so close to the rest of Centrum, but the quietness of the neighborhood makes it the perfect spot for a sunset stroll.

GETTING THERE

The Western Islands are about 1.8 kilometers (1.1 miles) or a 20-minute walk from Dam Square. After following the signs toward Amsterdam Central Train Station, make a left onto Haarlemmerdijk. Make a right onto Grote Bickersstraat to cross onto the Western Islands.

countless books, and dark wooden bookshelves. Many also enjoy the miniature ships on the first floor.

The museum has many amenities, including baggage storage, and its many working elevators are remarkably friendly for people with disabilities. It's particularly crowded on weekend afternoons, but if you opt for a weekday visit closer to closing, you'll have the museum mostly to yourself. The Rijksmuseum can feel a bit overwhelming because of its many exhibition rooms; if you have limited time, pick up a map and decide what pieces interest you.

1: Rijksmuseum 2: Museum The Ship

Moco Museum

Honthorststraat 20; tel. 020 370 1997; https://mocomuseum.com; 9am-7pm Mon.-Thurs., 9am-8pm Fri.-Sun.; adults €18.50, youth 13-17 €15.50, children 0-12 free

Moco is Amsterdam's newest art museum, set in a beautiful 1904 villa designed by Pierre Cuypers, the designer of the Rijksmuseum, and dedicated to "new" art that challenges and entertains. Featuring artists such as Banksy in its modern collection and interactive exhibitions where visitors are allowed to take photos, the permanent collection includes favorites from Salvador Dalí, Jeff Koons, Keith Haring, Yayoi Kusama, Roy Lichtenstein, and Damien Hirst. There is also a garden inspired by *Alice in Wonderland*. Book online for a discount.

Museumkwartier and Oud Zuid

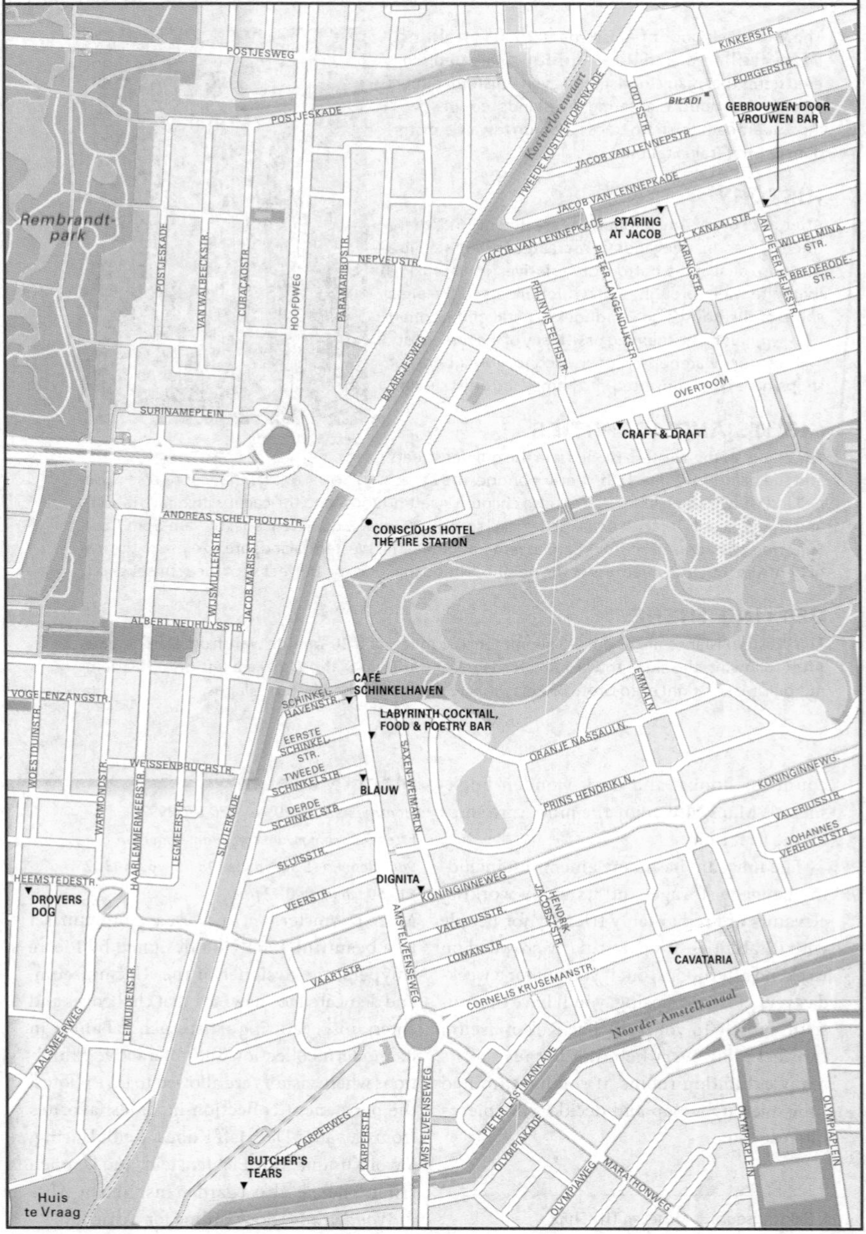

Rembrandt-park
BILADI
GEBROUWEN DOOR VROUWEN BAR
STARING AT JACOB
CRAFT & DRAFT
CONSCIOUS HOTEL THE TIRE STATION
CAFÉ SCHINKELHAVEN
LABYRINTH COCKTAIL, FOOD & POETRY BAR
BLAUW
DIGNITA
DROVERS DOG
CAVATARIA
BUTCHER'S TEARS
Huis te Vraag
Kostverlorenvaart
Noorder Amstelkanaal
POSTJESWEG
POSTJESKADE
KINKERSTR.
BORGERSTR.
LOOTSSTR.
TWEEDE KOSTVERLORENKADE
JACOB VAN LENNEPSTR.
JACOB VAN LENNEPKADE
KANAALSTR.
JAN PIETER HEIJESTR.
WILHELMINA-STR.
BREDERODE-STR.
STARINGSTR.
PIETER LANGENDIJKSTR.
RHIJNVIS FEITHSTR.
NEPVEUSTR.
POSTJESKADE
VAN WALBEECKSTR.
CURAÇAOSTR.
HOOFDWEG
PARAMARIBOSTR.
BAARSJESWEG
OVERTOOM
SURINAMEPLEIN
ANDREAS SCHELFHOUTSTR.
WIJSMULLERSTR.
JACOB MARISSTR.
ALBERT NEUHUYSSTR.
VOGELENZANGSTR.
SCHINKELHAVENSTR.
EERSTE SCHINKELSTR.
TWEEDE SCHINKELSTR.
DERDE SCHINKELSTR.
SAXEN-WEIMARLN.
EMMALN.
ORANJE NASSAULN.
KONINGINNEWEG
PRINS HENDRIKLN.
VALERIUSSTR.
JOHANNES VERHULSTSTR.
WOESTDUINSTR.
WEISSENBRUCHSTR.
WARMONDSTR.
HAARLEMMERMEERSTR.
LEGMEERSTR.
SLOTERKADE
SLUISSTR.
HEEMSTEDESTR.
VEERSTR.
AMSTELVEENSEWEG
JACOBSZSTR.
HENDRIK
LOMANSTR.
VAARTSTR.
CORNELIS KRUSEMANSTR.
LEIMUIDENSTR.
AALSMEERWEG
KARPERWEG
KARPERSTR.
PIETER LASTMANKADE
OLYMPIAKADE
OLYMPIAWEG
MARATHONWEG
OLYMPIAPLEIN

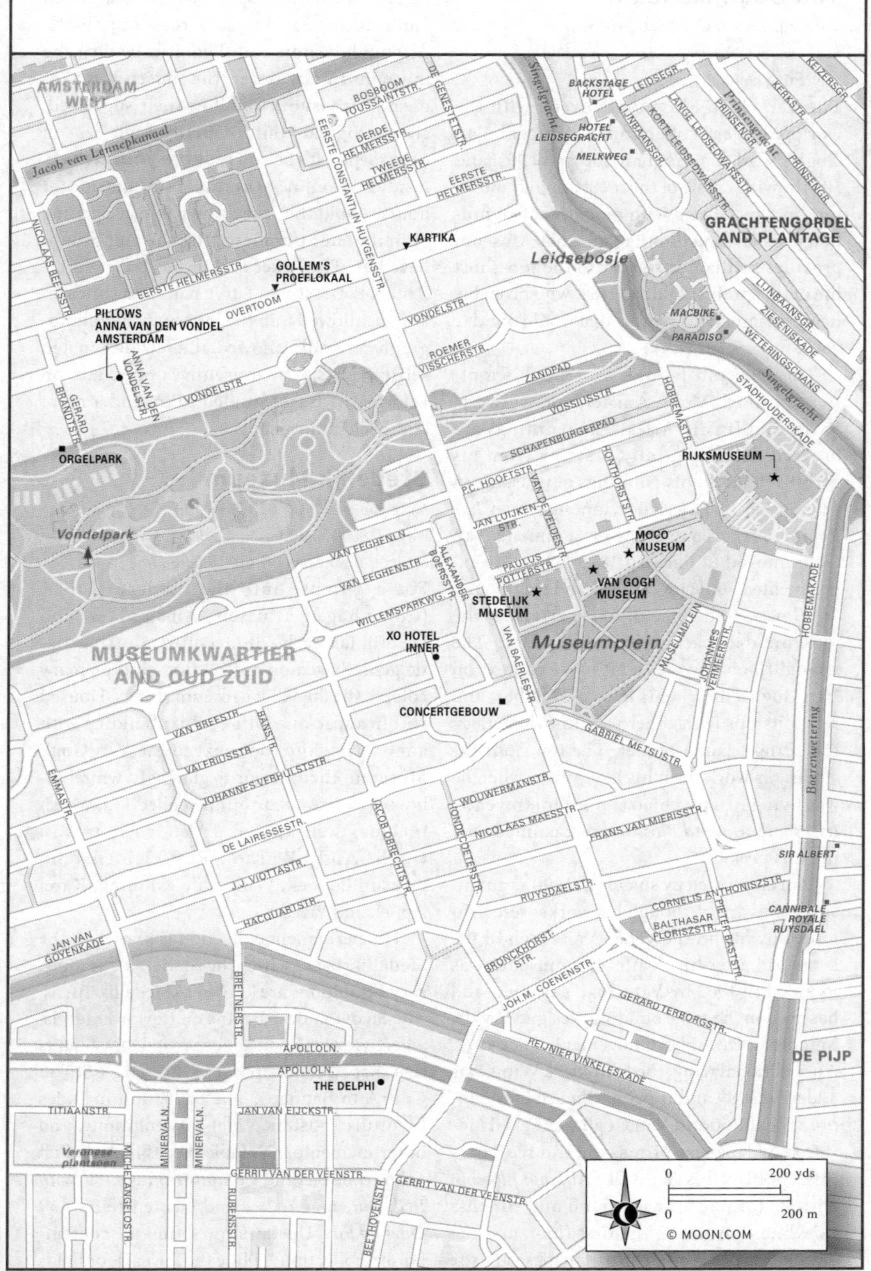
AMSTERDAM WEST
Jacob van Lennepkanaal
BOSBOOM TOUSSAINTSTR.
DERDE HELMERSSTR.
TWEEDE HELMERSSTR.
EERSTE HELMERSSTR.
DE GENESTETSTR.
EERSTE CONSTANTIJN HUYGENSSTR.
Singelgracht
BACKSTAGE HOTEL
HOTEL LEIDSEGRACHT
MELKWEG
LEIDSEGR.
LIJNBAANSGR.
KORTE LEIDSEDWARSSTR.
LANGE LEIDSEDWARSSTR.
PRINSENGR.
Prinsengracht
KERKSTR.
KEIZERSGR.
GRACHTENGORDEL AND PLANTAGE
NICOLAAS BEETSSTR.
KARTIKA
GOLLEM'S PROEFLOKAAL
Leidsebosje
OVERTOOM
PILLOWS ANNA VAN DEN VONDEL AMSTERDAM
ANNA VAN DEN VONDELSTR.
VONDELSTR.
ROEMER VISSCHERSTR.
ZANDPAD
MACBIKE
PARADISO
LIJNBAANSGR.
ZIESENISKADE
WETERINGSCHANS
STADHOUDERSKADE
GERARD BRANDTSTR.
VOSSIUSSTR.
HOBBEMASTR.
SCHAPENBURGERPAD
ORGELPARK
P.C. HOOFTSTR.
HONTHORSTSTR.
RIJKSMUSEUM
VAN DE VELDESTR.
JAN LUIJKENSTR.
Vondelpark
MOCO MUSEUM
VAN EEGHENLN.
VAN EEGHENSTR.
ALEXANDER BOERSSTR.
PAULUS POTTERSTR.
VAN GOGH MUSEUM
STEDELIJK MUSEUM
WILLEMSPARKWG.
XO HOTEL INNER
MUSEUMKWARTIER AND OUD ZUID
Museumplein
MUSEUMPLEIN
JOHANNES VERMEERSTR.
HOBBEMAKADE
VAN BAERLESTR.
CONCERTGEBOUW
VAN BREESTR.
BANSTR.
GABRIEL METSUSTR.
Boerenwetering
VALERIUSSTR.
JOHANNES VERHULSTSTR.
EMMASTR.
WOUWERMANSTR.
HONDECOETERSTR.
JACOB OBRECHTSTR.
DE LAIRESSESTR.
NICOLAAS MAESSTR.
FRANS VAN MIERISSTR.
SIR ALBERT
J.J. VIOTTASTR.
RUYSDAELSTR.
CORNELIS ANTHONISZSTR.
HACQUARTSTR.
BALTHASAR FLORISZSTR.
PIETER BASTSTR.
CANNIBALE ROYALE RUYSDAEL
JAN VAN GOYENKADE
BRONCKHORSTSTR.
BREITNERSTR.
JOH.M. COENENSTR.
GERARD TERBORGSTR.
REIJNIER VINKELESKADE
APOLLOLN.
APOLLOLN.
DE PIJP
THE DELPHI
TITIAANSTR.
JAN VAN EIJCKSTR.
MINERVALN.
MINERVALN.
Veronese-plantsoen
MICHELANGELOSTR.
GERRIT VAN DER VEENSTR.
GERRIT VAN DER VEENSTR.
RUBENSSTR.
BEETHOVENSTR.
0
200 yds
0
200 m
© MOON.COM

Van Gogh Museum

Museumplein 6; tel. 020 570 5200; www.vangoghmuseum.nl; 9am-6pm daily; adults €19, children free

The Van Gogh Museum delivers, with the world's largest collection of Vincent Van Gogh's works: more than 200 paintings and 500 drawings. One of the most popular museums in Amsterdam with more than two million visitors annually, the Van Gogh Museum provides brilliant insight into the too-short life of this prolific Dutch artist, who probably never imagined the crowds that would one day come to view his work.

The museum follows Van Gogh's footsteps, through Mons, Amsterdam, Antwerp, Paris, and finally Arles. The paintings are ordered chronologically, starting from his early sketches to his paintings of peasants in the southern Netherlands, among which *The Potato Eaters* is one of the most famous. Van Gogh moved to Paris in 1886, where he experimented with new subjects and techniques. *Sunflowers* and some of his portraits at the museum date back to his Paris period. The second floor provides a bit more context on Van Gogh's life via his letters, sketches, and relationships with other well-known artists, including Claude Monet. The top floor includes his work from his later years, when he was living in a psychiatric ward in Provence; *Irises* and *Almond Blossom* were painted during this period.

Van Gogh died by suicide in 1890 as an unsuccessful artist, though his works were promoted by his brother Theo Van Gogh in the art world after his death. The museum was founded in 1962 by Van Gogh's nephew and has been in the same building, designed by the founder of De Stijl art movement, since 1973. An additional wing, the Kurokawa Wing, was added in 1999 and is primarily used for temporary exhibitions. Van Gogh was heavily inspired by Japanese prints; you can see works influenced by this genre, like *Almond Blossom* with its turquoise background and simplistic white flowers, on the first floor, and the Kurokawa Wing often hosts Japanese artists.

The museum is spacious, with artwork and information spread across four floors. Although visitors can theoretically visit the museum in any order, the museum makes it easy for visitors to follow their suggested, chronological route. During high season (Apr.-Sept.), it's best to **reserve your tickets** in advance online to avoid waiting outside for hours. Avoid the crowds by going at opening or in the late afternoon, after the tour groups have left. The ticket desk is located right off Paulus Potterstraat. Large bags and suitcases are not allowed into the museum, and photographs are only allowed at a few designated selfie points. The museum is open late on Fridays, with free guided tours and a more laid-back atmosphere.

Stedelijk Museum

Museumplein 10; tel. 020 573 2911; www.stedelijk.nl; 10am-6pm daily; adults €18.50, students €10, children free

For a glimpse into the modern CoBrA (Copenhagen, Brussels, Amsterdam) and De Stijl (an early-20th century Dutch artistic genre based on abstraction, and primary colors), the Stedelijk Museum shines. Housed within a spacious 19th-century building with a modern white roof next to the Van Gogh Museum, the interior is glaringly white, allowing you to focus on the collection, which includes well-known artists such as Van Gogh, Andy Warhol, Roy Lichtenstein, Jackson Pollock, Willem de Kooning, Karel Appel, and Picasso.

The permanent collection is known as the Stedelijk Base, while the Stedelijk's temporary exhibitions are known as Stedelijk Turns. The Stedelijk Base begins on the lower levels, where viewers learn about pivotal movements that shaped contemporary art, from De Stijl to CoBrA to Bauhaus. The collection includes furniture, posters, videos, typography, and other mementos. Notable pieces include Piet Mondrian's iconic *Composition No. IV with Red, Blue and Yellow* and Lichtenstein's *As I Opened Fire*. Upstairs you'll find the contemporary collections, while the lower floor holds

The Most Beautiful Sunset Spots in Amsterdam

sunset over Amstel River

With ample canals and well-preserved 17th-century architecture, Amsterdam has many lovely places to enjoy a picturesque sunset. Though the city is famous for its rainy weather, the clouds create a beautiful sunset if the cloud coverage is under 90 percent and it's not raining.

- Of course, you can take a cruise or find a nice place along a canal, such as **Herengracht** or **Brouwersgracht,** to enjoy the sunset.
- For an iconic photo of Amsterdam, head to a bench at the famous photo spot **7 Bridges** (Keizersgracht 661) at sunset for a glimpse of Amsterdam's canals in every direction. Though you can't see all these bridges lined up if you're on foot, it is possible to see them from a canal boat on the water, stopping at the intersection of Keizersgracht and Reguliersgracht!
- You can also do like an Amsterdammer and find a nice terrace along a canal, such as the one at **Café P96** (page 109) to sit at.
- In summer, any spot along the **Amstel River** is always lovely.
- On the other side of the IJ river, **Pllek** (page 104) is a favorite for sunset with a drink in hand from its rocky spot along the river.

temporary exhibitions that often include big names in the art world, from Matisse to Keith Haring to Surinamese artists.

As early as 1905, the Stedelijk Museum proudly promoted Van Gogh's artwork shortly after his death—the curators have always had a sharp eye for upcoming artists and have nurtured artists such as Nam June Paik. There is an audio tour available for those interested in more information about the pieces and the movements that influenced them. The museum is accessible to people with disabilities.

DE PIJP

Heineken Experience

Stadhouderskade 78; tel. 020 721 5300; www.heineken.com/heineken-experience; 12:30pm-7:30pm daily; adults €18

The Heineken Experience is one of Amsterdam's most popular attractions; it's

De Pijp

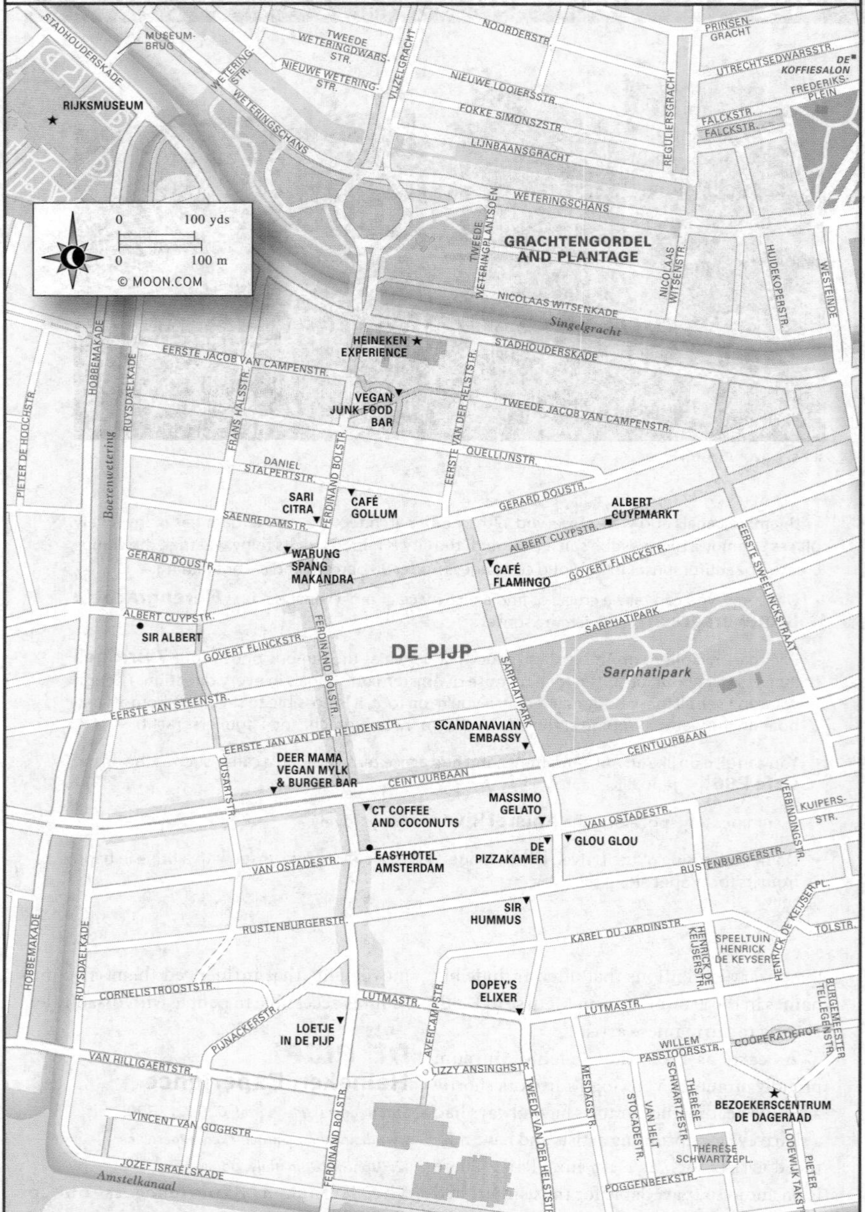

DE PIJP

GRACHTENGORDEL AND PLANTAGE

RIJKSMUSEUM

HEINEKEN EXPERIENCE

VEGAN JUNK FOOD BAR

SARI CITRA

CAFÉ GOLLUM

ALBERT CUYPMARKT

WARUNG SPANG MAKANDRA

CAFÉ FLAMINGO

SIR ALBERT

SCANDANAVIAN EMBASSY

DEER MAMA VEGAN MYLK & BURGER BAR

CT COFFEE AND COCONUTS

MASSIMO GELATO

GLOU GLOU

DE PIZZAKAMER

EASYHOTEL AMSTERDAM

SIR HUMMUS

DOPEY'S ELIXER

LOETJE IN DE PIJP

SPEELTUIN HENRICK DE KEYSER

BEZOEKERSCENTRUM DE DAGERAAD

DE KOFFIESALON

Sarphatipark

Singelgracht

Boerenwetering

Amstelkanaal

STADHOUDERSKADE, MUSEUMBRUG, WETERING STR., WETERINGSCHANS, TWEEDE WETERINGDWARSSTR., NIEUWE WETERING STR., VIJZELGRACHT, NOORDERSTR., NIEUWE LOOIERSSTR., FOKKE SIMONSZSTR., LIJNBAANSGRACHT, REGULIERSGRACHT, PRINSENGRACHT, UTRECHTSEDWARSSTR., FREDERIKSPLEIN, FALCKSTR., TWEEDE WETERINGPLANTSOEN, NICOLAAS WITSENSTR., HUIDEKOPERSTR., WESTEINDE, NICOLAAS WITSENKADE, EERSTE JACOB VAN CAMPENSTR., TWEEDE JACOB VAN CAMPENSTR., HOBBEMAKADE, RUYSDAELKADE, PIETER DE HOOCHSTR., FRANS HALSSTR., FERDINAND BOLSTR., EERSTE VAN DER HELSTSTR., QUELLIJNSTR., DANIEL STALPERTSTR., GERARD DOUSTR., SAENREDAMSTR., ALBERT CUYPSTR., GOVERT FLINCKSTR., EERSTE SWEELINCKSTRAAT, SARPHATIPARK, EERSTE JAN STEENSTR., EERSTE JAN VAN DER HEIJDENSTR., CEINTUURBAAN, DUSARTSTR., VAN OSTADESTR., VERBINDINGSTR., KUIPERSSTR., RUSTENBURGERSTR., HENRICK DE KEIJSERPL., TOLSTR., KAREL DU JARDINSTR., HENRICK DE KEIJSERSTR., CORNELIS TROOSTSTR., LUTMASTR., AVERCAMPSTR., BURGEMEESTER TELLEGENSTR., COOPERATIEHOF, WILLEM PASSTOORSSTR., PIJNACKERSTR., VAN HILLIGAERTSTR., LIZZY ANSINGHSTR., MESDAGSTR., STOCADESTR., VAN HELT, THÉRÈSE SCHWARTZESTR., THÉRÈSE SCHWARTZEPL., TWEEDE VAN DER HELSTSTR., LODEWIJK TAKSTR., PIETER, VINCENT VAN GOGHSTR., JOZEF ISRAËLSKADE, POGGENBEEKSTR.

0 100 yds

0 100 m

certainly true that Heineken tastes much better from the source. In the first Heineken brewery, the Experience teaches visitors about the history of Heineken, and beer in general, over the past 150 years. After your tour, you'll be invited to enjoy a cold Heineken that you pour yourself. If you're a fan of Heineken, it is a fun stop, but if you're more interested in having drinks, you can opt for beer at a nearby café for a fraction of the price.

Bezoekerscentrum de Dageraad

Burgemeester Tellegenstraat 128; tel. 020 686 8595; www.hetschip.nl/over-het-museum/locaties/de-dageraad; 1-5pm Thurs.-Sun.; adults €9.50, students €7

De Dageraad is a must-see for lovers of the Amsterdam School of architecture. Known as the most beautiful social housing project in the Netherlands, the complex with bricks and roof tiles was built by a socialist housing association to ensure that shopworkers had access to comfortable homes. First built as six separate buildings, the building fits together perfectly with curved edges. A guided tour offers a peek into the intricacies of the building, and a larger tour of the neighborhood is included if you opt for the walking tour.

AMSTERDAM OOST

National Maritime Museum (Het Scheepvaartmuseum)

Kattenburgerplein 1; tel. 020 523 2222; www.hetscheepvaartmuseum.nl; 10am-5pm daily; adults €16.50, youth 4-17 €8, children 0-3 free

The Dutch National Maritime Museum is a great family-friendly pick, with its large historical collection and interactive exhibits. The main gallery tells the story of the Netherlands' seafaring past, with a large collection of historic maps, navigational instruments, and ship decorations—surprisingly thought-provoking thanks to the well-written explanations for each item. Outside is the impressive golden Royal Barge used by the Dutch royal family on special occasions, and a full-size replica of a 1749 VOC (Dutch East India Company) ship that was lost at sea, with interactive exhibitions that give visitors insight into what life on the sea was really like; part of the ship is accessible for people with disabilities. The museum is rarely too crowded compared to other museums, and it has a cloakroom for larger bags.

Tropenmuseum

Linnaeusstraat 2; tel. 088 004 2800; www.tropenmuseum.nl; 10am-5pm Tues.-Sun.; adults €16, youth 4-18 €8, students €10, children 0-3 free

The Tropenmuseum began as part of the Dutch Colonial Institute for showcasing objects from Indonesia and other Dutch colonies at the time. This large museum spent considerable resources studying Indonesian society as a means of increasing profits from their colonies. In 1926, the spacious building along Linnaeusstraat was opened to the public to showcase its nearly 30,000 objects. Following Indonesian independence in 1945, the museum has expanded its collection to cover a wider swath of the world beyond Indonesia, including collections from Africa, South America, and Asia.

Compared to similar museums, its curators have worked hard to confront its colonial past while showcasing the richness of contemporary art from societies around the world, by featuring upcoming artists from the cultures historically colonized by the Netherlands. Their temporary exhibitions—such as *What a Genderful World*—are particularly impressive in their depiction of complex cultural issues in a nuanced way, and their core collection of masks, sculptures, furniture, and many other pieces of artwork is worth a visit if you're interested in Indonesian history and culture. There is a wing built specifically for kids called the Tropenmuseum Junior, which includes interactive exhibitions. No photos are allowed.

Amsterdam Oost

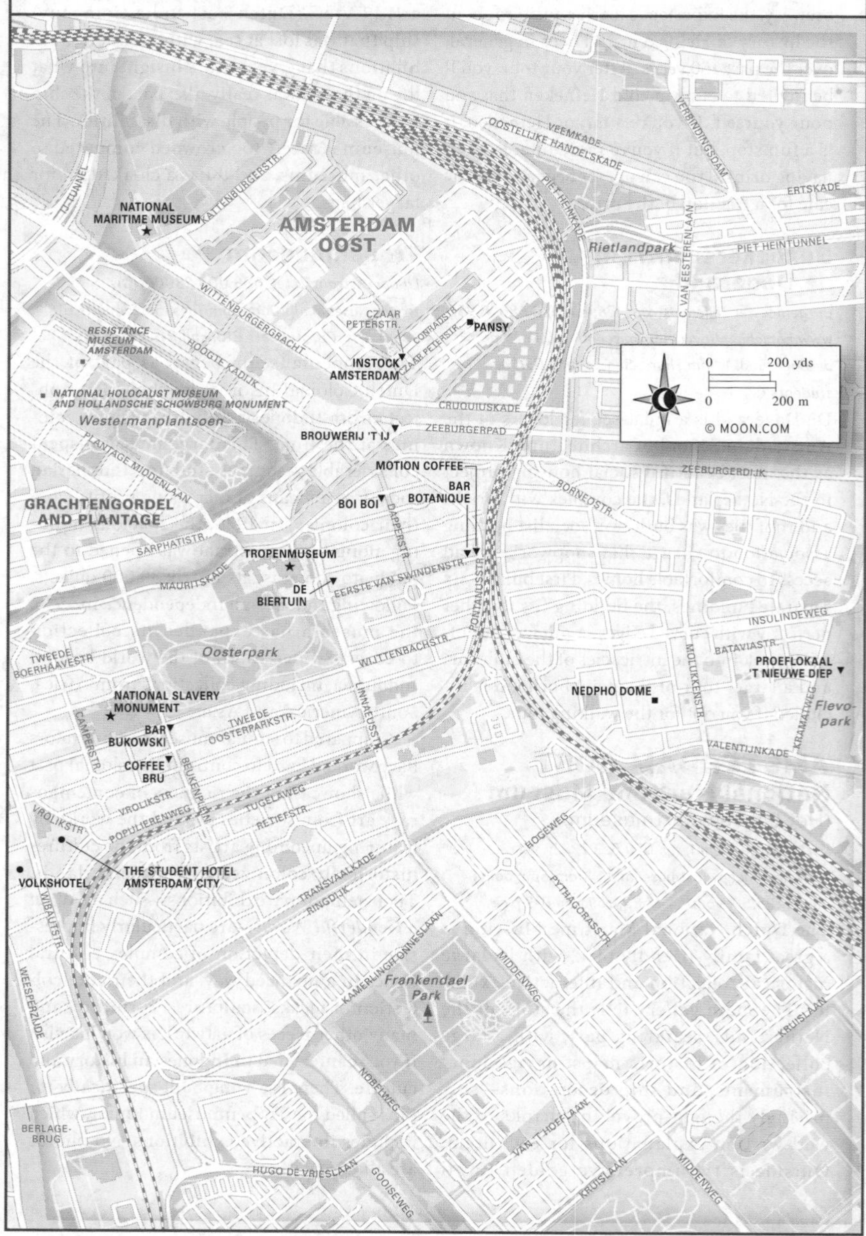

Sports and Recreation

PARKS

Amsterdam West

WESTERPARK

open 24/7

Not as well known as Vondelpark, Westerpark is still a popular spot for picnics and a wander outside central Amsterdam. Once polluted by factories in Amsterdam West, the park was first conceptualized in the 1800s, but it was only in the 1980s that the park was cleaned and renovated to make it friendlier to visitors. Westerpark is larger than many realize, at 5.6 hectares (14 acres), and in summer, people sit along the banks of the many ponds enjoying good weather. Along the park's southern border, former factory buildings have been repurposed into restaurants, bars, shops, and event venues, known as **Westergasfabriek** (Pazzanistraat 37; tel. 020 586 0710; https://westergas.nl; 8am-8pm daily), which also has a lively **Sunday market** and the park is a favorite location for outdoor festivals, including **Rolling Kitchens.**

Museumkwartier and Oud Zuid

VONDELPARK

open 24/7

Vondelpark is as iconic to Amsterdam as Hyde Park is to London. More than 10 million people visit this lush 47-hectare (116-acre) green space yearly, to roller-skate, bike, walk, exercise, or just sit and picnic with friends in the grass. Two kilometers (1 mile) long, with a 2-kilometer (1-mile) car-free asphalt path for bikers and walkers, the park is also home to several smaller pedestrian-only paths that loop around the lakes.

Vondelpark was created in 1865 by a group of citizens who wanted a park for members of their association (and others, with a fee). First called "The New Park," the park's name changed after a statue of Dutch writer Joost van den Vondel was displayed here—it still stands in a quieter section of the park. On the southern side of the park, you'll find an original sculpture by Pablo Picasso.

Built in the English garden style, with small ponds, tree-lined lawns, and bridges to stroll along, the park is full of picturesque, watery landscapes; you can also admire a landscape closer to Amsterdam's original grassy swamp beyond the fence closer to the west end of the park, near Amstelveenseweg.

From June to August, there are free open-air concerts at the **Vondel Openluchttheater** (www.openluchttheater.nl), and on **King's Day,** Vondelpark is filled with performances and markets. The main entrances to Vondelpark are along Stadhouderskade and Amstelveenseweg.

Amsterdam Oost

FRANKENDAEL PARK

Middenweg 72; sunrise-sunset

This fairly small park (3 hectares/7 acres) is a very charming spot away from the crowds in Amsterdam Oost. Originally intended as an escape from the bustle of the city, the Frankendael estate is one of the only remaining houses of more than 40 that were built in what was formerly countryside. The impressive 17th-century **manor** (Middenweg 72; tel. 020 423 3930; https://huizefrankendael.nl; noon-5pm Sun. or by appointment; free) is mainly used for events and as a restaurant, although an hour-long **tour** (in Dutch, also free) is held each Sunday starting at noon. Until 1930 the estate was private; the nursery was converted into a park in the late 1990s. It's literally a breath of fresh air, with picturesque stone paths lined with flowers, tree-lined canals, and an impressive brick gate that feels like it's straight out of *Pride and Prejudice.* The manor's restaurant, **Restaurant Merkelbach** (Middenweg 72; tel. 020 665 0880; www.restaurantmerkelbach.nl; 8:30am-6pm daily; €12), is part of the slow-food movement.

1

2

3

Amsterdam Outskirts

AMSTERDAM FOREST (Amsterdamse Bos)

open 24/7

Farther outside Amsterdam's city center (10 kilometers/6 miles, about 1 hour by public transit, 40 minutes by bike), you'll find the Amsterdam Forest, an impressive park three times the size of Central Park. Created by a botanist with the idea of creating a green place for Amsterdammers to escape the city without going too far, the park was built during the Great Depression with more than 20,000 employees planting numerous trees. It features several large ponds, playgrounds, picturesque streams, and rolling meadows intended for picnics, and there is also a goat farm, **Goatfarm Ridammerhoeve** (Nieuwe Meerlaan 4; www.geitenboerderij.nl; 10am-5pm Mon. and Wed.-Sun.) in the middle of the park that serves up goat milk ice cream. A section of the park with 400 cherry trees was gifted by the Japan Women's Club to honor the friendship between the Netherlands and Japan; the trees bloom between March and April, a favorite time among photographers and families. Like Amsterdam Noord, this is another great place to see a polder landscape; people also love biking through the Amsterdamse Bos in order to find the hairy Highland cattle that live in the forest.

It's easiest to get here by **bike,** a 40-minute (9.9-kilometer/6.1-mile) ride. To get here by public transit, take **Bus N47** to Amstelveen bus station, a 25-minute ride. From here, it's about a 20-minute (1.7-kilometer/1-mile) walk to the edge of Amsterdamse Bos.

CYCLING

Cycling in Amsterdam sounds much dreamier than it is, but it is one of the best ways to see Amsterdam if you dare. There are more than 400 kilometers (250 miles) of bike paths around Amsterdam, and it's often faster to bike than walk or take public transit. That said, biking in Amsterdam is not for the fainthearted. It is truly city biking: bikers can be outright aggressive—and impatient. If you're an inexperienced biker, it's best to take a biking tour first to learn the rules. Many bike rental locations are also happy to lecture you on the basics. The outer neighborhoods (**Amsterdam West, Amsterdam Oost,** and **Amsterdam Noord**) away from tourist attractions tend to be the best places to bike.

1: Westerpark 2: cycling in Vondelpark
3: Amsterdam Noord Ferry

Bike Paths and Routes

HIGHLIGHTS OF AMSTERDAM

Cycling Distance: *10.6 kilometers (6.5 miles) round-trip*
Cycling Time: *1-2 hours round-trip*
Trailhead: *Anne Frank House*
Information and Maps: *https://goo.gl/maps/h2fjU3ji9mjTp6y8A*

This route is intended to help first-time tourists see some of the highlights of Amsterdam by bike. It skips over some parts of the city center, but is still best biked closer to sunset on quieter evenings out of peak season, when you don't have to worry as much about breaking for pedestrians. Start off at the **Anne Frank House** and cross the bridge over **Prinsengracht** toward Rozengracht. You'll bike through the heart of the Jordaan, crossing over two bridges. Make a left onto Nassaukade and continue along the bike path for 1.3 kilometers (0.8 miles). You'll see signs for **Vondelpark** and make a right into the park via its grand gate. Cycle around Vondelpark in a 1-kilometer (0.6-mile) loop for a kilometer before returning to the entrance.

Make a right onto Stadhouderskade and continue for 350 meters (1,100 feet). Once you see the **Rijksmuseum,** make a left and right underneath the museum via the tunnel. You'll see the vast **Museumplein.** Once you're done, return to the bike path infront of the Rijksmuseum on Stadhouderskade. Cross over the canal and continue for 450 meters (1,500 feet) before making a right onto Ferdninand Bolstraat. (If the **Albert Cuypmarkt** is going

Cycling Safety

Though cycling in Amsterdam isn't for the faint of heart, there are a few rules of the road that can make your experience safer and more pleasant.

- In the Red Light District and close to Amsterdam Central Train Station, biking can be particularly difficult given the number of tourists who cross the street without looking, which can be a recipe for disaster. Be sure to **use your bell** to notify pedestrians who walk into the bike lane of your presence.
- **Helmets** are not required for bikers, but you can rent a helmet for yourself or children at bike rentals.
- Bikers are supposed to **stay in the right lane** of the road, which is often a red paved path that is one-directional. A bicycle image should appear in the same direction as your bike. If the image appears upside-down, you're going the wrong way! On smaller streets, bikes must stay to the right, even if there's not a bike path. Be cautious of cars or trucks opening their doors onto the bike lane.
- If you see a **sign with a red circle and a bicycle** in the center, this means that bikes are not allowed on the street/square. There is a fine for biking on the sidewalk and in pedestrian zones.
- **Illegal bike actions** include using your phone while biking, failing to stop at a pedestrian crossing, going through a bike light while it's red, biking while intoxicated or stoned, and not using bike lights at night.
- Other important rules include cycling single file if biking with a group, **allowing others to pass you on the left,** and **signaling that you are turning** by holding your arm straight out in the direction of your turn.
- If you intend to pull over, be sure to **hold out your arm to indicate to you will be stopping.** Do not stop randomly without signaling, as this is how bike accidents happen.
- Amsterdam cyclists tend to be aggressive and short-fused, especially with tourist bikers. Don't take this personally, and if possible, **don't bike close to rush hour** (8am-9am, 4pm-7pm) to avoid bikers in the biggest rush.

If you get into a bike accident, **exchange information with the cyclist or pedestrian** as you would in a car accident. It would be best to notify your bike rental as damage might not be covered depending on whether it's your fault.

on, you'll need to dismount to walk down the street.)

Cycle 350 meters (1,100 feet) toward the **Heineken Experience** before crossing over the water. At the roundabout, you'll take the second right onto Weteringschans. Continue for almost 1 kilometer (0.6 miles) until you cross the **Amstel River.** On the other side of the bridge, you'll make a left onto Amstel to head North and cross over another bridge and make a left onto the Blauwbrug. Keep right after the bridge to continue along the Amstel. After 350 meters (1,100 feet), you'll turn left at Halvemaansteeg before making an immediately right at **Rembrandtplein,** a busy nightlife square, onto Reguliersdwarsstraat. After 500 meters (1,600 feet), you have the option of walking one street over to see the **Flower Market,** but biking is not allowed on this street. At **Koningsplein,** make a left and cotninue on the bike path over Heregracht canal and turn right. After 100 meters (300 feet), you'll see Huidenstraat, which is one of the **9 Streets.** Make a right at Keizersgracht before ending behind the Anne Frank House.

TOP EXPERIENCE

★ AMSTERDAM NOORD CYCLING ROUTE

Cycling Distance: *20.3 kilometers (12.6 miles) round-trip*
Cycling Time: *1-2 hours round-trip*
Trailhead: *Pontplein (reachable via the Amsterdam Noord IJplein Ferry from behind Amsterdam Central Train Station, on the southwest tip of Amsterdam Noord facing Centrum)*

This scenic cycling route is a far more relaxing experience than biking through the city center. It passes through a few former villages that are now part of Amsterdam, with plenty of opportunities to stop and admire an open polder landscape that feels miles from Amsterdam. Staying on the path is easy: Just follow signs toward the charming villages along the bike route, which include (in order) Nieuwendam, Schellingwoude, Durgerdam, Ransdorp, and Zunderdorp. On the way back, look for the sign for the Amsterdam Centrum ferry stop.

Start off your bike ride at **Pontplein,** which you can reach with your bike via the free **Amsterdam Noord Ferry** from Amsterdam Central Train Station to IJPlein (10 minutes, free). You'll follow a road called Meeuwenlaan north until you turn right onto Nieuwendammerdijk, which takes you through the most picturesque part of the former village of **Nieuwendam.** After this, you'll notice many of the roads lead toward their eponymous villages: Schellingwouderdijk leads to **Schellingwoude;** this road turns into Durgerdammerdijk, which leads to **Durgerdam;** after Durgerdam, you'll make a left onto Durgerdammergouw, which leads to **Ransdorp,** where you'll make a left onto Nieuwe Gouw to cycle west toward **Zunderdorp.** Once you reach Zunderdorp, make a left onto Zunderdorpergouw, and continue heading south until this street turns into Beemsterstraat. Make a left onto Nieuwendammerdijk to head back toward the ferry via Meeuwenlaan, the way that you came. If you want to stop off on the way back, you can turn left onto Motorkade to **Oedipus Brewing** (www.oedipus.com), a trendy Dutch microbrewery that produces some of the most delicious craft beers in Amsterdam. They have a nice tasting room/terrace perfect for enjoying a beer after a long cycle.

Bike Tours and Rentals

Dutch bikes come in a few varieties. The cheapest is typically the footbrake bike, which requires pedaling backward to stop. Some basic bikes with no gears and a foot pedal are referred to as ***omafiets,*** or "grandma bikes," for their comfortable low entry. You can also rent a bike with handbrakes and limited gears. Many bike rentals also offer seats to strap in young children. Finally, those not as used to biking might want to consider renting an **electric bike. Helmets** are typically rented separately, as they're surprisingly not required in the Netherlands. It might be worthwhile to rent a bike with a basket to make it easy to transport your belongings.

When you're not using your bike, you'll need to park it at a **bike rack** and use chains to properly lock the bike up. Typically, you'll be provided two **locks** as part of your rental, one with a key over the wheel and a secondary lock for the bike frame. Amsterdam's reputation for bike theft is well deserved, and the city may tow your bike if you leave it somewhere it shouldn't be. Luckily, there are many designated bike parking spots throughout the city.

All rates in this section are for the most inexpensive bike for a full day.

STAR BIKES

De Ruijterkade 143; tel. 020 620 3215; www.starbikesrental.com; 8am-7pm Mon.-Fri., 9am-7pm Sat.-Sun.; €7

If you're looking for a bike that doesn't scream that you're a tourist, Star Bikes's rentals help you blend in with the locals at an affordable rate. Their location, close to Centraal underneath the underpass, is a little difficult to find, but besides that, the only disadvantage of having a typically Dutch bike is that the local cyclists will expect you to know the rules of the road.

Amsterdam Noord

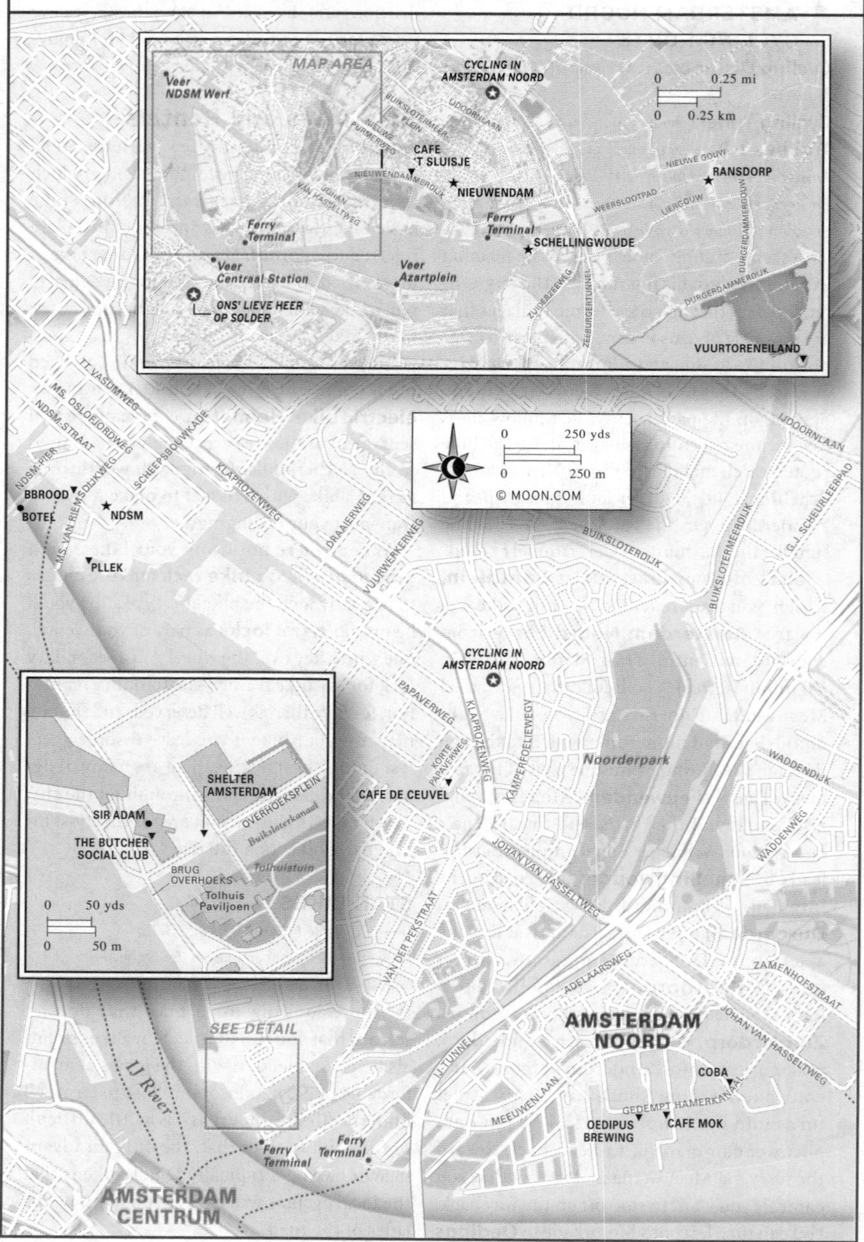

MACBIKE

Weteringschans 2; tel. 020 528 7688; www.macbike.nl; 9am-6pm daily; €9.75

Macbike is the best-known bike rental company in Amsterdam, with a large variety of options from e-bikes and *bakfiets* (bikes with a front area for young children) to normal bikes. Most locals can quickly pick out a tourist on these bikes, thanks to their clear label and bright-red color, which means that people will be a bit more forgiving of your mistakes. They have multiple locations throughout Amsterdam, including one next to Amsterdam Central Train Station (De Ruijterkade 34; www.macbike.nl; daily 9am-6pm), but the most convenient location in Amsterdam's center is on Weteringschans.

RENT A BIKE

Damstraat 20; tel. 020 625 5029; www.rentabike.nl; 9am-6pm daily; €8.50

Rent a Bike rents out typical tourist bikes, from standard bikes to tandem bikes and kids' bikes with a basket and sticker. Their bikes can be identified by their blue logo. They also rent out e-bikes and cargo bikes for those with kids. Their location near Dam Square is useful for Centrum.

BLACK BIKES

Reguliersbreestraat 41; tel. 085 273 7454; https://black-bikes.com/location/rembrandtplein; 8am-8pm Mon.-Fri., 9am-7pm Sat.-Sun.; €8.50

If you're looking to blend in like a local, Black Bikes rents nondescript bikes with a variety of options, from standard "oma" bikes without a hand brake to bikes with a clog-shaped cargo section in the front. They also rent out tandem bikes, e-bikes, and children's bikes. This bike shop is located close to Grachtengordel Oost.

BOATING

Amsterdam's many waterways are beautiful for boating, whether it's on your own or with a tour company. One of the most enjoy able ways to see Amsterdam is by renting a well-equipped electric boat to pilot yourself. These boats require few skills beyond what one would need for driving—simply keep your eyes on the waterway. It's hard to get truly lost as you're likely to end up in the Amstel River or pass a major landmark you recognize. Those less keen on piloting can opt for one of the many canal cruises, whether to sightsee during the day or enjoy a drink/dinner close to sunset.

CANAL MOTORBOATS

Zandhoek 10A; tel. 020 422 7007; www.canalmotorboats.com; 10am-10pm daily; €90 for 2 hours

Canal Motorboats is a small boat company in the Western Islands for those looking to steer themselves around Amsterdam. Their aluminum boats come with an electric motor that is fairly easy to use if you fancy yourself a captain. Their rates decrease by the hour depending on how long you intend to rent—and you're allowed to picnic on the way. A boat rental requires a €150 deposit and a valid ID. They provide a few easy-to-follow routes depending on how much time you have.

AMSTERDAM BOAT CENTER

Singel 315; tel. 020 428 2725; https://amsterdamboatcenter.com; 9am-6pm Mon.-Sat., 10am-3:30pm Sun.; €175/hour

Amsterdam Boat Center's beautiful historic wooden canal boats are perfect for those looking for the classic Amsterdam boat experience. You can opt for an open boat, or a covered "salon" boat in case of bad weather. The boats are a bit better suited to larger groups, as the rentals are more expensive, but you'll get the benefit of an experienced skipper to tell you about the attractions; you can also opt for unlimited drinks on board for €25 extra. This is a great way to kick back and relax as you see Amsterdam. Reservations recommended.

THOSE DAM BOAT GUYS

Nieuwe Leliestraat 2; tel. 020 210 1669; www.thosedamboatguys.com; 2pm-5pm Mon.-Fri., noon-5pm Sat.-Sun.; €27.50 pp

Those Dam Boat Guys is a friendly boat tour outlet run by Amsterdam expats who will

The Dutch and the Color Orange

Many people associate orange with the Netherlands and are surprised when they remember that the color is not in the red, white, and blue Dutch flag. Some historians say that orange was intended in place of the red, but that the orange dye was too unstable.

THE HISTORY

The popularity of orange can be traced back to Willem I van Oranje, otherwise known as William the Silent, who lead the Dutch revolt against the Spanish (1568-1584). His title came from the county of Orange, an area now located in the Rhône Valley, which the Orange family has historically held as a reward for their services to the Holy Roman Empire. Willem became the Prince of Orange after his cousin named him heir of the noble family. He was the first of the Dutch monarchs of the Nassau-Orange linage that continues today with King Willem-Alexander.

WHEN TO WEAR IT

Each year since the ascension of King Willem-Alexander, the entirety of the Netherlands celebrates his birthday by proudly wearing orange as they revel in the streets and on the canals. The Dutch are so proud of their royal family, it's said they started cultivating orange carrots in their honor. Orange fever has also seeped into Dutch sports culture—and many Dutchies own at least one piece of orange clothing as a result. Whether or not you find it a flattering color on yourself, it's not a bad idea to pack an orange item if you'll be in town for King's Day, or if you're lucky enough to be attending a football game.

make you laugh as you learn about the history of the city, cruise the canals, and drink or snack on whatever you choose to bring with you from the supermarket. The 90-minute tours are highly personalized, with questions highly encouraged—you won't be getting a standard recording here. It's best to reserve your place ahead on their website as they limit their tours to 10 people at most.

REDERIJ KOOIJ

Oude Turfmarkt 125; tel. 020 623 3810; www.rederijkooij.nl; 10am-9pm daily; €13 pp

Rederij Kooij is the oldest family-run boat company in Amsterdam, with almost 100 years of experience showing tourists around the city. Even if you're short on time, try to squeeze in a one-hour canal cruise from one of their boats, which depart on the half hour close to Centraal Station. Their guides are fairly standardized with an auto recording that comes in 10 different languages. Their boats include a toilet and heating on board for those cold Amsterdam nights. You typically don't need to reserve ahead unless you want a spot for a nighttime cruise for the Amsterdam Light Festival. They also offer a candlelit cruise, on which you can enjoy cheese and a glass of wine as you cruise the canals for a bit of romance for a bit extra close to sunset.

SPECTATOR SPORTS

The Dutch are obsessed with **football** (soccer in American English), as many Europeans are; most Dutch people have a favorite local team. Amsterdam is known for the **Ajax** football team, named after the Greek hero. Their stadium is southeast of the city center, in the outer neighborhood of Bijlmer, about 25 minutes by Metro from Dam Square.

JOHAN CRUIJFF ARENA

Arena Boulevard 1; www.johancruijffarena.nl/home-1.htm

Ajax, the main football club in Amsterdam, plays at the Johan Cruijff Arena, a large stadium that can hold more than 50,000 people for football games and large-scale concerts. It can be very difficult to get tickets for Ajax games, and visitors will need to vie with local superfans for a chance to sit in the stands, especially during popular matches. Tickets begin close to €150. The season is usually August-May. Most fans opt for orange and cheers such as *Hup Holland Hup* or *Viva Hollandia*. Visitors can reach the stadium by Metro (M54, 25 minutes).

Entertainment and Events

Support for the arts comes quite naturally to the Dutch, for everything from the avant-garde to classical favorites. Many of the churches in the Amsterdam area are dedicated to preserving the art of organ playing and the carillon in particular, often performed for the public at no or low cost. Event-wise, there's something going on almost constantly—the feeling of FOMO (fear of missing out) is very real for many Amsterdammers, whose calendars are often full of cultural events and weekend festivals, celebrating everything from tulips to ships to electronic music. Be sure to buy tickets in advance for events that you're interested in attending, as they often sell out quickly.

THE ARTS

Classical Music

ROYAL CONCERTGEBOUW

Concertgebouwplein 10; tel. 020 671 8345; www.concertgebouw.nl

Across from the Rijksmuseum on Museumplein, it's hard not to notice the striking neoclassical building that has been Amsterdam's premier spot for classical music since 1888. The Concertgebouw has stellar acoustics for non-amplified music, refined as the building has been renovated over the years. The Main Hall (Grote Zaal) is stunning, with 2,000 velvet seats and an organ in the center of the stage. There is also a smaller room that seats less than 500. More than 900 well-attended events and concerts occur annually at the Royal Concertgebouw, making it one of the most popular concert halls in the world. Notably, Led Zeppelin played here in the 1960s, but you'll mostly find orchestral, choir, and jazz concerts here today. **Free concerts** are held Wednesdays at 12:30pm from September-June.

MUZIEKGEBOUW AAN 'T IJ

Piet Heinkade 1; tel. 020 788 2000; www.muziekgebouw.nl

Jutting out into the IJ river, the Muziekgebouw aan 't IJ makes quite a statement. With a square roof, the glass-paned building looks out on the river—if you attend a concert, the views from the café after the show as the sun sets are worth lingering for. The main hall, built in 2005, is mostly made of concrete and wood, a not as aesthetically pleasing as a historic building, but allowing for a lot of flexibility, as everything is movable. The hall has been well calibrated for amplified music, from experimental classical music to quartets to world music. The institution also hosts a **lunch concert** throughout the year with young musicians that is free to attend.

NEDPHO DOME (NedPhO-Koepel)

Batjanstraat 3; tel. 020 521 75 00; https://orkest.nl/nl/over/nedphokoepel

The NedPhO Dome in Amsterdam Oost is the home of the Netherlands Philharmonic Orchestra and Netherlands Chamber Orchestra. This former Catholic church dates back to 1926. Its distinctive shape is inspired by Byzantine churches in Palestine and Turkey; the church was decommissioned in 1992, restored with public funds, and since 2012 has been filled with beautiful classical music. The setting, with its wide windows and spacious stage, makes it a wonderful place to enjoy a classical concert.

Muziekgebouw
BIMHUIS
1
2
CONCERT-GEBOUW
ZORG GOED VOOR ELKAAR
3
4

Open Monument Weekends

If you're interested in historical architecture, there are three weekends throughout the year when private buildings are opened up for the public to enjoy.

OPEN MONUMENT DAY

www.openmonumentendag.nl; Sept.

The largest event of all, Open Monument Day occurs in the middle of September, when more than 50 buildings open to the public and many host events to honor the building's history. Most musums with historic buildings are open for free on this day, and other rare gems include a historic theater (**De Kleine Komedie**), historic canal houses, and some buildings from **the Amsterdam School.**

OPEN TOWER DAY

(Open Toren Dag)

https://opentorendag.nl; Mar.

If you enjoy getting "high"—literally—the seocnd such holiday, Open Tower Day occurs in March. Many modern and historic viewpoints are open to the public with a tour on this day for a few euros. Open towers include the **Posthoornkerk** in the Jordaan and rare access to some hotel rooftops.

AMSTERDAM OPEN GARDEN DAYS

(Open Tuinen Dagen)

www.opentuinendagen.nl; June

For those interested in greenery, the Amsterdam Open Garden Days occur in June. In order to attend, pick up a ticket along with a pamphlet with addresses at **Museum van Loon** (page 60) for €20. There is a biking and walking route through the private gardens that open to the public.

ORGELPARK

Gerard Brandtstraat 28; tel. 020 515 8111; www.orgelpark.nl

Fans of the organ should check the agenda at the Orgelpark, a concert venue within a beautiful restored 20th-century church. Several organs are proudly displayed and often played for an eager audience. Concerts held here often combine the organ with other art forms, and you'll also find jazz, theater, and dance performances here.

Theater, Dance, and Opera

DUTCH NATIONAL OPERA

Amstel 3; tel. 020 625 5455; https://operaballet.nl

The Dutch National Opera is a modern white building adjoined with Amsterdam City Hall. More than 1,600 patrons can enjoy ballet and operas, from classic to modern, underneath the subtle ceiling lights. About 11 productions are put on annually here with subtitles/information in both English and Dutch.

ROYAL THEATER CARRÉ

Amstel 115-125; tel. 900 252 5255; https://carre.nl

Along the IJ river, this elaborate neo-Renaissance building stands apart from the rest. Originally intended as a building for a circus, it has become a popular venue for artists from comedians to pop stars. The theater has preserved much of its original layout, with elegant ringed rows surrounding the floor seats, as you'd expect for a circus. As a result, no matter where you sit, you'll have a great view of the show.

1: Muziekgebouw aan 't IJ **2:** Museumplein **3:** Royal Concertgebouw **4:** Amsterdam Pride

FESTIVALS AND EVENTS

Spring

KING'S DAY

Throughout the city; www.amsterdam.nl/toerisme-vrije-tijd/evenementen/koningsdag; Apr. 27

The highlight of April for many Dutchies and visitors has to be King's Day, which celebrates the birthday of Dutch King Willem-Alexander. Locals and visitors deck themselves out in orange, the official color of the Orange Royal Family, as well as Dutch flag colors (red, white, and blue) as they roam the streets. All Amsterdam turns into a *vrijmarkt*, where people can sell their favorite items, baked goods, and even alcohol without a license; **Vondelpark** is a popular start for these makeshift shops. Those with boats cruise down the canals with friends, blasting music.

Many festivals and parties take place both on King's Day as well as the night before, known as **King's Night.** Many concerts are free to attend, but popular festivals and parties at bars and clubs are best reserved in advance. Most of the fun of King's Day and King's Night is getting dressed up in your finest orange and wandering the streets with the rest of the Netherlands. The Amsterdam website often lists large-scale events on King's Day, but some private events with tickets might only be on the websites for venues.

ROLLING KITCHENS FOOD FESTIVAL

Westerpark; https://rollendekeukens.amsterdam; May

More than 100 food stalls fill Westerpark over a weekend for this popular festival, which grew from humble beginnings as a neighborhood party. If you attend, be sure to bring some cash, as not all of the food trucks accept cards. On a nice summer day or evening, large groups split a bottle of wine and a tapas style meal with food from all over the world. The festival is free, but food must be paid for.

REMEMBRANCE DAY/ LIBERATION DAY

Dam Square and across the Netherlands; www.4en5mei.nl; May 4-5

On May 4, all of the Dutch victims of World War II and other conflicts around the world are remembered with a nationwide two-minute silence at 8pm. There are ceremonies all around the Netherlands, including in Dam Square. On May 5, the Netherlands celebrates the end of World War II and the day that the Netherlands was freed from Nazi occupation with festivals and free concerts around the country.

Summer

SAIL

Amsterdam Central/IJ river; www.sail.nl; every four years in Aug.

Every four years, thousands of sailors and vintage ship lovers congregate at the annual SAIL festival. Since 1975, tall ships from around the world have come to Amsterdam to celebrate the city's watery history with a moving flotilla. SAIL is generally free to attend, and visitors are welcome upon some ships (generally with reservations via the SAIL website).

GRACHTENFESTIVAL

Throughout the city; www.grachtenfestival.nl; Aug.

Lovers of live music, especially jazz, classical, and international music, will want to check the agenda of the Grachtenfestival, or Canal Festival, where rising stars of the music world perform at churches and public spaces around the city. Some of the more than 250 concerts are along the canals, but it's best to check the agenda beforehand and to reserve tickets ahead for popular concerts. The festival takes place over about 2 weeks.

AMSTERDAM PRIDE

Canals of Amsterdam; https://pride.amsterdam; Aug.

The Netherlands was the first country in the world to recognize gay marriage, and since 1996, this annual parade celebrating the freedom to be who you are has been one of

Winter Holidays in Amsterdam

Christmas is not as big of a deal in the Netherlands as it is in neighboring countries, like Germany; a traditional holiday called Sinterklaas tends to be more popular with families with children. Amsterdammers do still celebrate Christmas with markets, but many see it as a holiday to catch up with family members and maybe go on vacation, so shops and restaurants are often closed during this time of year in addition to being closed on Christmas Day itself. It's best to plan well for Christmas dinner on Christmas if you'll be visiting then—expect a lot of quiet!

SINTERKLAAS

Perhaps the most controversial holiday in the Netherlands, Sinterklaas (www.sintinamsterdam.nl) is a big holiday for Dutch families, although the last 10 years have brought significant changes.

It's based around the figure of Saint Nicholas, who supposedly lives in Spain and arrives by boat with his "helpers" and a horse. His helpers, known as Zwarte Piet (Black Pete), are the subject of significant criticism because of the blackface worn for their traditional costume. In recent years, Amsterdam has banned the use of blackface, and the traditional Piet has been phased out of the national celebrations. Today, many Pieten are known as "Chimney Piet," their faces marked with a small amount of soot meant to symbolize going down the chimney to deliver presents, and many Dutch cities are experimenting with other versions. That said, it is still quite common to see images of Zwarte Piet in full blackface during this time, especially in more rural towns and private establishments.

There is a big **parade** to mark Saint Nicholas's arrival, usually in mid-November, and Dutch children lay out their shoes to receive *pepernoten* (cinnamon cookies). December 5 is when Dutch children traditionally receive presents from their family members, write poems, and eat traditional Dutch sweets. On December 6, Sinterklaas leaves until the next year.

CHRISTMAS MARKETS

You'll find a few markets in Amsterdam with stalls selling gifts, including the **Ice Amsterdam** skating rink with a small Christmas market outside the Museumplein from late November until January. Much of the charm can be found at the smaller markets that only happen over one weekend in mid-December, including the **Haarlemmerstraat Christmas Market** and the Christmas Market at **Westergasfabriek.**

NEW YEAR'S EVE

The sound of New Year's Eve in Amsterdam has oft been compared to that of a war zone, as the ban on fireworks gets lifted for one day. It's a free-for-all as families and locals set off sizable fireworks from their homes. If you're a visitor and you wish to dance the night away, there are many **parties** throughout the city, which often require tickets that you'll need to reserve ahead. ***Oliebol,*** a fried ball similar to a donut, is a traditional New Year's treat that you'll find at stands throughout the city.

AMSTERDAM LIGHT FESTIVAL

To brighten up the dark winter nights in Amsterdam, where the sun can set quite early, the city has commissioned artists from around the world to create **light-filled installations** along Grachtengordel canal and the Amstel and IJ Rivers. From December-January, take a **boat cruise** or walk down the canals to take in the stunning, annually changing sculptures that make winter just a little brighter.

the biggest holidays in Amsterdam. Themed decorated boats cruise down the canals in the **Canal Parade,** and the surrounding canals become packed with locals and tourists decked out in rainbow colors, making for a joyous celebration. There are other related events, including dance parties and film screenings. Pride typically lasts a week, and the Canal Parade generally falls on a weekend.

Fall

AMSTERDAM DANCE EVENT

Thoughout the city; www.amsterdam-dance-event.nl; Oct.

For the last 25 years, Amsterdam has hosted one of the largest club festivals in Europe, known as ADE for short. It takes place over five days in more than 200 locations across Amsterdam with more than 2,500 artists, and there is also a conference to discuss the music industry as a whole. Tickets are generally affordable if purchased in advance, although some concerts sell out quickly. Some concerts are as cheap as €20, while popular shows can cost in the hundreds.

Winter

NATIONAL TULIP DAY

Dam Square; third Sat. of Jan.

Every January, Dam Square becomes a lot more colorful when it's filled with more than 200,000 tulips donated by Dutch farmers. A bouquet of tulips is free to enjoy and take back to your hotel room with you, and it's a great break from the gloomy Amsterdam winter. The bouquet is unlikely to keep beyond a day.

Shopping

A few great Amsterdam souvenirs are **tulips** from the Flower Market and **Delft pottery** from the Nieuwe Spiegelstraat antique shops. Certain bulb varieties from the Flower Market may not be allowed back into some countries, including the United States, so it's best to check the entry restrictions for your country with bulb sellers, who often designate bulbs safe for countries with tougher plant restrictions in a separate section. Some more beautiful and rare tulips might not be available.

In Amsterdam Centrum, **Spui** is the main commercial shopping street, with chain retailers and high street shops. It's perpendicular to **Kalverstraat,** the city's main artery, as well as **Rokin** a block farther east, where some retailers prefer to have their massive shops.

GRACHTENGORDEL AND PLANTAGE

For independent shopping in Gractengordel West, the **9 Streets (9 Straatjes)** are the place to be. This rectangular neighborhood of Amsterdam—which is, not surprisingly, made up of nine streets—boxed in by Singel, Herengracht, Keizersgracht, and Prinsengracht makes for the complete shopping experience, with small concept stores next to well-curated vintage stores and design studios.

To the southeast, **Utrechtsestraat** is another popular street for clothing shopping and upscale interior goods.

Clothing

SCOTCH & SODA

Wolvenstraat 14; tel. 020 788 2633; www.scotch-soda.com; noon-6pm Sun.-Mon., 10am-6pm Tues.-Sat

With several locations throughout Amsterdam, including no less than four in the Grachtengordel, Scotch & Soda is the most famous Dutch fashion brand, known for their colorful, stylish, and classic designs for women and men. Created in Amsterdam in 1985, the brand had been producing wholesale garments before selling directly consumers.

Best Bookstores in Amsterdam

Amsterdam is full of wonderful bookstores, many of which have at least a small English section where you're bound to find a wonderful book to bring home with you. Don't forget to visit Oudemanhuispoort (page 50), an atmospheric covered passage where secondhand books are sold.

AMERICAN BOOK CENTER

Spui 12; tel. 020 625 5537; https://abc.nl; 11am-7pm Mon.-Sat., 11am-6pm Sun.

The American Book Center is a three-story independent bookstore in Amsterdam Centrum that specializes in all forms of English literature, from comics to travel to fiction. They have a wonderful section specifically about the Netherlands in English as well. On Friday, there is an open-air book market during the day (10am-6pm) in front of the American Book Center on Spui. Typically the selection is in Dutch, but you might find some English literature if you dig!

ATHENAEUM BOEKHANDEL

Spui 14; tel. 020 514 1460; www.athenaeum.nl; 10am-7pm Mon.-Sat., noon-5:30pm Sun.

Across the street from the American Book Center in Amsertdam Centrum, Athenaeum Boekhandel specializes in magazines, academic publications, and periodicals if you're missing your favorite newspaper from home.

BOEKHANDEL DE DOLFIJN

Haarlemmerdijk 92; tel. 020 422 3945; www.libris.nl/boekholtboekhandels/de-dolfijn; 11am-6pm Mon., 9:30am-6pm Tues.-Fri., 9:30am-5:30pm Sat., noon-5pm Sun.

Along Haarlemmerstraat, Boekhandel De Dolfijn is a cozy bookstore that specializes mostly in children's and young adult books, but you'll also find kid-friendly favorites in English.

THE BOOK EXCHANGE

Kloveniersburgwal 58; tel. 020 626 6266; http://bookexchange.nl; noon-4pm daily

If you're willing to dig deep, the Book Exchange in Centrum is packed with used English titles; it's hard to leave this three-story bookstore without finding something.

SCHELTEMA

Rokin 9; tel. 020 523 1411; www.scheltema.nl; 10am-7pm daily

Lastly, Scheltema close to Dam Square in Centrum is known for its massive location with more than 125,000 titles. Since the 19th century, this major Dutch purveyor of books has been stocking books in multiple languages.

WE ARE LABELS

Herengracht 356; tel. 20 620 5254; www.wearelabels.com; noon-6:30pm Mon., 10:30am-6:30pm Tues.-Fri., 10am-6pm Sat., noon-6pm Sun.

We Are Labels is another popular Dutch brand with a few locations in the Grachtengordel as well as some in De Pijp to the south. The ethos is style on a budget with a dose of Dutch simplicity; most of the store's chic clothes for both men and women are capped at €80.

Home Goods

THINGS I LIKE THINGS I LOVE

Haarlemmerdijk 124; tel. 020 786 7817; www.thingsilikethingsilove.com; 1pm-6pm Mon., 11am-6pm Tues.-Sat., noon-6pm Sun.

With six locations throughout Amsterdam, Things I Like Things I Love started as a pop-up sale, and is now a trendy concept store featuring household items, chic clothes, art, and Dutch-inspired décor. The interior is airy and bright, and it's hard to resist the urge to pick up at least one item for a closer look.

Tasty Souvenirs

Food from the Netherlands is probably the best souvenir to bring home with you, whether to keep for yourself or give as a gift.

CHEESE

The most obvious gift is cheese, which can be purchased at specialty independent cheese shops such as **Kaasland** (page 95). When purchasing cheese to bring home with you, ask for your cheese to be vacuum-sealed for freshness while traveling. (In case you forget to buy cheese while sightseeing, you can often buy sealed cheese balls at the Albert Heijn in Schiphol Airport.)

OTHER FOODS

Most of the following food souvenirs can be found at the Dutch supermarket **Albert Heijn** and the Dutch all-purpose store **HEMA,** which can be found within Amsterdam and at Schiphol Airport.

- ***Stroopwafels*** (Dutch wafers with caramel) are absolutely delicious, but they don't necessarily travel well. If you want to bring some back with you, visit Albert Heijn to find their made-for-travel *stroopwafel* tins.
- A lesser-known Dutch favorite, especially for kids, is ***hagelslag,*** or chocolate sprinkles that can be spread on buttered toast.
- From November-December, you can find **chocolate letters** with the first initial of your name, a treat associated with the winter holidays.
- Another winter favorite is ***pepernoten,*** a miniature cookie made with cloves and spices.
- Although not everyone is a fan of licorice, the Dutch call licorice ***drop*** and eat it up in all different shapes.

Jewelry

ALL THE LUCK IN THE WORLD

Berenstraat 2; www.alltheluckintheworld.nl; 11am-6pm Thurs.-Sun.

In their airy, light-filled shop in the 9 Straatjes neighborhood, All the Luck in the World focuses on showcasing their smart yet minimalist jewelry pieces, which are perfect for any budget. Their pins and rings are favorites among local fashionistas. The shop also features their self-made quirky prints, cards, and postcards for every occasion. You'll find other locations in De Pijp and Amsterdam Oost.

Markets

FLOWER MARKET (Bloemenmarkt)

Singel between Muntplein and Koningsplein; www.iamsterdam.com/en/see-and-do/shopping/amsterdam-markets/flower-market; 9am-5:30pm daily

Amsterdam has the world's only floating flower market, where you can pick up plants and flowers to bring home as souvenirs. The market is certainly touristy, and most stalls specialize in seeds and tulip bulbs packaged for tourists. Nevertheless, there's something quite nice about picking out flowers along such a scenic canal-side spot. Prices are higher than at other similar stores, but it's worth a browse for specialty tulip bulbs that are manufactured for countries with more restrictive plant regulations. When buying tulips, be sure to check that they can be legally imported into your home country.

1: 9 Streets **2:** Pansy art gallery **3:** Amsterdam Flower Market **4:** Nieuwe Spiegelstraat (antique shopping street)

402
LOCAL SERVIC
1
2
3
4
SALE

Antique Shopping in Amsterdam

De IJ-hallen flea market

Although you'll certainly find many antique stores in Amsterdam, **Nieuwe Spiegelstraat** between Prinsengracht and Herengracht is a favorite spot for high-end antiques from clocks to Delftware. As you wander through the city, you'll definitely want to peek into the various shops along the way.

- There are a few notable shops if you head down Spiegelstraat toward the Rijksmuseum, including **Prints & Maps Hoogkamp** (Spiegelgracht 27; https://antiquariaat-hoogkamp.business.site; 1pm-6:30pm daily), with antique maps and prints perfect for displaying on your wall.
- The best place to find curiosities on a budget is at the monthly **De IJ-hallen flea market** (https://ijhallen.nl) in Amsterdam Noord.
- Lastly, for serious buyers with the budget to match, The **Antiques Center Amsterdam** (Elandsgracht 109; tel. 020 624 9038; www.antiekcentrumamsterdam.nl/en/antiekcentrum; 11am-6pm Mon. and Wed.-Fri., 11am-5pm Sat.-Sun.) is home to more than 55 antique dealers who sell everything from antique jewelry to paintings in a large maze of stalls.

DE JORDAAN AND HAARLEMMERDIJK

In De Jordaan, **Haarlemmerdijk** and **Haarlemmerstraat** are full of beautiful, atmospheric indie shops selling everything from jewelry to books.

Clothing

THE DARLING

Runstraat 4; tel. 020 422 3142; www.thedarlingamsterdam.com; 1pm-6pm Mon., 11am-6pm Tues.-Sat., noon-6pm Sun.

The Darling stocks affordable clothing with that quintessential European cool-girl style. Their cozy store is filled with vintage furniture and other thoughtful touches that make shopping special.

JUTKA & RISKA

Haarlemmerdijk 143; tel. 020 618 8021; www.jutkaenriska.com; 10am-6:30pm Mon.-Sat., noon-6pm Sun.

Started by Dutch sisters, Jutka & Riska highlights new designers while encouraging shoppers to find their own unique style. The store features an eclectic mix of vintage meets cool girl if you're looking for a statement piece or a wardrobe staple.

MARBLES VINTAGE

Haarlemmerdijk 64; tel. 020 750 8146; 11am-7pm

One of the best-known vintage shops in Amsterdam, Marbles Vintage curates their ever-changing collection of vintage pieces with a slight bias toward the '70s and '80s. Their two-story shop on Haarlemmerdijk features an impressive collection of shoes—even cowboy boots—bags, dresses, and other staples in great condition.

SIX AND SONS

Haarlemmerdijk 31; tel. 020 655 8888; www.sixandsons.com; 11am-6pm Tues.-Sat., noon-6pm Sun.

Six and Sons specializes in sustainable clothing for women, men, and children. Their quirky selection of organic and eco-friendly brands is displayed in a charming yet airy store, with a coffee shop that specializes in fair-trade raw cacao downstairs.

Souvenirs

HET MUIZENHUIS

Eerste Tuindwarsstraat 1HS; www.hetmuizenhuis.nl; 11am-5pm Wed.-Sun.

Part museum and part shop, Het Muizenhuis is the creation of Dutch artist Karina Schaapman, who decided to write a children's book in 2008 using photographed dioramas rather than drawings. She created a 3-meter-high (10-foot-high) house to document the adventures of her mice, Sam and Julia. The books were a hit and she was able to open up a dedicated shop for both adults and children with art pieces and DIY dioramas for purchase. All of her creations include tiny furniture and props made with love.

AMSTERDAM WEST

Markets

SUNDAY MARKET WESTERGAS

Gosschalklaan, Pazzanistraat 7; www.sundaymarket.nl; noon-6pm Sun.

The Sunday market at Westergas, a collection of shops, restaurants, and bars in the city's former gasworks, is lively, with everything from housewares, ceramics, fashion, accessories, and artwork for sale from colorful booths.

AMSTERDAM OOST

Czaar Peterstraat, the new hip shopping street of Amsterdam, is being developed with sustainability in mind. This street in Amsterdam Oost, named after Peter the Great, is tree-lined, with countless independent shops, cozy cafés, and many unique places to buy a gift.

Souvenirs

PANSY

Czaar Peterstraat 104; 10am-6pm Wed.-Sat.

A great spot for souvenirs, Pansy is an art shop dedicated to the prints of Aussie artist Alina Tang, who creates cheerful and adorable paintings inspired by her life in Amsterdam. There are prints of tulips and of Amsterdam's charming houses with all of their intricacies.

Clothing

DREAMBOAT

Czaar Peterstraat 145; 11am-6pm Wed.-Fri., 11am-5pm Sat.

Dreamboat is a combination of a studio and store selling cutting-edge designs in women's wear, lifestyle items, and accessories.

Food

Although you're unlikely to hear about Dutch food abroad, you're going to want to try it while traveling in the Netherlands. Typical dishes range from the austere potato-based ***stamppot*** to savory Javanese ***saoto*** soup that came to the Netherlands via Suriname and Indonesia, former Dutch colonies. For lunch, try **raw herring with onions** from the local herring stand, or a sandwich from the local cheese shop made with **Gouda cheese.** Cheese is a true point of national pride, even in Amsterdam, and you're likely to pass cheese shops where wheels of cheese are stacked from floor to ceiling.

A popular dinner out with friends is ***rijsttafel,*** Dutch for "rice table." Rooted in the Dutch colonization of Indonesia, this is a great way to sample Indonesian food if you're unsure where to start, as you're likely to try at least eight dishes at minimum.

Around 4pm-5pm, especially on Fridays, Dutch snacks are likely to come out alongside beer. ***Bitterballen,*** fried beef balls traditionally dipped in mustard, are the perfect snack to enjoy with a blonde or triple beer. **Fries** are also a national obsession. If none of this sounds appetizing, don't worry: Amsterdam's diverse and rich culinary scene has attracted restaurateurs and chefs from around the world.

Visitors are sometimes surprised by the casualness of many Amsterdam restaurants, where service can be slow—if you want the bill, it's often best to walk up to the register to pay. Many Dutch restaurants do not accept credit cards from abroad, so it's best to have some cash with you. In the center along major squares, such as **Leidseplein** and **Dam Square,** you'll see prices that will make your eyes swell for basics like a glass of Heineken or Dutch pancakes. There are many other spots throughout Amsterdam where you'll find places to get your Dutch food experience while paying substantially less.

AMSTERDAM CENTRUM

Dutch

PANCAKES AMSTERDAM

Prins Hendrikkade 48; tel. 020 820 4240; https://pancakes.amsterdam; 8:30am-6pm daily; €15

Dutch pancakes differ quite a bit from American pancakes—and many tourists flock to one of the locations of Pancakes Amsterdam to have a taste of the slightly flatter Dutch pancake with a sweet or savory addition. One notable difference between this restaurant and some other pancake restaurants is that they also cater to those with food restrictions. There's often a line and prices are higher here than at some other cafés that also offer pancakes, but the friendly staff makes enjoying a pancake a great experience for all.

Brunch

GREENWOODS SINGEL

Singel 103; tel. 020 623 7071; http://greenwoods.eu; 9am-4pm daily; €13

Greenwoods Singel is a friendly Aussie-run lunch/brunch spot with all-day breakfast that is popular with expats looking for a taste of home with a perfectly-done eggs Benedict and other comfort foods. The interior is cozy, with wooden tables, and the terrace along the Singel canal is nice on a warm day.

Cafés and Light Bites

VAN STAPELE KOEKMAKERIJ

Heisteeg 4; tel. 020 777 9327; www.vanstapele.com; 10am-3pm or earlier if they sell out daily; €3

For delectable chocolate cookies that melt in your mouth, don't be afraid to arrive early to get to Van Stapele before they sell out of their famous chocolate cookies, typically in the early afternoon. The cookies have an exterior made with Valrhona dark chocolate and a gooey white chocolate interior. There's always a short line into the charming shop, and their decorative tins make a great gift if you can resist the urge to open the box.

NAKED ESPRESSO

Warmoesstraat 46; tel. 020 774 1593; http://nakedespresso.nl; 9am-9pm daily; €4

Naked Espresso is a bit touristy, but the specialty coffee bar has an incredibly convenient location right off Dam Square. Compared to the many chain cafés and restaurants in the area, Naked Espresso is a nice change with well-done specialty coffee and tasty pastries.

BLUE AMSTERDAM

Winkelcentrum Kalverpassage, Singel 457; tel. 020 427 3901; www.blue-amsterdam.nl; 11am-6:30pm Sun.-Mon., 10am-6:30pm Tues.-Wed., 10am-8pm Thurs., 10am-6:30pm Fri.; €10

Blue Amsterdam is hidden within a fairly anonymous shopping mall, but if you can manage to find the elevator that leads to this rooftop restaurant with 360-degree views of Amsterdam, you'll be excited to sit down for a coffee. Their lunch sandwiches, including healthier salad options, are thoughtfully done—and it's a nice spot near the Amsterdam Flower Market for a reasonable lunch.

International

SURINAAMS CHINEES RESTAURANT KAM YIN

Warmoesstraat 6; tel. 020 625 3115; https://kamyin.nl; noon-midnight daily; €9

In the heart of Amsterdam's Chinatown, sample Surinamese Chinese food at Kam Yin. The interior is modern and the portions are hearty. For meat eaters, their marinated and roasted pork cooked *cha sieuw* style is quite good, with brown beans and rice or noodles depending on how hungry you are. They also offer a set menu for curious eaters looking to sample a few dishes at once.

THE FOOD DEPARTMENT

Nieuwezijds Voorburgwal 182; www.thefooddepartment.nl; noon-8pm Mon.-Fri., noon-9pm Sat.-Sun.; €10-15

Amsterdam's newest food hall is the Food Department, which is a great affordable option for anyone stuck in the Red Light District during the day amid the endless steak restaurants. The food court is on the second floor of the neoclassical Magna Plaza shopping mall, which is spread across 1,100 square meters (12,000 square feet) of space with more than nine stalls offering options from dim sum to burgers. This is a good pick for groups as everyone can share a table—and opt to choose their own lunch/dinner from the stall of their choice. Cards only!

D'VIJFF VLIEGHEN

Spuistraat 294-302; tel. 020 530 4060; www.vijffvlieghen.nl; 6pm-10pm daily; €24

For atmosphere, it's hard to rival d'Vijff Vlieghen's location within five 17th-century canal houses, including one room with sketches from Rembrandt. Although the restaurant's name, which translates as The Five Flies, might not inspire confidence, the restaurant is a beautiful spot for a date night, showcasing Dutch food at its finest using seasonal local ingredients. A mix of well-dressed couples and business travelers dine next to authentic Delft tiles on chairs inscribed with the names of famous diners.

GRACHTENGORDEL AND PLANTAGE

Dutch

THE PANTRY

Leidsekruisstraat 21; tel. 020 6200 922; www.thepantry.nl; 10am-11pm daily; €14.50

The Pantry is a great spot for old-school traditional food close to Museumplein and Vondelpark. You'll find wintertime favorites such as warming stews (*hutspot*), fish, shrimp croquettes made with Dutch shrimp, and pea soups. With warm brown wood, elaborate chandeliers, Delft landscape paintings, and Delftware on the walls, this is a tourist favorite, so be sure to make a reservation.

Cafés and Light Bites

TOKI

Binnen Dommersstraat 15; tel. 020 363 6009; www.tokiho.amsterdam; 8am-5pm Mon.-Fri., 9am-5pm Sat.-Sun.; €4

Toki is a charming specialty café just off

Haarlemmerstraat popular with freelancers and young professionals catching up over a perfectly made coffee with sustainably sourced beans made however you want it. Their tempting sweets (that change by the season and ample seating make it easy to get comfortable.

DE KOFFIESALON

Utrechtsestraat 130-BG; tel. 020 226 8994; www.dekoffiesalon.nl; 7am-7pm daily; €4

De Koffiesalon's location on Utrechtsestraat blends the chic coffeehouse with a modern, hip café thanks to its minimalistic interior, black-and-white photographs, and elegant original wooden beams on the ceiling. The coffee is always good, and the balcony is a magical place to read a book or people-watch from above. The buzz of Amsterdam settles down a little here.

ZUIVERE KOFFIE

Utrechtsestraat 39; tel. 020 624 9999; 8am-5pm Mon.-Fri., 9am-5pm Sat., 9:30am-4pm Sun.; €5

Zuivere Koffie is a charming independent coffee shop with a cute green terrace, friendly service, sleepy cat, and beautiful stained glass windows. The interior feels homey and relaxed, and the limited space caters to creatives and neighborhood locals who pop in to take a break from the busyness of Amsterdam while chatting with the friendly baristas. It feels like an oasis of calm.

PATISSERIE KUYT

Utrechtsestraat 109-111; tel. 020 623 4833; www.patisseriekuyt.nl; 8am-1pm Mon., 8am-5:30pm Tues.-Sat.; €5

Although the debate over the best apple pie will never be fully settled in Amsterdam, Patisserie Kuyt is known for being one of the best bakeries in Amsterdam. Even if you don't opt for a high tea in their modern tearoom, their delectable cakes and pastries are a favorite of many Amsterdammers with a serious sweet tooth.

VAN SOEST AMSTERDAM

Frederiksplein 1a; tel. 020 620 8025; www.vansoest-amsterdam.nl; noon-10pm Sun., 8:30am-10pm Tues.-Sat.; €10

For chocolate lovers, the van Soest chocolatier is a must-see with a great assortment of bonbons, truffles, and chocolate bars made with fair-trade chocolate that they source themselves. If you're not crazy about chocolate, they also serve Italian-style ice cream—which often comes with a chocolate added to the top for an additional sweet touch. The interior is beautifully decorated with marble, hardwood floors, and a cabinet that showcases their sweets. You can also buy pralines as a gift.

International

WATER AND BROOD

Nieuwe Kerkstraat 84; tel. 06 41078060; www.waterenbrood.com; 11am-7pm Wed.-Fri., 11am-4pm Sat.-Sun.; €7.50

Water and Brood is a Black-owned fusion restaurant and one of Amsterdam's best brunch spots. They serve everything from Southern-style fried chicken and waffles to Surinamese favorites such as *moksi alesi* at dinner. On weekends, they offer all-day brunch for late risers craving waffles after many other lunch spots stop serving breakfast. The interior is clean and modern, but the café still feels quite cozy and intimate. Reservations recommended.

TEMPO DOELOE

Utrechtsestraat 75; tel. 020 625 6718; www.tempodoeloerestaurant.nl; 6pm-midnight Mon.-Thurs., midnight-4pm and 6pm-midnight Fri.-Sat.; €40

This Dutch-Indonesian run restaurant serves Michelin-recognized *rijsttafel* in a chic environment with white tablecloths and antique wood. The restaurant has been around for more than 30 years, and their *rijsttafel* with 10-plus dishes is considered one of the best in Amsterdam. Their food is known for being spicy, so order carefully. Reservations recommended.

DE JORDAAN AND HAARLEMMERDIJK

Dutch

KAASLAND

Haarlemmerdijk 1; tel. 020 625 7945; www.kaasland.eu; 8am-8pm Mon., 8am-6:30pm Tues.-Wed., 8am-8pm Thurs.-Fri., 8am-6pm Sat., 9am-7pm Sun.; €4

Kaasland is an independently run cheese shop on Haarlemmerdijk that is a favorite among office workers who wait in line at lunchtime for sandwiches made with freshly cut cheese of their choice and bread baked fresh daily. There are no seats, but you can enjoy your sandwich sitting by the Prinsengracht canal. Their selection of Dutch cheeses is great if you're looking for cheese to bring home with you, or simply take as a snack for later. The staff is happy to let you sample cheese to find your favorite.

★ HET PAPENEILAND

Prinsengracht 2; tel. 020 624 1989; www.papeneiland.nl; 10am-1am Mon.-Thurs., 10am-3am Fri.-Sat, noon-1am Sun.; €5

Het Papeneiland is one of the most iconic cafés in Amsterdam, with its beautiful Delft-tiled wall filled with mementos of the past. The café is your classic brown bar with Amsterdammers tucking into apple pie slices and cups of coffee underneath the wood-beamed ceiling. The name of the café (Papists' Island) derives from the fact that there was a tunnel that lead to a secret church for Catholics to attend mass without attracting attention. (This was during the Protestant Reformation when Catholicism was functionally outlawed.) The remains of the tunnel sit behind a green gate in the basement, but the café's beautiful brick exterior with stained glass windows that date back to 1642 can be admired from across the water from the Papiermolensluis bridge at Korte Prinsengracht 109. Even if you're not a history buff, Het Papeneiland's beautiful wooden interior with brown walls and bronze chandeliers can charm the grumpiest of guests. It's a wonderful spot to sit and enjoy a coffee or beer.

PIQNIQ

Lindengracht 59HS; tel. 020 320 3669; https://piqniq.nl; 9am-4pm Mon.-Fri., 9am-5pm Sat.-Sun.; €7

PIQNIQ is a cozy little Dutch spot for breakfast and lunch. Their sandwiches are pretty standard fare, but the café's cozy modern interior makes everyone, including those with food allergies, welcome. Their café cat is often snoozing in the window, and it's a great spot to enjoy a book on a rainy day.

MOEDERS

Rozengracht 251; tel. 020 626 7957; www.moeders.com; noon-10:30pm daily; €19

Moeders is a favorite among tourists for trying traditional Dutch comfort food from green pea soup to *stamppot*. The interior is full of kitschy Dutch sayings and photos, which makes it feel a little like a time capsule. Although you can certainly find these dishes elsewhere for less, most of the charm is in the homey feeling where nothing matches. This is a great spot for public holidays when other restaurants are closed, as they often host holiday meals. Reservations recommended.

Cafés and Light Bites

WINKEL 43

Noordermarkt 43; tel. 020 623 0223; https://winkel43.nl; 7am-1am Mon., 8am-1am Tues.-Thurs., 8am-3am Fri., 7am-3am Sat., 10am-1am Sun.; €4

Winkel 43 is Amsterdam's best-known spot for divine apple pie, routinely brought up from their basement kitchen. With its charming terrace overlooking the Noordermarkt and wood-filled interior, it's a staple for Amsterdammers; it can be hard to find a seat, especially on weekends and on market days in the Jordaan.

MONTE PELMO

Tweede Anjeliersdwarsstraat 17; tel. 020 623 0959; http://montepelmo.nl; 1pm-10pm daily; €4

On a warm day, there's typically a long line for Monte Pelmo, which is known for having the best ice cream in Amsterdam since 1957. They specialize in gelato and sorbet, which can be

amsterdam
15.95
40.00
1
2
3

served with an additional mini waffle cone (if you ask). Cash only.

GOOD BEANS

Binnen Oranjestraat 4; tel. 06 24471218; www.goodbeans.nl; 9am-5pm daily; €4

Good Beans is a small coffee shop that is as tiny as they come. If you're claustrophobic, it might be best to grab a coffee to go, but much of the charm is in sitting in this postage-stamp-sized café to chat with the friendly locals who pop in for a coffee and a chat.

International

LE SUD

Haarlemmerdijk 118; tel. 020 622 5888; http://lesud.nl; 10am-7pm Mon.-Sat., 10am-5pm Sun.; €4

One of the best spots on Haarlemmerdijk for a great lunch is this unassuming, casual all-vegetarian café. The interior is nothing special, but their endless section of dishes available in either to-go containers, wraps, or sandwiches make it a tempting choice for lovers of Middle Eastern food looking for a quick meal or a picnic to bring to Westerpark. The owners are Iranian, and they offer Mediterranean favorites from hummus to tabbouleh. Their eggplant wrap is a very safe bet for a tasty lunch. Bring cash!

AFHAALCENTRUM TERANG BOELAN

Tweede Lindendwarsstraat 3; tel. 020 620 9974; www.terangboelan.nl; 3pm-9pm Mon.-Fri.; €12

Afhaalcentrum Terang Boelan is a small Indonesian takeaway *toko* restaurant deep in the Jordaan that serves up big flavors without big prices. The friendly owners are happy to explain the various dishes; *rames* (a plate with rice or noodles and several dishes of your choice) is a good deal if you're hungry and indecisive. The interior is fairly plain besides a few photos of Indonesia; they let the food be the star of the show. It's a great place to get delivery or take-out if you're staying in the neighborhood and looking for a taste of Indonesian cooking, but there are only a few tables inside if your hotel is too far.

MEN IMPOSSIBLE

Hazenstraat 19H; tel. 06 82439199; https://men-impossible.business.site; 5-9pm Fri., 11:45am-2:15pm and 5pm-9pm Sat.; lunch €14, dinner €25

Men Impossible is a play on the fact that many thought that it would be impossible to create a ramen that was 100 percent vegan that tasted so good. Although only open on weekends, Men Impossible serves ramen at a large communal dining table. Their meal special comes with unlimited tea or water. If you're serious about ramen and open to trying this acclaimed vegan take on it, make a reservation as their small dining room fills up on Saturdays.

★ Markets

On Monday and Saturday, the streets of De Jordaan, particularly Lindengracht, Westerstraat, and Noordermarkt, fill up with locals doing their weekly shopping as they go stall-to-stall buying fresh bread, fruit, and other groceries for the week. Many stands at these markets are cash-only or accept only Dutch debit cards, so be sure to stop at the ATM before you come.

NOORDERMARKT

Noordermarkt; https://noordermarkt-amsterdam.nl; 9am-1pm Mon., 9am-5pm Sat.

A market has long taken place on Saturdays at the foot of the Noorderkerk church. Today, the market offers everything from street food to clothing to antiques to books. Most stalls are cash-only.

WESTERSTRAAT MARKET

Westerstraat, next to Noordermarkt; 9am-1pm Mon., 9am-4pm Sat.

On Monday, Westerstraat turns into a busy market 9am-1pm, with more than 160 vendors selling fruits, veggies, cloth, flowers, and other necessities for those living in the

---

1: Kaasland **2:** Van Stapele cookies
3: Het Papeneiland café

☆ Indonesian and Surinamese Cuisine

Some of the best food in Amsterdam is not traditional Dutch, and comes with a complicated legacy: Dutch colonialism in Indonesia and Suriname from the 16th-century on eventually led to mass migration of Indonesians and Surinamese to the Netherlands. Sampling these cuisines with clear eyes about their complicated histories is an experience not to be missed on a visit to the city.

INDONESIAN

The Dutch and other Europeans colonized in Indonesia in the 16th century to take advantage of the many spices, including nutmeg and cloves, produced there, using Batavia (now Jakarta), as their base. Mass migration of Indonesians to the Netherlands following Indonesian independence in 1945 means that it's easy to find Indonesian food all throughout the country.

Indonesian food varies quite a bit depending on where the chef in the kitchen is from; the most common regional cuisine you'll find in Amsterdam is Javanese. Many regional dishes can be found at ***tokos,*** cozy Indonesian takeaway restaurants. Many *tokos* have a few tables or chairs, but the food shines brighter than the décor. **Sari Citra** (page 102) in De Pijp is a great example of a classic *toko,* where you'll find typical *rames* dishes, or rice with a protein (fish, tofu, chicken, egg, etc.) and 1-2 vegetable sides of your choice. It's best to ask the owner what they recommend given your spice tolerance. You can always ask for *sambal* (chili paste) to add to your meal if it's not spicy enough!

One famous Indonesian-inspired dish is ***rijsttafel,*** but the history of this dish is complex. Indonesia is made of hundreds of islands, so generally 40-plus dishes from various islands are presented alongside tables of rice. It's said that *rijsttafel* was invented when the Dutch came to Indonesia and demanded to try the local food, only to be told that there was no single specialty; it changed from island to island. The *rijsttafel* emerged as a product of colonialism as a way of impressing visitors with the abundance of foods available. Today, this meal is extremely common

neighborhood. On Saturday, in front of the Noorderkerk, a farmers market takes place 9am-4pm with fresh cheese brought in from the nearby region, freshly made sausage, organic vegetables, and other sustainable food items.

Around the corner on some Monday mornings, you'll also find a **flea market** with vintage dresses, jackets, rugs, and other unexpected delights. Having a market of some kind has been a tradition since 1618—and there's no sin in taking a break to enjoy a coffee (and slice of apple pie) at **Winkel 43** after hard work browsing the stands.

LINDENGRACHT MARKET

Lindengracht; 9am-4pm Sat.

Just two streets up, Lindengracht hosts a sizable market with everything from cheese to plants. The market began in 1894 in this working-class Amsterdam neighborhood, and it remains a weekly tradition to walk along the former canal-turned-street as part of a stroll almost a kilometer long down the market. More than 200 stalls set up shop for the day, which makes the Lindengracht Market a great spot for a pastry for breakfast—and for scouting for souvenirs to bring home.

AMSTERDAM WEST

Cafés and Lite Bites

WHITE LABEL COFFEE

Jan Evertsenstraat 136; tel. 020 737 1359; https://whitelabelcoffee.nl; 8am-6pm Mon.-Fri., 8:30am-6pm Sat.-Sun.; €4

White Label Coffee is known for some of the best coffee in Amsterdam. This specialty café roasts their own coffee, and their lattes with elaborate designs are best enjoyed in the urban interior filled with creatives catching up. Their banana bread is also worthwhile.

in the Netherlands, but increasingly rare in Indonesia in the modern-era; **Blauw** (page 101) is great place to try *rijsttafel* while in Amsterdam.

SURINAMESE

Surinamese food may lesser known than Indonesian, but its complex flavors, influenced by cuisines from China to India, make it an unexpected delight. Suriname, in South America, was an English colony with plantations as early as 1663. The colony became Dutch after the English traded Suriname for New York, and the Dutch West India Company brought thousands of enslaved Africans to work the plantations. Shortly before this period, the Dutch aggressively recruited contract workers of Chinese, Indian, and Indonesian (Javanese) origins to work the plantations. The descendants of these workers were Dutch citizens until Suriname wasn't a colony anymore, at which point, many Surinamese people had to emigrate to the Netherlands keep their Dutch citizenship. This history of immigration has resulted in an interesting combination of dishes influenced by each culture; you'll find subcategories like Chinese Surinamese, Javanese Surinamese, Creole Surinamese, and Indian Surinamese throughout the Netherlands.

New Draver (page 104) is one of the best spots to try Creole Surinamese food, which includes dishes like *herie herie,* a dish with Portuguese influences that includes cassava, banana, and potatoes. A Javanese Surinamese dish, *telo terie* is small salted fish cooked and fried with spices as well as the influence of serving *nasi* or Indonesian fried rice with a meal. From Indian Surinamese food, you cannot go wrong with *bara,* a fried donut-esque bread made with mung bean flour that can be cut open to have a filling added. You'll also find *roti* served with a potatoes, vegetables, or meat. Lastly, Chinese Surinamese food includes many Cantonese influences. *Moksi meti* is Chinese Surinamese-style sliced pork. For lunch, you can often find dishes like these served Dutch-style in a sandwich.

International

BILADI

Borgerstraat 189; tel. 020 412 5796; www.restaurantbiladi.nl; 11am-11pm Mon.-Sat., 1pm-11pm Sun.; €11.50

Since 2006, Biladi has been inviting customers into their atmospheric café filled with beautiful Moroccan tiles and lanterns. It's sometimes hard to get a seat, as loyal customers come here to sip tea, snack on their delicious "Fingers of Fatima," and talk for hours. If you're a fan of flavorful Moroccan *tajines* and couscous dishes, you'll find plenty of options. For a lighter meal, opt for their soups and Moroccan sandwiches. Cash only.

FOODHALLEN

Bellamyplein 41; tel. 020 254 6437; www.amsterdam.nl/parkeren-verkeer/parkeergarages/overzicht/de-hallen; noon-11pm Sun.-Thurs., noon-1am Fri.-Sat.; €12

Since 2014, the Foodhallen has offered up 20-plus different food stalls with options from around the world to lively groups of tourists and locals. It's situated within De Hallen, a former tram depot dating back to 1902 that has been transformed into a cultural center. Despite the crowds, the food options stay fresh, and you're likely to find everything from dim sum to tacos along with food hall favorites such as burgers. It can be difficult to find a table, especially with a larger group, and the venue tends to be quite loud, but the fun atmosphere, often with a DJ playing, makes the Foodhallen a great place to start off a night in Amsterdam. Their bar serves a well-curated list of local craft beers.

ORONTES WEST

Hugo de Grootplein 8; tel. 020 684 7758; www.restaurantorontes.nl; 2pm-11pm daily; €20

Named after the river that runs through Turkey, Lebanon, and Syria, Orontes is a Turkish restaurant that serves up delicious

Turkish *mezzes* underneath colorful lanterns in a beautiful, atmospheric space. Orontes is a great late-night option, especially for couples and groups thanks to their shared platters and hearty portions.

MUSEUMKWARTIER AND OUD ZUID

Dutch

CAFÉ SCHINKELHAVEN

Amstelveenseweg 126; tel. 020 671 9509; www.cafeschinkelhaven.nl; 10am-1am daily; lunch €8, dinner €16.75

Café Schinkelhaven is a friendly Dutch pub outside the entrance to Vondelpark that is the perfect escape if it starts raining in the park. Their lunch and dinner are typically Dutch, with grilled cheese sandwiches (*tostis* in Dutch), croquettes, salads, and burgers. The café attracts families as well as couples enjoying a lazy weekend or drinks on a Friday on the pleasant patio. If the weather doesn't cooperate, the interior of the café is cozy enough—and the staff is quite friendly. Cards only.

Brunch

DIGNITA

Koninginneweg 218; tel. 020 221 4458; https://eatwelldogood.nl; 8:30am-5pm daily; €12.50

Keep a clean conscience and enjoy a meal at Dignita, a brunch spot that donates its profits to stop modern slavery and provide opportunities for vulnerable people. Their delicious all-day brunch, including their American-style pancakes served with rose, rhubarb, and chocolate, make doing good tastier than you can imagine. It's often hard to get a seat during lunch on weekends at their busy location close to Vondelpark, but it's much easier early in the day and with a reservation.

STARING AT JACOB

Jacob Van Lennepkade 215; tel. 020 223 7498; https://staringatjacob.nl; 9am-4pm daily; €13

Staring at Jacob is a trendy brunch restaurant that is packed on the weekend with young professionals who line up for lunch with a Bloody Mary on the side. They're best known for their chicken and waffles, but the smashed avocado toast is also a favorite.

International

VONDELPARK3

Vondelpark 3; tel. 020 639 2589; www.vondelpark3.nl; 10am-11pm daily; €9

One of the easiest places to meet up with friends or simply take a break is Vondelpark3, a café and cultural center in a beautiful neo-Renaissance building that overlooks Vondelpark. An upscale crowd, along with hungry tourists, often stops off to enjoy the spacious terrace with umbrella-covered tables, perfect for watching the skaters, tourists, bikers, and runners as they pass by. Many visitors end up grazing on their mixed appetizer plates or their *bitterballen* along with other Dutch *borrel* snacks. Salads as well as entrees are available for both lunch and dinner.

DROVERS DOG

Heemstedestraat 25; tel. 020 669 2233; http://drovers-dog.com; 9am-11pm Tues.-Sun.; €14

Drovers Dog is an Aussie-run brunch and dinner joint that is a favorite of English-speaking expats and internationally minded Dutchies. The café (their second branch) prides itself on its friendliness, delicious burgers, tasty pancakes, and poached eggs made with locally sourced ingredients. If you're lucky, you'll spot their friendly canine mascot! The café is quite family-friendly, with a children's play area close to a table where parents can relax.

KARTIKA

Overtoom 68H; www.restaurantkartika.com; 3pm-10pm Mon.-Sat.; €18.90

Kartika's walls are lined with wooden puppets from Java, reflecting the roots of the proud owners of this Indonesian restaurant who have been serving *rijsttafel* for the last 50 years. Their 13-dish *rijsttafel* is said to be one of the quicker rice tables in Amsterdam—which is a considerable boast—but still, don't rush out of this intimate restaurant. Reservations recommended.

CAVATARIA

Cornelis Krusemanstraat 15; tel. 020 237 4337; https://cavataria.nl; 4pm-midnight; €11.50, set menu €29.50

Cavataria is a friendly Spanish restaurant that aims to elevate Spanish wine and tapas to the next level. It's a perfect spot for couples and groups who enjoy sparkling wine (cava). For a nice date night, opt for their daily three-dish set menu with whatever is on special, although *patatas bravas* are a popular side. The interior is cozy yet playful, with some surprises including a confession booth.

★ BLAUW

Amstelveenseweg 158-160; tel. 020 675 5000; https://restaurantblauw.nl; 5:30pm-10:30pm Mon.-Fri., 5pm-10:30pm Sat., 5pm-10pm Sun.; €23, rijsttafel €34

Transport yourself directly to Jakarta at Blauw, Amsterdam's premier high-end Indonesian restaurant. Smartly dressed business travelers, expats, and locals tuck into Blauw's beautifully presented dishes made with East Javanese recipes handed down by the owner's grandmother, as well as modern Indonesian recipes that take inspiration from other Indonesian islands and street food. The interior is modern, with a giant blown-up black-and-white photo of the owner's family.

Many first-time visitors opt for the sizable *rijsttafel* featuring delicious dishes such as mackerel in candlenut sauce. Those looking for bold flavors won't be disappointed, as Blauw does not shy away from putting a twist on familiar favorites or perfecting mainstays like *rendang* (slow-cooked beef). Vegetarians will also find many options. Reservations recommended.

DE PIJP

Dutch

VEGAN JUNK FOOD BAR

Marie Heinekenplein 9; www.veganjunkfoodbar.com/locations/marie-heinekenplein; 11am-midnight daily; €13

Amsterdam's best-known vegan restaurant proudly serves up animal-free Dutch food, including favorites such as fries, *bitterballen*, and *kapsalon*. The graffiti-style décor with a millennial feel is trendy, and their vegan renditions of Dutch favorites pair well with beers from Amsterdam. Warning: The "burgers" are huge.

LOETJE IN DE PIJP

Ferdinand Bolstraat 188A; tel. 020 237 4321; https://indepijp.loetje.nl; 10am-10:30pm daily; €20

One of the best-known Dutch restaurants in Amsterdam, in business for more than 40 years, Loetje in De Pijp is famous for perfectly-grilled tenderloin steaks. Although this location isn't the original, the café has maintained a warm atmosphere where you can enjoy a beer and *bitterballen* with friends around 5pm, or a have a quieter dinner with family.

Cafés and Light Bites

MASSIMO GELATO

Van Ostadestraat 147; tel. 06 25208610; 11am-11pm daily; €4

Massimo Gelato is one of the best-known ice cream parlors in Amsterdam, serving up inventive flavors of rich gelato ice cream made with natural ingredients. Amsterdammers line up around the block in summer. Massimo produces vegan sorbet and gelato, along with traditional Italian gelato flavors like *gianduja* for true chocolate lovers.

SCANDINAVIAN EMBASSY

Sarphatipark 34; tel. 06 81600140; http://scandinavianembassy.nl; 8am-6pm Mon.-Fri., 9am-6pm Sat.-Sun.; €5

For a taste of *fika* in Amsterdam, Scandinavian Embassy is the perfect stop. Their small yet homey café in De Pijp is cozy enough that you'll want to sit down on the bench outside as you enjoy a cinnamon roll with a perfectly brewed coffee.

International

WARUNG SPANG MAKANDRA

Gerard Doustraat 39; tel. 020 670 5081; www.spangmakandra.nl; 11am-10pm Mon.-Sat., 1pm-10pm Sun.; €10

Warung Spang Makandra is proudly the first Javanese Surinamese eatery in the Netherlands, established in 1978. The family behind the business has continued serving up their delicious *saoto* soup along with *roti,* Javanese tempeh, and other delicious dishes that represent the richness of flavors in Javanese Surinamese food. If you cannot handle spiciness, inform the staff! Cash only.

CT COFFEE AND COCONUTS

Ceintuurbaan 282-284; tel. 020 354 1104; https://coffeeandcoconuts.com; 8am-5pm daily; €10

CT Coffee and Coconuts is housed in a beautiful former movie theater from the 1920s that looks quite unassuming on the outside. Once you walk in, you feel transported to Bali, the inspiration for the owners of this leafy café that focuses on incorporating coconuts and other healthy ingredients into many of their dishes. No reservations are accepted, which can make it a tough place to visit on weekends without waiting in line, but their refreshing salads, sandwiches, and smoothie bowls are worth the wait.

DE PIZZAKAMER

Tweede van der Helststraat 16; tel. 020 221 1457; www.pizzakamer.nl; 5pm-10pm Sun.-Thurs., 5pm-11pm Fri.-Sat.; €10

De Pizzakamer keeps things simple with scrumptious personal pizzas served fresh out of the oven with top-quality buffalo mozzarella. It can be challenging to find a seat, but if you can't get a table on their lovely terrace in summertime, get a pizza to-go and it's just a 10-minute walk to the Amstel River.

SIR HUMMUS

Van der Helstplein 2; tel. 020 664 7055; www.sirhummus.nl; noon-9pm Wed.-Sat., noon-5pm Sun.; €11

Founded by Israeli cooks in Amsterdam, Sir Hummus proudly perfects hummus and falafel at their *hummusiya.* Their airy take-out restaurant has a just a few tables. They focus on hummus, perfectly roasted beans and nuts, and other vegetables cooked to perfection with delicious pita bread on the side. Cards are accepted, and a healthy meal is a guarantee here.

DEER MAMA VEGAN MYLK & BURGER BAR

Ceintuurbaan 71; tel. 020 233 4882; www.deermama.nl; 11am-10pm daily; €12

Vegan food doesn't need to be boring. Deer Mama proudly serves the first vegan softserve ice cream in the Netherlands along with other vegan shakes. However, the main attractions here are their delicious "burgers" with an international twist (think Tex Mex and Thai), especially with their meat substitutes that taste as good as the real thing.

SARI CITRA

Ferdinand Bolstraat 52; tel. 020 675 4102; www.saricitra.nl; 2pm-8pm daily; €13

Although many tourists flock to high-end Indonesian restaurants for *rijsttafel,* budget-savvy locals often stop off for a quick dinner at Sari Citra, a cozy *toko* close to the Heineken Experience. Don't be discouraged by the plastic tablecloths and retro décor; this is one of the most popular Indonesian take-out restaurants in De Pijp. Head to the buffet to choose from a smorgasbord of choices, which generally include a few vegetables and meats along with noodles or rice, to fill up a plate for €10. Specify your spice level if you can take the heat! There is limited seating, but you can always take your food to-go to enjoy while sitting on Museumplein.

Markets

ALBERT CUYPMARKT

Albert Cuypstraat; https://albertcuyp-markt.amsterdam; 8am-5pm Mon.-Sat.

Albert Cuypmarkt is one of the largest markets in Amsterdam with more than 260 stalls selling everything from fabric to *stroopwafels.* It takes up most of Albert Cuypstraat in De Pijp during the week.

1: Scandinavian Embassy **2:** Albert Cuypmarkt **3:** apple pie at Winkel 43

SCANDINAVIAN EMBASS
Queue behind
Queue behind
1

Vlaardingse
Haringhandel
2

3

AMSTERDAM OOST

Dutch

INSTOCK AMSTERDAM

Czaar Peterstraat 21; tel. 020 363 5765; www.instock.nl; 11am-11pm Tues.-Sat.; lunch €7, dinner €26

Instock is a sustainable restaurant that uses leftover supermarket produce to create delicious dishes with a bit of creativity and some culinary magic. Their sizable restaurant serves a very reasonable lunch as well as an ever-changing dinner menu, where you can choose from a few dishes made with seasonal ingredients. Although food waste isn't sexy, their dishes are always served beautifully.

Cafés and Light Bites

COFFEE BRU

Beukenplein 14; tel. 020 751 9956; www.coffeebru.nl; 8am-6pm Mon. -Fri., 9am-6pm Sat.-Sun.; €4

Coffee Bru was the first specialty coffee bar to open in the rapidly generifying Amsterdam Oost. The modern café, decorated with a heavy dosage of greenery, attracts a hip, creative crowd. There are a few tables outside, but the interior is far more atmospheric.

MOTION COFFEE

Eerste Van Swindenstraat 547; tel. 06 57544293; https://eerstevanswindenstraat.amsterdam/motion-coffee; 8:30am-5pm Mon.-Sat.; €4

Motion Coffee is a vintage-themed coffee bar with a cheerful interior out of a Wes Anderson movie. Their beans are roasted locally and are popular with laptop workers who come here for a bit of inspiration. The service is friendly and the cakes are tasty.

International

NEW DRAVER

Tweede Oosterparkstraat 2-4; tel. 020 663 0230; www.newdraver.nl; 2pm-11pm daily; €12

For more than 30 years, New Draver has been serving Creole Surinamese dishes, and it's well known throughout the Surinamese community for its authentic Surinamese food. The interior is plain with various tables and stools, but people come here for the daily specials and the great atmosphere inside. There's a terrace outside for warmer days.

BOI BOI

Dapperstraat 12HS; tel. 020 233 9499; https://boiboi.com; 3pm-10pm daily; €13

If you end up spending a bit too long at Brouwerij 't IJ, you might end up seeking a quick place for dinner. Although Boi Boi can certainly get busy, their reasonable Thai dinner specials are a great detour. They boldly claim that they have the best pad thai noodles in Amsterdam, and their spice levels aren't a joke. The interior is playful and modern, and their beer selection is impressive.

AMSTERDAM NOORD

Dutch

CAFÉ DE CEUVEL

Korte Papaverweg 4; tel. 020 229 6210; http://deceuvel.nl; 11am-midnight Tues.-Sun.; lunch €7, dinner €15

Café De Ceuvel is one of the most unique waterside cafés in Amsterdam. The café feels a bit like a seaside cabin thanks to its sustainable architecture assembled from recycled materials. It's not too far from the Noord ferry, but it's easy to get lost in the easygoing atmosphere, especially in summer, when the terrace is packed with young couples and groups of friends who come for both the cool vibes and the vegan-friendly menu.

PLLEK

T.T. Neveritaweg 59; tel. 020 290 0020; www.pllek.nl; 9:30am-1am Sun.-Thurs., 9:30am-3am Fri.-Sat.; lunch €9, dinner €19

Pllek is the place to be in Amsterdam Noord. This bar's interior is made up entirely of former shipping containers, while its terrace sits directly on the IJ river with an artificial beach. A solid beer selection and vegetarian-friendly menu attracts a young, trendy crowd that comes to sunbathe in summer, cheers with friends, snack, and occasionally take a dip in the river.

THE BUTCHER SOCIAL CLUB

Overhoeksplein 1; tel. 020 215 9515; https://the-butcher.com/socialclub; 8am-1am Mon.-Thurs., open 24 hours Fri.-Sat., 8am-1am Sun.; €11

At the Butcher Social Club, the restaurant-bar at the Sir Adam Hotel, all are welcome to eat, drink, and be merry, with nice views of Amsterdam's Central Train Station. The Butcher is known for their hamburgers, but they also do brunch along with snacks for those who aren't burger-crazy. The interior is plain and modern. Most people come here for the weekend buzz, which picks up on Friday and Saturday with well-dressed professionals planning to go out at Shelter and other clubs in Amsterdam Noord.

VUURTORENEILAND

Vuurtoreneiland; tel. 020 362 1664; http://vuurtoreneiland.nl; by appointment/ferry schedule Tues.-Sat.; lunch €82.50, dinner €90

When was the last time that you were on your own private island for a dinner? Vuurtoreneiland is a small island with a lighthouse that is generally closed to the public. Savvy entrepreneurs have set up a restaurant here that feels like a truly special occasion: You'll be able to take a private ferry from the Lloyd Hotel for a five-hour meal and exploration of the island with your reservation. In summer, meals created with seasonal regional ingredients are served in a glass house to allow you enjoy the stillness of your surroundings. In winter, diners eat inside surrounding an open fire. Booking required, with a maximum of two months ahead, although you might have luck with a last-minute reservation.

Cafés and Light Bites

CAFÉ MOK

Gedempt Hamerkanaal 75; https://mok.amsterdam; 9am-6pm Mon.-Fri., 11am-5pm Sat.-Sun.; €3

Café Mok is a cozy living room for residents of Amsterdam Noord in an area full of former warehouses. Although the interior is slightly industrial, the bar has a friendly feel; you'll find residents catching up over a coffee or slice of cake.

BBROOD

Ms. van Riemsdijkweg 30; tel. 020 633 1089; www.bbrood.nl; 7:30am-6pm daily; €4

Bbrood is a good quick option for breakfast or lunch once you get off the NDSM ferry. The two-story bakery sits across from the ferry stop, and it's a good location for sweets or a sandwich made with their namesake bread. You can enjoy views of the IJ river—and the ferry from their upper terrace—alongside your coffee.

International

COBA

Schaafstraat 4; tel. 06 40848875; www.coba-taqueria.com; 6pm-midnight Thurs.-Sun.; €11

Around the corner from Oedipus Brewing, Coba is a great spot for tacos. The Mexican chef pairs traditional favorites with killer cocktails and drinks that are all made in-house. The ever-changing tacos, made with ingredients sourced from Mexico, are delicious.

Bars and Nightlife

Amsterdam's nightlife is known for its electronic music and infamous coffeeshops, but the Dutch capital has much more to offer, from high-end cocktail bars to old-fashioned cafés. Many tourists go out in Amsterdam Centrum, particularly the **Red Light District,** or main club districts **Leidseplein** and **Rembrandtplein** in Grachtengordel Oost. But you'll find stellar clubs elsewhere in Amsterdam, too, and drinks farther from the center aren't as overpriced.

If you're looking for a quieter night out, you can opt for Amsterdam's **brown bars,** the Dutch answer to the English pub, where wood-lined cafés welcome tourists and locals alike with a cold beer from the tap. In these neighborhood spots, the volume allows for conversation and the tap lists feature great craft beers produced within the city limits. In summer, Amsterdammers flock to the terraces along the canals and outside cafés to people-watch—and slurp down G&Ts, a favorite among millennials. No matter your nightlife preference, from speakeasy to divey, you'll find something to your taste.

For live music, it's best to buy tickets, as many popular shows at De School, Melkweg, and Paradiso sell out, especially during the Amsterdam Dance Event (ADE).

AMSTERDAM CENTRUM

Bars

CAFÉ DE JAREN

Nieuwe Doelenstraat 20-20; tel. 020 625 5771; https://cafedejaren.nl; 8:30am-1am Sun.-Thurs., 8:30am-2am Fri.-Sat.

It's easy to walk past Café de Jaren without realizing how charming this riverfront café on the Amstel truly is. It's grand and beautiful with tasteful modern art, free Wi-Fi, and a reasonable menu; it's worth waiting for a seat outside even if it's just for a coffee to watch the boats cruise past on the river.

★ IN 'T AEPJEN

Zeedijk 15-1; tel. 020 626 8401; noon-1pm Sun.-Thurs., noon-3am Fri.-Sat.

In the heart of Amsterdam's Red Light District, you'll find a beautiful 16th-century building hiding In 't Aepjen, a bar whose name refers to the café's past as an inn popular with sailors who would return from their travels with monkeys that they acquired as souvenirs. After spending all of their hard-earned money on drinks, the sailors would offer to pay their bills with the monkeys or be forced to sleep with them in the attic. (The monkeys were eventually donated to what became the Amsterdam Zoo.) Thus, in Dutch the phrase "You spent the night in the monkey" means that you've gotten yourself in trouble.

Despite its former seedy reputation, the bar is now a quiet establishment where Amsterdammers have a drink or read the newspaper while sipping on a coffee or beer. You'll find monkey-related paintings, stuffed animals, and statues throughout the bar, but there are no live monkeys to be found. The interior is *gezellig* in the truest Dutch sense with old Delftware, jenever bottles from its past, bronze chandeliers, a wood-beamed ceiling that shows the café's true age, and candle-lit tables. If only these walls could talk.

HIDING IN PLAIN SIGHT

Rapenburg 18; tel. 06 25293620; www.hpsamsterdam.com; 6pm-1am Sun.-Thurs., 6pm-3am Fri.-Sat.

Hiding in Plain Sight is a "secret" cocktail bar that is hardly a secret anymore, but that doesn't take away from its charm. It's a great stop for smartly dressed individuals looking for one last nightcap before heading back to their hotel.

CAFE DE DOELEN

Kloveniersburgwal 125; tel. 020 624 9023; www.cafededoelen.com; 9am-1am Sun.-Thurs., 9am-3am Fri.-Sat.

Café De Doelen is a favorite brown bar in the Red Light District that dates back to 1895. Its wooden interior and tables along Kloveniersburgwal canal make it a nice spot for a quick drink with friendly locals, including a bar cat, and tourists. It's a strange mix of divey and upscale, with a goat head, sand on the floor, and stained glass lamps.

MR. PORTER

Spuistraat 175; tel. 020 811 3399; www.mrportersteakhouse.com; noon-1am Mon.-Thurs., noon-2am Fri, 7pm-2am Sat., 7pm-1am Sun.

Mr. Porter is a cosmopolitan bar with an incredible view of Dam Square thanks to its position on top of the W Hotel. Although not for every traveler, the hotel caters well to a well-dressed group of locals and tourists who are happy to open a bottle of champagne with a view. The bar is especially known for its ticketed events for Dutch public holidays, especially King's Day.

BEER TEMPLE

Nieuwezijds Voorburgwal 250; tel. 020 627 1427; www.beertemple.nl; noon-midnight Mon.-Thurs., noon-2am Fri.-Sat.

As the name suggests, the Beer Temple is part of a pilgrimage for beer lovers visiting Amsterdam. The bar offers 35 craft beers on tap from local favorites to imported beers, from the United States in particular. It's a great place to start off your night and a favorite of local American expats.

Clubs

TONTON CLUB CENTRUM

Sint Annendwarsstraat 6; tel. 020 244 4633; https://tontonclub.nl; 4pm-midnight Mon.-Fri., noon-midnight Sat.-Sun.

TonTon Club Centrum is not your typical Amsterdam nightlife venue, as it's quite friendly to non-drinkers looking for a bit of fun. It's full of board games, pool tables, pinball, and air hockey. You have to pass through one of the narrowest streets of the Red Light District to find it, but it's a surprisingly innocent late-night café for good old-fashioned fun.

Distilleries

WYNAND FOCKINK PROEFLOKAAL AND SPIRITS

Pijlsteeg 31; tel. 020 639 2695; https://wynand-fockink.nl; 2pm-9pm daily

Wynand Fockink is a true Amsterdam institution and one of the best places to try some Dutch liquors. The distillery's small yet atmospheric tasting room holds a maximum of seven people and is located off an alleyway just off Dam Square in a beautiful 17th-century building. The distillery dates back to 1724, when Wynand Fockink took over, before leaving the business in his family's hands. The liquors sold here are still made in small batches using copper stills, as they have been for centuries.

The friendly staff behind the counter speak a number of languages and are happy to educate you on the history of every drink you're tasting. Their most interesting liquors are the Singelburger herbal bitter and the floral Volmaakt Geluk liqueur. There is a **distillery tour** and tasting for €17.50 on weekends, but it's not necessary if you're lucky enough to get into the tasting room.

DE DRIE FLESCHJES

Gravenstraat 18; tel. 020 624 8443; http://dedriefleschjes.nl; 2pm-8:30pm Mon.-Sat., 3pm-7pm Sun.

Since 1650, De Drie Fleschjes (The Three Little Bottles) has been serving up jenever to guests, including Anthony Bourdain once, with barrels lining the walls and Amsterdammers of all ages crowding in to enjoy miniature cocktails in jenever glasses. Be sure to admire the historic bottles with former Amsterdam mayors painted on them, and ask about the miniature cocktail of the month.

GRACHTENGORDEL AND PLANTAGE

Bars

PROEFLOKAAL ARENDSNEST

Herengracht 90; tel. 020 421 2057; www.arendsnest.nl; noon-midnight Sun.-Thurs., noon-2am Fri.-Sat.

Proeflokaal Arendsnest is a classic Dutch brown bar that has been a bit of an Amsterdam institution during its 20 years along Herengracht. The bar only stocks Dutch beer and there are more than 50 beers on draft—and more than 100 bottles available to buy. The beautiful wooden interior overflows onto a canal-front terrace with classic views of the city.

BAR LEMPICKA

Sarphatistraat 23; tel. 020 622 0209; www.barlempicka.com; 9am-1am Sun.-Thurs., 9am-3am Fri.-Sat.

Bar Lempicka is a beautiful art deco bar, named after Polish art deco artist Tamara de Lempicka, with big leather couches perfect for sharing drinks with a small group. The bar serves both breakfast and cocktails, so no matter the time, you can enjoy the lovely views of the Amstel from the terrace. Young couples, alongside couples their parents' age, cozy up on the terrace to catch up with friends, especially after shows at the nearby Royal Theater Carré.

DOOR 74

Reguliersdwarsstraat 74; tel. 06 34045122; www.door74.net; 6:30pm-1am Sun.-Thurs., 6:30pm-3am Fri.-Sat.

For a step into the past, Door 74 is a prohibition-style cocktail bar with an art deco twist. The bar is quite small, so it typically runs on the reservation system to ensure that patrons have a special experience. (You'll need to text or save your place via their website.) The décor embraces their prohibition influences with no clear sign on the door and retro-inspired furniture.

Clubs

PARADISO

Weteringschans 6-8; tel. 020 626 4521; www.paradiso.nl; hours vary by event

Paradiso is a beautiful music venue in Amsterdam with several locations, although the best-known location is in a 19th-century church on Weteringschans. The church was converted in the 1960s by hippies, but it became a favorite location for raves in the 1990s. Today, their weekly club nights and regular concert agenda cater to 1,500 visitors under the church's beautiful stained glass windows, with music tastes ranging from electronic to rock. Many of their popular events sell out in advance.

DUKE OF TOKYO

Reguliersdwarsstraat 37; tel. 020 777 9332; https://dukeoftokyo.com; 5pm-1am Mon. and Wed.-Fri., 2pm-3am Sat.

Duke of Tokyo is a fun karaoke bar, with eight karaoke booths. A slot for two hours of singing and dancing with friends starts at €12 per person and increases on weekends/evenings. The interior is colorful and decorated with Japanese banners, and if you're looking for a true party atmosphere, you'll love the Ikebukuro room with its disco ball. Reserve ahead online.

MELKWEG

Lijnbaansgracht 234A; tel. 020 531 8181; www.melkweg.nl; noon-3am when events occur

Melkweg is a former sugar refinery/milk producer that has been converted into cultural center, best known for its concerts and club nights. One stage might be playing indie pop while the other plays metal; it's best to check the agenda to ensure that you go to the right stage for your music taste. The largest stage holds up to 1,500 and has hosted international acts along with upcoming artists.

DE JORDAAN AND HAARLEMMERDIJK

Bars

CAFÉ THIJSSEN

Brouwersgracht 107; tel. 020 623 8994; http://cafethijssen.nl; 8am-midnight Sun., 8am-1am Mon.-Thurs., 8am-3am Fri., 7:30am-3am Sat.

Café Thijssen is a favorite among millennial Amsterdammers who crowd into this fairly modern café with a good beer selection, known for music on weekends and bilingual English-style pub quiz on Monday nights at 8pm. It's always crowded with groups here, so finding a table can be a challenge on weekends.

BAR OLDENHOF

Elandsgracht 84; tel. 020 751 3273; www.bar-oldenhof.com; 11am-1am Sun.-Thurs., 11am-3am Fri.-Sat.

For a quiet spot away from the crowds where you can enjoy a neat Scottish whiskey or cocktail, ring the doorbell and head beyond the black curtains to this speakeasy-style café with comfortable leather chairs, a fireplace, and a beautiful interior straight out of *The Great Gatsby*. The staff greet you at the door—and take your jacket before charming you with stories. It attracts an elegant yet interesting crowd often deep in conversations.

TOP EXPERIENCE

☆ Find Your Favorite Brown Bar

beer at a brown bar

As much as people associate the classic pub with the English, the Dutch have perfected the brown bar, a neighborhood bar where virtually every inch is covered in dark wood. Contrary to what you may think, the name has nothing to do with marijuana. Some say that it comes from the walls, stained from years of smoking inside before it was prohibited, but you can decide for yourself.

Brown bars are often visited during the day as cafés, where older locals often catch up on the news with friends over a cup of coffee. Some cafés have hardly changed for 100 years, besides an ever-rotating bar cat. At these cafés, you can truly experience the *gezellig* side of Amsterdam's nightlife. Have a small glass of beer on tap, though be warned: Many of these cafés do not accept foreign cards, so be sure to bring **cash.** Here are some of the city's best brown bars:

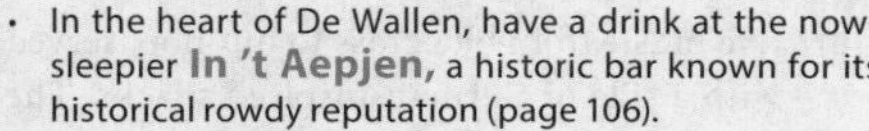

- In the heart of De Wallen, have a drink at the now-sleepier **In 't Aepjen,** a historic bar known for its historical rowdy reputation (page 106).
- At the always packed **De Drie Fleschjes,** natives crowd in for miniature cocktails made with traditional Dutch liquors (page 107).
- Just a little outside the Red Light District, you'll find the always charming **'t Blaauwhooft,** a neighborhood bar where it's easy to lose track of time and get lost in conversation (page 110).
- For a quieter beer in the Jordaan, **Café 't Smalle** offers stunning canal views with a modern beer menu (page 110).
- **Café Chris** is a sure bet for a memorable night of meeting interesting locals in a café from the 1600s (page 109).
- For a proper education on Dutch craft beer, **Proeflokaal Arendsnest** offers a beautiful location along the scenic Herengracht canal (page 107).

CAFÉ CHRIS

Bloemstraat 42; tel. 020 624 5942; www.cafechris.nl; 3pm-11pm Mon. and Wed.-Sat, 3pm-9pm Sun.

Café Chris is the oldest café in the Jordaan—and possibly one of the oldest continually existing brown bars in Amsterdam—dating back to 1624. The bar's ancient interior, including its stained glass windows advertising various liquors, wooden beams, and earthenware mugs from the past century, make it feel like a museum, but it's far from one. Despite the Jordaan slowly gentrifying, the bar is a favorite among an older local crowd, although tourists are eagerly embraced and chatted up by the regulars. Cash only.

CAFÉ P96

Prinsengracht 96; tel. 020 622 1864; http://p96.nl; 11am-3am Sun.-Thurs., 11am-4am Fri.-Sat.

Prinsengracht is one of Amsterdam's best-known canals, but Café P96 kills the pretense within their cozy brown bar that has been serving up beer and apple pie since 1975. Notably, they have a beautiful terrace on an old houseboat with one of the best spots to enjoy the sunset over Prinsengracht in warmer weather. It's also a great bar after last call elsewhere.

VESPER

Vinkenstraat 57; www.vesperbar.nl; 6pm-1am Tues.-Thurs., 5pm-3am Fri.-Sat.

Vesper is a tiny cocktail bar with a full-on James Bond theme, with creative drinks that occasionally come out smoking. The frequently well-dressed crowds, often on dates, are known to trust bartenders with their preferences and wait to be surprised. Despite its high-quality cocktails, it's not the kind of bar where there's a velvet rope of young 20-somethings; the staff makes the bar feel like your friend's beautiful living room where all are welcome. They change their menu frequently.

CAFÉ 'T SMALLE

Egelantiersgracht 12; tel. 020 623 9617; 10am-1am Sun.-Thurs., 10am-2am Fri.-Sat.

Café 't Smalle sits on one of the prettiest and greenest canals of the Jordaan, a spot that many tourists can't resist admiring from the bridge. Step into Café 't Smalle, a neighborhood café that embraces both tourists and locals on an old boat, one of the prettiest sunset spots in Amsterdam. It's never too loud this café that dates back to 1786, which makes it a great spot for long conversations over a drink, especially in winter when they serve *glühwein* (mulled wine) to you on wooden tables next to stained glass windows.

'T BLAAUWHOOFT

Hendrik Jonkerplein 1; tel. 020 623 8721; http://blaauwhooft.nl; 11am-1pm daily

'T Blaauwhooft is a typical Amsterdam brown bar hidden in the Western Islands. This neighborhood has a beautiful wooden interior with stained glass windows, and locals drop in to make conversation with the bartenders while sipping local craft beer. In summer the bar expands its terrace in the nearby square, while in colder seasons, most people dine inside at candlelit tables. Maupie, the bar's sometimes-friendly cat, often steals tables and seats from customers. Bring cash as foreign cards aren't accepted.

AMSTERDAM WEST

Bars

CHECKPOINT CHARLIE

Nassaukade 48; tel. 020 370 8728; www.cafecheckpointcharlie.nl; 1pm-1am Sun.-Thurs., 1pm-3am Fri.-Sat.

Checkpoint Charlie, named after the famous checkpoint in Berlin, is a hipster bar in Amsterdam West that can be immediately recognized by the David Bowie mural outside. The friendly, typically mixed crowd in their 20s and 30s dances along with alternative music from bluegrass to hip-hop, served with a side of German-inspired snacks. The bar also hosts comedy, live music, and other events weekly. The interior is trendy with pool, pinball, and high tables.

CAFÉ NASSAU

De Wittenkade 105A; tel. 020 684 3562; https://cafenassau.com; 11am-midnight Mon.-Thurs. and Sun., noon-1am Fri., 11am-1am Sat.

Café Nassau is a locals' secret thanks to its location in the unassuming and relatively unknown Wittenkade, a canal outside the center. At this charming café/restaurant, you're likely to find young couples and small groups of friends enjoying a meal before having a quiet drink on the sunny terrace in summer.

Clubs

DE SCHOOL

Doctor Jan van Breemenstraat 1; tel. 020 737 3197; open 24/7

Go back to school in a very different way at this former technical school turned 24-hour club/cultural space that is one of Amsterdam's best spots to dance the night away to electronic music and emerge in time for brunch.

Dutch Drinking Culture

If you don't drink alcohol, don't fret, as nobody judges you for your choice of drink in Dutch cafés: it's acceptable to order a coffee or tea at almost any hour. On cold days, you're likely to find the Dutch enjoying a warm drink, whether it's a fresh mint tea or a coffee. Of course, most tourists prefer to unwind with a beer while on vacation, which you'll certainly find plenty of thanks to a long history of brewing in the Netherlands. At the higher end of alcohol content, you'll find strong **jenevers** or **herbal bitters,** which are generally consumed within their own specialized glasses.

BEER

If you're looking to take it easy, it's best to stick to beer. But be sure to look at the percentage first, as many a tourist has ordered a few triples (***tripel***) before realizing that these heavier beers start at 7.1 percent ABV. A lighter option is the white beer (***witbier***), typically a maximum of 5 percent ABV. Many Dutchies often stick to cheaper Belgian and Dutch beers on tap behind the bar such as **Heineken** and **Jupiler** when drinking socially. You'll also find craft beers produced in Amsterdam including the female-led brewery **Gebrouwen door Vrouwen Bar** (page 112).

LIQUORS

For those looking for something a bit heavier, there are plenty of options, including **jenever,** a liquor brewed with juniper berries and malt. There are two kinds of jenever, old (*oude*) and young (*jonge*); old jenever is closer to a whiskey, aged in oak barrels, while young jenever is closer to a vodka. Jenever is traditionally drunk in a tulip-shaped glass filled to the brim, best sipped at the beginning while leaning down toward the counter before picking up the glass. You'll often see the ***kopstoot*** on the menu, which means having a jenever with a beer as a chaser. For those looking for something different, herbal bitters (***kruidenbitters***) are favorite drinks for sipping. These are typically jenevers that have been spiced with a secret blend that will make you curious about the recipe. (Most distilleries aren't eager to tell.)

COCKTAILS

In winter, a favorite Dutch remedy to warm oneself up is ***glühwein,*** typically made with red wine, cloves, anise, rum, cinnamon, and oranges, found at most cafés and winter markets. ***Oranjebitter*** is another favorite, especially on King's Day, made of brandy, oranges, and sugar.

TEA

One unique Dutch offering is fresh mint tea (***verse muntthee***), which isn't the mint tea that you're used to. The Dutch dunk an entire handful of fresh mint leaves into hot water and serve it with honey. It's a surprisingly warming beverage in winter that pairs well with a *stroopwafel,* best warmed up sitting on the rim of the glass. You'll also find standard teas available at every Dutch café.

COFFEE

Coffee has a long history in the Netherlands, and the Dutch are some of the heaviest coffee drinkers in the world at four cups daily. Coffee in the Netherlands tends to be black by default, but you can request milk if it suits you. ***Koffie verkeerd,*** which means "coffee wrong" in Dutch, is a milky alternative that adds 50 percent milk to your glass for those less keen on a black coffee.

The venue can hold up to 500 people within its three stages, including one underground stage. Beyond the club, live music and art events are hosted here. The rules are strict with no photos allowed inside and no groups larger than four. Ages 21 and up only.

DE MARKTKANTINE

Jan van Galenstraat 6; tel. 020 723 1760; https://marktkantine.nl; 8pm-5am Fri.-Sat.

De Marktkantine has come a long way from serving lunch to wholesale market sellers after converting its space into a theater. It's now primarily an industrial-feeling club with a large room that holds up to 1,200 dancers who come for everything from electronic headliners to hip-hop. If you're a fan of deep house, be sure to check the agenda for who is playing while you're in town. Ages 21 and up only.

KARAKTER

De Clercqstraat 75 H; tel. 020 737 0843; http://bar-karakter.nl; 5pm-1am Thurs.-Sun., 5pm-3am Fri.-Sat.

Karakter is a popular bar for lovers of song, who flock to the bar for great cocktails and dim sum, while wannabe singers can pick from 3,000 songs in their two private karaoke booths equipped with a tap by the hour. The friendly staff combined with the stylish retro-inspired interior makes it a popular spot for young professionals and friends looking to dance, sing, and have a good time.

MUSEUMKWARTIER AND OUD ZUID

Bars

LABYRINTH COCKTAIL, FOOD & POETRY BAR

Amstelveenseweg 53; tel. 020 845 0972; https://labyrinthamsterdam.nl; 4pm-midnight Sun.-Mon. and Wed.-Thurs., 4pm-2am Fri.-Sat

Labyrinth is a Black-owned bar, restaurant, and event space created by Cameroonian-born mixologist and poet Sam Kingue Ebelle who has won several awards for his delicious drinks. The bar has an artistic atmosphere thanks to its status as the only poetry bar in Amsterdam (at the time of writing) where spoken word performances coincide with drinking delicious cocktails named after poems. It's very much an intellectual bar, but all are welcome to enjoy the jazz, open mics, and poetry nights.

GOLLEM'S PROEFLOKAAL

Overtoom 160-162; tel. 020 612 9444; 11am-1am Sun.-Thurs., 11am-3pm Fri.-Sat.

Gollem's Proeflokaal is great for beer lovers with its 22 taps and more than 180 bottles available behind the counter. Don't be intimidated by the menu, as the staff is always happy to find something suitable for you; their house beers are a sure bet. The café has its own bar cat, Hondje, who eagerly introduces itself to customers enjoying the terrace outside or the typical brown bar interior.

BUTCHER'S TEARS

Karperweg 45; tel. 06 48955332; https://butchers-tears.com; 4pm-9pm Wed.-Thurs., 4pm-11pm Fri.-Sat., 2pm-7pm Sun.

Butcher's Tears is one of Amsterdam's most interesting upcoming breweries, known for its experimental beers. Despite being technically in Amsterdam Zuid, the brewery is hidden down an industrial street about 1 kilometer away from the entrance to Vondelpark (a 4-minute bike ride). The space feels unfinished and unpolished, but you'll definitely feel like an insider once you step in for a beer that you'll be drinking in something akin to a parking lot. You can also catch alternative music shows here.

GEBROUWEN DOOR VROUWEN BAR

Jan Pieter Heijestraat 119D; tel. 020 854 5277; https://gebrouwendoorvrouwen.nl/bar; 3:30pm-midnight Mon.-Thurs., 2pm-1:30am Fri.-Sat., 2pm-midnight Sun.

Amsterdam's first exclusively female-run brewery serves favorites including a gin-infused beer inspired by jenever. Started by two sisters, the name means "Brewed by

Amsterdam's Craft Breweries

Beer has long been a Dutch tradition, but don't horrify the locals by telling them that Heineken is the best beer you've ever had. (To be fair, a fresh Heineken off the tap is much better than the ones sold abroad.) For the best beer in Amsterdam, head to Amsterdam's many craft breweries.

- For experimental beer, **Oedipus Brewing** produces a great range of beers with a twist, from IPAs to sours (page 115).
- **Butcher's Tears** in Amsterdam Zuid is always prepared to surprise craft beer lovers up for a challenge (page 112).
- For Dutch standards perfected, you don't need to look any further than the female-run **Gebrouwen door Vrouwen Bar** (page 112).
- **Brouwerij 't IJ** is known for its location within an old pool underneath a windmill. The seasonal selection, only available at the brewery, certainly makes it worth the trip (page 114). They've now opened a second location in Vondelpark.
- **Walhalla** is a newcomer to the scene, and it's likely to impress with its Nordic-inspired beers. They have a physical location in Noord (Spijkerkade 10; tel. 06 11391675; www.walhallacraftbeer.nl; 4pm-11pm Thurs., 2pm-11pm Fri., 2pm-11pm Sat., 2pm-8pm Sun.) and you can often find their beers at bars.

Women" in Dutch. It's a hip neighborhood bar where young and old are welcome.

CRAFT & DRAFT

Overtoom 417; tel. 020 223 0725; www.craftanddraft.nl; 4pm-midnight Mon.-Thurs., 4pm-2am Fri., 2pm-2am Sat., 2pm-midnight Sun.

Lovers of variety will love Craft & Draft, which, not surprisingly, has an impressive list of 40 craft beers from around the world on draft. The brick-lined café is a quieter destination for beer lovers to soak up the great beers from throughout the Netherlands and beyond. Their patio is a particularly popular place to people-watch in summer and on weekends.

DE PIJP

Bars

CAFÉ GOLLUM

Daniël Stalpertstraat 74; tel. 020 737 0273; https://cafegollem.nl; 4pm-1am Mon.-Wed., 4pm-3am Thurs.-Fri., 2pm-3am Sat., 2pm-1am Sun

Café Gollum is a small craft beer spot that is truly for beer lovers looking for something new—or a hard-to-find beer. Their Belgian beer selection is quite impressive, and the bar feels cozy. There's always someone to debate the world's best beer with inside the bar or on their mini terrace outside. (There is another Café Gollum in the center, but this one tends to be a bit quieter.)

DOPEY'S ELIXER

Lutmastraat 49; tel. 020 671 6946; www.dopeyselixer.nl; 1pm-1am Mon.-Fri., 4pm-2am Sat., 4pm-11pm Sun.

Established in 1973, Dopey's Elixer is an intellectual brown and one of the last brown bars in the De Pijp, where you're likely to get into conversations with the people on the stools next to you. Don't be fooled by its aged appearance; you're bound to find a great selection of Dutch and international beers on their handwritten chalkboard.

CAFÉ FLAMINGO

Eerste van der Helststraat 37; tel. 020 670 9007; http://cafeflamingo.nl; 10am-1am Sun.-Thurs., 10am-3am Fri.-Sat.

Café Flamingo is a hip neighborhood café on the pedestrian-only street of Eerste van der Helststraat, with a terrace that provides the perfect opportunity for people-watching after shopping at the Albert Cuypmarkt. The café stocks a great selection of local Amsterdam beers along with juices.

GLOU GLOU

Tweede van der Helststraat 3; tel. 020 233 8642; https://glouglou.nl; 4pm-midnight Mon.-Thurs., 3pm-1am Fri., 2pm-1am Sat., 3pm-midnight Sun.

Glou Glou takes its name from the French for drinking down wine at a fast pace, but the bar isn't as wild as the name suggests. It's mostly a neighborhood wine bar that specializes in organic wines by the glass (or bottle), but on Friday nights, you're likely to be among groups of well-dressed professionals who happily drink their wine as they celebrate the start of the weekend.

AMSTERDAM OOST

Bars

BROUWERIJ 'T IJ

Funenkade 7; tel. 020 261 9800; www.brouwerijhetij.nl; noon-8pm daily

The city's best-known brewery was founded in 1985. You're likely to spot their eight standard beers, with an ostrich on the bottle, at bars throughout Amsterdam. Their flagship taproom is in a former bathhouse underneath the **De Gooyer windmill,** dating back 1725. Even if you're not a big beer drinker, the knowledgeable bartenders always have recommendations, and it's worth coming just to drink see the windmill. The bar accepts international cards, but finding a table after 5pm can be difficult, especially on weekends. Their limited-edition beers are certainly worth a taste as some aren't served outside the brewery, and few can find fault in the IJwit.

DE BIERTUIN

Linnaeusstraat 29; tel. 020 665 0956; https://debiertuin.nl; 11am-1am Sun.-Thurs., 11am-3pm Fri.-Sat.

De Biertuin is a German-style beer garden that attracts a diverse crowd thanks to a nice list of Dutch and international craft beers. It's a favorite among the *borrel* time crowd who come here with colleagues after work to enjoy *bitterballen* and a beer. In winter, they put up heated lamps to make sitting outside a bit more bearable, although there are always seats indoors.

BAR BOTANIQUE

Eerste Van Swindenstraat 581; tel. 020 358 6553; www.barbotanique.nl; 9am-1am Sun.-Thurs., 9am-3am Fri.-Sat.

Bar Botanique is the greenest place in Amsterdam outside the Hortus Botanicus thanks to an all-green interior filled with tropical plants. Many young Amsterdammers flock to the bar to share pitchers full of sangria with friends, but the staff won't judge if you opt for a Heineken fresh off the tap as you imagine yourself somewhere a bit warmer. The bar also stocks a great selection of local craft beers, nonalcoholic beers, and wine.

BAR BUKOWSKI

Oosterpark 10; tel. 020 370 1685; www.barbukowski.nl; 9am-1am Sun.-Thurs., 9am-3am Fri.-Sat.

Bar Bukowski's name does not match up well with its image. The elegant wood-filled interior with tall windows is a great place to enjoy a cocktail or a quieter beer away from the crowds. The music doesn't get loud until quite late—and it's the perfect place to debate Bukowski with friends during the day and early evening, even if this would not be his scene.

Distilleries

PROEFLOKAAL 'T NIEUWE DIEP

Flevopark 13a; www.nwediep.nl; 3pm-8pm Tues.-Sun. Apr.-Sept., 3pm-6pm Wed.-Sun. Oct.-Mar.

For a taste of a truly local liquor, you can head deep into the unassuming Flevopark to find this charming distillery that opened up in an old pumping station that looks far more attractive than you'd imagine. The distillery has a tasting room where you can sample their 100-plus drinks, which include jenevers, herbal bitters, liquors, and gins, in a plain yet unpretentious setting, and an attractive terrace with views of the park. All the liquors are made with old recipes using organic ingredients. Cash only.

LGBTQ Nightlife

The Netherlands is proudly the first country in the world to legalize gay marriage—and the LGBTQ community is quite strong in Amsterdam. One of the centers for LGBTQ nightlife in Amsterdam is **Reguliersdwarsstraat,** a quieter street tucked behind the Amsterdam Flower Market where rainbow flags fly proudly.

Reguliersdwarsstraat with pride flags

CLUB NYX

Reguliersdwarsstraat 42; tel. 068 236 3649; http://clubnyx.nl; 10pm-5am Fri.-Sat.

Club NYX is a popular club that hosts an LGBTQ-friendly Saturday night party starting around 11pm called 3XNYX, with three different floors with different music genres from '90s to house.

BAR BLEND

Reguliersdwarsstraat 41; tel. 062 955 7092; www.barblend.nl; 3pm-10pm Tues.-Sun.

On the same street, you'll find Bar BLEND, which hosts drag nights and bingo nights in a cozy two-story bar.

PRIK

Spuistraat 109; tel. 020 320 0002; www.prikamsterdam.nl; 4pm-1am Mon.-Fri., noon-3am Sat.-Sun.

Nearby, you'll find Prik, a proudly gay bar with a bright-pink interior that focuses on cocktails and an intimate atmosphere where visitors are welcome.

CAFÉ SAAREIN

Elandstraat 119; tel. 020 623 4901; www.saarein2.nl; 4pm-1am Tues.-Sun.

For lesbians, Café Saarein in the Jordaan is a favorite, with a pretty, typical brown bar exterior. Started in 1978 by a group of women as a collective who wanted to create a safe space, the café is now inclusive of all queer-minded people.

DE TRUT

Bilderdijkstraat 165; www.trutfonds.nl; 10pm-2:45am Sun.

De Trut is a safe space and disco where your phone must be shut off, with once-a-week parties run by volunteers.

AMSTERDAM NOORD

Bars

CAFÉ 'T SLUISJE

Nieuwendammerdijk 297; tel. 020 636 1712; www.cafehetsluisje.nl; 10am-midnight Mon.-Thurs. and Sat.-Sun., 10am-1am Fri.

Café 't Sluisje is a more than 100-year-old picturesque brown bar with a beautiful wooden interior. It's a great stop as you bike through Amsterdam Noord, especially on a sunny day when you can sit on the terrace overlooking the *sluis* (canal lock) or the picturesque houses along Nieuwendammerdijk while enjoying a coffee or cold beer. Cash only.

OEDIPUS BREWING

Gedempt Hamerkanaal 85; tel. 020 244 1673; https://oedipus.com; 5pm-10pm Thurs., 2pm-11pm Fri.-Sat., 2pm-7:30pm Sun.

Oedipus Brewing's tap room in an old warehouse is surprisingly cozy despite the industrial feeling of the neighborhood about 20 minutes (2 kilometers/1 mile) from the ferry stop from Amsterdam Centraal. If you're already biking around Amsterdam Noord, be sure to pop in for their experimental beers, especially the risqué-named Polyamorie mango sour and the Swingers lemon gose. The atmosphere is very casual, though it skews more hipster and intellectual than other craft breweries in Amsterdam.

Clubs

SHELTER AMSTERDAM

Overhoeksplein 3; https://shelteramsterdam.nl; 11pm-8am daily

The entrance to Shelter Amsterdam is straight out of sci-fi movie, with a trapdoor that rises straight out of the concrete down into the abyss, which happens to be the former basement of the Shell tower. The nights start late here, but it's not abnormal to dance the night away in their dark, smoky underground space until morning to top electronic acts who often take the reins during ADE and other events. There is no dress code besides dressing for your personality, however dark or bright it may be. Ages 21 and up only.

Accommodations

Accommodations in Amsterdam range from basic hostels to swanky boutique hotels to quirky bridge houses along the waterways. Depending on your taste—and your budget—there's something for everyone, although finding accommodation for less than €150 in peak season can be a challenge.

Most of the well-known accommodations are clustered in Amsterdam Centrum, although many tourists also opt for the beautiful Grachtengordel for canal views from their balcony. For the tourist looking for a more off-the-beaten-path experience, De Pijp, Amsterdam Oost, Amsterdam Noord, and Amsterdam West have more affordable rooms (by Amsterdam standards), with good access to more trendy restaurants and nightlife.

To cut costs even further, a lot of travelers opt for accommodations outside Amsterdam's main neighborhoods, or even the adjoining nearby towns. **Amsterdam Bijlmer** is a popular choice due to its good Metro and train connections with Amsterdam's center and its location next to the Amsterdam ArenA, for those planning to attend concerts. There are also hotels in residential neighborhoods farther from the center, including New West (**Nieuwe West**) and **Amstelveen.** Another popular choice is **Haarlem,** which is just 15 minutes from Amsterdam and a charming Dutch city in itself. **Zaandam** is also a popular choice with good train connections. You can cut the cost of a hotel by around 30 percent by leaving Amsterdam.

AMSTERDAM CENTRUM

Under €100

ST CHRISTOPHER'S AT THE WINSTON

Warmoesstraat 129; tel. 020 623 1380; www.st-christophers.co.uk/amsterdam/winston-hostel; €70

Best suited to younger travelers, St Christopher's at the Winston is a hip hostel with private rooms for those looking for a centrally located place to crash and meet fellow travelers. The social feeling extends to the friendly hostel bar, free breakfast with booking, a 24-hour desk for travelers arriving late, a smoking room, and a terrace garden. The rooms are basic, but it's a good value for a quick overnight on a budget. Some of the rooms feature art from local artists.

1: Brouwerij 't IJ 2: Café 't Sluisje 3: Sir Albert hotel 4: boats in front of the Amsterdam Central Train Station

Brouwerij't IJ
1
2
3
SiR
IZAKAYA
4

Over €200

INK HOTEL AMSTERDAM - MGALLERY

Nieuwezijds Voorburgwal 67; tel. 020 627 5900; www.ink-hotel-amsterdam.com; €208

With more than 149 rooms, the Ink Hotel Amsterdam is inspired by the history of one of the canal houses that make up the hotel, the former home of the Dutch newspaper/magazine *De Tijd*. The hotel includes a 24-hour gym for night owls, a cozy bar known for its high-quality coffee, a chic restaurant, and meeting rooms for business travelers. The lobby features lettering in keeping with the newspaper theme. Despite its central location, the hotel has good sound isolation. The rooms have an open layout best suited to couples or solo travelers. Extras include an espresso machine, kettle, flat-screen TV, rainfall shower, bathrobes, and air conditioning.

GRACHTENGORDEL AND PLANTAGE

Under €100

HOTEL LEIDSEGRACHT

Leidsegracht 117; tel. 06 54932477; www.hotelleidsegracht.com; €66

Hotel Leidsegracht is a small seven-room hotel right on the canal. The hotel is no-frills (although some higher-priced rooms include canal views), but the location is great, a few steps from Leidseplein. The lobby operates 24 hours a day with coffee, Wi-Fi, and luggage storage upon checkout. Most of the appeal of the hotel comes from the central location, though this can make it noisy.

Over €200

MAX BROWN HOTEL CANAL DISTRICT

Herengracht 13; tel. 020 710 7288; https://maxbrownhotels.com/canal-district-amsterdam; €209

The dreamiest accommodation along the canals is Max Brown, located in three historic canal houses about 10-minutes from the Anne Frank House. The interior of the hotel's café is filled with warm wooden furniture and a book wall made up of covers to make you feel at home. Every room features a wooden wall and a rustic feel, including quilted blankets. Breakfast is standard with a Max Brown reservation, which is a nice addition. Guests can also enjoy the board game collection, grab a book from the book swap library, and relax in the private garden.

DE JORDAAN AND HAARLEMMERDIJK

€100-200

BACKSTAGE HOTEL

Leidsegracht 114; tel. 020 624 4044; www.backstagehotel.com; €111

Backstage Hotel is a music-themed hotel right in the heart of Amsterdam's nightlife district, footsteps from Leidseplein. Best suited to traveling musicians or those traveling to Amsterdam for concerts/nightlife, Backstage features hip rooms decked out in stage- and music-themed decorations. The rooms are comfy enough, although noise can be an issue due to the location close to many bars. Rooms feature a lighted vanity mirror like you would find backstage, and you can borrow a guitar or record player if you fancy yourself to be a musician for a night. Their staff stays up to date on the local music gigs, and the lobby/bar is filled with signatures if you want to leave your mark.

MR. JORDAAN

Bloemgracht 102; tel. 020 626 5801; https://mrjordaan.nl; €150

Design lovers will adore Mr. Jordaan, started by a born-and-raised Amsterdammer with a great sense of hospitality. Housed within a canal house a bit off the beaten path, Mr. Jordaan is one of the few accommodation options in this sleepier residential neighborhood. If you're looking to truly live like a local, you'll love this friendly hotel. The rooms are thoughtfully designed with cutouts of Amsterdam canal houses on the headboards and lots of wood. The hotel has air-conditioning, a rarity in Amsterdam canal houses.

AMSTERDAM WEST

Under €100

HOTEL NOT HOTEL

Piri Reïsplein 34; tel. 020 820 4538; www.hotelnothotel.com; €95

Located footsteps away from Amsterdam West's coolest street, Kinkerkstraat, Hotel Not Hotel is a bold experiment in design, with rooms that make you feel like you're sleeping in an art museum. They feature everything from a converted tram car and rooms hidden behind bookshelves, to one room that includes its own crow's nest reading spot. The rooms themselves are comfortable and minimal, and in some cases lacking a private bathroom. The restaurant features a trendy bar with killer cocktails named after Kevin Bacon.

MUSEUMKWARTIER AND OUD ZUID

Under €100

XO HOTEL INNER

Wanningstraat 1; tel. 020 400 4187; www.flyingpig.nl; €80

XO Hotel Inner is just footsteps from Museumplein along a beautiful and posh street in Oud Zuid, an ideal location. Their rooms are small and basic. Cat lovers will be excited to meet the assistant part-time manager who sleeps behind the manager's desk.

€100-200

THE DELPHI

Apollolaan 101-105; tel. 020 679 5152; www.delphihotel.nl; €110-150

In a typical Amsterdam townhouse 10 minutes from Museumplein, the Delphi is an elegant independent hotel with 50 thoughtfully furnished rooms. Their rooms come with a safe, hairdryer, air-conditioning, coffee/teamaker, Wi-Fi, and television. There's a cozy living room where you can meet other guests or plan your day. The hotel is great for couples looking for a nice place to relax.

CONSCIOUS HOTEL THE TIRE STATION

Amstelveenseweg 5; tel. 020 820 3333; www.conscioushotels.com; €136

The Tire Station is located in a more modern part of town, in an eco-friendly hotel with 112 rooms just a block from Vondelpark. In what used to be an auto repair shop, today, expect trendy 20- and 30-somethings dining at the hotel's restaurant and separate café serving up organic and vegan-friendly options. The rooms are basic yet have a hipster sense of design, with a corkboard headboard and playful signs in the bathroom. The hotel has self-check-in 24/7 and a boardroom available for business travelers.

Over €200

PILLOWS ANNA VAN DEN VONDEL AMSTERDAM

Anna van Den Vondelstraat 6; tel. 020 683 3013; www.pillowshotels.com/amsterdam-vondel; €303

Pillows Anna van den Vondel Amsterdam was featured in the novel *The Fault in Our Stars* under its previous name, Hotel Filosoof. It's made up of three beautiful 19th-century houses, with a smart exterior that fits into the neighborhood perfectly. There's a private garden where guests can sit outside with a drink from the lounge on the ground floor. Some of its 30 rooms include a garden view. The rooms are built for a luxurious stay thanks to thoughtful touches like a walk-in shower, smart TV, and an iPad in the room.

DE PIJP

€100-200

SIR ALBERT

Albert Cuypstraat 2-6; tel. 020 710 7258; www.sirhotels.com/en/albert; €120

Housed within a 19th-century diamond factory, Sir Albert pulls out all the stops for the tourist looking for immersion in Amsterdam's coolest neighborhood, De Pijp. The 90-room hotel features high ceilings, ultra-modern design touches, Illy espresso machines, rain showers, and high thread counts. A few rooms have a balcony. The hotel amenities include a small gym, meeting room, and a study with a fireplace and comfy leather chairs to relax in.

EASYHOTEL AMSTERDAM

Van Ostadestraat 9; tel. 020 846 8100; www.easyhotel.com/hotels/netherlands/amsterdam; €139

Certainly not the most glamorous hotel option in Amsterdam, Easyhotel Amsterdam's location in De Pijp offers a great location and value for budget travelers looking for a comfortable place to crash. The exterior is uninspiring and particularly gray, but the interior is bright with orange touches. The rooms are basic, but comfy enough for a quick weekend trip. The hotel sits within the heart of De Pijp's trendiest area, so it will be easy to find great meals here.

AMSTERDAM OOST

Under €100

THE STUDENT HOTEL AMSTERDAM CITY

Wibautstraat 129; tel. 020 214 9999; www.thestudenthotel.com/amsterdam-city; €100

The Student Hotel Amsterdam is not just for students.It offers hip, cute college-inspired rooms with air-conditioning and all the perks, from a café with events to a coworking space to fast Wi-Fi. Housed within a former office complex, the rooms feature playful college banners alongside a gym, game room, laundry, and bike rentals. Even business travelers will feel at home at this grown-up hotel. In Amsterdam Oost, it's still walking distance from Amsterdam's center.

€100-200

VOLKSHOTEL

Wibautstraat 150; tel. 020 261 2100; www.volkshotel.nl; €149

Once a newspaper headquarters, the Volkshotel is a trendy hotel whose interior hides much of its charm. The smallest rooms are quite small, but much of the appeal of staying at the Volkshotel is taking advantage of its close location to Amsterdam, its lively rooftop bar and sauna, and many activities, including yoga. This is a great hotel for solo travelers and trendy couples looking to experience the liveliness of Amsterdam.

AMSTERDAM NOORD

Under €100

BOTEL

NDSM-Pier 3; tel. 020 626 4247; https://botel-nl.book.direct/n; €90

Botel is one of the more unusual budget-friendly hotels in Amsterdam. With more than 175 no-frills rooms, Botel is housed on a former cruise ship. Guests can unwind in the on-site bar with games, or opt to disembark to explore the rest of NDSM, the trendiest part of Amsterdam Noord. There are also some ultra-modern themed lofts within the letters that display the hotel's name from afar.

€100-200

SIR ADAM

Overhoeksplein 7; tel. 020 215 9510; www.sirhotels.com/en/adam; €110-130

Housed in a 22-story building with stunning floor-to-ceiling windows, Sir Adam has a great view of the Amsterdam waterfront from across the IJ, especially from the 360-degree rooftop, which features a swing. The rooms include high-thread-count sheets, an Illy machine, a rain shower, a guitar, and a record player. The hotel has its own vinyl library for dancing in your room, along with a lounge for relaxing or getting ready for a big night out. There is also a gym available for guests. Within the building, there are two restaurants, including a rotating restaurant and a popular bar/restaurant known for its burgers.

Information and Services

TOURIST INFORMATION

IAMSTERDAM VISITOR CENTRE STATIONSPLEIN

Stationsplein 10, 1012 AB; www.iamsterdam.com; 10am-7pm Mon.-Fri., 9am-6pm Sat.-Sun.

For a map or to buy a GVB (public transit pass) or **iAmsterdam card,** you can head to the convenient, friendly iAmsterdam visitor center right outside the Amsterdam Central Train Station.

LUGGAGE STORAGE

DROP & GO

Prins Hendrikkade 86; tel. 020 223 36 48; http://dropandgo.nl; 9am-10pm daily

Just around the corner from the Amsterdam Central Train Station, you'll find Drop & Go. Its location makes it useful if you have to check out of your hotel earlier despite having a later flight in the evening. They charge by number of luggage pieces and their sizes.

AMSTERDAM CENTRAAL

5am-1am daily

Close to Track 1 at the Amsterdam Central Train Station, you'll find a small luggage storage area that is a good option for smaller bags. There are a limited number of lockers—and suitcases may not fit inside. This storage area is better suited for smaller backpacks and other smaller pieces of luggage. Credit cards are accepted.

SAFETY

Amsterdam is a safe city to explore, although pickpocketing incidents can occur in the city center, on public transit, and by bike. (Some thieves will pluck valuables out of your basket before zooming off, so be sure to secure your valuables before cycling.) Bike theft is also a big issue.

In case of an emergency, call **112** for the **police, fire brigade,** or an **ambulance.** For those who are deaf or hard of hearing, you can also call 0800-8112. There are **police stations** all throughout the city, including in Amsterdam Central Train Station. If you have a non-urgent emergency, you can call the Amsterdam Police at 0900-8844.

In the Netherlands, it's typical to get an **appointment** to speak to the police—and it's best not to show up at police stations for minor crimes such as lost items without calling first. Be sure to bring your passport and ID forms with you. The Dutch police speak good English on average.

HEALTH

For toiletries, tampons, and other over-the-counter medicines, you can head to the popular Dutch drugstore chains **Etos** and **Kruidvat** all throughout Amsterdam. In a pinch, **Hema** carries some toiletries, with locations with extended hours at its location within Amsterdam Central Train Station and on Nieuwendijk 174 (9am-9pm Mon.-Sat., 10am-7pm Sun.).

OLVG EAST

Oosterpark 9; tel. 020 599 9111; www.olvg.nl

For urgent care, the closest hospital is OLVG, which has two branches: East and West. OLVG East is the closest hospital to Amsterdam city center. Staff members in Amsterdam hospitals generally speak good English and are used to non-Dutch-speaking patients. The hospitals in Amsterdam also have 24/7 **pharmacies** for patients.

AMSTERDAM TOURIST DOCTORS

Nieuwe Passeerdersstraat 8; tel. 020 237 3654; www.amsterdamtouristdoctors.nl; 8am-8pm Mon.-Fri., 9am-6pm Sat., 9am-5pm Sun.

If you need to see a doctor while in Amsterdam, this is a group of doctors who cater to visitors with a walk-in clinic as well as pre-booked appointments.

LEIDSESTRAAT PHARMACY

Leidsestraat 74-76; tel. 020 422 0210; www.leidsestraatapotheek.nl; 9am-12:30pm and 2pm-7pm Mon.-Fri., noon-5pm Sat.-Sun.

If you need to pick up a prescription as prescribed by a Dutch doctor, you can ask the doctor for the nearest pharmacy or head to the Leidsestraat Pharmacy. Many Dutch pharmacies tend to be closed after 5pm and on weekends, so be sure to check the hours before agreeing to have your prescription sent to a pharmacy.

CONSULATES

The **United States Consulate** (Museumplein 19; tel. 020 575 5309; https://nl.usembassy.gov/embassy-consulate/amsterdam; by appointment) in Amsterdam requires appointments; if you lose your passport and/or require emergency services, it's best to contact the consulate by phone or online.

Other embassies in Amsterdam include the **UK Embassy** (Koningslaan 44; tel. 070 4270 427; www.gov.uk/world/organisations/british-consulate-general-amsterdam) and **Australian Embassy** (Carnegielaan 4; tel. 070 310 8200; https://netherlands.embassy.gov.au). The embassies for Canada and New Zealand are located in the Hague rather than in Amsterdam. For emergencies, contact the embassy by phone or email.

Transportation

GETTING THERE

The best way to arrive in Amsterdam if you're not flying is undoubtably by train. The Netherlands is well connected with Belgium, France, and Germany, and a few hours on the Thalys (a high speed train from Paris and Brussels) will land you right in the heart of Amsterdam's city center. Once you arrive, there's no need to fret about a car while exploring the larger area, as the bus and train network runs reliably and distances between cities are small.

Air

SCHIPHOL AIRPORT

Evert van de Beekstraat 202; tel. 020 794 0800; www.schiphol.nl

Schiphol Airport (AMS) is the main international airport for the Netherlands, with numerous international flights. It's about 20 kilometers (12 miles) outside Amsterdam.

Schiphol Airport has routinely been rated one of the world's best airports year after year. And it's well deserved: From the moment you arrive, you'll be delighted by the airport's many food and souvenir options in the pre-security area. Do like the Dutch and stop off at **Albert Heijn** for a light snack if you have a bit of time. Schiphol Airport technically has just one passenger terminal, but there are several departure halls and a general division between EU and non-EU destinations. All the halls are well connected with each other, with pedestrianized moving walkways. There are numerous food options past security, too. Despite the size of Schiphol, the clear signage and laid-back feeling of the airport makes it one of the smoothest places to fly into Western Europe.

The most efficient and cheapest way to get to Amsterdam from the airport is by **train.** From any train station in Amsterdam, there are connections to Schiphol Airport, with a train running every 10-15 minutes 5am-midnight. The journey takes just 10-15 minutes and costs €4.50 per ride.

Another option to travel from Amsterdam to Schiphol Airport is by **bus,** which is included in the GVB transit pass and iAmsterdam card. There are many options for buses throughout the day and evening, including the **397/N97** bus that runs between Schiphol Airport and Leidesplein every 20-30 minutes. From Leidesplein, it is possible to transfer to another bus or the Metro to other locations in Amsterdam. A single-trip costs €6.50 each way.

A registered **taxi** from the airport to Amsterdam Center stand should cost about €45 and take about 30 minutes depending on traffic. Fake taxis are a particular issue by Schiphol Airport. Always go with a taxi that is lined up at a proper taxi stand. Be sure to check that the meter is on!

EINDHOVEN AIRPORT

Luchthavenweg 25; tel. 0900-9505; www.eindhovenairport.nl

If you're a fan of budget flights, you might see flights to the Netherlands via Eindhoven (EIN) pop up, but Eindhoven is about 1.5 hours' drive from Amsterdam (123 kilometers/76 miles). This is not as convenient as Schiphol Airport—and you might also find budget flights that go into Schiphol Airport as well. Be sure to plan well to give yourself enough time beforehand if you catch a flight from Eindhoven.

From Eindhoven, you can opt for taking the **train** to Amsterdam, which takes 1 hour 15 minutes and costs €25 total each way, including the 400/401 **airport shuttle bus** from Eindhoven Train Station (Eindhoven Centraal) to the airport. You can purchase an Airport Eindhoven Single Ticket, which includes the bus fare to the airport, via the www.ns.nl public transit website.

For a more direct route, you can also book a ticket on the **AirExpressBus** that runs between Eindhoven Airport and Amsterdam approximately every hour (www.airexpressbus.com; €22.40 online, €24 in person one-way) during business hour with extra hours on weekends. The bus takes 1.5 hours, and you can catch the bus across from Lovers Canal Cruises.

Train

Amsterdam is well connected with other European cities by train. In the coming year, there will be increased numbers of overnight trains to encourage travelers to take the train instead of flying. Coming from **Paris** or **Brussels,** you can opt for the Thalys or Intercity trains that run about once an hour. The Thalys takes just a little over 3 hours from Paris, while Brussels to Amsterdam takes about 2 hours. There are also daily trains to Germany, including **Berlin** (6 hours 20 minutes). The Eurostar runs between Amsterdam and **London** (4 hours 10 minutes). You can purchase train tickets on the **NS International website** (www.nsinternational.nl) as well as at the NS International kiosk in Amsterdam Central. Tickets tend to be cheaper about two months in advance, and a reservation is generally required on international trains. It is possible to catch the Thalys directly from Schiphol Airport; however, other international trains might need to be caught at Amsterdam Central Train Station.

AMSTERDAM CENTRAL STATION (Amsterdam Centraal)

Stationsplein 15; tel. 030 751 5155; www.ns.nl; open 24/7

Amsterdam Centraal's distinctive neo-Gothic facade was designed by Pierre Cuypers in the late 1800s. The station is spacious with a lot of amenities, including a first-class lounge and numerous eateries. Some parts of the station, including the main row of restaurants close to the tracks, require a valid ticket to access. With the Dutch train system, you generally need to scan your ticket on the way into the station, as well as on the way out to exit.

Bus

AMSTERDAM SLOTERDIJK STATION

Zaventemweg 1; tel. 030 751 5155; www.ns.nl; open 24/7

The largest bus company that operates out of Amsterdam is **Flixbus** (https://global.flixbus.com), which operates of the Amsterdam Sloterdijk train station, with daily journeys to Paris, Berlin, London, Antwerp, and Brussels. For travel to smaller towns in Europe or farther destinations, **Eurolines** (www.eurolines.eu) offers buses to Paris, Antwerp, London, Prague, Berlin, and Frankfurt. Most trips tend to take a similar amount of time as on the trains (not high-speed), provided there isn't traffic, which is unavoidable. Overall, the buses tend to be substantially cheaper than the trains when booked in advance.

Car

Amsterdam allows cars within the city, but **parking** is an issue. It is possible to park for an hour or two after paying at a machine in some parts of Amsterdam, but parking is reserved for residents by permit in much of the city. If you choose to visit Amsterdam by car, the best option is to park at one of the P+R (Park and Ride) parking lots near public transit locations, where rates are as low as €8 per day for a maximum of 4 days. Most locations are at least 15-30 minutes outside of Amsterdam Center and require a transfer. There are two convenient locations in **Zeeburg** (Zuiderzeeweg 46; Zuiderzeeweg 8). Zeeburg is an outer neighborhood of Amsterdam, and you can take tram 26 or 14 in the direction of Amsterdam Centraal (Centrum).

If you plan to park in the center, underground parking garages generally cost €0.21 per 2 minutes, or a maximum of €63 per day. The most central lots are located at **Ruysdaelkade 100** in De Pijp and **Waterlooplein 28** in the Plantage. Privately owned parking garages are mostly run by **Q-Park** (www.amsterdam.nl/parkeren-verkeer/parkeergarages/parkeergarages); locations include Museumplein, Westergasfabriek, Amsterdam Central Train Station, Rembrandtplein, and Waterlooplein.

GETTING AROUND

Amsterdam has a good public transit network, although in the city center, it's often faster to walk or bike than wait for public transit.

Public Transit

The public transit agency in Amsterdam, **GVB,** operates a network of buses, trams, and a Metro in the larger Amsterdam region, though not to other cities like Rotterdam or the Hague. As soon as you arrive into Amsterdam Schiphol or Centraal, you'll see a clear map posted of the GVB network, and maps are available at kiosks. There are also ticket machines next to major transfer points (e.g. metro stations and train stations). Generally, trams are more tourist-friendly, as there's typically a kiosk manned by a person on board and announcements often note nearby attractions. This is not true for the bus and Metro, although the whole GVB is fairly straightforward as long as you know your stop and direction of the tram/bus/Metro. Announcements are in both English and Dutch. People are eager enough to help out if you're unsure.

It is important to note that public transit in the Netherlands requires checking out when you exit—if you forget to check out, you may invalidate your pass. You can purchase a ticket on a bus, or from a GVB kiosk or vending machine in Amsterdam or Schiphol Airport. A one-way ticket valid for 90 minutes (including transfers) costs €3.20. It's easy to look up public transit in Amsterdam on Google Maps as well as on the GVB app/website.

Public transit after midnight (12:30am-7am) is more limited in Amsterdam. After midnight, GVB operates **night buses** that take a bit longer and cover multiple routes. A 90-minute night bus ticket that includes transfers costs €4.70 per person. They mainly originate from Rembrandtplein and Leidesplein.

If you're using public transit, the **day pass** is a steal at €8 per 24 hours for adults. These passes are also often sold at many Amsterdam hotels. It is also possible to buy a 72-hour GVB ticket (€19). The **iAmsterdam card** includes a GVB pass.

Ferry

A free ferry run by GVB connects Amsterdam's main city center with Amsterdam Noord across the IJ river (https://reisinfo.gvb.nl/en/lijnen). It is possible to bring a bike, scooter, or wheelchair onto the ferry as long as you stick to the correct section. The most trafficked routes across the river are the **907/902/901** routes, which originate behind Amsterdam Central Train Station and run directly across the river, running to either **IJplein** or **Buiksloterweg,** which are directly across from Centraal across the water. IJplein is slightly southwest just footsteps from the Eye Museum. Buiksloterweg is a 2-minute walk away, and it doesn't matter much which stop you take the ferry to. These ferry lines run approximately every 5-15 minutes 6am-midnight. After midnight, the 907 ferry runs approximately every 15 minutes from Amsterdam Central Train Station to Buiksloterweg station.

For those staying in the NDSM neighborhood or wishing to visit Amsterdam Noord, there is also a less-frequent ferry that runs every 15 minutes 7:30am-midnight between Amsterdam Central Station and NDSM. Past midnight, these ferries run approximately once an hour.

Cycling

Even Dutchies who don't live in Amsterdam often don't dare to bike here, as it involves a lot of defensive biking that's far from stress-free. The closest analogy for inexperienced bikers would be if you learned to drive and opted to head to New York City to drive through Times Square after years of not driving. Simply, think carefully before renting a bike. Maybe wait until you've been in Amsterdam for a day or two, or go on a cycling tour **outside the city center** first. There are a number of **bike tours,** including tours that offer **e-bikes** for those who aren't used to biking for longer periods.

If you're brave enough to rent a bike, it does provide a significant amount of mobility throughout Amsterdam compared to taking public transit or walking. That said, if you intend to stay in the heart of Amsterdam Centrum, it's unlikely that you will need a bike.

Taxi

Taxis in Amsterdam have a less-than-stellar reputation among tourists and locals, so make sure you are in a registered taxi, which includes a roof light with a Taxi symbol and the name of the operator, and a blue numbered license plate. A short taxi ride should cost a maximum of €15-20. Taxis *must* have the meter running, provide a receipt, take the shortest route possible, and accept trips of *any* length. There are no official fixed prices in place for taxi rides at the time of writing, so do not agree to a fixed price. I strongly recommend keeping Google Maps running during your ride.

Taxis cannot idle around the city or pick up passengers off the street, but rather in defined spots, so be sure to ask your hotel for the nearest taxi stand or to call a taxi in advance if needed. **Taxi stands** can be found at several points throughout the city including Amsterdam Central Train Station, Dam Square, and the Van Gogh Museum. A full map of the various taxi stands can be found here: www.amsterdam.nl/parkeren-verkeer/taxi/standplaatsen/kaart.

There are several taxi operators in Amsterdam, but the largest and most dependable taxi company is **Taxicentrale Amsterdam** (www.tcataxi.nl; tel. 020 650 6505), with more than 1,500 drivers and their own app. You can look for their cabs with the distinctive TCA sign at taxi stands throughout the city or preorder a taxi by phone.

It's best to ask before you get into a taxi, even a licensed one, whether they accept non-Dutch cards, as some drivers will ask for cash later, claiming their machines are broken to avoid giving a receipt and getting fined for violating taxi operating laws. If you are severely ripped off by a taxi driver, you can file a complaint via the **Taxi Complaints Commission** (www.taxiklacht.nl), which includes a filing fee of about €52, or contact the police in case of an illegal taxi scam. Be sure to note the time that you got into the taxi, the license plate, and the date, which should be on your receipt, along with your taxi's license/driver's ID (should be displayed in the cab).

Uber also operates in Amsterdam. Rates tend to be slightly lower than the taxis, but there are fewer Ubers operating.

Vicinity of Amsterdam

A quick bus ride allows you to step away from the city and get fresh air as you explore the Amsterdam area's most beautiful castle—and iconic windmills that are straight out of a postcard. Those looking for a scenic workout may also enjoy the longer bike ride through the countryside and Amsterdam's outer neighborhoods along perfectly maintained bike paths.

MUIDEN

Muiden is a cute fortified city just 15 kilometers (9 miles) southeast of Amsterdam with historical castles and forts. Despite the seemingly small distance, leaving Amsterdam for Muiden feels like getting a breath of fresh air and a taste of small-town Holland. Muiden's cobblestoned streets, rustic brown bars with a whiff of a seafaring past, and picturesque buildings make it an easy day trip from Amsterdam that requires minimal planning beyond keeping an eye on the once-an-hour bus schedule.

Muiden is best known for Muiderslot, an impressive medieval castle that guards the entrance to the Vecht river, one of the key transport routes. The fortifications served as a way of protecting Holland from invaders. One of the key defense points is Fort Pampus, a human-made fortress island just off Muiden by ferry, from the late 19th century. Although the island was never actively used in war and was stripped for parts during World War II, the fortress generally welcomes those interested in military history. For the next few years, renovations will be occurring at Pampus to turn it into the first 100 percent self-sufficient and fossil-free UNESCO World Heritage Site.

★ Muiderslot Castle

Herengracht 1; tel. 0294 256 262; www.muiderslot.nl; 10am-5pm daily; adults €15.50, children 4-11 €9, children 0-3 free

Muiderslot is one of the Netherlands' most scenic castles, straight out of a fairy tale, with a moat, ramparts, four towers, and everything that makes a castle feel epic.

HISTORY

This medieval castle dates back to 1285, when it was acquired by Count Floris V. It served as a fortress on the banks of the busy Vecht river that lead into the Zuiderzee, a former bay that was important for trade. Floris's castle turned out to be bad luck, as he was imprisoned and murdered shortly after building it. The castle was demolished, but much of the castle's shape was retained when it was rebuilt in 1363, including four corner towers that you can imagine Rapunzel leaning out of.

Since the medieval period, there have been more renovations, but the castle has retained its medieval shell. In the 17th century, ramparts were added in order to protect the fortress from attackers—and fortunately, the castle managed to avoid being destroyed by attackers for much of its history. As you walk around the castle, you'll notice various defensive features including a spot where hot tar could be poured onto intruders.

A group of intellectuals called the Muiderkring regularly met here to discuss everything from poetry to the sciences. They were known to sip on an herbal bitter with a secret recipe during their discussions, named for their only female member. (You can find the herbal bitter Tesseltje at the gift shop if you're curious.)

VISITING THE CASTLE

The interior has now been restored to reflect life in the 16th and 17th centuries, which was an important period for the castle. The Knights' Hall has been restored to its 17th-century glory with beautifully carved wooden furniture, Delft tiles, and 16th-century portraits. In the bedroom, you can see a rare

17th-century bed engraved with flowers and animals.

Admission comes with a free audio tour, and if you time your visit well, you can catch medieval-themed events such as dueling and **tours** of the castle with a live guide.

Admission includes access to the beautiful sculpted gardens, which include a green tunnel where feudal lords would stroll away from the sun, as well as an herb and vegetable garden used for growing food and medicinal plants for the castle. On weekends, the falconry also showcases birds of prey used by the lords of the castle for hunting. The castle has a number of kid-friendly exhibitions and even offers costumes for eager young royals.

Be sure to walk the fortifications surrounding the castle for a beautiful view of the IJsselmeer and the castle with its moat from above. It should be noted that the castle is not accessible for people in wheelchairs or people with mobility issues because of its steep winding stairs and narrow hallways. Admission is free with the iAmsterdam card. There's a **café** inside.

Food

OME KO

Herengracht 71; tel. 0294 262 333; www.omekomuiden.nl; 8am-noon Sun.-Mon., 8am-1am Tues-Sat; €13

Ome Ko is an old sailors' bar turned friendly neighborhood brown bar with a pretty terrace that overlooks one of the main locks boats must pass through to get out toward the IJsselmeer (formerly the Zuiderzee). You'll find all kinds of sailors' mementos from its past as a sailors' café, although today the café is a friendly spot for a quick lunch or drink after seeing the castle.

Getting There

The most convenient way to get to Muiden involves taking the **train** from the Amsterdam Central Train Station to Weesp, a nearby suburb, before transferring to the **110 bus** toward Bussum via Muiden that drops you off in Muiden Centrum. The bus goes once an hour and will leave you directly in the Muiden city center, which is about 10 minutes from the castle on foot (1 kilometer/0.6 mi). The trip costs €5.41 total each way—€3.60 for the train and €1.81 for the bus—and takes 40 minutes.

If you have the iAmsterdam pass, the easiest way is to take the **Metro/tram/bus** to Amsterdam Amstel Station, a lesser-known commuter station within Amsterdam, before catching the **322** or **327** bus to Almere. From the P+R Muiden bus stop, it's a scenic, 30-minute, 2-kilometer (1-mile) walk through Muiden's cute city center. The trip costs €5.46 total each way total—€3 for the bus, €2.40 for the train—and takes 50 minutes.

A taxi would take 20-30 minutes but would cost €50 at minimum.

★ ZAANSE SCHANS

Holland's most famous village is just 30 minutes outside Amsterdam. More than a million visitors come here to stroll along the Kalverpolder, a 170-hectare (420-acre) polder with typically Dutch dikes that connect the various villages, and admire the iconic windmills housed within a picturesque village that appears to be from 1850. But Zaanse Schans is not exactly what it appears to be: the village itself is made up of authentic houses from the 17th-19th centuries, in the distinctive style with a lovely green color. But these houses are not originally from this village, but rather were gathered from the larger region.

Zaanse Schans was conceptualized by a young architect who hoped to save historic buildings and mills from demolition as part of a graduate project in the 1950s. Today, the village itself is a slightly kitschy representation of Dutch life in the olden days, but don't let the kitsch put you off from enjoying the atmospheric village.

A clearly marked path takes visitors in the direction of various windmills and museum. The path is about a 20-minute walk in one direction, and there's a map at the entry.

Sights

WINDMILLS

Kalverringdijk; tel. 075 204 7510; www.dezaanseschans.nl; €5 per windmill entry

The iconic windmills of Zaanse Schans never cease draw crowds. Although not all of the mills are open to the public, they have been largely restored to their former glory, producing spices, paint pigments, and oil. Of the seven windmills, two are accessible to the public. Entry, paid in cash at the windmills, includes climbing up the steep stairs to view the higher levels and the view of the other windmills. One of the most impressive aspects of Zaanse Schans is arriving and seeing a neat row of windmills in the distance across a flat landscape punctuated with dark green buildings. Once the banks of the Zaan river held around 1,000 windmills that processed everything from wood to paints to grains. We think of windmills as quaint today, but the Zaan region was a powerhouse of industry in the 1600s. Today, only 13 of these windmills remain with names often inspired by animals.

Paintmill The Cat (Verfmolen De Kat) was first built in 1781, and it functions as a mill for grinding up chalk that is used to create paint pigments, the same way they were produced historically, making this one of the last remaining traditional pigment mills in the world. Art museums including the Rijksmuseum and the Vatican source their paints from this small mill—if you're lucky, you can talk to the miller about the process of working this renovated mill, which has burned down and been rebuilt several times.

The other open windmill is a sawmill called the **Young Sheep (Het Jonge Schaap)**, a replica of the original mill that was demolished in 1942. Although the windmill is relatively new, it is one of the only hexagonal mills in the Netherlands and a working sawmill. Visitors can explore the dark green windmill to potentially find its resident cat—and see how wood can be cut without the use of electricity, just water and wind.

MUSEUM SHOP ALBERT HEIJN

Kalverringdijk 5; tel. 075 616 9619; https://albertheijnerfgoed.nl; 10am-4:30pm daily; free

It's hard not to notice the most common supermarket in the Netherlands as you explore the country, but this popular supermarket has humble roots. In 1887, Albert Heijn established his namesake shop in a tiny historic storefront in the nearby town of Oostzaan. Today, this shop has been moved to the Zaanse Schans village, where you can view the original interior along with historic products sold at the time.

ZAANS MUSEUM

Schansend 7; tel. 075 681 0000; https://zaansmuseum.nl; 10am-5pm daily; adults €12.50, seniors/students €10, children €6.50

To learn more about the history of the Zaan region and its iconic products, spend a few hours exploring the Zaans Museum, which includes a nice collection of antiquities and paintings of the region. The highlight for many visitors is the exhibition on Verkade, a well-known Dutch manufacturer of biscuits, tea lights, and chocolate, with interactive games.

WOODEN SHOE WORKSHOP OF ZAANSE SCHANS

Kraaienest 4; tel. 075 617 7121; www.woodenshoes.nl; 9am-5pm daily; free

Set within an old warehouse from 1750, the Zaanse Schans clog factory is definitely not what you'd expect. As soon as you enter, you can admire historic clogs from all over the Netherlands and the world before watching live workshops showcasing the craft of making clogs. They sell souvenir clogs along with handmade clog souvenirs, perfect for a gift or wall decoration.

1: Muiderslot Castle **2:** Zaanse Schans

1

2

Food

RESTAURANT DE KRAAI

Kraaienpad 1; tel. 075 615 6403; https://dekraai.nl; 9am-5pm daily Nov.-Feb., 9am-6pm daily Mar.-Oct.; €10

The Dutch are extremely proud of their pancakes, and despite the central location in the center of Zaanse Schans's tourist village, Restaurant De Kraai has reasonable prices for Dutch staples from pancakes to sandwiches and soups. The oversized pancakes combined with the sunny terrace make it a great spot to take a break from sightseeing.

BROUWERIJ HOOP

Lagedijk 71; tel. 075 204 7000; www.brouwerijhoop.nl; Sun.-Thurs. 11am-11pm, Fri.-Sat. 11am-12:30am; €17.50

If you came to Zaanse Schans by train and choose to make a full day of walking around the picturesque village, consider stopping off at Brouwerij Hoop's restaurant and café for a drink or a dinner after a long day of sightseeing. Be sure to try their award-winning bocks or lighter seasonal beers. The restaurant has a few options for vegetarians and vegans along with steaks and burgers.

Getting There

The best way to get to Zaanse Schans is by bus, which is included in the iAmsterdam card. The **391 bus** runs every 15 minutes between Amsterdam Central Train Station and Zaanse Schans. The trip takes 40 minutes and drops you off directly in front of the Zaanse Museum. The bus costs €4 each way. E-tickets can be purchased at www.connexxion.nl.

It is also possible to come by train into the nearby **Zaandijk-Zaanse Schans train station.** This train station is 1.5 kilometers (0.9 miles) from the main village; the walk should take 15 minutes on a nice day. The train journey from Amsterdam Central Train Station takes about 17 minutes on the **Sprinter train** toward Alkmaar or Uitgeest. The journey costs €6.80 round-trip.

Day Trips from Amsterdam

In what seems like the blink of an eye, you can travel to so many places in the Netherlands from Amsterdam using the efficient and clean Dutch NS train system, which connects one of the densest countries on Earth. Sailing by polders, pastures full of sheep, blooming fields of tulips, and small towns on the train, you'll quickly realize how small the Netherlands really is.

As you visit more Dutch cities, you'll also discover that even though many have an old church in common, each has its own unique character, from laid-back to daring. Although windmills and tulips may be a Holland stereotype, there's no shame in marveling at Dutch ingenuity in agriculture and architecture. Within Keukenhof and the surrounding bulb region, it's hard to resist taking a photo of the endless

Highlights

Look for ★ to find recommended sights, activities, dining, and lodging.

★ **Teylers Museum:** Appreciate the scientific advances of yore at the oldest museum in the Netherlands, still bringing wonder to visitors (page 138).

★ **Alkmaar Cheese Market:** Enjoy a slice of cheesy history at the most famous cheese market in the Netherlands (page 141).

★ **Keukenhof:** Step into a fantasy of endless flowers in the Netherlands' most impressive garden in spring (page 146).

★ **Canals of Utrecht:** Picnic along or cruise down Utrecht's 13-century two-story canals (page 151).

★ **Binnenhof:** Learn about Dutch government, past and present, up close at the world's oldest parliament building (page 159).

★ **Cube Houses:** Peek behind the scenes of one of Rotterdam's wildest pieces of architecture: a cube house turned on its side (page 177).

rows of colorful flower fields that fill your vision in April. At Kinderdijk, the ability of the Dutch to transform a swamp into a UNESCO-recognized polder landscape using windmills and dikes is as impressive as it is beautiful.

Although not all of these cities require a full day trip, there's something relaxing about leaving behind the choked crowds of Dam Square for a quieter city whose past is just as storied as Amsterdam's. Some cities, such as Alkmaar, allow you to experience living history as you watch cheese carriers in their pristine whites run through a square just as they have for hundreds of years. The Hague is a particularly interesting city for lovers of history, politics, and a bit of sun. Head to modern Rotterdam for a taste of contemporary Dutch culture and cutting-edge architecture. You may find yourself tempted to delay your train back to Amsterdam, or even opting for an overnight stay, while you're discovering the best of what the rest of the Netherlands has to offer.

ORIENTATION

Haarlem is approximately 21 kilometers (13 miles) east of Amsterdam, while **Alkmaar** sits about 40 kilometers (25 miles) northwest of Amsterdam in Noord Holland. The picturesque tulip fields of **Lisse,** home to **Keukenhof** gardens, are about 39 kilometers (24 miles) southwest of Amsterdam, close to Schiphol Airport. Continuing south along the North Sea, you'll find the major Dutch cities of **the Hague** and **Rotterdam.** Finally, about 30 minutes south of Amsterdam by train, you'll find the beautiful city of **Utrecht.**

PLANNING YOUR TIME

The best way to travel around the Netherlands is by **train,** thanks to the well-connected and relatively high-speed network that connects all major cities in the Netherlands with each other. (The only exception here is **Keukenhof,** which is only accessible by bus, as it's not close to a train station.) Compared to other regions and countries, the Netherlands is relatively small, making some of the day trips here less than an hour away from Amsterdam by train. Still, the cost of a round-trip fare for day trips can quickly add up, to as much as €20 euros per person per day. If you want to tack some of these day trips on to one another, you may find cheaper costs in between cities that are very close together (e.g. the **Hague** and **Rotterdam**). If you're open to adding more time, opt to stay overnight to minimize travel in between cities. Many visitors also find that staying overnight outside of Amsterdam lowers accommodation costs and provides an opportunity to experience the local nightlife.

When taking the train, remember to hold onto your ticket after boarding in case the conductor comes around, and to **tap your ticket on the way out.** Unlike neighboring European countries, there are not reserved seats on Dutch trains as long as you're in the correct class for your ticket. (If you want to ensure that you have a seat, especially in rush hour, opt for first class.)

Once you leave Amsterdam, things are much less crowded, requiring less planning ahead as much. Due to COVID-19, at the time of writing many museums and attractions in the Netherlands have shifted to an **appointment-only system;** you can often book your spot the same day using your smartphone if you forget to make a reservation. The only museum in Utrecht that is harder to get reservations for is the **Rietveld Schröderhuis.** In the Hague, for some of the international institutions, such as the **Peace Palace** or the **International Criminal Court,** it's best to check the website for a tour schedule as well as potential court dates prior to your visit.

Previous: the Teylers Museum in Haarlem; Utrecht canals with Domkerk in the distance; Keukenhof gardens in the spring.

Where to Go from Amsterdam

Destination	Why Go	Getting There from Amsterdam	How Long to Stay
Haarlem (page 136)	Stroll a friendlier, more intimate version of Amsterdam's squares and monumental buildings	Train: 19 minutes	Half a day
Alkmaar (page 141)	Taste the best Dutch cheese in a picturesque city with historic canals	Train: 35 minutes	One day
Lisse (page 146)	Bike along fields filled with red, purple, and yellow tulips	Metro + bus transfer: 1 hour	Half a day
Utrecht (page 151)	Escape from the crowds in what some call the most beautiful canal city in Europe	Train: 27 minutes	Overnight
The Hague (page 157)	Political intrigue, world-class art, and the Netherlands' beach, all with a cosmopolitan feel	Train: 50 minutes	One day
Delft (page 168)	Charming markets and a chance to buy Delftware, traditional Dutch pottery, and see how it's made	Train: 1 hour	One day
Rotterdam (page 175)	View cutting-edge architecture and the modern side of Dutch culture in this exciting river city	Train: 40 minutes (nonstop train)-1 hour 15 minutes (with stops)	Overnight

The most crowded time of year is the typical **peak period,** (April-August). To avoid the crowds, especially at Keukenhof, arrive early or later in the afternoon, or midweek instead of on a weekend. Some attractions and museums, including Keukenhof, stay open late on certain days (often Thursdays). Note that public transit is often less frequent on holidays and Sundays.

Trains make **driving** completely unnecessary. Traffic during the work week at rush hour (8am-9:30am/4-6pm) can be quite bad, and parking will likely run up the biggest bill. The cheapest parking lots tend to be on the city outskirts, which is why it's often better to take the train to a location closer to the city center. Most travelers rent their cars at Schiphol if needed.

Day Trips from Amsterdam

Haarlem

From the moment you arrive at Haarlem's Grote Markt, the main market square, you'll immediately feel a sense of calm. Full of monumental buildings with elaborate stepped gables, all the chairs in the cafés face the square so locals and tourists alike can people-watch with a coffee or beer. Despite the grandeur and the importance of Haarlem's role in Dutch art history, its historic center feels smaller and more intimate. Walking down the picturesque streets, locals will greet you as you admire their 17th-century houses.

The neighborhood of Harlem in New York was named for this city in the Netherlands, although the Dutch version has an extra a. Haarlem was one of the earlier Dutch cities to obtain city rights, which allowed it to flourish in the medieval period. The residents notably rose against the Spanish in 1573, which resulted in the majority of the city population being executed. Following Dutch independence, Haarlem rebounded as a major trader of fabric, beer, and tulips, which made it into a cultural hub during the Golden Age. Today, these industries play a less significant role in Haarlem's prosperity; however, lovers of beer will want to stop by the Jopenkerk, a former church turned brewery, where some of the beer is brewed from original recipes from this period.

Even with limited time, you can easily cover many of Haarlem's highlights, including the impressive Müller organ in St. Bavo Church, the wonder of the Teylers Museum, hidden courtyards funded by wealthy patrons, and the Ten Boom house for a bit of World War II history. Haarlem also has several market days, and it's hard to resist the urge to browse.

SIGHTS

Grote Markt

open 24/7; free

In Haarlem's grand, well-preserved market square, 13th-17th century buildings blend in perfectly with 19th-century neo-Gothic buildings, a beautiful view everywhere you look.

The impressive St. Bavo Church stands in the heart of the square. At the foot of the church, you'll notice a few historic looking stalls, which were used as the city's fish market until 1941. Today, they're used for art exhibitions. You'll also spy the elaborate **Vleeshal** (Grote Markt 16), now part of the Frans Hals Museum, a beautiful Dutch Renaissance building from 1603 with an elaborate stepped gable facade. You can identify it from the ox heads in front, which indicate that meat was once sold here. Another elaborate building is the **Hoofdwacht** (Grote Markt 17), the oldest building in Haarlem. There's an old Dutch plaque over the door noting that the count established his court here. The building served as the city hall of Haarlem until the new city hall was built. After, it was used for everything from a headquarters for the civil guard to town jail to a sentinel post to watch for city fires. Today, the building is occupied by the Haarlem Historic Society and it's open on some weekends in the summer (1pm-5pm).

STADHUIS HAARLEM

Grote Markt 2; www.haarlem.nl

You can't miss Haarlem's opulent city hall, Stadhuis Haarlem, commissioned in 1250 as a count's manor. The original building was lost in a fire, but today's beautiful city hall was completed in 1602; the tower was added more recently. The interior includes original stained glass windows, tapestries, and even a dungeon. Peek inside on **Open Monument Day** (www.iamsterdam.com/en/see-and-do/whats-on/festivals/overview-cultural-festivals/open-monuments-day-amsterdam),

1: St. Bavo Church **2:** Windmill de Adriaan on Haarlem's riverfront **3:** Grote Markt in Haarlem

1

2

3

the first week of September; access is limited to official ceremonies the rest of the year.

ST. BAVO CHURCH

Grote Markt 22; tel. 023 553 2040; www.bavo.nl; 10am -5pm Mon.-Sat., noon-4pm Sun. July; adults €2.50, children €1.25

From almost anywhere in Haarlem, you can spot the imposing spire of St. Bavo Church, which sits in the center of Grote Markt. The building has roots in a 13th-century church that was continuously built upon until it became a grand cathedral in 1559. Much of the medieval interior was destroyed or looted during the Great Iconoclasm, but the church is certainly very grand; its massive organ, created by Christian Müller in 1738, was even referenced in *Moby-Dick*. On Tuesdays (and some Sundays) May-October, you can enjoy a free **concert** played on this very organ, a truly holy experience for classical music lovers. Check the schedule online.

★ Teylers Museum

Spaarne 16; tel. 023 516 0960; www.teylersmuseum.nl; 10am-5pm Tues.-Fri., 11am-5pm Sat.-Sun.; adults €14, children 6-18 €2

Lovers of science and curiosities will adore the quirky Teylers Museum, one of the most surprising museums in the Netherlands. Housed in a stunning neoclassical building, the oldest museum in the country was founded by a wealthy merchant in 1778. This science museum explores the concept of scientific advancement through a self-guided study of artifacts, books, drawings, and fossils. Unlike many museums that arrange fossils by what we know today, the museum has intentionally left some pieces of its impressive fossil collection in the same order as they were originally thought to be arranged in.

The most striking room in the museum has to be the impressive 18th-century oval room, used for scientific experiments throughout history. Today, it's a magnificent wood-filled room that feels like a step back to the time of the Enlightenment. The museum has supplemented its original collection of early microscopes, barometers, scientific literature, fossils, and stones with drawings by famous artists, including Michelangelo and Rembrandt, as well as other scientific instruments, including a large electrical machine, that have enabled major discoveries. It all serves as a powerful reminder of how much we've learned in such a short period of time.

Take a few hours to see the whole museum. Although not as interactive as some other science museums, it does have a number of kid-friendly exhibitions, workshops, and activities. There's a **café** in the back of the museum overlooking a sculpted lawn, as well as a gift shop with fossil-themed items and other science-related gifts for all ages.

Ten Boom Museum

Barteljorisstraat 19; tel. 023 531 0823; www.corrietenboom.com; 10am-3:30pm Tues.-Sat.; donation

Much lesser known than the Anne Frank House, many people outside the Netherlands haven't heard of the Ten Boom house, one of the highlights of Haarlem. This small museum above a jewelry shop on one of Haarlem's busiest streets holds a secret. The family that ran the shop hid Jews as well as members of the Dutch resistance here from the Nazis until they were betrayed in 1944. Corrie ten Boom wrote about her role in the resistance in her best-selling book *The Hiding Place*. For an English-language **tour,** reserve at least a week ahead on their website, or arrive extra early for their morning tours, as only 20 people are allowed. Be sure to bring euros to donate to keep this museum, run by volunteers, afloat.

Frans Hals Museum

Groot Heiligland 62; tel. 023 511 5775; www.franshalsmuseum.nl; 11am-5pm Tues.-Sat., noon-5pm Sun.; adults €16, children free

Noted Flemish-Dutch painter Frans Hals happily called Haarlem his home and even made his customers come to him here. Today, lovers of the Dutch masters can view Hals's work in this unique museum dedicated to

Haarlem's *Hofjes*

Scattered throughout Haarlem, and in cities in towns throughout this region, you'll find the remnants of former almshouses for the elderly and the poor, known as *hofjes* in the Netherlands and *godshuizen* in Belgium. Many of them were privately financed by wealthy families, a very visble way of providing charity to those in need, thought to get the giver into heaven at the time. Some of these private courtyards remain relatively untouched today, hidden throughout the city. They courtyards of most *hofjes,* despite being private property, tend to be open Monday-Saturday during business hours (9am-5pm) to the quiet visitor who respects the everyday citizens who live in these beautiful homes. Residents welcome visitors who appreciate the history of where they live. Seeking out a city's *hofjes* and *godshuizen* is a great way to explore off-the-beaten-path.

HOFJE VAN NOBLET

Nieuwe Gracht 2

The most stunning *hofje* in Haarlem has to be Hofje van Noblet, which dates back to 1761. It was built as part of the lasting legacy of the Noblet family, who had no legal heirs, for elderly members of the Dutch Reformed Church. It's still lived in today.

HOFJE VAN DEN GROENEN TUIN

Warmoesstraat 23

Hofje van den Groenen Tuin is a beautiful green courtyard filled with 19th-century white houses, built when this 17th-century courtyard was renovated. In the past, renters had to turn over their entire life savings upon death and bring their own bed, but today, the landlords are a bit more reasonable. The courtyard remains privately run. Curious visitors can visit 10am-noon on weekdays.

TEYLERS HOFJE

Koudenhorn 64

Teylers Hofje is a beautiful *hofje* that sits about a block away from the Teylers Museum. This courtyard dating back to 1787 is reserved for older women on a limited income without pets or children. Twenty-two picturesque single houses sit behind the impressive neoclassical gate that is open weekdays and Saturdays 9am-5pm.

his work, which includes viewing some of his group portraits in their original location at Groot Heiligland 62, a former almshouse. Admission to the Frans Hals Museum also includes admission to a secondary museum on Grote Markt 16, where you can enjoy the Dutch masters, including many of Hals's own works, and modern Dutch art.

SHOPPING

GROTE MARKT

https://visithaarlem.org/haarlem-markets; Mon. and Sat.; 9am-4pm

Several markets occupy Haarlem's main square throughout the week. On Mondays, there's a charming market dedicated to furniture, fabrics, and clothing. Sewers will love the beautiful fabrics with traditional Dutch designs for purchase (generally in cash). The most bustling market is on Saturdays, when seemingly all of Haarlem comes to buy fresh vegetables, fruit, and other household goods. The atmosphere is relatively laid back and the market is a nice spot to look for cheeses and sample regional products.

FOOD

HOFJE ZONDER ZORGEN

Grote Houtstraat 142A; tel. 023 531 0607; https://hofjezonderzorgen.nl; 10am-5pm Sun.-Fri., 10am-6pm Sat.; €9

Within a beautiful 15th-century building overlooking a hidden courtyard, Hofje Zonder Zorgen serves beautiful organic breakfast and lunches alongside delicious cakes, even for those with dietary restrictions. It definitely lives up to its name, which means "courtyard without worries" in Dutch; you'll see what I mean when you dine with family or friends at this relaxed lunch spot. Reservations are recommended for weekends.

★ JOPENKERK

Gedempte Voldersgracht 2; tel. 023 533 4114; www.jopenkerk.nl; noon-1am daily; lunch €13, dinner €24

Even if you're not particularly religious, you'll want to at least stop by for a pint at the Jopen Church, the name given to the church taken over by the Jopen brewery, a popular Dutch craft brewery that has revived Haarlem's brewing tradition. It was formerly known as the Vestekerk, which dates back to 1910 but ceased being used as a church in 1975. Today, Jopen serves up beer made according to traditional Haarlem recipes and techniques as well as lunch, dinner, and typical Dutch beer snacks. The stained glass windows and ruby red walls make for a special touch as you enjoy Dutch snacks and meals from burgers to hearty stews. The dinner entrees are made specifically to pair with certain beers, so be sure to ask for the right beer to go with your meal.

SPECKTAKEL WERELDSE KEUKEN

Spekstraat 4; tel. 023 532 3841; https://specktakel.nl; 5:30pm-10pm Thurs.-Fri., 5pm-10pm Sat.-Sun.; €37

You don't need to travel the world to have a taste of it at this trendy Haarlem restaurant that prides itself on seasonal fare and a changing menu that will make your mouth water. They offer a three-course meal that allows you to pick your favorites from their menu—a hard choice. The menu varies seasonally, but expect everything from Thai-influenced vegetarian dishes to Sicilian dishes with seafood. There are just a few tables, but the restaurant maintains a cozy yet upscale atmosphere with a big emphasis on presentation. Reservations recommended.

GETTING THERE

Train

HAARLEM TRAIN STATION

Stationsplein 11 L; tel. 900 202 1163; www.ns.nl

Haarlem is only 15 minutes away from Amsterdam Centraal (Stationsplein 1; www.ns.nl/stationsinformatie/asd/amsterdam-centraal) by train; trains depart up to six times an hour. A round-trip ticket costs €9. The Haarlem Train Station is 1 kilometer (0.6 mi) north of the center of Haarlem, a 13-minute walk. From the train station, walk down Kruisweg, following clear signs to Grote Markt.

Bus

If you have the **iAmsterdam card** (www.iamsterdam.com), you can opt to use the **Connexxion bus 80** from the bus stop at **Elandsgracht** in the Grachtengordel neighborhood of Amsterdam to travel to Haarlem. The journey by bus takes about 40 minutes and drops you off in the heart of the city center. A single-use ticket on the bus costs €4.

Car

It's ill-advised to drive from Amsterdam to Haarlem given how great the train and bus connection is. There's often traffic on the A5 highway that connects the two cities, and parking can be a headache. The 25-kilometer (15-mile) drive should take 22 minutes without traffic, but it usually takes about 45 during rush hour, mostly via the **A5** or **A9.**

Paid **parking** is available on the outskirts of the city center, as many parts of Haarlem are closed to cars. The largest is **Parkgarage Houtplein** (Wagenmakerslaan 1), near the Frans Hals Museum. A parking garage just 300 meters (1,000 feet) from the Teylers Museum is ParkBee De Koepel (Harmenjansweg 4).

GETTING AROUND

Haarlem's city center, which is where most tourists remain and where all the tourist attractions are located, is very walkable. From Grote Markt, it's very hard to get lost thanks to the signage that points to Haarlem's main sights. People with disabilities will also find Haarlem fairly accessible due to minimal cobblestones.

Bike

Haarlem is bike-friendly, like many Dutch cities. The center and shopping streets might be a bit too busy for inexperienced bikers, but there are dedicated bike lanes all throughout the city.

RENT A BIKE HAARLEM

Lange Herenstraat 36; tel. 023 542 1195; www.rentabikehaarlem.nl; €8

Rent a Bike Haarlem rents everything from basic Dutch bikes to electric bikes and tandem bikes. In spring when Keukenhof is open, they offer a Keukenhof special that includes entry to Keukenhof, a map of the fields, a bottle of water, and a bike for the day (€27).

Alkmaar

Harken back to the days of yore in Alkmaar. If you're a cheese lover, you can't miss the 30-minute train journey to this beautiful city north of Amsterdam. On Fridays throughout spring and summer, cheese bearers here wear white as they run cheese-shaped barrows (weighing up to 160 kilos/350 pounds) to the scale before delivering the cheese to sellers. Although the cheese market can certainly get crowded and it is touristy, cheese is so engrained in the city of Alkmaar that the residents call themselves *kaaskoppen,* for the wooden cheese molds that soldiers of Alkmaar used in place of helmets in a battle against the Spanish in the 16th century. This event is reenacted annually during Kaeskoppenstad in early June.

Beyond the cheese market, Alkmaar is an attractive, historic city with beautiful canals running through the city center and charming shopping streets where you can browse for local cheeses and souvenirs. Alkmaar's food options are well priced and surprisingly accommodating for those with dietary restrictions, considering this is a city built on cheese. A half day with lunch is enough to see the best of Alkmaar without breaking a sweat.

SIGHTS

★ Cheese Market

Houttil 26; tel. 072 511 4284; www.kaasmarkt.nl; 10am-1pm Fri. Apr.-Sept., plus 7pm-9pm Tues. July-Aug.; free

Cheese—Gouda, Edam, Beemster—runs in the lifeblood of Alkmaar, where it has been traded since medieval times. Since 1593, the cheese carriers have been running around this bustling Dutch cheese market, which takes place during peak season (July-Aug.) on Friday mornings. The Alkmaar cheese market is one of the oldest cheese markets in the Netherlands, and it is certainly the most tourist-friendly: The market activities are narrated in Dutch, German, English, and sometimes Spanish.

Like nearly all cheese markets in the Netherlands today, the market in Alkmaar is now staged. Cheese isn't actually sold at the market, although samples of locally produced cheeses are occasionally given out. In the post-war period, Dutch cheese producers came together to sell and set prices more efficiently, a decision that made the traditional cheese markets slightly obsolete. However, the locals wanted to preserve their traditions, and somehow, these staged cheese markets have a nostalgic charm, and an unironic delight to watch. Any cheese lover will get a kick from seeing the elaborate process of how cheese was bought and sold in the Netherlands for centuries, and there are numerous shops that sell cheesy products surrounding the market to get your cheese fix.

Here's how the cheese running works: Members of the cheese guild, which still operates today, begin by ringing the cheese bell at 10am sharp on Fridays. They then organize

Say Cheese: A Dutch Cheese Primer

Alkmaar cheese market

The Netherlands has become a slice of paradise for cheese lovers, with an impressive collection of cheeses known around the world. Cheeses from the region have been lauded since Julius Caesar, and today the Dutch are one of the world's leading producers of cheese, exporting more than 650,000 kilos (1.4 million pounds) annually. Even if you are only a little familiar with some cheeses, such as Gouda, you'll be delighted to discover the local selection, from savory goat cheeses to sharper aged cheeses. If you go to a Dutch supermarket, you'll understand immediately how beloved cheese is—the cheese section is truly massive. And once you have a taste, you'll understand why the Dutch are so proud of their dairy.

in teams to quickly transport "cheese" (today wood pallets meant to approximate the weight) throughout the market from sellers to buyers with a stop-off at the weighing scales. Cheese carriers dress all in white as they run throughout the market, and sometimes even let tourists try it out, which is more challenging than it looks! For a good spot, it's best to arrive early, as the square often fills up with tour groups from all over the world who vie for a spot near the front.

There is also an **evening cheese market** in July and August. For those with children ages 6-12, the market has a special **tour** on Fridays in summer that allows kids to try out the cheese-weighing scale and even bring a weighing certificate home. The market lasts about two hours before the square returns to normal, quiet and filled with cafés.

St. Laurens Church (Sint Laurenskerk)

Koortstraat 2; tel. 072 548 9999; https://grotekerk-alkmaar.nl; 11am-5pm daily summer; free

St. Laurens Church is one of the largest medieval churches in Holland, dating back to 1440. Today, this massive church is an open-air museum in summer, where visitors can take in the high ceilings with no less than 26 freestanding columns that support a massive vault and canopy. Within the former church, you can take in art by local artists as well as admire the beautiful 16th-century choir organ with its painted case.

CHEESE TYPES

Dutch cheeses are generally distinguished by origin, milk fat content, and age. Most Dutch cheeses are named for the marketplace where they were once sold—for example, Gouda is often produced in region surrounding its eponymous town. The number on a package typically indicates the fat content, rather than the age; if you want to know the age of your cheese, it's helpful to know a few Dutch terms.

- ***Jong*** cheeses have ripened just four weeks and tend to be smoother.
- ***Oude*** cheese (aged 10-12 months) tends to be sharper with more complex notes, perfect for those who love a stronger cheese.
- ***Belegen,*** at 16-18 weeks, is a good balance between the two.

The most famous cheeses include, of course, **Gouda** (pronounced with a hard G, closer to g-how-da), as well as **Beemster** and **Edam.** But you'll find many other varieties: Be sure to look out for **Graskaas,** which debuts in summer and is made with the first milk of the season-ing. It's a more subtle and complex cheese that is rarely exported. You should also ask about the **Boerenkaas,** which is simply cheese produced by smaller farms.

WHERE TO TRY IT

In every Dutch city, you're likely to find at least a few ***kaaswinkels,*** or cheese shops. Although you might see tourist traps like Henri Willig or Cheese & More throughout major Dutch cities, you're best off going to an independently run shop, which will offer more varieties with plentiful samples. You can also opt to head to the **supermarket** for cheese to enjoy on a picnic. At many Dutch **cafés,** you'll find dishes with cheese, such as the savory *tosti,* a grilled cheese sandwich. Many **bars** also serve locally made cheeses with drinks. No matter where you go in the Netherlands, there will be a delicious local cheese, so simply ask for samples, as they're always given out freely at cheese shops! The best places in Alkmaar to try Dutch cheese include **Kaan's Kaashandel** and **Kaaswinkel Alkmaarse Notenbranderij.**

National Beer Museum De Boom

Houttil 1; tel. 072 511 3801; www.biermuseum.nl; 1pm-4pm Mon.-Sat.; adults €5, children €2.50

Beer lovers might want to check out the small yet informative National Beer Museum, where you can learn about beer production in the last 200 years via antique brewing equipment. Set on the grounds of a historic now-defunct brewery, the museum's main highlight for many visitors is enjoying a cold beer on the floating terrace of the in-house old-timey **café,** *Proeflokaal De Boom,* after a tour.

ENTERTAINMENT AND EVENTS

KAESKOPPENSTAD

Throughout the city; tel. 06 19966241; www.kaeskoppenstad.nl; first weekend in June; €4

The Kaeskoppenstad is a historical weekend in which the entire city is transported back to 1573, after it was liberated from the Spanish. Hundreds of actors in period clothing reenact daily life during the era, as well as showcase traditional crafts and arts (such as sword-fighting and storytelling.) The event, held throughout the city, is very kid-friendly, and it's educational. Though much of the event is more geared toward the Dutch, some things are translated into English.

SHOPPING

Shop along **Fnidsen** and **Hekelstraat** for Alkmaar's section of independently owned shops, from old-timey sweets to cool household goods. These two streets, as well as **Koorstraat** in the heart of Alkmaar's city center, are just 130 meters (430 feet) from the famous Alkmaar cheese market.

DAY WOMAN

Fnidsen 85; tel. 072 582 5846; https://daywoman.nl; 10am-5:30pm Tues.-Sat.

Day Woman is a 15-year-old Alkmaar-created shop that sells original fashion, home, and lifestyle designs, in addition to stocking brands from across the Netherlands and Scandinavia. Their combination shop on Fnidsen showcases their simple yet fashionable clothing brands alongside stylish home goods in a beautiful shop within a historic building.

KAAN'S KAASHANDEL

Koorstraat 11; tel. 072 220 1995; www.echtfood.nl; 1pm-6pm Mon., 9am-6pm Tues.-Fri., 8:30am-5pm Sat.

If you're looking to bring home local cheeses from Alkmaar, head to Kaan's Kaashandel, which was started in nearby Hoorn more than 100 years ago. This family-run business specializes in locally made farmers cheeses, and they happily vacuum-seal unique cheeses, including their lavender cheese, for clients from around the world. Samples are abundant, and their friendly staff is always happy to make recommendations.

FOOD

KAASWINKEL ALKMAARSE NOTENBRANDERIJ

Magdalenenstraat 8; tel. 072 512 6452; www.kaaswinkel-alkmaar.nl; 8am-6pm Mon.-Fri., 7am-5pm Sat.

Just off the cheese market, you'll find the Alkmaar Nut Distillery (in English) where you can taste and purchase Dutch favorite cheeses from North Holland paired with nuts, tapenades, and other local food products. The store has been in business for 18 years, and the owners are always delighted to educate you on the perfect pairing for when you head home.

IJSSALON LAAN ALKMAAR

Koorstraat 45; tel. 072 511 5685; www.laanijsalkmaar.nl; 10am-6pm daily Mar.-Apr., 10am-9pm daily May.-Sept.; €2

This favorite ice cream parlor often has a line out the door for their only flavor, vanilla. Don't be discouraged by the lack of choice; they've won an award for the best ice cream salon in the Netherlands. This old-school shop was founded after World War II, and not much has changed inside since.

ALKMAARS KOFFIEHUIS

Aan de Gedempte Nieuwesloot 42; tel. 072 531 8712; www.alkmaarskoffiehuis.nl; noon-midnight Wed.-Sun.; lunch €5

Set within a beautiful building that blends in perfectly with its surroundings, Alkmaars Koffiehuis oozes charm from morning to night. In addition to coffee, they also serve up Zeglis, a popular local craft beer, throughout the day, along with affordable Dutch sandwiches and snacks. It's the kind of café where you'll immediately feel at home with a cup of your favorite beverage.

ECHT

Marktstraat 4; tel. 072 220 1995; www.echtfood.nl; 8:30am-5:30pm Fri.-Mon.; €7.75

Echt is a trendy restaurant serving up organic versions of Dutch favorites (*tostis*, or grilled cheese, and cheesy croquettes), along with vegan-friendly sandwiches. Just a few footsteps from the cheese market, Echt lives up to its name, which means "authentic" or "real" in Dutch, as an accessible restaurant for both adults and kids. It fills up for casual lunches along with high tea. Be sure to save room for their cakes if you can!

1: view of Alkmaar **2:** tulip fields in the Lisse region **3:** sightseeing

1
2
3
Jazzy

ACCOMMODATIONS

Staying overnight in Alkmaar is not necessary, but if you prefer a small town over a big city, you might enjoy the quiet. Things get very quiet in the evenings, but if you enjoy good cheese and beer, you'll feel right at home in this friendly city.

WOLF HOTEL

Mient 3; tel. 072 520 5969; www.wolf-alkmaar.nl; €89

In the heart of the Alkmaar city center, Wolf is a boutique hotel combined with a restaurant of the same name only a block away from the famous cheese market. A stay includes a clean, modern room with an up-to-date bathroom at a fraction of the price of staying in Amsterdam.

GETTING THERE AND AROUND

Walking is sufficient for getting around Alkmaar, as the city center is relatively compact. Thanks to the many day-trippers who come by train, there are clear signs as soon as you leave the train station, often marked with cheese (in some form) showing the way to the cheese market.

Train

ALKMAAR TRAIN STATION

Stationsweg 43c; www.ns.nl

Trains run 1-3 times per hour from **Amsterdam Centraal** (Stationsplein 1; www.ns.nl/stationsinformatie/asd/amsterdam-centraal) to Alkmaar. The trip is direct and takes about 30 minutes; the direction is typically Hoorn, Alkmaar, or Den Helder. A one-way ticket costs €8.10. The train station is located 1 kilometer (0.6 miles) northeast of the city historic center, a 15-minute walk.

Car

Driving from **Amsterdam** to Alkmaar should take about 35 minutes (50 kilometers/30 miles), mostly via the **A9** motorway. But given Alkmaar's compact size and pedestrianized streets, driving is unnecessary here. There's paid parking throughout the city center, although the four-story **Singelgarage** (Ritsevoort 70; 24 hours; €1.82/hour), with over 350 spots, is the best option.

Lisse

In late March through April, the Dune and Bulb Region of the Netherlands, just south of Schiphol Airport, explodes in colorful rows of flowers. The region is named for these blooms, as well as the many dunes that protect the land from flooding from the nearby sea, and many tulip farms here sit on the sandy soil where former dunes used to be.

The Dutch dominate the global flower industry, and you can easily spot the flowers soon to be distributed all over the world on a bus or train traveling through this area, the best known and closest to Amsterdam of the Netherlands' flower-growing regions. It's renowned for its tulips, but you'll also find many other kinds of flowers, including hyacinths and daffodils, in the fields surrounding the famous Keukenhof gardens. Lisse itself is an average small Dutch town, the main hub for tourists visiting Keukenhof, where seven million flowers are planted annually. Getting a photo of this gardening masterpiece without people in it is tough, especially toward the end of April. For a taste of the fields beyond Keukenhof, bike or drive along narrow country roads, often shared with tractors and farmers.

SIGHTS

★ Keukenhof

Stationsweg 166A; tel. 025 246 5555; https://keukenhof.nl; 8am-7:30pm daily Mar.-May; adults €19

In 2019, more than 1.5 million visitors from

around the world headed to the Keukenhof's 32 hectares (79 acres) of sculpted gardens, wowed by more than seven million flower bulbs planted by hand. Although people associate Keukenhof with tulips, the park hosts more than nine gardens, including an impressive orchid display. At the heart of the estate is a 17th-century castle, built on the spot where laborers once grew fruit and vegetables for the Dutch nobility who lived in the house and gave the estate its name. After World War II, local flower growers decided to open the estate to the public as a means of promoting tourism and the flower industry. Keukenhof was opened to the public in 1950, and it's been a success ever since.

If tulips are what you want, Keukenhof may not actually be the right place, though you do have a view of tulip fields surrounding the park from some edges of the property and as you approach Keukenhof by bike, bus, or car. But don't let that discourage you. Keukenhof's paved paths lined with flowers lead to nine pavilions with various flower themes. All displays are thought through to ensure that flowers beautifully contrast with their neighbors. Each year, Keukenhof chooses a new theme for the park, which sometimes corresponds to the theme of the **Dutch Flower Parade** held close to King's Day (late Apr.) that ends in Lisse.

To avoid the crowds, it's recommended to buy your ticket in advance and arrive early or closer to closing when most tourists have gone home. In April, the sun sets after 8pm, which provides ample opportunity for those arriving around dinnertime to enjoy the quiet grounds without groups coming off tour buses. If you get hungry, you can bring a picnic into the park from the supermarkets in Lisse's town center, or you'll find a variety of options at Keukenhof's four restaurants and stands, serving Dutch favorites including pancakes and herring alongside international options. There are cheaper options like sandwiches, too.

Keukenhof is only open between mid-March and early May; exact opening and closing dates vary annually. Keukenhof offers a **combination ticket** with public transit (€32.50). To cut out the extra effort, you can also purchase a ticket that includes taking a direct bus from **Schiphol Airport** (bus 858; €27.50) or **Amsterdam** (Station RAI in Amsterdam Zuid; bus 852; about 8 times an hour 8:35am-6:53pm; €39).

FAM Flower Farm

Address provided upon reservation; www.famflowerfarm.com; by appointment only; adults €40, children 4-12 €20, children 0-4 free

For those looking for the ultimate tulip photoshoot, head to FAM Flower Farm, run by two friends who own two family-run farms that grow dahlias and tulips. One of the farms has been continuously owned by the same family for more than 200 years.

At a time when growers are not allowing tourists into the fields, the FAM Flower Farm has opened its doors to small groups to take photos on their grounds for a set fee. They will also teach you about life on the farm behind the scenes. The entrance fee includes the chance to take photos, plus coffee, *stroopwafels,* and some tulips as a souvenir of your visit. You must reserve your slot ahead using their website—and the owners will then provide their address, which is about 4 kilometers (2 miles) outside Lisse. It's best come by bike.

CYCLING

Plan on a few hours on your bike to spot flowers in the fields. Every bike rental comes with a **map** of different recommended routes; many will have you follow the ***knooppunten,*** numbered signs along roads that allow cyclists to follow directions without checking road names constantly. It's also helpful to have a working phone that you can place on your bike to provide turn-by-turn directions. Many farmers put a self-service stand with tulip bunches out on the corners, so don't forget to bring a little cash to buy tulips!

In addition to Rent-a-Bike Van Dam in the Keukenhof parking lot, which often

Tulip Field Etiquette

tulips in Keukenhof

Throughout the Dune and Bulb Region, a relatively small area between Leiden and Haarlem, in April, the typically brown and sometimes green fields bloom with flowers that range in color from orange to purple, with many variations in pattern, from the elaborate parrot tulip to the standard Darwin Hybrid. As you drive, bike, or walk along the provincial roads that lead past many of the tulip farms, you'll see that they are often separated by a watery dyke to prevent interlopers from walking in the fields. The success of Keukenhof has brought many tourists to Lisse and the towns surrounding it, causing destruction to the fields; as such, farmers from the region have limited access without payment.

WHERE TO SEE TULIPS

To view the tulip fields outside Keukenhof, driving or biking is best, as the most beautiful fields

runs out of bikes, it is also possible to rent a bike from **Rent a Bike Haarlem** (www.rentabikehaarlem.nl) if you're up for a longer bike ride. It's a picturesque 1-hour ride from either city toward Keukenhof. If you choose to bike from Haarlem, be sure to wear rain-proof clothing; Dutch weather can be surprising and damp in spring.

RENT-A-BIKE VAN DAM

Keukenhof parking lot; tel. 025 225 1144; www.rentabikevandam-keukenhof.com; €10 per bike for 3 hours, €9 for kids bikes

If you wish to explore the tulip fields on your own, you can rent a bike from the Keukenhof parking lot. It is highly recommended to reserve your bike in advance online or arrive early, as the bike rentals are limited in quantity and go fast.

HAARLEM TO KEUKENHOF RIDE

Cycling Distance: *19 kilometers (12 miles) one-way*

Cycling Time: *1 hour one-way*

Trailhead: *Rent a Bike Haarlem*

Information and maps: *www.rentabikehaarlem.nl*

On this pleasant ride, roads and bike paths will take you out of Haarlem's center and past the famous **Jopenkerk brewery,** over canals and through picturesque fields. Eventually, you'll reach Loosterweg Noord, one of the are often too far away to walk. The roads are often narrow, or two lanes, so it's important that visitors stopping to take photos—whether they're on a bike, walking, or driving—are aware of traffic in front of and behind them, including passing tractors. Those coming by car should find a parking spot and walk back to admire the fields instead of pulling onto private property or stopping traffic. If you're biking and you see a good vantage point, it's best to pull off the road to find a good point to stop.

The most beautiful fields vary each year, but the roads of **Loosterweg Noord** (1 kilometer/0.6 miles from Keukenhof's entrance) and **Zwartelaan** (2 kilometers/1.2 miles from Keukenhof's entrance) are favorites due to their proximity to Keukenhof. About 5 kilometers (3.1 miles) south of Keukenhof, you'll find **Johan Speelmanweg,** which has a high concentration of tulip farms.

WHEN THEY BLOOM

Seeing the tulips in bloom is often a matter of luck, as tulips can bloom earlier depending on the year; a bit of research can pay off. April, especially **late April,** tends to be the most popular time to visit the tulip fields, although many locals prefer **mid-April,** when the fields are often at their most vibrant. If you come too early, you'll see mostly hyacinths rather than tulips. They're still lovely, but it can be a disappointment to some. Similarly, many fields tend to be cut, or past their prime, around the end of April. The flower farmers in the region catalog their blooms daily with photos via **www.flowerradar.com,** which allows visitors to discover spots in bloom.

RULES FOR VISITING THE FIELDS

After significant economic damage to tulip fields caused by visitors tramping over them in 2018, **visitors are no longer allowed to step into the fields.** Nearly all farmers in the Bulb region have cordoned them off from visitors. Tulip fields are private property, and it's considered trespassing to enter fields that are closed off. Even if you see an open field, do not enter it. It's very easy to get photos from the often-elevated roads. It should also be noted that **visitors are not allowed to fly drones** in this area without the permission of the farmers whose property is being filmed.

prettiest streets to cycle just north of the Keukenhof, before reaching the parking lot for the gardens.

ENTERTAINMENT AND EVENTS

DUTCH FLOWER PARADE

throughout the Dune and Bulb Region; tel. 025 242 8237; www.bloemencorso-bollenstreek.nl; second or third Sat. in Apr.; free

The floats of the Dutch Flower Parade, made with various flowers from the Dune and Bulb region, runs 42 kilometers (26 miles) through the towns of Noordwijk, Voorhout, Sassenheim, Lisse, Hillegom, Bennebroek, and Haarlem on a Saturday in mid-April. The towns join together to celebrate the Dutch flower with live music performed by local bands. This is the only parade in the world where all the floats are made entirely of flowers. Viewing the parade is free, though you can pay for a seat in the stands (€24.95).

The most popular spot to watch the parade is certainly in **Lisse,** about 2 kilometers (1 mile) from Keukenhof, but there are also covered stands with seats that can be reserved in advance along the route in Lisse, Hillegom, and Sassenheim. Following the parade, all the floats are parked overnight in **Haarlem,** which makes for an easier way of viewing the floats without waiting in line.

FOOD

BROUWERIJ KLEIN DUIMPJE

Hyacintenlaan 2A, Hillegom; tel. 025 253 1186; https://kleinduimpje.nl; 1pm-8pm Fri.-Sat., 1pm-6pm Sun.; beer €3.30, tour with drink €6

If you're biking through the Bulb Region, consider stopping off in the picturesque town of Hillegom. Brouwerij Klein Duimpje is a nice stop post-Keukenhof. On weekends, this popular Dutch brewery opens its doors to visitors for an occasional beer as well as fried snacks (*bitterballen*).

PANNENKOE LISSE

Kanaalstraat 22A, Lisse; tel. 025 241 3739; www.pannenkoe.nl/locatie-lisse; 11am-8:30pm Tues.-Sat., 2pm-8:30pm Sun.; €9

A short walk into town brings you to a charming house with red and white shutters where savory and sweet pancakes are served to anyone who steps in, families and tourists alike.

GETTING THERE

Train

To get to Lisse and Keukenhof from **Amsterdam Centraal** (Stationsplein 17a; www.ns.nl/stationsinformatie/asd/amsterdam-centraal), visitors must take the train to **Leiden Station** (Stationsplein 3; www.ns.nl/stationsinformatie/ledn/leiden-centraal; €19.60) or **Haarlem Station** (Stationsplein 1; www.ns.nl/stationsinformatie/hlm/haarlem; €17.80) before getting on a bus. You can also combine an overnight trip to Haarlem or Leiden with a half day in Keukenhof.

Bus

From Haarlem Station, **bus 50** runs to Keukenhof (40 minutes; €5 one-way). Similarly, outside of Leiden Station, you'll find **bus 854,** which departs for Keukenhof (25 minutes; €5 one-way).

If you want to opt for the entire route by bus, you can pick up a special ticket for entrance to Keukenhof sold at various shops in Amsterdam, Haarlem, Schiphol, and Leiden that includes a bus ticket (adults €32.50, children €14 from Amsterdam; adults €27.50 from Haarlem, Schiphol, or Leiden). Within Amsterdam, **bus 397** runs from Leidseplein, Museumplein, and next to the Rijksmuseum and brings visitors to Hoofddorp Station outside Amsterdam, where they'll transfer to **bus 859** to Keukenhof. From Hoofddorp, it only takes 15 minutes to get to Keukenhof. From **Schiphol Airport,** tourists can follow the workers in colorful vests to **bus 858,** which brings you directly to Keukenhof in 30 minutes.

Car

Although **parking** at Keukenhof is a bit pricey (€6), a car is a great way to see the surrounding tulip fields if you're not a fan of cycling. The drive from **Amsterdam Centrum** to Lisse (40 kilometers/25 miles), mostly on the **A4,** should take 30 minutes, but the drive can take up to an hour with traffic.

Utrecht

Utrecht has one of the best-preserved medieval city centers in the Netherlands and has been named the most beautiful canal city in Europe. Even if you think that you've seen enough canals in Amsterdam, the two-story canals of Utrecht, dating back to the 13th century, leave a lasting impression. Unlike Venice, you don't need to fight crowds to take a dreamy photo of the iconic Dom Tower that sits in the city center, the former site of a Roman fort that gave Utrecht its name.

Among Dutchies, Utrecht is best known for its fine restaurants, as well as its lively café scene, partially thanks to Utrecht University (UU), which gives the city a young student population. Utrecht has something for everyone, from those with young children to serious architecture lovers, who will want to reserve tickets at the modern, minimalistic Rietveld Schröder house. Grab a coffee, take a walk along the canals, and find your ideal spot to sit. Luckily, there's not too much competition, even on the most beautiful days.

SIGHTS

TOP EXPERIENCE

★ Canals

throughout central Utrecht; open 24/7

Utrecht's loveliest feature has to be the two-story canals in the city center. In the heart of Utrecht, you'll quickly spot the **Oudegracht** canal, which was built in the 12th century to ensure that trade ships could enter the city. As you cruise down the brick-lined canals, you'll understand quickly why so many fall in love with Utrecht. The best-known viewpoint is from the **Maartensbrug,** which overlooks Oudegracht in front of the Domtoren. Just below **Keek** (https://keekutrecht.nl), a bakery, you'll find a way down to the pedestrianized lower level, **Oudegracht aan de Werf,** where you can watch boats passing at the same level as the water. Another popular viewpoint is the **Stadhuisbrug,** a pedestrian square that overlooks a pretty curve in Oudegracht with the Domtoren on the left side. A lookout on Pausdam provides picturesque views of **Nieuwegracht,** with houses and water as far as the eye can see.

The ancient **cellars** that you'll spot, either from above or within many of Utrecht's many waterfront restaurants and cafés, largely date back to the 13th century. These cellars were storage spaces for the shipyards that once lined the canals of Utrecht. Locks were added to Utrecht's canals to ensure that the cellars and wharves did not get flooded as the water level changed. Today, these cellars are privately owned, but you'll find more than few restaurants, including **Ted's** (http://tedsplace.nl), have a cellar underneath.

The best way to explore the canals is **on foot,** although it's also wonderful to cruise down Utrecht's canals by **boat,** or even **kayak.**

Ganzenmarkt Tunnel

Ganzenmarkt 3; www.trajectumlumen.nl/en/locations/1865954738/ganzenmarkt-tunnel; open 24/7; free

This quiet brick tunnel was once used by horses and buggies for loading up their carriages with freight from incoming ships reaching the Oudegracht wharf. Today, the not-so-dark tunnel is a modern art installation known as *Trajectum Lumen* by eco-friendly artist Erik Groen, designed to challenge your ideas about light and darkness via shifting lights within the darkest spot of the tunnel. It doesn't take long to walk through the tunnel, but it is a nice surprise to find as you wander around Utrecht.

Dom Tower and St. Martin's Cathedral
(Domtoren and Domkerk)

Domplein; tel. 030 231 0403; http://domtoren.nl; 10am-5pm daily; adults €10, children under 12 €4

The Dom Tower is one of the enduring symbols of Utrecht. Built on top of a Roman fortress dating back to AD 47, the first chapel in Utrecht was destroyed before being rebuilt in the name of St. Martin. Although the original chapel dating back to the 9th century was destroyed again by fire, the massive church (www.domkerk.nl) that sits on the spot today dates back to 1254. Construction on the Domtoren was completed in the 14th century, to most of the height that the tower has today. The tower became separated from the church in the 1600s following a tornado through the center of Utrecht.

Be sure to leave enough time to walk around the enclosed inner courtyard of the church, called the **Pandhof** (10am-4pm Mon.-Fri., noon-5pm Sat.-Sun.; free) which is one of Utrecht's loveliest places to sit outside. The lush green courtyard surrounded by a medieval cloister dates back to 1390 when it was used as a medieval herb garden for the monastery.

In the 1900s, the Dom Tower was finally restored to its former glory by noted Dutch architect Pierre Cuypers. Today, the tower is 112 meters (367 feet) high. The only way to reach the top is with a guide, via an elevator or 465 steps each way. **Tours,** given on the hour, last approximately an hour. It's certainly worth the climb to learn more about the history of Utrecht and to enjoy the view from the top. The carillon is played for an hour on Saturday mornings at 11am and on Fridays at 12:30pm (Apr.-Dec.).

Miffy Museum
(Nijntje Museum)

Agnietenstraat 2; tel. 030 236 2399; https://nijntjemuseum.nl; 10am-5pm Tue.-Sun.; adults and youth 7-17 €6.50, children 2-6 €10, children 0-1 free, family ticket €25

The Miffy museum, known as the Nijntje Museum in the Netherlands, is dedicated to children who love the Utrecht-born cartoon character Miffy (or Nijntje in Dutch) by Dick Bruna. The museum's many interactive exhibitions are primarily geared toward kids under the age of 6. To avoid disappointment, as the museum has limited capacity, reserve your appointment for your family in advance on their website.

Museum Speelklok

Steenweg 6; tel. 030 231 2789; www.museumspeelklok.nl; 10am-5pm Tues.-Sun.; adults €14, children €7.50, family ticket (2 adults, 2 kids) €39, combination ticket with Domtoren available

For those who are young at heart or families looking for a museum with something for older kids past the age of Miffy, Museum Speelklok has it all. The Netherlands has a very proud tradition of self-playing instruments, including street organs that can often be spotted on the streets of Dutch cities. This unusual museum displays hundreds of self-playing instruments including violins, organs, and clocks, many of which you can try out for yourself. There are free tours on the half hour with an enthusiastic tour guide.

Museum Catherijneconvent

Lange Nieuwstraat 38; tel. 030 231 3835; www.catharijneconvent.nl; 10am-5pm Tues.-Fri., 11am-5pm Sat.-Sun.; adults €14, seniors €12.50, children €7

The largest collection of religious art in the Netherlands is held at Museum Catherijneconvent, a former medieval convent. The museum educates visitors on the history of Christianity in the Netherlands with art, altarpieces, manuscripts, and relics from both Catholics and Protestants. The museum also houses religious paintings by Rembrandt, Frans Hals, and other Dutch masters.

1: the Dom Tower **2:** Rietveld Schröder house **3:** Utrecht canal

1
2
3

Rietveld Schröderhuis

Prins Hendriklaan 50; tel. 030 236 2310; www.rietveldschroderhuis.nl; 11am-5pm Tues.-Sun. Oct.-Mar., 11am-9pm Tues.-Sun. Apr.-Sept.; adults €18, children €9.50

In the middle of a seemingly average Utrecht neighborhood on the outskirts of town, you'll find the innovative Rietveld Schröder house. Built in 1924, it's a unique collaboration between owner and architect. Its minimalist interior has innumerable brilliant hidden features that will be revealed during a **tour,** including sliding walls that create the feeling of privacy. Rietveld is considered to be one of the founders of the De Stijl design movement, and the house is his masterpiece, showcasing his love of abstract shapes, primary colors, and reducing objects to their basic forms. The interior remains fully preserved, and even for non-interior design geeks, the guided tours are likely to elicit a gasp.

It's best to **bike** to the house, a 3-kilometer (2-mile), 10-minute cycle from Utrecht's center. Or, you can take **bus 8** from the bus stop on the Jaarbeurszijde of **Utrecht Central Train Station** toward Utrecht Prins (www.u-ov.info; €2.90, ticket can be purchased from the driver). A **cab** should cost about €14.50 euros one-way (UTC; https://utc.nl).

Castle De Haar (Kasteel De Haar)

Kasteellaan 1 Haarzuilens; tel. 030 677 8515; www.kasteeldehaar.nl; 9am-5pm daily; adults €17, children €11

Easily the most beautiful castle in the Netherlands, Kasteel De Haar is an impressive medieval castle renovated by architect Pierre Cuypers in the late 1800s with no detail spared. From every angle, the castle's Gothic turrets surrounded by a moat is out of a fairy tale. The castle and all its surrounding buildings bear the distinctive red and white colors of the van Zuylen family coat of arms. It's named after the de Haar family, former feudal lords, whose family died out, passing the castle to the van Zuylen family, wealthy aristocrats linked to the Rothchilds. If you don't want to take a tour of the the castle (adults €6, children €4).

That said, the **tours** are worthwhile. Fully modernized despite the castle's historic appearance, the standard 45-minute tour through most of the rooms on the lower floors will impress, especially the church-inspired main hall. Tours of the castle take place in the morning prior to 11:15am and after 3:30pm every day besides Christmas, New Years, and a brief period in September which varies year to year, when the owners make use of the property.

De Haar is located in Kasteellaan, 12 kilometers (7 miles) west of Utrecht, a 24-minute drive. Getting to Kasteel De Haar is a bit of a challenge without a car, even from Utrecht, but the dedicated traveler can manage with a bit of patience. It's only a 45-minute **cycle.** Public transit takes nearly an hour, requiring taking the **train** toward Den Haag Centraal to Vleuten (www.ns.nl; 10 minutes, train every 20 minutes; €2.40) and transferring to **bus 127** (www.u-ov.info; 40 minutes, 1 bus per hour; €2.90).

CYCLING

Utrecht has a well-developed bike path system that makes it easy to navigate the city on two wheels, although inexperienced bikers might be uncomfortable biking on the narrower cobblestone streets within the city center. The Utrecht tourism board, **VVV Utretcht** (Domplein 9), can provide you with quieter biking routes, but the prettiest place to cycle is along Oudegracht.

Bike Shops and Rentals

BLACK BIKES BIKE RENTAL UTRECHT

Vredenburg 29; tel. 085 273 7454; https://black-bikes.com; 8am-8pm Mon.-Fri.; €9 for 24 hours

Just around the corner from Utrecht Central Train Station, you'll find a branch of Black Bikes, where they rent everything from handbrake adult bikes to tandem bikes for adults. Bikes with a pedal brake begin at €9 per day.

Bike Routes

KASTEEL DE HAAR CYCLING ROUTE

Cycling Distance: *13 kilometers (8 miles) one-way*

Cycling Time: *45 minutes one-way*

Trailhead: *Black Bikes (Vredenburg 29)*

Cycling is one of the best ways to get to Kasteel de Haar, though the best way to navigate is to have a phone with Google Maps enabled: there are quite a few turns on this route, and the way to the castle isn't specifically marked. You'll pass green fields, canals, and small villages, with the dramatic walls of the castle being a great reward for your efforts.

WATER SPORTS

The waterways of Utrecht can be a little busy, but they're considerably calmer than those of Amsterdam. A number of boat companies rent boats on Utrecht's canals by the hour, as well as provide tours with a captain. It's important to note that some waterways are two-way (Oudegracht) while others are one-way (Nieuwegracht), but if you're sticking to these two canals, it's hard to get lost. If you end up navigating yourself, your boat rental will provide a map with beginner-friendly routes.

CANOE RENTAL UTRECHT (Kanoverhuur Utrecht)

Oudegracht 275; tel. 06 15602823; https://kanoverhuurutrecht.nl; 10am-8pm Tues.-Sun., 1pm-8pm Mon.; €6 per hour

If you're interested in boating through Utrecht on your own and burning off some extra calories, you can opt for kayaking. The kayaks here are well maintained, and every rental comes with a waterproof map showing a pleasant one-hour kayaking route on Oudegracht and Nieuwegracht.

REDERIJ SCHUTTEVAER

Oudegracht 85; tel. 06 15602823; www.schuttevaer.com; 10:30am-6pm Mon.-Sat., 11am-6pm Sun.; adults €13.95, children 4-12 €9.75 kids

For a more relaxed way to see Utrecht by boat, you can opt for a boat cruise with Rederij Schuttevaer, which runs tours almost every half hour 11am-5pm. Their boat tours, which they've been giving for the last 50 years, last an hour and have a prerecorded message that plays during the tour. Although it's not a highly customized option, it's an affordable way to see the city.

GREENJOY UTRECHT

Oudegracht 275; tel. 06 15602823; https://greenjoy.nl; 10am-8pm Tues.-Sun., 1pm-8pm Mon.; €30-50 per hour (minimum 2 hours)

Not everyone enjoys taking a backseat when it comes to boating, and you'll be piloting your own boat with Greenjoy. If you'll be with a large group, one of the best experiences is renting an larger boat and enjoying a picnic while you cruise around Utrecht. These boats are eco-friendly as well as quiet.

FOOD

Utrecht has a lively food scene that has attracted many innovative Dutch and international chefs. You'll find everything from Dutch favorites to international food, as well as a bustling café and bar scene where you can linger over a coffee or a beer.

Dutch

FIRMA PICKLES BURGERS & WINES

Drieharingstraat 1; tel. 030 231 7971; https://firmapickles.nl; 4pm-10pm Mon.-Wed., noon-10pm Thurs. and Sun., noon-11pm Fri.-Sat.; €16

Drieharingstraat is one of Utrecht's most charming streets. This narrow street is home to many restaurants, including Firma Pickles, which doesn't pull any punches when it comes to their specialties: burgers and wine. Their sizable burgers seem expensive but are well worth the price if you're seeking a filling dinner after a day of sightseeing.

BELGISCH BIERCAFE OLIVIER

Achter Clarenburg 6A; tel. 030 236 7876; https://utrecht.cafe-olivier.be; 11am-midnight Mon., 10am-midnight Tues.-Wed., 10am-2am Thurs.-Sat., 11am-midnight Sun.; lunch €8-10, dinner €20, snacks €7

It's easy to miss Belgisch Biercafe Olivier (Belgian Beer Café Olivier) as you walk toward the train station in Utrecht, but once you step into this former secret church, whose entrance is hidden by a typical Dutch house with the words "Maria-minor" above the door, you'll understand why Utrecht residents crowd into this café for *borrels,* the typical hour in the afternoon when people grab a beer with friends. The convenient location en route to the station, beautiful interior that mostly dates back to 1860, and good hours make it a handy spot to remember for a meal or drink—if you can find it.

Cafés and Light Bites

KEEK

Twijnstraat 23; tel. 030 233 3299; https://keekutrecht.nl; 8:30am-5pm Mon.-Fri., 9am-6pm Sat.-Sun.; lunch €9, breakfast €6

This is one of Utrecht's favorite bakeries and lunch spots, known for its organic products and delicious coffee. There are two locations: Twijnstraat 23 is a dedicated lunchroom for a quiet meal featuring one of their trademark *desem* breads, and there's also a bakery/store at Oudegracht 262.

International

TED'S

Lichte Gaard 8; tel. 030 743 7599; http://teds-place.nl; 9am-5pm Mon.-Sun.; €12

Ted's is one of Utrecht's favorite brunch and breakfast places. This American-style restaurant has stunning views of the canals, especially from its waterfront terrace. Their banana pancakes will melt in your mouth!

RESTAURANT SYR

Lange Nieuwstraat 71; tel. 030 233 1104; http://restaurantsyr.nl; 5:30pm-10pm Mon.-Sat., 11:30am-4pm Sun.; lunch €7.50, 3-course dinner €30

Syr is the result of a successful crowdfunding initiative to help former refugees to find their bearings with a good job. The restaurant serves up Syrian food with a side of hospitality. Reservations recommended.

ACCOMMODATIONS

Utrecht is close enough to Amsterdam that staying overnight is not necessary, but it is a more frugal option since accommodations are cheaper here. Stay overnight to enjoy the magic of walking back along Oudegracht or Nieuwegracht in the evening.

BUNK HOTEL UTRECHT

Catharijnekade 9; tel. 088 696 9869; https://bunkhotels.com/utrecht; €54 rooms €24 pods

Bunk Hotel is a budget-friendly hotel housed in a 19th-century converted church with private rooms and private pods. It has an enviable location canal-side in Utrecht's center, just five minutes from Utrecht Central Train Station. Amenities include night-time organ concerts, communal dining (not during COVID), and many events to meet fellow travelers. The bathrooms include rain showers and blackout curtains. There is plenty of room for families and larger groups.

★ MOTHER GOOSE HOTEL

Ganzenmarkt 26; tel. 030 303 6300; www.mothergoosehotel.com; €90

Mother Goose is a cozy boutique hotel in the heart of Utrecht's city center. Housed within a 17th-century building-turned-mattress-factory, the hotel has four floors with different themes. Some of the higher-tier rooms feature exposed stone walls and views of the Domkerk; all rooms include sustainable, eco-friendly products.

INFORMATION AND SERVICES

VVV UTRECHT

Domplein 9; tel. 030 236 0004; www.bezoek-utrecht.nl; 10am-8:30pm daily

Right underneath the Domtower, you'll find the tourist center, where you can ask for maps, biking routes, tips, and souvenirs. You can also purchase tickets to select attractions and the **Utrecht Region Pass** (https://utrechtregionpass.com; €6.50 plus additional costs as incurred). This program provides cheaper bike rentals and train reservations, making it easy to explore the region.

GETTING THERE

Train

UTRECHT CENTRAL TRAIN STATION (Utrecht Centraal)

Stationshal 305; www.ns.nl/stationsinformatie/ut/utrecht-centraal

Utrecht's main train station is right in the heart of the city, although in order to exit the station, you'll need to walk 500 meters (1,600 feet) through the indoor shopping mall Hoog Catharijne. There's clear signage toward the city center (Centrum in Dutch). There is a direct train between **Amsterdam Centraal** (Stationsplein 1; www.ns.nl/stationsinformatie/asd/amsterdam-centraal) and Utrecht; the journey takes 27 minutes. A round-trip train ticket from Amsterdam costs €16.20 for adults.

Car

Considering the ease of taking the train, it only makes sense to rent a car if you'll be visiting Kasteel de Haar. The 42-kilometer (26-mile) drive from **Amsterdam** to Utrecht should take 40 minutes, although it might take longer during rush hour, mostly via the **A2.**

Driving in Utrecht is limited within the historic city center, so it's best to leave your car at one of Utrecht's parking garages. The modern **Hoog Catherine** mall (Spoorstraat 22) next to the Utrecht Central Train Station has more than 3,500 spots across six parking lots. Although it's not the cheapest parking option (https://parkerencentrumutrecht.nl; €15 for the day reserved in advance), it's a 5-minute walk to the city center.

GETTING AROUND

Utrecht is a fairly walkable and easy-to-navigate city. Within the historic city center, you should be able to walk to most places of interest within 15-20 minutes. Sidewalks and pedestrianized sections are common throughout the city; however some caution should be taken on smaller streets, often shared with cars as well as bikers. Utrecht has clear signage along its major streets, making it hard to get truly lost within the historic city center.

Still, if you intend to leave the main city center to visit less central attractions, you might want to **cycle** (Black Bikes; https://black-bikes.com), take a **taxi** (UTC; tel. 030 230 0400; https://utc.nl), or take a **bus** (www.u-ov.info; adults €2.90).

The Hague

The Hague, or Den Haag, is one of Holland's most regal cities, both figuratively and literally. Home to what many call the grandest street in Holland (Lange Voorhout), the Hague certainly has its charms, which have lured many politicians to this former village turned political powerhouse. The Dutch royal family happily calls the Hague home, with multiple palaces within the city limits. Although the Hague is not the capital of the Netherlands anymore, what happens in the Hague shapes politics both inside and outside the country, as the Hague holds many of the United Nations's most influential buildings. As you stroll down the well-maintained streets, you'll want to step into the many independent shops, international restaurants, and cozy cafés.

The Hague's full name in Dutch, *'s-Gravenhage,* can be a handful to say; it means "the Count's Woods" in old Dutch. Since 1358, the Hague has been an important place for politics and the residence of the Count of Holland, exercising power over

The Hague

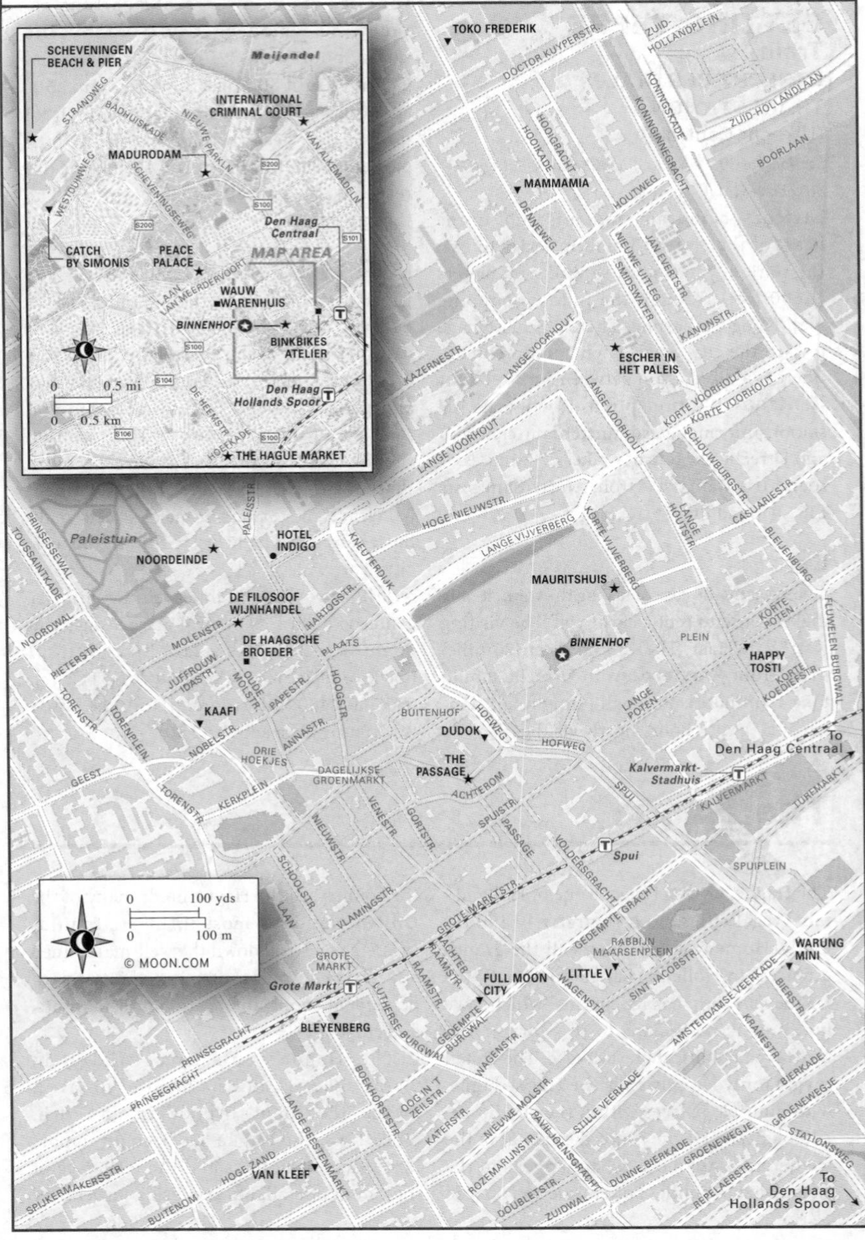
SCHEVENINGEN BEACH & PIER
Meijendel
INTERNATIONAL CRIMINAL COURT
MADURODAM
Den Haag Centraal
MAP AREA
CATCH BY SIMONIS
PEACE PALACE
WAUW WARENHUIS
BINNENHOF
BINKBIKES ATELIER
Den Haag Hollands Spoor
THE HAGUE MARKET
0 0.5 mi
0 0.5 km
TOKO FREDERIK
MAMMAMIA
ESCHER IN HET PALEIS
HOTEL INDIGO
NOORDEINDE
Paleistuin
DE FILOSOOF WIJNHANDEL
DE HAAGSCHE BROEDER
MAURITSHUIS
BINNENHOF
HAPPY TOSTI
KAAFI
DUDOK
THE PASSAGE
To Den Haag Centraal
Kalvermarkt-Stadhuis
Spui
0 100 yds
0 100 m
© MOON.COM
WARUNG MINI
LITTLE V
FULL MOON CITY
Grote Markt
BLEYENBERG
VAN KLEEF
To Den Haag Hollands Spoor

much of the region through its councils, and making the Binnenhof the oldest continually used parliament building in the world. Next to the Binnenhof, you'll find the world-class Mauritshuis art museum, which holds Vermeer's *Girl with a Pearl Earring.*

Beyond the politics, the Hague is the only city in the Netherlands with a beach; it annexed the nearby beachside village of Scheveningen, which is popular with summer tourists. Scheveningen's kitsch definitely stands at odds with the well-curated shopping streets of Noordeinde, Denneweg, and the Passage, but it also lends an air of breeziness to this cosmopolitan city.

ORIENTATION

A full day in the Hague is enough to cover a handful of the major attractions. Though the Hague is a fairly large city, most tourists end up staying relatively close to the **Centrum,** with the **Binnenhof** and the **Mauritshuis** museum just around the corner form each other, and many of the best shops and restaurants. All throughout the Hague's city center, you'll be able to spot the tall tower of the **Grote Kerk,** a historic church, which serves as a good orientation point. Six kilometers (4 miles) west is **Scheveningen,** the Hague's famous beach, with the **Peace Palace** and **Madurodam** located about halfway between. The only other sights farther away are the **International Criminal Court,** about 2 kilometers (1 mile) east of Madurodam, and **the Hague Market,** about 2.5 kilometers (1.5 miles) southeast of the city center.

The Hague has two main train stations: **Den Haag Central Train Station,** 1 kilometer (0.6 miles) east of the center, and **Den Haag HS,** 1 kilometer (0.6 miles) south of the center. Although the Hague has a large public transit network known as HTM (www.htm.nl), which includes trams, buses, and a Metro (shared with Rotterdam), the tram is the easiest system to navigate. Most trams pass through either Den Haag HS or Den Haag Centraal. You will need to know the direction (with the final destination), but it's possible to hop onto the tram and purchase a ticket once you get on. Useful routes include **Tram 1,** which links the Hague's center with Delft via Centrum or Den Haag HS, and **Tram 9,** which links the Hague's center with Scheveningen via Den Haag Central Train Station.

SIGHTS

Centrum

★ BINNENHOF

Lange Poten 4; tel. 070 318 2211; www.houseofrepresentatives.nl, www.prodemos.nl/binnenhof; 9am-5pm Mon.-Fri.; Tweede Kamer (Dutch Parliament) visit free, general tour with ProDemos €9.50 per person

Although the capital of the Netherlands is in Amsterdam, the government meets in the Hague, in the oldest house of parliament in the world. Since the 13th century, a castle has stood on this exact spot, thanks to Floris IV, who created a hunting lodge in the middle of a forest. The only remaining part of that original building is the **Knight's Hall** (Ridderzaal), the castle-like structure that still stands at the heart of this government complex. Although the moat and orchards don't exist anymore, you can still spot the former gate, the **Gevangenpoort** (Buitenhof 33), which was used as both an entryway and a prison in medieval times. Later palaces from various periods in Dutch history, from the 16th century on, surround the Knight's Hall. In the 1990s, a modern wing was added to accommodate the House of Representatives.

It is possible to walk or cycle through the gates to admire the outside of the buildings, but to go inside, you'll need to book a **tour** in advance with ProDemos, House for Democracy and the Rule of Law, an organization that aims to inform citizens and encourage them to play an active role in their government. There are four different tour options, ranging from 50-90 minutes, from €5.50-11 per person. The tours start in the reception area of the **Visitor Center** (Hofweg 1). Even if you don't have time for a tour, don't be afraid to take a 15-minute walk around the Binnenhof to enjoy the jaw-dropping view from across the **Hofvijver,** the pond on one side of the building. Look for the small tower from the 14th century, which is used as the prime minister's office.

MAURITSHUIS

Plein 29; tel. 070 302 3456; www.mauritshuis.nl; 1pm-6pm Mon., 10am-6pm Tues.-Wed. and Fri.-Sun., 10am-8pm Thurs.; adults €15.50, children free

For a glimpse of *Girl with a Pearl Earring* by Johannes Vermeer, stop by the Mauritshuis, next to the Binnenhof. This world-class museum, on par with the Rijksmuseum, focuses on Dutch painters primarily out of the Golden Age, within a beautiful Dutch Classicist building that sits on the edge of the picturesque Hofvijver pond. The interior is straight out of a painting itself, with plush velvet, grand staircases, and elaborate period wallpapers.

The real entrance to the museum is down the clear elevator on the left of the building. Be sure to head upstairs (via the stairs close to the museum **café,** behind the ticket/coat check booths) for special exhibitions after seeing the permanent collection. Today, the museum has been examining its roots more critically—including its namesake, John Maurice, the former governor of Dutch Brazil during a period when the transatlantic slave trade was still occurring—with more exhibitions examining its own past links with colonialism. A ticket also provides access to the **Prince William V Gallery** in the center of the Hague (Buitenhof 33), which houses more works by Jan Steen and Peter Paul Rubens.

NOORDEINDE

Noordeinde 68; not open to the public

In the center of the Hague, you'll find the working palace of King Willem-Alexander. This building has belonged to the Orange family since 1609, when a former medieval farmhouse was expanded into a palace. Although it's not open to the public, you can admire it from outside the beautiful gates with the Royal Coat of Arms on the not-so-surprisingly-named Noordeinde street that leads to the palace. Many royals have lived in the palace part-time; however the current royal family lives elsewhere in the Hague. It's said that if the flag is up, the king is in his office working.

ESCHER IN HET PALEIS

Lange Voorhout 74; tel. 070 427 7730; www.escherinhetpaleis.nl; 11am-5pm Tues.-Sun.; adults €10 euros, children €6.50, combination tickets available with Madurodam (adults €22.25, children €18.75)

Housed in a former palace along one of the grandest streets of the Hague, Escher in Het Paleis is a great museum for people of all ages. It houses the works of famed 20th-century artist M. C. Escher, who is known for his woodcuts and lithographs that often include optical illusions. The museum does a great job of telling the story of Escher's life via his work, while the top floor involves fun modern-day optical illusions.

West of Centrum

PEACE PALACE

Carnegieplein 2; tel. 070 302 42 42; www.vredespaleis.nl; 10am-5pm Tues.-Sun. Apr.-Oct., 11-4pm Tues.-Sun. Nov.-Mar.; tour €11, visitors center free

The impressive Peace Palace was partially funded by American businessman Andrew Carnegie, who hoped to create a better world at the turn of the 20th century. With the permission of the Dutch queen, the building was designed with gifts from various countries, including a Swiss clock and Italian marble. The Peace Palace was completed in 1913, before the outbreak of World War I, and although it did not prevent war in the 20th century, many wars have been stopped within its walls thanks to mediation.

This grand structure is not so much a palace as much as a court, used for the Permanent Court of Arbitration and the

---

1: Binnenhof **2:** Peace Palace **3:** Grote Markt in the Hague **4:** Scheveningen Beach & Pier

1
2
3
4

International Court of Justice. This building and the **International Criminal Court,** 3 kilometers (2 miles) east, are often misunderstood to be one and the same, but this building is where countries discuss amicable agreements, legal disputes, and humanitarian issues, while the Criminal Court prosecutes war criminals.

It is possible to be a witness for some of the cases with some prior notice, business-appropriate clothing, and luck; however, this building is often closed to the public. Public **tours** are available, typically in the off-hours of the court, such as weekends and evenings (95 minutes; palace €14.50, €11 exterior). Even if you're not able to reserve a tour in advance, you can still admire the court's grand appearance from the outside gates and learn about the history within the free **visitors center.** Be sure not to miss the eternal flame burning outside the building.

To visit the Peace Palace, you can opt to take **Tram 1** toward Scheveningen (www.htm.nl; €4) from **Spui** (Spui 6). The ride takes only 10 minutes and drops you off at the Peace Palace via the Vredespaleis/Peace Palace tram stop. Otherwise, it's a 45-minute (3.6-kilometer/2.2-mile) walk west from the city center.

MADURODAM

George Maduroplein 1; tel. 070 416 2400; www.madurodam.nl; 11am-5pm daily Jan-Mar., 9am-8pm daily Mar.-Aug., 9am-7pm daily Aug.-Oct., 11am-5pm daily Oct.-Dec.; adults €19.50, children 0-3 free

Madurodam might be the most cheerful war memorial you've ever seen. This miniature version of the Netherlands dates back to the post-World War II period, when a family sought to memorialize their fallen soldier, George Maduro, who was captured as a prisoner of war before being sent to a Nazi death camp. His family raised funds for a living memorial to inspire the Netherlands to rebuild at a time when the country was struggling. Within the memorial, you'll find famous buildings from throughout the Netherlands built at a 1/25 scale. No matter your age, it's a delight to admire the small details and interact with the exhibitions that help you learn more about the Netherlands. How often can you say that you've traveled around the entire country in just an hour?

Madurodam is about halfway (3 kilometers/2 miles) between the Hague city center and Scheveningen. To get to Madurodam from the city center by public transit, take **Tram 9** (www.htm.nl; €4) from Den Haag Central Train Station toward Scheveningen Noord. The journey takes 11 minutes and drops you right in front of Madurodam via the Madurodam tram stop. The tram runs every 10 minutes or more during the day.

INTERNATIONAL CRIMINAL COURT (ICC)

Oude Waalsdorperweg 10; tel. 070 515 8515; www.icc-cpi.int/visit; 8am-6pm Mon.-Fri.; free

For a bit of international intrigue, head to the International Criminal Court during their office hours to learn about the workings of this often-controversial court, which prosecutes war criminals. Only in existence since 2002, the International Criminal Court (known as the ICC) has famously indicted Omar al-Bashir (former president of Sudan), Muammar Gaddafi, and Joseph Kony. Visitors can register for a **tour** in advance online or check the agenda on their website for the hearing schedule for a chance to be in the audience for a real-life international criminal trial (free; 2 hours).

Note that a **passport** is obligatory for entry, and all phones/personal items must go into lockers downstairs. There are clothing restrictions, so be sure to dress professionally if you're curious about the inner workings of the court. Some sessions end early, so don't arrive too late in the day if you want to attend a hearing. They provide live translations into English using headsets.

The International Criminal Court is 4 kilometers (2 miles) northwest of the city center. Take **bus 20** from Den Haag Central Train Station toward Duinzigt (www.htm.nl; 10 minutes; €4) before getting off at

Waalsdorperweg, where the court is across the street.

BEACHES

SCHEVENINGEN BEACH & PIER

Strandweg 150-154; tel. 06 10386859; www.pier.nl; pier 10am-10pm daily; free

Although many don't associate the Netherlands with the beach, the Hague has a lovely one about 3 kilometers (2 miles) from the city center. The water isn't very warm, so most of the appeal comes from strolling along the boardwalk or enjoying activities along the pier, including bungee jumping and a Ferris wheel. In summer, the beach is lined with countless cafés, bars, and nightclubs, where you can listen to the waves and music from the cafés. **Tram 9** toward Scheveningen will bring you from the Spui/Centrum tram stop. You'll take the tram to the last stop (Kurhaus), which will take 23 minutes. The tram goes every 15 minutes.

SHOPPING

The Hague is known for being posh, and you'll certainly find your fill of exclusive streets for shopping high-end Dutch brands on **Noordeinde** and within **the Passage** shopping center close to Noordeinde Palace. Just off Noordeinde, you'll find many skinny pedestrian-friendly streets, including **Papestraat, Prinsestraat,** and **Oude Molstraat,** home to independent stores selling specialty items from organic soaps to wine. Many of the Hague's main high street shops are clustered on **Spui,** which is just a 15-minute walk from The Hague Central Station, close to the Binnenhof.

Malls

THE PASSAGE

Passage 72; https://depassage.nl; noon-6pm Mon., 10am-6pm Tues.-Wed. and Fri.-Sat., 10am-9pm Thurs., noon-5pm Sun.

Although the Hague is pretty far from Paris or Milan, you'll find a beautiful arcade from 1882 in the center of the city, just footsteps from the Binnenhof, that is the oldest shopping center in the Netherlands. Today, the Passage is still a functioning shopping center with more than 20 stores and cafés, including an Apple Store, antique stores, a gift shop, and clothing shops. **Hop & Stork** (70 345 5455; www.hopenstork.com; 10am-5:30pm daily) is a great spot for a coffee with a handmade chocolate. Be sure to look up to admire the glass dome in the center.

Wine

DE FILOSOOF WIJNHANDEL

Papestraat 5; www.defilosoof.eu; 11am-7pm Tues.-Sun.

Papestraat is an atmospheric shopping street close to Noordeinde Palace. Visitors to de Filosoof (the Philosopher) often end up admiring Socrates, the owner's fluffy Persian cat, who can be found sleeping at the cash register or within the window of this wine store that specializes in Persian-style wines created in Bulgaria as well as imported wines from the Caucasus region, the Balkans, and other lesser-known wine locales. Many cat lovers can't resist bringing home the Socrates Dry Gin, which is a bespoke gin brand with Socrates's image on it. The owner Ofran does wine tastings on weekends.

Souvenirs

DE HAAGSCHE BROEDER

Oude Molstraat 35; https://haagschebroeder.nl; 1pm-4:30pm Wed.-Sat.

Although a monastic concept store might be a first for you, if you're lucky enough to be on Molstraat in the afternoon on one of the open days, you might notice a handsome building with a large circular window that resembles a church. The wooden door leads into the Monastic Shop of the Hague Brothers, an order of monks who inhabit this monastery in the middle of the Hague, which is a protected monument dating back to the 1920s. Their shop, which accepts cash and Dutch debit cards, sells goods produced by monks and nuns in Europe as well as handmade clay mugs and some of the best small-batch beer brewed in the Hague. If you're a fan of organic products, this is an affordable spot to stock up on lotions and soaps.

WAUW WARENHUIS

Piet Heinstraat 51a; www.wauwwarenhuis.nl; 11am-6pm Tues.-Sat., noon-5pm Sun.-Mon.

Wauw is a wild warehouse where you have no idea what you'll find (hence the *Wauw*, meaning Wow in Dutch). This shop is filled with unexpected delights, from jewelry to plants to handmade woven items to quirky gifts. From the moment you peer into the shop, which is filled with colorful tropical plants, you're likely to find something that will catch your eye.

Clothing and Accessories

OMAR MUNIE CLOTHING

Noordeinde 64; https://omarmunie.com; 11am-5:30pm Mon.-Fri., 10am-5:30pm Sat., noon-5pm Sun.

Omar Munie is a Somali-Dutch designer who arrived in the Netherlands as a refugee. Today one of the best respected designers in the Netherlands, he owns one of the most exclusive locations in the Hague just footsteps from Noordeinde Palace. Within a beautifully decorated shop, Omar Munie showcases his beautifully designed purses and accessories for both men and women that are handcrafted partially in the Hague. Even if his handbags are out of your price range, his accessories make a unique gift or souvenir.

FOOD

The Hague's food scene is quite lively, with options from numerous countries represented. The many UN and Dutch governmental institutional have attracted a professional and well-traveled set of residents who appreciate everything from American-style brunches to Chinese dim sum. Whether you're looking for a nice meal by the beach, a casual herring, a flavor-rich Javanese-style *rijsttafel,* or just a friendly cup of coffee, the Hague offers something for everyone.

The Hague's deep connection to Indonesia is rooted in the fact that the Indonesian colony was largely governed from the Hague, which brought many middle-class civil servants to the Hague in the postcolonial era. As a result, the Hague is one of the best places in the Netherlands to sample Indonesian food.

Cafés and Light Bites

DUDOK

Hofweg 1A; tel. 070 890 0100; https://dudok.nl; 9:30am-11pm Sun.-Wed., 9:30am-midnight Thurs.-Sat.; €5

The most famous spot in the Hague for apple pie is Dudok, which sits across from the Binnenhof. Whether you're looking for a fresh cup of coffee or just a delicious piece of cake, this favorite café is a great place to take a breather from sightseeing.

HAPPY TOSTI

Korte Poten 5; tel. 070 744 0544; www.happytosti.nl; 8am-5pm Mon.-Fri., 9am-5:30pm Sat., 9am-5pm Sun.; €7

A favorite lunch spot not far from the Mauritshuis is Happy Tosti, a casual restaurant that works to provide good jobs for people with disabilities. Their sandwiches are delicious, large, and a steal for the price.

Indonesian

TOKO FREDERIK

Frederikstraat 225; tel. 070 360 3125; www.tokofrederik.nl; noon-9pm Mon.-Sat., 4pm-9pm Sun.; lunch €10, dinner €15

Due to the historic role of the Hague in governing the Netherlands, and the fact that Indonesia was once a Dutch colony, many Indonesians live in the Hague. Although you'll find countless *tokos* throughout the city, one of my favorites has to be Toko Frederick, which has been serving up Indonesian specialties since 1984. If it's a nice day you can do takeout, or opt to sit down for lunch or dinner. It's best to reserve ahead. Although you can choose from their menu or even opt for the rice table (if you're hungry!), I recommend the Rames daily specials, with a mix of dishes by spice level (non-spicy is an option), if you're unsure what to order.

International

WARUNG MINI

Amsterdamse Veerkade 57; tel. 070 365 4628; https://warungminidenhaag.nl; 11am-11pm Mon.-Fri., noon-11pm Sat.-Sun.; sandwiches €3.50, roti €7.50, mains €10

Warung Mini is a short walk from Den Haag Central Train Station, and it's a great place to pick up a quick dinner. This Surinamese-Javanese restaurant is almost always packed with a line snaking out the door during lunch and dinner, but it's certainly worth the wait. They're well known among office workers for their sandwiches, but their *saoto* soup and dishes with *pom* (a Surinamese vegetable) are a highlight if you're hungry. Bring cash, as credit cards are not accepted.

KAAFI

Prinsestrat 25; tel. 06 11776610; https://kaafi.nl; 10am-6pm (kitchen closed by 3pm) Mon.-Sun.; €9

The Hague is very international thanks to its many embassies and United Nations institutions, and Kaafi is the perfect representation of the city's diversity. Its American owner pulls from various international cuisines, including Pakistani, to create a delicious and surprising brunch or lunch served with the perfect cup of coffee.

LITTLE V

Rabbijn Maarsenplein 21; tel. 070 392 1230; www.littlev.nl; noon-3:30pm and 4:30pm-9:30pm Tues.-Sun.; €13.50

The best Vietnamese food in the Hague can be found at Little V, which fills up each night with customers who come back weekly for their generous portions in a beautifully decorated restaurant.

MAMMAMIA

Denneweg 27; tel. 070 212 8061; www.mammamiadenhaag.nl; 5pm-11pm Mon.-Tues., noon-10pm Wed.-Thurs., noon-11pm Fri.-Sat., noon-10pm Sun.; pizza €14

Vegans and non-vegans can eat together at Mammamia, a pizzeria and Italian restaurant in the Hague serving up delicious organic Italian-style pizzas that don't compromise on quality.

FULL MOON CITY

Achter Raamstraat 75; tel. 070 356 2013; https://fullmooncity.nl; noon-11pm daily; €15

Hidden up an escalator on the side entrance of a building, Full Moon City is one of the most popular Chinese restaurants in the Hague's surprisingly sizable Chinatown, which is right in the Hague's city center. Once you reach the top of the escalator, you'll find round tables filled with families and couples enjoying dim sum, noodles, and other Chinese favorites. No reservations needed.

Markets

THE HAGUE MARKET (Haagse Markt)

Herman Costerstraat; https://dehaagsemarkt.nl; 9am-5pm Mon., Wed., and Fri.-Sat.

The Hague Market is a bit outside the city center, but it's worth the trek if you love browsing. This bustling market has been meeting on the same spot for over 80 years. Come armed with cash for fruit, veggies, fabrics, and other household favorites as the sellers shout their offerings. Even if you're not grocery shopping, it's always fun to come here to sample from the various food stalls serving up Surinamese *roti,* Caribbean snacks, and Turkish *burek.* In order to get to the Haagse Markt, you can catch **Tram 6** from the underground tram station underneath Grote Markt (Prinsegracht 1) or Den Haag Central Train Station toward Den Haag Leyenburg (www.htm.nl). The journey only takes 5-7 minutes on the tram; when you arrive, just cross the street toward the Haagse Markt following the many shoppers with carts.

Seafood

CATCH BY SIMONIS

Dr. Lelykade 43; tel. 070 338 7609; www.simonisvis.nl; 5pm-11pm Mon.-Thurs., noon-11pm Fri.-Sun.; €16-20

As the only Dutch city on the sea, the Hague enjoys great access to high-quality fish.

For the best-quality seafood meal, head to Simonis, a well-regarded local restaurant chain with multiple locations throughout the Hague. Catch, the location in Scheveningen, has been praised by Michelin for its fresh ingredients and good cooking.

BARS AND NIGHTLIFE

VAN KLEEF

Lange Beestenmarkt 109; tel. 070 345 2273; www.museumvankleef.nl; 10am-6pm Tues.-Sat., 1pm-6pm Sun.

Once frequented by Vincent Van Gogh, this distillery is the last jenever distillery in the Hague, and they're still serving up liquors according to their recipes from the 1800s. The interior is all original, down to the vintage jenever bottles along the wall and the cash register. Visitors can reserve a place ahead for a guided tasting, or simply go up to the bar to sample liquors before making a purchase. The Kruìde Baggâh, a flavorful herbal bitter, has a colorful story behind it and a delightful taste.

BLEYENBERG

Grote Markt 10; tel. 070 800 2120; www.bleyenbergdenhaag.nl; 11am-1am Sun.-Wed., 11am-1:30am Thurs.-Sat.

Although the Hague isn't one for splashy nightlife, Bleyenberg is the perfect spot to enjoy a cocktail in summer. This restaurant/café transforms from a hip restaurant with reasonable lunch and dinner specials into a cool rooftop bar at night.

ACCOMMODATIONS

Although you don't need to stay over in the Hague for a day trip, it is a great base for traveling within the region to Delft or Rotterdam. In just 12 minutes you can be in Delft, and Rotterdam in 30.

HOTEL INDIGO

Noordeinde 33; tel. 070 209 9000; www.ihg.com/hotelindigo; €150

At the heart of the bustling city center across from Noordeinde Palace, you'll find Hotel Indigo. This former bank turned hotel has embraced the quirky details of the building, down to the art deco windows, vault-themed details, and brass lighting. Downstairs, you'll find a chic bar centered around the old bank vault.

GETTING THERE

Train

DEN HAAG CENTRAL TRAIN STATION

10 Koningin Julianaplein; www.ns.nl/stationsinformatie/gvc/den-haag-centraal

DEN HAAG HS TRAIN STATION

Stationsplein 44; www.ns.nl/stationsinformatie/gv/den-haag-hs

Both train stations in the Hague are 12-minute walks (1 kilometer/0.6 miles) away from the city center. It doesn't matter much which station you travel to, although it's often easier to find the train toward Den Haag Centraal at **Amsterdam Centraal** (Stationsplein 1; www.ns.nl/stationsinformatie/asd/amsterdam-centraal). It's an easy train ride from Amsterdam (50 minutes); trains depart approximately 2-4 times per hour. A round-trip ticket to the Hague costs €25 for adults and €2.50 for children under 12.

Car

Driving to the Hague can be a good option if you'll be traveling in the larger region. From **Amsterdam,** the 65-kilometer (40-mile) drive takes about 50 minutes, mostly on the **A4. Parking** and driving in the pedestrian city center are limited/prohibited on some streets, but you can find underground parking in a few points close to major tourist attractions as well as the city center. The area surrounding Den Haag HS Train Station has ample parking, including the Laakhaven QPark (Rijswijkseweg 27) with 1,338 parking spots. Parking closer to the city center is possible at the Plein parking garage behind the Mauritshuis museum (Plein 24), or close to Scheveningen beach at BKS Parking (Nieuwe

Parklaan 248). There are also 1,200 spots available close to Den Haag Central Train Station at Q-Park CS New Babylon at Prinses Irenestraat 1 (€2 per 30 minutes, €30 euros maximum for the day).

GETTING AROUND

For those staying in the Hague/Rotterdam metro area, there is a special **Tourist Day Pass** (https://touristdaytickets.com) that allows for unlimited transit on buses, trams, and metros in the region. This pass, which costs €14.50, can be purchased at subway stations in The Hague and Rotterdam region.

Public Transit

Once you arrive in the Hague, purchase a ticket for the **HTM** (Haagse Tram Maatschappij; www.htm.nl), the public transit provider within the city. A day pass costs €7.10 per adult and €1.50 for children under 13. This gives you access to buses and the tram and metro system within the greater Hague region. It's not necessary if you're staying strictly in the center, but if you intend to visit Scheveningen or one of the UN institutions, the tram is a great option.

Many tourists stick to Trams 1 and 9, which run between Den Haag Central Train Station and Scheveningen. **Tram 1** stops outside of the Binnenhof entrance in the Hague center, although it's also easy to catch it at **Spui 6** in the heart of the city center. This tram passes the Peace Palace as well. **Tram 9** is best caught at Den Haag Central Train Station and stops at Madurodam.

HTM has a booth within Den Haag Central Train Station and Den Haag HS Train Station where you can purchase a day pass as well as receive information about public transit. You can check the HTM website or download the HTM app in advance to purchase a ticket/day pass on your phone. There are machines available on the trams where you can purchase a ticket, and most stops have a map and a schedule.

Bike

The Hague is laid-back in terms of cycling, with a well-established set of bike paths that are largely separate from cars throughout the city. Due to the size of the Hague and how spread out some of the attractions are, biking is a great way to get around, especially in the case of farther attractions like the International Criminal Court and the Hague Market. The Hague is calmer for biking than Amsterdam, as many of the roads tend to be wider. Most major bike paths have clear signage leading to museums and attractions.

BINKBIKES ATELIER

Herengracht 56A; tel. 070 4062201; www.binkbikes.nl; 10am-7pm daily; €15

BINKBIKES has a convenient location about one block away from Den Haag Central Train Station. They offer a small selection of well-maintained city bikes as well as electric bikes that are a step above your average bike rental in Amsterdam. Their bikes can be retrofitted with children's seats (€10) for families with young children.

Delft

Delft is one of the most iconic cities in the Netherlands, known for its well-preserved city center and beautiful Delftware pottery. The name Delft comes from an old Dutch word, *delven,* that is related to digging a canal. Not surprisingly, Delft is full of pretty canals to explore, especially the Oude Delft canal and the tiny Voldersgracht canal.

Much of visiting Delft involves soaking up the charm, especially on its bustling market days in summer, where you can find lunch as well as antiques. Lovers of history will want to step back in time at the Royal Delft Factory or either of the city's well-known churches to learn about their storied past, retracing the steps of famous son Johannes Vermeer, buried underneath the Old Church.

Despite its beautiful old center, Delft is very much a modern city at heart, home to leading Dutch university Delft University of Technology (TU Delft). The large student population and the many alums who stick around after graduation in the tech industry allow Delft to support a wide range of independent restaurants and cafés that might surprise visitors.

A half day is enough to get a good feeling for Delft by walking around aimlessly, stopping at cafés, and pausing far too often to admire the view. If you intend to visit the Royal Delft Factory or the Paauw Delft Blue Factory, you might want to opt for a full day.

ORIENTATION

The main historic city center of Delft is fairly compact, surrounded by canals. It's small enough that it's hard to truly get lost. Use the towers of the iconic **New Church** and **Old Church** for navigating; you're always likely to be able to spot one of them in the distance. **Markt Square** is the main square where most events and the weekly Thursday market occur, although on Saturdays, the more commercial **Brabantse Turfmarkt,** a few blocks south of Markt Square, takes the stage as the main market.

The former city walls are largely gone aside from a handful of towers; the only real remnant is the **Eastern Gate** in the southern part of the historic city center. Next to the **train station,** you'll spot **Windmill The Rose** as you walk eastward toward the city center.

SIGHTS

Delft Center

Delft's canals originally served as method for flood prevention; however, water and a lot of digging eventually allowed Delft to transport its wares via human-made waterways to the larger port town of Delftshaven (now Rotterdam). The canals crisscross the city center, ranging from large and spacious to cramped canals that are better suited to birds than boats.

Oude Delft is the most iconic canal thanks to the leaning Old Church. Lined with the beautiful facades of a mixture of 17th- and 18th-century buildings, it's the first canal you pass over when coming from the train station. The best viewpoint is from the bridge on Nieuwstraat. The rest of the canals form a watery boundary around the city center.

NEW CHURCH (Nieuwe Kerk)

Markt 80; tel. 015 212 3025; http://oudeennieuwekerkdelft.nl; 11am-4pm Mon.-Fri., 10am-5pm Sat. Nov.-Jan., 10am-5pm Mon.-Sat. Feb.-Mar., 9am-6pm Mon.-Sat. Apr.-Oct.; New and Old Churches adults €5.50, children €4, New Church tower only adults €4.50, children €2.50, combination churches and New Church tower adults €8.50, children €3.50 (children under 5 not allowed in the tower)

It feels a bit ironic to call this very historic and important church the "new" church, but comparatively speaking, it is new for the city, not completed until 1655. Although construction

The Lowdown on Delftware

Delftware at Paauw

Even if you don't consider yourself an aficionado of fancy vases or dishes, you'll likely recognize the striking blue-and-white-patterned ceramics that have made Delft famous.

HISTORY AND DESIGN

The base material for Delftware (also known as *Delft Blauw,* or Delft Blue) is typically marl, a clay from Germany and Belgium, which is coated with a tin glaze prior to a ceramic glaze. Around the time that the Dutch began trading with China, Chinese pottery became a popular commodity, which spawned Delftware with scenes inspired by traditional Chinese art. Delft was once at the center of this industry, but due only two factories remain in Delft today.

Designs on the ceramics range from ornate portraits of typically Dutch scenes, to more minimalistic flowers and flourishes and ornately drawn flowers. The most distinctive shape is the tulip vase, a stacked vase with many spouts for holding individual tulips.

DETERMINING AUTHENTICITY

When buying Delftware, it's important to check the bottom carefully to find out if the item is authentic. All items produced within the Netherlands must be stamped and signed by the manufacturer. Many items produced abroad, including some of the cheaper items by the Royal Delft Factory, are not authentic; if a price seems too good to be true, it's probably because it is. These are generally mass-produced by a machine in a factory rather than hand-painted by artisans, which is why the real thing is so expensive.

BUYING DELFTWARE

In the Netherlands, secondhand shops are known as ***kringloops,*** and these are a great place to look for Delftware on a budget. You can also browse **flea markets,** including the one in Delft and the IJhallen in Amsterdam for secondhand Delftware. You can purchase Delftware from the source at **Royal Delft Factory** and **Paauw: The Delft Blue Factory by Heinen Delfts Blauw** (page 172).

Authentic Delftware can be found secondhand for as little as €5-10, but at reputable shops, there's no limit to what you might pay depending on the size and complexity of design, up to €100 for nicer plates and vases. But you'll also find smaller items, such as Christmas ornaments, for less.

One final note: Be careful with packing your Delftware in your suitcase, as it's quite fragile!

began much earlier (as early as 1381), a series of unfortunate events prevented the completion of the church until much later. Today, the church is one of the most significant in the Netherlands, due to its links to the Dutch royal family. William of Orange, who was murdered in Delft in 1584, has a mausoleum built in his honor within this church. Since then, the Dutch royal family has used the crypts underneath for burying family members. The crypts are not open to the public, but if you visit, you can learn about the history of the church and admire some of the memorials above ground.

The church itself is nice, but the main attraction for many visitors is the stunning view of Delft that you get from the impressive 85-meter (280-foot) tower after climbing 376 steps to the top. The spire of the tower that you see today was designed by Pierre Cuypers, the same architect who designed the Rijksmuseum, after the tower was struck by lightning several times. On a clear day, you might be able to see the Hague. As you climb to the top, you'll also pass by the carillon room, which houses 48 bells. You can hear the bells played by the carillon master for free on Fridays (7pm-8pm) and on market days (11am-noon Tues. and Sat.).

OLD CHURCH
(Oude Kerk)

HH Geestkerkhof 25; tel. 015 212 3025; http://oudeennieuwekerkdelft.nl; 11am-4pm Mon.-Fri., 10am-5pm Sat. Nov.-Jan., 10am-5pm Mon.-Sat. Feb.-Mar., 9am-6pm Mon.-Sat. Apr.-Oct.; New and Old Churches adults €5.50, children €4, combination churches and New Church tower adults €8.50, children €3.50

The Old Church is fairly ancient, even by Dutch standards. Built upon the site of a smaller basilica, St. Bartholomew's Church was first constructed in 1236 as a Catholic church. The tower was a later addition, which was a misstep given that the foundations of the tower were on top of an old canal. Since the 14th century, the tower, known as Crooked Jan, has been leaning precariously to the left. Luckily, renovations have stabilized the 75-meter (250-foot) tower, but it's still hard to ignore this church when walking down the Oude Delft canal.

Unfortunately, the tower is not open to the public at this time, but visitors can take a walk around the church's interior, which is a mix of periods. It was expanded in the medieval period into a gothic basilica and rededicated to St. Hippolytus. Following the Protestant Reformation, the church was modified and largely stripped of its decorations. Still, today, the Old Church is a fascinating medieval church that reflects the evolution of Christianity throughout Dutch history. Be sure to look down at the floors, which include the graves of notable people including pirate Piet Hein, scientist Anton van Leeuwenhoek, and famous Delftian Johannes Vermeer.

WINDMILL THE ROSE
(Molen de Roos)

Phoenixstraat 111; tel. 015 887 1162; www.delftsemolen.nl; 10am-4pm Wed.-Sat.; donation

Walking from the train station toward the city center, you'll immediately spot the De Roos Windmill, the last remaining windmill in Delft. Although it wasn't always on this exact spot, as it was moved to allow for the train station to be renovated, the current stone windmill dates back to 1679. Today, the windmill is open to the public to explore, provided they give a donation. On the ground floor, you'll find a **shop** that sells organic flours that are ground by the windmill. The higher floors are reached by climbing several steep staircases that require some dexterity to navigate, especially on the way down. The view from the top of Delft's 17th-century skyline is certainly worth the climb if you're not afraid of heights and confined spaces.

1: Nieuwe Kerk **2:** Molen de Roos **3:** Ramen Nikkou **4:** popular eatery Kek

1
2
3
CHECK OUT OUR INSTAGRAM
4
kek

EASTERN GATE
(Oostpoort)

Oostpoort 1; not open to public, but viewable 24/7; free

The Eastern Gate of Delft is easily one of the most iconic places in the city. This beautiful gate is the last remaining city gate in Delft, with a building that dates back to the 1400s and has impressive spires from the 16th century. There's a small park and drawbridge, but the best view is from across the water, after you walk through the gates. The building itself is not open to the public.

Delft Outskirts

ROYAL DELFT FACTORY TOUR

Rotterdamseweg 196; tel. 015 760 0800; www.royaldelft.com; 9am-5pm Mon.-Fri.; adults €14, teens €8.75, children free

If you're crazy about pottery, you might be interested in the full experience of the Royal Delft Factory Tour. The factory is the last remaining Delftware factory from the 16th century, and their tour provides more than just a quick overview of the process. The factory provides a significant look into the history of Delftware over the last 400 years and a peek at priceless Delftware worthy of a museum. Visitors can also watch the process of an artist creating Delftware.

The factory is about 20 minutes on foot outside the Delft historic city center. From Delft Train Station, turn right and follow the canal underneath the tunnel. After the tunnel, turn left onto Hooikade. Keep walking along the canal for 450 meters (1,500 feet) before turning left onto Abtswoudsebrug, a bridge over the canal. Follow the bike path for 230 meters (750 feet). You'll see a modern building that says Haagse Hogeschool (Delft), and the Royal Delft Factory is across the street on the side closest to you.

During high season (Apr.-Aug.), there is a miniature **shuttle** that holds 4-6 people and costs €3 (children under 12 free) for a one-way trip, departing every 2 minutes, that will take you from the Tourist Office in front of the New Church (Kerkstraat 3) to the factory. You can purchase a ticket within the tourism office 10am-5pm. The ride should take 10 minutes at most.

PAAUW: THE DELFT BLUE FACTORY BY HEINEN DELFTS BLAUW

Delftweg 133; tel. 015 212 4920; https://dedelftsblauwfabriek.nl; 9am-4:30pm Mon.-Fri., 10am-4pm Sat., 11am-1pm Sun.; free

One of Delft's hidden gems, the Paauw Delft Blue Factory is a working Delftware factory that provides free tours every 10 minutes in a multitude of languages. It's a small workspace where artists draw elaborate designs on a ceramic base. Unlike a conventional tour, you can stop to ask questions about the process. After the tour, you'll end up in their small souvenir **shop** where you can buy authentic Delftware pottery and other collectibles. The factory is about 25 minutes outside the city center, a 2-kilometer (1-mile) walk. Tram 19 stops close by, and the tram ride from the Delft Train Station only takes 15 minutes if you get lucky with the schedule.

From Delft Train Station, **Tram 19** (www.htm.nl; adults one-way €4, day ticket €7.10, children 4-12 day ticket €1.50) toward Leidschendam departs approximately every 20 minutes. From the Delft, Brasserskade tram stop, it's a 6-minute (500-meter/1,600-foot) walk. You'll cross at the intersection onto the sidewalk on the left-hand side and continue in the direction away from Delft before making a left on Pauwhof. The road curves, so continue right along Pauwhof before making a left onto Pauwenstein. (After your visit, you can take **Tram 1** in the direction of the Hague to head to the Den Haag Central Train Station if you're not interested in returning to Delft. The journey takes about 33 minutes and the tram runs every 15 minutes.)

Market Days in Delft

flower market in Delft

ANTIQUES MARKET DELFT
(Antiekmarkt Delft)

On Saturdays in summer 9am-5pm, Delft hosts a charming flea market along the canals on the western side of Markt Square. Come armed with cash as you browse vintage posters, pottery (including authentic Delftware), and other curiosities. Elsewhere in the city, you'll find more than 60 stands selling food and other household items on Brabantse Turfmarkt.

FLOWER MARKET

On Thursdays, the weekly flower market is held on Brabantse Turfmarkt. This small market has a number of stalls selling beautiful seasonal flowers, household plants, and occasionally some sweets such fresh *stroopwafels*. From 9am-5pm, a lively local market with more than 160 stalls selling fruits, veggies, fabrics, and other items sits in the center of Delft on Markt Square underneath the New Church.

SHOPPING

SECOND STORY TWEEDEHANDS BOEKEN EN SPELLEN

Vrouwjuttenland 25; tel. 015 212 6101; www.secondstory.nl; noon-5pm Tues.-Wed., 11-5pm Sat.

Hidden on a back canal of Delft, you'll know Second Story by the racks of quirky and charming postcards outside the door. Once you step inside, you'll see floor-to-ceiling bookcases stocked with books in English and Dutch. Their collection is surprisingly well curated for small shop, with popular titles as well as upcoming literary stars. Be sure to say hello to the shop cat!

LOCO LAMA

Molslaan 35; tel. 06 23037443; www.locolamadesign.com; 10am-6pm Tues.-Thurs. and Sat., 10am-9pm Fri., noon-5pm Sun.

Loco Lama is a quirky gift and household store that stocks wild and creative ornaments for your home. Whether you're looking for a gift to put a smile on someone's face or a unique souvenir to bring home with you, it's always fun browsing here.

FOOD

Dutch

THUIS BY LADERA

Oosteinde 123; tel. 015 212 5950; www.facebook.com/thuisbyladera; 6pm-8pm Mon.-Fri.; €7.50

It's surprisingly hard to find certain Dutch favorites that you often find in a typical Dutch home. Thuis prides itself on cooking up simple and delicious Dutch dinner specials that won't break your budget. The small restaurant is decorated with cute Holland kitsch, perfect for immersing yourself in a bit of the Netherlands. Call to make a reservation—and remember to bring cash.

Cafés and Light Bites

VAN DER BURGH CHOCOLAAD

Vrouwenregt 2; tel. 015 364 8273; www.vanderburghchocolaad.nl; 10am-6pm Mon.-Sat.; €6

Van der Burgh is a family-run artisanal chocolatier in the heart of Delft. They pride themselves on creating delicious chocolate shaped by hand, which you can sometimes watch being made in the back of the shop. Their flavors range from standard popular options to creative combinations with pepper and strawberries.

KEK

Voldersgracht 27; tel. 015 750 3253; https://kekdelft.nl; 8am-6pm Wed.-Mon.; €15

Kek is a favorite of Delft's students and professionals with its wide variety of elaborate lattes, open-faced sandwiches, and trendy interior. It's not possible to make a reservation, but if you're willing to wait a little while for lunch, you'll be able to enjoy your meal underneath artwork produced by Belgian and Dutch artists. International credit cards are accepted.

International

HUMMUS

Molslaan 39; tel. 015 879 5252; https://ilovehummus.nl; noon-9pm Wed.-Thurs., noon-10pm Fri.-Sat., noon-9pm Sun.; €10

Hummus is a popular Middle Eastern restaurant that serves up vegan food without comprising on flavor. Reserve for a table, especially close to dinnertime, and be sure to sample their namesake hummus and their shawarma made with vegan meat substitutes.

RAMEN NIKKOU

Oosteinde 199; 5pm-9pm Tues.-Wed., noon-2pm and 5pm-9pm Thurs.-Sat.; €13

For authentic Japanese ramen in the middle of Delft, look no further than Ramen Nikkou, a ramen shop run by a Japanese entrepreneur who wanted to create the feeling of an intimate ramen shop in the Netherlands. His ramen is made fresh to order, with daily specials that sell out. Larger groups and reservations are not accepted.

HILLS & MILLS

Oude Langendijk 6; tel. 015 212 3930; www.hillsmills.nl; 11:30am-10pm Wed.-Thurs., 11am-10pm Fri. and Sun., 10am-10pm Sat.; lunch €12, dinner €18

Hills & Mills is a restaurant that perfectly embodies the roots of its owner. This restaurant close to the main market square prides itself on healthy food that takes inspiration from both East and West with a modern Indian kitchen. Their naan specials are a favorite among diners.

ACCOMMODATIONS

Although a day trip to Delft from Amsterdam is definitely a possibility, staying the night is a great option, as many of the day-trippers depart by 5pm. There's nothing more magical than enjoying a sunset on Markt underneath the New Church or at a canal-side café once all the tour groups have gone home. Hotel options are fairly limited in Delft, so it's best to reserve ahead in peak season. You'll find more options in the nearby city of the Hague.

HOTEL DE EMAUSPOORT

Vrouwenregt 9; tel. 015 219 0219; www.emauspoort.nl; €135

For a night away from the chaos, consider staying at De Emauspoort, a small guesthouse in the center of Delft. Although they have standard rooms, their themed rooms are more interesting, including one inspired by Vermeer and a cozy wooden caravan in the middle of their courtyard. All rooms include a delicious breakfast.

GETTING THERE

Delft is 1 hour from Amsterdam by car or train. For those staying in the Hague/Rotterdam metro area, there is a special transit pass, **Tourist Day Pass** (https://touristdaytickets.com; €14.50), that allows for unlimited transit on buses, trams, and metros in the region. This pass can be purchased at subway stations in the Hague and Rotterdam region.

Train

DELFT TRAIN STATION

Stationsplein 16; www.ns.nl/stationsinformatie/dt/delft

The Delft train station is very close to the city center, about 5 minutes on foot (400 meters/1,300 feet). There are about four hourly trains (direct and indirect) to Delft from **Amsterdam Centraal** (Stationsplein 1; www.ns.nl/stationsinformatie/asd/

amsterdam-centraal). A round-trip ticket costs €28.80 per adult.

From **the Hague,** Tram 1 (www.htm.nl/en/timetable/tram-1; adults €4, children 4-12 €1.50) departs regularly for Delft, a 30-minute trip. A 2-hour pass costs €4 per person and can be purchased on the tram. From **Rotterdam** (Stationsplein 8a; www.ns.nl/stationsinformatie/rtd/rotterdam-centraal), the journey is easiest by train; it takes 12 minutes to get to Delft Central Train Station (€3.60 one-way).

Car

There's no reason to drive to Delft; the historic city center is largely car-free, and Delft's narrow streets make navigating with a car difficult. If you do drive, the 67.5 kilometers (42 miles) from Amsterdam should take 50 minutes, mostly on the **A4.** You're best off leaving your car at the **Zuidpoort Garage** (Zuidwal 14; open 24/7; €3/hour) on the southern part of town. It's a brief 8-minute walk (650 meters/2,100 feet) to the New Church from the parking lot.

GETTING AROUND

Delft's city center is very walkable. Aside from the Delft factories, most of the attractions are within a 15-minute walk of each other. Most main streets have clear signs courtesy of the tourism board with signage toward popular tourist attractions and major squares.

Rotterdam

Rotterdam is one of the most vibrant cities in the Netherlands, often called Manhattan on the Maas thanks to its location on the Nieuwe Maas river and its cutting-edge architecture, exciting nightlife, and world-class museums. Rotterdam's name is simple: It comes from the former estuary Rotte and the subsequent dam that protected Rotterdam from flooding. Long a center of trade, industry, and shipping, in 1940 Rotterdam was destroyed almost entirely by the Nazis, trying to force a Dutch surrender. Following World War II, Rotterdam rebuilt itself in a new form: The blank blueprint for the city allowed for building innovations and skyscrapers that were not allowed in other Dutch cities, which still have height restrictions in their city centers. The experimental Cube Houses have become symbols for a city that never stopped dreaming up new ideas.

Rotterdam's innovation can be easily seen within its many cutting-edge museums, trendy cafés, and lively nightlife, although a taste of the past can still be found in the historic Delftshaven district. If you thought the Netherlands was windmills and historic houses, you're in for a shock once you arrive in Rotterdam's train station with its shiny roof.

If you're interested in visiting Rotterdam for its architecture, a full day is needed, as the city has a larger blueprint than many other Dutch cities. If you intend to visit the nearby polder-and-windmill landscape of Kinderdijk, a masterpiece of Dutch water management, it's best to spend the night.

ORIENTATION

Rotterdam's city center is sprawling, but most of the attractions are quite accessible by public transit. Most day-trippers stay within **Rotterdam Centrum,** aside from a trip to Delftshaven. The heart of Rotterdam's center is a neighborhood called **Stadsdriehoek,** where you'll find the **Markthal,** the **Cube Houses, St. Laurenskerk,** views of the **Nieuwe Maas river,** and **Rotterdam Blaak Train Station.** The only main attraction farther away is the neighborhood of **Delftshaven,** formerly a separate town with a picturesque harbor and 17th-century architecture. It's about 4 kilometers (2 miles) west of the Cube Houses.

Rotterdam Centrum

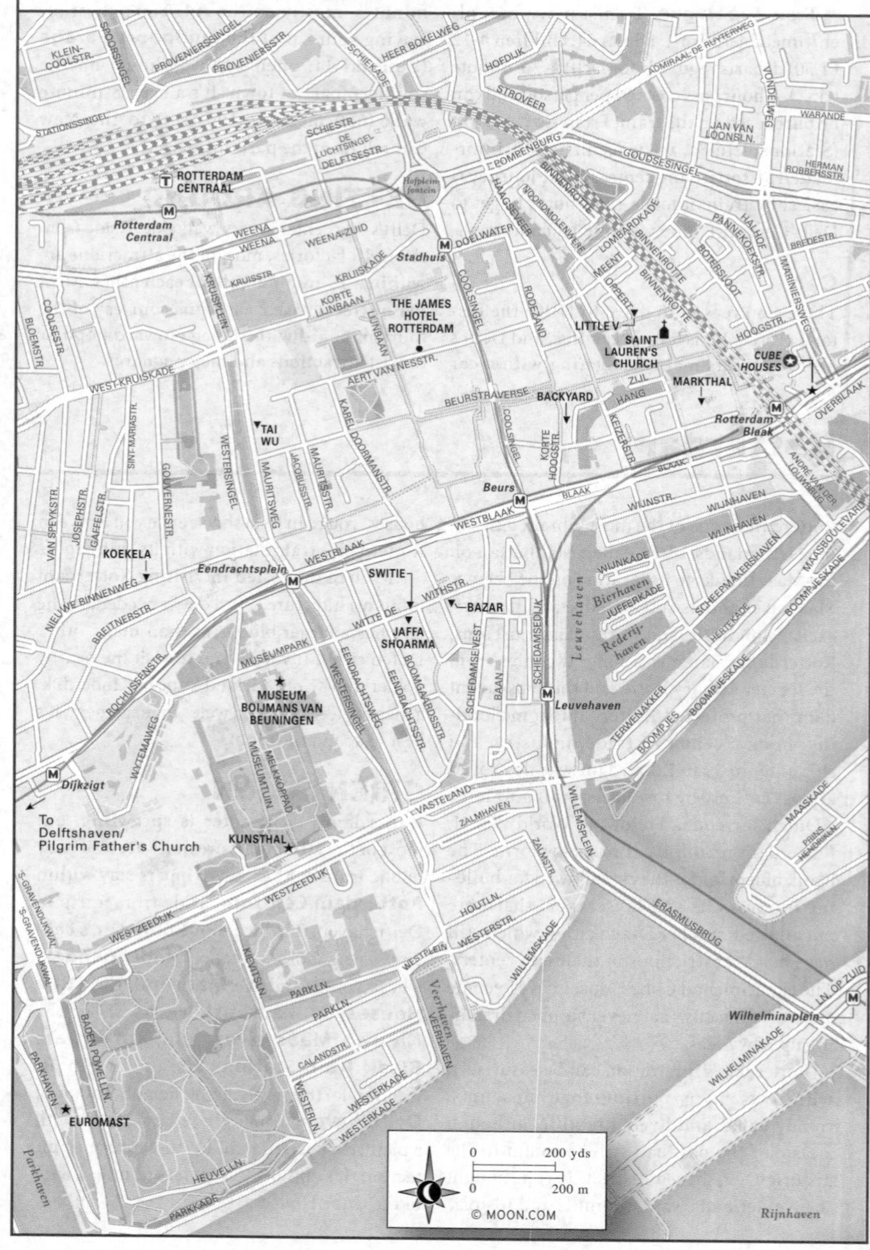

SIGHTS

Rotterdam Centrum

★ CUBE HOUSES
(Kijk-Kubus)

Overblaak 70; tel. 010 414 2285; https://kubuswoning.nl; 10am-6pm daily; adults €3, children €1.50

Rotterdam's most famous landmark has to be the Cube Houses designed by innovative Dutch architect Piet Blom in the 1970s. At a time when Rotterdam was rapidly expanding in the post-World War II era, Blom envisioned these bright yellow and gray tilted 45-degree cube houses, to be part of their own architectural forest. (The architect envisioned the houses to be like trees thanks to a strong "trunk" or foundation underneath and wider shape on top, which also solved a city-planning issue in terms of minimizing space on the ground while maximizing living space.) There are 38 cubes that connect with a courtyard in the center that's a magnificent point to stop and enjoy this untraditional architectural installation.

Today, two of the Cube houses are open to the public, one of them as a hostel (Stayokay Hostel Rotterdam) and the other as a museum. The low ceilings and steep staircases make the houses a challenge to navigate. For a few euros, you can explore the 1,080-square-meter (11,600-square-foot) cube, including some of the original furnishings intended to make this unique house slightly more livable—conventional furniture would be at odds with the walls. Still, the shape renders some of the space unusable due to the angles. From the interior of the show house, you can peer into others' houses thanks to the ample windows that often lean down toward the ground. The interior feels very 1970s thanks to the groovy palette and accents, and furniture that feels straight out of *The Jetsons*.

Each house has three stories, although you'll need to go up a steep staircase in order to get to the first floor, where you'll typically find a living room and kitchen. On the second floor, you'll find bedrooms and a bathroom. The top floor is typically a sunroof or garden. (The entry staircase makes the Cube Houses a bit infeasible for people who have trouble with stairs.) It's best not to look down too much once you enter the houses as vertigo from the shape of the windows can unnerve some visitors.

ST. LAURENSKERK
(Sint-Laurenskerk)

Grotekerkplein 27; tel. 010 413 1494; https://laurenskerkrotterdam.nl; 10am-5pm Tues.-Sat. Mar.-Oct., 11am-5pm Tues.-Sat. Nov.-Feb.; church only adults €3, children free, tower adults €6, children €3.50

The St. Laurenskerk is one of the enduring symbols of Rotterdam and one of the only remnants of the beautiful medieval city that remained after World War II. The church dates back to 1449 and was renovated several times during the medieval period. After the Protestant Reformation, it was converted from a Catholic church into a Protestant church, which it remains to this day. The church was badly damaged in World War II, but it was restored in the 1950s. Today, the church allows visitors for a small fee. A visit includes an overview of the church's history, but it's certainly worth paying for the tower climb for stunning views of Rotterdam. The tower with its 300-plus steps is climbable in peak season (Mar.-Oct.). Ask at the reception for the next tower climb appointment before purchasing a ticket.

MUSEUM BOIJMANS VAN BEUNINGEN

Museumpark 18; tel. 010 441 9400; www.boijmans.nl; 11am-5pm Tues.-Sun.; adults €17.50 adults, children €8.75

Museum Boijmans van Beuningen holds one of the most impressive art collections in the Netherlands outside Amsterdam. Within its private collection, visitors can enjoy works from European artists ranging in eras from van Eyck to van Gogh to Dalí. Whether you're more interested in modern art or the classics—including *The Tower of Babel* by Pieter

1
2
3

Bruegel the Elder—the museum is certainly one art lovers shouldn't miss.

KUNSTHAL

Westzeedijk 341; tel. 010 4400 300; www.kunsthal.nl; 10am-5pm Tues.-Sun.; adults €14 adults, children free

For cutting-edge art, head to the Kunsthal, a taste of Rotterdam's more daring side. This spacious museum changes its exhibitions regularly to both entertain and challenge the visitor. Not all the exhibitions may be your cup of tea, so check their website for the latest before committing.

EUROMAST

Parkhaven 20; tel. 010 436 4811; www.euromast.nl; 9:30am-10pm daily Apr.-Sept., 10am-10pm daily Oct.-Mar.; adults €10.25 adults, children €6.75

Rotterdam's well-known tower is a favorite of height lovers, who can enjoy the view from 185 meters (607 feet) up. An elevator goes most of the way up (100 meters/328 feet); however, a staircase is required for the remaining 85 meters (279 feet) for a 360-degree view of Rotterdam. It's pricey, but the tower is enjoyed by photographers who love to capture the sunset from the top.

Delftshaven

One of Rotterdam's cutest districts has to be the largely forgotten former town of Delftshaven on the outskirts of Rotterdam, west of the city center. Created as a port, this small neighborhood survived World War II largely intact. It's a joy to retrace the footsteps of the Pilgrims here: After a spell in Leiden, the Pilgrims (who once attended church at the Oude Kerk, now known as the **Pilgrim Father's Church;** Aelbrechtskolk 20; tel. 010 477 4156; www.oudeofpelgrimvaderskerk.nl; noon-4pm Fri.-Sat.; donations appreciated) set sail from this very harbor in 1620 on the *Speedwell* for the United Kingdom to get permission to settle in the colonies that later became the United States.

Delftshaven is a picturesque area to explore on foot. You can walk a maximum of 2 kilometers (1 mile) along **Voorhaven** and **Achterhaven,** the two main streets along the water. An hour is enough to see the neighborhood. To get here, take the **Metro C** from Blaak (next to the Cube Houses) in the direction of De Akkers to the Delftshaven stop (www.ret.nl; 20 minutes; €4, tickets available at the machines by the metro entrance).

1: Cube Houses **2:** view of Rotterdam from the Euromast **3:** the iconic food hall Markthal

FOOD

Cafés and Light Bites

KOEKELA

Nieuwe Binnenweg 79A; tel. 010 436 4774; www.koekela.nl; 8am-6pm Mon.-Fri., 8:30am-6pm Sat., 9:30am-5pm Sun.; €5

Rotterdam locals go crazy for Koekela's scrumptious cakes and cookies, paired with a freshly made cappuccino. Be sure to ask about their ever-changing seasonal specialties and homemade muffins. Koekela is close to Museum Boijmans van Beuningen, making it a nice spot to stop for a coffee.

International

SWITIE

Witte de Withstraat 43A; tel. 010 230 8442; noon-10pm Tues.-Sun.; €6

With the perfect blend of cultures and cuisines, this casual Chinese-Surinamese restaurant with limited seating is a popular lunch spot. Their sandwiches, including favorites like fish, Chinese-style barbequed pork, and curried eggs. The length of the menu can be a bit intimidating, but if you're hungry, you might want to opt for their noodle (*bami*) dishes or chicken broth (*saoto*) soup.

TAI WU

Mauritsweg 24-25; tel. 010 433 0818; https://tai-wu.nl; noon-midnight Mon.-Sat., noon-11pm Sun.; €13

A staple restaurant in Rotterdam's Chinese community, serving up fresh dim sum and other Cantonese-style food for over 25 years. Their circular tables make it easy to share a multitude of delicious dishes from their seemingly endless menu with friends or family.

Day Trip from a Day Trip: Kinderdijk

Kinderdijk at sunset

Nederwaard 1; www.kinderdijk.com; 9am-5:30pm daily Mar.-Oct., 10am-4pm daily Jan.-Feb. and Nov.-Dec.; summer adults €9, youth 5-17 €5.50, children 0-4 free, winter adults €4.50, youth €2

Kinderdijk, with its 19 picturesque windmills, is easily one of the most beautiful day trips in the Netherlands. About 15 kilometers (9 miles) south of Rotterdam, this UNESCO World Heritage Site with more than 19 windmills along a polder is a perfectly preserved village dating back to the 13th century. You can enjoy views of reeds often blowing in the wind and the windmills turning

LITTLE V

Grotekerkplein 109; tel. 010 413 1191; www.littlev.nl; noon-10pm Tues.-Thurs., noon-10:30pm Fri.-Sat. noon-9:30pm Sun.; €14

Rotterdam's best Vietnamese place is hands-down Little V, which is perfect for groups looking for a shared dining experience. Little V's beautiful interior combined with its thoughtful service has made it a staple hot spot for a nice dinner out. Be sure to reserve ahead.

BAZAR

Witte de Withstraat 16; tel. 010 206 5151; www.hotelbazar.nl; 8am-midnight Mon.-Thurs., 8am-1am Fri.-Sat., 9am-midnight Sun.; lunch €10, dinner €14

From the moment you step into Bazar, your eyes will be feasting on the interior, which is chock-full of beautiful hanging lights, colorful tiles, and elaborate wallpapers. The food at Bazar is Middle Eastern-inspired and incredibly well priced given the large portion sizes. It can be hard to get a table in the evenings without a reservation, but if you're looking for a quick meal with an extra touch of ambiance, Bazar is a great option.

Markets

★ MARKTHAL

Dominee Jan Scharpstraat 298; tel. 030 234 6468; www.markthal.nl; 10am-8pm Mon.-Thurs. and Sat., 10am-9pm Fri., noon-6pm Sun.; €8

The Markthal is hard to miss. This iconic food hall is the largest in the Netherlands, and it certainly impresses with its chic 21st-century mixed-use design. The ceiling of the as bikers pass by on the narrow path. The site is named after a folk tale called *Kinderdijk* (children's dike), when a child was found floating in a cradle after the infamous Saint Elizabeth flood in 1421.

The site has been recognized by UNESCO for the way it showcases Dutch water management throughout history. The Dutch have long battled water encroaching on their land, and this complex system of windmills, pumping stations, polders, and sluices created in the medieval period has prevented flooding in the lowlands. As you walk around the grounds of Kinderdijk, marvel at the variety of windmills, many of which are still lived in and actively operated throughout the year.

Anyone can bike or walk past the windmills and explore the 322 hectares (796 acres) without paying the entry fee; however, admission includes access to two of the windmills-cum-museums and the **visitor center.** If you're lucky enough to come in winter, you'll want to stop to enjoy the reeds rustling in the wind as you watch the sunset. You can rent a bike just outside of Kinderdijk at **Café De Klok** (Molenstraat 117; tel. 078 691 2597; www.deklok.com; 11am-closing daily; €8) to enjoy a scenic cycle through this landscape.

GETTING THERE

Those who are good independent planners may want to opt for two days in Rotterdam to provide enough time to see Kinderdijk. If you are spending the day or evening in **Rotterdam,** Ferry 20 (www.waterbus.nl/haltes/de-schans; €4) runs about 2 times per hour 7am-6pm between Rotterdam and Kinderdijk from the Veer Erasmusbrug ferry stop on Willemskade underneath the Erasmusbrug. The journey takes about 30 minutes. By car, it's a 24-minute drive (24 kilometers/15 miles) on the **A15.**

To visit Kinderdijk from **Amsterdam,** it's best to rent a car (96 kilometers/60 miles; just over an hour on the **A2**) or go with a tour company. **Tour Company** (www.tourcompany.nl; tel. 020 218 4218, €89-159/person) offers small group bus tours to Kinderdijk, with daily departures on most days at 9am. Another option is the tour company **Choose Your Tour** (www.chooseyourtour.com), which offers a whirlwind Dutch tour including Kinderdijk, the Hague, Madurodam, and Delft for €110 on Thursdays and Saturdays from April/May-August. There is limited paid parking at Kinderdijk, although visitors can park for free on weekends.

hall notably has the world's largest mural—taking up more than 11,000 square meters (118,000 square feet)—featuring digital images of fruits, vegetables, flowers, and insects, created by artists Arno Coenen and Iris Roskam.

While admiring the artwork you'll notice the windows, which belong to residential apartments, including some that even have a view of the hall from their floor. Next to the central staircases, you'll find the **Time Stairs** (*Tijdtrap*), which allow you to admire historical findings from the 14th-century village that once sat upon this very spot.

The hall has a multitude of options, with 70-plus food stalls, from Dutch croquettes to Turkish food. Most stalls accept cards only. Seating within the hall is limited, but there are plenty of scenic spots outside with a view of the Cube Houses. You'll also find a few supermarkets in the basement, including a specialty Asian supermarket and Albert Heijn, where you can grab ingredients for a picnic.

Street Food

JAFFA SHOARMA

Witte de Withstraat 44; tel. 010 414 0326; noon-4am Sun.-Thurs., noon-6am Fri.-Sat.; €9

Rotterdam's most famous dish, *kapsalon,* is served up at this popular casual kebab shop along Witte de Withstraat. This late-night comfort food is made with shawarma/doner kebab meat, fries, Gouda cheese, lettuce, garlic sauce, and hot sauce. It's incredibly indulgent; if you're particularly hungry after drinks, a *kapsalon* is a must. Jaffa also sells staples such as falafels, shawarma wraps, and sandwiches for a quick bite. Non-Dutch cards not accepted.

Vegan

BACKYARD

Korte Hoogstraat 14; tel. 010 842 8263; www.backyardrotterdam.nl; 9am-6pm Mon.-Tues., 9am-9pm Wed.-Sun.; €9

Backyard shows off the best of sustainable food at their lunch restaurant in the heart of the city center. Whether you're vegan, flexitarian, or simply curious about greener meals, Backyard has many delicious options that will make you wonder whether what you've ordered really is vegan!

ACCOMMODATIONS

If you intend to visit Kinderdijk or want to sample the nightlife in Rotterdam, it's best to opt for an overnight stay for convenience's sake. If you intend to visit the Hague, Delft, or Kinderdijk, Rotterdam can make a good base for day trips within the region.

THE JAMES HOTEL ROTTERDAM

Aert van Nesstraat 25; tel. 010 760 5070; https://thejames.nl; €80

This trendy hotel in the heart of the hip Coolsingel district of Rotterdam is just footsteps from many of the city's well-known attractions. Its modern interior and vintage-inspired touches are aesthetically pleasing, and the hotel also hosts useful amenities including a 24-hour supermarket, a coffee machine, a fitness center, air-conditioning, and a lounge. Some of their top-billed rooms feature lovely views.

HOTEL NEW YORK

Koninginnenhoofd 1; tel. 010 439 05 00; https://hotelnewyork.com; €140

Hotel New York sits directly on the Nieuwe Maas river. The building, built in 1901 with a neoclassical facade and now a listed monument, once served as the headquarters of the Holland America Line, a prominent shipping line that transported thousands of people to the United States in the early 20th century. The rooms are fairly spacious, although you'll need to pay more for a waterfront view. The hotel is across the water from the city center, but it's accessible via the bridge, water taxi (every 15 minutes to Leuvehaven/Centrum; www.watertaxirotterdam.nl; adults €4.50, children €2.75), and metro (Wilhelminaplein; lines D and E). Parking costs €17.50 per day, and their breakfast buffet is extra (€19.50 per adult).

GETTING THERE

In addition to being well connected to Amsterdam, Rotterdam is close to Belgium, with high-speed train connections to Antwerpen and Brussels. For those staying in the Hague/Rotterdam metro area, there is a special transit pass, the **Tourist Day Pass** (https://touristdaytickets.com; €14.50), that allows for unlimited transit on buses, trams, and metros in the region. This pass can be purchased at subway stations in the Hague and Rotterdam region.

Public Transportation

ROTTERDAM CENTRAL TRAIN STATION

Stationsplein 8a; www.ns.nl/stationsinformatie/rtd/rotterdam-centraal

Rotterdam is a 1 hour 15 minutes away from Amsterdam by train. More than seven trains depart for Rotterdam hourly from **Amsterdam Centraal** (Stationsplein 1; www.ns.nl/stationsinformatie/asd/amsterdam-centraal). A round-trip second-class ticket costs €32.80 from Amsterdam Centraal. A special high-speed direct train called the **NS Intercity Direct** costs €2.60 on top of the normal fare. You can purchase your ticket at the station or by using the NS website or app (www.ns.nl).

Rotterdam Centraal Train Station is a 2-kilometer (1-mile) walk to the main attractions of Rotterdam, such as the Cube Houses. After exiting the station, follow the signs toward the center. To minimize walking, you can also route yourself to the smaller **Rotterdam Blaak** station (Blaak 1; www.

ns.nl/stationsinformatie/rtb/rotterdam-blaak), which is directly across the street from the Cube Houses.

Car

A car is certainly not a necessity thanks to the high-speed train connection between **Amsterdam** and Rotterdam, but it will give you more flexibility if you want to visit Kinderdijk. Driving from Amsterdam to Rotterdam should take 1 hour without traffic. It's an 80-kilometer (50-mile) drive, mostly on the **A4.**

There is more parking in Rotterdam than many Dutch cities. Parking garages tend to be pricier as you get closer to the city center. The **Markthal parking lot** (Dominee Jan Scharpstraat 306; https://parkereninmarkthal.nl) is very convenient, located in the center of Rotterdam with more than 1,000 parking spots. You can save on parking costs by reserving your parking at least a day in advance with a set maximum of €12.50 (Mon.-Fri.) or €15 on weekends.

GETTING AROUND

Rotterdam is a fairly walkable city because of its modern layout: Most of the attractions and businesses are within walking distance (1 kilometer/0.6 miles) of the center. If you're not keen on walking, Rotterdam has a well-connected public transit network with trams, metros, and buses, all part of the RET public transit system (www.ret.nl).

There are five metro lines in Rotterdam, which traverse the city primarily underground. Metro line E connects the Hague (Den Haag Centraal Train Station) with Rotterdam center (Beurs train station). At Beurs, you can catch any of the five metro lines as they all connect here. For traveling between Rotterdam Centrum and Delfshaven, you can take either metro line A, B, or C from Blaak or Beurs. Metro D and E connect Rotterdam Centrum (Beurs) with the other side of the Nieuwe Maas river.

All train and metro stations have a RET kiosk prior to entry where you can purchase a ticket. Compared to many cities, Rotterdam's metro system is laid out in an easy-to-navigate cross pattern. Tickets cost €4 for a two-hour valid ticket, but if you will be taking the Metro more than once, it's best to purchase a 1-day RET pass, which costs €8.50. A children's day ticket (ages 4-11) costs €4.50.

Brussels

The world truly meets in Brussels, a complex puzzle of a city at the center of Belgium's cultural multiplicity—and of the country geographically. Once a small village in the marshes near the Senne River, an important trade route as early as the 12th century, some parts of Brussels still feel like villages today, especially on market days.

Brussels rose to prominence due to its mastery of the lace and luxury fabric industry during the medieval period. This and its central location made it a logical place for administration; Charles V, the Holy Roman emperor, made it his capital during his rule. The city's importance rose and faded over the years as it fell under the rule of different empires and kingdoms, from France to the Netherlands, but

Highlights

Look for ★ to find recommended sights, activities, dining, and lodging.

★ **Grand Place:** Take in Brussels's magnificent square, which truly lives up to its name, lined with imposing 17th-century buildings (page 195).

★ **Royal Museums of Fine Arts of Belgium:** Housing art that ranges from modern to ancient, the Royal Museums of Fine Arts of Belgium rank among the world's best art museums (page 199).

★ **Horta Museum:** Transport yourself to the grandeur of the turn of the century in one of art nouveau's greatest masterpieces (page 205).

★ **Leuven:** Soak up the architectural splendors of Flanders's most beautiful university town (page 238).

★ **Villers Abbey:** The gorgeous, otherworldly ruins at Villers Abbey merit a long stroll (page 243).

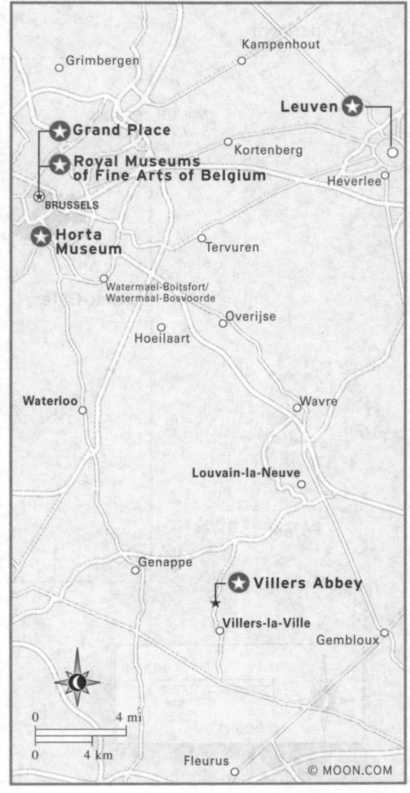

Brussels

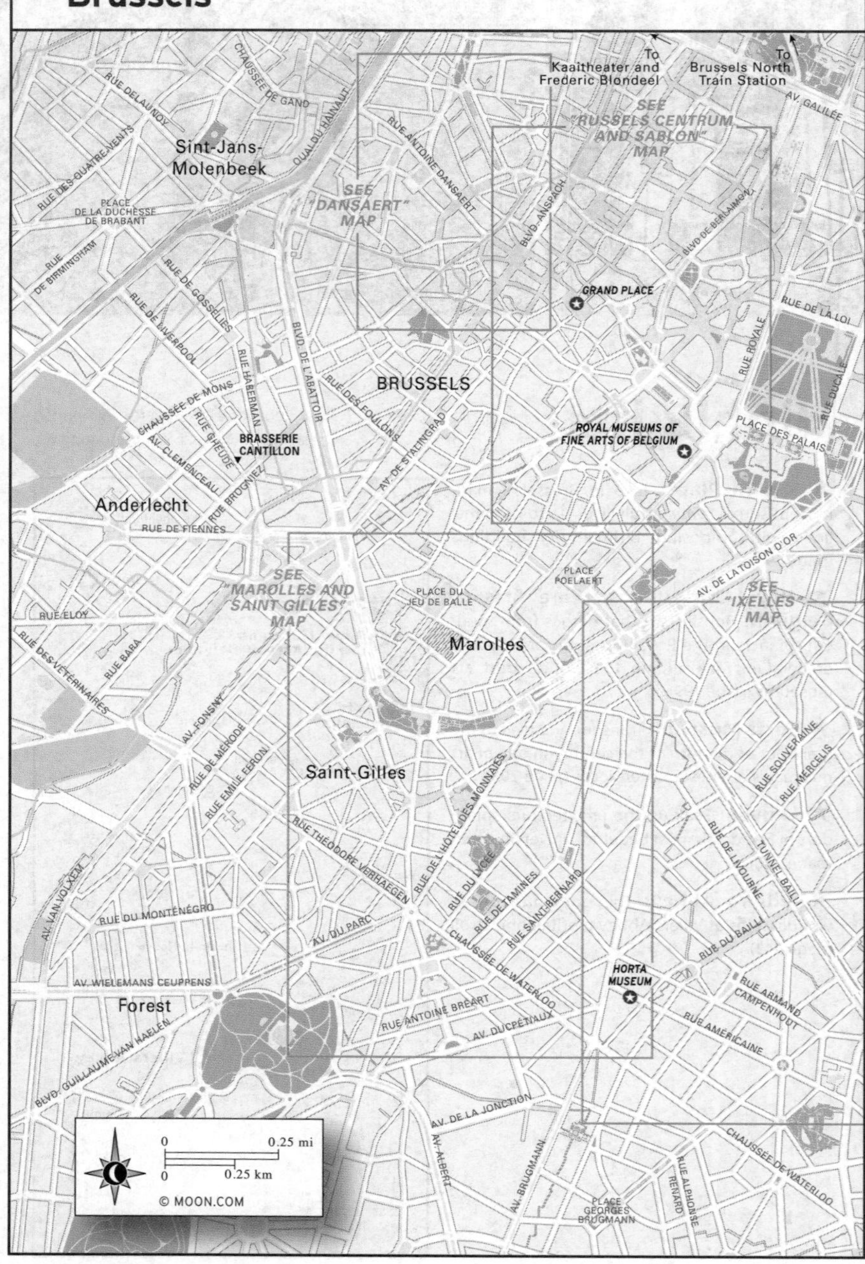
To
Kaaitheater and
Frederic Blondeel
To
Brussels North
Train Station
SEE "RUSSELS CENTRUM AND SABLON" MAP
SEE "DANSAERT" MAP
SEE "MAROLLES AND SAINT GILLES" MAP
SEE "IXELLES" MAP
Sint-Jans-
Molenbeek
BRUSSELS
Anderlecht
Marolles
Saint-Gilles
Forest
GRAND PLACE
ROYAL MUSEUMS OF
FINE ARTS OF BELGIUM
BRASSERIE
CANTILLON
HORTA
MUSEUM
RUE DELAUNOY
CHAUSSÉE DE GAND
QUAI DU HAINAUT
RUE ANTOINE DANSAERT
BLVD. ANSPACH
AV. GALILÉE
BLVD DE BERLAIMONT
RUE DE LA LOI
RUE ROYALE
RUE DUCALE
PLACE DES PALAIS
RUE DES QUATRE-VENTS
PLACE
DE LA DUCHESSE
DE BRABANT
RUE
DE BIRMINGHAM
RUE DE GOSSELIES
RUE DE LIVERPOOL
RUE HABERMAN
BLVD. DE L'ABATTOIR
RUE DES FOULONS
AV. DE STALINGRAD
CHAUSSÉE DE MONS
RUE GHEUDE
AV. CLEMENCEAU
RUE BROGNIEZ
RUE DE FIENNES
AV. DE LA TOISON D'OR
PLACE
POELAERT
PLACE DU
JEU DE BALLE
RUE ELOY
RUE BARA
RUE DES VÉTÉRINAIRES
AV. FONSNY
RUE DE MÉRODE
RUE EMILE FÉRON
RUE DE L'HÔTEL DES MONNAIES
RUE THÉODORE VERHAEGEN
RUE DU LYCÉE
RUE DE TAMINES
RUE SAINT-BERNARD
RUE SOUVERAINE
RUE MERCELIS
RUE DE LIVOURNE
TUNNEL BAILLI
RUE DU BAILLI
AV. VAN VOLXEM
RUE DU MONTÉNÉGRO
AV. DU PARC
CHAUSSÉE DE WATERLOO
AV. WIELEMANS CEUPPENS
RUE ANTOINE BRÉART
AV. DUCPÉTIAUX
RUE ARMAND
CAMPENHOUT
RUE AMÉRICAINE
BLVD. GUILLAUME VAN HAELEN
AV. DE LA JONCTION
AV. ALBERT
AV. BRUGMANN
RUE
RENARD
RUE ALPHONSE
PLACE
GEORGES
BRUGMANN
CHAUSSÉE DE WATERLOO
0 0.25 mi
0 0.25 km
© MOON.COM

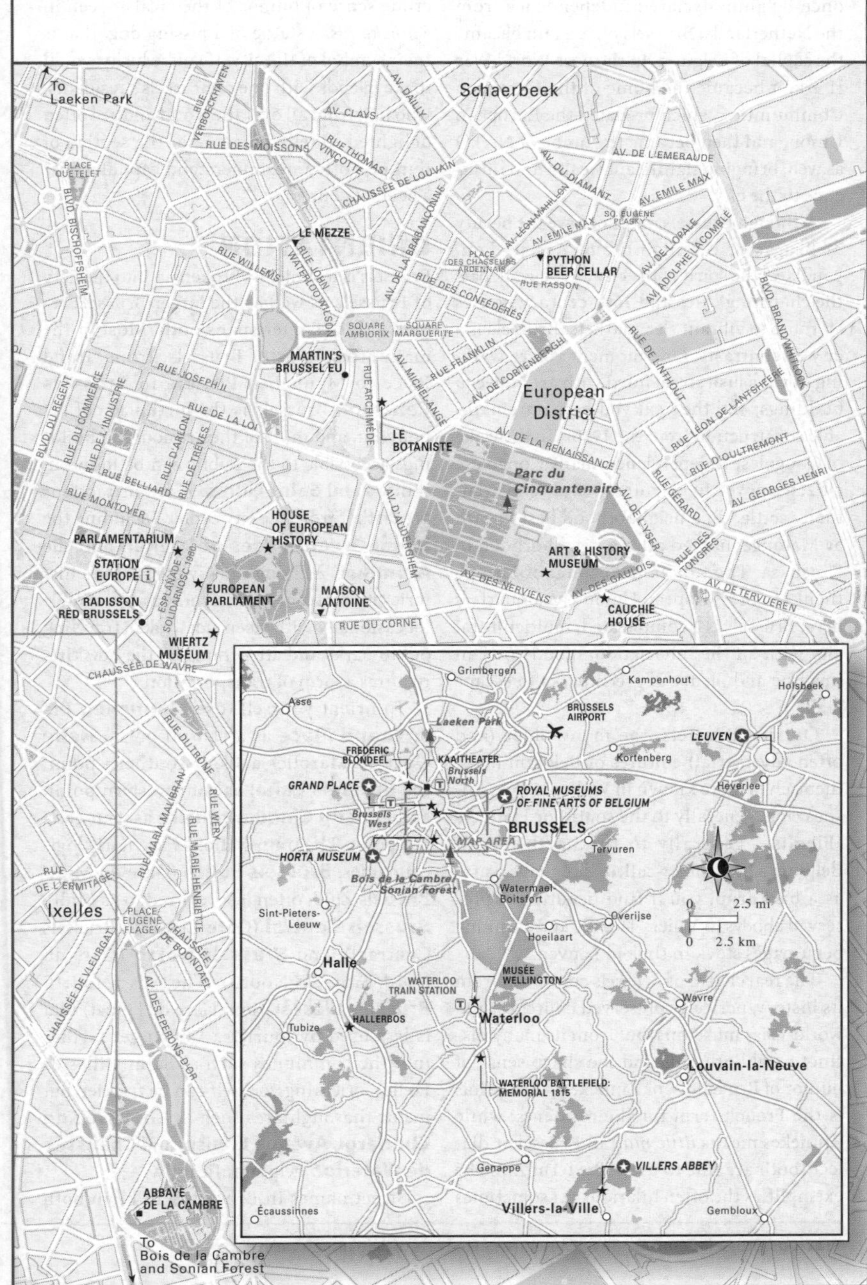
To
Laeken Park
Schaerbeek
European
District
Parc du
Cinquantenaire
Ixelles
LE MEZZE
PYTHON
BEER CELLAR
MARTIN'S
BRUSSEL EU
LE
BOTANISTE
HOUSE
OF EUROPEAN
HISTORY
PARLAMENTARIUM
STATION
EUROPE
RADISSON
RED BRUSSELS
EUROPEAN
PARLIAMENT
MAISON
ANTOINE
WIERTZ
MUSEUM
ART & HISTORY
MUSEUM
CAUCHIE
HOUSE
ABBAYE
DE LA CAMBRE
To
Bois de la Cambre
and Sonian Forest
Grimbergen
Kampenhout
Holsbeek
Asse
BRUSSELS
AIRPORT
Laeken Park
LEUVEN
FREDERIC
BLONDEEL
KAAITHEATER
Brussels
North
Kortenberg
GRAND PLACE
ROYAL MUSEUMS
OF FINE ARTS OF BELGIUM
Heverlee
Brussels
West
BRUSSELS
MAP AREA
Tervuren
HORTA MUSEUM
Bois de la Cambre/
Sonian Forest
Watermael-
Boitsfort
Sint-Pieters-
Leeuw
Overijse
Hoeilaart
0 2.5 mi
0 2.5 km
Halle
MUSÉE
WELLINGTON
WATERLOO
TRAIN STATION
Waterloo
HALLERBOS
Tubize
Wavre
Louvain-la-Neuve
WATERLOO BATTLEFIELD:
MEMORIAL 1815
Genappe
VILLERS ABBEY
Écaussinnes
Villers-la-Ville
Gembloux

once Belgium declared independence from the Netherlands, Brussels once again became the capital of Belgium. In the post-World War II era, it became the home of the European Communities, which predated the European Union, and then became the home of NATO as well, bringing significant wealth and influence to the city.

Although Brussels may not have the beauty of Bruges or the nightlife of Amsterdam, you'll feel the spirit of the city as you walk past the charming cafés and 16th-century houses en route to vibrant flea markets. Brussels is a city of contrasts: One moment you're walking down a lush street lined with art nouveau buildings, and the next you pass unremarkable construction from the 1970s. In the wake of Congolese independence, many Congolese citizens moved to Belgium to study and eventually settled in a neighborhood best known as Matonge, named after a neighborhood of Kinshasa. The functional capital of Europe thanks to the European Union's headquarters here, Brussels is a complicated, multicultural city with all the international food you can imagine and plenty of green parks to escape it all.

Outside Brussels, the many older (and often adversarial) cultures of Belgium make themselves more known in Wallonia (French-speaking, generally to the south) or Flanders (Flemish, generally to the north). With Belgium's ancient so-called "language wars" as a backdrop, you'll find beautifully preserved abbeys in Villers-la-Ville and stunning beguinages stuck in time in Leuven.

The real charm of Brussels comes not from its history, perfectly preserved churches, and world-class museums, but from its many distinct neighborhoods and the sharp sense of humor of Bruxellois, or Zinnekes—Bruxellois is the French term for the residents, while Zinnekes means *little mutt* in Brusseleir dialect (both are fine to use). The term Zinneke exemplifies the often hilarious yet sometimes crude sense of humor of the locals—seen in *Zinneke Pis,* a statue of a pissing dog, that is their symbol of the city. If you're lucky, you'll make friends with one of Brussels's residents, who hail from all over the world and are often delighted to tell you some of the secrets of Europe's often misunderstood capital—over a beer, of course.

ORIENTATION

Brussels is technically broken up into the City of Brussels as well as the larger Brussels region—this chapter spans both. Most of the main attractions of Brussels, from Grand Place to Manneken Pis, are in **Brussels Centrum.** Brussels is the birthplace of art nouveau, and most of the art nouveau buildings accessible to the public can be found in **Ixelles** and **Saint Gilles.** A few attractions are farther from the city center, including the **Royal Greenhouses of Laeken** and the **Atomium.** Although many parts of the historic city center of Brussels are easily walkable (occasionally with steep sidewalks), traveling out to parks and attractions on the outskirts requires a form of transportation.

To orient yourself, use **Manneken Pis** or **Grand Place** as a central point, **Halle Gate** in Marolles as your southern point, the **Brussels Canal** as your western point, and **Parc du Cinquantenaire** as your eastern point. The train stations have fairly logical names: **Brussels South** (Gare du Midi/ Brussels Zuid, often just referred to as Midi), **Brussels Central** (Gare Centrale/Brussels Centraal), and **Brussels North** (Gare du Nord/Brussels Noord). There is a fourth **Brussels West** station (Gare de l'Ouet) that is less used by tourists. As you get farther into the communes such as Saint Gilles or Ixelles, orienting yourself can be trickier, but major thoroughfares such as **Chaussée de Charleroi, Avenue Louise,** and **Chaussée de Waterloo** help significantly.

Street names in Brussels will be in both

Previous: Brussels Centrum; Royal Museums of Fine Arts of Belgium; Zinneke Pis.

French and **Dutch.** It's more common to use the French names when asking for directions, so this chapter primarily uses the French street names. Although Brussels is bilingual, the vast majority (90 percent) of its residents speak French fluently, if not also Dutch and English. This is due to a larger population of Francophone immigrants and strong French education throughout Belgium; Dutch was prohibited for various periods throughout Brussels's history, so the ability to speak Dutch freely is not taken for granted among Flemish-speaking residents who fought hard for Brussels's full bilingual status in the 1960s. That said, French is often the de facto language within the city center, and it's now a bit rarer to hear Dutch outside certain neighborhoods (e.g. Dansaert). If you ask for directions, it's often best to stick with the names in French, although it cannot hurt to know the name in Dutch, too. Language can be a touchy subject, but Bruxellois are happy to speak the language most convenient to the visitor (when possible).

Brussels Centrum

In the center, you'll find **Grand Place;** most of Brussels's museums, including the **Royal Galleries of Saint Hubert;** the spunky **Manneken Pis,** an irreverent city symbol; the best-known bars in the city; and Brussels's spectacular **Saint Michael and Saint Gudula Cathedral.** It's hard to get truly lost as the gleaming white tower of the **Brussels Town Hall** is often visible from various points in the center; it's bordered to the east by Rue Royale, which runs parallel to the **Royal Palace of Brussels** and the **Royal Museums of Fine Arts of Belgium.** The main commercial street is **Nieuwestraat,** running northeast a few blocks north of Grand Place.

Sablon

Just south of the Royal Quarter, the Sablon is one of Brussels's chicest neighborhoods. This small yet beautiful area is home to many of Brussels's poshest cafés lining well-maintained streets, from the scenic and hilly Rue de Rollebeek to **Place du Grand Sablon,** the neighborhood's central square, with the green **Square du Petite Sablon** on the Grand Sablon's southeast corner. You'll find some of Brussels's finest chocolatiers here. To navigate this area, just locate the black roof of the **Chapel Church,** downhill from the dramatic **Church of Our Lady of Victories** on Place du Grand Sablon. Don't be afraid to duck down the picturesque alleyways found in this quarter.

Marolles

A small quarter south of the Sablon, Les Marolles feels like Paris's Montmartre with its **artsy, bohemian vibe.** This homey neighborhood is quickly gentrifying, with hip **international food** and atmospheric cafés along the steep Rue des Renards. If you're a lover of bargain hunting, you can't miss the daily **Marolles Flea Market,** which takes place in the Place du Jeu de Balle in the neighborhood's center.

Dansaert

West of Brussels Centrum, Dansaert is one of Brussels's upcoming neighborhoods, with a growing population that prefers Dutch to French. Lovers of books, **gourmet restaurants, indie shopping,** or just sitting at a café and **people-watching** will feel like they're in the right place. The district is ordered by **Saint Catherine Church,** on Place Sainte-Catherine, to the east and the **Brussels Canal** to the west, a trendy spot for a craft beer.

European District

East of Centrum, the relatively large area of the European District is the center of Brussels politics. It's the headquarters for the **European Parliament,** but also a great spot for museum-hopping for those interested in European history, especially at the **House of European History** and the **Parlamentarium.** The European District is also home to some art nouveau gems.

Ixelles

South of the European District and the Sablon, Ixelles is one of Brussels's most interesting neighborhoods, where beautiful neoclassical houses mix with African shops and restaurants in the sub-neighborhood of **Matonge.** The birthplace of fashion icon Audrey Hepburn, this is also where you'll find some of the city's **high-end shopping** on Avenue Louise; be sure to end your day in time for some sophisticated **cocktails.**

Saint Gilles

Moving west, wedged between Ixelles to the east and Marolles to the north broken up by Brussels South, Saint Gilles is a former village that became part of Brussels in the late 1200s. It's now home to many art nouveau homes including the **Horta Museum,** charming **street markets,** a beautiful **city hall,** and a host of lovely local cafés that will make you feel like the ultimate insider. It's also one of the best spots to browse independent shops.

Laeken

A bit removed from central Belgium, Laeken is a quiet residential neighborhood about 30-40 minutes north via Metro that is home to the **Royal Greenhouses of Laeken,** the **Castle of Laeken** (the home of the Belgian royals), the iconic stainless steel **Atomium** sculpture, built for the 1958 World's Fair, and the lush, green, lake-filled **Laeken Park.**

PLANNING YOUR TIME

For those looking to quickly cover the main attractions, **one day** is enough for an overview. But for a deeper dive, give yourself at least a **weekend** to sightsee, eat, drink, stroll through Brussels's leafy parks, and take in farther-flung communes like Saint Gilles.

Most of the city's attractions are concentrated in **Brussels Centrum,** but you'll find some of the best art deco houses in **Saint Gilles** and **Ixelles.** The **European Quarter** also holds European Union-related buildings of interest to many travelers. The most crowded spot is certainly **Grand Place,** but once you leave the heart of center and the area around the central train station, you'll find that Brussels is relatively quiet. You'll certainly see groups following tour guides with flags, but this is most often right on the streets surrounding Grand Place and Manneken Pis. This can make exploring Brussels an unexpected joy, as locals are quite friendly toward the relatively rare tourist who veers off the beaten path.

European Parliament

Your base in Brussels doesn't matter as much as you'd imagine, as the city center and many of the surrounding communes are fairly **walkable.** Whether you chose to stay in Centrum, European District, hip Dansaert, or get away from the crowds in Saint Gilles, you'll discover it's not hard to find your way around. **Public transit** in Brussels is generally reliable, although buying a ticket can take a bit of effort for the uninitiated.

Although Grand Place is certainly worthwhile, take some caution in Brussels's most touristy spots, as **pickpocketing** does occur. Though many flock to the World's Fair exhibitions of the Atomium and "Mini-Europe" out in **Laeken,** they may be a bit of disappointment given the length of the journey. If the weather is good (a big if in the Benelux region), it's worthwhile to get away from Brussels's occasionally gritty streets and head for the lush **parks** on the outskirts.

Brussels is best enjoyed outside of general European travel peak season and around the **Christmas Market. Shoulder season** is great for experiencing Brussels without the crowds but when it's still warm enough to enjoy sitting on a terrace. **Hours** in Brussels tend to be better than many other Belgian cities, although many shops and cafés open late, around 9am-10am, and close in time for dinner. Hours on Sundays, Mondays, and Tuesdays may be more limited. Fridays and Saturdays tend to be the best days to explore Brussels, as most things tend to be open and cafés tend to be hopping.

The main attractions that should be booked in advance include the **Atomium,** the **Parlamentarium,** tours at **Brasserie Cantillon** and **Brussels Town Hall,** and the **Horta Museum.** The popular **Royal Greenhouses of Laeken** are only open for a small window each year (Apr.-May).

Many use Brussels as a base for **day trips** through Belgium, a worthwhile idea if you find an affordable hotel in Brussels and prefer to keep one base. Brussels enjoys a fairly central location, and the easy Belgian train system means that no reservation is necessary to hop onto a train to another city, whether it's Leuven or Antwerpen.

Sightseeing Passes

Visitors to Brussels might want to invest in the useful **Brussels Card** (https://visit.brussels/en/sites/brusselscard; €28-44), which provides free entry to 39 museums throughout Brussels for 24, 48, or 72 hours. For a little more, you can also add unlimited public transit within the Brussels region on the STIB system (€7.50-18). The biggest perk is that visitors with the Brussels card can purchase a skip-the-line ticket for the Atomium (adults €12). Children under 12 do not require a Brussels card, as they already receive often free or heavily discounted admission to most attractions. Brussels Cards are available for purchase online and at Visit Brussels offices around the city.

For visitors spending more time in Belgium, the **Museum Pass Belgium** (www.museumpassmusees.be/nl/english; €59) can provide significant value with entry into 170 museums throughout Belgium for an entire year. The pass is available for purchase only in person at museums, as the online system requires a Belgian address to ship the card to.

Itinerary Ideas

DAY 1: BEST OF BRUSSELS CENTRUM AND DANSAERT

1 Start with an offbeat introduction to the city at the **Comics Art Museum,** a testament to Belgium's creativity in art and comics.

2 Walk 7 minutes down Rue du Marais and you'll find yourself in the **Royal Galleries of Saint Hubert,** beautiful covered passages that house shops and some of Brussels's most notable chocolatiers—try Neuhaus.

3 Leave the Royal Galleries to enjoy the beauty of **Grand Place's** shining guild houses before it becomes too busy.

4 Exit Grand Place on the left of Brussels's impressive City Hall along Rue Charles Buls, where you'll find some of the city's famous comic book walls, including Hergé's iconic Tintin, en route to **Manneken Pis,** another toungue-in-cheek symbol of the city.

5 From here, stroll down beautiful Rue des Grands Carmes, heading northwest in the direction of Dansaert. You'll find many independent shops, including **Passa Porta,** one of Brussels's best bookstores.

6 Time for another snack: Head to Place Sainte-Catherine for a bit of champagne with a side of shrimp croquettes at **Noordzee,** a food stand at the foot of Saint Catherine Church.

7 Satisfied, wander Dansaert's charming side streets, heading west past the canal toward Rue de Flandre in search of the **Brussels Beer Project,** the city's most notable craft brewery.

8 After a few beers, head back toward Saint Catherine to enjoy dinner at **Dam Sum Place Sainte-Catherine,** a beautifully decorated Chinese restaurant.

DAY 2: MUSEUMS, PARKS, AND CULTURE

1 Begin your day at one of the most stunning viewpoints in the city, **Mont des Arts,** overlooking the entire city, located just south of Brussels's center.

2 On your way down from the viewpoint, step into **Galerie Bortier,** a covered passage filled with antiquarian bookstores.

3 Next, head to the **Royal Museums of Fine Arts of Belgium** to enjoy world-class art, from the old masters to Magritte.

4 After the museum, step into the atelier of **Laurent Gerbaud,** one of Brussels's most talented chocolatiers, for a cup of coffee and some of his masterful chocolates.

5 Walk off the sweets with a short stroll through **Parc de Bruxelles,** where you'll find impressive views of the Royal Palace exterior.

6 Walk down Rue Royale toward Sablon, where you'll find **La Pizza è Bella,** one of the best pizzerias in Brussels. In good weather, enjoy your pizza in Square du Petit Sablon, a charming park nearby.

7 After your meal, take Tram 92 from Petit Sablon toward Fort-Jabo to Janson in the Ixelles neighborhood. The **Horta Museum,** the house and former studio of one of the

Itinerary Ideas

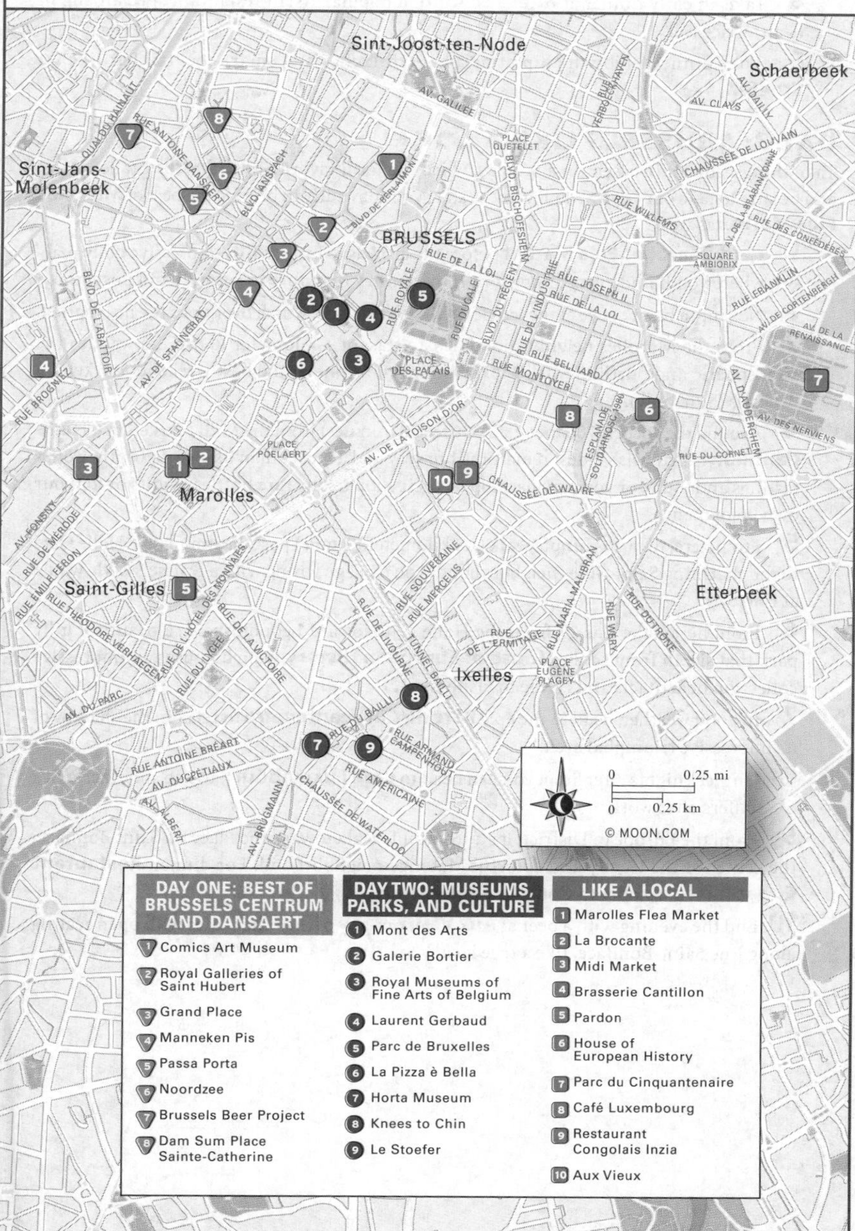

founders of art nouveau, is one of the genre's masterpieces. There are countless art nouveau houses surrounding the museum, especially on Rue Defacqz and Rue Paul Emile Janson.

8 Take an early dinner at **Knees to Chin,** a popular Asian restaurant specializing in healthy rice rolls.

9 After dinner, enjoy the hip atmosphere of Ixelles at a smart cocktail bar like **Le Stoefer.**

DAY 3: BRUSSELS LIKE A LOCAL

Take things slow in Brussels on a Sunday, when the local favorite **Midi Market** takes place, and be sure to take out **cash.** You'll want to start your day early to browse the best of **Marolles Flea Market** as well.

1 Get to **Marolles Flea Market** before the crowds to browse this impressive daily market, where you'll find everything from 18th-century furniture to secondhand postcards.

2 Next up: a bit of coffee at the iconic **La Brocante** café, which overlooks the flea market.

3 From the Marolles neighborhood, it's a pleasant 1-kilometer (0.6-mile) walk to the atmospheric and bustling **Midi Market,** known as one of the best weekend markets in Brussels (Sun. only).

4 Around the corner (700 meters/2,300 feet; 8 minutes) from the Midi Market, **Brasserie Cantillon** is Brussels's oldest remaining brewery and a museum in its own right. They offer tastings and tours, or you can just stop by their shop to buy rare bottles as gifts or for your own enjoyment.

5 From here, it's a 20-minute walk (1.5 kilometers/1 mile) past the impressive Halle Gate to the charming Saint Gilles neighborhood. You can't go wrong with a Brussels-style waffle at **Pardon.**

6 From here, take Bus 27 from the Halle Gate toward Leopoldspark, a beautiful hilly park that sits in front of the **House of European History,** which houses an impressive collection of artifacts and is free to visitors.

7 In good weather, head to the epic **Parc du Cinquantenaire** to relax in the shadow of its impressive triumphal arch.

8 On weeknights after 5pm, you can head to **Café Luxembourg** to rub shoulders with EU staffers after work.

9 From the European District, it's a 15-minute walk toward the Place du Saint Boniface, the center of the trendy and colorful Matonge neighborhood. For dinner, **Restaurant Congolais Inzia** offers a Congolese buffet.

10 End the evening with a beer at **Aux Vieux** or any of the other cafés with open seating along Rue Saint-Boniface, like a true local.

Sights

BRUSSELS CENTRUM

★ Grand Place/Grote Markt

open 24/7; free

Grand Place, or Grote Markt in Dutch, has long been the economic center of Brussels, and it remains so to this day in its current form as a tourist mecca. The square has been a marketplace since the 12th century and increased in stature alongside Brussels's wealth and prosperity, reflected in the glittering gold inlays decorating the grand buildings, once guild houses for Brussels's industries, from haberdashery to baking. Today, these buildings are taken up largely by commercial shops and cafés, some of which have tables on the square for a drink, though #10 remains inhabited by the Belgian beer brewers guild, as it has for centuries.

During the Bombardment of Brussels in 1695, when the troops of France's Louis XIV hammered the square for 36 hours, many of the beautiful buildings in the square were destroyed, but the square was largely restored to its former glory. If you study the historic paintings at the **Brussels City Museum,** right on Grand Place, it's almost impossible to tell the difference between the square centuries ago and now, though the buildings were rebuilt in stone rather than wood to help make them last. Surviving medieval buildings include #3, which was once the guild house for tallow merchants dating back to 1644, and #5, which belonged to the archers guild (the phoenix on the facade was added as a testament to the square's rebirth from the ashes). Grand Place is recognized as a UNESCO World Heritage Site for its representation of 17th-century Belgian social and cultural life.

BRUSSELS TOWN HALL (Hotel de Ville)

Grand Place 1; tel. 02 279 23 43; www.brussels.be/city-hall; 8:30am-5:30pm Mon.-Fri.; €7

It's hard to miss the Hotel de Ville, or Brussels Town Hall, with its soaring tower, first built in the 15th century in the Gothic style and reconstructed based on paintings from medieval times; following the Bombardment, only the facade of the building remained. It's been considered one of the masterpieces of Gothic architecture since its restoration. The 96-meter (315-foot) tower, which replaced a belfry, is topped with a statue of Michael the Archangel. Most of the interior is a bit more recent, but it's hard not to admire the impressive marriage hall and the not-so-Gothic Gothic Hall. English **tours** of town hall are available on select days (2pm Wed., 2pm, 3pm, and 4pm Sun.; purchase tickets at the Visit Brussels office in Grand Place up to five days ahead).

BRUSSELS CITY MUSEUM

Grand Place 2; tel. 02 279 43 50; www.brusselscitymuseum.brussels; 10am-5pm Tues.-Sun.; €8, seniors €6, students €4, under 18 free

The Brussels City Museum is a beautiful museum right on Grand Place that regales visitors with the history of Brussels. The relatively modest museum depicts the development of the city over time through plaques in Dutch and French and a few rare paintings depicting Brussels through the centuries. (There is an audio guide for English speakers.) Also on display are examples of pottery, tapestries, lace, and other pieces of city history. The most interesting piece is definitely the original Manneken Pis, stored here in the museum for safekeeping along with some of his most interesting outfits.

Saint Nicholas Church

Rue au Beurre 1; www.upbxlcentre.be/eglises/saint-nicolas; 10am-6:30pm outside of services; free

As you exit Grand Place you'll pass this church, which seems fairly unremarkable from the outside. The facade largely dates back to 1956, but this church is one of the oldest in

Brussels Centrum and Sablon

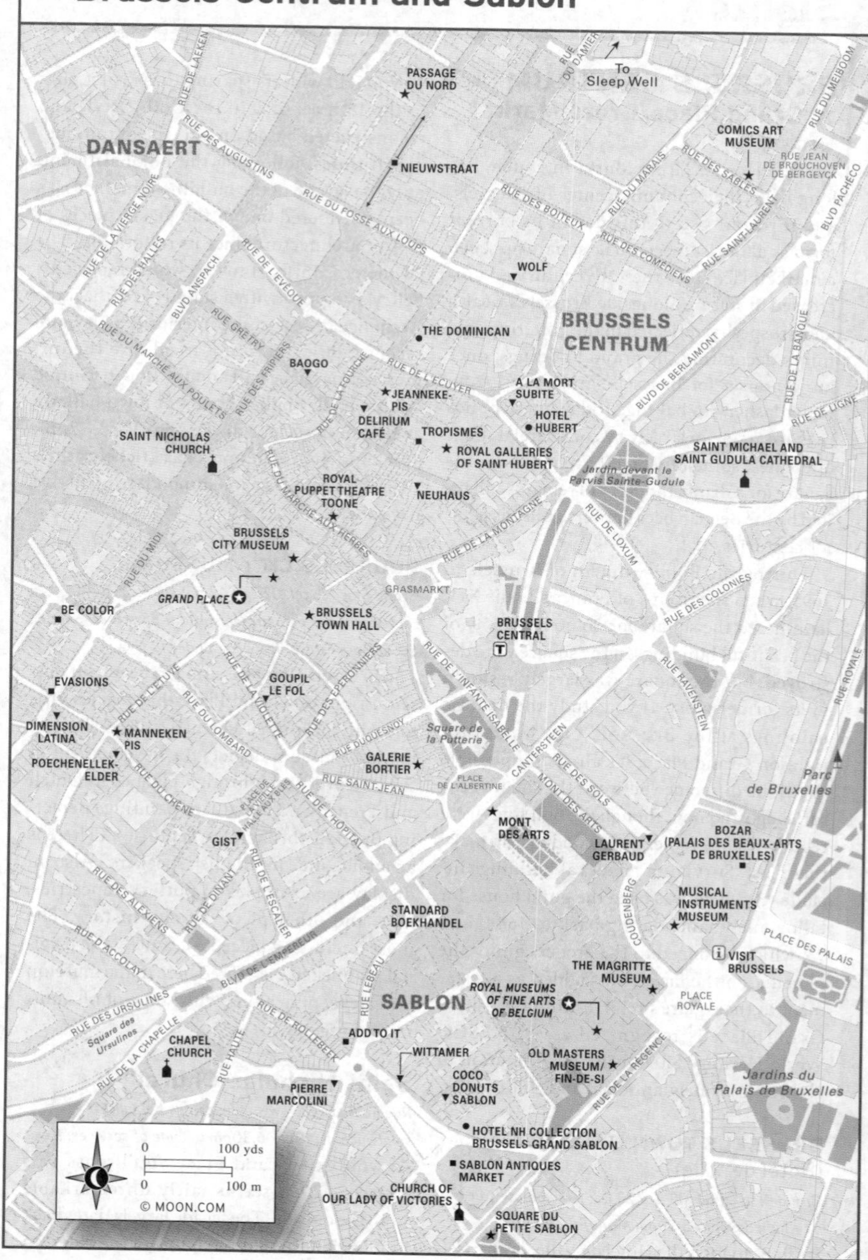

To Sleep Well
PASSAGE DU NORD
DANSAERT
NIEUWSTRAAT
COMICS ART MUSEUM
RUE JEAN DE BROUCHOVEN DE BERGEYCK
WOLF
BRUSSELS CENTRUM
THE DOMINICAN
BAOGO
JEANNEKE-PIS
A LA MORT SUBITE
HOTEL HUBERT
DELIRIUM CAFÉ
TROPISMES
SAINT NICHOLAS CHURCH
ROYAL GALLERIES OF SAINT HUBERT
SAINT MICHAEL AND SAINT GUDULA CATHEDRAL
Jardin devant le Parvis Sainte-Gudule
ROYAL PUPPET THEATRE TOONE
NEUHAUS
BRUSSELS CITY MUSEUM
GRAND PLACE
GRASMARKT
BE COLOR
BRUSSELS TOWN HALL
BRUSSELS CENTRAL
EVASIONS
GOUPIL LE FOL
DIMENSION LATINA
MANNEKEN PIS
POECHENELLEK-ELDER
Square de la Putterie
GALERIE BORTIER
PLACE DE L'ALBERTINE
Parc de Bruxelles
MONT DES ARTS
GIST
LAURENT GERBAUD
BOZAR (PALAIS DES BEAUX-ARTS DE BRUXELLES)
MUSICAL INSTRUMENTS MUSEUM
STANDARD BOEKHANDEL
VISIT BRUSSELS
THE MAGRITTE MUSEUM
PLACE ROYALE
SABLON
ROYAL MUSEUMS OF FINE ARTS OF BELGIUM
Square des Ursulines
CHAPEL CHURCH
ADD TO IT
WITTAMER
OLD MASTERS MUSEUM/ FIN-DE-SI
PIERRE MARCOLINI
COCO DONUTS SABLON
Jardins du Palais de Bruxelles
HOTEL NH COLLECTION BRUSSELS GRAND SABLON
SABLON ANTIQUES MARKET
CHURCH OF OUR LADY OF VICTORIES
SQUARE DU PETITE SABLON
0 100 yds
0 100 m
© MOON.COM

Brussels. It was first built in 1125 and added to throughout the centuries, resulting in a mix of elements from Romanesque to Gothic to modern that make the church particularly interesting. The oldest visible element is the choir, dating back to 1381. You can also see works by one of Pieter Paul Rubens's prodigies and other Flemish painters, as well as the remains of a cannonball from the 1695 Bombardment of Brussels.

Royal Puppet Theatre Toone
(Théâtre Royal de Toone)

Rue du Marché Aux Herbes 66; tel. 02 511 71 37; www.toone.be; shows 8:30pm Thurs., Fri., 4pm and 8:30pm Sat., closed Jan.; €12

Since the 1830s, generations of the Toone family have been showcasing their puppets along with plays performed in the traditional dialect of Brussels. Today, the Théâtre Royal is the last puppet theater still operating in Brussels, now offering shows in English, Spanish, and German. Shows take place at least four times a week within the original theater, located on a skinny alley off Grand Place marked by the word *Toone*. Even if you miss the show, you can soak up the atmosphere and admire the marionettes at their cash-only Estaminet Café in the evenings. At the time of writing, the theater was closed due to COVID-19, and it was unclear when it would reopen.

Royal Galleries of Saint Hubert
(Galeries Royales Saint Hubert)

Galerie du Roi 5; tel. 02 545 09 90; www.grsh.be; open 24/7, shop hours vary; free

The Royal Galleries of Saint Hubert was the first "mall," or arcade, in Europe. Although arcades are often associated with Paris, these beautiful vaulted-glass-covered passages are actually older, built in 1847. There are a few entrances, one closer to Grand Place, another just off Rue d'Arenberg, and it's hard not to spend a moment taking in the grand windows, luxurious stores, and marble decorations upon entry.

There are technically three passages, known as Gallery of the King, Gallery of the Queen, and Gallery of the Prince. Within the galleries, you'll find several notable shops including the **Neuhaus,** the pharmacy-turned-chocolatier that created the praline, as well as **Tropismes,** a beautiful bookstore that stocks primarily French titles.

Manneken Pis

intersection of Rue du Chêne and Rue de l'Étuve; www.brussels.be/manneken-pis; open 24/7; free

Since the reputation of Manneken Pis is larger than life, many visitors to Brussels are often disappointed seeing him in person. This small bronze statue, whose name translates to "Little Man Peeing" in the Brussels Flemish dialect, has become an unlikely symbol of Brussels. The site of a water fountain since the 13th century, the statue in the shape that we know it today was created in 1619 by Jérôme Duquesnoy to replace the earlier version with a baroque version. It has been stolen and thrown in the canal quite a few times over the course of its history; in fact, the version on the corner of van de Stoofstraat and de Eikstraat is a copy, to protect the original (now kept in the **Brussels City Museum**) from this very fate. The resilience of the Manneken Pis to remain peeing on top of a fountain plays into the typical Brussels sense of humor, the lore of Brussels itself, and the ability of Brussels to laugh at itself.

It says a lot about Brussels's sense of humor that the locals proudly have a peeing young boy as their city symbol. About a third of the year, the statue is dressed up in costume by the official dresser of Manneken Pis (generally an appointed role). Interesting costumes include the earliest costume to date, a costume provided by Louis XV him as an elegant 17th-century gentleman, a samurai robe to mark the friendship between Belgium and Japan, and educational costumes to symbolize different roles in Belgian society.

Manneken Pis has two sister statues: **Jeanneke Pis** (Impasse de la Fidélité 10-12) and **Zinneke Pis** (Rue des Chartreux 35). Jeanneke Pis, Mannekin Pis's female

TOONE
1
2
3

counterpart, was installed in 1987 and sits in an alleyway near Grand Place. Zinneke Pis, installed in 1998 in Dansaert, is Manneken Pis's pet, modeled after a real dog that belonged to the sculptor.

Mont des Arts

https://visit.brussels/site/en/place/Mont-des-Arts-Gardens; open 24/7; free

Brussels's most beautiful lookout is known as the "Hill of Art" in French. The hill was once a neighborhood known as Quartier Saint-Roch, designated an arts quarter by King Leopold II. In the end, the project did not amount to much, but a beautiful staircase and park were built in 1910. The park has since been rebuilt, but the spirit of this original project remains—and the view is now just as beautiful as the art found in museums in Brussels today. It's one of the best spots in the city to enjoy the sunset.

Saint Michael and Saint Gudula Cathedral (Brussels Cathedral)

(Cathédrale des Sts Michel et Gudule, Bruxelles)

Place Sainte-Gudule; tel. 02 217 83 45; https://cathedralisbruxellensis.be; 7:30am-6pm daily; free

Just around the corner from Brussels Central Train Station, you'll find a grand Gothic Cathedral atop a hill so steep that you need stairs to ascend it. This cathedral is the main church used by the Belgian royals for weddings. It's thought that a chapel was first built here in the 8th century, but the chapel was turned into a Romanesque church and dedicated to Saint Gudula, the patron saint of Brussels, in 1047. The elaborate white Gothic facade along with the towers, once admired by Victor Hugo, were built in the 15th century. Inside, you'll find an impressive marble altarpiece and a beautiful baroque pulpit carved by Hendrik Frans Verbruggen. There's a small **treasury** in the back for fans of relics and church art (€2). Even without paying admission, you can still admire the church's Brabantine Gothic nave and beautiful stained glass windows, some of which date back to the 16th century. There is also a **crypt** (€3) where you can see the remains of the previous Romanesque church.

Musical Instruments Museum

(Musée des Instruments de Musique)

Rue Montagne de la Cour 2; tel. 02 545 01 30; www.mim.be; adults €10

Known as one of the most beautiful examples of art nouveau in Brussels, the Musical Instruments Museum documents the development of musical instruments over time, both within Europe and elsewhere in the world. The collection is sorted by region/country, and they have a few astounding pieces including the world's oldest saxophone. The **café** on the top floor has some of the best views of Brussels you'll find, just for the cost of a cup of coffee.

★ Royal Museums of Fine Arts of Belgium

(Musées Royaux des Beaux-Arts de Belgique)

Rue de la Régence 3; tel. 02 508 32 11; www.fine-arts-museum.be; 10am-5pm Tues.-Fri., 11am-6pm Sat.-Sun.; €10 per exhibition

Fine art lovers cannot miss a visit to the three museums that make up the Royal Museums of Fine Arts of Belgium, an incredible collection beginning with the 15th-century Flemish old masters to the art nouveau of the early 20th century. Depending on your taste, you may want to pick just one of the museums to visit, or all three; each requires a separate ticket, though admission to all of them is included with the **Brussels Card.**

There is technically a fourth museum included in the Royal Museums, the **Wiertz Museum** (Rue Vautier 62; tel. 02 648 17 18; https://fine-arts-museum.be/en/museums/musee-wiertz-museum; 10am-noon and 12:45pm-5pm Tues.-Fri.; free), dedicated to one of Brussels's most intriguing and

1: Brussels Centrum **2:** Brussels Town Hall **3:** Grand Place

1
2
3
4

polarizing artists, Antoine Wiertz, who was part of the Belgian Romantic school of art. The museum is housed within his former workshop in the European Quarter. Though the museum is interesting to fans of Wiertz, it's definitely the least visited of Brussels's Royal Museums.

OLD MASTERS MUSEUM

The Old Masters Museum focuses on paintings by the Flemish Primitives and from the Flemish Renaissance and the baroque period. This very impressive collection was established in 1801 by Napoleon Bonaparte, composed mostly of works that were seized during the French Revolution. There is an entire room dedicated to the work of Pieter Bruegel the Elder and another dedicated to Peter Paul Rubens. Highlights of the collection include *The Fall of the Rebel Angels* by Bruegel, *Portrait of Anthony of Burgundy* by Rogier van der Weyden, and *The Road to Calvary* by Rubens, along with works by Hieronymus Bosch, Hans Memling, and Jacob Jordaens. The collection included almost no female or minority artists at the time of writing, with the exception of Michaelina Wautier, a baroque painter from Mons whose work was often misattributed to her brother. It takes a few hours to go through this museum, which has one of the most complete collections in Europe. It is accessible for people with disabilities.

THE MAGRITTE MUSEUM

René Magritte, one of Brussels's best-known artists, was active in the early 20th century, creating surrealist paintings that often commented on society and poked fun at popular concepts. But the Magritte Museum holds 230 of his works, the most complete collection in the world. Connected to the Old Masters by an underground tunnel, the museum is otherwise quite recent, established in 2009. *Empire of Light* is housed here, along with many of the artist's sketches, displayed chronically to provide more context into Magritte's process—and his life. Magritte lived in Brussels for many years—the house is now a smaller museum, **Musée René Magritte** (Rue Essegham 135; tel. 02 428 26 26; www.magrittemuseum.be; 10am-6pm Wed.-Sun.; €10, under 18 free).

FIN-DE-SIÈCLE MUSEUM

Dedicated to impressionism and art nouveau, this collection houses works from the end of the 19th century and early 20th century, ranging from ornate sculptures by Auguste Rodin to wild and symbolic paintings like *The Caress* by Fernand Khnopff. You'll also find paintings by Georges Seurat and Paul Gauguin, and designs by Victor Horta, one of the founders of art nouveau. The museum has a large collection of sketches from Anna Boch, an artist influenced by impressionism who often used pastels and drawing as a medium. Although becoming an artist was quite difficult for women at the time, a number of female artists received recognition, including Cécile Douard, Alix d'Anethan, and Paule Deman.

Royal Palace of Brussels
(Palais de Bruxelles)

Rue Brederode 16; tel. 02 551 20 20; www.monarchie.be/en/heritage/royal-palace-of-brussels; 10:30am-5pm Tues. late July-Sept.; free

The Royal Palace of Belgium is owned by the Belgian royal family, although it's generally not inhabited and only used for special occasions. Notably, its facade is 50 percent longer than the one at Buckingham Palace (the palace itself is quite a bit smaller). The palace is filled with beautiful rooms decked out in period furniture and many portraits of nobility. It's best known for its Hall of Mirrors, whose brilliant green ceiling was created using more than 1.6 million jewel beetles by Jan Fabre, but a lucky few get to see it: The palace is only open to the public by appointment during the summer.

1: exterior of Saint Michael and Saint Gudula Cathedral **2:** interior of Saint Michael and Saint Gudula Cathedral **3:** Manneken Pis **4:** Royal Galleries of Saint Hubert

Passages of Brussels

Although the covered passages of Brussels are certainly not as famous as those of Paris, the city does have some lovely arcades, beyond the **Royal Galleries of Saint Hubert.**

Galerie Bortier

GALERIE BORTIER

Rue da la Madeleine 55; https://visit.brussels/en/place/Galerie-Bortier-shopping; 9am-6pm Mon.-Sat.

Galerie Bortier, like the Royal Galleries of Saint Hubert, is a covered market near Mont des Arts, a beautiful neo-renaissance building with a baroque facade. The interior is now full of antique bookstores. Most of the books are in French or Dutch, but you'll find English books if you look hard enough through the racks.

PASSAGE DU NORD

Rue Neuve 40; tel. 02 218 50 68; https://passage-du-nord.business.site; 8am-8pm Mon.-Sat.

Passage du Nord is the other main historic covered passage of Brussels, a 10-minute walk north of Grand Place. Part of King Leopold's campaign to cover up the river that once ran through Brussels, Passage du Nord was conceptualized as a way to tear down industrial areas that were considered unsightly. It was built in 1881 by Henri Rieck and remains a shopping street today.

Comics Art Museum (Musée Belge da la Bande Dessinée)

Rue des Sables 20; tel. 02 219 19 80; www.comicscenter.net; 10am-6pm Tues.-Sun.; €8

Nobody can put their finger on exactly why Belgium has become one of the world's leading producers of comic books, but many suspect the Belgian sense of humor plays into it. Whether you're a fan of Hergé's famous Tintin or interested in more contemporary comics, the Comics Art Museum is engaging for all ages. It's housed in a beautiful former warehouse from 1906 designed by Belgian art nouveau architect Victor Horta, spectacular in itself to explore as you soak up the history of the comics on display. It takes a few hours to go through the entire museum, which is accessible for people with disabilities. The museum also has a beautiful **gift shop** selling comic books and related souvenirs.

SABLON

Chapel Church (Église Notre Dame de la Chapelle)

Place de la Chapelle; 9am-6:30pm Mon.-Fri., 10am-6:30pm Sat.-Sun.; free

The Chapel Church is the heart of the Sablon neighborhood, and you can see its iconic black roof throughout the city. The church itself is an impressive blend of Romanesque and Gothic, likely dating back to the 12th century when it was a Benedictine abbey. The neighborhood grew around the church, and it was one of the most important churches in Brussels in the medieval period. After the church partially burned down in the 15th century, it was rebuilt in the Gothic style with a baroque bell tower. Notably, painter Pieter Bruegel the Elder was married here and was later buried within the church: There's a small memorial near the confessional. Today it's a Polish Catholic church.

Church of Our Lady of Victories at the Sablon
(Église Notre Dame des Victoires au Sablon)

Rue des Sablons; 10am-6pm daily; free

This 15th-century Roman Catholic church dominates the magnificent Grand Sablon square, with imposing baroque and Gothic architectural features. With its tall nave and chapels housing sculptures made by some of the most celebrated artists of the 17th-century, the Church of our Lady of Victories was traditionally patronized by Brussels's elite.

MAROLLES

Halle Gate
(Porte de Hal)

Boulevard du Midi 150; tel. 02 534 15 18; www.kmkg-mrah.be; 9:30am-5pm Mon.-Thurs., 10am-6pm Sat.-Sun.; €12

The Halle Gate is a fortified gate so impressive you might wonder from afar if it's a castle. The last of Brussels's medieval city gates, first built in 1381, the gate was intended to protect what is now Saint Gilles via a moat, portcullis, and drawbridge. The gate did not always have turrets; these were part of an upgrade in the late 19th century, with neo-Gothic touches. In the museum inside, you can admire armor that once belonged to Albert of Austria dating back to the 16th century. Even if you don't go inside, the gate is surrounded by a lovely park where beautiful bluebells bloom.

DANSAERT

Saint Catherine Church
(Église Sainte-Catherine de Bruxelles)

Place Sainte-Catherine 50; tel. 0492 76 66 17; http://eglisesaintecatherine.be; 9am-7pm Mon.-Fri., 9am-8pm Sat.-Sun.; free

Saint Catherine Church is one of the key landmarks of Dansaert. It dates back to the 15th century, but most of the church you see today was designed in the 17th-19th centuries. The main reason people come here is to visit the food stands in front of the church, including perennial favorite **Noordzee,** or sit with friends near the fountain behind the church on warm summer nights. But the church is still quite pretty inside thanks to art and a baroque pulpit.

Saint John the Baptist at the Béguinage
(Église Saint Jean Baptiste au Béguinage)

Place du Béguinage 2062; tel. 32 483 60 72 10; 11am-5:30pm Tues.-Sun.; free

Brussels, like many cities in Belgium and the Netherlands, was home to a community of Beguines, a lay religious order whose members lived lives of poverty and chastity. A Beguine community was established here close to 1250, along with a Gothic church in the 14th century, which are both lost to history after being burned by Calvinists. The current church was rebuilt in the 17th century in the Flemish baroque style and is considered of the most beautiful in Belgium, with its Gothic interior with high vaults.

EUROPEAN DISTRICT

European Parliament

Rue Wiertz 60; www.europarl.europa.eu/visiting/en; 10am-4pm Mon.-Thurs., 10am-1pm Fri.; free with advance reservation

The European Parliament was created in the hopes of promoting economic growth strengthening ties between European countries in the post-World War II landscape. Brussels was chosen as a headquarters early on thanks to its central location between the original six member states, quieter city center, good links with other countries, affordable housing, and space for building.

The building used for European Parliament, known as the **Hemicycle,** is open to visitors for free on a 60-minute **tour** (with advance reservation). The building itself is circular and modern, with a dome shape, a mirror-like blue exterior, and the flags of the member countries displayed outside. The chance to follow debates and simply view the meeting space is reason enough to visit. A multimedia guide is

Dansaert

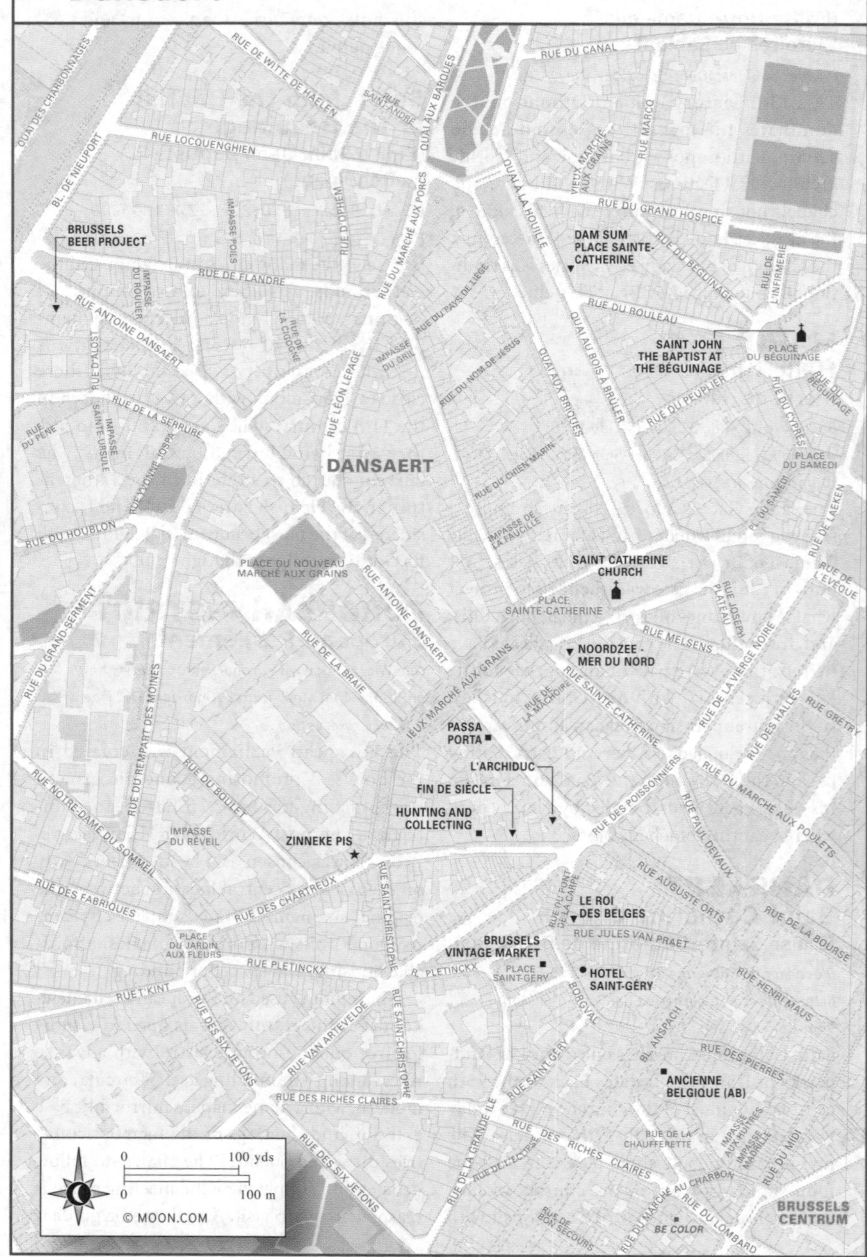
BRUSSELS BEER PROJECT
DAM SUM PLACE SAINTE-CATHERINE
SAINT JOHN THE BAPTIST AT THE BÉGUINAGE
DANSAERT
SAINT CATHERINE CHURCH
NOORDZEE - MER DU NORD
PASSA PORTA
L'ARCHIDUC
FIN DE SIÈCLE
HUNTING AND COLLECTING
ZINNEKE PIS
LE ROI DES BELGES
BRUSSELS VINTAGE MARKET
HOTEL SAINT-GÉRY
ANCIENNE BELGIQUE (AB)
BE COLOR
BRUSSELS CENTRUM
PLACE DU NOUVEAU MARCHÉ AUX GRAINS
PLACE SAINTE-CATHERINE
PLACE DU BÉGUINAGE
PLACE DU SAMEDI
PLACE DU JARDIN AUX FLEURS
PLACE SAINT-GÉRY
0 100 yds
0 100 m
© MOON.COM

provided, and there are also special options for attending talks or plenary sessions.

Parlamentarium

Place du Luxembourg 100; tel. 02 284 36 48; https://europarl.europa.eu/visiting; 1pm-6pm Mon., 9am-6pm Tues.-Fri., 10am-6pm Sat.-Sun.; free

The Parlamentarium is a museum dedicated to the workings of the European Parliament. Even if you're not a politics junkie, the museum educates the visitor on the formation of the European Union, workings of the European Parliament, key issues that have plagued the European Union, and even the difficulty of finding a solution via interactive debates. Each visitor is given an interactive audio guide prior to exploring the exhibitions; you can also imagine yourself within the European Parliament thanks to the 360-degree interactive film. Prepare for airport-style security: You must carry your ID or passport.

House of European History (Maison de l'Histoire Européenne)

Rue Belliard 135; tel. 02 283 12 20; https://historia-europa.ep.eu; 1pm-6pm Mon., 9am-6pm Tues.-Fri., 10am-6pm Sat.-Sun.; free

The House of European History is a bit of a hidden gem, with more than 4,000 square meters (43,000 square feet) of exhibitions that walk the visitor through important historical periods in Europe, as well as key ideas that reshaped history as we know it. Covering Greek history through the development of the EU, notable pieces include ancient Greek antiquities, the gun that started World War I, and documentation of life under communism. It's a surprisingly intellectual museum that's easy to spend hours in, and a great spot to pick up EU souvenirs.

Art & History Museum (Musée Art & Histoire)

10 Parc du Cinquantenaire; tel. 02 741 73 31; www.artandhistory.museum; 9:30am-5pm Tues.-Fri., 10am-5pm Sat.-Sun.; €10, seniors €8, students €4, under 18 free

The Art & History Museum has a simple name, but it houses an impressive collection of art from all over the world, from Greece to modern-day Peru. The museum's exhibitions also dive into Belgian prehistory and European art from various periods. If you love the Met in New York, you're likely to find something to admire at this underappreciated museum.

The museum is unfortunately not accessible to people with disabilities, as visitors will be climbing the original staircases of the house after entering through the home next door. Photography is prohibited, but you can purchase cards and books with images at the **gift shop.** Only 45 visitors are allowed in at a time, as the house is fairly small, but it's certainly worth the wait, if there is one, to see the beauty of art nouveau up close, as so few buildings in Brussels are open to the public.

SAINT GILLES

★ Horta Museum

Rue Américaine 27; tel. 02 543 04 90; www.hortamuseum.be; 2pm-5:30pm Tues.-Fri., 11am-5:30pm Sat.-Sun.; €10, students €5

One of the most magnificent art nouveau sights in Brussels is the Horta Museum, the home and studio of the grandfather of art nouveau, Victor Horta. The house has been perfectly preserved, with its original furniture, stained glass windows, architectural fixtures, and even decorations, supplemented with period pieces.

Victor Horta was born in Ghent in 1861. His father was a shoemaker, and after being expelled from the Ghent Conservatory while studying music, he went to the Royal Academy of Fine Arts instead. He moved to Brussels in 1880 and began studying architecture at the Academie Royale des Beaux-Arts, and was inspired by influences as diverse as the British Arts and Crafts Movement and the royal greenhouses, which he brought together in his first art nouveau buildings, constructed in the late 19th century. The open floor plans, generous light, and curved lines and decoration

Marolles and Saint Gilles

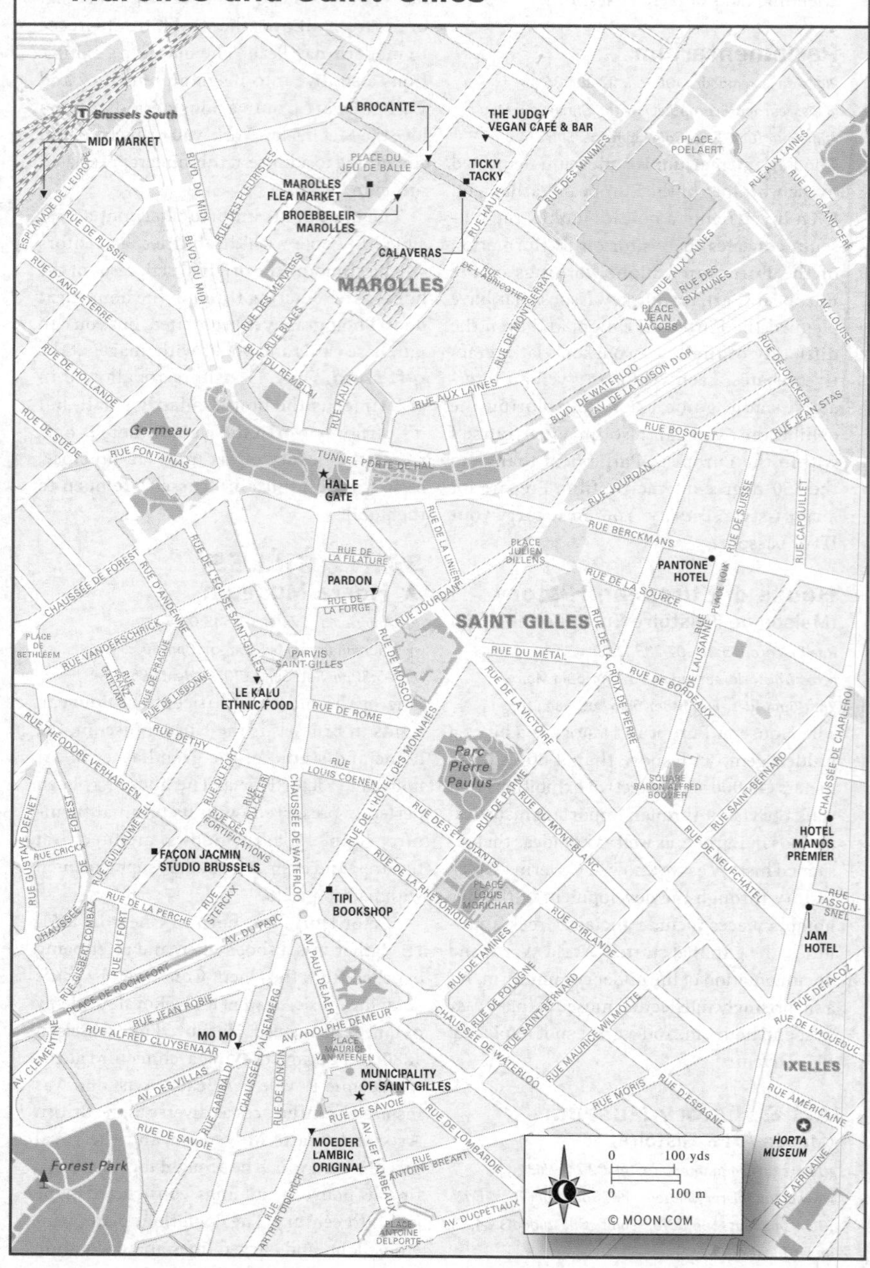
Brussels South
MIDI MARKET
LA BROCANTE
THE JUDGY VEGAN CAFÉ & BAR
TICKY TACKY
MAROLLES FLEA MARKET
BROEBBELEIR MAROLLES
CALAVERAS
MAROLLES
Germeau
HALLE GATE
PARDON
SAINT GILLES
PANTONE HOTEL
LE KALU ETHNIC FOOD
Parc Pierre Paulus
HOTEL MANOS PREMIER
FAÇON JACMIN STUDIO BRUSSELS
TIPI BOOKSHOP
JAM HOTEL
MO MO
MUNICIPALITY OF SAINT GILLES
IXELLES
MOEDER LAMBIC ORIGINAL
HORTA MUSEUM
Forest Park
0 100 yds
0 100 m
© MOON.COM

TOP EXPERIENCE

Art Nouveau in Brussels

Art nouveau is a unique form of art that originated in Brussels in the late 19th century. It focuses on flowing curved lines and depicting forms seen in nature, incorporating designs from butterflies to birds. Compared to art deco, another popular form that came about 30 years later, art nouveau is all about the flourishes, while art deco focuses on straight lines. Most of the art nouveau houses in Brussels are unfortunately largely private residences, but a few are open to the public on select days, and a handful are museums. Here are few of the best examples to look out for while in Brussels:

Cauchie House

- The first art nouveau house can be found at **71 Rue Defacqz** in Saint Gille. It was the residence of Paul Hankar, a Belgian architect who was inspired by glass, iron, and sculpture. The front of the house is a great example of sgraffito, a technique that uses plaster layers with pastel colors to create beautiful floral designs.
- **Hotel Tassel** (Rue Paul-Emile Janson 6) is a beautiful curved house designed by Victor Horta, with an elaborate steel-and-glass facade. The interior, like all of Horta's designs, includes his own furniture, woodwork, windows, doors, and even doorknobs.
- The **Cauchie House** (Le Maison Cauchie Bruxelles, Rue des Francs 5; tel. +027 33 86 84; www.cauchie.be; 10am-1pm and 2pm-5pm first weekend of every month) in the European District has a beautiful sgraffito design on its exterior and houses a museum dedicated to architect Paul Cauchie's designs.
- Similarly, the **Musical Instruments Museum** (page 199) is a beautiful example of art nouveau.
- True art nouveau enthusiasts will not want to miss Horta's workshop and residence at the **Horta Museum** (page 205).
- Another great opportunity to see Art Nouveau is **BANAD,** the Brussels Art Nouveau and Art Deco Festival (www.banad.brussels), one of the few times when many buildings are open to the public. So if you're into art nouveau, be sure to visit in March!

have had long-lasting impact on the architecture of Brussels and the world.

Every detail of the house, from the curvature of the banister that hides a heater to a swiveling urinal, is thought out to maximize beauty and functionality simultaneously—the philosophy behind art nouveau. The staircase is certainly a highlight, especially as you reach the top floor, with its impressive Chinese-inspired skylight that allows natural light into the home. As you move through the house, don't hesitate to take time to inspect everything, from the light fixtures to the hand-printed English wallpaper to the dish warmer hidden within the dining room table.

Municipality of Saint-Gilles (Administration de Saint-Gilles)

Place Maurice van Meenen 39; tel. 02 536 02 11; https://stgilles.brussels; 8am-noon Mon., Wed.-Fri., 8am-noon, 3pm-6pm Tues.; free

The Hôtel de Ville Saint Giles is an impressive

French neoclassical building that was constructed around 1900 to help Brussels manage its growing population. The building's iconic tower, styled like a belfry, can be seen throughout Saint Gilles. No expense was spared in the construction of this building; note the elaborately carved statues representing various public works housed inside.

LAEKEN

The huge green space that is Laeken Park, in the suburb of Laeken north of Central Brussels, is home to the 18th-century **Castle of Laeken** (Château de Laeken, Avenue du Parc Royal), an official residence to the Belgian royals that is not open to the public.

Royal Greenhouses of Laeken

Rue Brederode 16; tel. 02 551 20 20; www.monarchie.be/en/heritage; 9:30am-5pm Apr.-May; €2.50

Once a year, you can transport yourself from an often-rainy Brussels to a dreamy tropical paradise with a troubled past. The Royal Greenhouses of Laeken were built during the tenure of Leopold II, one of Belgium's most infamous monarchs.

When much of Africa was being carved up by European powers, Leopold II colonized the Congo Basin, what is now the Democratic Republic of the Congo, parts of Rwanda, and parts of Burundi. His rule of Congo was marked by brutality, exploitation, violence, and genocide in search of resources such as rubber, minerals, and ivory, giving him the nickname "Butcher of the Congo." It is estimated than nearly 10 million Congolese died during this brief 23-year period; overt racism and continued exploitation led to an independence movement and the failure of the Republic of the Congo in 1960. The Royal Greenhouses were built in part to showcase the extent of King Leopold II's wealth extracted from the Congo and feature Congolese plants.

In spite the difficult history, Belgians have long flocked to the greenhouses and wait in long lines to see this rarely opened attraction. In recent years, people are becoming more critical of this remnant of Belgium's colonialist past, but it's a hard conversation that many aren't eager to have. As of 2020, the Belgian king had sent his deep regrets for the abuses that took place in Congo.

Like many of the difficult vestiges of colonialism, the greenhouses are a beautiful landmark, with curved steel and glass that complements the rare plant collection within seven buildings that took over 30 years to complete. The complex is more than 2.5 hectares (6.2 acres), and many of the plants were sourced from seedlings from Leopold's original collection dating back to the 1860s.

Visitors must follow a fixed route through the greenhouses; avoid the crowds by visiting on weekdays. The first greenhouse is the Theatre Greenhouse, which holds camellias, an iconic Belgian flower and a favorite of the king. One of the most romantic passages, the Great Gallery houses 200 meters (650 feet) of geraniums and fuchsias. The Winter Garden showcases beautiful flowers in bloom under an impressive 30-meter-high (100-foot-high) domed ceiling. A Japanese pavilion is especially beautiful in spring when the cherry blossoms bloom.

Not all the buildings are open to visitors, but the ones that are cost less than the price of a cup of a coffee. There is a small **snack bar** in one of the greenhouses, along with a souvenir kiosk.

Atomium

Atomiumplein 1; tel. 02 475 47 75; https://atomium.be; 10am-6pm daily; €16, students €8.50, children free

First built for the Brussels World Fair in 1958, the Atomium was meant to showcase the Atomic Age, or the post-World War II period, with its atom shape. Interestingly, the Atomium is taller than the Brussels Town Hall at 102 meters (335 feet). Today, the exterior has LED lights and a stainless-steel facade. Within

1: Sablon **2:** Saint Catherine Church **3:** alley in Dansaert **4:** Horta Museum

1

2

3

4

the structure, a lift (once the fastest elevator in Europe at 5 m/s/11 mph!) takes visitors to the top, where they can enjoy views over the surrounding Parc de Laeken. The first floor discusses the history of the World's Fair, while the second and third spheres usually house temporary exhibitions. Today, the Atomium has become a symbol of the city, although only the truly dedicated take the 30-45-minute trip to Heysel station.

Sports and Recreation

TOURS

Like many cities, Brussels has an option for a **hop-on/hop-off bus** (www.citysightseeingbrussel.be) for easy sightseeing with minimal work in terms of transportation. Those on a budget can also opt for the cheaper free walking tours of the main attractions via the likes of **Sandemans** (www.neweuropetours.eu/brussels-walking-tours; donation).

GROOVY BRUSSELS

www.groovybrussels.com; €39

Groovy Brussels is a popular small-group Brussels-based tour operator that operates well-regarded bike, beer, and chocolate tours throughout Brussels.

BAJA BIKES

www.bajabikes.eu/en/brussels-bike-tour; 3.5 hours; €24

Baja Bikes operates a popular biking tour that brings you all over Brussels.

PARKS

Brussels is a remarkably green city, with 28 square meters (300 square feet) of parks for each resident, most of it outside the historic center, with the exception of **Parc de Bruxelles.** Parks were intended for weekend recreation as the city expanded, and in good weather, people head to the parks to enjoy picnics with friends and quiet walks. For the most part, Brussels's parks require public transit to get to.

Brussels Centrum

PARC DE BRUXELLES

Rue Royale; tel. 32 2 279 61 00; www.brussel.be

Once known as the Royal Park, Parc de Bruxelles is now a park for all of Brussels. The park was used as a hunting ground for nobility until 1770, when it was transformed into a park with sculpted gardens and fountains. This was Brussels's first park, offering a lovely view of the Royal Palace and a favorite spot for runners and families. It's a short walk (500 meters/1,600 feet; 5 minutes) from Brussels Central Train Station, making it a nice spot to enjoy lunch before catching a train elsewhere.

European District

PARC DU CINQUANTENAIRE

Avenue de la Renaissance

Parc du Cinquantenaire is one of Brussels's most iconic parks because of the dramatic triumphal arch that can be seen from virtually every corner of the park. The park was built in honor of the 50th anniversary of Belgium and is full of green spots to sit. History lovers might be interested in visiting the museums, including the **Art & History Museum,** adjacent to the park. You'll also find the **Horta-Lambeaux Pavillion,** of art nouveau design by the grandfather of the genre himself. This park is located east of Brussels's city center, about 15 minutes on foot from the European Parliament building.

1: Parc de Bruxelles **2:** Bois de la Cambre **3:** a statue in the Royal Greenhouses **4:** Parc du Cinquantenaire

Ixelles

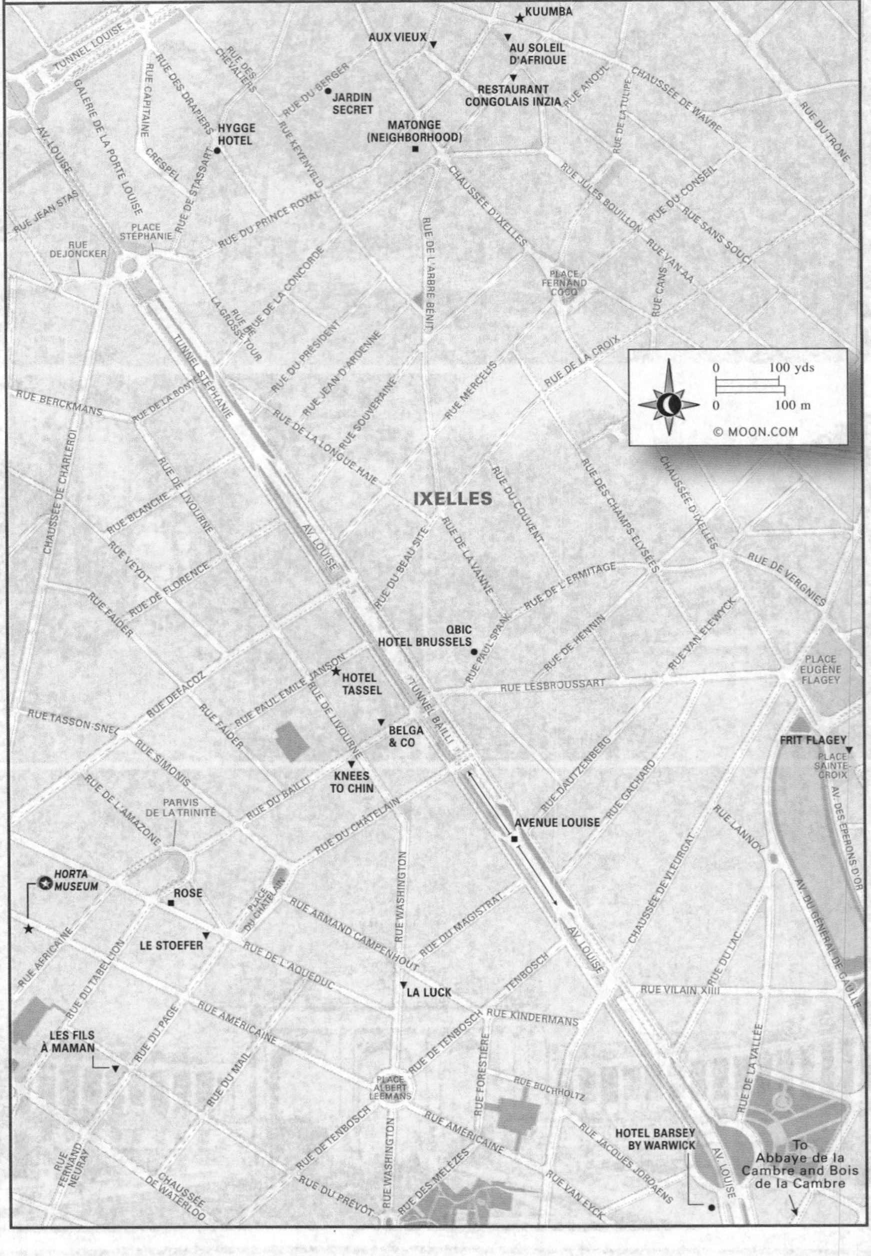

KUUMBA
AUX VIEUX
AU SOLEIL D'AFRIQUE
RESTAURANT CONGOLAIS INZIA
JARDIN SECRET
HYGGE HOTEL
MATONGE (NEIGHBORHOOD)
IXELLES
QBIC HOTEL BRUSSELS
HOTEL TASSEL
BELGA & CO
KNEES TO CHIN
AVENUE LOUISE
FRIT FLAGEY
HORTA MUSEUM
ROSE
LE STOEFER
LA LUCK
LES FILS À MAMAN
HOTEL BARSEY BY WARWICK
To Abbaye de la Cambre and Bois de la Cambre

0 100 yds
0 100 m
© MOON.COM

Ixelles

ABBAYE DE LA CAMBRE

www.premontres-lacambre.be

This beautiful park located in the south of Brussels is the grounds of a 13th-century abbey that was rebuilt in the 18th century, now actively used for other purposes, such as an arts school and mapping institute. Coming here feels like transporting yourself to the countryside, with trimmed hedges, leafy laws, and views of the remaining church. It's a lovely spot to sit and read on a nice day. If you continue southeast from La Cambre, you'll enter **Bois de la Cambre.** Bus 71 toward Delta runs from the center (stop: De Brouckère) to Géo Bernier. Trams 8 and 93 also stop nearby.

BOIS DE LA CAMBRE

www.brussel.be/parken-en-tuinen

Bois de la Cambre is a public park on the southeast edge of Brussels from the late 19th century, a longtime hunting ground for Hapsburgs, and today a beautiful place for a leisurely stroll or intense cycle through beech and oak forest. It's a beautifully sculpted park with a small lake complete with paddleboats. Admire the dreamy **Chalet Robinson** (Sentier de l'Embarcadère 1; tel. 02 372 92 92; www.chaletrobinson.be; noon-11pm daily; €14-24), a rebuilt wooden chalet with a restaurant inside. On weekends, the park is closed to cars. The park is accessible via multiple transfers (about 50 minutes) via the same bus stop as Abbaye de la Cambre with a 5-minute walk. Bus 71 toward Delta runs from the center (stop: De Brouckère) to Géo Bernier. Trams 8 and 93 also stop nearby.

Laeken

LAEKEN PARK

https://visit.brussels/site/en/place/Laeken-Park

Parc de Laeken is a beautiful park in the northwest part of Brussels, close to the Atomium and the Royal Greenhouses. The park sits across from the Castle of Laeken, a closed-off estate belonging to the Belgian Royal family, and was constructed in the late 19th century by the same landscape architect who designed Bois de la Cambre, in the French style. The park's wide avenues and winding paths make for a lovely wander in good weather, with more than 20 kinds of magnolias that bloom throughout the year. It's one of Brussels's quieter parks due to its residential location. Tram 3 toward Esplanade runs between center (stop: Beurs) and a stop just outside of the park, De Wand (33 minutes).

Entertainment and Events

THE ARTS

As the capital of Belgium, Brussels hosts a lot of top-quality music and theater. At the time of writing, COVID-19 had forced many of these institutions to close temporarily.

Brussels Centrum

BOZAR (PALAIS DES BEAUX-ARTS DE BRUXELLES)

Rue Ravenstein 23; tel. 02 507 82 00; www.bozar.be

BOZAR is Brussels's Center for Fine Art, where literature, music, art, and architectural interests meet in an airy, open space. It's housed in a 1928 art nouveau building designed by Horta, a difficult project given its size, but now art patrons have the benefit of being able to watch performances within the **Horta Hall,** the **Henry Le Boeuf Hall,** or the smaller **Chamber Music Hall.** The agenda changes frequently, and BOZAR is also known for its temporary art exhibitions, which frequently sell out in advance.

Dansaert

ANCIENNE BELGIQUE (AB)

Boulevard Anspach 110; tel. 02 548 24 84; www.abconcerts.be

The Ancienne Belgique (AB) is a well-known

Street Art in Brussels

Brussels is known for its vibrant street art. Images from Belgian comics adorn the sides of buildings throughout the city, from Tintin to Lucky Luke. The city has encouraged artists, both local and foreign, to decorate the city of Brussels. Every month, more pieces of artwork in eclectic styles crop up.

TOURS AND MAPS

Most of the murals are located within the city center, but dedicated fans can actively search the streets on foot for farther-flung art with the help of a handy **map** from the Brussels Tourism Board (www.brussels.be/comic-book-route). The **Visit Brussels** website (https://visit.brussels/en/article/Street-Art-in-Brussels) is another place to find an up-to-date list of street art the city, as well as information on local artists. Beyond the comics, you'll find commissioned murals all throughout the city featuring social messages, and others just livening up the streets, made by famous street artists from around the world. The **Belgian Comics Art Museum** offers guided themed walking tours showcasing cartoons and street art upon request (www.comicscenter.net/en/guided-tours; €140 per group). It is also possible to take a tour of the Matonge neighborhood via the **Kuumba** cultural center (www.kuumba.be).

BEST STREETS

Great streets to see murals include **Lollepotstraat** and **Rue de la Chaufferette,** south of Grand Place, which feature colorful stories and messages promoting the acceptance of LGBTQ people in society. One of Brussels's most famous street artists is **Bonom,** who has works throughout the city, including a mural of wildlife in the urban jungle. His most famous work, *Unbridled Talent,* is on the intersection of Rue Fontainas and Avenue de la Porte de Hal. Several murals can be seen along **Rue Charles Buls,** a skinny pedestrian-only street that begins at Grand Place.

concert hall in the center of Brussels that can hold more than 2,000 people in its Main Hall with perfect acoustics, making it a favorite of traveling bands. The roster skews toward indie and rock. Despite being named "ancient," the building itself is just over 100 years old.

KAAITHEATER

Square Sainctelette 20; tel. 02 201 59 59; www.kaaitheater.be

The Kaaitheater is an art center that focuses on dance, theater, and other performances such as stand-up comedy. It developed from an experimental art festival in 1977, whose popularity allowed the organizers to find a more permanent exhibition to promote avant-garde events.

FESTIVALS AND EVENTS

Brussels is a major hub for festivals, especially when Christmas markets brighten up the city. Most festivals are free, unless you want to shell out for special access or seating; see event websites for more details. Visit Brussels, the Brussels Tourism Board, keeps an active calendar on events on their website (https://visit.brussels/en/article/gah-agenda).

Spring

BELGIAN PRIDE

Brussels Centrum; www.pride.be; May

Brussels is proudly an inclusive and LGBTQ-friendly city, and the annual Belgian Pride parade is dynamic proof of this. The weekend is filled with rainbow flags, with parties at bars across the city center, especially close to Grand Place.

BRUSSELS JAZZ WEEKEND

throughout the city; www.brusselsjazzweekend.be; May

Brussels Jazz Weekend typically takes place over a long weekend at the end of May. More than 200 free concerts take place across the city, from large concerts in Grand Place to intimate nights showcasing newer jazz compositions at bars throughout Brussels.

Summer

BRUSSELS OMMEGANG

Brussels Centrum; www.brussels.be/ommegang; June

Brussels Ommegang is a medieval tradition maintained today, which reenacts the royal entry of Charles V into the city in 1549, a proper and traditional welcome fit for a Holy Roman emperor. The festival has roots from the 14th century in a local legend, when a woman had a vision that the Virgin Mary instructed her to steal a statue from Antwerpen and bring it back to Brussels. The dates celebrating the miracle of her obtaining the statue and the entry of Charles V got combined into one event over the years.

During the Ommegang, more than 1,400 participants dress up as notable figures from Belgian history, such as Saint Gudula and the emperor himself. The procession begins in Sablon and ends in Grand Place. Visitors can enjoy the procession from the sidelines.

HELLO SUMMER

through the city; www.bruxelleslesbains.be; July/Aug.

Although Brussels is quite far from the beach, you can pretend you're on the coast via a series of pop-up "beaches" throughout the city in July and August, when real sand and performances celebrate summer in all its forms. Some of the beaches are along the Brussels Canal while others are placed on random squares throughout the city.

FOIRE DU MIDI

Boulevard du Midi; www.foiredumidi.site; July/Aug.

Brussels's Carnival is one of the biggest events of the year. For about a month, rides, food, and fun fill up Boulevard du Midi between Halle Gate and Anderlecht Gate in the center of Brussels.

BRUSSELS FLOWER CARPET

Grand Place; www.flowercarpet.brussels; every other Aug.

Tourists flock to Brussels for the distinctive Brussels Flower Carpet, a biennial event in which a carpet-like tapestry of more than a million flowers is spread across the ground of Grand Place. Since 1971, the festival has taken place with concerts and other entertainment, each year with a newly inspired theme.

MEYBOOM

throughout Brussels; Aug. 9

Meyboom is a charming Brussels tradition that dates back to 1308, one of the oldest customs in the region. Each August 9, a beech tree is planted at Rue des Sables and Rue du Marais. Similar to the maypole tradition, the tree is meant to mark the beginning of harvest festivals. It's said this specific tradition began with a festival dedicated to the Roman goddess Flora, where a tree taken from a nearby forest became the center of revelry. Today, a tree is still transported through the communes of Brussels in a long procession, which circles around Grand Place and other spots before being planted at 5pm, and is then removed the next day. Meyboom is footnote in the long feud between Brussels and Leuven, which also holds a version of the holiday. It's a fascinating insight into a tradition that has been maintained throughout the centuries.

Fall

BELGIAN BEER WEEKEND

Grand Place; www.belgianbrewers.be/en/events; first weekend in Sept.; €30

Beer lovers will not want to miss Belgian Beer Weekend. During the first weekend of September, more than 60,000 visitors come to Grand Place to celebrate Belgium's most famous export with breweries from all around Belgium.

HERITAGE DAYS BRUSSELS

throughout the city; https://visit.brussels/en/sites/heritage; Sept.

On Heritage Weekend, museums, European Parliament institutions, and lesser-known buildings usually closed to the public open their doors to visitors. Check the schedule for buildings that might strike your interest, or opt for a **walking tour** to learn more about the history of individual neighborhoods.

Winter

WINTER WONDERS/BRUSSELS CHRISTMAS MARKET

Grand Place; www.brussels.be/winter-wonders; end of Nov.-early Jan.

Brussels hosts one of Belgium's largest Christmas markets, running from the end of November through the first week of January. Streets surrounding Grand Place, and Grand Place itself, are pedestrianized and filled with more than 200 chalets selling food, drinks, and souvenirs. After dark, an hourly sound and light show plays against the backdrop of Grand Place.

Shopping

Brussels is a great destination for shopping, whether you love browsing flea markets or shopping independent labels at cozy high-end shops. The city has a number of glitzy neighborhoods home to world-famous designers, but you'll also find more affordable commercial streets, with charming stores selling gifts and stationery.

The most well-known spot for luxury shopping is certainly Avenue Louise in **Ixelles,** but the neighborhood also hosts more approachable shops, as does **Dansaert.** You'll also find quite a few **flea markets** throughout the city center during the week.

BRUSSELS CENTRUM

Running northeast starting a few blocks north of Grand Place, **Nieuwestraat,** or Rue Neuve, is the commercial heart of Brussels, with chain stores, budget-friendly clothing brands, and electronics stores in case you've forgotten your phone charger. And there are still a few hidden gems in this area if you know where to look! In addition to the upscale shops in the **Royal Galleries of Saint Hubert,** the art nouveau arcade **Passage du Nord** is just off Rue Neuve, and you'll find some charming boutiques and vintage shops on **Rue du Midi** between Rue des Grand Carmes and Rue du Lombard/Rue des Teinturiers.

Books

STANDARD BOEKHANDEL

Boulevard Anspach 28; www.standaardboekhandel.be; 9am-7pm Mon.-Thurs., 9am-7:30pm Fri., 9am-7pm Sat.

Standard Boekhandel is one of the best Belgian bookstores, with a great selection of books in both Dutch and English at their main location here in Brussels. Located in a modern mall northwest of Grand Place, it's worth the detour if you're looking for English books about Belgium; their English selection is well curated and the staff speaks three languages.

EVASIONS

Rue du Midi 89; www.evasions-livres.eu; 10am-8pm daily

Lovers of secondhand books will spend hours digging through the slightly musty, still charming Evasions bookshop. The multistory bookshop is filled from top to bottom with books in an assortment of languages, including English. The fiction section is

1: Ticky Tacky **2:** Marolles Flea Market **3:** Rose **4:** chocolates from Laurent Gerbaud

1
2
3
4
Kitty
FIGHT LIKE A GIRL
CUTE BUT PSYCHO
MONDAY YOU BASTARD
chérie

TOP EXPERIENCE

Brussels's Best Chocolatiers

Pierre Marcolini chocolates

Many of Belgium's best-known chocolatiers have their roots in Brussels, making the city a chocolate lover's paradise. The praline was invented here, by a pharmacist who hoped to disguise the terrible taste of some medicines with delicious chocolate, and Brussels's chocolatiers have worked hard to refine and improve upon the classics with sustainable sources and wild flavors ever since.

Though Belgian chocolate is famous all over the world, lesser known is that in each bite are layers of history, exploration, trade and exploitation. Cocoa beans were first brought to Belgium in the 17th century, when it was still ruled by the Spanish, who brought them from South American colonies. But it wasn't until the Belgians colonized the Congo that the country gained access to large quantities of the beans; by the late 19th and early 20th centuries, Belgium had gained the

quite impressive, and its prices are even better. Reaching the books can be a challenge in some cases, requiring a ladder, but that's part of the fun.

TROPISMES

Galerie des Princes 11; tel. 02 512 88 52; www.tropismes.com; 10am-6:30pm daily

One of Brussels's most beautiful bookstores is a nondescript shop just off a passage of the Royal Gallery of Saint Hubert. Once you enter, you can admire the ornate 19th-century ceiling, which is straight out of a period drama. The bookstore mainly carries French-language books and gifts, but it's a worthwhile trip if you are a bibliophile.

Souvenirs

BE COLOR

Rue du Lombard 5-9; www.becolor.be; 11am-7pm Tues.-Sat.

Be Color is a cute gift shop with quirky stationery, home décor, plants, and Brussels-themed decorations. Step into the roomy shop filled with colorful accents, and you're bound to find something that makes you smile.

SABLON

Flea Market

SABLON ANTIQUES MARKET (Antiekmarkt van de Zavel)

Place du Grand Sablon; 9am-6pm Sat., 9am-2pm Sun.

The Sablon Antiques Market is one of the best

upper hand in the cocoa and chocolate trade. Though a taste of rich Belgian chocolate can be a highlight of any trip to the country, it's important to remember that that sweet bite wouldn't be possible without access to the best cocoa beans, still often harvested by farmers in the former Congolese territory. Happily, the best Belgian chocolatiers are now obsessed with transparent and ethical sourcing of their cocoa beans.

Here are some of the best places to taste chocolate in Brussels:

NEUHAUS

Galerie de la Reine 25-27; tel. 02 512 63 59; www.neuhauschocolates.com; 11am-7pm Mon.-Fri., noon-8pm Sat.-Sun.

With locations all over Brussels, visit the Neuhaus shop in the Royal Galleries if you want to try a piece of history. This is the original location, where in 1857 Jean Neuhaus opened a pharmacy and covered his medicines in chocolate to make them go down easier.

LAURENT GERBAUD

Rue Ravenstein 2D; tel. 02 511 16 02; www.chocolatsgerbaud.be; noon-6pm Tues.-Thurs., noon-6:30pm Fri.-Sun.

Laurent Gerbaud operates a small shop close to BOZAR, creating delicious chocolates that are influenced by Belgian traditions as well as Asian ingredients.

PIERRE MARCOLINI

Rue des Tongres 69, tel. 02 733 03 62; https://eu.marcolini.com; 10:30am-6:30pm Tues.-Sat.

In the center of Sablon, Pierre Marcolini has become a household name in Brussels. It's hard to miss his flashy shop where chocolates are made with care.

WITTAMER

12 Place du Grand Sablon; tel. 02 512 37 42; www.wittamer.com; 9am-6pm Mon., 8am-7pm Tues., 7am-7pm Wed.-Sat., 7am-6:30pm Sun.

You'll also find Wittamer in Sablon, a family-owned chocolatier well known for desserts.

in Brussels, for high-end antiques from paintings to ceramics. Antiques dealers have been selling their wares here since the 1960s. The market is fairly small—just 64 stalls—with a laid-back yet sophisticated feel.

MAROLLES

Flea Market

MAROLLES FLEA MARKET

(Marché aux Puces des Marolles)

Place du Jeu de Balle; www.marcheauxpuces.be; 6am-2pm daily

If you're a bargain hunter, you'll want to rise early to browse the goods at Brussels's main flea market, which occurs daily at Place du Jeu de Balle. Laid out on the sidewalk in the center of the Marolles neighborhood, treasures mingle with junk galore, patrolled by both casual browsers and serious antique hunters. There has long been a market here, dating back to a secondhand clothing market in the 17th century. It's easy to spend a few hours here, marveling at finds from beautiful Louis XV furniture to delightful postcards. You're more likely to find rare pieces on weekends, though Thursdays and Fridays are also popular days for the sellers to bring extras. Most items don't have a price on them, so don't be afraid to ask—and to try your luck at haggling. The market is **cash only.**

Galleries

CALAVERAS

Rue des Renards 15; tel. 02 833 68 68; www.calaveras.be; 1pm-6pm Wed., 10am-6pm Thurs.-Sun.

Calaveras hosts a collective of Mexican and Belgian artists, who sell prints and stickers as well as bonefide art.

Souvenirs

TICKY TACKY

Rue des Renards 28; tel. 02 502 88 61; 10:30am-6pm Wed.-Mon.

Ticky Tacky is a retro-inspired home décor and stationery store in the heart of Marolles. The shop has a cheerful and eclectic interior, with goods from quirky cards and stationery to retro-inspired maps. Downstairs they sell furniture and home goods, some of which are decorated with retro images of Brussels and make a lovely souvenir.

DANSAERT

Dansaert is a great place to find independent shops, one of the hippest areas in Brussels for local brands and concept stores. You'll find everything here, from high-end clothing brands to one of Brussels's best bookstores, to an excellent monthly flea market.

Books

PASSA PORTA

Rue Antoine Dansaert 46; tel. 02 502 94 60; www.passaporta.be; 11am-7pm Mon.-Sat., noon-6pm Sun.

Passa Porta is the largest independent bookstore in Brussels. It's very much the intellectual's bookstore, the place to come for thoughtfully picked books in English, Dutch, and French and to rub shoulders with Brussels's writing community at workshops and readings.

Clothing and Accessories

HUNTING AND COLLECTING

Rue des Chartreux 17; tel. 02 512 74 77; www.huntingandcollecting.com; 2pm-6pm Mon., 11am-7pm Tues.-Sat.

Hunting and Collecting is a Brussels-born concept store with a stylish selection of more than 30 clothing brands for adults and children along with lifestyle accessories. The interior is beautifully designed, almost like an art exhibition. For true fashionistas, this stylish store is likely to have some unusual pieces that you won't find as easily elsewhere.

Flea Markets

BRUSSELS VINTAGE MARKET

Place Saint-Géry 1; https://brusselsvintagemarket.be; noon-7pm first Sun. of each month

Lovers of secondhand clothing should time their visit with the Sunday Brussels Vintage Market, which occurs once a month throughout the city, typically within the spacious **Halles Saint-Géry** (Place Saint-Géry 1, tel. 02 502 44 24; www.sintgorikshallen.be; 10am-midnight daily), which also hosts a bar and sometimes art shows and other events. The ambiance skews heavily hipster and millennial, with DJs playing sets while people browse retro favorites from different eras, from stereos to cozy sweaters. The market is **cash only.**

IXELLES

Louizalaan, or **Avenue Louise,** is one of Brussels's grandest streets for shopping, a tree-lined avenue with wide sidewalks. You'll find high-end brands from Chanel to Zadig & Voltaire here.

Souvenirs

LULU HOME INTERIOR & CAFÉ

Rue du Page 101; tel. 02 537 25 03; www.luluhomeinterior.be; 10:30am-7pm Tues.-Sat., 10:30am-6pm Sun.

Lulu Home Interior & Café is a unique concept store and café where you can enjoy a coffee while you shop for modern and trendy home goods within a spacious brick-lined shop.

ROSE

Rue de l'Aqueduc 56; tel. 0474 36 88 57; 10:30am-6pm Mon., 10:30am-6:30pm Tues.-Sat.

Rose is one of the most charming gift shops in Brussels, where you're likely to find that perfect present for your friend who is impossible to shop for. Their rotating selection skews satirical, smart, and feminist, but you'll also find items with uniquely Belgian designs from the popular Belgian brand Bshirt.

SAINT GILLES

Books

TIPI BOOKSHOP

Rue de l'Hôtel des Monnaies 186; tel. 0478 95 68 41; https://tipi-bookshop.be; 10am-5pm Mon.-Tues., 10am-5pm Thurs.-Sat.

Artists and art lovers should stop by Tipi Bookshop, a small independent bookstore specializing in photography books, especially ones that are self-published or from small publishers. With ladders to reach the higher shelves, it's a small but charming stop in Saint Gilles.

Clothing and Accessories

FAÇON JACMIN STUDIO BRUSSELS

Rue du Fort 67; tel. 0474 33 02 55; www.faconjacmin.com; 10:30am-12:30pm and 2pm-6pm Mon.-Fri.

Façon Jacmin is a Belgian fashion brand that focuses on sustainability and denim with a nod to the 1970s. Run by two sisters, the brand is a favorite among Brussels fashionistas.

Food

Just as much as Paris or London, Brussels is truly a foodie capital, from its fine dining, to Congolese food and Asian favorites, to Belgian *frites* served fresh from the local fries stand. No matter what you love, you're likely to find it here, thanks to Brussels's extremely international population that loves an excuse for a nice meal out. If you're a chocolate lover, you will be spoiled for choices among Brussels's chocolatiers. The best restaurants in Brussels require **reservations,** especially on the weekends.

As the Belgian capital, Brussels is a great spot to find typical Belgian foods as well. At snack bars and pubs, you'll find ***frikandel,*** a traditional, deep fried sausage. Another hearty favorite, ***carbonnade*** (sometimes spelled carbonade) is a traditional beef stew, made with dark beer. Crispy **shrimp croquettes** are ubiquitous on menus across the capital, as are Belgian-style mussels, or ***moules-frites,*** usually stewed in white wine.

One of the hallmarks of any Brussels park is the ever-present waffle truck. Bring a bit of cash, as these are some of the best, freshest **waffles** you'll find throughout the city, and they won't break the bank at €2.50-3 per piece. Most of the appeal is in taking the waffle to enjoy in a scenic point of your choice.

BRUSSELS CENTRUM

International

DIMENSION LATINA

Rue du Midi 96; tel. 02 512 27 79; noon-2:30pm, 6:30pm-9pm Mon.-Thurs, noon-2:30pm, 7pm-10pm Fri., noon-2:30pm, 6:30pm-10pm Sat.; €7-12

Dimension Latina is a casual Peruvian restaurant best known for its affordable lunch specials, one of the best deals in the center of Brussels. How often can you find a delicious chicken sandwich served with sweet potato chips for just €5? For a little extra, you can add soup and a drink. The establishment is cash-only and a favorite of area locals who skip the many touristy restaurant in favor of this cozy establishment.

★ WOLF

Wolvengracht 50; https://wolf.brussels; noon-10pm Sun.-Thurs., noon-11pm Fri.-Sat.; €10

Wolf is a new food court in Brussels that hosts an assortment of affordable dining options, from Syrian to authentic Italian pizza. With modern light fixtures and a Scandinavian aesthetic, it's a great spot for groups due to its many options and affordable drinks (including house-brewed beverages). It's just 500 meters (1,600 feet) from Brussels Central Train Station and the city center.

BAOGO

Rue Grétry 48/50; tel. 02 203 07 33; www.baogo.be; noon-10:30pm daily; €12

BaoGo is a concept restaurant that combines delicious burgers with steamed bao buns. Despite its location in the center of Brussels around the corner from the famous Delirium Café and the Royal Galleries of Saint Hubert, Baogo offers affordable meals with a side of fries. It's an uncommonly good value for the location.

SABLON

Cafés and Light Bites

COCO DONUTS SABLON

Rue Sainte-Anne 36; tel. 02 513 24 60; https://sablon.cocodonutsbrussels.be; 10:30am-6pm daily; €4

Coco Donuts is a cheerful donut shop in Sablon with beautiful flower displays, photogenic quotes, and a great selection of donuts, from standard flavors to wild innovations. Hidden down one of Sablon's charming streets, Rue Sainte-Anne, Coco is a cozy spot in the neighborhood to stop for a coffee

International

★ LA PIZZA È BELLA

Rue Lebeau 75; tel. 02 512 01 70; https://lapizzaebella.be; noon-2:30pm, 6pm-10pm Tues.-Thurs., noon-2:30pm, 6pm-10:30pm Fri.-Sun.; €12-15

If you ask around for the best pizzeria in Brussels, if not Belgium, many will name La Pizza è Bella. Portions are hearty, and pizzas have a beautiful, crisp crust. The Neapolitan owner comes from a family of pizza makers, and he imports the ingredients from Naples for that authentic taste of Italy in each bite.

MAROLLES

You'll find a concentration of atmospheric cafés along romantic **Rue des Renards.**

Belgian

BROEBBELEIR MAROLLES

Place du Jeu de Balle 62; https://lesvignesduliban.be; 11am-3pm, 5pm-10pm Mon.-Thurs., 11am-3pm, 5pm-11pm Fri., 11am-11pm Sat., 11am-10pm Sun.; €5

A good *fritterie* is beloved by every Belgian. Broebbeleir Marolles serves up organic *frites* and organic mayo with local Brussels-made beers and other fried Belgian foods, like *frikandel,* a pork sausage. Just across from the Marolles Flea Market, Broebbeleir serves up their delicious fries in a beautiful building, a former 19th-century fire station. The top stories of the building provide pretty views over the flea market with skylights and wide windows.

Cafés and Light Bites

THE JUDGY VEGAN CAFÉ & BAR

Rue des Capucins 55; tel. 02 540 80 38; www.thejudgyvegan.com; 6pm-10:30pm Thurs.-Fri., 11am-10:30pm Sat., 11am-6:30pm Sun.; €14

Despite its name, the Judgy Vegan is an inclusive and friendly café with delicious vegetarian and vegan meals that will please even meat-eaters. With a hippie vibe inside, it's a great spot lunch after perusing the flea market.

DANSAERT

Belgian

FIN DE SIÈCLE

Rue des Chartreux 9; tel. 02 732 74 34; 6pm-midnight daily; €17

For no-frills Belgian favorites, head to the ever-popular Fin de Siècle, a Belgian bistro best known for their beef slow-cooked in beer (*carbonnade,* also spelled *carbonade*) as well as other meat dishes that are literally soaked in beer. Despite being a few blocks from Brussels Center, the prices at this cozy bistro make it a steal for sampling some Belgian favorites. Reservations are not accepted.

International

★ DAM SUM PLACE SAINTE-CATHERINE

Quai au Bois à Brûler 51; tel. 02 446 07 86; www.damsum.com; 6:30pm-10:30pm Wed.-Sat.; €21

Dam Sum is a well-known Chinese restaurant

1: La Pizza è Bella **2:** *frites* at Broebbeleir Marolles **3:** Noordzee **4:** mussels at Aux Vieux

1
100 % MADE IN
2
3
ABC
4

that serves fresh dim sum favorites made with local ingredients à la carte. It's beautifully decorated with modern design elements, a perfect place for a group dinner. Dam Sum is best known for their filled xiao long bao, or soup dumplings.

Seafood

★ NOORDZEE - MER DU NORD

Place Sainte-Catherine 50; tel. 02 513 11 92; https://noordzeemerdunord.be; 11am-6pm Tues.-Sat., 11am-4pm Sun.; €10-15

Noordzee is a Brussels institution in the vicinity of Saint Catherine Church. If you love fish, don't miss it fresh off the fryer here, along with North Sea shrimp croquettes at their best. Many Brusselois come here for brunch to start off the weekend with a bit of seafood and a glass of champagne to wash it down, on the steps of Saint Catherine or seated underneath their tent in poor weather.

EUROPEAN DISTRICT

Belgian

MAISON ANTOINE

Place Jourdan 1; tel. 02 230 54 56; www.maisonantoine.be; noon-10pm daily; €3

Classic snack hut Maison Antoine is a *frites* mainstay, serving up deliciously crispy fried potatoes since 1948, alongside other quick and satisfying snacks like burgers and croquettes.

International

LE MEZZE

Chaussée de Louvain 228; tel. 02 361 43 56; www.le-mezze.be; 11am-2pm, 6pm-9pm Mon.-Sat.; €14-20

Le Mezze is a Syrian Lebanese restaurant that's known, not surprisingly, for their hearty mixed appetizer platter, or *mezze,* well suited to couples or groups. Alongside a set menu that mixes *mezzes* and an appetizer for €20, they also offer à la carte entrees. The dining area typically fills up quickly on weekends.

Vegan and Vegetarian

LE BOTANISTE

Rue Franklin 2; tel. 02 646 44 47; http://lebotaniste.be; noon-3pm, 6pm-9:30pm Mon.-Sat.; €14.50

Le Botaniste is a trendy vegan-friendly, gluten-free restaurant that provides healthy and delicious vegan versions of popular dishes from around the world, from Morocco to Tibet. You'll also find salads and glasses of wine to pair with your meal. Their small space is a great spot for a meal close to Parc du Cinquantenaire.

IXELLES

Belgian

FRIT FLAGEY

Place Eugène Flagey; 11:30am-midnight Tues.-Sun.; €3

Of the countless food trucks selling *frites* scattered around Brussels, Frit Flagey is a perennial favorite, simply selling *frites* with a variety of sauces, from mayonnaise to aioli and doing it well.

★ AUX VIEUX

Rue Saint-Boniface 35; tel. 02 503 31 11; www.auvieuxbruxelles.com; 6pm-11:30pm Mon.-Thurs., 6pm-midnight Fri.-Sat., 6pm-11pm Sun.; €27

For a taste of Brussels-style mussels, Aux Vieux is one of the most atmospheric options. This old-time café has been serving up delicious Belgian cuisine since 1881, and within the café, you'll find tables that wouldn't look out of place in a small village outside Brussels. Despite sitting on one of the city's hippest squares with a lovely terrace, the café feels like a time capsule from the past. Credit cards accepted.

Brunch

BELGA & CO

Rue du Bailli 7A; tel. 02 644 14 98; www.belgacoffee.com; 8am-5:30pm Mon.-Fri., 9am-5:30pm Sat.-Sun.; €7

Belga & Co is a popular Brussels café and breakfast spot for a slow lunch or brunch while chatting with friends or reading a newspaper. The interior is minimalistic with a hidden terrace in the back for a bit of air in good weather. With great coffee, Belga & Co is an affordable option for brunch on weekends, with favorites like smoked salmon sandwiches and an assortment of jams, meats, and bread.

Matonge, Brussels's African Neighborhood

The year 2020 marked 60 years of independence from Belgian colonial rule for the Demographic Republic of the Congo (DRC). During this time, Matonge, a neighborhood in the eastern part of Brussels named for a lively part of Kinshasa, has attracted visitors and residents from the DRC, who often moved to Belgium to study, often staying in hostels that provided a home away from home for African students. A neighborhood has grown along Chausée de Wavre with everything from African grocery shops to restaurants offering pan-African foods. Be sure spend a few hours strolling, browsing, and tasting this vibrant neighborhood.

- Try Congolese food at the well-known **Restaurant Congolais Inzia,** often with live music (page 225).
- The Senegalese chicken at **Au Soleil d'Afrique** is definitely worth a stop (page 226).
- To learn more, visit the **Kuumba** cultural center (Chaussée de Wavre 78; tel. 0476 71 37 92; www.kuumba.be; 4pm-9pm Wed.-Fri.; tours €90/group), which offers tours of Matonge's African culture, food, and music as well as concerts and workshops.

Matonge neighborhood with Place du Saint Boniface

International

KNEES TO CHIN

Rue de Livourne 125; tel. 02 644 18 11; www.kneestochin.com; 11:30am-2pm, 6pm-9pm Mon.-Sat.; €9-11.50

Knees to Chin is a Vietnamese restaurant specializing in rice rolls. The female-led chef team comes exclusively from Vietnam, and their menu is inspired by street food. Two to three rolls is enough for a meal, served alongside dishes and soups. You'll recognize their shop by the bright neon sign outside. It's a fairly casual place and a great option for takeout.

LES FILS À MAMAN

Rue Fourmois 29; tel. 02 534 56 26; www.lesfilsamaman.com; noon-2:30pm, 7pm-11pm Mon.-Fri., noon-3pm, 7pm-11pm Sat., 11:30am-3pm Sun.; €12-25

For a taste of homestyle French food, head to Les Fils à Maman, which means "the mother's sons," a popular French chain that serves hearty fixed-price meals that won't break your budget. Their menu changes regularly using seasonal ingredients, and it's a favorite for weekend brunch. The interior is eclectic, with red booths and nostalgic décor, and the service is friendly.

RESTAURANT CONGOLAIS INZIA

Rue de la Paix 37; tel. 0485 06 97 37; https://lapiolapizza.com; noon-3pm, 6:30pm-11:30pm Tues.-Sat.; €16

If you're visiting Matonge, you have to try Congolese food. Restaurant Congolais Inzia, serves a Congolese buffet along with a friendly explanation of traditional Congolese cuisine. The palm and peanut chicken (Moambe Chicken) is a highlight. Be sure to come hungry as the portions are large and the staff provides a warm welcome even for first-time visitors.

AU SOLEIL D'AFRIQUE

Rue Longue Vie 10; tel. 0486 30 26 40; 5:30pm-midnight Mon.-Sat., 5:30pm-11:30pm Sun.; €7-9

This brightly decorated little Senegalese restaurant serves delicious platters of traditional dishes at an affordable price; the chicken is excellent, though vegetarian options are also available.

SAINT GILLES

Belgian

PARDON

Rue de Moscou 36; tel. 0479 16 40 17; www.facebook.com/pardonbrussels; 11am-6pm Wed.-Mon.; €5-8

For the best waffles in Brussels, head to Pardon, a café that focuses on perfecting the Belgian waffle with organic ingredients. All their Brussels-style waffles are served fresh, which is how a waffle should be served. You can top your waffle with sweet or savory ingredients, but powdered sugar is the classic. They also serve a variation on the Liege-style waffle, which is a bit sweeter and fluffier than Brussels-style. Try both side by side, possibly with Nutella, to taste the difference. Brunch and lunch on weekends are delicious—with plenty of waffles, of course.

International

MO MO

Avenue des Villas 7; tel. 02 850 72 48; https://mo-mo.eu; noon-2pm, 7pm-10pm Tues.-Wed., noon-3pm, 7pm-10pm Thurs.-Sat.; €10

Momo is a cozy Tibetan restaurant in the heart of Saint Gilles that serves up hearty vegetarian Tibetan dumplings, soup, and steamed vegetables in a modern space with a lovely terrace, overlooking a residential part of Saint Gilles. In the evenings, prices go up a little, but Mo Mo remains a Saint Gilles staple for affordable vegan food. Dinner reservations are recommended, especially on Saturdays.

LE KALU ETHNIC FOOD

83 Rue de l'église; tel. 0488 23 66 42; www.facebook.com/LeKaluEthnic; 2pm-9:30pm Mon.-Sat.; €15

Le Kalu is an Afro-Caribbean restaurant serving delicious food from Trinidad and Tobago at reasonable prices, a great option for takeout—the restaurant itself is fairly cramped. They're best known for their chicken and beef, but the crispy banana balls and mac and cheese are also not to be missed.

Markets

MIDI MARKET (Marché du Midi)

Avenue Fonsny; www.brusselslife.be/en/article/midi-market; 6am-2pm Sun.

On Sunday mornings, more than 450 stalls showcase their wares to visitors at this this often intense and loud, but fun to explore, market with food, spices, and other specialty items near Midi station. The market's ready-to-eat stalls that serve food is a favorite weekend spot among locals for a quick yet filling lunch. The Moroccan pancakes are the best-known option for lunch!

LAEKEN

International

BROOKLYN FOOD

Rue de Wand 45; tel. 0494 08 68 88; noon-11pm Mon.-Sat., 4pm-10:30pm Sun.; €9

There aren't many food options close to the Royal Greenhouses, but Brooklyn Food is one of the best. It's classic American with burgers served in a space that's clearly inspired by American diners. It's a good option for lunch.

1: Mo Mo **2:** Congolese food **3:** Pardon brunch

1

2

3

Bars and Nightlife

Although Brussels certainly does not have the nightlife of Amsterdam, the bar scene here may surprise you, from perfectly paired beer served at restaurants to beautiful and unique bars with unparalleled atmosphere and history. You'll also find cozy, divey brown bars, often called *estaminets* in Brussels, along with a new breed of craft beer bars that celebrate the ingenuity of Belgium's beer culture. Brussels certainly has clubs, too, and many bars turn into a dance party a certain hour. The most atmospheric bars tend to be outside the city center, but you can still find a number of establishments here that are not overrun by tourists.

Brussels is known for **lambic** style beers, produced much in the same way since the 13th century. Lambics can range from sweet to sour and mouth puckering to smooth and complex. The best-known variety is the **geuze,** which is a mix of aged lambics. **Kriek** is a popular style of lambic brewed with cherries, which are traditionally grown in the region. Not all lambics are the same quality, as many are artificially sweetened with syrups rather than traditionally brewed. For those not a fan of sour beers, **witbier,** a cloudy white beer, is a favorite.

One of the beers that you'll see all over Brussel is the **Brasserie de la Senne** (www.brasseriedelasenne.be), which is produced right outside the city center. They specialize in unfiltered craft beers inspired by classic Belgian varieties. Newbies to Belgian beer might enjoy the traditional **Zinne Bier** pale ale, which is sold at restaurants all around Brussels.

BRUSSELS CENTRUM

Bars

POECHENELLEKELDER

Rue du Chêne 5; tel. 02 511 92 62; https://poechenellekelder.be; 11am-1am Tues-Sun.

You'd expect a bar across from Manneken Pis to be complete tourist trap, but the Poechenellekelder is a bit of a surprise. The bar, on top of a staircase with windows overlooking the surrounding street, is a quiet place to taste favorite local beers and snack on Brussels's cheese. The main attraction is the over-the-top decorations, with puppets and wall-to-ceiling framed Brussels memorabilia.

★ GIST

Place de la Vieille Halle aux Blés 30; tel. 02 512 70 06; https://gistbeerandco.business.site; 4pm-11pm Tues.-Sun.

Gist is a hip Belgian beer bar for lovers of vinyl, craft beer, and local culture. Despite being a short walk away from Mannekin Pis, the bar feels very much like a neighborhood spot due to its friendly owners, who make everyone feel at home. The inside is no frills, with a small terrace outside for warmer nights. Come for the beer and the company!

A LA MORT SUBITE

Rue Montagne aux Herbes Potagères 7; tel. 02 513 13 18; www.alamortsubite.com; 11am-1am Mon.-Sat, noon-midnight Sun.

A la Morte Subite is a classic Belgian café best known for its fruity *kriek* beers, named after a dice game called Sudden Death. The interior is a beautiful example of a Louis XVI-style interior from the early 20th century, with giant mirrors and gold accents. The café is still family-owned and is a beautiful place to enjoy a beer after exploring Brussels Centrum.

GOUPIL LE FOL

Rue de la Violette 22; tel. 02 511 13 96; www.goupillefol.com; 4pm-2am daily

Goupil Le Fol might be the strangest wine bar you'll find in Brussels. It's easy to get lost in this maze of a café, with furniture that looks

1: Poechenellekelder **2:** Brussels Beer Project **3:** Brasserie Cantillon

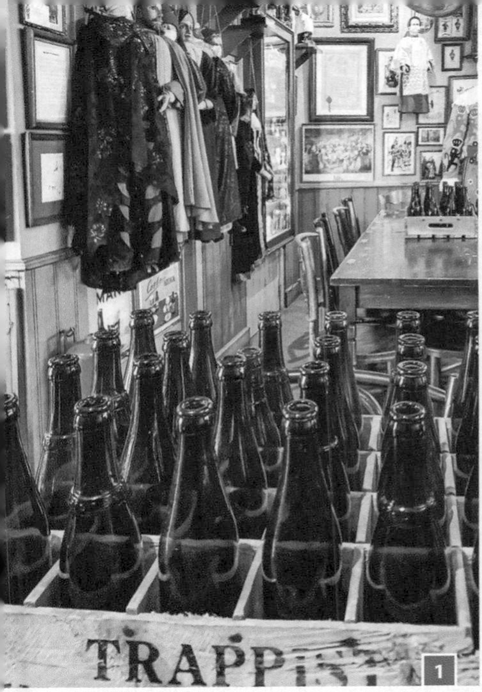

TRAPPIST
1
DELTA IPA 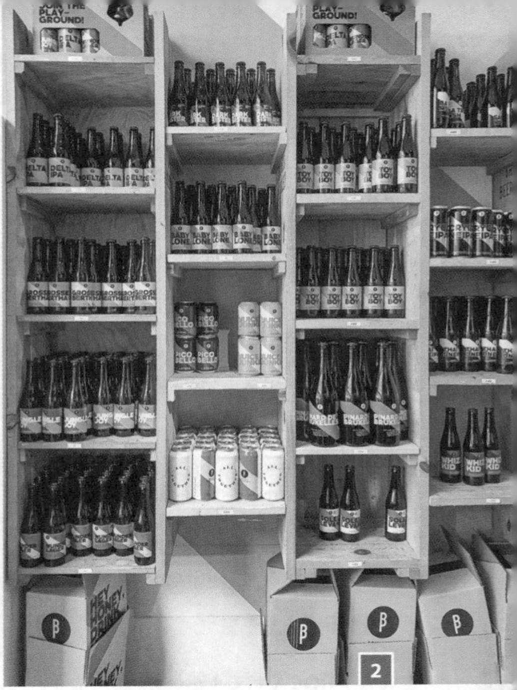
DARK SISTER
TOY BOY
BABY LONE
GROSSE BERTHA
JUICY BELLE
JUNGLE JOY
PINARD BRUXELLES
WHIZ KID
HEY HONEY DRINK
2 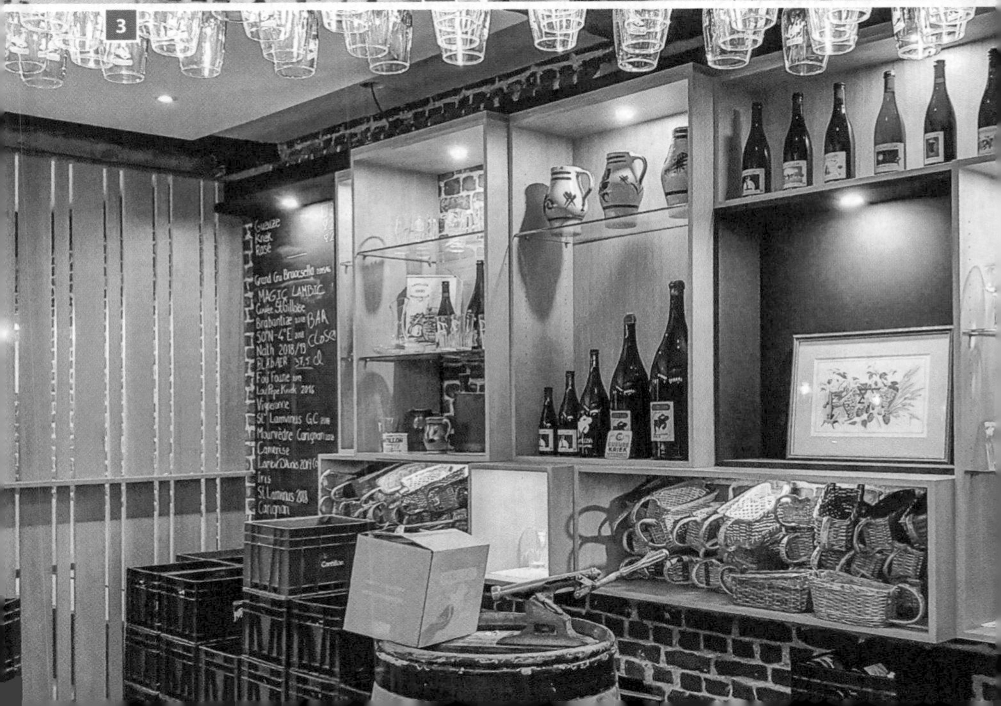
3
Gueuze
Kriek
Rosé
Grand Cru Bruocsella
MAGIC LAMBIC
Cuvée St Gilloise
Lou Pepe Kriek 2016
Vigneronne
Camerise
Iris
St Lamvinus 2018
Carignan

like it belongs to a grandmother and paintings practically stacked on top of each other, with no corner left untouched. It's a great experience away from the crowds of Grand Place.

DELIRIUM CAFÉ

Impasse de la Fidélité 4; tel. 02 514 44 34; www.deliriumvillage.com; 3pm-11pm Mon.-Thurs., 2pm-11pm Fri.-Sun.

Delirium Café is a spacious bar at the end of the alleyway home to Jeanneke Pis, as well as eight other bars in the "Delirium Village" family. The Café holds the world's record for the most beers available at a café (2,004). A checklist for many travelers, it's a surprisingly decent place to step in for a drink, especially in the late afternoons before it gets too busy. You'll of course find Delirium on tap, but the Trappist beer selection is also worth studying. There is live music on Thursday nights.

MAROLLES

Bars

LA BROCANTE

Rue Blaes 170; tel. 02 512 13 43; 6am-10pm daily

Located on the square overlooking the Marolles Flea Market, the cozy and lovingly dated bar La Brocante has more than 200 beers available and a friendly cat to greet you. The interior has not changed much in the last 30 years, and they feature beer from a number of local breweries, including Brasserie de la Senne. It's a cozy, cash-only spot for a drink after browsing the flea market. Coffee and tea along with typical Belgian foods (meatloaf and *stoemp*, mashed potatoes with vegetables) are available.

DANSAERT

Bars

LE ROI DES BELGES

Rue Jules Van Praet 35; tel. 02 503 43 00; 9am-1am daily

Le Roi des Belges is a cozy two-story bar on the Place Saint-Géry. The main attraction is their classic Belgian beer menu and a seat facing the sidewalk, a great spot to people-watch in the open air without spending a fortune not far from Brussels's Centrum.

Breweries

BRUSSELS BEER PROJECT

Rue Antoine Dansaert 188; tel. 02 502 28 56; www.beerproject.be; 2pm-8pm Wed.-Sat., 1pm-6pm Sun.

Brussels Beer Project is a crowdsourced brewery begun by two amateur beer lovers who simply wanted to make alternatives to traditional Belgian beers—hard to find in Brussels. The project has been a smashing success, and you can sample their latest and greatest at the surprisingly spacious café with a large seating area in the back and a small sidewalk terrace.

Live Music

★ L'ARCHIDUC

Rue Antoine Dansaert 6; www.archiduc.net; 4pm-1am daily

L'Archiduc is a classic Belgian establishment best known for its live music and its beautiful art deco interior with smooth lines. A place for brokers and secretaries to have a drink together in private after work, in the 1950s, this bar became part of jazz history thanks to Nat King Cole and Miles Davis, who were friends of the late owner. The café continues its proud jazz tradition while serving up delicious cocktails. Stepping inside feels like entering a time machine.

EUROPEAN DISTRICT

Bars

CAFÉ LUXEMBOURG

Place du Luxembourg 10; tel. 02 721 57 15; www.cafeluxembourg.be; 4pm-10pm Mon.-Fri.

If you're interested in catching up on European Parliament politics, the Café Luxembourg is the place to be on Thursday night, Parliament's after-work party. The café serves everything from cocktails to juices for those on a health kick. It's a surprisingly fun spot despite the seemingly buttoned-up crowd.

PYTHON BEER CELLAR

Avenue Emile Max 55; www.facebook.com/PythonCraftBeer; 4pm-midnight daily

Python is a modern beer shop/café/bar, with an open terrace that spills onto the sidewalk. It's a quiet oasis with a chill atmosphere amid the business of the European District. The staff know their beers extremely well, which make this a great place to try new beers; they often have 8-10 on tap.

IXELLES

Bars

★ LA LUCK

Rue Washington 74; tel. 0476 17 45 28; https://la-luck.com; 6pm-midnight Tues.-Thurs., 6pm-1am Fri., noon-1am Sat.,11am-10pm Sun.

La Luck is a board game bar and café with more than 1,000 games, ranging from modern to classic. They serve a selection of local beers, nonalcoholic drinks, and some delicious food if you get hungry. There's a cute cobblestone-lined terrace in the summer.

Cocktail Bars

LE STOEFER

Rue de l'Aqueduc 103; tel. 02 851 70 09; https://lestoefer.be; 5pm-8pm Wed.-Sat.

Le Stoefer, or "the braggart," is one of the city's best cocktail bars, located in a trendy district of Ixelles. The interior is richly decorated with leather sofas, a wood-paneled bar, and a brick-lined wall. Although the cocktails are certainly pricey, the choice of liquors is almost unlimited, and the flavor combinations range from traditional to complex.

SAINT GILLES

Bars

MOEDER LAMBIC ORIGINAL

Rue de Savoie 68; tel. 02 544 16 99; www.moederlambic.com; 4pm-midnight daily

Moeder Lambic Original is Brussels's best-known craft beer bar, where you'll find a fantastic seasonal selection of Belgian beers. Beer lovers flock to this unpretentious corner café to get into spirited debates over the best beers with the staff and other patrons. As may be expected, they carry an impressive collection of lambics, a strong sour beer.

Breweries

★ BRASSERIE CANTILLON

Rue Gheude 56; tel. 02 521 49 28; www.cantillon.be; 10am-5pm Mon.-Tues., 10am-5pm Thurs.-Sat.

In the heart of a working-class neighborhood a short walk (500 meters/1,600 feet) from Brussels South, you'll find an ancient relic from Brussels's brewing past. Cantillon is a family-run brewery established in 1900, still brewing in Brussels using original methods. Geuze beers, their specialty, utilize spontaneous fermentation, a tricky process that can be seen by the public here at the last traditional brewery in Brussels. You can also purchase rare bottles at their shop, or tour the historic brewery on Mondays, Tuesdays, Thursdays, and Fridays (€7), as well as on Saturdays (€9.50).

Accommodations

Brussels has surprisingly affordable hotels compared to many cities in Belgium. In this major hub for business and government, hotels tend to be clustered in the city center and European District, but more indie options have opened in upcoming communes like Dansaert as more weekend tourists discover Brussels's charm. Unusually, rooms tend to be cheaper on weekends than weekdays due to the prevalence of business travelers, who often return home before the weekend.

The location of your hotel doesn't matter so much, thanks to Brussels's very walkable center and efficient Metro. Saint Gilles and Ixelles are great neighborhoods for visitors who want the local experience and access to Brussels's best food.

BRUSSELS CENTRUM

Under €100

SLEEP WELL

Rue du Damier 23; tel. 02 218 50 50; www.sleepwell.be; €55

Sleep Well is a one-star hotel and hostel on the northern side of Brussels Center, on a fairly quiet commercial street about two blocks from the comic book museum. The rooms are nothing to write home about, but for the price and the surprisingly social lounge, it's a great place to crash if you're only in Brussels for a short time. They offer individual rooms as well as shared accommodations.

€100-200

★ THE DOMINICAN

Rue Léopold 9; tel. 02 203 08 08; www.carlton.nl; €166

Named after the 15th-century abbey that once stood on this site, this 150-room boutique hotel has retained much of its monastic charm thanks to atmospheric arches and the Gregorian chanting that plays in the background of the elevator rides. The hotel's facade is early 19th century, the former home of painter Jacques-Louis David. The interior has luxury touches, from a boxing room, a spa, a private courtyard, and a built-in restaurant/café.

Over €200

HOTEL HUBERT

Rue d'Arenberg 18; tel. 02 548 18 18; www.hotelhubert-brussels.be; €215

Hotel Hubert is a well-located hotel inspired by Brussels's art nouveau past, just around the corner from the Royal Galleries of Saint Hubert. If you're looking for a central hotel for a weekend away in Brussels, this one offers a number of amenities, including 24/7 gym access, a modern lobby, self-check-in/out, and air-conditioning. Only one room is handicap accessible.

SABLON

Over €200

HOTEL NH COLLECTION BRUSSELS GRAND SABLON

Rue Bodenbroek 2; tel. 02 518 11 00; www.nh-hotels.nl; €208

NH Collection Brussels Grand Sablon is a four-star hotel with 196 rooms in the heart of Sablon, with a gym, meeting rooms, air-conditioning, on-site parking (€30/day), 24-hour reception, and a beautiful view of one of Brussels's most beautiful districts, close to the Royal Museums of Fine Arts of Belgium.

DANSAERT

€100-200

HOTEL SAINT-GÉRY

29-32 Place Saint-Géry; tel. 02 204 06 20; www.hotelstgery.com; €103

This small boutique hotel a very short walk from Grand Place is located next to the buzzing Halles Saint Géry (Place Saint-Géry 1; tel. 02 502 44 24; www.sintgorikshallen.be; 10am-midnight daily), a bar and exhibition space. The interior is modern, and each room is artist-designed. The hotel is also known for its jazz bar, **De Belmonte** (tel. 02 204 06 22; www.debelmonte.be; 3pm-1am Thurs.-Sat.), where you can enjoy a cocktail and some blues.

EUROPEAN DISTRICT

Under €100

★ MARTIN'S BRUSSELS EU

Boulevard Charlemagne 80; tel. 02 230 85 55; www.martinshotels.com; €89

Martin's is a popular Belgian hotel chain that specializes in comfortable rooms for business travelers. This location is a short walk from EU headquarters, which makes it more affordable on weekends when the business travelers go home. The rooms, often dressed in red, feature a desk, high-speed Wi-Fi, a mini fridge with a complimentary beverage, air-conditioning, and access to a fitness club. The hotel is about 10 minutes from the center by Metro.

€100-200

RADISSON RED BRUSSELS

Rue d'Idalie 35; tel. 02 626 81 11; www.radissonhotels.com; €176

The Radisson Red caters to both business and leisure travelers. Rooms are decorated with a bright and modern red-and-yellow palette with business hotel amenities like a fitness center and restaurant.

IXELLES

Under €100

JARDIN SECRET

Rue du Berger 22; tel. 02 510 83 49; https://jardinsecrethotel.be; €91

Jardin Secret is one of Brussels's best-kept secrets for a romantic weekend away. This small boutique hotel has a hidden entrance behind a fake plant shop that leads to a leafy garden, which many of the hotel's modern rooms look out onto. A bit of serenity in the heart of the trendy Saint Boniface area.

€100-200

★ MADE IN LOUISE

Rue Veydt 40; tel. 02 537 40 33; www.madeinlouise.com; €126

Made in Louise is one of Brussels's best-known boutique hotels with just 48 rooms, some of which overlook the courtyard and others with views of the Ixelles neighborhood. The rooms all have different quirks to them, but in general expect comfortable appointments and upscale decorations at this thoughtful hotel footsteps from the chic Avenue Louise. There's a private courtyard, a bar where you can enjoy a Belgian beer, and a lounge with a fireplace for colder nights.

HYGGE HOTEL

Rue des Drapiers 31-33; tel. 02 274 28 00; www.hyggehotel.be; €149

Named after the Scandinavian concept of coziness, *hygge*, this hotel in the heart of Ixelles aims to make its guests feel at home. The interior is well designed, with neutral colors, a beautiful staircase that feels straight out of a movie, and modern Scandinavian décor. There's a lovely private garden/terrace to enjoy in good weather.

QBIC HOTELS BRUSSELS

Rue Paul Spaak 15; tel. 02 645 61 11; https://qbichotels.com; €162

Get all the perks of a four-star hotel and more for a bargain at Qbic, a trendy pet-friendly hotel that offers amenities including a private cinema, a gym, and karaoke. Their rooms are eco-friendly with comfortable beds, perfect for a good night's sleep between going out for dinner along Rue du Bailli and enjoying the art nouveau on the surrounding streets.

HOTEL BARSEY BY WARWICK

381-383 Avenue Louise; tel. 02 641 51 30; www.warwickhotels.com; €178

Hotel Barsey by Warwick is a four-star

hotel with an understated elegance perfect for luxury or business travelers looking for extra comfort. This notably family- and pet-friendly hotel with a fitness center and private underground parking is about 15 minutes outside of central Ixelles's most popular streets, but only footsteps from the charming Abbaye de la Cambre and Bois de la Cambre parks.

SAINT GILLES

Under €100

★ JAM HOTEL

Chaussée de Charleroi 132; tel. 02 537 17 87; www.jamhotel.be; €60

Jam Hotel is a hip and affordable option, decorated with wood almost everywhere. Access to Saint Gilles makes this trendy hotel popular with twenty- and thirtysomethings. The top floor offers stunning views of Brussels along with a long, skinny pool where you can sip a cocktail from their hotel bar. The rooms can be noisy due to traffic.

€100-200

PANTONE HOTEL

Place Loix 1; tel. 02 541 48 98; www.pantonehotel.com; €109

If you're often inspired by colors, you will love the Pantone Hotel, where each floor is themed with a different hue. Each room offers a unique color palette along with artwork by photographer Victor Levy depending on the purpose of your stay. The rooftop has a fantastic view of Brussels.

HOTEL MANOS PREMIER

Charleroise Steenweg 100/106; tel. 02 537 96 82; www.manospremier.com; €110

Hotel Manos Premier is a beautiful five-star boutique hotel with comfortable rooms, a facade covered in ivy, and an upscale interior with gold-framed portraits, elegant Louis XV and XVI period furniture, and grand chandeliers. There's a Moroccan-style hammam (access included with Deluxe rooms) with beautiful mosaics as well as a fitness center.

Information and Services

TOURIST INFORMATION

VISIT.BRUSSELS

Rue Royale 2; tel. 02 513 89 40; https://visit.brussels; 9:30am-5:30pm Mon.-Fri., 10am-6pm Sat.

Brussels Tourism Board, visit.brussels, has several offices where you can get information about Brussels in person, in addition to their exhaustive website. Their main office is located on top of the Mont des Arts. There is a smaller tourist information booth located within the **Town Hall of Brussels** (Grand Place; tel. 02 513 89 40; 9am-6pm daily).

STATION EUROPE

Place Du Luxembourg; https://europarl.europa.eu/visiting/en/visitor-offer/brussels/station-europe; 9am-6pm Mon.-Fri., 10am-6pm Sat.-Sun.

The European Parliament also has an info point in Station Europe, in front of the European Parliament building.

SAFETY

Brussels is as safe as other European capitals; like with any city, you should stay alert and keep a close eye on your belongings on crowded streets and squares or while sitting at cafés. Scams are fairly commonplace in around Grand Place and train stations. Theft from cars can also be an issue: Be sure to leave your valuables out of view.

There are a few spots to be wary of at night, including the area around Brussels North and Brussels South. Still, the train stations are well patrolled by police and military to protect civilians. For young women in particular, street harassment can be an issue. When possible, it's best to take a taxi back instead of walking far distances late at night.

Brussels has four **police stations** that are open 24 hours a day (www.brussels.be/police-stations); the one at Rue du Marché au

Charbon 30 is the closest to the center. The police speak French, Dutch, and English. The general emergency number is **112** in Belgium; this will connect you to an operator who speaks English.

HEALTH

Travelers can call to make an appointment with any Belgian GP during normal business hours (generally 9am-5pm Mon.-Fri.; for a full list of GPs in Brussels, go to www.bhak.be). In the case of non-urgent medical issues on evenings and weekends, travelers can head to six **medical centers** for assistance; the Brusselse Wachtdienst closest to the center is located at Rue de Brouchoven de Bergeyckstraat 2 (tel. 02 201 22 22; www.gbbw.be/index.php/en; 7pm-midnight Mon.-Fri, 8am-noon Sat.-Sun). If you have a medical emergency, you can call **112** for an ambulance.

Pharmacies are typically open during normal business hours, but you can look for pharmacies open later at www.pharmacie.be. Near the center, try **Pharmacy Fripiers** (Rue des Fripiers 24; 9:30am-7pm Mon.-Fri.).

Brussels has a large network of private and public hospitals, and Belgian healthcare is generally well regarded and affordable. Visitors to Belgium might need to pay out of pocket for services if they do not have European residency. There are five major hospitals in Brussels, including **Institut Jules Bordet** (Boulevard de Waterloo 121; www.bordet.be; tel. 0322 541 31 11) near the Halle Gate, **Clinique Saint Jean** (Boulevard du Jardin Botanique 32; www.clstjean.be; tel. 0322 221 91 11) near Brussels North, and **Brugmann University Hospital** (Place A.Van Gehuchten; www.chu-brugmann.be/en/virtu/horta-go.asp; tel. 0322 477 22 11) near European Parliament.

For psychiatric help, call the **Community Help Service** (tel. 02 648 40 14) or chat online at www.chs-belgium.org for English-speaking assistance.

CONSULATES

- **US Embassy:** Boulevard du Régent 27; tel. 0322 811 40 00; https://be.usembassy.gov; 8am-noon, 2pm-4pm Mon.-Thurs., 8am-noon Fri. Appointments are required to enter the embassy; it's best to call right when they open at 8am for consular services.
- **Canadian Embassy:** Avenue des Arts 58; tel. 02 741 06 11; www.canadainternational.gc.ca/belgium-belgique/offices-bureaux/embassy-ambassade.aspx?lang=eng. Emergencies should be reported 9am-noon or 2pm-4pm Mon.-Fri.
- **Australian Embassy:** Avenue des Arts 56; tel. 02 286 05 00, emergency tel. +612 6261 3305; https://belgium.embassy.gov.au; appointment required.
- **New Zealand Embassy:** Avenue des Nerviens 9; tel. 02 512 10 40; www.mfat.govt.nz/en/countries-and-regions/europe/belgium/new-zealand-embassy; 9am-1pm, 2pm-5pm Mon.-Fri.
- **South African Embassy:** Rue Montoyer 19; tel. 02 285 44 00; www.southafrica.be. Hours are limited and it's best to contact the embassy for appointments; the emergency phone number after hours is 0475 76 02 70.

Transportation

GETTING THERE

Brussels is in the center of Belgium, often a convenient stopping point for travelers passing between Paris and Amsterdam. Most roads, trains, and buses in Belgium will at least pass close to Brussels, and travelers entering Belgium from outside the European Union are likely to fly into Brussels Airport, a major international hub.

Air

BRUSSELS AIRPORT

BRU; Leopoldlaan, 1930 Zaventem; www.brusselsairport.be

Brussels Airport is located 15 kilometers (9 miles) northeast of Brussels Centrum in the nearby town of Zaventem. Medium-sized, at least compared to Amsterdam Schiphol Airport, its single terminal is easy to navigate, divided into two concourses: one for Schengen flights and one for non-Schengen flights. Brussels Airlines, United, and Delft fly direct to New York (7.5-8.5 hours; €500-700 round-trip) as well as London (1 hour; €80-100 round-trip). There are also frequent international flights to other major European cities as well as the Middle East (Dubai) for connections to Australia (usually about 30 hours total travel time; €1,000 round-trip).

A train station directly under the airport links to Brussels city center; the ride takes less than 30 minutes on the slow train and just 16 minutes on faster trains (€9.10 one-way). Trains depart about every 10 minutes. Given the terrible traffic often encountered in the Brussels region and limited parking in Brussels, this is the best way to get to the city from the airport. You can always opt for a taxi or bus/tram from Brussels Centrum to reach your hotel.

BRUSSELS SOUTH CHARLEROI AIRPORT

CRL; Rue des Frères Wright 8, 6041 Charleroi; www.brussels-charleroi-airport.com

Despite the name, Brussels Charleroi Airport is definitely not in Brussels, a mistake made by many travelers. Rather, it's in the industrial city of Charleroi, about 60 kilometers (37 miles) to the south. Charleroi, as it's often called by locals, has two terminals, although one is only used in peak periods, and is small enough that it's hard to get lost. Flights from Charleroi tend to be more regional, from other European cities as well as some destinations in North Africa and Turkey. The main appeal of Charleroi is the price—often half what it costs to fly to Brussels Airport, with some flights costing as little as €20—but it comes at the cost of time and often limited customer service on budget airlines.

A **shuttle** (www.flibco.com; €15) connects Brussels Charleroi to Brussels South in 50 minutes, departing every 30 minutes. If you intend to fly into Charleroi and arrive late at night or have an early flight in the morning, it might be wiser to stay closer to the airport rather than in Brussels. A taxi from Charleroi costs approximately €100 booked in advance; those traveling more broadly around Belgium beyond Brussels might find it more convenient to rent a car.

Train

Brussels is served by four main train stations, logically named according to their location within the city. All the stations are well connected by local trains, so if you make a mistake with your station, you should be able to get to the correct one fairly easily.

From Brussels Midi and Brussels Central, trains run approximately once every 20 minutes to Bruges (€14.30; 1 hour).

BRUSSELS CENTRAL

(Gare Centrale/Brussels Centraal)

Carrefour de l'Europe

The most central station, Gare Central is just 500 meters (1,600 feet) from Grand Place.

BRUSSELS NORTH

(Gare du Nord/Brussels-Noord)

Rue du Progrès 76

Gare du Nord is a popular stop for international buses heading to the Netherlands and France. The station is about 2 kilometers (1 mile) north of Brussels center.

BRUSSELS WEST

(Gare de l'Ouest/Brussels-West)

Chaussée de Ninove; www.belgianrail.be/fr/gares/recherche-gares/1/bruxelles-ouest.aspx

Brussels West is about 2 kilometers (1 mile) west of the city center.

BRUSSELS SOUTH

(Gare du Midi/Brussels-Zuid)

Avenue Fonsny 47B

Gare du Midi, located 2 kilometers (1 mile) south of the city center, is where high-speed trains from Amsterdam, London, and Paris arrive. It's well equipped with luggage lockers and ample food options; the **ticket office** is open 4am-1am daily.

Trains connect Brussels with Amsterdam (www.thalys.com/nl/en/info-services/timetable/brussels/Amsterdam; 2 hours; €29-100) once an hour. There's also a direct hourly train from Rotterdam (www.thalys.com/nl/en/info-services/timetable/brussels/Rotterdam; 1 hour 10 minutes; €29-100).

Bus

Brussels is well connected by bus to Amsterdam, but unfortunately not to Bruges. **Flixbus** runs buses about eight times per day between Amsterdam Sloterdijk (Zaventemweg 1; www.ns.nl/stationsinformatie/ass/amsterdam-sloterdijk) and Brussels Noord that must be booked online in advance (https://global.flixbus.com/bus-routes/bus-amsterdam-brussels; €15). Be sure to check your ticket for relevant bus information and to bring your passport/ID with you.

Car

The **E19** forms a loop around Brussels. **Bruges** is located 98 kilometers (61 miles) northwest of Brussels via the **E40.** From **Amsterdam,** the 200-kilometer (124-mile) drive takes closer to 2.5 hours, not including traffic, driving south via the **A4.** Brussels is quite infamous for its traffic, with many daily commuters from Wallonia and Flanders.

Parking in Brussels is limited during the day; it's best to opt for paid parking at a garage (typically €1.50/hour) unless parking is available at your hotel. Parking is free overnight (6pm-8am), but you'll be fighting with the locals for a free space, and busier streets may limit parking to two-hour periods.

GETTING AROUND

The best way to see Brussels city center is **on foot.** Brussels has many short streets that often change name after 1-2 blocks; get your bearings by memorizing the location of Grand Place or Mannekin Pis. Beyond the city center, it's best to take **public transit,** known as STIB/MIVB. If you'll be exploring the countryside surrounding Brussels, a car might be useful, but the constant traffic and difficulty of parking is discouraging. Cycling in Brussels is fairly dangerous and should be reserved for experienced urban bikers.

Public Transit

STIB, or **MIVB** in Dutch (www.stib-mivb.be), is the main public transit agency in Brussels, responsible for buses, trams, and the Metro. The metro in particular is very easy to navigate, with an easy-to-understand circular shape. If you intend to spend time in Brussels, it might be worth investing in a refillable MOBIB card (€5); you can add value to it at kiosks throughout the city, similar to a MetroCard in New York. There are booths with employees on site to help you purchase tickets at all major train stations.

A one-way fare valid for 60 minutes on all forms of transit costs €2.10, and a 24-hour pass costs €7.50, with unlimited transfers. If you purchase a ticket on a bus, you will be charged more, so it's best to purchase five-pack of tickets whenever you find a ticket machine. As of July 1, 2020, at STIB-MIVB Metro, tram, and bus booths, you can pay for your ticket via contactless payments using Google Pay, Apple Pay, and other contactless cards, a notable improvement.

Cycling

Cycling in Brussels is tricky, with occasionally steep hills and limited biking lanes criss-crossed with tram tracks. Although there are ample bike rentals through the **Blue Bike** program (www.blue-bike.be) outside of Brussels South, Brussels is still in the process of making the city more bicycle friendly. Biking is not allowed on the sidewalks.

Taxi

There are a number of taxi stands throughout the city center where licensed taxis wait for riders (www.brussels.be/taxi), including outside Brussels Central and on the roads outside the pedestrian zones in the city center. Taxis begin at €1.80/kilometer within the city center and €2.70/kilometer outside Brussels. There is an evening surcharge of €2. Ensure that the meter is turned on when you get in; it is your right to ask for a ticket documenting the trip details. **Taxis Verts** (https://taxisverts.be; tel. 02 349 49 49) is a popular taxi service. **Taxi Hendriks** (tel. 02 752 98 00; www.hendriks.be) provides wheelchair-friendly taxis.

Brussels also has a collective shared service called **Collecto** (https://mobilite-mobiliteit.brussels/en/collecto), which picks you up at any public transit stop or train station within Brussels between 11pm-6am for €6. Users should download the app in advance. Ride-hailing services such as **Uber** are also available.

Vicinity of Brussels

Brussels is surrounded by lush green parks and beautiful towns that are often overlooked by travelers, perhaps because the larger Brussels region is particularly unfriendly toward those without an automobile. But with a car, you'll find that it's very easy to combine multiple stops within one day.

If you're a fan of museums, nature, and the occasional sour beer, you'll find something to love away from the crowds of Grand Place. Notable stops including the haunting Villers Abbey, an abandoned medieval complex an hour south of Brussels; the Hergé Museum, for lovers of the *Tintin* comic book series; the purple carpet of bluebells in bloom at the psychedelic Hallerbos forest; the famed battlefield of Waterloo; and the lively university city of Leuven. Villers Abbey and the Hergé Museum are within 15 minutes' drive of one another if you want to combine the two stops. Note that some of the destinations are within Flemish Brabant, where Dutch will be the primary language.

★ LEUVEN

Leuven is a beautiful university city just 15 minutes outside Brussels, in Flemish Brabant. Pronounced "Low-ven," the city is full of beautiful, well-preserved Flemish architecture, and it's small enough that a pleasant afternoon of walking is enough to enjoy its main attractions, including its extraordinary city hall and the biggest beguinage in Belgium. Thanks to Leuven University, KU Leuven, one of Belgium's leading universities, the city has thrived throughout the centuries as a center for intellectual thought and religion.

The center of Leuven is marked by a large square, known as **Grote Markt,** site of Leuven's city hall and some buildings belonging to KU Leuven. The **Dijle River** flows to the west of Grote Markt, and the **train station** is to the east.

Sights

GROTE MARKT

www.visitleuven.be; open 24/7

Leuven's Grote Markt is like Brussels's Grand Place in miniature, with grand brick-and-glass guild houses facing the wildly ornate Leuven City Hall in the center of the square. It's the place in Leuven to people-watch from one of the charming café tables covering the cobblestones. To the south, **Oude Markt** is one long bar street, where the lively, youthful spirit of this university town is evident in abundance.

CITY HALL (Historisch Stadhuis van Leuven)

Grote Markt 9; www.visitleuven.be/nl/stadhuis; tours 4pm Fri.-Sun.; €4

Leuven's best-known building is its beautiful and ornate city hall that sits in the center of Grote Markt. This 15th-century beauty sits across from the impressive 15th-century **Sint-Pieterskerk Cathedral** (Grote Markt 1; tel. 016 29 51 33; www.mleuven.be; 10am-4:30pm Thurs.-Tues.), which was built by the same architects. The exterior is in the typical Brabantine Gothic style, with sharp turrets that line the roof. In between the building's niches, 236 elaborate statues (mostly from the 19th century) sit symbolizing the city and region's history. It's the only building in Leuven to survive World War I.

Weekend **tours** in English (4pm Fri.-Sun.; €4) allow you to step into the Stadhuis (as it is called in Dutch); the original Gothic Hall with its exquisite original star-vaulted ceiling is worth the visit.

M LEUVEN

Leopold Vanderkelenstraat 28; tel. 016 27 29 29; www.mleuven.be; 11am-6pm Thurs.-Tues; €12

The M Leuven is an innovative art museum, housed in a hyper-modern building built on top of a neoclassical home belonging to a former major. It's an impressive collection of art made since 1945, along with historical artifacts from Leuven's past. The museum strives to bring in young talented artists for temporary exhibitions for an intriguing mix of modern and old.

GROOT BEGIJNHOF LEUVEN

Groot Begijnhof; www.visitleuven.be/nl/groot-begijnhof; open 24/7; free

The Groot Begijnhof might be the most beautiful dorm you've ever seen. This tiny village within Leuven is about 10 minutes on foot from the city center, but once you enter the streets of the Groot Begijnhof, it feels like another world. As early as the 13th century, a community of Beguines lived in Leuven, but only a few of the current houses are older than the 16th century—theses notably have timber frames, a rarity for existing buildings this old. The rest of the buildings are from the 17th century, generally built in sandstone. All 81 houses—one of the largest collections of the like in the Benelux region—are technically the private property of Leuven University, but anyone can take a stroll down the cobblestone streets. Unfortunately, is not accessible to people with disabilities.

Sports and Recreation

SINT-DONATUS PARK

Vlamingenstraat; tel. 016 27 20 00; 7am-9:30pm daily

South of the Leuven city center, you'll find a charming park in the English landscaping style straight out of a Victorian folly, decorated by the ruins of the city's medieval walls. It's a popular picnic spot in summer.

Food

GREENWAY LEUVEN

Parijsstraat 1; tel. 016 30 97 35; https://greenway.be; 11am-9pm daily; €14

Greenway Leuven is a vegan restaurant founded by a progressive vegan brand that pioneered vegan burgers in Leuven. Even for carnivores, the large assortment of healthy options as well as indulgent burgers make

Greenway a great spot for lunch or dinner after walking around. They have a small terrace along a scenic street off Grote Markt.

DOMUS BEER

Tiensestraat 8; tel. 016 20 14 49; https://domusleuven.be; 11am-2:30pm, 5:30pm-10pm Tues.-Thurs., 11am-10pm Fri.-Sun.; €20

This small brewery/restaurant serves house beers alongside a rich assortment of Flemish favorites, from stews to meatballs. The restaurant has a charming brick-lined interior with atmospheric wooden beams, completing the brasserie experience.

Information and Services

Tourist information is available at the official **Visit Leuven** office (Naamsestraat 3; tel. 16 20 30 20; 10am-5pm daily).

Getting There

LEUVEN TRAIN STATION

Martelarenplein 16

The direct train between **Brussels Central** and Leuven leaves approximately every 15 minutes (22 minutes; €5.50 one-way).

WATERLOO

Waterloo is a history junkie's dream, site of a pivotal battle in the Napoleonic Wars, after which Napoleon was forced into exile for the last time and the Congress of Vienna fundamentally redrew the map of Europe. The battlefield of Waterloo sits about 40 minutes outside Brussels, and history buffs come to learn about the battle at dedicated museums.

The **Pass 1815** (www.waterloo1815.be/visiter-waterloo; adults €22, students and seniors €21, youth 10-17 €13, children under 10 free) is a combination ticket that includes entry to the Waterloo Battlefield as well as other sites in the region.

Sights

MUSÉE WELLINGTON

Chaussée de Bruxelles 147; tel. 02 357 28 60; www.museewellington.be; 10am-5pm daily; adults €7.50, youth €6.50, children under 10 free, free with Pass 1815

Musée Wellington is a former lodge built in 1777 that was used as the headquarters for the British during the Waterloo campaign. Notable guests included the namesake Duke of Wellington. The building now houses a small museum including original items from the battle. Although the museum is truly for die-hard military history fans, it's free with the Pass 1815.

WATERLOO BATTLEFIELD: MEMORIAL 1815

Route du Lion 1815; tel. 02 385 19 12; www.waterloo1815.be; 9:30am-6:30pm daily Sept.-Oct. and Apr.-June, 9:30am-5:30pm daily Nov.- Mar., 9:30am-7:30pm daily July-Aug.; adults €18, seniors and students €17, youth 10-17 €9, children uner 10 free, free with Pass 1815

The real reason people visit Waterloo is to see the Waterloo 1815 Memorial, the sprawling site of the 1815 battle. The highlight for many is climbing the Lion's Mount for a bird's-eye view of the battlefield. Today, the battlefield is covered up by often green flat pastoral fields, although a map of the positions is visible from the top where you can imagine approximately 185,000 soldiers from both sides pitted against each other. It was built to commemorate the famous battle and requires climbing 226 steps to reach the top. A giant lion statue sits atop the hill, which represents the crests of the United Kingdom as well as the coat of arms of the Netherlands, as it was the Prince of Orange, William II, who was wounded at this exact spot, and whose father built the hill.

To learn more about the Battle of Waterloo, the underground Memorial 1815 museum walks you through interactive exhibitions (worth the €2 extra for the realistic 3D movie!). With the Pass 1815 ticket, on select days, you can also visit the nearby **Hougoumont Farm** (Musée de la Ferme d'Hougoumont, Chemin du Goumont; tel. 02 385 19 12;

1: Groot Begijnhof Leuven **2:** Waterloo Battlefield: 1815 Memorial **3:** Villers Abbey

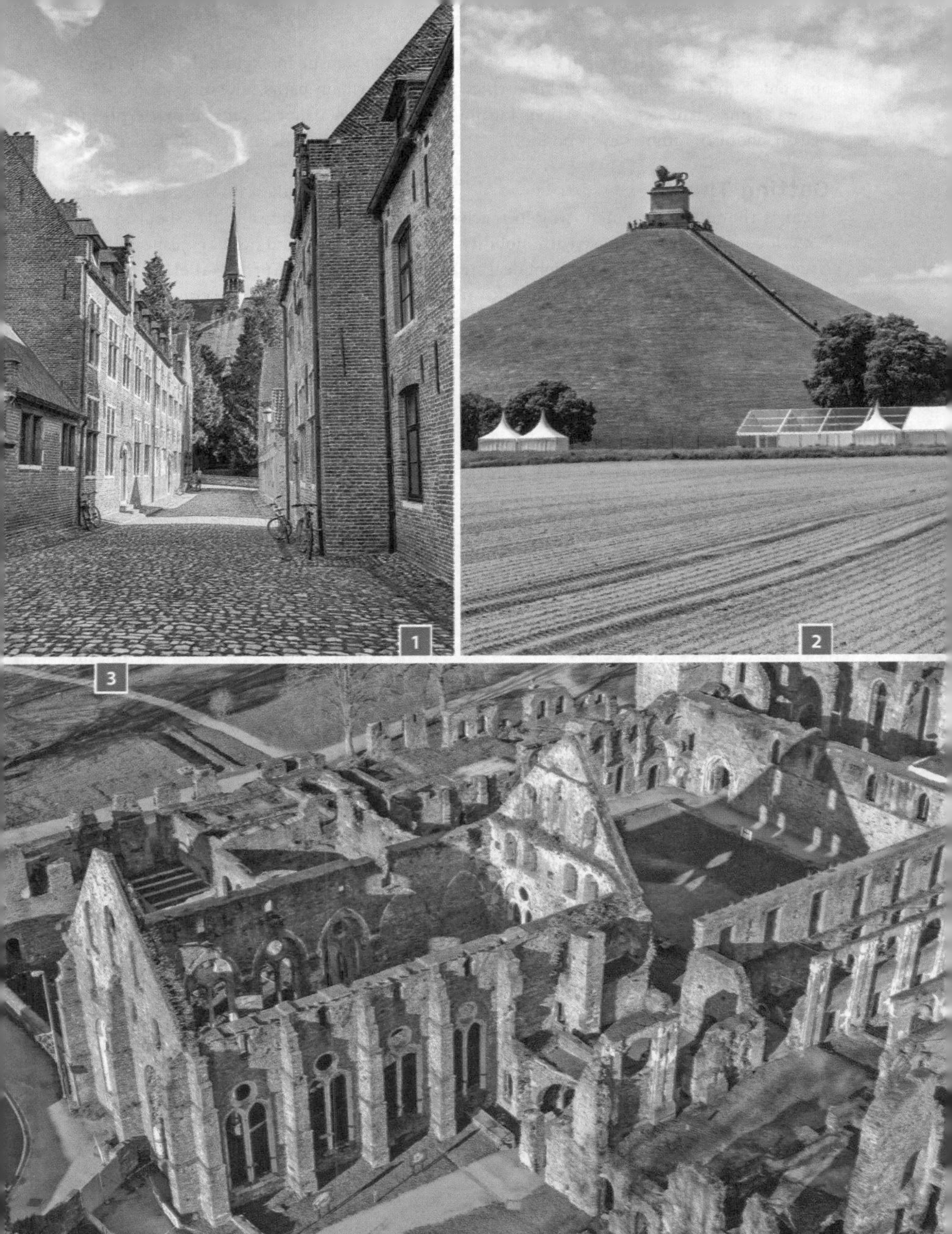
1
2
3

www.waterloo1815.be; 1pm-6pm Wed., 10am-6pm Sat.-Sun.; free with 1815 ticket), which served as one of the defense locations for the British, about 20 minutes away on foot.

Getting There

A car is the most convenient way to reach Waterloo, especially for those with mobility issues—and those who are impatient dealing with the limited bus schedule. Free **parking** is available at the memorial, which is only 35 minutes by car from Brussels (21 kilometers/13 miles); take **N24** south toward Bois de la Cambre before continuing onto **N5,** and drive south for 10 kilometers (6 miles) in the direction of Waterloo.

Bus #365 (www.letec.be; €10) departs from Brussels South in the direction of Chareloi, stopping at the battlefield. The journey takes about 50 minutes, and the bus runs every 2 hours.

WATERLOO TRAIN STATION

Place de la Gare; www.belgiantrain.be

There is a train every 30 minutes from Brussels Central Train Station toward Nivelles that stops over in Waterloo. The train ride takes 30 minutes and costs €3.80 per adult each way (children €2.50). From Waterloo station, you can take **bus W** (www.letec.be) from the bus stop across from the train station, toward Route de Nivelles. A one-way ticket costs €2.10. The 6-kilometer (4-mile) journey takes about 10 minutes.

HALLERBOS

Vlasmarktdreef 4 Halle; tel. 02 658 24 60; www.hallerbos.be; sunrise-sunset daily; free

Toward the end of April (the timing varies each year!), an otherwise unknown forest explodes with beautiful bluebells—and visitors—for about 10 days. This is a public forest outside Brussels with beautiful walking paths that makes for a lovely day trip from the city, especially in fall with the changing leaves, although it's most famous for its bluebells. You can download a free walking guide from the website to explore the paths. There are not so many paths, buut the park spans 555 hectares (1,400 acres). The **Yellow Walking Path** (Reebokwandeling) is a particularly picturesque 7-kilometer (4-mile) stroll on a dirt path in between endless flowers and redwoods from California. The walk takes about an hour.

On weekends and holidays, especially toward the end of April, Hallerbos can get busy, but you can avoid the crowds by checking Hallerbos's website for detailed updates on the process of the forest's blooms—some years, they bloom earlier than others.

Getting There

A great way to get to the Hallerbos is via a combination of train and bike. Take the train from **Brussels Central** to Halle (23 minutes; €3.70 one-way), where you can rent a **Blue Bike** (www.blue-bike.be/en/discover; €3.15; best to have your subscription purchased before your trip). It's a 5-kilometer (3-mile) ride from the station (20 minutes); follow Nijvelsesteenweg south away from the city center before following the signs toward Hallerbos.

On weekdays, it's also possible to take a bus from Halle train station to **Vlasmarkt** (bus 114; www.letec.be; 9 minutes), from where you can follow a footpath to the forest. On weekends and holidays during the blooming period, you can take **De Lijn bus 155** (www.delijn.be; 50 minutes; €1.80) to the bus stop at **Hallerbossttraat,** right near the forest's car park.

It's also possible to drive to Hallerbos, although during the bloom period, some nearby roads are closed off. Instead, you can route yourself to **Vlasmarktdreef** (Halle), which will take you straight to the **parking lot** near the forest (32 minutes; 22.8 kilometers/14.2 miles; take the N266 out of Brussels before taking the E19 toward Namur to Exit 21. Merge onto 203a for 1.3 kilometers/0.8 miles and make a left onto N28/Nijvelsesteenweg. Continue for 2.7 kilometers/1.7 miles until you reach Vlasmarktdreef).

HERGÉ MUSEUM

Rue du Labrador 26, Louvain-la-Neueve; tel. 10 48 84 21; www.museeherge.com; 10:30am-5pm Tues.-Fri., 10:30am-6pm Sat.-Sun.; adults €12, children 7-12 €5, children under 7 free

Fans of Georges Remi, aka Hergé, and his adventurous character Tintin might want to make the trip out to the address of Tintin's first house in the comics, turned into a futuristic museum in the town of Louvain-la-Neueve just outside Brussels. The museum is more geared toward adults who grew up with the comics, with three floors detailing Hergé's life and the characters of the book. It's particularly interesting to understand Tintin within the context of the period, and the notable shift in the comic books as the plots moved from Hergé's imagination to ones inspired by his travels and research; one room is dedicated to all the places Tintin visited, linked to Hergé's notes. The museum does not allow photographs. It is accessible for visitors with disabilities.

Getting There

The easiest way to get to the Hergé museum is by car. There is paid **parking** underneath the museum, and the journey along the **E411** (33 kilometers/20 miles) takes about 40 minutes.

Trains in the direction of Namur run about twice per hour from **Brussels Central,** stopping in Louvain-la-Neuve, where the station is right next to the museum (1 hour; €5.50 one-way). A combination ticket that includes admission and trains from Belgium costs €12.40 (www.belgiantrain.be/en/leisure/b-excursions/art-culture/herge-museum).

★ VILLERS ABBEY

(Abbaye de Villers)

Rue de l'Abbaye 55 Villers-la-Ville; tel. 071 88 09 80; https://villers.be; 10am-5pm daily Nov.-Mar., 10am-6pm daily Apr.-Oct.; adults €9, students and seniors €7, children 6-12 €4, children under 6 free

Although Belgium certainly is full of beautiful abbeys, many of them are in use and don't allow tourists to visit freely. Villers Abbey south of Brussels is a particularly gorgeous abbey, frozen in time since it was abandoned around the French Revolution, with epic Cistercian stone arches untouched for centuries. Today, the abbey is a hauntingly lovely site, a place to wander, take photos under the serene remains of flying buttresses, and imagine yourself stepping into the past as you explore gardens, chapels, and the many paths that traverse property. Bring lunch for the most picturesque picnic you've ever had.

A Romanesque abbey was built on this spot as early as 1146, but the bulk of the current abbey dates back to a 1197 Gothic-style building, with construction continuing for more than 100 years. The current garden was built in the early 1700s, only to be abandoned after the abbey was pillaged during the French Revolution, leaving the abbey largely undisturbed and rotting in place, even drawing the attention of Victor Hugo. Nearly 300 years after the abbey was abandoned, the Belgian government began restoring the site, including adding medicinal plant gardens. Be sure to check the abbey's **gift shop** and **café** for their beers brewed according to monks' ancient recipes.

Getting There

It's easiest to get to Villers Abbey with your own vehicle, with free **parking** for cars. From Brussels, it's a 30-50-minute drive (50 kilometers/31 miles) depending on traffic, along the **E411** highway. It's close to the Hergé Museum (15 minutes; 14 kilometers/9 miles), in case you chose to combine the two into one day.

Bruges

Bruges (in Flemish: Brugge) charms you from the moment you get off the train. Cobblestone streets lead you past swans floating by in Minnewater Park, stunning stepped gable houses, ancient windmills, busy squares, and impressive towers (including the hard-to-miss Belfry of Bruges).

You can take in most of Bruges's compact, historic city center, recognized by UNESCO, on a leisurely walk of just a few hours. But outside the busy Burg neighborhood, it's easy to lose track of the days in the quieter Sint Anna and Langestraat Quarters, with perfectly worn-down brick buildings, reflective canals, and towers straight out of a fairy tale.

Bruges is incredibly rich culturally, with countless festivals, art history, a proud lacemaking tradition, and excellent gastronomy. The city's

Highlights

Look for ★ to find recommended sights, activities, dining, and lodging.

★ **Markt:** Enjoy the beautiful guild houses of Bruges's most famous square, shop for fruit at the Wednesday market, and take in Bruges from above from its highest point, the Belfry of Bruges (page 252).

★ **Gruuthusemuseum:** For those short on time, this hidden gem of a museum provides great insight into Bruges's history (page 259).

★ ***Godshuizen:*** Step back in time by stepping into one of Bruges's many medieval almshouses scattered throughout the city center (page 264).

★ **Chocolate Shops:** Scoop up the best chocolate that Bruges has to offer from its many specialty chocolatiers (page 276).

★ **Brouwerij De Halve Maan:** Don't miss sampling a fresh beer from Bruges's most famous brewery, known for its beer pipeline (page 287).

Bruges

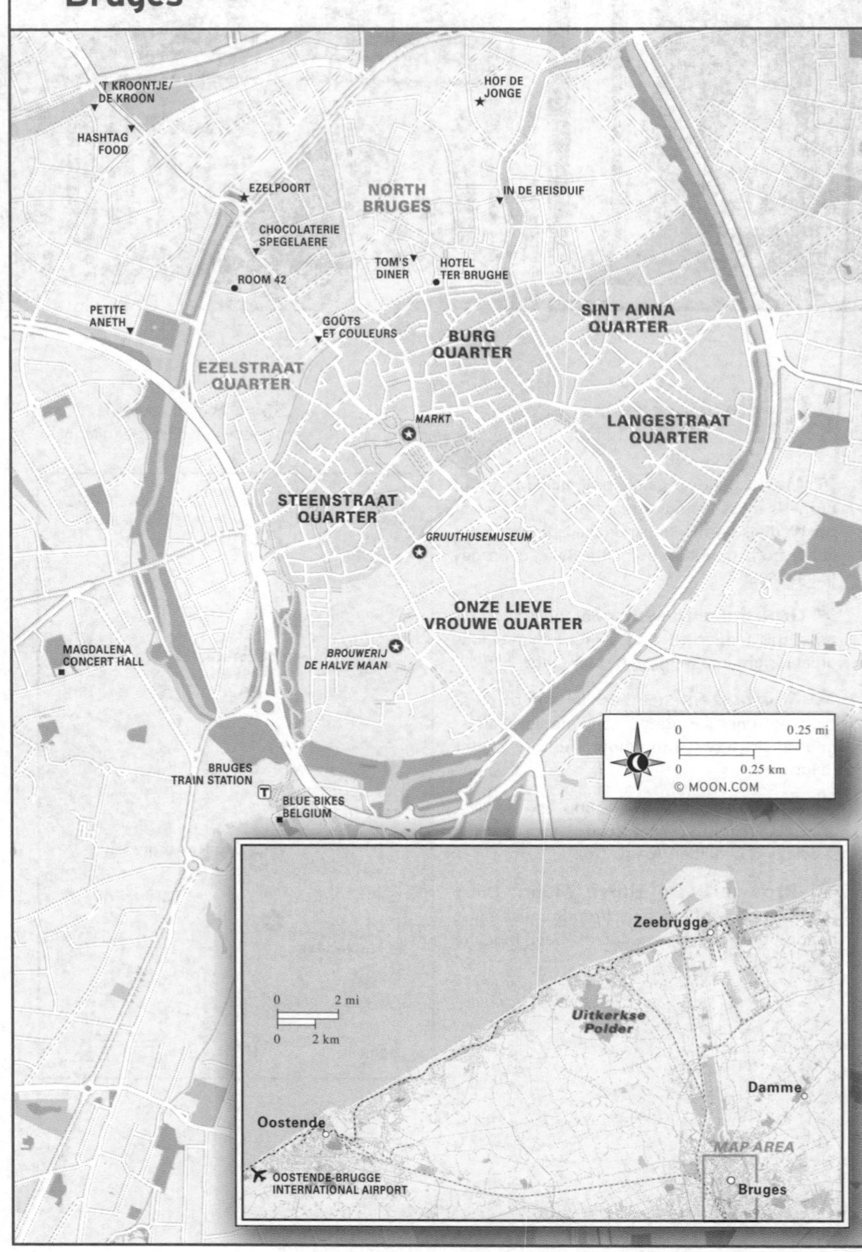

'T KROONTJE/ DE KROON
HASHTAG FOOD
HOF DE JONGE
EZELPOORT
NORTH BRUGES
IN DE REISDUIF
CHOCOLATERIE SPEGELAERE
TOM'S DINER
HOTEL TER BRUGHE
ROOM 42
PETITE ANETH
GOÛTS ET COULEURS
SINT ANNA QUARTER
BURG QUARTER
EZELSTRAAT QUARTER
MARKT
LANGESTRAAT QUARTER
STEENSTRAAT QUARTER
GRUUTHUSEMUSEUM
ONZE LIEVE VROUWE QUARTER
MAGDALENA CONCERT HALL
BROUWERIJ DE HALVE MAAN
0
0.25 mi
0
0.25 km
© MOON.COM
BRUGES TRAIN STATION
BLUE BIKES BELGIUM
Zeebrugge
0
2 mi
0
2 km
Uitkerkse Polder
Damme
Oostende
MAP AREA
OOSTENDE-BRUGGE INTERNATIONAL AIRPORT
Bruges

creativity can be seen in its world-class chefs, chocolatiers, and artists showcasing their heritage with a twist. Throughout the city, many shopkeepers are also carving out a new path, focusing on sustainability and promoting regional products and brands. This creative side can also sometimes make visiting chaotic, with somewhat inconsistent opening hours and unpredictable closures, but rolling with the punches, being flexible, and going with the flow make this part of the city's charm.

With the growth of social media and the desire to snap that iconic photo (often the Rozenhoedkaai viewpoint at sunset), Bruges is at a critical turning point as it copes with more than 9 million yearly visitors to a city of only 200,000. More changes to cap the number of cruisers allowed to explore the city, spreading out city events, and restrictions on building new hotels are meant to help mitigate the impact of over-tourism. Learning a bit of Flemish is truly appreciated here, and making your trip a mix of cultural appreciation and fun goes a long way. Hopefully, this glimpse behind the lace curtains will lure you back to Bruges for more.

ORIENTATION

Bruges is known for its picturesque medieval city center, which is one of the best-preserved in Belgium. Although you cannot miss the busy **Burg** and **Onze Lieve Vrouwe Quarters,** get a better feeling for Bruges through its quieter neighborhoods of **Sint Anna, Langestraat,** and **North Bruges.**

It's hard to get truly lost in the city center of Bruges; the churches serve as good landmarks. If you're unsure of the center, look for the Belfry's clock tower and octagonal top. **Onze Lieve Vrouwe's** iconic spire-topped tower leads you toward the Onze Lieve Vrouwe Quarter, and the **Jerusalemkerk's** ornate yellow tower will help you find the Sint Anna and Langestraat Quarters. Nearly all the locations mentioned in this book are located within the oval of Bruges's widest canal, formerly fortified. The exception is **Bruges Train Station,** which is located south of the oval across the canal.

A great escape from the tour groups, the historic town of **Damme** is less than 7 kilometers (4 mi) to the northeast, a nice bike ride on a warmer day.

Burg Quarter

No tourist to Bruges can miss the small yet regal Burg Quarter, the oldest part of Bruges, which holds some of the city's most famous attractions, including **Markt** square, the **Belfry of Bruges,** the **Basilica of the Holy Blood,** and **Jan van Eyck Square.** Full of cobblestone streets and ornate buildings with stepped gable roofs, the Burg Quarter is also one of Bruges's busiest neighborhoods, making it hard to take a photo without other tourists.

Steenstraat Quarter

West of the Burg Quarter, the Steenstraat Quarter is the main district for hotels, shopping, bars, and restaurants in Bruges. Here, you'll find quieter cobblestone streets, epic churches, cozy beer cafés, the popular **'t Zand** square with the modern **Concertgebouw** concert hall, and some of Bruges's most popular and best-value restaurants.

Onze Lieve Vrouwe Quarter

This popular neighborhood south of the Burg and Steenstraat Quarters sits in the shadow of Onze Lieve Vrouwe church, or the **Church of Our Lady,** one of Bruges's most impressive. Many popular attractions, from the historic **Begijnhof** courtyard to the **Halve Maan brewery** to the **Gruuthusemuseum** of applied arts, are a short walk away from Onze Lieve Vrouwe. The crowds mostly congregate along on the western part of Katelijnestraat and neighboring Wijngaardstraat, some of Bruges's most popular shopping streets,

Previous: iconic Bonifacius Bridge; Church of Our Lady Madonna; waffle on Markt square.

while many tourists miss the historic almshouses (*godshuizen*) scattered throughout this neighborhood.

Sint Anna and Langestraat Quarters

The quiet cobblestone streets of Sint Anna and Langestraat, east of the Burg and Onze Lieve Vrouwe Quarters, feel far away from the hustle and bustle of other neighborhoods; this former working-class area is one of Bruges's best-kept-secrets with its many tucked-away almshouses. It's only a 20-minute walk from the famous Jan van Eyck Square to **Café Vlissinghe,** Bruges's oldest café, but you'll wonder why the tourists quickly melt away. Visitors interested in history, lace, and antiques will enjoy the many antique shops in the area as well as the private museums such as the **Adornes Domain,** a preserved medieval estate, and the **Folklife Museum,** which preserves daily life in Bruges during the 19th and early 20th centuries.

North Bruges

North Bruges is still relatively undiscovered compared to many other parts of the city. As locals say, it's *quiet,* which is half the appeal in peak season. **Ezelstraat** to the west continues to grow as a hot spot for cool boutiques, low-key Flemish cafés, and high-quality restaurants geared toward locals. Locals flock to the scenic parks, such as **Hof de Jonge,** for a respite from the crowds. However, North Bruges has relatively few accommodation options compared to other neighborhoods.

PLANNING YOUR TIME

Many visit Bruges on a day trip, which is a bit of a shame. Bruges is best seen over a long weekend, enough time to get a sense of the city, visit its museums, and take an afternoon cycle to nearby **Damme.** Bruges is well-connected to other cities in Belgium by train; it's only 1 hour from Brussels, with trains departing at least once an hour.

Peak season in Bruges starts around Easter and goes through summer. December's Christmas markets, re also crowded. Hotel rates will be higher during these times, but be careful of traveling in January and February, the **low season,** when attractions and businesses may be closed or have shorter hours. If you want to avoid larger groups during busy times, when possible, opt for smaller streets instead of main thoroughfares.

There are plenty of high-quality museums in Bruges, so choose wisely to avoid **tourist**

Belfry with Markt square

traps, such as the Torture Museum and the Historium. Although it is possible to go to museums dedicated to beer (Bruges Beer Experience), fries (Fritesmuseum), and chocolate (Choco-Story Bruges), you can just as well visit any of the high-quality sellers to learn about these popular Belgian drinks and foods for only the cost of a pint or chocolate bar.

Given its compact size, practically any accommodation in Bruges city center makes a good base for exploring the city. Those open to walking or seeking a quieter neighborhood might want to stay outside the city center in the **Sint Anna and Langestraat Quarters** or **North Bruges.** Bruges is best seen **on foot,** although people with mobility issues might find the cobblestones difficult.

Sightseeing Passes

The **Musea Brugge Card** (www.discoverbruges.com/en/attractions-museums/pp/musea-brugge-card-2) provides three-day access to most of Bruges's museums for only €28 for adults, a steal considering that some museums cost upward of €12. If you'll be visiting many museums in Belgium, it might be worth it to buy the **Museum Pass Belgium** (www.museumpassmesses.be), which provides access to more than 140 museums for a year for only €50, available at most museums.

Itinerary Ideas

DAY 1: CLASSIC BRUGES

It only takes 3 kilometers (2 miles) of walking to wander through most of Bruges's city center, with stops for shopping, eating, museums, and even a boat tour.

1 Start off with a healthy breakfast at **That's Toast,** a casual local all-day breakfast spot.

2 Take a slow stroll down Noordzandstraat, popping into cute independent shops such as **Juttu,** a Scandinavian-inspired boutique.

3 Be sure to stop off for mouthwatering specialty chocolates at **Chocolatier Dumon;** try to save a few to eat later!

4 To continue building your picnic, head to **Diksmuids Boterhuis** armed with cash to pick up made-to-order sandwiches with Wallonian sausage and Flemish cheese. (Vegetarians might prefer the unpretentious and modern Potato Bar for veggie-friendly burgers and *frites* made from, you guessed it, potatoes.) There are a few benches on nearby Muntplein.

5 Next, make your way to the **Basilica of the Holy Blood** to witness the veneration of the relic of the Holy Blood before the lunch pause at noon.

6 For the best views over Bruges and to learn about the Belgian tradition of belfries, climb the slightly claustrophobic 366 steps to the top of the **Belfry of Bruges.**

7 Stroll over to the famous **Rozenhoedkaai viewpoint** for the iconic view of the Bruges Belfry.

8 Hop on a boat tour with Boottochten Brugge from the nearby **Gruuthuse** departure point to discover Bruges by boat.

9 Disembark at the Gruuthuse and learn about the history of Bruges in the **Gruuthusemuseum,** a former palace.

10 Afterward, walk a few steps over to explore the incredibly ornate **Church of Our Lady**

Itinerary Ideas

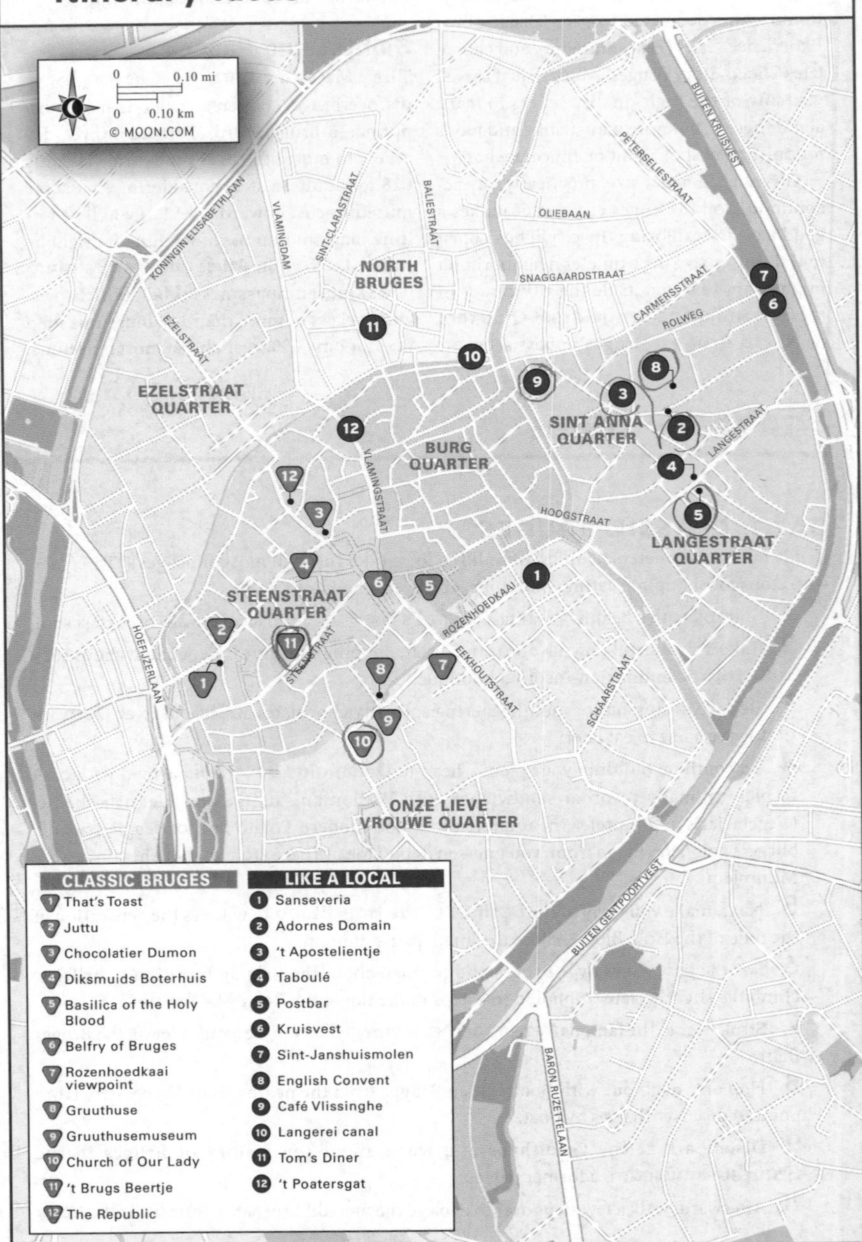
0 0.10 mi
0 0.10 km
© MOON.COM
NORTH BRUGES
EZELSTRAAT QUARTER
BURG QUARTER
SINT ANNA QUARTER
LANGESTRAAT QUARTER
STEENSTRAAT QUARTER
ONZE LIEVE VROUWE QUARTER
KONINGIN ELISABETHLAAN
EZELSTRAAT
VLAMINGDAM
SINT-CLARASTRAAT
BALIESTRAAT
PETERSELIESTRAAT
BUITEN KRUISVEST
OLIEBAAN
SNAGGAARDSTRAAT
CARMERSSTRAAT
ROLWEG
LANGESTRAAT
VLAMINGSTRAAT
HOOGSTRAAT
ROZENHOEDKAAI
EEKHOUTSTRAAT
SCHAARSTRAAT
STEENSTRAAT
HOEFIJZERLAAN
BUITEN GENTPOORTVEST
BARON RUZETTELAAN
CLASSIC BRUGES
1 That's Toast
2 Juttu
3 Chocolatier Dumon
4 Diksmuids Boterhuis
5 Basilica of the Holy Blood
6 Belfry of Bruges
7 Rozenhoedkaai viewpoint
8 Gruuthuse
9 Gruuthusemuseum
10 Church of Our Lady
11 't Brugs Beertje
12 The Republic
LIKE A LOCAL
1 Sanseveria
2 Adornes Domain
3 't Apostelientje
4 Taboulé
5 Postbar
6 Kruisvest
7 Sint-Janshuismolen
8 English Convent
9 Café Vlissinghe
10 Langerei canal
11 Tom's Diner
12 't Poatersgat

to see Michelangelo's *Madonna of Bruges.* (A combination ticket gets you into both the Gruuthusemuseum and the Church of Our Lady.)

11 Head down the quiet alleyway of Kemelstraat to find one of Bruges's best beer bars, **'t Brugs Beertje.** Sit down in one of the wooden chairs and leaf through the massive beer book to pick a Belgian beer to enjoy.

12 After a couple of beers, head to **The Republic** (ideally after making a reservation) for a modern Belgian dinner.

DAY 2: BRUGES LIKE A LOCAL

Today brings you to some of the quieter parts the city, in North Bruges and Sint Anna and Langestraat Quarters.

1 Bagels aren't Belgian, but getting one for breakfast at **Sanseveria** is a great start to a day.

2 Escape the crowds by exploring the quieter streets of the Sint Anna Quarter and entering the private **Adornes Domain** museum to visit the stunning Jerusalemkerk.

3 Walk down Balstraat with its beautiful whitewashed former almshouses that look straight out of a fairy tale. It's easy to miss the ivy-covered exterior of the **'t Apostelientje,** but those interested in the history of lace in Bruges will want to peek into this antique store that specializes in Flemish lace.

4 Walk down Rodestraat before turning onto Langestraat to find **Taboulé,** a casual eatery serving fresh and affordable Syrian-Lebanese food.

5 Afterward, cross the street to buy a souvenir postcard along with a coffee at **Postbar.**

6 Follow Langestraat to **Kruisvest,** a park housing part of Bruges's former fortified walls.

7 Head north to find Bruges's famous windmills, including **Sint-Janshuismolen,** which can be toured in the summer.

8 History enthusiasts will love the picturesque walk along Rolweg en route to the **English Convent.** If you're lucky enough to visit when they're open, be sure to ring the doorbell to enter the working cloister to get a glimpse of their stunning private chapel.

9 Reward yourself with a beer at **Café Vlissinghe,** Bruges's longest operating café.

10 Follow this with a scenic stroll along the quieter **Langerei canal.**

11 Be sure to reserve ahead for dinner at **Tom's Diner,** a cozy restaurant in North Bruges that uses locally sourced ingredients that won't break your budget.

12 End your night at Bruges's most famous late-night bar, **'t Poatersgat,** where you can sip Belgian beers and play foosball until 3am.

Sights

BURG QUARTER

★ Markt

Markt 1; open 24/7; free

This ancient heart of Bruges is one of its most classic views, with the Belfry rising in the east. For a millennium, this square has been the city's main marketplace, and still today, on Wednesday mornings, the square transforms into a bustling local **market** with fruit, vegetables, flowers, and cheeses. Markt is easily the most touristic place in Bruges, with countless cafés in former guild houses vying for tourists' money, horses and carriages, and tour groups regularly passing by. Avoid the crowds by coming early in the morning before day-trippers arrive, or by waiting until after dark to admire the Belfry up close.

Not all of the buildings in Markt are originals from the 15th century; it can be fun to pick out neo-Gothic additions. Hint: The imposing, palatial **Provinciaal Court** on the eastern side of the square is not so historic. It dates back to the 19th century, though it was built in the Gothic Revival style to replace a building that burned down. The **Historium** (Markt 1) is a tourist trap housed in a neo-Gothic building with a striking tower next to the Provinciaal Hof. You may want drop in for the tourist information available inside.

Be wary of pickpockets here, and avoid the tourist trap restaurants along the square. If you're looking for somewhere to sit, head to **Grand Café Craenenburg** (Markt 16; tel. 050 33 34 02; www.craenenburg.be; 8am-10pm daily) housed in a 14th-century building that used to be a smokers room. One of the other highlights of the square is Bruges's oldest bookshop, **De Reyghere Bookstore**, which has been in the same location for more than 100 years.

BELFRY OF BRUGES

Markt 7; tel. 050 44 87 11; www.visitbruges.be/en/belfort-belfry; 9:30am-6pm daily; €12

The Belfry is an iconic symbol of Bruges, and this 13th-century tower with an octagonal upper stage is a must-see for lovers of history, cultural heritage, and a good photo. Throughout the region, having a belfry represented a sort of freedom, asserting the power of the local government at a time when nobility and the church dominated the lives of regular people. Belfries also helped keep daily life on schedule by signaling the passing of time. In Bruges, the Belfry housed various government functions, from treasury to outpost to archives. It was once even higher thanks to a wooden spire, which burned down in the 1700s. It may be hard to tell, but the tower is leaning ever so much (87 centimeters/34 inches).

The steep and winding 366 steps up the skinny 83-meter (272-foot) tower can leave you out of breath, but the view of the medieval city of Bruges from the top will take your breath away. The **carillon,** installed in the 16th century with 47 bells, is played by the Bruges carillon master a few days a week and still keeps time for the city. It's better appreciated from the bottom than the top, where the bells can be deafening. Hear the carillon Wednesday, Saturday, and Sunday at 11am, and 9pm on Monday and Wednesday during peak season (June-Sept.). You can find the agenda online (www.carillon-brugge.be).

The line can take a while in peak season, but the many stopping points with small displays help you take advantage of pauses in the climb. The narrow staircase is not for those afraid of tightly enclosed spaces, and the addition of chicken wire at the top can unfortunately make taking photos difficult. Be sure to admire the large Triumphant Bell dating

Burg Quarter

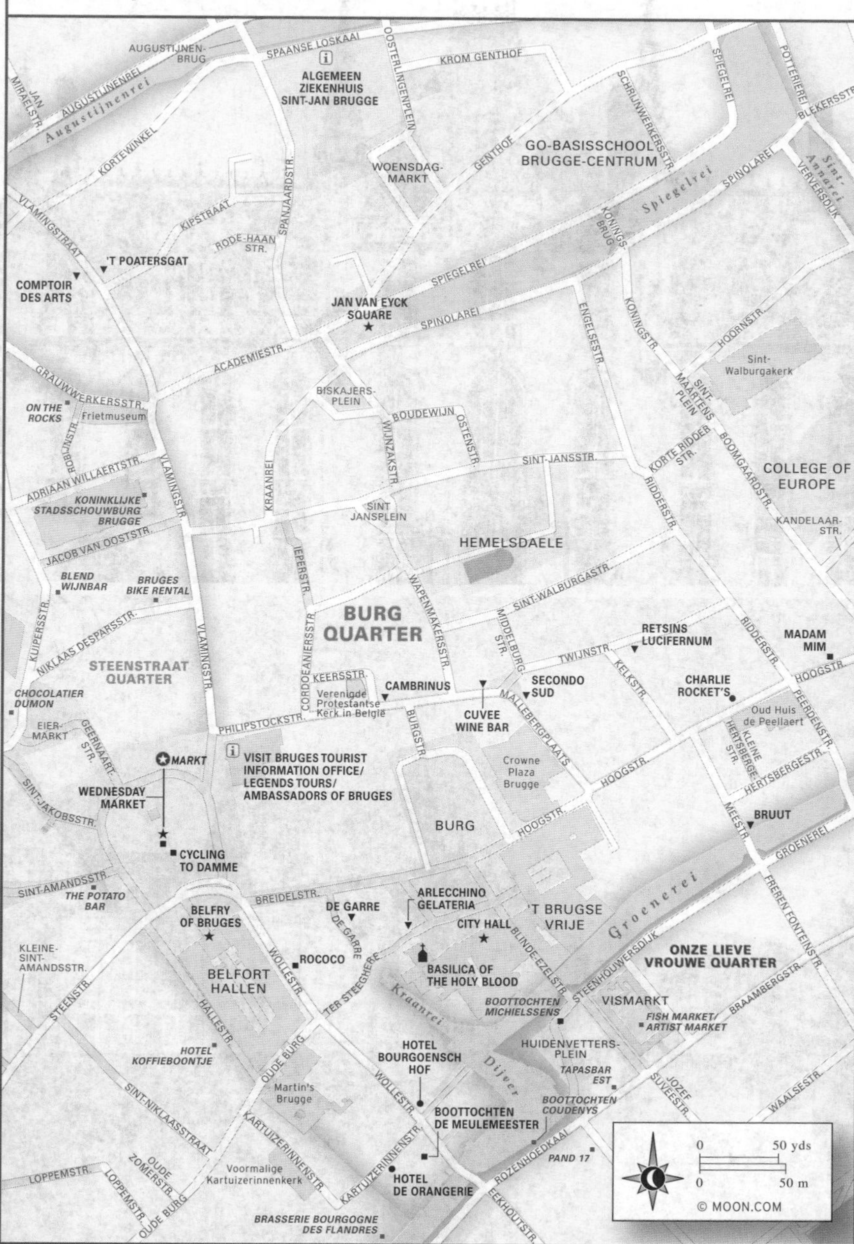

AUGUSTIJNENBRUG
SPAANSE LOSKAAI
ALGEMEEN ZIEKENHUIS SINT-JAN BRUGGE
OOSTERLINGENPLEIN
KROM GENTHOF
SPIEGELREI
POTTERIEREI
BLEKERSSTR.
JAN MIRAELSTR.
AUGUSTIJNENREI
Augustijnenrei
KORTEWINKEL
SCHRIJNWERKERSSTR.
GO-BASISSCHOOL BRUGGE-CENTRUM
GENTHOF
WOENSDAGMARKT
SPANJAARDSTR.
Spiegelrei
SPINOLAREI
Sint-Annarei
VERVERSDIJK
KONINGSBRUG
KIPSTRAAT
RODE-HAAN STR.
VLAMINGSTRAAT
'T POATERSGAT
COMPTOIR DES ARTS
JAN VAN EYCK SQUARE
ENGELSESTR.
KONINGSTR.
HOORNSTR.
ACADEMIESTR.
Sint-Walburgakerk
GRAUWWERKERSSTR.
BISKAJERSPLEIN
SINT-MAARTENSPLEIN
ON THE ROCKS
Frietmuseum
ROBIJNSTR.
BOUDEWIJN OSTENSTR.
WIJNZAKSTR.
KORTE RIDDERSTR.
BOOMGAARDSTR.
ADRIAAN WILLAERTSTR.
SINT-JANSSTR.
COLLEGE OF EUROPE
KONINKLIJKE STADSSCHOUWBURG BRUGGE
KRAANREI
SINT JANSPLEIN
RIDDERSTR.
KANDELAARSTR.
JACOB VAN OOSTSTR.
HEMELSDAELE
IEPERSTR.
BLEND WIJNBAR
BRUGES BIKE RENTAL
SINT-WALBURGASTR.
WAPENMAKERSSTR.
KUIPERSSTR.
BURG QUARTER
MIDDELBURGSTR.
RETSINS LUCIFERNUM
MADAM MIM
NIKLAAS DESPARSSTR.
STEENSTRAAT QUARTER
TWIJNSTR.
KELKSTR.
CORDOEANIERSSTR.
KEERSSTR.
CAMBRINUS
SECONDO SUD
CHARLIE ROCKET'S
HOOGSTR.
CHOCOLATIER DUMON
Verenigde Protestantse Kerk in België
CUVEE WINE BAR
MALLEBERGPLAATS
Oud Huis de Peellaert
PEERDENSTR.
EIERMARKT
GEERNAARTSTR.
PHILIPSTOCKSTR.
BURGSTR.
KLEINE HERTSBERGESTR.
MARKT
VISIT BRUGES TOURIST INFORMATION OFFICE/ LEGENDS TOURS/ AMBASSADORS OF BRUGES
Crowne Plaza Brugge
HERTSBERGESTR.
WEDNESDAY MARKET
SINT-JAKOBSSTR.
BURG
MEESTR.
BRUUT
GROENEREI
CYCLING TO DAMME
SINT-AMANDSSTR.
THE POTATO BAR
BREIDELSTR.
ARLECCHINO GELATERIA
DE GARRE
'T BRUGSE VRIJE
Groenerei
BELFRY OF BRUGES
CITY HALL
FREREN FONTEINSTR.
KLEINE-SINT-AMANDSSTR.
BLINDE-EZELSTR.
STEENHOUWERSDIJK
ONZE LIEVE VROUWE QUARTER
ROCOCO
TER STEEGHERE
BASILICA OF THE HOLY BLOOD
BELFORT HALLEN
WOLLESTR.
Kraanrei
BOOTTOCHTEN MICHIELSSENS
VISMARKT
BRAAMBERGSTR.
STEENSTR.
HALLESTR.
FISH MARKET/ ARTIST MARKET
HOTEL BOURGOENSCH HOF
HUIDENVETTERSPLEIN
HOTEL KOFFIEBOONTJE
OUDE BURG
Dijver
TAPASBAR EST
Martin's Brugge
JOZEF SUVEESTR.
WAALSESTR.
SINT-NIKLAASSTRAAT
BOOTTOCHTEN DE MEULEMEESTER
BOOTTOCHTEN COUDENYS
KARTUIZERINNENSTR.
ROZENHOEDKAAI
0 50 yds
PAND 17
OUDE ZOMERSTR.
Voormalige Kartuizerinnenkerk
HOTEL DE ORANGERIE
0 50 m
LOPPEMSTR.
EEKHOUTSTR.
© MOON.COM
BRASSERIE BOURGOGNE DES FLANDRES

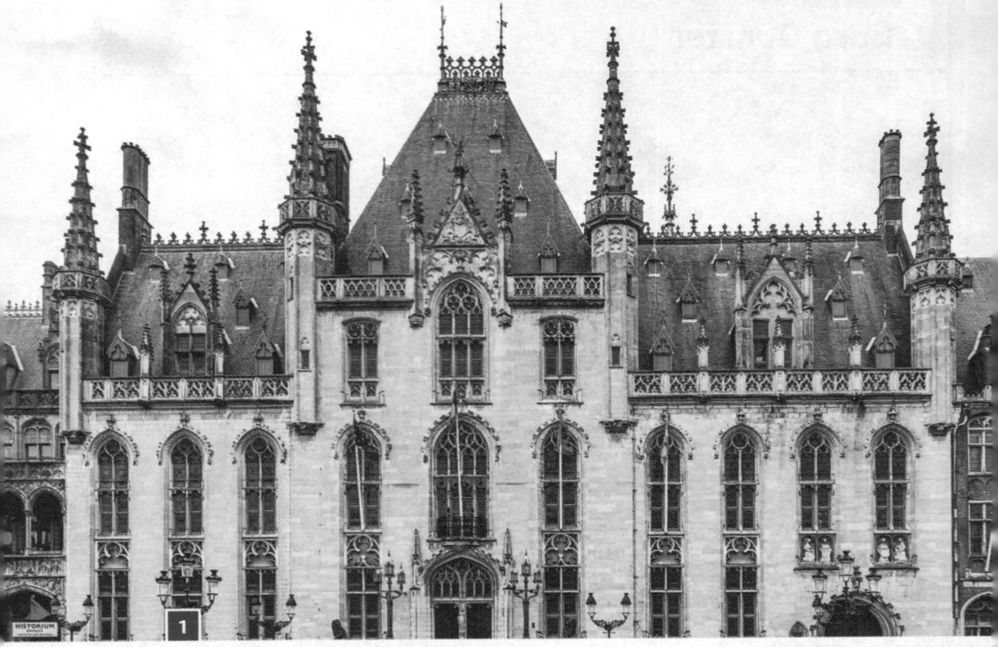
HISTORIUM
1

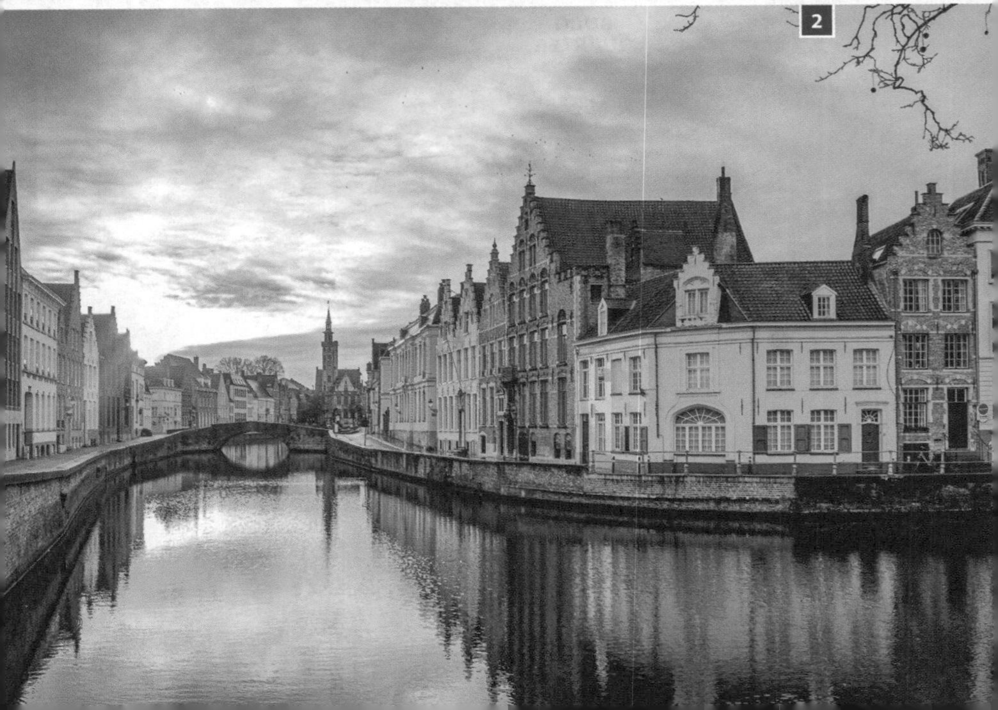
2

Bruges's Most Stunning Churches

sunset over Church of Our Lady

Bruges's key location close to the North Sea enabled this once small port to quickly grow from a town to a city in its own right in the 12th century. The number of churches in Bruges grew steadily alongside its wealth throughout the medieval period. Churches in Bruges vary in style, from Romanesque to Gothic to baroque, with some neo-Gothic additions from the 18th and 19th centuries, often decorated with works from Flanders's greatest painters. Stepping into a church in Bruges is almost like entering a museum, as most churches have their own art collections. Some churches require an admission fee for the museum section of the church, where you can see these priceless works of art on display. Here are some of the city's most stunning churches:

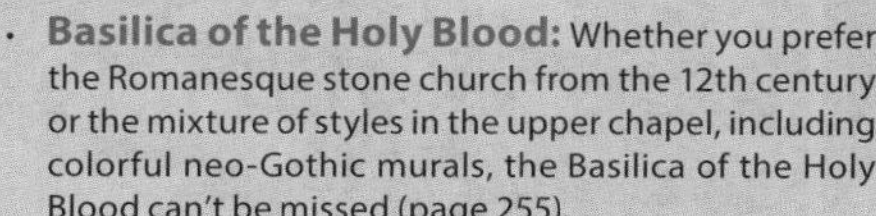

- **Basilica of the Holy Blood:** Whether you prefer the Romanesque stone church from the 12th century or the mixture of styles in the upper chapel, including colorful neo-Gothic murals, the Basilica of the Holy Blood can't be missed (page 255).
- **Church of Our Lady:** Bruges's most famous church, with its own Michelangelo statue, is resplendent with flying buttresses, Flemish masterpieces, and royal tombs (page 261).
- **Jeruzalemkerk** (in the Adornes Domain): The private chapel of the Adornes family, the Jeruzalemkerk is a Gothic replica of the Church of the Holy Sepulchre in Jerusalem, with ornate stained glass windows of and a skull-and-ladders covered altarpiece (page 262).
- **English Convent:** The chapel of this convent has a beautiful dome that carries sound perfectly and a stunning altar made with 22 kinds of marble (page 264).
- **Saint Salvator Cathedral:** The oldest parish church in Bruges is located in the Steenstraat Quarter. It has rich tapestries, tall stained glass windows, and Flemish primitives (page 257).

back to 1748 and a take a peek into the carillon room about three quarters of the way up.

Burg Square

BASILICA OF THE HOLY BLOOD

Burg 13; tel. 050 33 67 92; www.holyblood.com; 9:30am-12:30pm and 2pm-5:30pm daily; free

This well-known basilica in the heart of Bruges is famous for the relic of the Holy Blood. It's filled with elaborated stained glass windows and Gothic Revival murals. Devout Catholics, as well as the simply curious, wait in line to view the relic of the Holy Blood, encased in an ornate golden case, an object of pilgrimage for centuries. Though the bible doesn't mention anyone saving the blood Christ, legends assert that Joseph of Arimathea was able to save some on a cloth. During the crusades, this relic fell into the hands of the king of Jerusalem, who gifted it to the count of Flanders, who in turn brought it to Bruges. So the legends go, although recent research has shown that the unopened vial holding the cloth is likely a Byzantine perfume bottle from the 11th century.

Even for non-Catholics, the church's various chapels, built over the course of centuries, provide interesting insights into the history of Christianity. The lower chapel dates back

1: Provinciaal Court on Markt square **2:** canal with Jan van Eyck Square in the distance

1
2
3
4

to 1134, and the chapel of Saint Basil remains one of the best-preserved Romanesque churches in Belgium. Be sure to walk through the right nave to see the carved wooden sculpture of Madonna and her child and to climb the impressive medieval stone staircase to the Chapel of the Holy Blood. There is a small museum (€2.50) showcasing religious art; however, it's best to save your euros to donate to help preserve this stunning private church.

The main reason that visitors come is to see the upper chapel, which is where the veneration of the relic of the Holy Blood occurs, daily 11:30am-noon and 2-4pm. Visitors may need to wait for up to an hour during busy periods to see the relic up close. It's also possible to see the relic paraded through the streets of Bruges on **Ascension Day**, an annual tradition since 1291. Photos and talking are not allowed while the relic is on view.

CITY HALL
(Stadhuis)

Burg 12; tel. 050 44 81 11; www.visitbruges.be/en/stadhuis-city-hall; 9:30am-5pm daily; €6

Bruges's City Hall is one of the oldest in the region, dating back to 1376, and it has been the meeting place for the city ever since. This beautiful Gothic building sits on the location of the former castle of Bruges. The upstairs chamber (Gothic Hall), complete with a vaulted ceiling and 19th-century murals, is a showstopper of Gothic architecture in all its splendor; be sure to pick up a headset to learn more about the room. There is also a small museum on the history of Bruges, though many descriptions are only in Dutch. Your ticket to the Bruges City Hall also includes access to the decorated former **Court of Justice of Bruges** (Brugse Vrije, Burg 11a) and its impressive carved fireplace dating back to 1528, around the corner if you have time to burn. Access to the City Hall is free with the Musea Brugge Card.

1: horse carriage on Markt square **2:** sunset view of Church of Our Lady from Belfry **3:** iconic Rozenhoedkaai view of Bruges **4:** view from Gruuthusemuseum

Jan van Eyck Square
(Jan van Eyckplein)

open 24/7; free

A statue of the painter Jan van Eyck keeps a watchful eye over the iconic Spiegelrei canal, heavily featured in the cult classic *In Bruges.* Once the main harbor for the city of Bruges, Jan van Eyckplein is now a quiet square with a few benches and beautifully ornate houses. It's a lovely place to enjoy the sunset.

STEENSTRAAT QUARTER

Saint Salvator Cathedral
(Sint-Salvatorskathedraal)

Sint-Salvatorskoorstraat 8; tel. 050 33 68 41; http://sintsalvator.be; 10am-1pm and 2pm-5:30pm Mon.-Fr.i; 10am-1pm and 2pm-3:30pm Sat., 11:30am-noon and 2-5pm Sun.; free

The main cathedral of Bruges, dating back to 1280, rises above the Steenstraat. After a fire damaged the roof in the 1800s, a flat neo-Romanesque tower was added, differing considerably from the rest of the church and more reminiscent of a castle, to the chagrin of locals at the time.

ONZE LIEVE VROUWE QUARTER

Groeninge Museum

Kartuizerinnenstraat 6; tel. 050 44 87 11; www.museabrugge.be; 9:30am-5pm Tues.-Sat.; €12

Art lovers flock to Bruges for the Groeninge Museum, known for its collection of Netherlandish painters and Flemish Primitives, a group of Belgian artists who focused on reproducing the world as best they could in oil paintings. Subjects are often religious; paintings intended for churches (e.g. altarpieces) were often painted on triptychs, a three-part panel that can be closed.

Take a moment to admire the handmade 16th-century detailed Brussels tapestries, based on paintings, as soon as you enter. Saint Salvator is one of the best churches in Bruges to visit for **organ performances** (www.kathedraalconcerten.be; various times June-Oct.; €9-12), as the organ has been rebuilt

Steenstraat Quarter

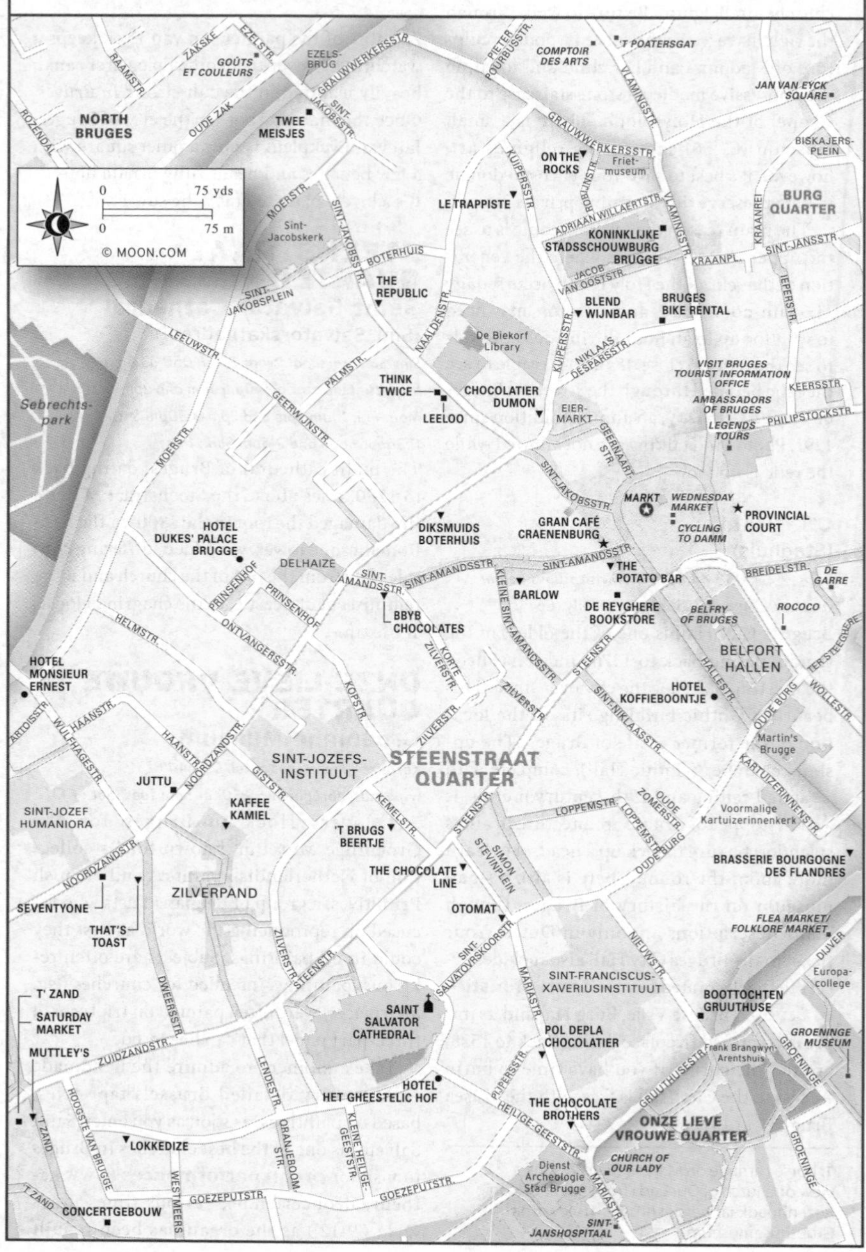
NORTH BRUGES
BURG QUARTER
STEENSTRAAT QUARTER
ONZE LIEVE VROUWE QUARTER
0 75 yds
0 75 m
© MOON.COM
GOÛTS ET COULEURS
EZELS-BRUG
TWEE MEISJES
COMPTOIR DES ARTS
'T POATERSGAT
JAN VAN EYCK SQUARE
ON THE ROCKS
Friet-museum
LE TRAPPISTE
KONINKLIJKE STADSSCHOUWBURG BRUGGE
BISKAJERS-PLEIN
Sint-Jacobskerk
THE REPUBLIC
BLEND WIJNBAR
BRUGES BIKE RENTAL
De Biekorf Library
Sebrechts-park
THINK TWICE
LEELOO
CHOCOLATIER DUMON
EIER-MARKT
VISIT BRUGES TOURIST INFORMATION OFFICE
AMBASSADORS OF BRUGES
LEGENDS TOURS
MARKT
WEDNESDAY MARKET
CYCLING TO DAMM
PROVINCIAL COURT
GRAN CAFÉ CRAENENBURG
HOTEL DUKES' PALACE BRUGGE
DIKSMUIDS BOTERHUIS
DELHAIZE
THE POTATO BAR
BARLOW
DE REYGHERE BOOKSTORE
BELFRY OF BRUGES
ROCOCO
DE GARRE
BBYB CHOCOLATES
BELFORT HALLEN
HOTEL MONSIEUR ERNEST
HOTEL KOFFIEBOONTJE
Martin's Brugge
SINT-JOZEFS-INSTITUUT
JUTTU
SINT-JOZEF HUMANIORA
KAFFEE KAMIEL
'T BRUGS BEERTJE
Voormalige Kartuizerinnenkerk
BRASSERIE BOURGOGNE DES FLANDRES
THE CHOCOLATE LINE
ZILVERPAND
SEVENTYONE
THAT'S TOAST
OTOMAT
FLEA MARKET/ FOLKLORE MARKET
Europa-college
SINT-FRANCISCUS-XAVERIUSINSTITUUT
T' ZAND
SATURDAY MARKET
SAINT SALVATOR CATHEDRAL
BOOTTOCHTEN GRUUTHUSE
MUTTLEY'S
POL DEPLA CHOCOLATIER
GROENINGE MUSEUM
Frank Brangwyn-Arentshuis
HOTEL HET GHEESTELIC HOF
THE CHOCOLATE BROTHERS
LOKKEDIZE
CHURCH OF OUR LADY
Dienst Archeologie Stad Brugge
CONCERTGEBOUW
SINT-JANSHOSPITAAL
ZAKSKE
RAAMSTR.
EZELSTR.
GRAUWWERKERSSTR.
ROZENDAL
OUDE ZAK
SINT-JAKOBSSTR.
PIETER POURBUSSTR.
VLAMINGSTR.
KUIPERSSTR.
ROBIJNSTR.
MOERSTR.
ADRIAAN WILLAERTSTR.
KRAANREI
BOTERHUIS
SINT-JANSSTR.
KRAANPL.
JACOB VAN OOSTSTR.
IEPERSTR.
SINT-JAKOBSPLEIN
NAALDENSTR.
NIKLAAS DESPARSSTR.
LEEUWSTR.
PALMSTR.
KEERSSTR.
GEERWIJNSTR.
PHILIPSTOCKSTR.
GEERNAART STR.
SINT-JAKOBSSTR.
SINT-AMANDSSTR.
BREIDELSTR.
PRINSENHOF
HELMSTR.
ONTVANGERSSTR.
KLEINE SINT-AMANDSSTR.
STEENSTR.
KORTE ZILVERSTR.
ZILVERSTR.
KOPSTR.
HALLESTR.
SINT-NIKLAASSTR.
OUDE BURG
WOLLESTR.
TER STEEGHERE
HAANSTR.
ARTOISSTR.
WULFHAGESTR.
NOORDZANDSTR.
GISTSTR.
KEMELSTR.
KARTUIZERINNENSTR.
LOPPEMSTR.
OUDE ZOMERSTR.
SIMON STEVINPLEIN
DWEERSSTR.
NIEUWSTR.
DIJVER
SINT-SALVATORSKOORSTR.
MARIASTR.
ZUIDZANDSTR.
LENDESTR.
PIJPERSSTR.
GRUUTHUSESTR.
GROENINGE
HEILIGE-GEESTSTR.
HOOGSTE VAN BRUGGE
ORANJEBOOM. STR.
KLEINE HEILIGE-GEESTSTR.
WESTMEERS
GOEZEPUTSTR.

multiple times to accommodate up to 60 stops. Medieval tombs, reliquaries, triptychs, and collection of Flemish paintings only add to the reasons to step inside.

The Groeninge Museum includes the Moreel Triptych by Hans Memling and famous works from Jan van Eyck, a well-known Flemish Primitive painter who worked in Bruges before his death in 1441. Beyond the Flemish Primitives, the museum also showcases six centuries of Flemish paintings up to the modern era. This museum is a must, and considering the sizable collection, it's a good value for the price of admission.

Rozenhoedkaai Viewpoint

Rozenhoedkaai; open 24/7; free

The most iconic photo of Bruges is often taken from the Rozenhoedkaai viewpoint along the Dijver canal. From here, you can enjoy the passing boats, the Belfry, and a few of the picturesque buildings in the medieval style that line the Kraanrei canal. Getting a photo without people can be a challenge here; it's much easier when traveling in the off-season. Early birds will also find the spot deserted prior to the arrival of day-trippers.

If you can imagine the arrival of ships in the Middle Ages, it's thought that salt was unloaded here before being sent to the houses of nobility. In the 18th century, rosaries were sold along this canal—and since that time, the locals have referred to it as the Quay of the Rosaries. It's certainly touristy, but it's a useful spot to catch a canal cruise.

Bonifacius Bridge

Groeninge 6, Arentshof; www.visitbruges.be/en/bonifaciusbrug-bonifaciusbridge; open 24/7; fre

Bruges's most famous bridge certainly has to be the Bonifacius Bridge, a picturesque stone bridge in the middle of Arentshof park with stunning views of the Church of Our Lady's stained glass windows. The bridge dates back to 1910 despite its older appearance; the stone was chosen to fit in with the surrounding buildings. It's a favorite spot for photos, but if you visit around sunrise, you're likely to have the bridge to yourself.

★ Gruuthusemuseum

Dijver 17; www.museabrugge.be; 9:30am-5pm daily; €12, €14 combo ticket with Church of Our Lady

The Gruuthusemuseum, one of the most underrated in Bruges, concisely takes the visitor on a journey through the city's history through textiles, maps, and other antiques. Recent renovations make the museum even more interactive and engaging than before. Besides the collection, the building, a former palace, is breathtaking inside. On the ground floor, you'll find early maps of Bruges along with decorative tapestries and early coins. On the second floor, you'll find beautiful examples of Bruges's lace in abundant amounts and pristinely preserved ceramics and glassware that look practically new.

Don't miss the majestic view of the Bonifacius Bridge on the third floor, up a steep stairwell, and the wing that connects the palace with the Church of Our Lady, allowing the lords of Gruuthuse to pray without leaving their home. If you have limited time, the Gruuthusemuseum covers a lot: the art of making lace, life throughout the centuries, and museum-quality tapestries. Even if you're not much of a history buff, you can still enter the courtyard for fairy tale views of the palace for free.

Sint-Janshospitaal

Mariastraat 38; www.museabrugge.be; 9:30am-5pm Tues.-Sat.; €12

Lovers of the strange and unusual should pay a visit to Sint-Janshospitaal, one of the oldest hospitals in Europe. Founded in the 12th century, Saint John's Hospital gives insight into the brutal reality of medicine in medieval times and its impressive progress over the ages. (The medieval equivalent of an ambulance is particularly fascinating.) Beyond medical instruments, the museum holds six paintings by Hans Memling, a well-known German painter who lived in Bruges, and the beautiful Shrine of St. Ursula, painted by Memling himself and

Onze Lieve Vrouwe Quarter

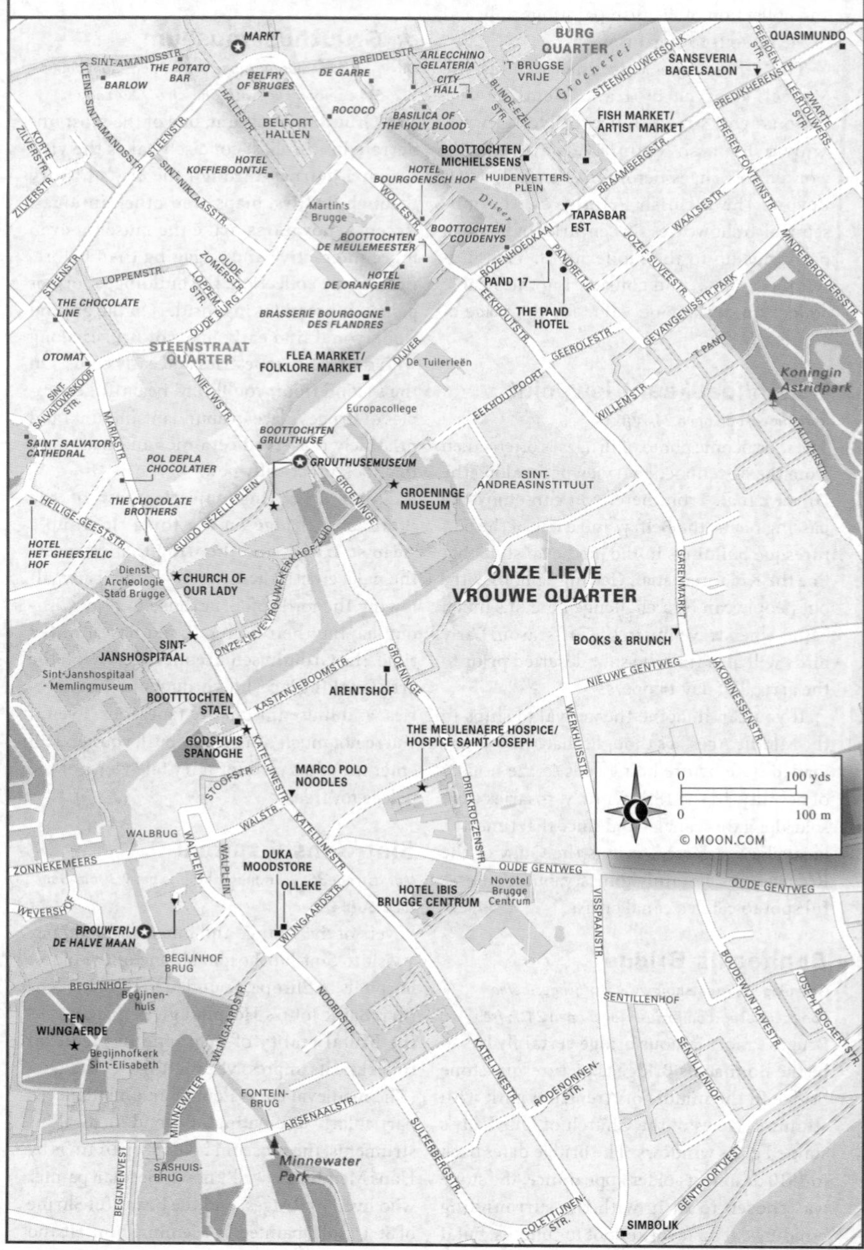
MARKT
BURG QUARTER
QUASIMUNDO
SINT-AMANDSSTR.
THE POTATO BAR
BARLOW
BREIDELSTR.
ARLECCHINO GELATERIA
'T BRUGSE VRIJE
SANSEVERIA BAGELSALON
BELFRY OF BRUGES
DE GARRE
CITY HALL
Groenerei
STEENHOUWERSDIJK
PEERDEN-STR.
PREDIKHERENSTR.
ZWARTE LEERTOUWERS-STR.
KLEINE SINT-AMANDSSTR.
HALLESTR.
ROCOCO
BASILICA OF THE HOLY BLOOD
BLINDE-EZEL-STR.
FISH MARKET/ ARTIST MARKET
BELFORT HALLEN
KORTE ZILVERSTR.
STEENSTR.
BOOTTOCHTEN MICHIELSSENS
BRAAMBERGSTR.
FRERE FONTEINSTR.
HOTEL KOFFIEBOONTJE
SINT-NIKLAASSTR.
HOTEL BOURGOENSCH HOF
HUIDENVETTERS-PLEIN
ZILVERSTR.
Martin's Brugge
WOLLESTR.
Dijver
TAPASBAR EST
WAALSESTR.
BOOTTOCHTEN DE MEULEMEESTER
BOOTTOCHTEN COUDENYS
ROZENHOEDKAAI
JOZEF SUVEESTR.
MINDERBROEDERSSTR.
OUDE ZOMERSTR.
PANDREITJE
STEENSTR.
LOPPEMSTR.
LOPPEM-STR.
HOTEL DE ORANGERIE
PAND 17
GEVANGENISSTR.
PARK
THE CHOCOLATE LINE
OUDE BURG
BRASSERIE BOURGOGNE DES FLANDRES
EEKHOUTSTR.
THE PAND HOTEL
STEENSTRAAT QUARTER
GEEROLFSTR.
'T PAND
OTOMAT
DIJVER
FLEA MARKET/ FOLKLORE MARKET
De Tuilerleën
Koningin Astridpark
SINT-SALVATORSKOOR-STR.
NIEUWSTR.
WILLEMSTR.
Europacollege
EEKHOUTPOORT
MARIASTR.
BOOTTOCHTEN GRUUTHUSE
STALIJZERSTR.
SAINT SALVATOR CATHEDRAL
POL DEPLA CHOCOLATIER
GRUUTHUSEMUSEUM
GROENINGE
SINT-ANDREASINSTITUUT
GROENINGE MUSEUM
HEILIGE-GEESTSTR.
THE CHOCOLATE BROTHERS
GUIDO GEZELLEPLEIN
HOTEL HET GHEESTELIC HOF
Dienst Archeologie Stad Brugge
ONZE-LIEVE-VROUWEKERKHOF-ZUID
CHURCH OF OUR LADY
ONZE LIEVE VROUWE QUARTER
GARENMARKT
SINT-JANSHOSPITAAL
BOOKS & BRUNCH
Sint-Janshospitaal - Memlingmuseum
KASTANJEBOOMSTR.
GROENINGE
NIEUWE GENTWEG
JAKOBINESSENSTR.
ARENTSHOF
BOOTTTOCHTEN STAEL
GODSHUIS SPANOGHE
THE MEULENAERE HOSPICE/ HOSPICE SAINT JOSEPH
WERKHUISSTR.
STOOFSTR.
KATELIJNESTR.
MARCO POLO NOODLES
DRIEKROEZENSTR.
100 yds
100 m
0
© MOON.COM
WALBRUG
WALSTR.
WALPLEIN
ZONNEKEMEERS
DUKA MOODSTORE
OLLEKE
OUDE GENTWEG
HOTEL IBIS BRUGGE CENTRUM
Novotel Brugge Centrum
WEVERSHOF
WIJNGAARDSTR.
BROUWERIJ DE HALVE MAAN
VISSPAANSTR.
BEGIJNHOF BRUG
BEGIJNHOF
Begijnenhuis
TEN WIJNGAERDE
Begijnhofkerk Sint-Elisabeth
NOORDSTR.
SENTILLENHOF
BOUDEWIJN RAVESTR.
JOSEPH BOGAERT STR.
MINNEWATER
RODENONNEN-STR.
FONTEIN-BRUG
ARSENAALSTR.
SULFERBERGSTR.
SASHUIS-BRUG
Minnewater Park
BEGIJNENVEST
GENTPOORTVEST
COLETTIJNEN-STR.
SIMBOLIK

In Bruges Filming Locations

In Bruges is a black comedy about two Irish hitmen who await their next orders while sightseeing in Bruges, starring Colin Farrell, Brendan Gleeson, and Ralph Fiennes. Since it came out in 2008, it's become a cult classic for its dark sense of humor, cheeky dialogue, and surprisingly insightful discussion of humanity's darkest moments. Even if you're not waiting for your next hit job, you can easily find many of the filming locations throughout the city center.

- The **Bruges Belfry** plays an important role in the climax of the movie (page 252).
- **Jeruzalemkerk** (Adornes Domain) was included in the film as a substitute for the Basilica of the Holy Blood (page 262).
- The courtyard of the **Gruuthusemuseum** is also featured prominently at the end of the film (page 259).
- The hitmen admire artworks by Flemish Primitives at the **Groeninge Museum** (page 257).
- On **Jan van Eyck Square,** the hitmen discuss their lives on a bench overlooking the square (page 257).

encased in shiny gold. Don't miss the small room holding Memling's triptych of St. John the Baptist and St. John the Evangelist, and be sure to head up the stairs to admire one of the oldest remaining vaulted ceilings in the world.

The most interesting part of the museum, arguably, is a perfectly preserved pharmacy dating back to 1634 and in use until the 1970s. In this separate building, you can learn about medicinal plants and see how medical prescriptions were filled in the past.

Church of Our Lady

(Onze-Lieve-Vrouwekerk)

Mariastraat; tel. 050 44 87 43; www.museabrugge.be; 9am-5pm Mon.-Sat., 1:30pm-5pm Sun.; €6, €14 combo ticket with Gruuthusemuseum

Onze-Lieve-Vrouwekerk has long been an important place for prayer in Bruges. Since 875, a chapel has sat on this exact spot. In the 13th century, the church grew and expanded into the Gothic-style building you see today. The church is the tallest building in Bruges thanks to its 115.6-meter (379.3-foot) brick tower, which serves as a good landmark for navigating the city.

Although visitors can easily step into the church for free, paid admission provides access to the impressive nave and choir, along with a view of Michelangelo's ***Madonna of Bruges*** statue. Don't miss the impressive tombs of Mary of Burgundy and her father Charles the Bold (although his corpse is missing and has never been found). The vibrant and well-preserved triptych in front of their tombs was painted by well-known Flemish painters Bernard van Orley and Marcus Gheeraerts I. Be sure to look up to see the window close to the altar, where the lords of the Gruuthuse would attend mass without leaving the many creature comforts of their palace.

Many come to the church to see *Madonna of Bruges,* the only Michelangelo statue sold outside of Italy during his lifetime. Purchased by a Bruges merchant in the 1500s, it has been twice removed from the city; it was famously recovered from the Nazis by the Monuments Men, a group of art historians, museum curators, and art professors working for the Allies during World War II.

SINT ANNA AND LANGESTRAAT QUARTERS

Folklife Museum (Volkskundemuseum)

Balstraat 43; tel. 050 44 87 43; www.museabrugge.be; 9:30am-5pm daily; adults €6, children free

For a step back into the past or to escape the crowds, head to the Volkskundemuseum. The small museum is housed within a former almshouse, allowing visitors a peek into what life was like for Bruges residents 100 years ago. Different houses showcase different aspects of Belgian culture, including a classroom, a home, a pharmacy, and a shoe repair shop. There is a cozy museum **café** aptly named for the friendly black cat that sleeps around the bar. Bring a few euros to enjoy a beer or coffee.

Sint-Janshuismolen and Koeleweimolen Windmills

Kruisvest 3 and 11; tel. 050 44 87 43; www.visitbruges.be/en/koeleweimolen-koeleweimill-2; 9:30am-12:30pm and 1:30pm-5pm Tues.-Sun. Apr.-Sept.; adults €4, children free

Medieval Bruges must have been a sight to behold, with its many towers and windmills. Much of that same skyline is still visible from the raised ramparts of Bruges, once part of the medieval walls dating back to the 1300s that protected the city from invaders. Today, what remains of the walls and the windmills that top them are part of a long, thin park called **Kruisvest.** A tree-lined, 19th-century promenade along the canal leads to steeper (sometimes slippery, with stairs) uphill paths that allow a closer look at the windmills on top of what were once heavily fortified walls, and are now lush, green, smooth hills.

The Bruges ramparts were built in several stages, the first stage being 14th-century earthen walls and canals with centralized ports for entry into the city. Approximately 100 years later, walls were added as an extra defense. In the 17th century, bastions (projecting, angular corners built into the walls) and ravelins (a triangular fortification forcing opponents to spread out) were added to reinforce the edges. In the late 18th century, as Bruges transformed into a major port city and no longer required fortifications, the walls were disassembled. Shortly after, the fortifications were transformed into a greenway. You need to use your imagination a bit to imagine the many soldiers who protected the walls beyond the ramparts-turned-rolling-green-hills today.

Nearly 25 windmills once stood here. Today Bruges has only four windmills, with just two of these open to the public in peak season. **Sint-Janshuismolen** was constructed in 1770 and stands in the place of an even earlier windmill. The **Koeleweimolen** was built in 1765 and still grinds grains into flour today. Unlike Sint-Janshuismolen, which stands in the place it was first constructed, the Koeleweimolen was moved to its current site close to Dampoort, the road named after the former city gate at this location. Both windmills hold small museums open during peak season that give you a glimpse into their history. Those without a fear of vertigo can climb the slightly terrifying stairs to see the windmills in action, but it's not necessary to climb the windmill to appreciate the history here. Be aware that the steps up to the windmills can be slippery in the rain. Even if you're not able to enter the windmills outside peak season, you can still admire them from outside the gates or from the ramparts.

Adornes Domain

Peperstraat 3; tel. 050 33 88 83; www.adornes.org; 10am-5pm Mon.-Sat.; €8

This private chapel and museum is still the property of the 17th generation of the Adornes, a wealthy Belgian family whose storied ancestor led an extraordinary life that included exploring Jerusalem, Egypt, and Scotland in the 1400s. The private chapel, **Jeruzalemkerk,** modeled off the Holy Sepulchre Church in Jerusalem, is truly one

Sint Anna and Langestraat Quarters

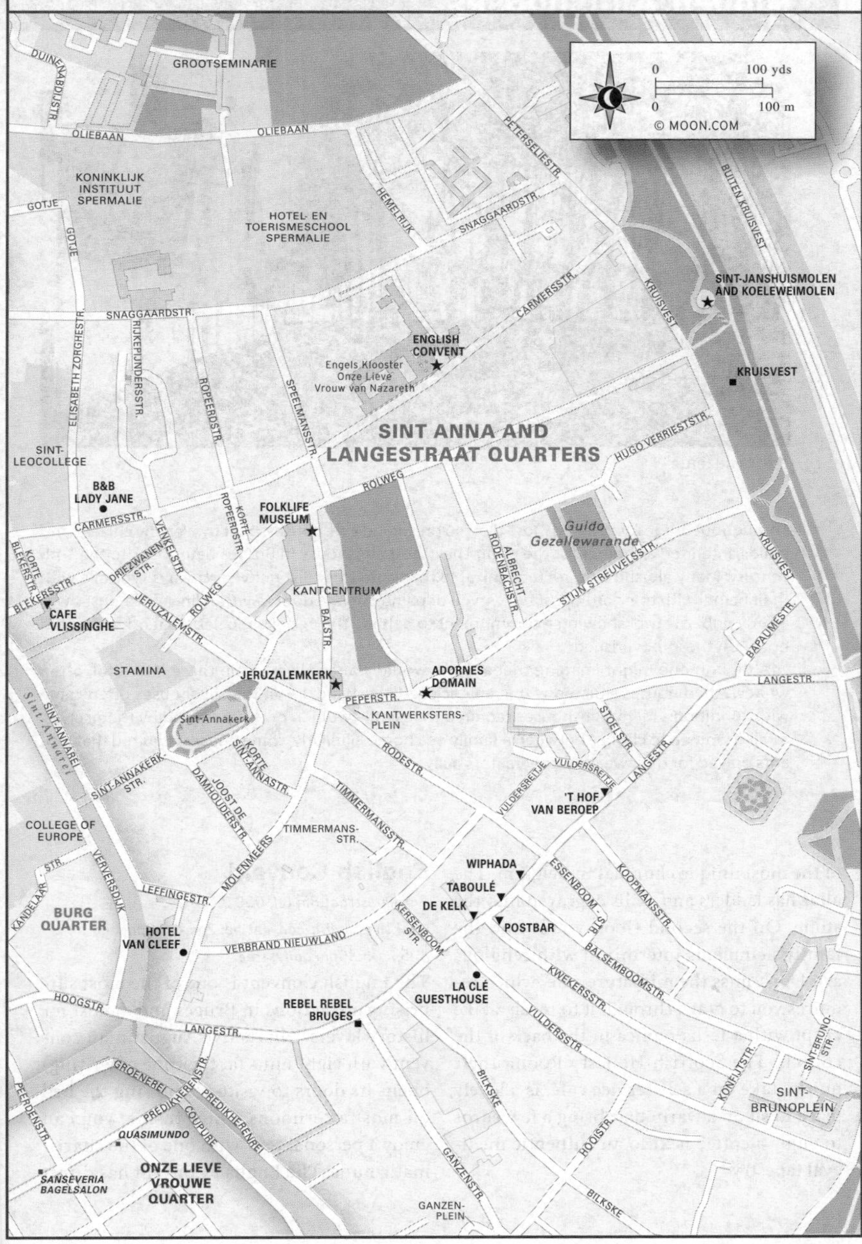
0
100 yds
0
100 m
© MOON.COM
GROOTSEMINARIE
OLIEBAAN
KONINKLIJK INSTITUUT SPERMALIE
HOTEL- EN TOERISMESCHOOL SPERMALIE
SNAGGAARDSTR.
ENGLISH CONVENT
Engels Klooster Onze Lieve Vrouw van Nazareth
SINT-JANSHUISMOLEN AND KOELEWEIMOLEN
KRUISVEST
SINT ANNA AND LANGESTRAAT QUARTERS
SINT-LEOCOLLEGE
B&B LADY JANE
FOLKLIFE MUSEUM
Guido Gezellewarande
KANTCENTRUM
CAFE VLISSINGHE
STAMINA
JERUZALEMKERK
ADORNES DOMAIN
Sint-Annakerk
KANTWERKSTERS-PLEIN
'T HOF VAN BEROEP
COLLEGE OF EUROPE
TIMMERMANS-STR.
WIPHADA
TABOULÉ
DE KELK
POSTBAR
BURG QUARTER
HOTEL VAN CLEEF
LA CLÉ GUESTHOUSE
REBEL REBEL BRUGES
SINT-BRUNOPLEIN
QUASIMUNDO
SANSEVERIA BAGELSALON
ONZE LIEVE VROUWE QUARTER
GANZEN-PLEIN

☆ *Godshuizen:* Bruges's Hidden Almshouses

Ten Wijngaerde

Throughout Bruges, you'll find more than 46 preserved almshouses, built by wealthy citizens and guilds, intended as homes for the poor. The oldest almshouse in Bruges dates back to the 14th century. Many almshouses are recognizable thanks to their distinctive archways typically with their name (with the word *Godshuis*) carved or painted in the doorway. Building almshouses was a fairly public way of showing a commitment to helping the poor in a society that otherwise did not assist the impoverished.

Although one might imagine that anyone would want to live within these beautiful, often whitewashed houses situated within an enclosed courtyard, life in the almshouses often came with conditions. Many almshouses required that single women or widows lived by themselves, forcing women to choose between a family or a home. Similarly, some houses required that tenants prayed for their wealthy benefactors daily.

of the most unique churches in Belgium. The altar has ladders and skills engraved into the stone. On the second floor, you'll find the family's emblems intermixed with religious art. Don't miss the miniature gate, which requires you to crawl through it to reach a fake crypt with a Jesus replica in the back of the church. The Scottish Honesty Room, their quirky take on a self-service café, is a lovely place to sit on a warm day; bring a few euros to enjoy a coffee next to an authentic medieval tapestry.

English Convent

Carmersstraat 85; tel. 050 33 24 24; www.the-english-convent.be; 2pm-3:30pm and 4:15pm-5:30pm daily; free

The English Convent is one of the most surprising attractions in Bruges and a must for history lovers. This active Augustinian convent with eight nuns (at the time of writing) opens its doors to visitors who ring the bell on most afternoons. Once inside, you can enjoy a personal tour with one of the charismatic nuns. The English Convent has direct

Today, many of the *godshuizen* are still in use as affordable housing for the elderly, still owned by the same wealthy families. They're easy to pass if you are just wandering around, so don't be afraid to try the door if you pass one. There's something magical about walking from a street through a nondescript door and into these beautiful, quiet courtyards. It should be noted that almshouses are generally private property, so it's best to be quiet and respectful if you visit. The doors are typically open during the day (9am-5pm) and locked at night.

TEN WIJNGAERDE

Begijnhof 24; www.visitbruges.be/religieuserfgoed/begijnhof; courtyard 6:30am-6:30pm daily, Begijnenhuisje 10am-5pm daily

Ten Wijngaerde has a slightly different history than other almshouses, as it was populated by single women and widows who wished to devote their lives to the church without taking formal vows. The almshouses vary in age but generally date back to the 16th-18th centuries. In order to get here, you'll need to cross over the impressive stone Wijngaard Bridge. Today, Ten Wijngaerde functions as a Benedictine convent, with a small museum open to tourists. Enjoy the spacious courtyard filled with daffodils in spring.

GODSHUIS SPANOGHE

Katelijnestraat 8; 9am-5pm daily

Smaller than other almshouses in the area, Godshuis Spanoghe was established in 1680 as a home for poor women. Don't be nervous about the dark alleyway leading to this almshouse, signed clearly from the street. You'll be rewarded with views of the ancient Sint-Janshospitaal across the canal.

THE MEULENAERE HOSPICE/HOSPICE SAINT JOSEPH

Nieuwe Gentweg 8-22; 9am-5pm daily

The impressive entryway of the Meulenaere Hospice with the date of establishment written on the wall (1613) makes you wonder what's beyond the gates. Once the home of poor widows, the almshouse now holds a perfectly manicured courtyard surrounded by whitewashed houses. Look for the old water pump in the garden.

links to Sir Thomas More, whose adopted kin helped found this convent in 1629 (take a close look at the vertebrae of More's neck enclosed in the frame of his original portrait). Even if you're not into church history, the domed chapel with its impressive altar—made with 22 kinds of marble—is truly spectacular. If you're lucky, you'll also get to see a liturgical prayer performed by the sisters. Be sure to carry a few euros to buy a souvenir postcard or booklet to support the church's upkeep.

NORTH BRUGES

Ezelpoort

open 24/7; free

The Ezelpoort is one of the most beautiful city gates still standing in Bruges. The gate was first built in 1297 before being rebuilt less than 100 years later as part of the early city ramparts. Passing through the Ezelpoort by bike or foot, you can admire the swans in the water on the right of the gate. The cobblestone view of Ezelstraat behind the gate creates a stunning welcome into Bruges.

Sports and Recreation

PARKS

Onze Lieve Vrouwe Quarter

KONINGIN ASTRIDPARK

Stalijzerstraat 11; open 24/7

Koningin Astridpark is a small, well-landscaped park in the Onze Lieve Vrouwe Quarter, mostly used by locals. A monastery garden for over 500 years, it became a park in 1796. In the middle of the park is an elegant bust of Astrid, a beloved Belgian queen who died in a tragic car accident. Enjoy the picturesque landscaping and the pagoda, perfect for enjoying a herring from the nearby Vismarkt.

ARENTSHOF

Groeninge 2/4; open 24/7

One of the smallest green spaces in Bruges, entered through an ornate stone archway, this park is located on the northern edge of the Onze Lieve Vrouwe Quarter. Many tourists rush away after taking an iconic photo of the Bonifacius Bridge, but the beauty of this small park shines close to sunset when the windows of Church of Our Lady begin to be illuminated and the day-trippers are gone. The views from the benches of the impressive Gruuthusemuseum are worth a pause.

MINNEWATER PARK

Minnewater 1; open 24/7

Minnewater Park is easily Bruges's most romantic park, with spacious trails where lovers often walk hand-in-hand along the reservoir. The park sits along the south medieval boundaries of the city, in the Onze Lieve Vrouwe Quarter. The story of the park, known for its "Lake of Love," dates back to Roman times, when a young man, Stomberg, fell in love with a girl named Minna, who refused to marry someone else and ran off into the forest where her Romeo found her and she died in his arms. There are different versions of the story, but it's said that the picturesque stone Minnewater bridge is where her grave is today. If you're a couple, it's said that you will be in eternal love if you walk over this bridge with your partner.

There are several **cycling paths** throughout the park, as well as **walking trails** that weave through scenic tree-covered paths. To cruise through the park, you'll need to catch a boat tour elsewhere in the city. Minnewater can get crowded on a nice day. Be careful of the swans, which can get aggressive looking for food.

Sint Anna and Langestraat Quarters

KRUISVEST

Kruisvest; open 24/7

On the eastern outskirts of Bruges in the Sint Anna and Langestraat Quarters, you'll find the quiet Kruisvest, a long park home to four windmills including the **Sint-Janshuismolen** and **Koeleweimolen.** It's a picturesque place to enjoy a sunrise or sunset away from the crowds. Runners looking for a challenge may enjoy the hilly terrain, although it's best to use caution on rainy days as the steep path can be slippery. It's worth climbing the hills for a glimpse of Bruges's medieval skyline.

North Bruges

HOF DE JONGHE

Hof de Jonghe; sunrise-sunset

In good weather, consider following the mysterious sign from Langerei to Hof de Jonghe. This hidden park in Bruges has three friendly sheep that roam the park, grazing in the grass. It's a nice quiet place to get away from the crowds while enjoying a bit of greenery. Dog lovers will also meet many friendly dogs as this small park is a favorite among dog walkers.

1: Minnewater Park **2:** Gruuthusemuseum **3:** view from Sint-Janshuismolen (Kruisvest park)

CYCLING

Bruges is a fairly bike-friendly city. Although locals cycle within the medieval city center, its narrow streets, shared with cars, can be difficult for cycling. A popular trip is cycling to **Damme,** less than 10 kilometers (6.2 miles) northeast of Bruges.

There are a number of bike rental agencies in Bruges. For those who want more flexibility, **Hotel Koffieboontje** has longer hours for rentals. Though not necessary for confident bikers, a **tour** can be helpful, usually providing a helmet (not always included with rentals), a rain jacket for weather changes, and insurance in case of any accidents. Independent travelers looking for value will be a fan of the bike-sharing initiative **Blue Bikes,** though using this service requires a bit of effort beforehand.

Bike Paths

CITY WALLS BIKE PATH

(Fietspad Vestingen)

Cycling Distance: *9 kilometers (5.5 miles) round-trip*

Cycling Time: *1 hour*

Trailhead: *Bruges Train Station or Ezelpoort*

Information and Maps: *www.brugge.be/fietsroute-vestingen*

Indulge yourself in an idyllic cycle along the old city walls of Bruges, starting from the train station or Ezelpoort. Follow the blue signs for the Vestingroute to sail past Bruges's windmills, the Ezelpoort, and a reconstructed crane used in medieval times. Although the route is sometimes shared with cars, this bike route avoids the worst of the crowds and cobblestones of the city center. The cycle should take around an hour at a leisurely pace; it's hard to get lost, as you simply need to ensure that the city walls are in plain sight.

FIETSROUTE 10

Cycling Distance: *9 kilometers (5.5 miles) round-trip*

Cycling Time: *1 hour*

Trailhead: *Bloedput, North Bruges*

Information and Maps: *www.brugge.be/fietsroute-9-en-10*

Get away from the hustle and bustle of the crowds in peak season along this scenic bike path following Fietsroute 10 (Koude Keuken-Bloedput). Signage is very clear as long as you start next to signs for Bloedput. This route brings you to a picturesque estate, Koude Keuken, with a dreamy castle that dates back to 1328, and the lush Coppietersbos Forest to bring you back to Bruges city center.

Bike Rentals and Tours

BLUE BIKES BELGIUM

Hendrik Brugmansstraaat 3/002; tel. 050 39 68 26; www.blue-bike.be; 7am-7pm Mon.-Fri.; €12 membership fee, €1.15 daily

Blue Bikes Belgium is a regional bike-sharing initiative, one of the most affordable options for regular travelers to Belgium. The bikes are well-maintained seven-gear bikes with hand breaks, rented via an automatic machine that requires a bit of legwork ahead. You'll need to order card, which comes in the mail, before your trip. From each machine, you'll receive pin to check out a bike, which will be assigned from the available bikes at the station. In theory, it's possible to rent a bike the same day with a deposit (€18.30) during office hours, but true bike lovers should request a Blue Bike card in advance (at least three weeks ahead of their travels). With a membership card, members can rent bikes 24 hours a day at incredibly affordable rates.

BRUGES BIKE RENTAL

Niklaas Desparsstraat 17; tel. 050 61 61 08; www.brugesbikerental.be; 10am-8pm daily; €13/day single bike

The best-known bike shop in Bruges shares its location with a hairdresser. It's a strange combination, but the location close to Markt square makes Bruges Bike Rental a popular choice. Each bike rental includes a colored city map with routes, a basket, panniers for storage, child seats, and straps to hold down your bags. Tandem bikes (€30/day), multiday, and shorter rentals are also possible.

HOTEL KOFFIEBOONTJE

Hallestraat 4; tel. 050 33 80 27; www.bikerentalkoffieboontje.be; 9am-10pm daily; €15/day single bike

For those planning a longer cycle and concerned about closing hours of the bike rental shops, Hotel Koffieboontje is a great option, as the hotel hours offer more flexibility. This hotel offers a variety of bikes regardless of whether you're staying at the hotel, including child seats and trailers for children's bikes. Tandem bikes (€25/day), multiday, and shorter rentals are also possible.

QUASIMUNDO

Predikherenstraat 28; tel. 050 330 775; www.quasimundo.com; tours 1:30pm daily Apr.-Oct.; adults €33, students €28, children 6-12 €1, children under 5 free

QuasiMundo is a popular Belgian bike tour agency that regularly takes tourists on day trips on the scenic bike path between Damme and Bruges. Reserve ahead and show up on time for this local tour company to show you the best of greater Bruges by bike. Tour price includes bike rental, local guide, rain jacket, insurance, and helmet. Bike tours depart daily in peak season along the scenic bike route to Damme, with a pit stop for a drink. You'll arrive back by 5:30pm.

TOURS

Walking Tours

LEGENDS TOURS

Markt 1; tel. 0498 69 37 79; https://legendstours.be; tour times vary; €0-50

Legends Tours is one of the longest-running Bruges tour outfits with daily tours for every budget, from daily free walking tours to higher-priced beer tours in the evenings. One of their best-value tours for those visiting by ship is their Day Tour of Bruges, including transport to and from the Zeebrugge port.

AMBASSADORS OF BRUGES

Markt 1; tel. 0484 93 58 78; https://ambassadorsofbruges.com; tour times vary; €0-16

Run by a knowledgeable Dutchman living in Bruges, Ambassadors of Bruges is a small company that offers history tours of Bruges in English and Spanish. They have a daily free tour that is pay-what-you-want, although for those looking for something a bit more engaging, their other history tour offers good value. In Markt square, look for a yellow umbrella.

Boat Tours

There's nothing like seeing Bruges's famous bridges from the canals. Unfortunately, it's not possible to rent a boat to navigate for yourself, as boating is quite regulated. Soon, all boats cruising through Bruges will be electric, too.

BOOTTOCHTEN BRUGGE

boottochten-brugge.be; 10am-6pm daily; adults €10, children 3-11 €6, children under 3 free

Enjoy a half-hour scenic boat tour through Bruges from five different starting points as your captain tells you about the city. Bring cash for payment. The starting points are:

- Michielssens, Huidenvettersplein 13; tel. 050 33 00 41
- Coudenys, Rozenhoedkaai; tel. 050 33 13 75
- De Meulemeester, Wollestraat 32; tel. 050 33 41 20
- Gruuthuse, Nieuwstraat 11; tel. 050 33 32 93
- Stael, Katelijnestraat 4; tel. 050 33 27 71

Entertainment and Events

PERFORMING ARTS

Despite its small size, Bruges shines when it comes to the performing arts, particularly in terms of classical music. Summer is the best time to come to Bruges for arts-related performances.

CONCERTGEBOUW

't Zand 34; www.concertgebouw.be; box office 2pm-5pm Mon.-Fri.; tickets €22-55

Not everything in Bruges is historic. The Concertgebouw is a cutting-edge modern building built in 2002 by architecture firm Robbrecht en Daem. It can hold up to 12,900 guests in a large, rather sparse concert hall and 320 guests in the cozier chamber music hall. Those curious about the building itself can take a **tour** (2pm-6pm Wed.-Sat., 10am-2pm Sun.; €8; free tour 3pm Sat.), which takes you behind the scenes to show off the advanced acoustics and a lesser-known viewpoint of Bruges's medieval city center from the top of the building. The performances vary, from comedians to classical quartets to modern pop music.

KONINKLIJKE STADSSCHOUWBURG BRUGGE

Vlamingstraat 29; www.ccbrugge.be; 1pm-5pm Tues.-Fri., 4pm-7pm Sat.; tickets €0-50

Bruges's most elegant theater is surprisingly unknown to many visitors to the city. The Royal Stadsschouwburg is a beautiful neo-renaissance theater built in 1869, with more than 700 seats decked out in plush red velvet and gold. The theater showcases cultural lectures, theater products, and dance performances.

MAGDALENA CONCERT HALL (Magdalenazaal)

Magdalenastraat 27; www.ccbrugge.be; 1pm-5pm Tues.-Fri., 4pm-7pm Sat.; tickets €0-50

The Magdalenastaal is just outside the historic city center, very close to the train station. Don't let the plain modern exterior discourage you from booking a concert here, as it regularly hosts pop and rock concerts by artists from all around the world.

BELFRY OF BRUGES CARILLON CONCERTS

Belfry of Bruges; www.carillon-brugge.be/concerten.htm; 11am-noon Wed. and Sat.-Sun. year-round, 9pm-10pm Mon. and Wed. June-Sept.; free

Sit under the Belfry or close to Markt square year-round to experience the magic of the carillon's 47 bells played by Bruges's carillon master and other carillon players, especially close to sunset in peak season. Unlike other concerts, it's free to listen, wrapping the Markt in an elegant sound that makes Bruges feel even more magical.

SAINT SALVATOR CATHEDRAL CONCERTS

Sint-Salvatorskathedraal Brugge; www.kathedraalconcerten.be; June-Oct.; €9-12

Listen to heavenly music in the stunning Saint Salvator Cathedral as musicians from all over the world perform classical pieces on the organ and other accompanying instruments. Tickets in summer can sell out for these popular events, so be sure to reserve ahead.

FESTIVALS AND EVENTS

Spring

MAY FAIR (Meifoor)

't Zand; www.brugge.be/meifoor; Apr./May; free

There's nothing like a carnival to make you feel like a kid again. Each year, Bruges hosts a three-week-long carnival along the 't Zand square (and other locations in Bruges), with more than 90 rides, a parade for kids, and fireworks. Despite the modern rides, the carnival has a long tradition in Bruges dating back to 1200, when Bruges was given the right to host an annual fair. Despite the name, the fair begins on the third Friday after Easter, which can be in April depending on the year, and ends after Ascension Day.

Summer

ASCENSION DAY/PROCESSION OF THE HOLY BLOOD

Locations vary; www.bloedprocessiebrugge.be; May; free, seats €4-12

One of the most important events of the year has to be the Procession of the Holy Blood (Dutch: Heilig Bloedprocesie) when the Relic of the Holy Blood is paraded around Bruges as it has been since 1304. Today the UNESCO-recognized parade is reenacted by more than 1,700 residents of Bruges, complete with costumes, music, dances, and small plays (including a passion play). The schedule of the parade is listed online and visitors can watch for free from various points throughout the city center; however, seats in the stands cost a marginal amount of money (€4 for benches and €12 for seats in the stands).

MAFESTIVAL BRUGES

Locations vary; www.mafestival.be; July/Aug.; prices vary

For lovers of early music and musical history, the MAFestival is a delight, showcasing organ, harpsichord, singing, recorder, and other classical instruments through a series of lectures, performances, and meetings. Since 1960, music lovers, as well as those in the music industry, have been gathering to learn about the past through themed visits and competitions. Tickets are sold per event, and the events are spread throughout Bruges.

ZANDFEESTEN

't Zand; http://brugsezandfeesten.be; first Sun. in July, first Sun. in Aug., third Sun. in Sept.; free

Antique lovers will want to come to Bruges over the summer to visit the largest antique and flea market in Flanders. This is a great place to pick up quality Flemish antiques for a fair price, or just to browse. The main location is on 't Zand square.

Fall

OPEN MONUMENT DAY (Open Monumentendag)

throughout the city; www.bruggeomd.be; mid-Sept.; free

You might pass many beautiful buildings in Bruges that seem quite closed to the public, but during one weekend in September, many private institutions housed in historic buildings as well as museums open their doors to the public for free. If you're lucky enough to be in Bruges over this weekend, pick up an Open Monumentendag booklet for a few euros at the main library, the city archive, or various other public institutions to find out where you can take a sneak peek into many places often not open to tourists.

Winter

WINTERGLOED CHRISTMAS MARKET

Locations vary; www.brugge.be/wintergloed; Nov.-Jan.; free

Don't let the cold deter you from Bruges's famous winter markets, which will warm you up with their cozy atmosphere and *gluhwein* (mulled wine). Bruges's winter markets have recently gone green, with LED lights and eco-friendly attractions spread throughout the city center. The real appeal is snacking on Belgian delicacies and sipping warm drinks with such a splendid view. If you're cold, get your hands on a glass of *gluhkriek*, which is traditional warm, sour Belgian beer.

BRUGES BEER FESTIVAL

Locations vary; www.brugsbierfestival.be; first weekend in Feb.; €15 starter pack

The Bruges Beer Festival is one of the premier beer festivals in Belgium. It has gained international fame among beer connoisseurs for its wide selection of 90-plus breweries from across Belgium, including traditional makers brewing hundred-year-old recipes alongside some of Belgium's most exciting new microbreweries. Tickets can go quickly, so buy a ticket ahead on the website. A starter pack includes a tasting glass, a few tokens, and a guide.

Shopping

BURG QUARTER

ROCOCO

Wollestraat 9; tel. 050 34 04 72; www.rococobrugge.be/index-nl.aspx; 11am-6pm Mon.-Tues. and Thurs., 11am-5pm Wed. and Sun., 10:30am-6pm Fri.-Sat.

Rococo is a family-run lace shop in the heart of Bruges that sells lace for every budget, from small souvenirs to elaborate tablecloths to face masks. Their lace is mostly new, but they also stock vintage lace for those with higher budgets. The shop is crammed with lace, with every wall lined with lace patterns. Their staff speaks multiple languages and is happy to educate visitors about lace.

DE REYGHERE BOOKSTORE

Markt 12-13; tel. 050 33 34 03; https://dereyghere.be; 9am-6pm daily

De Reyghere is the oldest bookstore in operation in Bruges, in business for 129 years. They also own the shop next door, which specializes in travel-related books. The bookstore specializes in books in Dutch, but you'll also find a thoughtful selection of English and French books, from fiction to Belgian nonfiction about the region. The interior is cozy with creamy white wooden bookshelves. This is a great spot to pick up regional maps.

STEENSTRAAT QUARTER

Steenstraat and **Noordzandstraat** are the main shopping veins of Bruges, with countless international brands as well as popular Belgian chains such as Kruidvat for picking up necessities. Discerning shoppers will also find smaller independent Belgian boutiques showcasing sustainable clothing, leather shoes, and vintage-inspired statement pieces.

Clothing

SEVENTYONE

Noordzandstraat 75; tel. 0468 04 87 41; www.seventyone.be; 10am-6pm Mon.-Sat.

Fans of vintage-style clothing will love the retro-inspired designs featuring many Belgian and Dutch designers in this airy store filled with Marilyn Monroe-inspired accents and fantastic rugs.

THINK TWICE

Sint-Jakobsstraat 21; tel. 0495 36 39 08; https://thinktwice-secondhand.be; 10am-6pm Mon.-Sat., 1pm-6pm Sun.

Not everything needs to be new to make a statement. Think Twice is a popular Belgian secondhand clothing store with a keen eye for high-quality vintage pieces at an affordable price. It's a favorite among Bruges fashionistas. In their one-of-a-kind selection, you can count on a well-curated mix of '80s jackets, high-rise jeans, thick coats, and vintage statement pieces. Watch for their €1 sales!

TWEE MEISJES

Sint-Jakobsstraat 61; tel. 050 33 16 61; https://tweemeisjes.be; 2pm-6pm Tues. and Sun., 11am-7pm Wed.-Sat.

Color lovers, unite! Twee Meisjes is a fun clothing shop focusing on colorful dresses, fun prints, and classic cuts with a mix of international brands. Their vintage-inspired clothing selection is restocked weekly, and the focus here is not on trends, but rather expressing yourself.

LEELOO

Sint-Jakobsstraat 19; tel. 050 34 04 55; www.leeloo.be; 10pm-6pm Mon.-Sat.

Bruges's first animal-friendly clothing shop has been creating cute T-shirts, sweatshirts, socks, and other clothing for more than 20 years. Within Leeloo, you'll find more than 25 European eco-friendly clothing brands including the owners' own brand that features

---

1: Goûts et Couleurs **2:** Wednesday Market on Markt square **3:** Duka Moodstore

1

2

3

Lace in Bruges

'T Apostelientje

The Flemish tradition of lace-making has brought great wealth to Bruges for generations. Since the 16th century, Flemish lace has been synonymous with wealth and luxury. The popularity of lace collars and other lace pieces among aristocrats resulted in numerous lace-making schools within Bruges and other Flemish provinces in the 19th century.

The Bruges style of lace-making is incredibly time-consuming, using up to 200 needles (known as bobbins) and 1,500 threads at once for more elaborate pieces. The decline of the lace industry came in the mid-1900s when the value of lace dipped due to the popularization of machine-made lace. Today, there are still an estimated 1,000 lace-makers in Bruges who produce pieces by hand, mostly as a hobby. But don't walk into just any shop in Bruges that boasts lace. The shops selling high-quality lace are few and far between, with many tourist shops passing off machine-made versions as the original. The following shops are great places to learn about the delicate art of lace-making:

- **Rococo** is a lace shop close to Markt square owned by a fifth-generation lace-maker. As you explore her beautiful shop, you'll learn about the history of lace and see beautiful handmade pieces (page 272).
- True lace aficionados will want to visit **'t Apostelientje** (Balstraat 11; tel. 050 33 78 60; www.apostelientje.be; 1pm-5pm Tues.-Sat.), an antique shop specializing in Flemish lace within a beautiful almshouse. The shop is beautifully organized, almost like a museum, and has something for every budget. The shopkeeper, Anna, is a true connoisseur, and it's worth dropping by her shop during its opening hours if you're in the Sint Anna Quarter.

modern and novelty pattern designs along with great customer service.

JUTTU

Noordzandstraat 54; tel. 050 33 10 06; www.juttu.be; 10am-6pm Mon.-Fri., 10am-6:30pm Sat.

One of the shopping highlights of Bruges, Juttu features sustainably made clothing, gifts, and books in a unique urban concept store with items for women, men, and children. Even if their minimalistic clothes aren't your favorite, their emphasis on local designers makes Juttu a great place to find surprising souvenirs, from handwoven scarves to adorable kitchenware. This Scandinavian-inspired shop truly has something for everyone, so don't hesitate to take 20 minutes to browse the ever-changing selection.

ONZE LIEVE VROUWE QUARTER

Katelijnestraat and neighboring **Wijngaardstraat** can feel like a tourist trap closer to Onze-Lieve-Vrouwekerk, but Katelijnestraat quiets down quickly farther south. You'll find shops catering to locals, from hardware stores to hobby stores, but you'll also find studios showcasing some of the best handmade products from Bruges as well as fun lifestyle stores perfect for gifts.

Home Goods

DUKA MOODSTORE

Wijngaardstraat 14; tel. 0478 98 79 10; www.duka-store.be; 11am-6pm Tues.-Fri., 10:30am-6pm Sat., 1:30pm-6pm Sun.

As soon as you head up the stairs to Duka's homey and light-filled second floor, complete with pillows and blankets, you'll want to move into this eco-friendly yet stylish gift, clothing, and home goods store within walking distance of the Halve Maan Brewery. Owner Katrien is happy to tell you the origins of every piece in the store, including their adorable minimalist jewelry.

Souvenirs

OLLEKE

Wijngaardstraat 12; tel. 085 105 0459; https://desprookjeswinkel.be; 11am-5pm Mon.-Fri., 11am-6pm Sat.-Sun.

Although *Alohomora* may not work to open the door of Olleke, a Harry Potter-inspired store, millennials and anyone who has grown up with Harry Potter will enjoy browsing this "wizardry" shop that also stocks favorites inspired by movie and television series such as *Game of Thrones*. Items on sale include Bertie Bott's beans, wands, delightful cards, and even wizarding robes.

SIMBOLIK

Katelijnestraat 139; tel. 0495 30 70 56; www.simbolik.be; 10am-6pm Thurs.-Sat.

Local artist Nathalie Beelprez's studio gives you a small glimpse into her creative world. Her shop showcases her creative calligraphy, often with inspiring quotes, and ceramic bowls engraved with beautiful lettering. If you're lucky, you'll meet her friendly cats snoozing in the window or running through the shop.

SINT ANNA AND LANGESTRAAT QUARTERS

Langestraat is full of charming antique stores where patient collectors can find countless goodies for less than a night out in Bruges. Even for visitors less keen on antiques, Langestraat is a popular spot for alternative shops selling specialty items, from beautiful postcards to eco-friendly gifts. Many stores are cash-only.

Antiques

MADAM MIM

Hoogstraat 29; tel. 050 61 55 05; www.madammim.be; 11am-6pm Wed.-Sun.

You can easily spend an eternity browsing the crowded shop of Madam Mim where you can pick up handmade lace for a steal, beautiful flapper dresses, well-curated vintage home goods, and even vintage-inspired clothing created with original materials by owner Mim. Every corner is a vintage lover's dream. The narrow aisles are best navigated with minimal bags.

Clothing

REBEL REBEL BRUGES

Langestraat 50; tel. 050 34 83 40; https://rebelrebel.be; noon-6pm Wed.-Sat.; 12:30pm-5pm Sun.

A new dress can make you feel like a new person. Rebel Rebel is your best bet for vintage-inspired clothing featuring fun novelty prints and quirky gifts.

TOP EXPERIENCE

☆ Best Chocolatiers in Bruges

Bruges's reputation as a giant in the chocolate world is something of a happy accident; high-quality, often family-run chocolatiers have charmed tourists, who have spread the word. There are many great chocolatiers in Bruges, but there are also many shops happy to rip off tourists who don't know better. Your average store advertising chocolates will not be selling high-quality chocolates made in Bruges, but rather chocolates made in factories elsewhere in Belgium. Save your money for the good stuff or head to the supermarket for a better value.

Don't come hungry to any of these chocolatiers, or you'll end up making a dent in your wallet. A small box of chocolate at a high-quality chocolatier typically costs a little under €10. Pralines tend to be popular here (compared to Brussels, where truffles reign). Keep an eye out for the **Bruges's Swan** (*het Brugsch Swaentje*), a praline specific to the city made with a secret recipe of almonds, biscuits, and a spice mix used for beer brewing.

STEENSTRAAT QUARTER

Chocolatier Dumon

Eiermarkt 6; tel. 050 22 16 22; www.chocolatierdumon.be; 10am-6pm Wed.-Sat., 10am-5pm Sun.; €10 small box

Creating high-quality chocolates since 1992, this chocolatier was exclusively family-run until 2020, and despite new ownership, the chocolatier continues to produce high-quality Belgian chocolates, which are the favorite of many Bruges locals.

Pol Depla Chocolatier

Mariastraat 20; tel. 050 33 49 53; www.poldepla.be; 10am-6pm daily; €10 small box

One of Bruges's premiere chocolatiers, opened in 1958. Their experimental and single-origin chocolates with a focus on sustainability make Pol Depla a great choice for true chocolate lovers.

BbyB Chocolates

Sint-Amandsstraat 39; tel. 014 49 02 47; www.bbyb.be; 10:30am-6:30pm Tues.-Sat.; €6 small box

Started by Michelin-starred chefs, this smaller chocolate shop has some interesting flavors that are packaged perfectly for gifts. Their premade boxes vary from standard to adventurous. Be sure to try the babbalaar, a popular caramel flavor originating from the Belgian coast.

The Chocolate Brothers

Mariastraat 34; 10am-6pm daily; €7 small box

This no-frills family-run chocolate shop has a convenient location close to Onze-Lieve-Vrouwekerk. Bring cash to buy surprisingly affordable high-quality chocolates by weight. Chocolate aficionados will want to try their single-origin chocolates. The Bruges Mouse is a popular crunchy milk chocolate praline.

NORTH BRUGES

Ezelstraat and **Sint-Jakobsstraat** are currently the coolest streets in Bruges, with many up-and-coming boutiques focusing on high-quality Belgian brands, sustainability, Scandinavian design, and home goods. Expect a pleasant mix of locals and tourists within the often-minimalistic shops along these picturesque streets lined with gabled houses.

Chocolate Brothers

The Chocolate Line

Simon Stevinplein 19; tel. 050 34 10 90; www.thechocolateline.be; 10:30am-6:30pm Sun.-Mon., 9:30am-6:30pm Tues.-Sat.; €10 small box

Local hero Dominique Persoone and his wife Fabienne run this beloved Bruges chocolate shop known for its experimental flavors made with sustainably made chocolate, the famous chocolate shooter, and well-done traditional Belgian pralines.

NORTH BRUGES

Chocolaterie Spegelaere

Ezelstraat 92; tel. 050 33 60 52; www.sweetchocolatedreams.be; 8:30am-noon and 1:30pm-6:30pm Tues.-Sat., 9am-1pm Sun.; €9.50-12 box

This friendly family-run chocolate shop has been focusing on high-quality chocolates since 1952. Spegelaere feels much like a mom-and-pop shop; you'll get personal service from members of the family pointing out the numerous options (even for non-chocolate lovers!), which makes it worth the trip. Payment by card is possible for amounts over €15.

Home Goods

GOÛTS ET COULEURS

Ezelstraat 1 and 5 ;tel. 050 69 82 83; www.gouts-et-couleurs.be; 10:30am-6pm Tues.-Sat.

For interior design inspiration and winsome home goods to brighten up your house, ask Ester, the owner of Goûts et Couleurs and an interior designer, for her helpful advice. Her empire is spread across two stores on the block, one focusing on cute home goods, funny cards, gifts, and delightful items for children's rooms sourced from European designers. The other is a little more serious, with an emphasis on the Scandinavian modern aesthetic combined with clever Belgian statement pieces.

TOP EXPERIENCE

Best Local Markets

Bruges is very passionate about its local markets. Many locals get up at sunrise, even in winter, to get the first pick, whether of antiques or food. If you have a sweet tooth, be sure to look out for the bakery stalls, while those with a taste for the savory might want to stick to the herring stand at the fish market and the cheese stands at other markets. One great item to pick up at the food markets is the Brugge Oud cheese, an aged cheese that is produced just outside the city.

Saturday Market

TIPS FOR VISITING

- Locals crowd in from the nearby towns armed with their own trolleys, so **be careful where you step!**
- Be sure to carry **cash** on you as many stalls do not accept cards.
- Don't be afraid to **ask for a sample** of the goods and to stop for a friendly chat with the owners who generally speak fluent English, especially if it's a quieter time.
- It's best to be aware in busy markets, as many take place in busy public squares where there may be **pickpockets.**

FOOD

- **Saturday Market** ('t Zand; 8am-1:30am Sat.): Bruges's busiest weekly market is the Saturday market, where you can buy fruits, veggies, fabrics, meats, cheeses, and bread. There aren't many tourist stalls, but it's a great place to buy cheeses and other foods for a picnic.
- **Wednesday Market** (Markt; 8am-1:30am Wed.): The Wednesday market is a busy hustle and bustle of locals shopping for everyday goods such as fruits, veggies, flowers, cheeses, and plants in front of the Belfry. It's a great place to stop for a snack.
- **Fish Market** (Vismarkt; 8am-1:30pm Wed.-Sat.): This market is a favorite among tourists who come to admire shrimp from Zeebrugge and sample herring in summer. On other days, an art market occupies the same spot.

ARTS AND ANTIQUES

- **Flea Market/Folklore Market** (Dijver; 10am-6pm Sat.-Sun. and holidays Mar.-Nov., plus Fri. in summer): On a nice day, stroll along the Dijver to browse the many tents and blankets filled with antiques, household items, and curiosities that are more than 50 years old.
- **Artist Market** (Vismarkt; 9:30am-4pm daily Mar.-Nov., 10am-4pm daily Nov.-Mar.): If you love bringing back a piece of art from your trips, be sure to check out the paintings and artisan products sold to tourists at this small market.

Food

Food options in Bruges tend to skew more Belgian than other nearby cities, with local favorites such as ***frites*, shrimp croquettes** (*garnaalkroketten*), fish from the North Sea, Flemish **beef or rabbit stew** (*stoofvlees*), meats marinated in beer, and fresh **waffles.** Sandwiches are a mainstay of Belgian lunch, and many restaurants add their own creative spin with international ingredients. As in much of Belgium, you'll also find mussels with *frites* as well as oysters and shrimp croquettes from neighboring Zeeland in the Netherlands in the right season (July-mid-Apr. for mussels, Sept.-Apr. for oysters). If you're looking for something other than Belgian food, there are some international options serving up brunch, Middle Eastern food, pizza, and Asian food.

Most restaurants in Bruges tend to be clustered in the Steenstraat and Burg Quarters, but there are great affordable options in the surrounding Sint Anna and Langestraat Quarters as well as North Bruges. It's best to avoid eating very close to Markt, as prices are high and quality tends to be lower. There are good food options just a 10-minute walk away.

BURG QUARTER

Belgian

CAMBRINUS

Philipstockstraat 19; tel. 050 33 23 28; https://bierbrasseriecambrinus.eu; 11am-10pm daily; €11-25

One of the best spots for a long Belgian-style lunch in Bruges's city center, complete with local delicacies such as rabbit slow-cooked in beer and fresh Belgian beer off the tap, is Cambrinus. (Their beer list has more than 400 options!) The wood-heavy booths and high tables fill up quickly, so it's best to reserve for lunch on weekends.

BRUUT

Meestraat 9; tel. 050 69 55 09; www.bistrobruut.be; noon-1:30pm and 7pm-8:45pm Mon.-Fri.; lunch €40-55, dinner €76-86

Bruut is not a secret among lovers of fine dining; this Belgian restaurant has even captured the attention of the Michelin guide. Housed within a beautiful 17th-century building, Bruut uses fresh, local ingredients to twist traditional Belgian recipes on their head. The interior is sober and simple; chef Bruno Timperman lets his food be the true art. The menu changes often, and chef Bruno enjoys explaining his dishes to guests. There is a bespoke wine pairing for a little extra. Be sure to reserve ahead.

Cafés & Light Bites

ARLECCHINO GELATERIA

Burg 15; www.facebook.com/johnwaffless; 11am-5pm Wed.-Sun.; €3.50-4.50

The best waffles in Bruges are found at this small truck that sits quietly on Burg Square most days. The owner, John, creates fresh Liège-style waffles to-order with toppings for a bit extra. Though less showy than others, these waffles are certainly the most delicious and are best enjoyed in view of Bruges's beautiful City Hall. Be careful: He often sells out by 3pm in summer.

International

SECONDO SUD

Mallebergplaats 5; tel. 050 34 45 62; www.sudinbrugge.com; noon-2pm and 6:30pm-9pm Mon.-Tues. and Thurs.-Sat.; €19-29

Transport your taste buds to Italy for the evening at one of Bruges's best Italian restaurants, specializing in food from southern Italy. Their chef, who hails from Puglia, proudly showcases artisanal and organic ingredients imported from his home country. The interior is small with a few mismatched tables, so it's best to reserve your place. Ask about the dish of the day before you make a decision. Dishes are paired with a fitting Italian wine and best shared.

STEENSTRAAT QUARTER

Belgian

LOKKEDIZE

Korte Vuldersstraat 33; tel. 0496 69 26 62; http://bistrolokkedize.be; 6pm-1am Thurs.-Mon.; €10-17

Lokkedize is a local favorite focusing on Mediterranean food with a kitchen that is open late on Monday night, which can be hard to find in Bruges. The interior is dimly lit with old-school tables and musical instruments on the walls, which makes it a great spot for a romantic dinner or nightcap with a Belgian beer. Check their schedule for live music.

THE POTATO BAR

Sint-Amandsstraat 3; tel. 050 33 91 19; https://thepotatobar.be; noon-10pm daily; €10-20

Don't let the hipster modern interior skew your perception: The *garnaalkroketten* (shrimp croquettes) are delicious, and the prices at the Potato Bar won't break the bank. Those who are hungrier might want to try their delicious burgers. Some say that these are the best *frites* in Bruges, but you'll have to judge for yourself.

OTOMAT

Simon Stevinplein 12; tel. 050 66 21 21; https://otomat.be; 11am-10pm daily; €10-20

A hearty pizza can be very satisfying after spending a day walking around Bruges and sampling beer. Otomat is a popular Belgian pizzeria that uses Duvel's beer yeast in their dough, serving up pizzas perfect for sharing between two people. Their pizzas include vegan-friendly options, seasonally inspired pizzas, and uniquely Belgian pizza combinations. No reservations are needed, and it's a quick meal option compared to many restaurants.

THE REPUBLIC

Sint-Jakobsstraat 36; tel. 050 73 47 64; https://republiekbrugge.be; noon-midnight Sun.-Thurs., noon-2am Fri.-Sat.; €20-30

Those traveling in Belgium will often end up battling Belgian hours, which can force your holiday to be more time-oriented than you'd like. The Republic is one of Bruges's best options for food that offers flexibility to visitors, with a pretty exposed brick interior. Meal options include Belgian favorites along with international-inspired dishes served to perfection. Ask about the daily mains and check the beer list for a great selection of regional beers. Reservations are strongly recommended for dinner. Their garden is one of the hippest spots in Bruges in summer.

Cafés and Light Bites

DIKSMUIDS BOTERHUIS

Geldmuntstraat 23; tel. 050 33 32 43; www.diksmuidsboterhuis.be; 10am-12:30pm and 2pm-6:30pm Tues.-Sat.; €3-8

For a tasty Belgian lunch perfect for a picnic, stop by local institution Diksmuids Boterhuis for delicious sandwiches to-go made with local cheeses and your choice of meat, including Wallonian sausages. Although this cash-only deli is very far from vegan-friendly with its sausage decorations, it's a great stop-off for those looking to cut down on the costs of eating out in Bruges.

KAFFEE KAMIEL

Zilverpand 7; tel. 050 68 66 60; www.kaffeekamiel.be; 8:30am-5pm Mon.-Sat.; €3-15

Hidden down an alley next to a parking lot entrance, Kaffee Kamiel is easy to miss. It's one of Bruges's trendiest brunch/lunch addresses, serving up American-style brunch, fresh pastries, and hearty sandwiches on their signature bread. The interior with bold checkered floors is as close to Instagrammable as Bruges restaurants come, contrasting with old whitewashed brick outside.

1: That's Toast **2:** The Republic **3:** Syrian food at Taboulé **4:** Books & Brunch

1
2
3
4

THAT'S TOAST

Dweersstraat 4; tel. 050 68 82 27; www.thatstoast.com; 8:30am-4pm Wed.-Mon.; €7.50-14

For a lighter brunch or lunch, head to That's Toast, a bright and modern restaurant serving up all-day breakfast with good options for those with food sensitivities. Whether you're looking for healthy muesli, their classic toast with asparagus, or a creative Korean take on the traditional eggs and toast, there's an option for everyone. Seating can be limited, so arrive early on weekend mornings.

ONZE LIEVE VROUWE QUARTER

Belgian

BOOKS & BRUNCH

Garenmarkt 30; tel. 050 70 90 79; http://booksandbrunch.be; 9am-3pm Mon.-Fri.; €9-20

This cozy restaurant's modern interior filled with books is the stuff of dreams for anyone looking for a cozy place to curl up with a book. You'll find vegan-friendly drinks, tasty sandwiches, and sizeable portions (especially with the lunch specials!) among their many options. For something truly inspired, try the Harry Potter Butterbeer if it's available. Breakfast is only served on weekdays until noon, and brunch is also only available on weekdays.

International

SANSEVERIA BAGELSALON

Predikherenstraat 11; tel. 050 34 81 43; www.sanseveria.be; 8am-5pm Mon.-Sat., 10am-3pm Sun.; €10

Head to Sanseveria for hearty breakfast bagels. I especially like the Richard breakfast sandwich, which offers a taste of my childhood in New York. The interior is a modern eclectic mix of Bruges nostalgia and cacti. Reservations are recommended on weekends.

TAPASBAR EST

Braambergstraat 7; tel. 0478 45 05 55; https://tapasbar-est.business.site; 6:30pm-midnight Fri.-Tues.; €12

Finding authentic Mexican food in Bruges is quite a surprise, but Tapasbar Est has managed to pull this off thanks to an owner's wife who hails from Mexico. Expect Mexican small plates including nachos, tortillas with chicken, calamari, and other Mexican-influenced surprises using local ingredients. Formerly only a wine bar, Est still has a nice wine selection and an intimate atmosphere perfect for a romantic dinner. Reservations are required.

MARCO POLO NOODLES

Katelijnestraat 29; tel. 050 734 285; www.marco-polo-noodles.com; 11:30am-3pm and 5:30pm-9pm Thurs.-Tues.; €12-15

Just like their namesake, Marco Polo Noodles brings Asian influences to Bruges. Their menu is a mix of noodle-based dishes from Vietnam, Korea, and China. Their pho and ramen are particularly tasty and filling.

SINT ANNA AND LANGESTRAAT QUARTERS

Cafés and Light Bites

POSTBAR

Langestraat 82; tel. 0486 11 57 01; https://postbar-coffee-shop.business.site; 8am-5:30pm Wed.-Sun.; €3-5

So often we forget to pause to regroup ourselves, and Postbar is the perfect stop-off en route to Bruges's windmills. This modern coffee shop combined with a post office features cute cards and postcards made by local artists. Come for the phenomenal coffee, stay to scribble off a postcard to a friend to be delivered on the date of your choice, and to chat with the easygoing owners. Their baked goods are flaky, soft, and worth ordering.

International

TABOULÉ

Langestraat 81; tel. 050 33 87 01; www.facebook.com/taboulebrugge; 11:30am-2pm and 5pm-11pm daily; €7-10

For a break from Belgian food, head to Taboulé for Syrian-Lebanese dishes. The owner fled Syria and set up shop in Bruges to share his culture through food after immigrating to Belgium. This casual eatery has been serving up fresh pita bread, delicious hummus, baba ghanoush, and falafel at affordable prices to a mix of tourists and locals. The portions are generous, and reservations are recommended for dinner. Service can be a bit slow when it's full, but the food is definitely worth the wait.

WIPHADA

Langestraat 93; tel. 050 31 51 55; www.wiphada.be; noon-3pm and 6pm-9pm Thurs.-Mon.; €10-14

Wiphada is the first Thai restaurant along Langestraat, and it's been readily welcomed to the neighborhood. There are a few tables in the back, but Wiphada mostly does a brisk take-out business. It is possible to take a high chair by the door if you don't have a reservation to eat in. Opened by a Belgian-Thai couple, Wiphada serves up authentic Thai food with friendly service. Thai spicy truly means something here, so don't overestimate your spice tolerance.

NORTH BRUGES

Belgian

TOM'S DINER

West-Gistelhof 23; tel. 050 33 33 82; www.tomsdiner.be; 6pm-9pm Tues.-Sat.; €18-28

Housed in a stunning 16th-century building with exposed brick walls, this restaurant owned by local chef Tom Mestdagh serves a fun mix of Belgian and international flavors. Be sure to try the salmon. Reservations are recommended.

PETITE ANETH

Maria Van Bourgondiëlaan 1; tel. 050 31 11 89; www.aneth.be; 11:30am-4pm and 6pm-9:30pm Tues.-Sat., 11:30am-4pm Sun.; lunch €19, dinner €25-29

Compared to the tourist trap restaurants in the center of Bruges, Petite Aneth is a steal considering that the Belgian dishes with a French twist are prepared by chef Paul Hendrickx who chose to eschew his Michelin star in favor of more freedom. Reservations are a necessity within their small dining room that happily caters to local foodies. The restaurant is far enough off the beaten path that you won't be dealing with too many tourists.

HASHTAG FOOD

Scheepsdalelaan 37; tel. 050 70 76 70; https://hashtagfood.eatbu.com; noon-2pm and 5:30pm-8:30pm Thurs.-Fri., 5:30pm-8:30pm Sat.-Sun.; lunch €20, dinner €30-40

Vegans and others with food intolerances or allergies will fall in love with the diverse meal options at Hashtag Food, a trendy Belgian restaurant that prides itself on making something for everyone, whether they're vegan or gluten-intolerant. (They also offer meat options.) Their dishes are consistently beautiful. The restaurant is mostly frequented by Bruges locals looking for a nice meal out; however, tourists are also welcome with a reservation.

Bars and Nightlife

Bruges's nightlife tends to be on the quieter side despite its fame for beer. If you're one for a calmer night out, you'll find many bars where quieter conversation and sipping beers reign supreme. Most bars are located in the Burg and Steenstraat Quarters, besides the well-known **Brouwerij De Halve Maan** in Onze Lieve Vrouwe Quarter. If you're looking for a wilder night, you'll find a handful of livelier spots along **'t Zand** and surrounding **Markt.** Non-beer drinkers and those who don't drink will also find options at many cafés.

A typical night out in Bruges usually starts with a local beer, perhaps a Fort Lapin 8 or a Brugse Zot. Other favorite beers include Belgian Trappist ales, sour lambic beers, and many craft beers produced within the surrounding province of West Flanders (West

TOP EXPERIENCE

Bruges's Coziest Cafés

Bruges's many charming cafés add to the temptation to forgo serious sightseeing in favor of enjoying beers in a cozy atmosphere. One of the best experiences to have in Bruges has to be escaping the rain in a warmly lit bar, where you feel at home from the moment you walk in, and the staff can guide you through the best beer that Flanders has to offer. I'm partial to old Flemish cafés where the furniture is all wood, the curtains are made of Flemish lace, it's quiet enough to chat or figure out where you'll go next, and the bar list tilts heavily in favor of regional beer. Here are a few:

- **'t Brugs Beertje:** Tourists and locals alike settle into the tiny tables of this old bar to chat, play games, and browse its thick book filled with pages of Belgian beers (page 285).
- **De Kelk:** This local establishment on Langestraat 69 with a friendly pug gets lively on the weekends, with music and a great selection of drinks (page 287).
- **Café Vlissinghe:** Bruges's oldest café has barely changed over the decades (page 288).
- **Le Trappiste:** It's easy to miss Le Trappiste's stairwell, but it's a favorite late-night bar for locals and tourists who come here to sample Trappist beers and other local favorites (page 287).

Vlaanderen). Many bartenders are happy to educate you about Trappist beers if you're a newbie, and it's best to head to a brewery for a tour if you're interested in the process of making Belgian beer.

BURG QUARTER

BRASSERIE BOURGOGNE DES FLANDRES

Kartuizerinnenstraat 6; tel. 050 33 54 26; www.bourgognedesflandres.be; 10am-6pm daily

At Brasserie Bourgogne des Flandres, visitors can taste their popular Belgian lambic at the bar, open most days to the public. Although lambic styles aren't as famous as other Belgian styles, lambics are some of the most difficult styles to produce, and the brewery **tour** (€9-11) provides a glimpse into lambic production combined with a sample. Tours go throughout the day, but those keen on simply trying the beer can stop by the bar without a reservation for simply the cost of drinks. The interior of the brewery is fairly industrial, but the view from their canal-front terrace down the stairs is out of a painting. If a sample of the Timmermans Oude Gueuze is available, be sure to order it.

'T POATERSGAT

Vlamingstraat 82; tel. 0495 22 68 50; 5pm-3am Sun.-Thurs., 5pm-4am Fri.-Sat.

It's easy to pass by 't Poatersgat (The Priest's Hole) without noticing its cellar entrance during the day, but you'll want to stop here at night for a nightcap, as it's one of the only Brugge bars open very late most nights. During the late hours, the crowd is a lively mix of sociable locals and beer-loving tourists who drink mostly Belgian beers and play foosball under the beautiful stone crosses. The bar is cash-only, and it's best to be aware of the candles on the tables to avoid setting any fires.

DE GARRE

De Garre 1; tel. 050 34 10 29; www.degarre.be; noon-11:30pm Sun.-Thurs., noon-12:30am Fri., 11am-midnight Sat.

De Garre is one of Bruges's most hyped bars. Hidden down the smallest street in the city, you'll find this skinny two-story bar serving up their house beer along with beloved Belgian favorites on classic wooden tables. Despite the many tourists and cramped tables, De Garre has a small and intimate feeling thanks to classical music.

CUVEE WINE BAR

Philipstockstraat 41; tel. 050 33 33 28; www.cuvee.be; 11am-10pm Tues.-Sat.

Although beer is often the focus for many visitors to Bruges, wine lovers can head to Curvee Wine Bar for their impressive selection within their shop and their sleek wine bar in the back. The owners and staff know their drinks inside and out, and in summer, you can enjoy their cozy enclosed patio. Their small plates are beautifully prepared and delicious.

COMPTOIR DES ARTS

Vlamingstraat 53; tel. 0494 387 961; www.comptoirdesarts.be; 8pm-3am Wed.-Sun. May-Sept., 7pm-3am Sun.-Mon. and Wed.-Fri., 4pm-3am Sat. Oct.-Apr.

For live music, check the agenda at Comptoir Des Arts, one of Bruges's dedicated jazz, blues, and soul bars that regularly hosts bands. At a minimum, head downstairs to enjoy the warm fire on cold days and their good beer selection. The welcoming atmosphere is made complete with lots of wooden furniture and candles. Cash-only.

RETSINS LUCIFERNUM

Twijnstraat; https://lucifernum.be; 8pm-10pm Sun.

Bruges's strangest experience has to be at Retsins Lucifernum, a former masonic lodge turned pseudo-museum/bar by Willy Retsin, its owner who calls himself a vampire. Entry to the museum includes the ability to walk around the mansion and a drink at the bar once you've settled in. Take in the mix of spooky Gothic paintings, controversial statues meant to provoke, and erotic art. In summer, head out to the freemason cemetery turned bar patio. Most nights, Retsins entertains his guests with live music, conversation, and singing. Not for the faint of heart or haters of smoking, come on a sleepy Sunday to liven up your night and stay for the killer Cuba Libres. You'll be wondering if it was all a dream afterward.

STEENSTRAAT QUARTER

'T BRUGS BEERTJE

Kemelstraat 5; tel. 050 33 96 16; www.brugsbeertje.be; 4pm-midnight Sun.-Thurs., 4pm-1am Fri.-Sat.

Step back in time at this Flemish beer café with a continually updated menu of local craft beers from all around Flanders. The lively atmosphere, classical music, and knowledgeable bartenders make this one of the coziest bars in Bruges to sit back. Take a seat to chat in the slightly cramped café with a friendly mix of tourists and locals. Order the Fort Lapin beer if it's in stock.

MUTTLEY'S

't Zand 3; tel. 0479 39 14 78; https://muttleys.be; noon-1am Sun.-Thurs., noon-3am Fri.-Sat.

Muttley's is an English pub with a sublime spot on 't Zand, the place to be in Bruges past sunset for people-watching and going out. Belgian favorites are on tap, and it's a favorite spot in summer for its terrace.

ON THE ROCKS

Grauwwerkersstraat 5; tel. 0487 53 40 49; https://julesbrugge.wixsite.com/my-cafe; 8pm-4am Wed.-Sat., 8pm-3am Sun.

On the Rocks has a non-ironic retro '70s-style interior with disco lights and way too many mirrors. Come for the karaoke and stay because it's too late to go anywhere else. The owner and regulars are keen to chat with whoever dares to enter this slightly dark, cash-only Bruges institution.

BLEND WIJNBAR

Kuipersstraat 8/10; tel. 0497 17 20 85; www.blendwijnhandel.be; 11am-11pm Wed.-Sun.

Blend Wijnbar is a spacious and intimate wine bar/wine store a short walk from Markt. You can sample their thoughtful selection of wines with the help of their knowledgeable sommeliers, including a few who won the prestigious title of best sommelier in Belgium. The owners own part of a winery in Tuscany and source many of their organic wines from their

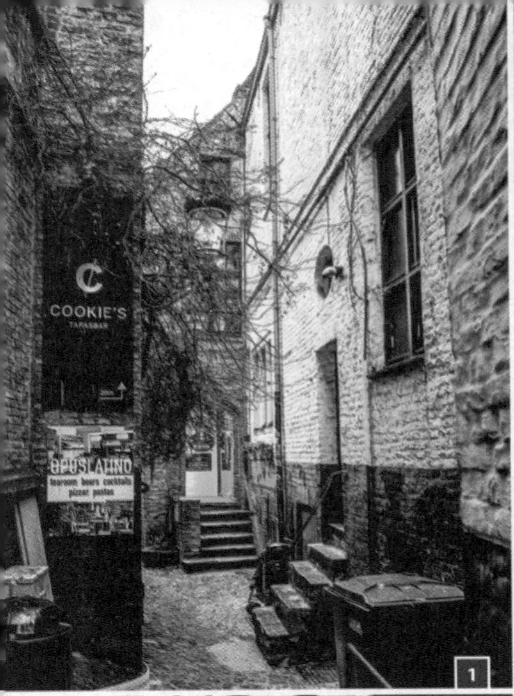

COOKIE'S
OPUSLATINO
tearoom beers cocktails pizzas pastas
1

Le Trappiste
2

Brouwerij
HENRI MAES
Brugge
3

4

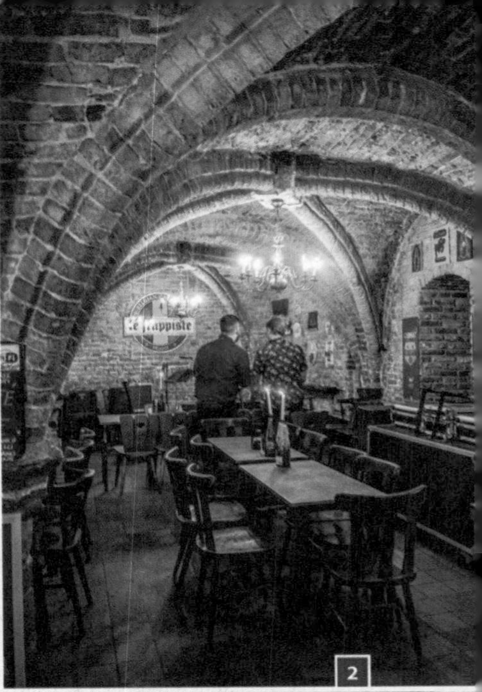

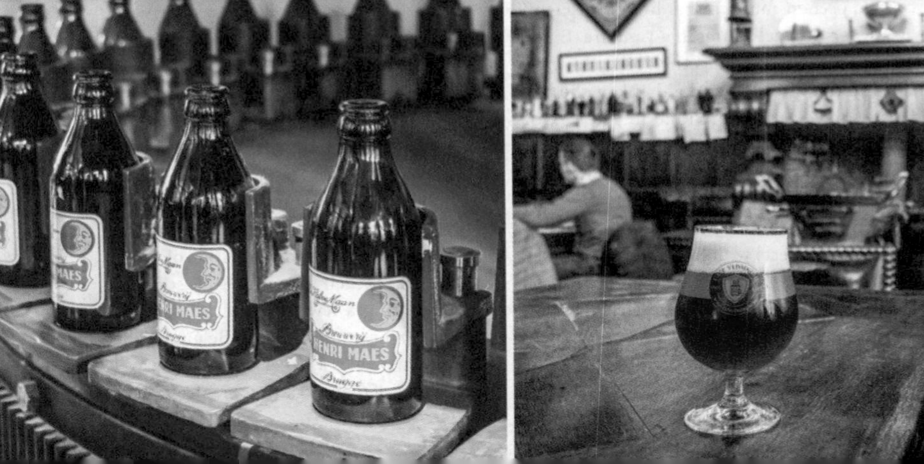

own winery. Take a seat at one of their high chairs within the Scandinavian-inspired bar and describe your ideal wine to one of their sommeliers.

BARLOW

Sint-Amandsstraat 11; www.barlowbrugge.be; 4pm-1am Mon.-Wed., 4pm-2am Thurs., 4pm-4am Fri.-Sat., 4pm-11pm Sun.

Barlow is a modern underground bar with a nice tap list featuring local microbreweries. It's easy to miss the staircase down to this dark bar filled with warm interior woods, leafy plants, and fun music. On weekends, this is a favorite among locals looking for a fun place to dance the night away. Non-beer drinkers will also feel at home here due to the thoughtful wine and cocktail list.

LE TRAPPISTE

Kuipersstraat 33; tel. 0475 45 50 66; www.letrappistebrugge.com; 5pm-1am Thurs.-Tues.

This well-known Belgian beer bar is hidden on a quiet street in a stone cellar. Le Trappiste has 25 high-quality and occasionally rare beers on tap, not including their massive beer list and private collection (including beers brewed by the owners). There's ample seating for larger groups, and the atmosphere of the bar is lighthearted thanks to the throwback music.

ONZE LIEVE VROUWE QUARTER

★ BROUWERIJ DE HALVE MAAN

Walplein 26; tel. 050 44 42 22; www.halvemaan.be; 10am-6pm Sun.-Wed., 10am-9pm Thurs.-Sat.

Beer has been brewed on the location of De Halve Maan Brewery for more than 500 years, but their highly popular Straffe Hendrik and Brugse Zot beers, which today can be found throughout Belgium, were developed fairly recently. Both beers became cult classics fairly quickly, leading to increased production by popular demand, but the brewery faced issues transporting their beer out of the city of Bruges without causing traffic. In 2016, the brewery famously constructed a 3.2-kilometer (2-mile) beer pipeline to ensure that their beer was still produced in its original location prior to being bottled in the Bruges suburbs.

The taproom of the brewery is housed in an airy open-plan building with a view of the beer tanks. Although there can be a bit of a wait on weekends (30-50 minutes), you'll have no problem getting a small table at the taproom without a reservation. Regular 45-minute **tours** (€12) are organized every hour 11am-4pm in Dutch, French, and English with an extra tour at 5pm on Saturdays. All tours end with a free unfiltered glass of beer in a private area away from the crowds and gorgeous views of Bruges from the rooftop. For true beer lovers, the once-a-day XL tour (€21) is double the length of the standard tour at 90 minutes and provides access to the brewery cellar. You'll have to earn the three beers included in the tour price by traversing their steep stairs. Reserve tours online.

BRUGES GIN CLUB

Jozef Suvéestraat 19; tel. 0472 62 82 43; www.brugseginclub.be; 6pm-midnight Fri., 6pm-2am Sat., 6pm-10:30pm Sun

True gin lovers will need to stop by Bruges Gin Club to sample one of the more than 375 gin bottles available at this intimate cocktail bar. The owner is keen to chat and make recommendations if you're indecisive. Reservations are not possible and tables are shared with other visitors, so try your luck earlier rather than later as many patrons stay until closing. Closed Sundays in low season.

SINT ANNA AND LANGESTRAAT QUARTERS

DE KELK

Langestraat 69; tel. 0479 85 38 22; www.dekelk.be; 5pm-1am Tues.-Thurs., 5pm-2am Fri.-Sat.

Beer lovers looking for something different will love the rock 'n' roll-inspired bar de Kelk along Langestraat. Owners Vincent and Lisa

1: De Garre **2:** Le Trappiste **3:** De Halve Maan Brewery **4:** Café Vlissinghe stand behind the bar serving up craft beers from all around the world along with killer cocktails. Their beer list from West Flanders is impressive, and Vincent is particularly talented at finding you the perfect beer. Nab a table early on Fridays and Saturdays as the bar fills up quickly with locals and can get noisy.

CAFÉ VLISSINGHE

Blekersstraat 2; tel. 050 34 37 37; www.cafevlissinghe.be; 11am-9pm Wed.-Thurs., 11am-10pm Fri.-Sat., 11am-7pm Sun.

Since 1515, Café Vlissinghe has been serving beer to regulars, which makes it the oldest café in Bruges. Sit down at one of the beautiful wooden tables next to the Flemish heater, pet Freddie (the owner's dog), and enjoy the house beer. Compared to many bars in Bruges, Café Vlissinghe feels very formal and elegant due to well-dressed locals reading the newspaper in the bar. Be sure to find the portrait of the first owner of the bar, Teunis, and wife on the right-hand wall of the bar.

'T HOF VAN BEROEP

Langestraat 125; tel. 0488 67 83 37; www.thofvanberoep.com; 5pm-1:30am Sun.-Tues., 5pm-2:30am Thurs., 4pm-3:30am Fri., 5pm-4am Sat.

This unpretentious bar close to the famous windmills is a favorite among those working at the nearby courthouse. If you're looking for a quieter spot to enjoy a beer, listen to retro music, or watch soccer, you're in the right place. If you get hungry, try their spaghetti.

NORTH BRUGES

'T KROONTJE / DE KROON

Houtkaai 2; tel. 050 31 53 89; 11am-10pm Tues.-Sat.

De Kroon is an old-school Flemish bar that fills up with locals enjoying standard as well as special beers. It's not everyone's cup of tea, but if you enjoy divey bars, you'll love it here.

IN DE REISDUIF

Langerei 30; tel. 0468 49 39 78; 3pm-1am Mon.-Fri., 2pm-1am Sat.

In the more touristy parts of Bruges, it's hard to find a place that feels like a true neighborhood pub. In De Reisduif is a small tavern where time has largely stood still, from the dried flowers to the lace curtains. Those in the neighborhood come here to chat, be merry, and have Belgian beers, so don't hesitate to introduce yourself to the surrounding tables when you come inside.

Accommodations

You'll find an accommodation for practically every budget in Bruges, which is known within the region for its excellence in hospitality. Whether you're looking for a beautiful boutique hotel, just a cheap room to crash in, or a cozy B&B, Bruges has great options within walking distance from the major tourist attractions. Most of the hotels are concentrated in the Steenstraat Quarter, which is just 10 minutes on foot from Markt and most museums. For more budget-friendly accommodations and access to more affordable dining, opt for the Sint Anna and Langestraat Quarters. Breakfast is not standard with most hotel rooms, but the abundance of brunch spots in Bruges makes up for that. Narrow and steep stairwells are all too common at smaller hotels, so do your research before booking a hotel if you require an elevator or don't pack light.

BURG QUARTER

Under €100

CHARLIE ROCKET'S

Hoogstraat 19; tel. 050 33 06 60; www.charlierockets.com; €43

Younger travelers (or those young at heart) looking for a fun weekend in Bruges and a no-frills hotel can nab a private room at this well-known hostel with a rock 'n' roll theme and a café underneath. Rooms include a free Bruges discount card, Wi-Fi, a walking tour, and a free beer with check-in. Once a movie theater, Charlie Rocket's is definitely one of the more social places to stay in Bruges for solo travelers.

€100-200

HOTEL BOURGOENSCH HOF

Wollestraat 35; tel. 050 33 16 45; http://hotelbh.be; €130

Despite its nondescript appearance on Wollestraat, Hotel Bourgoensch Hof has some of the most desired views of Bruges from its canal-side rooms—without a five-star price point. This small former brewery turned hotel has 34 rooms, comfortable beds, a functional elevator, and quick Wi-fi, and its location steps from Markt cannot be beaten. Reception isn't 24 hours (8:30am-11pm daily), so be sure to arrive early enough to check in and to note the night entrance/exits.

★ HOTEL DE ORANGERIE

Kartuizerinnenstraat 10; tel. 050 34 16 49; www.hotelorangerie.be; €200

For comfort without compromising on heritage, head to De Orangerie, a small luxury hotel on Den Dijver canal with 104 rooms. Although this former convent from the 15th century is very centrally located—footsteps away from Markt—it's on a quiet street. The feminine interior is a beautiful blend of modern and old elegance with pastel wallpapers, tapestries, and antiques scattered throughout the hotel. Don't miss the warm fireplace in the dining room and the stunning terrace where you can enjoy a high tea. Even comfort rooms feature air-conditioning, Nespresso machines, and a spacious modern bathroom.

STEENSTRAAT QUARTER

Under €100

HOTEL HET GHEESTELIC HOF

Heilige-Geeststraat 2; tel. 050 34 25 94; www.gheestelic-hof.be; €80

Het Gheestelic Hof is housed in a beautiful original building from the 16th century with an impressive Gothic facade. Despite the exterior, this hotel is one of the best value picks in the center of Bruges. Although the room décor featuring cartoon sketches of famous musicians is slightly dated and there is no elevator, the rooms are comfortable and offer good value for budget travelers. There is a small courtyard open in summer.

Hotel De Orangerie

€100-200

★ HOTEL MONSIEUR ERNEST

Wulfhagestraat 43; tel. 050 960 966; www.monsieurernest.com; €120-150

Only two blocks away from the busy Noordzandstraat shopping streets, Hotel Monsieur Ernest is perfect for visitors looking for a quieter time in Bruges. This beautiful hotel in a former brewery overlooks the Speelmansrei canal, one of the quieter canals in Bruges. Even if you don't splurge on a room with a view, you can enjoy breakfast, a coffee, or a cocktail in the evenings in their smart and modern "living room" available to guests. One of my favorite moments of my stay was watching the bikers cycle along the canal as I enjoyed a morning coffee. An elevator is available and rooms include USB ports.

Over €200

HOTEL DUKES' PALACE BRUGGE

Prinsenhof 8; tel. 050 44 78 88; https://hoteldukespalace.com; €200-580

No doubt one of Bruges's most luxurious properties, the Dukes' Palace Brugge is a true five-star hotel fit for royalty, with a central location close to attractions and beautiful neo-Gothic towers out of a fairy tale. This former school on the grounds of a former palace houses 110 thoughtfully furnished rooms that have been fully modernized. Its standard rooms are upgradable to a superior room with a city or garden view for a marginal amount more. The hotel has a sauna, a salt wall, and gym, and many rooms have a closet. Wheelchair-accessible rooms are available.

ONZE LIEVE VROUWE QUARTER

Under €100

HOTEL IBIS BRUGGE CENTRUM

Katelijnestraat 65 A; tel. 050 33 75 75; https://all.accor.com/hotel/1047/index.en.shtml; €88

Although the Ibis is not anything worth writing home about, the Ibis in Bruges offers great value, a convenient location near De Halve Maan Brewery, free Wi-Fi, an elevator, a private bathroom, and the basics you need. The Ibis hotel is housed in a former 15th-century cloister joined with a modern building, although all the rooms lack a historic touch.

€100-200

PAND 17

Pandreitje 17; tel. 050 34 06 66; www.pand17.com; €114

Guests looking for a small taste of luxury with a convenient location close to Bruges's museums will like the charming B&B Pand 17, which only has three small bedrooms. Staying here means you'll get private attention from the friendly owners who have outfitted this historic house with modern bathrooms and air-conditioning. There is no elevator.

Over €200

THE PAND HOTEL

Pandreitje 16; tel. 050 34 06 66; www.pandhotel.com; €208

The Pand Hotel is a small luxury boutique hotel with 26 rooms with a beautifully furnished interior complete with antiques, tapestries, and wood accents to give an old-world feeling. Once a carriage house, the hotel, which is just around the corner from the Rozenhoedkaai viewpoint, offers a lounge, a library, and breakfast cooked to your taste served with champagne.

SINT ANNA AND LANGESTRAAT QUARTERS

Under €100

B&B LADY JANE

Carmersstraat 11; tel. 0495 68 50 54; www.bb-bruges4u2.be; €85

Travelers looking for a personal touch will love B&B Lady Jane run by a friendly Belgian. The room decorations are inspired by different countries, and lovers of Japan will want to book the superior double room for beautiful Japanese-inspired décor. The Africa room

1: Hotel Monsieur Ernest view **2:** Hotel Ter Brughe **3:** Hotel Dukes' Palace

1
2
3

features steep stairs up to the loft. A minimum stay is two nights, and all stays include breakfast. For certain rooms, the bathroom is shared with other guests. Be sure to ask Hugo about his private wine cellar. Travelers not keen on steep stairs might want to pass on this B&B.

€100-200

LA CLÉ GUESTHOUSE

Vuldersstraat 2A; tel. 0476 48 93 32; www.lacle-brugge.com; €133

This modernized guesthouse in a 16th-century home has the perfect location for exploring the Sint Anna and Langestraat Quarters. The rooms have picturesque exposed brick walls, comfortable beds, and original wood-beam ceilings. Be sure to keep a few euros with you for the snack bar or drinks in the kitchen if you get hungry in the middle of the night!

Over €200

HOTEL VAN CLEEF

Molenmeers 11; tel. 050 34 64 14; www.hotelvancleef.be; €250

Although less famous than the Duke's Palace, Hotel Van Cleef is a great option for discerning travelers who want to escape the crowds while remaining close to the major attractions. Every room includes a bath, a flat-screen TV, free Wi-Fi, and access to the hotel's tearoom with a canal-side terrace. The staff is known for their friendliness, and the modern interior with luxurious details will please design lovers.

NORTH BRUGES

Under €100

ROOM 42

Gieterijstraat 42; www.booking.com/hotel/be/room-42.nl.html; €99

Room 42 offers a convenient and cozy room in North Bruges for those who prefer a B&B for personal recommendations. The owner Caroline and her two cats welcome you to their modern home. Although the stairs are not ideal for everyone, this B&B is consistently affordable throughout the year.

€100-200

HOTEL TER BRUGHE

Oost-Gistelhof 2; tel. 050 34 03 24; www.hotelterbrughe.com; €175

Hotel Ter Brughe is technically located in North Bruges, but its old-world charm and well-priced 46 rooms make it a favorite among repeat visitors. Not all rooms have canal views, but all rooms do have a bathtub. The building dates back to 1470, and guests can enjoy the beautiful vaulted cellar during breakfast. The hotel does not have an elevator, but the cozy main sitting area with its small bar and beer vending machine is perfect for groups traveling together or solo travelers interested in socializing. Some rooms have pretty canal views, and in summer you can enjoy their little private garden.

Information and Services

TOURIST INFORMATION

VISIT BRUGES TOURIST INFORMATION OFFICE

Markt 1; tel. 050 27 03 11; www.visitbruges.be; 10am-5pm daily

Visit Bruges has several tourist information offices located around the city center. Their website is a great source for planning your trip to Bruges, as it's full of information about the city, from top attractions to lesser-known spots. The main tourist information office is located within the **Historium** (Markt 1). You can pick up city maps, get recommendations, and learn about the city's museums.

There is a **secondary tourist information office** located in the main **Bruges Train Station** (Stationsplein 5; 10am-5pm daily) as well as a smaller office within the **Concertgebouw** ('t Zand 34; 10am-5pm Mon.-Sat., 10am-2pm Sun.) with limited hours on Sundays and public holidays.

HEALTH AND SAFETY

Bruges is a safe city to explore with a low crime rate, although pickpocketing incidents do occur around Markt and other crowded spots. Walking back to your hotel at night shouldn't be an issue, but use common sense.

For an ambulance, call **112.** If you're in need of urgent care, **Algemeen Ziekenhuis Sint-Jan Brugge** (Ruddershove 10 and Spaanse Loskaai 1; tel. 050 45 21 11; www.azsintjan.be) and **Algemeen Zienenhuis St. Lucas** (Sint-Lucaslaan 29; tel. 050 36 91 11; www.stlucas.be) are the main hospitals in Bruges. Most staff members will speak good English and French, but some medical terms might not be translated perfectly. The quality of medical care in Bruges is very well-regarded. Visitors may have to pay a fee for hospital services, although Belgium is known for having affordable healthcare.

For non-urgent medical issues on weekends, public holidays, and evenings, you can call **1733** to talk to a doctor.

Belgian pharmacies (known as *apotheek* in Dutch) typically operate 8am/10am-5pm/7pm, often with a pause for lunch. Most pharmacies are closed Sundays. There are many pharmacies in the city center, but I recommend **Apotheek Neyt** (Geldmuntstraat 32; tel. 050 3334 37; www.apotheekneyt.be) for its central location with fairly flexible hours. You can find a larger budget-friendly selection of over-the-counter items including tampons, Band-Aids, make-up, and toiletries at any of the location of the popular Belgian/Dutch drug store (known as *drogist* in Dutch) **Kruidvat** (the most central located at Markt 18; www.kruidvat.be).

Transportation

GETTING THERE

Train is by far the best way to get to Bruges within Belgium, as trains regularly run between Brussels and Bruges, and you don't need a car to get around Bruges. **Zeebrugge,** the major port of entry for ferries from the UK and cruise ships, is only 30-40 minutes (18 kilometers/11 miles) away from Bruges by car or taxi (€55 euros).

Air

If not arriving from elsewhere in Europe by train, most travelers to Bruges tend to fly into **Brussels Airport** (Leopoldlaan, Zaventem; tel. 02 753 77 53; www.brusselsairport.be), 110 kilometers (68 miles) to the east. You can then arrange your transpiration to the city, either by taxi, train, or, as a last resort, a rental car. The **train** (1 direct train per hour; 1.5 hours; €21.20) is the most economical option, although many chose to enjoy Brussels before heading to Bruges. A private transfer by taxi from Brussels Airport to Bruges (or vice versa) will cost €200 and take 75 minutes.

Oostende-Brugge International Airport is the closest airport to Bruges (33 kilometers/20 miles), serving limited flights to and from sunny destinations such as Turkey, Spain, and Greece. A taxi from Oostende-Brugge Airport to Bruges will cost approximately €70; it's also possible to travel from the airport to Bruges via the Coastal Tram (€3) to Ostend's train station, followed by taking a train to Bruges (€4.30); this journey takes 42 minutes.

Train

BRUGES TRAIN STATION

Stationsplein 5; tel. 02 528 28 28; www.belgianrail.be

The train station is about 1 kilometer (0.6 miles) southwest of the city center, with some useful amenities including a cute coffee shop and decent lunch/dinner options. There is also a supermarket just outside the station.

There are regular Intercity (IC) trains to Bruges from **Brussels** (1 hour; €14.30) and **Ghent** (26 minutes; €6.70). Other destinations may require a transfer. Direct trains depart at least hourly from Brussels, and there are trains at least once per hour from **Amsterdam** (3 hours; €29).

Bus

Those on a lower budget can take low-cost bus lines from other European cities, including Amsterdam and Brussels, to get to Bruges. Bus lines include **Flixbus** (https://global.flixbus.com), **BlaBlaBus** (https://ouibus.com), and **Eurolines** (www.eurolines.eu). Most buses depart behind the train station close to the **Oesterparking** (Koning Albert I-laan), but check your ticket for updated departure information. It is not always possible to buy your ticket on the bus, so be sure to book your ticket in advance. A direct bus ticket with Flixbus from **Amsterdam** to Bruges costs as little as €17 booked a few months in advance and takes 4-6 hours depending on traffic. Similarly, a bus ticket from **Brussels** to Bruges costs roughly €7 and takes about 1.5 hours.

Car

Bruges is well-connected with the rest of Belgium by highways. **Brussels** is 1 hour 20 minutes (100 kilometers/62 miles) away from Bruges by car on the **E40.** The drive from **Amsterdam** to Bruges (269 kilometers/167 miles) takes approximately 3 hours. Parking in Bruges and the cost of a rental may be pricey, but for those traveling in a larger group, it might make more sense to drive than take the train.

Those with a car are best off parking at one of the **free parking lots** outside the city center (Randsparking Magdalenastraat, Randsparking Bevrijdingslaan, and Randsparking Lodewijk Coiseaukaai). There are also free **park-and-ride** parking lots farther away from the city center, which may require a shuttle bus or bus ride, including P&R Waggelwater, P&R Steenbrugge, P&R Jan Breydel, and P&R Boogshutterslaan.

For those looking for more convenient parking without a hefty hourly rate, the Bruges Train Station offers the cheapest parking in Bruges. **Oesterparking,** a short walk from the station, costs €2.50 daily. Your next best options are the underground parking garages next to 't Zand, Zilverpand, Pandreitje, Katelijne, and Langestraat that cost between €1.10-1.80/hour, with lower overnight rates. These garages are all open 24 hours daily.

Street parking is possible for up to four hours, although rates are significantly higher than at the underground parking garages. Visitors must give their license plate when paying for street parking.

GETTING AROUND

Walking around Bruges is the best way to see the city. **Biking** is a possibility, but even experienced bikers often choose to skip biking in favor of walking as the cobblestones can make for a bumpy ride. Similarly, bikes often have to share the streets with cars, which can make for an unnerving experience on narrower streets.

Bruges allows **cars** to drive within the city, but parking is very limited, and the city center is so compact that it's unlikely you'll need to drive.

Bus

De Lijn (headquartered at the Bruges Train Station, Stationsplein 5; www.delijn.be) runs the public transit in the Flanders region. Public transit runs 5am-10pm/11 pm on weekdays. The night bus runs between the Bruges Train Station and city center on weekends until 2am. You can buy a ticket using De Lijn's app, at the Bruges Train Station during standard business hours (7:30am-5:45pm Mon.-Fri., 9am-5pm Sat., 10am-5:10pm Sun.), or on the bus in cash. One-way tickets costs €1.80 ahead and €3 on the bus. Day passes cost €7.50 ahead/€9 on the bus. If you intend to travel more in Flanders, it's best to buy a Lijn card for 10 journeys, which costs €15 on the app.

Traveling by bus in Bruges is mostly useful for traveling between the Stationplein (the area close to the Bruges Train Station) and the city center, though this is also an easy 20-minute walk. Buses 1, 2, 3 4, 6, 11, 12, 13, 14, 16, and 23 run between the train station and the city center with various ending destinations. All lines except 11 stop at 't Zand. Lines 4, 13, and 14 stop at Markt.

For the budget-conscious traveler, there is a small, handicap-accessible 16-seat **shuttle bus** (www.brugge.be/shuttlebus; 7:20am-7pm daily; free) that runs every 20 minutes between the Bruges Train Station and the city center daily. The bus also stops at Markt, along with a few other stops in the center.

Taxi

Taxis are not necessary to get around Bruges, but if you have a lot of luggage or limited mobility, it might be best to take a taxi between the Bruges Train Station and your hotel. It doesn't make much sense to take a taxi within the city center, but it is an option if you get tired of walking. Taxi stands can be found next to the Train Station, on Markt square, near Minnewater Park at Bargeweg, near the central library (Kuipersstraat 3), and next to the Koninklijke Stadsschouwburg Brugge (Vlamingstraat 29). Taxi rates are standardized for any journey within Brugge less than 2 kilometers (1.2 miles) costing €7 (+€2.50 for additional distances). Try **Taxi Snel** (tel. 050 36 36 49; www.taxisnel.be) or **Fredo Taxi** (tel. 0494 200 362).

Vicinity of Bruges

DAMME

Damme is a cute historic town a short cycle from Bruges, lovely in good weather. It's hard to imagine the importance of Damme in the medieval area as you cycle past farms, cows, and polders today, but it gained its city rights during the same period as Bruges. Damme was the main port of entry for products intended for Bruges due to its key location by the water. At one time, the city had exclusive importing rights, from French wine to herring from Sweden. These riches from abroad made Damme a wealthy town.

Although parts of the town were lost during the Eighty Years' War, Damme impresses with its quiet beauty with whitewashed houses, a Gothic city hall, and great restaurant options. Today, Damme is a favorite among day-trippers from Bruges as well as Belgian foodies who flock to Damme for high-quality restaurants.

Orientation

It doesn't take more than a few hours to see Damme, walking along the long-gone fortifications and stopping off for a meal. Damme technically incorporates a larger area including the surrounding farmland and polders, but most visitors stick to the boundaries of the historic fortified town itself. It's impossible to miss the **Schellemolen** windmill as you bike in from Bruges and the show-stopping **City Hall.** As you continue down **Kerkstraat,** you'll find the beautiful medieval **Onze-Lieve-Vrouwekerk.**

Sights

ONZE-LIEVE-VROUWEKERK

Kerkstraat 56-48; www.visitdamme.be; 1pm-5pm daily Apr.-Sept.; free, €2.50 tower

Damme's most impressive sight is its ancient church, dating back to 1210, just 5 minutes from the town's center. Although Onze-Lieve-Vrouwekerk is not as perfectly preserved as the churches in Bruges, it's worth taking a peek inside of the church when it's open. For a few euros in peak season, those not afraid of heights and a bit of bird feces can climb the tower (adults €2.50) for lovely views of Damme, Bruges, and the North Sea

if it's not too cloudy. You can always explore the church's spooky courtyard.

CITY HALL DAMME (Stadhuis Damme)

Markt 1; www.damme.be; not open to the public

Any visitor to Damme cannot miss the town hall, a beautiful example of a Brabant Gothic building, characterized by round pillars in the shape of cabbage leaves. The current town hall and its beautiful clock largely dates back to the 15th century and neo-Gothic renovations in the 1860s. Be sure to admire the images in the facade showing important figures for Damme's long history. If you're lucky enough to be allowed inside, take the opportunity.

SCHELLEMOLEN

Noorweegse Kaai 4; www.visitdamme.be; tel. 0470 90 10 90; 9:30am-12:30pm and 1pm-6pm Sat.-Sun. Apr.-Sept.; free

It's impossible to miss the charming white stone windmill that greets you as you enter the town. The windmill on the spot dates back to 1867. Those curious about the interior can stop off on weekends from April to September to peek inside. Compared to Bruges's windmills, this one is fairly recent, but the free admission makes this worthwhile for those interested.

Walking and Cycling

Serious bikers should pick up bike maps at the tourism office for routes farther into the Belgian countryside.

RAMPARTS WALK

Walking Distance: *800 meters (0.5 miles)*
Walking Time: *10 minutes*
Trailhead: *Damme Zuid parking lot*
Information and Maps: *Damme Tourist Information*

The whole landscape of the Damme area was changed by the outbreak of the Eighty Years' War. In 1609, Damme was fortified into a heptagon shape surrounded by water. Today, you can still find the remains these 16th- and 17th-century fortresses in the countryside on a short bike ride from the town center. Those willing to slow down can enjoy a quiet walk and some bird-watching. There is a footpath along the former ramparts (Zuidervaartjepad) that starts at the Damme Zuid parking lot and ends south of Onze-Lieve-Vrouwekerk.

CYCLING FROM BRUGES

Cycling Distance: *6.6 kilometers (4.1 miles) one-way*
Cycling Time: *21 minutes*
Trailhead: *Markt (under the Belfry)*
Information and Maps: *Damme Tourist Information*

The bike ride to Damme is a small workout, enough to make you feel good but not enough to cancel out all the chocolates you've consumed. From Markt, follow the signs toward Burg Square before continuing onto Hoogstraat. Hoogstraat will turn into Langestraat after you cross over the canal. You can easily pick up the trail by following the scenic Kruisvest park north until you see the Koeleweimolen windmill. From here, make a right to pass the Dampoort. Stay on the right side to get on the Damse Vaart-Zuid bike path. It's a scenic 5-kilometer (3-mile) flat cycle straight along the canal. You'll pass polders, historic farms, and countless sheep. On the way back, stay on the same side of the canal that you came on, as the other road is shared with cars and can be dangerous for cyclists. Most cycling tours of Bruges and cycling maps in Bruges will show the path to Damme. You can join **QuasiMundo**'s popular four-hour bike tour to Damme (www.quasimundo.com; €33) if you want a guided cycle.

You can rent a bike at the **Tourist Information Office** in Damme, but it's best to rent a bike before you leave Bruges. Try the **Blue Bikes** bikeshare system (www.blue-bike.be) or **Bruges Bike Rental** (www.brugesbikerental.be).

1: Schellemolen **2:** Onze-Lieve-Vrouwekerk **3:** Damme bike path

Shopping

GALERIE INDIGO DAMME

Kerkstraat 15; www.indigoartgallery.be; tel. 050 37 03 31; 11am-1pm and 2pm-6pm Fri.-Wed., 2pm-6pm Thurs.

Across from Damme's City Hall, Gallery Indigo Damme can be busy on weekends with visitors day-tripping from Bruges. You'll find textiles as well as artwork by contemporary Belgian and international arts on sale here.

TERRA FLAMMA

Jacob van Maerlantstraat 17; www.terraflamma.be; tel. 050 68 56 06; 11am-7pm Thurs.-Tues.

Damme is small enough that there aren't many shopping options, but if you're looking for a unique gift or souvenir (albeit one that is easy to break), you can stop by Terra Flamma for handmade pottery and ceramics.

DAMME BOOK MARKET

www.visitdamme.be/en/boekendorp; 10am-5pm second Sun. of the month

Damme's Book Market is well-known among antique book lovers. It takes place within the **town hall** in winter or on the **main square** April-September. The theme of the book market changes monthly, so check the calendar for the upcoming themes (e.g. travel, food).

Food and Bars

DE SMISSE

Kerkstraat 6; www.eetcafe-desmisse.be; tel. 050 35 12 46; 10am-midnight Wed.-Sun.; €3-5

A favorite among bikers doing long-haul rides, De Smisse is a great place to stop for a beer to chat with friendly locals. At the praatcafe, many locals and visitors grab an affordable and cold Jupiler and chat before heading out. Service is friendly, although it's best to head to another spot in Damme for a better value with food.

TIJL EN NELE

Jacob van Maerlantstraat 2; www.tijlennele-damme.be; tel. 050 35 71 92; 9:30am-6pm Sat.-Thurs. Apr.-Sept., 10am-5pm Sat.-Wed. Oct.-Apr.; €5-10

For a quick casual lunch and maybe a cute souvenir from Damme, Tijl en Nele is a great spot. This cute restaurant filled with cute gifts and candies sells large affordable sandwiches that use regional cheese and typical Belgian meats.

TANTE MARIE

Kerkstraat 38; www.tantemarie.be; tel. 050 35 45 03; 10am-6pm Mon.-Sat., 9am-6pm Sun.; €10-20

After a fight against the wind en route to Damme, you'll want to pop into the hyper-feminine Tante Marie to satisfy your sweet tooth. If you're ready for a sugar high, order their homemade pastries, ice cream, and pancakes. Lunch and other snacks (including shrimp croquettes) are available in the afternoon.

ESTAMINET SOETKIN

Kerkstraat 1; tel. 050 37 29 47; 10am-8:30pm Fri.-Tues.; €15-20

A popular tearoom, Estaminet Soetkin is a popular pick among Belgians looking for a light snack in a tasteful setting. Their terrace sits close to the departure point of the steamboat, making it an idyllic place to sit outside in summer.

MOUT

Jacob van Maerlantstraat 7; www.moutdamme.com; tel. 0479 99 00 40; noon-2pm and 6pm-10pm Thurs.-Mon.; €15-30

Plenty of great beer can be found in the region surrounding Bruges. One of the upcoming microbreweries is Damse Brouwers, and the concept of this restaurant is to serve guests tapas-style food along with high-quality beers in the shared space. How often do you get to see a beer master at work?

LA BOUFFÉE

Kerkstraat 26; www.labouffee.be; tel. 050 68 05 88; noon-2pm and 6:30-9pm Tues.-Sat.; €28

For something of a surprise, head to La Bouffée to enjoy chef Nik Van Belle's seasonally inspired dishes. He is regularly inspired by regional ingredients and focuses on bringing out these flavors with French-Belgian dishes. The interior feels comfortable, but the food is taken seriously here. Lunch at La Bouffée is a steal compared to many restaurants in the area.

Information and Services

TOURIST INFORMATION OFFICE

Jacob van Maerlantstraat 3; www.visitdamme.be; tel. 050 28 86 10; 9:30am-12:30pm and 1pm-5pm daily

Damme's Tourist Information Office is the best place to pick up cycling maps and town maps, and make reservations for any of the museums in town. The knowledgeable staff speaks English, French, and Dutch, and it is possible to rent a bike here in peak season.

Getting There

From Bruges, the **bike ride** to Damme is an easygoing cycle along the Damme-Bruges canal. **Bus 43** runs from the Bruges Train Station to Damme a few times a day on weekdays, but not on weekends (30 minutes; €3). Damme is a very short 12-15-minute ride (7 kilometers/4 miles) from Bruges if you have a **car. Parking** in Damme is limited within the historic city center, but you can park at the free **Damme Zuid** (Damse Vaart-Zuid 2) or **Damme Oost** (Oude Sluissedijk 6) parking lot, each only a few hundred meters from the city center. A car can be useful for seeing more of the larger Damme region, which is full of cute villages and pretty castles, and is not well connected by public transit.

But the best way to visit Damme if you don't want to break a sweat is by **steamboat.** During peak season (Apr.-Sept.), the steamboat **Lamme Goedzak** (www.visitdamme.be/lammegoedzak) traverses the Damme-Sluis canal starting between Damme and the outskirts of Bruges, four times daily Tuesday-Saturday. There's a bar on board where you can pick up a coffee as you enjoy the view of the polders during the 35-minute ride. Reservations are not required for smaller groups, and the fare should be paid in cash (€10.50 one-way, €14.50 round-trip). The starting point for the ferry (Noorweegsekaai 31) in Bruges is still quite far from the city center and best reached by bike; bikes are allowed on board.

Getting Around

Damme is very small; it's easy to see most of the town **on foot** within 45 minutes. Unlike Bruges, bike lanes aren't as well defined in Damme, and bikers need to share the road with cars within the town center. You will find helpful signs to nearby major attractions.

Day Trips in Belgium

Beyond Brussels and Bruges, the rest of Belgium

is too often overlooked by visitors. Despite Belgium's tiny size—1.4 times smaller than the Netherlands—it offers a lot of variety. A short train ride brings you from the heart of Brussels's busy Grand Place to the rolling hills surrounding the castle town of Dinant, where you can enjoy hiking, climbing, or cycling; or the flat fields of Ypres where you can pay homage to those who fought in World War I.

This compact country is chock full of history and culture: Often, as you step off the train in your day trip destination, you'll find the language has switch from French to Dutch or Dutch to French, reflecting a complex legacy of linguistic division predating Belgium's foundation. But no matter where you end up, you'll find it easy to discover sublime

Highlights

Look for ★ to find recommended sights, activities, dining, and lodging.

★ **Plantin-Moretus Museum:** Great for bibliophiles, this unique museum in Antwerpen gives you a glimpse into the day-to-day business of the most successful publisher in 16th-century Europe (page 312).

★ **Saint Bavo's Cathedral:** Impressive in its own right, Ghent's oldest cathedral is also home to the world's most stolen painting (page 315).

★ **In Flanders Fields Museum:** This museum in Ypres, set in the countryside that saw some of the worst of World War I's trench warfare, is a both a moving history lesson and a somber memorial (page 321).

★ **Outdoor Recreation in Dinant:** A playground for outdoorsy Europeans, the landscape in and around Dinant begs to be hiked, cycled, kayaked, and climbed (page 333).

Day Trips in Belgium

beer from Trappist abbeys, fine culinary experiences, and surprisingly vibrant Belgian second cities like Antwerp.

The serviceable Belgian train system connects many cities in what seems like the blink of an eye, and some of the routes are very scenic, passing castles that sit perched above rivers and pastoral agricultural fields. You'll see beautiful examples of Belgium's artistic diversity, from 16th-century beguinages in Mechelen, to the glittering guild houses of Antwerp and Ghent, to the impressive Dinant Citadel. Those interested in art and culture will be intrigued by Belgium's lesser-known cities, such as Ghent and its world-famous altarpiece, part of a fascinating saga of art thievery; Ypres and Mons, home to UNESCO-recognized festivals with medieval origins; and Mons, where you can follow in the footsteps of Van Gogh, who spent time

Previous: Ghent; a decorated tree in Flanders Fields; Dinant with the Citadel in the background.

in the region during a short-lived stint as a missionary. Whether you opt for a day trip or a more relaxed overnight stay, a taste of what Belgium has to offer beyond chocolate, beer, and mussels will surprise and delight you.

ORIENTATION

Belgium is a relatively small country with three major regions: Flanders, Wallonia, and Brussels. The majority of the cities mentioned in this chapter are located in **Flanders,** the northern Dutch-speaking region of Belgium, with **Brussels** in its center. Historic **Antwerpen,** Belgium's second-largest city, is a quick train ride north of Brussels, with the university town of **Mechelen** in between. To the west is the canal town of **Ghent,** and farther west still, the border town of **Ypres,** important in World War I.

Wallonia is the French-speaking region immediately to the south of Flanders, home to some of Belgium's most impressive natural landscapes, like **Dinant's** epic cliffs alongside the beautiful Meuse River, about halfway between Brussels and Luxembourg (Belgium's southern neighbor). **Mons,** with key sights related to Van Gogh and Neolithic and coal-mining history, is located in southwestern Wallonia, close to the French border.

It's usually immediately clear when you've crossed the boundary between Flanders and Wallonia, as the main language often changes quite dramatically from French to Dutch (known as Flemish in Belgium), or vice versa. Still, English is well spoken by Belgians in both parts, so visitors don't need to worry much about communicating, regardless of which cultural side of Belgium they find themselves in.

PLANNING YOUR TIME

All the cities covered in this chapter can be visited as **day trips** from a centrally located city like Brussels or Ghent. However, those looking to slow down might enjoy staying **overnight** in smaller cities. Hotel rates are reasonable, and if you opt to stay overnight, it's easy to fall into the rhythm of walking around, covering an attraction or two, wandering into some shops, and tasting the local specialties. Beyond reserving a good spot for **dinner** (especially on weekends), minimal planning is needed. As most of the cities mentioned here receive fewer tourists than Bruges and Brussels, locals are likely to be surprised and excited to meet independent travelers, whether you're at a brown bar in Ghent or a cozy family-run restaurant in Mons.

Like the Netherlands, Belgium's major cities are easily seen by **train** thanks to frequent connections that often center around major cities like **Brussels, Antwerp, Ghent,** and **Namur.** Tickets can be purchased in advance either online (www.belgiantrain.be) or at the train station, but reservations are really only needed for international trains between the Netherlands and Belgium. Belgium's train system is not as well maintained as the Netherlands', but the train fares are considerably cheaper. If you time your visit well, you can save quite a bit by using a **weekend ticket** that provides a 50 percent discount on return journeys across Belgium. (There are also deals for families and combined tickets with attractions throughout the region.) Though certainly not needed for most cities, a **car** is more flexible, especially around Dinant or Ypres. A car reservation is best booked in advance via major cities (Brussels) or airports, such as Charleroi or Brussels Airport.

Visitors are best taking day trips later in the week (Thurs. or Fri.) or on **weekends** when domestic tourism means that more cafés, shops, and attractions are open to the public. You're likely to find more closures early in the week, particularly on Mondays or Tuesdays. That said, you'll have the streets almost to yourself if you opt for a day trip midweek, and you'll also find inexpensive hotel options. It's best to check the opening hours of museums and other niche attractions before planning your trip, as there are often **limited opening hours during off-season.** Although you don't need to prebook

Where to Go from Bruges and Brussels

Destination	Why Go	Getting There from Brussels	Getting There from Bruges	How Long to Stay
Mechelen (page 305)	Beautiful traditional Flemish architecture lines the streets of this medieval university town less than 30 minutes from Brussels.	Train: 25 minutes	Train: 1 hour	Half a day
Antwerpen (page 310)	Find fascinating history, cutting-edge design, and a trendy food scene in Belgium's surprising second city.	Train: 40 minutes	Train: 1.5 hours	One day
Ghent (page 315)	Stroll canals, castles, and a beautiful medieval center without the crowds.	Train: 35 minutes	Train: 25 minutes	One day
Ypres (page 320)	Somber World War I history can be found all around Ypres, as along with what some consider to be the world's best beer.	Train: 2 hours Car: 1.5 hours	Train: 1.5 hours Car: 1 hour	Overnight
Mons (page 325)	Come here for quirky Belgian history, from Neolithic sites to medieval traditions to Van Gogh.	Train: 55 minutes	Train: 2 hours	One day
Dinant (page 330)	See how the Belgians get outside in this outdoor paradise strewn with castles.	Train: 1 hour 45 minutes Car: 1 hour 15 minutes	Train: 3 hours Car: 2 hours	Overnight

attractions—aside from exceptions during the coronavirus—planning your days to avoid church and museum closures will ensure that you cover more ground with your day trip or overnight stay. Bookmarking good food options open on Sunday evenings and Mondays is often a good idea as well.

High season in most Belgian cities corresponds with good weather, often in **summer** (May-Aug.), and Christmas markets in **December.** Antwerp and Ghent are well known for their festive Christmas markets that last for most of December, but even smaller Belgian cities, including Dinant, are likely to be popular during this time. Belgian cities can be popular with Dutch and French tourists on summer weekends, especially in Wallonia. **Booking ahead** by at least a few months is a good idea for hotels during high season.

Mechelen

Mechelen is an adorable Belgian town just 20 minutes from Brussels, its cohesive, traditional Flemish brick buildings a feast for the eyes after Brussels's often hodgepodge mix of architecture. Mechelen was an important trading town in the 15th century, especially for cloth (including tapestries and lace), boosted by its position on the Dyle (or Dijle) River, a tributary that connects Mechelen with the port city of Antwerp. The city became quite wealthy during this period and was a popular residence for royals. Today, the city offers plenty of opportunities for picturesque walks along this important trade artery, especially the renovated Haverwerf harbor area.

Mechelen's atmospheric city center is lined with colorfully painted houses and beautiful, well-preserved beguinages, or architectural complexes built to house communities of religious women. In the center of Mechelen, the Belfry of St. Rumbold's Cathedral rises above the rest of the city and its many churches. The historic center spans a distance of approximately 2 kilometers (1 mile) at its widest, making it easy to traverse from anywhere in Mechelen on foot back to scenic Haverwerf along the Dyle River. There is clear signage throughout the city center, so getting lost is almost impossible. Mechelen lends itself to a relaxing day trip for those looking to take in Flemish architecture and art, drink beer, and stroll the pretty streets.

SIGHTS

Grote Markt is Mechelen's central square, and it's one of the nicest spots to take in the city. On the square, you'll be able to take stock of some of Mechelen's most important buildings, decorated with lavish Gothic and neo-Gothic turrets and elegant Rococo facades, including the elaborate, 13th-century UNESCO-listed **City Hall** (Stadhuis) at Grote Markt 21.

Less than a kilometer south of Grote Markt, across the **Dyle River,** the former harbor of Mechelen is a haven for lovers of architecture. This miniature square, called the **Haverwerf,** has been renovated after some years of decay and is now a popular hub for cafés and restaurants. Admire the beautiful 16th- and 17th-century houses along the river, from the square or from the **Dijlepad,** a floating river walk built as part of the renovation of the old harbor.

St. Rumbold's Cathedral and Belfry

(Sint-Romboutskathedraal)

Onder-Den-Toren 12; https://toerisme.mechelen.be; 9am-4:30pm daily; church free (donations appreciated), belfry €8, youth €2.40, children under 4 free

Mechelen is home to no less than eight impressive churches, but if you have to pick one church not to miss, it's St. Rumbold's, whose Gothic architecture is certain to impress. Once the church of the archdiocese, the cathedral dates back to the 13th century, continually expanded for the next 300 years, until the iconoclastic conflicts that embroiled much of this region in the 16th century resulted in some large-scale damage. That said, it has been rebuilt and has survived much, including World War II, and the church's impressive art collection is still standing strong, including Flemish baroque master Anthony van Dyck's *Christ on a Cross.* You can learn a lot about the history of the church via paintings that you'll find on the right side of the altar.

St. Rumbold's belfry is one of Mechelen's main attractions, thanks to the 360-degree view from the top of the tower's Skywalk. Construction of the belfry began in 1452. The builders intended the tower to be taller, but construction was never completed because

Beguinages of Mechelen

The Beguines, an order of Christian laypeople who lived together in poverty but did not take formal religious vows, left an indelible mark upon Mechelen after their dwelling outside the city center was destroyed in 1560. They ended up creating their own village-within-a-village in Mechelen, which still remains one of its most picturesque quarters. Though most of the Beguines, who were prominent in Mechelen's lace industry, have died out, it's still possible to visit their beautiful former residence. Signs pointing west from Grote Markt and St. Rumbold's will lead you to the Large and Small Beguinages, called the Groot Begijnhof and Klein Begijnhof in Dutch. The beguinages are usually open from dawn to dusk and are free to enter, but please be considerate of the residents and be quiet and respectful during your visit.

LARGE BEGUINAGE

Groot Begijnhof, Nonnenstraat 13; tel. 02 553 16 50; www.groot-begijnhof-mechelen.be

The Large Beguinage was once an independent thriving community, with a bakery, hospital, brewery, and even a church, with whitewashed walls and cobblestone streets. Many of these buildings remain, and it's now a residential neighborhood. You can access the larger Beguinage via Nonnenstraat, a 6-minute walk from St. Rumbold's.

SMALL BEGUINAGE

Klein Begijnhof 1

Even closer to St. Rumbold's, the Small Beguinage is a 3-minute walk north from the cathedral. Dating to the 13th century and beautifully restored, the small square lined with whitewashed walls can be found via a series of narrow archways that lead down skinny alleyways, past ivy-covered brick homes.

of a fear of collapse and a lack of funds; it was eventually combined with the church to prevent it from collapsing. Renovations in 2009 added modern glass stairs that provide a bird's-eye view of Mechelen, as well as Antwerpen's and Brussels's skylines in the distance. In order to reach the top, you'll need to climb 538 steps. Entering the church is generally free, but if you wish to climb the Belfry, a UNESCO recognized moment, you'll have to pay a fee.

A bit over halfway up, you'll be able to see the Bell Chamber; the carillons are just a little higher, at 423 steps. St. Rumbold's belfry is the only one in Belgium with two full carillons, a unique feature; Mechelen even has a carillon school. Special **tours** allow you to accompany a carillonneur, who will perform a concert at the top (https://toerisme.mechelen.be/carillon-culture). You'll often hear the sound of the carillon from the Grote Markt on weekend afternoons.

Kazerne Dossin

Goswin de Stassartstraat 153; tel. 015 29 06 60; www.kazernedossin.eu; 9am-5pm Mon.-Fri., 9:30am-5pm Sat.-Sun.; permanent exhibition €10, temporary exhibitions €9, combination ticket €16, youth 10-21 €4, children under 10 free

A somber side of Mechelen history, the city was the main point of deportation for Belgian Jews, Roma, and Sinti during World War II due to its central location close to Antwerp and Brussels, both key locations of the Jewish community in Belgium. Old army barracks dating back to the 1750s were converted into a transit camp by the Nazis, to house victims before they were sent to their death in Auschwitz. After the war, the building was used for a variety of purposes, from barracks to social housing. Today, a portion of the former barracks remain apartments, but the

1: Mechelen Grote Markt **2:** Belgian chocolates from The Cacao Project **3:** Dijlepad Riverwalk

1

2

3

rest of the complex has been converted into a thoughtful Holocaust monument.

The museum tells the stories of the events leading up to the Holocaust and of its victims by giving an insight into the richness of Jewish and Roma life in Belgium before World War II, with audio guides and items that belonged to victims. Staff members often run guided **tours** that can be reserved in advance online.

HIKING

DIJLEPAD RIVERWALK

Hiking Distance: *700 meters (0.4 miles)*
Hiking Time: *10 minutes*
Trailhead: *Haverwerf*

For many, a highlight of Mechelen is this short, pedestrianized river walk, starting at the Haverwerf and continuing along the river, where much of the wooden path actually floats on the Dyle. From the Dijlepad, you can take in many of Mechelen's most magnificent guild houses, including the former fishmongers' guild house at Zoutwerf 5, with a giant fish on the outside.

FOOD

Mechelen has a small yet innovative food scene, where creativity thrives. You can find artisanal chocolate, American-style brunches, and twists on the Belgian stews made with the local beers. It's clear that Mecheleners appreciate the finer things in life—especially when you realize that your dinner reservation often lasts a few hours.

★ SISTER BEAN

Vismarkt 26; tel. 015 65 86 65; https://sisterbean.be; 9am-5pm Fri.-Tues.; €14

Sister Bean is a friendly breakfast and lunch spot, known for American-style brunches and hearty omelets. It's a cozy little place to sit and linger over a coffee, run by sisters Patty and Helena. Try the weekend brunch special for couples and families, with sweets, cheese, and quiche among other items for €20 per person.

FUNKY JUNGLE

Onder-Den-Toren 7; tel. 015 67 72 99; https://funkyjungle.be; noon-2pm and 6pm-9pm Wed.-Sat.; €14

Funky Jungle is a relative newcomer to Mechelen's trendy dining scene, but this cozy restaurant specializes in plant-based food. Even for those who aren't vegan, Funky Jungle's healthy and generous portions so close to Mechelen's main attractions, including St. Rumbold's, make it a great pick for dinner if you'll be staying overnight.

THE CACAO PROJECT

Bruul 89; tel. 015 43 07 30; www.thecacaoproject.be; 11am-6pm Mon.-Sat.; €15

If you've been lucky enough to try Dominique Personne's chocolates at the Chocolate Line in Bruges, you'll want to make a beeline for the Cacao Project, run by one of Personne's former students, Pieter Vaes. This tiny workshop showcases ethical and fair-trade chocolates made with wild flavors, like mango and bergamot.

ACCOMMODATIONS

MARTIN'S PATERHOF

Karmelietenstraat 4; tel. 015 46 46 46; www.martinshotels.com; €100

Martin's Paterhof is one of the most unique hotels in the region, a four-star hotel that is nothing less than the holy grail for its convenient location in city center as well as its impressive rooms, housed within a neo-Gothic church. Many of the rooms have elaborate, colorful stained glass windows; opt for a "Great" room to get a space that has more of these details. The hotel is eco-friendly, with exceptionally comfortable beds, good Wi-Fi, and an expresso machine. If you opt for **breakfast** (€18), you'll take it underneath the former altar.

GETTING THERE

Mechelen is easily accessible by train from multiple cities in Belgium, including Antwerp and Brussels. Traffic surrounding Brussels's

Historic Brews

Mechelen is known for its local brews, one of the most famous of which is the ***maneblusser,*** or "moon extinguisher." The story behind the name goes that in January 1687, someone (who may not have been sober) looked up and saw that St. Rumbold's tower was on fire. The entire city mobilized to bring buckets of water up the tower, only to realize that there was no fire: It was the moon in a reddish midst. Though the residents did their best to keep this incident a secret, people from Mechelen soon came to be known as "moon extinguishers." Today, the locals proudly call themselves *maneblussers*—and with such a delicious blonde beer with the same name, why wouldn't they?

One of the best place to try the *maneblusser* is **Brouwerij De Anker** (Guido Gezellelaan 49; tel. 015 28 71 41; www.hetanker.be; €11 tour), which boasts some fascinating history of its own, dating back to the hospital at the Large Beguinage, where beer used to be brewed. Today, this former hospital is part of part of De Anker's grounds. In 1872, the van Breedam family purchased the brewery and modernized it with a steam boiler while incorporating beers inspired by traditional recipes.

The most popular beer is the **Gouden Carolus,** a traditional Belgian dark ale (named the World's Best in 2012). It's named after the currency under Emperor Charles, who reduced the beer tax for the Beguines. If you're a beer lover, take a tour followed by a meal at the **brasserie** (10am-11pm Mon.-Fri., 10am-1:30am Sat., 10am-10pm Sun.; €16.50); many of their dishes utilize beer in the recipe.

highways often impacts Mechelen, so it's best not to drive to here if possible.

Train

MECHELEN TRAIN STATION (Malines)

Koning Albertplein 2

The train station is located 1 kilometer (0.6 miles) southeast of the city center. From **Brussels,** trains run directly to Mechelen approximately once every 15 minutes, if not more often. The journey takes 20-25 minutes and costs €4.70 one-way. Trains run just as frequently from **Antwerpen,** a 17-minute journey that costs €4.10 one-way. The train connection with **Bruges** is poor and takes about 1.5 hours, often via Brussels.

Car

Driving from **Brussels** will take approximately 30 minutes without traffic, a 31-kilometer (19-mile) drive, mostly on the **E19.** The 27-kilometer (17-mile) drive from **Antwerpen** also takes approximately 30 minutes, again mostly on the E19. Mechelen is about 1.5 hours by car (12 kilometers/7 miles) via the **E40** from **Bruges.**

Parking in the city center of Mechelen is limited and expensive, with mostly underground lots, but there are several affordable parking lots about 1 kilometer (0.6 miles; 10 minutes) outside the city center with free parking on weekends, including one at Zandpoortvest 2.

Antwerpen

Antwerpen is a city that surprises—you may know it better as Antwerp, a name curiously only used by English speakers—often stealing the spotlight from Brussels among visitors to both cities. It's the cultural capital of Flanders, Belgium's northern region, and Belgium's second largest city. Home to some of the country's most intriguing historical and cultural institutions and a beautiful 16th-market square, Antwerpen also has a young soul, constantly innovating its food, architecture, and hot spots for a drink. If you're not keen on modern architecture like the MAS, Antwerpen's polarizing glass-and-sandstone museum of objects, there are also some truly impressive historic museums, including the UNESCO-listed Plantin-Moretus, a former publishing house and a must for bibliophiles, and the Rubens House, with its collection of works by the famous Flemish artist Peter Paul Rubens. From your first step onto Grote Markt, with its wealth of baroque and Renaissance architecture, you'll be wondering why everyone flocks to Amsterdam instead of Antwerp.

Antwerp, situated on a wide section of the Scheldt River, which widens further as it heads northwest into the Netherlands and eventually the English Channel, is another historically important port city for Belgium. It spans a larger footprint than many other cities, expanding into the newer Eilandje area, a former warehouse neighborhood. It's still a walkable city for those fond of going on foot, but public transit might be preferred for those who aren't keen on the 2-plus kilometer distances (20-minute walk) between the train station and the center. The Scheldt River cuts Antwerp in half and sits on the western side of the historic city center, where you'll find the Cathedral Our Lady Antwerp and Grote Markt. (An underground tunnel connects the two sides of the river.)

SIGHTS

Grote Markt

Grote Markt 1; www.visitantwerpen.be; open 24/7; free

If you've seen a photo of Antwerp, you've likely seen the Grote Markt, the main market square. Like Grand Place in Brussels, the square is filled with impressive guild houses with gold accents, most rebuilt and restored after the Spanish Sack of Antwerp in 1576 during the Eighty Years' War; the only original guild houses that remain are at numbers 24, 38, and 40. The **city hall** (1 Suikerrui) was built at the peak of Antwerp's wealth, in the baroque and Renaissance styles. In the center of the market, you'll find Brabo Fountain, named after a figure from a Flemish folklore. Brabo is said to have defeated a giant who demanded a toll from all those crossing the Scheldt River, cutting off the hands of those who refused. After defeating the giant, Brabo cut off the giant's hand and threw it into the river; the name "Antwerpen" is said to have come from Flemish for hand-throwing.

Cathedral of Our Lady Antwerp (Onze-Lieve-Vrouwekathedraal Antwerpen)

Groenplaats 21; tel. 03 213 99 51; www.dekathedraal.be; 10am-5pm Mon.-Fri., 10am-3pm Sat., 1pm-4pm Sun.; €6

Antwerp's most impressive Cathedral boasts the tallest tower in the region, at 123 meters (404 feet), making it an easy landmark for orientating yourself in the city. The main church took more than 170 years to complete, beginning in 1352 and finishing in 1521, and is the largest Gothic cathedral in Belgium and the Netherlands. It holds four works by Peter Paul

1: guild houses on Antwerpen's Grote Markt **2:** Vlaaikensgang alley in the historic center of Antwerpen **3:** Antwerpen Centraal Railway Station

1
2
3

Rubens, among pieces from other well-known Flemish painters; there's *The Assumption of the Virgin Mary*, a specially commissioned piece that serves as the altarpiece, *The Resurrection of Christ, The Elevation of the Cross,* and *The Descent from the Cross.*

Although the church isn't as grand as some other churches, due to looting around the Great Iconoclasm (attacks on Catholic churches by Calvinists in the 1600s), it is still truly impressive. It's a functioning church with Roman Catholic services in English on Saturday evenings (5pm). The church has free daily **tours,** as well as audio guides upon entry, along with free **carillon concerts** on Mondays, Wednesdays, and Fridays noon-3pm. The café next door, **De Plek,** is housed in a former chapel, serving beer brewed by the church through a hidden door.

★ Plantin-Moretus Museum
(Museum Plantin-Moretus)

Vrijdagmarkt 22-23; tel. 03 221 14 50; www.museumplantinmoretus.be; 10am-5pm Tues.-Sun.; adults €8, seniors and students €6, children under 12 free, free for visitors on last Wed. of every month

The Plantin-Moretus Museum is unique, the world's only UNESCO-protected museum. It was once the home and workplace of Christophe Plantin, who was born in France in the 16th century and became the largest publisher in Europe at the time. After learning to print and marrying, Plantin settled in Antwerp. At the time, tensions between Calvinism and Catholicism made printing any religious text a dangerous task, which landed Plantin, who printed works friendly to both Catholics and Protestants, in hot water. He redeemed himself by printing the largest multilingual bible of the 16th century, known as the *Biblia Polyglotta,* which included five languages and eight volumes. Plantin printed more than 2,450 works over 34 years as a printer, an impressive task considering how individual pages had to be printed by hand at the time. The works ranged from biology to religion to music. After his death in 1589, Plantin's son-in-law Jan Moretus took over the publishing company. The company was eventually sold to the city of Antwerpen in the 19th century, and was almost immediately open for public viewing.

This home is the last surviving publishing house from the Renaissance and baroque period, known as the *Officina Plantiniana.* Transport yourself to the 16th century in this perfectly preserved workshop, with original printing equipment where Plantin's associates would line up sentences by hand, letter by letter. These are the oldest printing presses in the world. Beyond the printing room, the Plantin-Moretus house is home to more than 25 Flemish masterpieces, including portraits of Plantin's family by Rubens, as well as atmospheric rooms with distinctive leather walls. You can also admire priceless works of literature, including a Gutenberg Bible. Don't miss the ivy-covered courtyard on your way out of the museum, which also includes temporary exhibitions that showcase the work of modern-day publishers.

The Rubens House
(Rubenshuis)

Wapper 9-11; tel. 03 201 15 55; www.rubenshuis.be; 10am-5pm Tues.-Sun.; adults €8, seniors and students €6, children under 12 free

The Rubens House is one of the top attractions of Antwerp, especially for art lovers. Peter Paul Rubens, one of the best-known Flemish artists, lived in this building from 1611 until his death in 1640. He built the house with his wife in the style of an Italian palazzo, following their return from Italy. Largely restored, the only original elements that have been left mostly untouched are the garden pavilion and the Roman-inspired triumphal arch (portico) that leads out to the courtyard. The interior includes a re-creation of Rubens's studio, a personal art gallery (including self-portraits), and living quarters with period furniture. The museum also owns many works by other Flemish artists, including Rubens's apprentices. Only the ground floor and garden are accessible to wheelchair users. Admission includes an audio tour.

Museum aan de Stroom (MAS)

Hanzestedenplaats 1; tel. 03 338 44 00; www.mas.be; 10am-5pm Tues.-Sun.; adults €10, students and seniors €8, children under 12 free

This ultra-modern building, made of sandstone and curved glass and inspired by art deco architecture, is in Het Eilandje, a rapidly gentrifying neighborhood close to Antwerp's docks that feels miles from Antwerp's historic city center. Its unique, massive collection houses objects based on five themes: power politics and world ports, food and cities, life and death, people and gods, and the upper and under world. Exhibitions vary wildly, using the objects to tell stories about Antwerp history, or showcasing the work of local artists or experimental artists from abroad; you may want check their agenda for the latest exhibition before committing to a ticket.

The building itself is free to enter if you want to simply head to the rooftop terrace to enjoy the views of Antwerp—just take the elevator to the 10th floor. It's a leisurely 15-minute walk north of Grote Markt.

Antwerpen Centraal

Koningin Astridplein 27; www.belgianrail.be; open 24/7; free

Antwerp's impressive train station is an icon of the city. Much like New York's Grand Central Station, it serves as both a major transportation hub as well as a beautiful location in its own right. Constructed by Belgian architect Louis Delacenserie at the turn of the 20th century, it was inspired by neo-Renaissance architecture, built in iron and glass in order to accommodate the smoke from locomotives. Today, the high glass ceiling and large dome makes for a magical gaze upward, especially as you climb the stairs to admire the entrance hall. Antwerp Central has been regularly named one of Europe's most beautiful train stations throughout the years—as you catch a train to Ghent or Amsterdam, leave yourself enough time to enjoy coffee with a view of the station or to watch the bustling people below.

FOOD AND BARS

Traditionally, Antwerp is best known for **eel** (*paling*) and **tartars** (raw meat) often served at traditional cafés. However, vegans and those looking for more international-influenced options (such as poke and burgers) will all find something to enjoy within Antwerp's rich foodie scene.

BILLIE'S BIER KAFETARIA

Kammenstraat 1; tel. 03 226 31 83; 4pm-midnight Sun.-Mon. and Thurs., 4pm-12:59am Fri., 2pm-12:59am Sat.; €4

Billie's Bier Kafetaria is a visitor-friendly old-school Flemish brown bar where tourists and locals mix as they enjoy Belgium's best beers. Billie's prides itself on its beer selection, which includes 11 local beers on tap. Even if you're not a beer expert, the friendly staff are happy to help you with Belgian brews with curated tastings as well as their extensive beer list.

PLANT B

Oude Koornmarkt 64; tel. 03 648 01 77; www.plantb.co; 10am-6pm Thurs.-Sun.; €10

Plant B is a vegan café with a cozy interior and a sunny balcony in summer, where vegetarians and meat-lovers alike can enjoy a delicious plant-based brunch or coffee on weekends. Their menu is simple with some clever touches, from vegan *speculoos* spread to Italian-inspired paninis. If you can, save room for the cake. Seating is quite limited, so arrive early on weekends.

ELFDE GEBOD

Torfbrug 10; tel. 03 288 57 33; https://elfdegebod.com; noon-11pm daily; mains €19

Elfde Gebod, or the "Eleventh Commandment," is named for the so-called extra commandment that those in Antwerp drink beer. As you enjoy a honey blonde (the house specialty) and *frites*, you'll be watched approvingly by hundreds of religious statues and paintings that are crammed into every single nook in the walls. The café, which claims to be one of Antwerp's oldest restaurants, once belonged to the Cathedral of our

Lady Antwerp, but today less than holy things happen in this cozy brown bar with a good beer and drink menu. The food menu includes hearty Belgian favorites such as mussels and beef stews. Whether you're religious or simply a fan of the quirky, Elfde Gebod is an atmospheric place that is worth a drink at a minimum. A reservation for eating or drinking (they request that you specify in advance!) is recommended on weekends, especially during major events.

DE ARME DUIVEL

Armeduivelstraat 1; tel. 03 232 26 98; www.armeduivel.be; noon-10pm Mon.-Sat. Apr.-Sept., noon-2:30pm and 5:30pm-10pm Mon.-Fri., noon-10pm Sat. Oct.-Mar.; €20

De Arme Duivel is a small restaurant close to the Rubens House that serves up Belgian classics, from beef stews to croquettes, complemented by popular Belgian beers. Reservations are strongly recommended in this cozy café with old photos and wooden booths. They are known for their raw meat tartars, a popular dish in the region.

HET NIEUWE PALINGHUIS

Sint-Jansvliet 14; tel. 03 231 74 45; www.hetnieuwepalinghuis.be; noon-2pm and 6pm-9pm Wed.-Thurs. and Sat., noon-2pm and 6pm-8:30pm Sun.; €47

A fixture Antwerp's culinary scene, this well-known Belgian restaurant serves up Antwerp's most famous dish: smoked eel in a green herb sauce, known as *paling in 't groen.* You'll also find many other fish and seafood specialties, including homemade shrimp croquettes and mussels. The historic wood-paneled interior is filled with black-and-white photos of Antwerp, a great introduction to the city's fine dining. Reservations recommended.

ACCOMMODATIONS

HOTELO KATHEDRAL

Handschoenmarkt 3/5; tel. 03 500 89 50; https://hotelokathedral.com; €100

HotelO is a boutique hotel with views of Antwerp's cathedral. Many of their rooms have large-scale Rubens replicas on the walls—and even on the ceilings. Set within a modernized medieval building, each room has an open-plan bathroom and other mod cons. Best suited to couples, HotelO Kathedral has a great location just footsteps from Grote Markt.

GETTING THERE

Antwerp is easily accessible from the Netherlands and other Belgian cities, including Brussels, by train (high-speed trains if you're coming from Brussels and Rotterdam). The train and car journeys take about the same amount of time from Ghent and Brussels, but having a car might be stressful due to low-emissions zone driving restrictions and the challenge of finding parking.

Train

ANTWERPEN CENTRAAL

Koningin Astridplein 27; www.belgianrail.be; open 24/7; free

Trains run directly from **Brussels** to Antwerpen Centraal approximately once every 30 minutes (if not more often). The train journey takes 40 minutes to 1 hour, depending on the speed of the train/number of stops. A one-way ticket costs €7.50. Trains also run directly from **Ghent,** approximately once every 15 minutes, a 1-hour journey (€9.60 one-way). From **Bruges,** trains run Antwerpen Centraal approximately once every 30 minutes (1.5-2 hours; €15). Antwerpen Centraal Train Station is located about 2 kilometers (1 mile; 20 minutes) east of the historic city center next to the Diamond District.

There is a high-speed train connection (https://nsinternational.com; 1 hour 15 minutes; €50) with **Amsterdam** and **Rotterdam** that runs approximately once every 2-3 hours.

Car

Driving from **Brussels** takes approximately 50 minutes (46 kilometers/28.5 miles) without traffic, mostly on the **A12.** From **Ghent,** the drive is also about 50 minutes

(63 kilometers/39 miles), mostly on the **E17.** From **Bruges,** the drive is about an 1 hour 15 minutes (92 kilometers/57 miles) via the **E34.** Antwerp is only 1 hour 15 minutes from **Rotterdam,** the closest Dutch city, via the **A4** (103 kilometers/64 miles).

Street **parking** in Antwerp can be challenging due to much of the city historic center being closed off to cars that do not meet a specific emissions standard, so it's best to opt for a covered garage on the city outskirts for free Park and Ride parking (www.visitantwerpen.be/en/transport/parking-in-antwerp). There is parking available in the city center, such as near Meir Interparking (Eiermarkt 33; €1.40 per hour).

Ghent

Ghent (Gent in Flemish) is one of Belgium's most underrated cities, skipped by many tourists in favor of Bruges or Antwerp. But its beautiful canals, epic Gravensteen castle, lovely medieval center, and edgy design scene make for a charming daytrip or weekend (especially during the Christmas market season), a remarkable mix of old and new.

Ghent has a fraction of the tourists of Bruges, whether you're strolling down the Graslei quay on the Leie River, or heading to Staint Bavo's Cathedral, home of *The Adoration of the Mystic Lamb* by van Eyck, known worldwide as the Ghent Altarpiece and arguably Belgium's most famous work of art. Its relative lack of renown lends it a more bohemian, down-to-earth character, deeply felt as you're weaving your way through cobblestone streets on your way to some of Belgium's best restaurants. This is another university town, evident in the lively, youthful population and quirky bar scene.

Ghent is fairly walkable once you're within the city center, but the main train station is a decent walk (2.5 kilometers/1.5 miles) from the city center.

SIGHTS

The **Leie River** weaves through Ghent, dividing the central **Saint Bavo's Cathedral** from other prominent sights like **Gravensteen** and **Design Museum Gent.** While wandering the city, be sure to walk **Graslei** and **Korenlei,** Ghent's most stunning strolls, on the river banks with a view of medieval houses as far as the eye can see. Start your walk close to **St. Michael's Bridge (Sint-Michielsbrug)** and head north. Both sides of the Leie are beautiful, but you'll have the best views of Graslei's iconic buildings from the Korenlei side. On summer evenings, the canals' many places to sit along the water make it a favorite among students and couples on dates.

★ Saint Bavo's Cathedral (Sint-Baafskathedraal)

Sint-Baafsplein; https://sintbaafskathedraal.be; Ghent Altarpiece 9am-5pm Mon.-Sat., 1pm-5pm Sun., catheral 8:30am-6pm Mon.-Sat., 1pm-6pm Sun.; Ghent Altarpiece adults €5, children 6-12 €4, children under 4 free, cathedral free

Saint Bavo's Cathedral is Ghent's oldest church. First built as a chapel in the 10th century in honor of St. John the Baptist, it became a Gothic church in the 1200s and was almost continually built upon for the next 300 years. Some of its features, including its original stained glass windows, were destroyed in the iconoclastic fury that spread over the region in the 16th century, but thankfully, the famous Ghent Altarpiece was able to be saved. Otherwise known as *The Adoration of the Mystic Lamb,* it's one of the most well-known pieces of art in history, both due to its status as the world's most stolen painting, and the mastery of its creator, Jan van Eyck.

The painting was first stolen in 1794 by French soldiers, who plundered it for the Louvre after the French Revolution, and was

1
2
3
4

brought back to Ghent in 1815 following the French defeat after the Battle of Waterloo. It was then stolen by German forces during World War I and returned in 1920. Thieves took two panels in 1934, returning one—the other, *The Just Judges*, is still missing. In 1940, at the outbreak of World War II, the decision was made to move the painting to prevent theft by the Nazis, but this did not stop Hitler from seizing it in 1942. Finally, the painting was recovered by the Allied group known as the Monuments Men, who tracked down art stolen during World War II; it had been hidden in in a salt mine. Today, the painting is housed behind bulletproof glass in a separate wing, and for the first time in many years, you can view it in the most complete state that it's been in years.

The restored painting is in full color, showing the lamb (with a controversially humanoid face) said to symbolize Christ being adored by angels. The surrounding panels show the Virgin Mary, John the Baptist, groups of angels, Adam and Eve, and other figures from the Bible.

Although the church is free, entry to see the completed and restored *The Adoration of the Mystic Lamb* by van Eyck is not, and it's subject to more limited hours than the church. The larger cathedral is also worth exploring for its crypt and works by other well-known Flemish artists, including Peter Paul Rubens's *Saint Bavo enters the Convent at Ghent*. Services are held Sundays at 11am.

Ghent Belfry
(Het Belfort van Gent)

Sint-Baafsplein; tel. 09 233 39 54; https://visit.gent.be; 10am-6pm daily; adults €8, students €2.70, youth 13-18 €1.60, children free

The Ghent Belfry is the tallest in Belgium, at 91 meters (299 feet) high. It dates back to 1313; the dragon on top of the Belfry has been there since it was built, becoming a symbol for the city at large.

For the best view over Ghent, climb the Belfry's 366 steps, or bypass some of the worst of it by taking an elevator to the bell room, where you can view the 53-bell carillon at work (the bells can be heard throughout Ghent 11am Sun., 8pm first Fri. of the month, and Sat. evenings in summer). From here, you'll need to climb another 100 or so steps. Space at the top is limited, sometimes requiring you to squeeze past others close to the edge, so be sure to secure your belongings first. (Due to steps, the Belfry is largely not accessible to visitors with disabilities.) At the base of the building adjoined to the Belfry is the medieval Cloth Hall, dating back to 1441, also used as the city prison.

Graffiti Street

Werregarenstraat; open 24/7; free

A small alleyway in Ghent's centrum, Werregarenstraat has been filled with street art since 1995, when the city legalized graffiti in the hopes of stopping it elsewhere. The street is constantly in flux, and it's often possible to chat with the artists while they work. The street is open 24 hours, but it's best to come here during the day to admire the artwork at its most colorful.

Design Museum Gent

Jan Breydelstraat 5; tel. 09 267 99 99; www.designmuseumgent.be; 9:30am-5:30pm Mon.-Tues. and Thurs.-Fri., 10-6pm Sat.-Sun.; adults €10, students €2, children free

Design Museum Gent is one of Belgium's most innovative museums, a mecca for designers, art lovers, and architects with its impressive collection of art nouveau artwork and furniture, iconic international designs, and innovative work from emerging Belgian artists. The museum is housed within a modern building, in the process of expanding into a new, more accessible wing with interactive exhibitions. Until then, you should ask about the giant toilet paper roll in its famous bathroom wing, which will be destroyed once renovations begin.

1: view of Ghent at night **2:** guild houses in Graslei **3:** *cuberdon*, local candies **4:** Saint Bavo's Cathedral

Gravensteen

Sint-Veerleplein 11; tel. 09 225 93 06; https://historischehuizen.stad.gent/nl/gravensteen; 10am-6pm daily; adults €12, students 19-25 €7, youth 13-18 €2, children 0-12 free

In the middle of Ghent, Gravensteen castle was the medieval home of the Count of Flanders for 173 years, beginning in 1180; its medieval moat now sits next to modern tram stops. The castle was largely abandoned until the 18th century, when it was utilized by the city as a prison and court of law. The darkest and most interesting parts of Gravensteen's history come from this period. Many of the most fascinating stories are related with the castle's unexpectedly hilarious audio guide, hosted by a local Ghent comedian, that comes with every tour. It's a clever way to humanize its inhabitants over the centuries while still educating visitors.

The tour takes you through the castle's large, often cold rooms, impressive weaponry collection, dungeons, torture chambers, and upper ramparts where you'll find the best views of Ghent from above. The castle is largely not accessible to people with wheelchairs due to the stone-cut staircases that you'll need to follow as you explore the castle, but it is very family-friendly (besides the audio tour, which has some cursing).

FOOD AND BARS

Ghent is best known for a popular dish called ***Gentse waterzooi,*** which is a stew with carrots, leeks, potatoes, and cream traditionally made with fish, nowadays more commonly made with chicken. You'll also find ***cuberdon*** (also known as the *Gentse neus*), a soft cone-shaped candy made of gum arabic and a fruit filling that is best bought fresh at a specialized stand along the **Groentenmarkt.** Of course, Ghent also has some great **chocolatiers** and modern food, where you'll find options for any diet, including vegan.

GROENTENMARKT

Groentenmarkt, https://visit.gent.be/en/see-do/groentenmarkt, 7:30am-1pm Fri.

This little square just off the Leie River, not far from Gravensteen castle on the other side, hosts a lively organize market on Fridays, a great place to try local candies and produce. From 10am-6pm Saturdays and Sundays from April-September, there is also an **art market** for local artisan-made products, such as

Gravensteen castle

jewelry and other accessories and regionally made cookware and vases.

GHENT GRUUT BREWERY

Rembert Dodoensdreef 1; tel. 09 269 02 69; www.gruut.be; 2pm-6pm Mon.-Thurs., 11am-11pm Fri.-Sat., 2pm-7pm Sun.;€4

Though this brewery is relatively new (founded 2009), it draws on a long tradition of beer brewed in Ghent, thanks to a female head brewer who brews beer with spices instead of hops—the word *gruut* comes from herbs traditionally added to beers in Ghent (breweries were taxed based on the number of spices/herbs used in their beers). Although you can certainly try *gruut* throughout Ghent, this brewery is a great place to do it. The brewery does a few **tours,** including a brewery visit and tasting (€11, €16 with appetizers from Ghent), boat tours of Ghent combined with a beer tasting (€22 per person, minimum 10 people), and beer workshops.

DULLE GRIET

Vrijdagmarkt 50; tel. 09 224 24 55; www.dullegriet.be; 4:30pm-1am Mon., noon-1am Tues.-Sat., noon-7:30pm Sun.; €4

One of Ghent's most infamous and tourist-friendly cafés is Dulle Griet, home of the "shoe beer": the Maximum of the House beer requires a deposit of a shoe in order to get the skinny glass filled with 7.5 percent ABV beer attached to a wooden handle. Once you finish your beer, you'll get your shoe back, and you might even be done for the night. The café itself is quite atmospheric, with many old beer signs and an impressive Belgian beer list—choosing might be the hardest part if you're not up for the shoe challenge.

BOON

Geldmunt 6; tel. 0477 77 01 81; www.boon.gent; 11:30am-5pm Tues.-Sat.; €11

Boon is a vegetarian restaurant that creatively serves up vegan-friendly salads, coffee, and sweets in a retro-inspired café with an '80s vibe. The food is both hearty and wholesome.

WASBAR

Korenmarkt 37; tel. 09 311 69 08; www.wasbar.be; 9am-9pm; €14

Even if you don't have clothes to wash, this aptly named combination laundromat-café/bar serves up American-inspired brunch, all-day hearty bagel sandwiches, and burgers. It's a strange concept, but the relaxed vibe makes Wasbar a nice and convienent place to eat—that's walking distance from most attractions—if you miss dinner/lunch hours at other restaurants in Ghent.

MOSQUITO COAST

Hoogpoort 28; tel. 09 224 37 20; www.mosquitocoast.be; 3pm-1am Mon.-Fri. and Sun., 11am-1am Sat.; €17

With an internationally inspired menu and bookshelves filled with old travel guides, Mosquito Coast is straight out of a travel lover's dream. This cozy café/bar is also a backpacking mecca, where many a story begins with "When I was in . . ." Stop in for tapas as well as traditional Ghent dishes such as beef stew.

'T KLOKHUYS

Corduwaniersstraat 65; tel. 09 223 42 41; www.klokhuys.com; 6pm-10:30pm Tues.-Thurs., noon-2:45pm and 6pm-10:30pm Fri.-Sat., 5:30pm-10:30pm Sun.; €17.50

This is one of the best spots in Ghent to sample the local specialty *Gentse waterzooi*, a Flemish chicken stew. It's a cozy Belgian restaurant with beautiful displays of dried flowers.

ACCOMMODATIONS

HOTEL ONDERBERGEN

Onderbergen 69; tel. 09 223 62 00; www.hotelonderbergen.be; €118

Hotel Onderbergen is a cozy family-owned hotel that is about 500 meters (1,600 feet) from Ghent's picturesque riverfront and main attractions. The spacious rooms have high ceilings, complimentary drinks, and easy access to numerous restaurants. (Note: There's no elevator.) Breakfast is available for €11 extra.

GETTING THERE

Ghent is quite easy to access from other cities in Flanders and from Brussels itself by train. Although it's certainly possible to drive, limited car access to the historic city center and frequent train connections make taking the train a no-brainer.

Train

GENT SINT PIETERS STATION

www.belgiantrain.be

Trains run directly from **Brussels** to Ghent approximately once every 20 minutes, a 35-40-minute journey (€9.10 one-way). From **Antwerp,** trains run every 15 minutes; the train journey takes 1 hour (€9.60 one-way). From **Bruges,** trains run once every 20 minutes (25-40 minutes; €6.70 one-way). The main train station for Ghent is located about 2.5 kilometers (1.5 miles) south of Ghent's city center, although Gent Dampoort station is slightly closer to the city center at 1.5 kilometers (0.9 miles) east of the center.

Car

From **Brussels,** the 57-kilometer (35-mile) drive takes about 50 minutes, mostly on the **E40.** Driving from **Antwerp** takes about 1 hour, 60 kilometers (37 miles), mostly on the **E17.** From **Bruges,** it's a 35-minute (51-kilometer/32-mile) drive on the E40.

Parking in Ghent's city center, like many Belgian cities, is limited due to low-emissions regulations, but there is ample and free parking at the free Park and Ride centers on the city outskirts (P+R Gentbrugge Arsenaal; Brusselsesteenweg 602) with a tram connection to the city center (Tram 2; www.delijn.be/nl/lijnen/lijn/2/121/6/#dienstregeling; every 20 minutes).

Ypres

Ypres, or Ieper in Dutch (pronounced E-per), is a small city in West Flanders, closer to the French border than it is to Bruges, with an outsize role in world history, especially World War I. Many come to honor the soldiers who fought and died in the brutal trench warfare that occurred here.

Ypres became entangled in global warfare on October 7, 1914, when German forces arrived in the town and occupied it. Although the town remained mostly intact, the surrounding fields soon became what was known as Ypres Salient, a deadly point for trench warfare between the Allied and German armies. For years, the trenches rarely moved in either direction, despite many skirmishes. The unprecedented use of chlorine and mustard gases, as well as the outbreak of the 1918 Spanish Flu, made fighting here incredibly deadly. The region surrounding Ypres is now full of cemeteries and memorials, and it's thought that more than 500,000 soldiers and civilians perished in this region. Many farmers here still often find remnants of World War I, like bullets and shrapnel, while cultivating the now peaceful fields, once the scene of so much bloodshed.

Today, Ypres is a quiet town, a good stopoff if passing through the western region of Belgium for its somber history as well as its present. Many claim the best beer in the world can be found in the nearby town of Westvleteren, and the tall belfry has become infamous for its role in Ypres's quirky triennial Cat Festival.

SIGHTS

Ypres is quite small, and it's feasible to see most of the city itself on foot. However, if you wish to visit the battlefields beyond Ypres, a car rental offers more flexibility than the limited bus network that runs sporadically on the weekends to the surrounding towns.

★ In Flanders Fields Museum

Grote Markt 34; tel. 057 23 92 20; www.inflandersfields.be; 10am-6pm daily Apr.-Nov., 10am-5pm Tues.-Sun. Nov.-Mar.; adults €10, youth €6, children 7-18 €5, children under 7 free, family ticket €22, Belfry €2 extra

In Flanders Fields is a museum dedicated to the Great War, named after poem written by Canadian Lieutenant Colonel John McCrae in 1915, after the funeral of a friend in the Second Battle of Ypres. The museum's permanent exhibition focuses on telling the story of World War I and its soldiers. When you enter, you're given a bracelet with a poppy shape on it that unlocks personalized experiences related to your country of origin (available for most Western countries involved in World War I), language preference, and age throughout the museum. Red poppies have become a symbol of World War I as they grow naturally in Western Europe, and following the battles of 1914, red poppies bloomed on the barren fields turned battlefields. Mentioned in John McCrae's poem *In Flanders Field*, the red poppy has endured as a powerful symbol of the losses on both sides. The museum explains how the war started and describes major battles in a way that humanizes the participants.

The In Flanders Museum takes up the second floor of the Ypres Cloth Hall, or Lakenhalle, a reconstruction of an impressive medieval building dating back to 1304 that spans most of the impressive Grote Markt square. Wool and linen were once stored here, but the building has had many uses over the decades, and today also houses the **Yper Museum** (www.ypermuseum.be; same hours as In Flanders Fields; combination ticket with In Flanders Fields adults €13, youth €8, children 7-18 €6, children under 7 free, family ticket €30), a newer, kid-friendly museum that focuses on the non-war history of Ypres, including its Cat Festival.

When entering the museum, pay in advance if you intend to climb the **Belfry,** which provides impressive views after 231 steps to the top. At 70 meters (230 feet) high, the Belfry is one of the highest in Belgium.

Menin Gate (Menenpoort)

Menenstraat; www.toerismeieper.be/menentor; open 24/7; free

Menin Gate was once a city gate on the eastern side of Ypres, and many Allied soldiers marched through this gate before seeing their last battle during World War I. The triumphal white arch, adored with limestone lions (replicas of the originals, restored by the Australian government), was built as a memorial in 1921. It includes the names of 54,896 missing soldiers from the beginning of World War I until August 15, 1917. (The rest of the names, from August 16 until the end of the war, can be found at Tyne Cot Cemetery.)

Since 1928, missing British soldiers have been commemorated at Menenpoort in a nightly ceremony at 8pm called **The Last Post** (www.toerismeieper.be/lastpost), a traditional bugle call played by the British Army to mark the end of the day, now intended as a final goodbye for the missing soldiers. Attendees are expected to remain under the interior of the gate and quiet during the ceremony; applause is discouraged. If you wish to lay down a wreath, contact the nonprofit that continues this moving tradition ahead of time (www.lastpost.be/en/ceremonies/participation), and if you want a place near the front, it's best to arrive early.

TOP EXPERIENCE

World War I Cemeteries

There are dozens of cemeteries throughout the Ypres region; you can find a full list online (www.greatwar.co.uk/places/ypres-salient-monuments.htm). The easiest way to reach these cemeteries is with a rental car.

MEMORIAL MUSEUM PASSCHENDAELE 1917

Berten Pilstraat 5a, Zonnebeke; tel. 051 77 04 41; www.passchendaele.be; 9am-6pm daily, closed Dec. 16-Feb. 1; adults €10.50, students €6, youth 7-18 €5, children under 7 free

Memorial Museum Passchendaele is a war

museum housed in a beautiful historic chateau, Kasteel Zonnebeke; its large, peaceful grounds contrast with the history contained in the museum. Three stories of exhibitions include a re-creation of a dugout to allow visitors to experience the trenches. A free audio guide is included with admission, although you'll need to provide your own headphones. The museum is located in the small town of Zonnebeke, about a 10-minute (9-kilometer/6-mile) drive east of Ypres on the N37/N332.

TYNE COT CEMETERY

Vijfwegestraat, Zonnebeke; visitors center 10am-8pm daily Feb.-Nov.; free

Tyne Cot is the largest Commonwealth war cemetery in the world, with more than 11,954 soldiers buried here. It's a humbling place, with its endless rows of gravestones, mostly without names—instead, they're inscribed with "Known to God" and their division and country of origin.

Tyne Cot itself was a barn captured by Commonwealth Australian forces during the Battle of Passchendaele (July 31-November 10, 1971), which reminded British soldiers of a cottage in Tyneside in the UK. You can still see some of the concrete pill boxes, slightly underground concrete guard posts, which belonged to German soldiers. The Cross of Sacrifice in the center of the cemetery was built on top of one of the preserved pill boxes and provides a bird's-eye view, the German viewpoint during the battle.

There's a small **visitors center,** where you can hear the names of the fallen and learn more about the events that took place here. It's generally a very somber place. **Bus 94** toward Passendale Tyne Cot (www.delijn.be; tickets €1.80 via the app, €2.50 on the bus) that goes once an hour from Ieper Bascule, about 400 meters (1,300 feet) east of the Menin Gate, or it's a 15-minute (12-kilometer/7-mile) drive from Ypres on the N37/N332, 5 minutes or so past Memorial Museum Passchendaele in Zonnebeke.

LANGEMARK GERMAN WAR CEMETERY

Klerkenstraat 64, Poelkapelle; open 24/7; free

This fairly modest cemetery lined by oak trees is the first location where gas was used in World War I, and the location of the Second Battle of Ypres. Nearly 25,000 German servicemen are buried in a mass grave next to the entrance, along with more buried in flat graves nearby. It's one of four German

Tyne Cot Cemetery

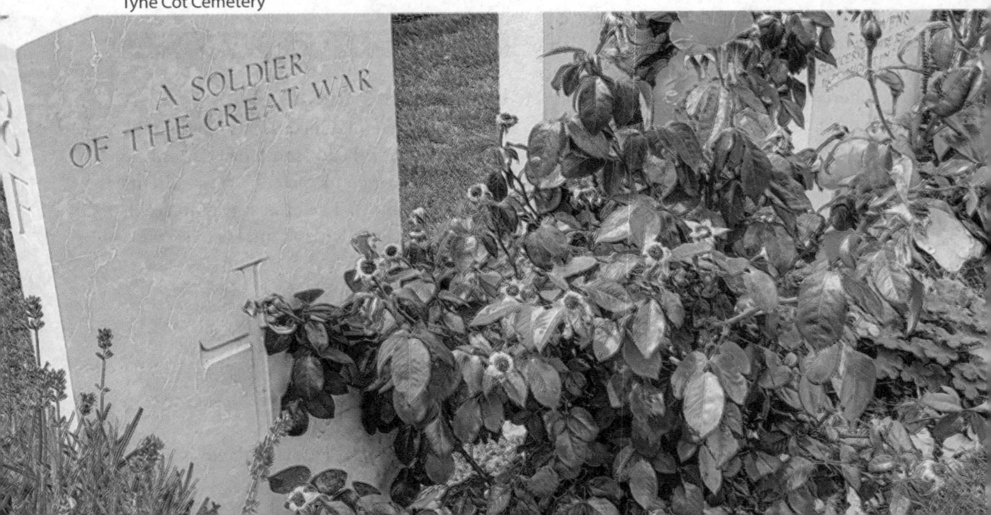

World War I cemeteries in the Ypres region. It's a 15-minute (12-kilometer/7-miles) drive from Ypres on Pilkemseweg, in the town of Poelkapelle.

ENTERTAINMENT AND EVENTS

CAT PARADE (Kattenstoet)

Cloth Hall; www.kattenstoet.be; second Sun. in May every three years

Although the Cat Parade sounds like a celebration of our feline friends, this triennial festival on the second Sunday of May wasn't always so feline-friendly. In the Middle Ages, people throughout Europe, including Ypres, believed that cats were linked to the devil and witchcraft, but Ypres's wool warehouses required many cats to police the rat and mouse population, and the number of feral cats exploded. As a population control measure, every so often on a day called "Cat Wednesday," cats were hurled out of the Cloth Hall **Belfry.** Luckily, this tradition ceased in the 1817, when one of the cats landed on its feet.

No live cats are harmed in the modern-day equivalent—today, cats are only celebrated, with music played on the church carillon, a cat-themed parade, and medieval costumes. It's one of Belgium's more bizarre traditions, but certainly a fun one for everyone (except for the stuffed animals thrown out of the Belfry in lieu of real cats). The next parade is set to take place in 2024.

FOOD

MARKTCAFÉ LES HALLES

Grote Markt 35; tel. 057 36 55 63; www.marktcafe-leshalles.be; 9am-midnight Mon.-Fri. and Sun., 8am-midnight Sat.; €18

It can be tough finding a meal in Belgium in the middle of the afternoon, but Marktcafé Les Halles serves food all day and most of the night. The café has an atmospheric location across from the Cloth Hall and a classic menu with Spanish flair. You can find something for everyone, including vegans, between their tapas, Belgian classics (like croquettes), and Italian-inspired pasta dishes. The café's brick-lined interior is quite spacious, and the beer menu is extensive enough to impress locals as well as visitors.

'T APPEL

Grote Markt 25; tel. 057 36 97 36; www.tappel.online; 11am-9am Mon-Sun; sandwiches €4, mains €13

This is a popular lunch spot with a small terrace where you can enjoy a reasonable lunch or dinner without breaking the bank. The cozy café with friendly service serves soups, sandwiches, waffles, pastas, and pizzas. The café enjoys impressive views of the Cloth Hall from across the Grote Markt square. It's a good place to grab takeout in good weather if you're keen on a picnic.

ACCOMMODATIONS

Ypres's limited accommodations will get booked up ahead of major events World War I memorial events. Staying overnight in Ypres may be advantageous if you arrive by train, due to the lengthy journey from other Belgian cities. Although there are other accommodation options (such as B&Bs) on the outskirts of Ypres in smaller towns closer to the World War I cemeteries, many of these accommodations may be difficult to access by public transportation. Book ahead if you intend to stay here!

NOVOTEL IEPER CENTRUM FLANDERS FIELDS HOTEL

Sint-Jacobsstraat 15; tel. 57 42 96 00; https://all.accor.com/hotel/3172/index.en.shtml; €100

Although a Novotel is not the most exciting option, this hotel's key location just 5 minutes from the In Flanders Fields Museum makes it a convenient hotel for a quick stay. Rooms are often decorated with red-accented pieces, including photos of the region's red poppies. The hotel features a 24-hour reception, modern rooms with no frills, a restaurant/bar, and online check-in.

Side Trip to Sint-Sixtus Brewery

If you're a beer lover traveling in Western Belgium, you have to make the pilgrimage to Sint-Sixtus (Abbey Brouwerij de Sint-Sixtusabdij van Westvleteren, Donkerstraat 12; tel. 057 40 03 77; www.trappistwestvleteren.be) in Westvleteren, a 20-minute drive northwest of Ypres. Beer enthusiasts will likely recognize their Quadruple Trappist Beer, known as the 12 (10 percent ABV) by aficionados, but this is just one of their offerings.

beer and snacks Sint-Sixtus

THE HISTORY

The abbey itself dates back to 1831, when a monk who intended to become a hermit settled in the forest not far from Ypres. In spite of his desire for solitude, he attracted a following. His community has grown so much that, to this day, the beer here is brewed entirely by monks, who only produce enough to fund their operations. Beer brewing began as a common practice in the Middle Ages, often as a means of fundraising, but also, it's said, as a means of extending a fast without eating, as drinking beer was not considered breaking your fast.

During World War I, while most abbeys were forced to give up their copper pans for use in the wartime effort, Sint-Sixtus was able to retain its original copper brewing equipment, as it served as an outpost for allied soldiers.

VISITING THE ABBEY

All the beer is made behind closed doors, but you at their visitors center, the **Claustrum** (2pm-5pm Sat.-Wed.; www.sintsixtus.be), you can learn more about the brewing process. The grounds are largely off limits to visitors, except for the modern chapel and an artificial cave used as another sanctuary for prayer. The main attraction for most visitors, of course, is enjoying a rare glass of the delicious beer, whether the Blonde (known as the 6) or the rich Quadruple 12, alongside a sandwich made with abbey-made bread and cheese or pate at the cafeteria, **In De Vrede** (10am-8:30pm Mon.-Thurs., 10am-9pm Sat.-Sun.; www.indevrede.be). Because the monks brew such limited quantities, what's available that day will be a matter of chance, but it's sure to be delicious. There's also a **gift shop** where you can purchase beers, mugs, shirts, and glasses.

GETTING THERE

This remote abbey around 16 kilometers (10 miles) northwest of Ypres is not the easiest place to get to, but it's certainly a scenic ride, through fields that were once the center of battle during World War I. From Ypres, it's a leisurely 20-minute drive down narrow country roads (it can take longer if you get struck behind a tractor), mostly on the N38, R33, and N321. Street parking near the abbey is generally free, although fairly limited. Due to the abbey's remoteness, you might choose to take away the beers to enjoy in your hotel, or have a single beer before a long lunch, so as not to drink and drive.

MAIN STREET HOTEL

Rijselstraat 136; tel. 57 46 96 33; https://mainstreet-hotel.be; €195

Main Street Hotel is a upscale boutique hotel off a cobblestone street in the heart of Ypres within an atmospheric red brick building from the 1930s. It's located in the city center and has six uniquely decorated rooms. All rooms feature air-conditioning, a filled minibar (free), a superior mattress, a Nespresso machine, a laptop safe, and a luxurious bathtub. The hotel's main hall features an honesty bar where you can pay based on what you drink, which is filled with local beers, board games, puzzles, knitting supplies, and even sweets. An organic and local breakfast is included with every stay.

GETTING THERE

Most people who come to Ypres are usually heading here from Bruges by car. Bruges is about 1 hour (70 kilometers/43 miles) from Ypres, and given that the train connection is not particularly good, a car makes a trip within this region considerably easier.

Train

IEPER TRAIN STATION

www.belgiantrain.be

The closest major Belgian city to Ypres is **Ghent,** with a direct train connection about once an hour in the direction of Poperinge. The train journey takes 1 hour 7 minutes and costs €11.60 each way for adults. From **Brussels,** the journey takes a bit longer as it requires a transfer in Ghent. A ticket costs €17.70 each way for adults and will take almost 2 hours. From **Bruges,** the train journey takes a little under 2 hours one-way with a transfer in Ghent or Kortrijk. An adult ticket costs €12.30. The Ieper Train Station is located about 1 kilometer (0.6 miles; 10-minute walk) west from the In Flanders Fields Museum.

Car

From **Brussels,** the drive takes approximately 1.5 hours (121 kilometers) via the E17 and E40. From **Bruges,** the drive is about 50 minutes (71 kilometers) southeast on the E403. From **Ghent,** it's an hour drive (79 kilometers) via E17.

If you drive to Ypres, 55 parking spots are available behind the train station at the **Mennepoort parking lot** (Hoornwerk 2; www.ieper.be/gratis-parkeren; €1 per hour). It's a 450-meter (1,500-foot) walk west along Menenstraat to the city center.

Mons

Mons (known as Bergen in Dutch) provides insight into many layers of Belgian history, from the nearby SILEX's Neolithic salt mines, to its perfectly preserved medieval town center, its industrial past, and even its connection to Vincent Van Gogh. Once a major hub for coal and other industries, today the town has a sleepy, friendly feel, with locals who are always excited to show visitors around. One unique view into Belgian culture can be found at the quirky annual Doudou festival, a re-creation of a medieval procession meant to save Mons residents from the plague. Outside the town proper, the land is peppered with small towns with links to Van Gogh as well as secrets underneath. One of the largest Neolithic mines ever discovered can be explored nearby. Mons is a beautiful city in Wallonia, the southern region of Belgium, to explore, even if just for a day.

Mons is a small city that is very walkable, but the larger region of the Borinage spans a larger footprint that is hard to navigate without a car. Luckily, the friendly Mons Tourist Information office is happy to help with arranging transportation by bike or bus to SILEX's or Le Grand Hornu.

SIGHTS

Grand Place

tel. 065 33 55 80; www.visitmons.be; open 24/7; free

Mons's Grand Place is a stunning sight, with its 15th-century town hall and many well-preserved medieval buildings. In front of the town hall, you'll see a statue of a monkey; rubbing its head is supposed to be good luck. It's the main location for events such as the Doudou Festival, and you'll find both tourists and locals dining at cafés overlooking this extremely grand square.

Belfry of Mons

Parc du Château; tel. 065 33 55 80; www.visitmons.be; 10am-6pm Tues.-Sun.; adults €9, students and seniors €6, children 6-12 €2, children under 6 free

The Belfry of Mons is a beautiful example of Belgian and French architecture, the only baroque belfry in Belgium. The 87-meter-tall (285-foot-tall) tower, constructed in 1669, sits on top of a hill overlooking Mons. Climbing the 360 steps to the top, near the Belfry's onion-shaped domes, gives great views. The 49-bell carillon rings every 15 minutes.

St. Waltrude's Collegiate Church

(Collégiale Sainte-Waudru de Mons)

Place du Chapitre; tel. 065 84 46 94; www.waudru.be; 9am-6pm daily; free

This impressive Catholic church a short walk from the center of Mons holds the shrine of Saint Waltrude, a female saint from medieval times. She is known for creating a convent after separating from her husband, which became the basis of the city of Mons. The women who joined her convent were referred to as the canonesses, generally noblewomen, who, unlike other nuns, were not forced to renounce their wealth. This gave the convent significant financial influence over the growing city, so much so that the canonesses were the functional heads of industry and conferred with the town council about affairs.

During the Black Plague, the canonesses famously arranged for a procession to circle Mons with the Shrine of Saint Waltrude, which is have said to have protected the town, and is the basis for today's Doudou Festival. The church itself is splendid, with original 16th-century stained glass windows, 15th-century statues of Saint Michael, and elaborate carvings by a local artist. Most importantly, you can admire the Golden Carriage, used to carry the Shrine of Saint Waltrude, while it's not in use for the festival. Guided **tours** of the church are available upon request at the Mons

Grand Place

Tourism office. The **treasury room** is open in the afternoons March-November.

Musée du Doudou

Grand Place; tel. 065 40 53 18; www.museedudoudou.mons.be; 10am-6pm Tues.-Sat.; €9

The Doudou is one of Belgium's most well-known regional festivals, recognized by UNESCO as a Masterpiece of the Oral and Intangible Heritage of Humanity. If you're fortunate enough to visit Mons on Trinity Sunday, you'll be able to experience the festival yourself, but for the rest of us, this museum beautifully tells the story of the Doudou's medieval origins and the famous uphill push of Saint Waltrude's Shrine.

Around Mons

SILEX'S (NEOLITHIC FLINT MINES AT SPIENNES)

Rue du Point du Jour; tel. 065 33 55 80; http://en.silexs.mons.be; 10am-4pm Tues.-Sun.; adults €6, children 10 and up €2 without a guided tour

During the Bronze Age (approximately 4,300-2,200 BC), this part of what is now Belgium was a major producer of flint, an important material in Neolithic times. The mines here were first discovered in 1843 during railway construction, and excavations have been taking place ever since. To date, this mine is the largest and earliest Neolithic flint mine to survive in northwest Europe, with an estimated 250 acres of mining pits. They show a high level of sophistication in mining techniques; some of the pits are as deep as 15 meters (49 feet).

SILEX's is not accessible to people with physical limitations, as you must descend a 10-meter (33-foot) vertical ladder (with a harness and helmet) to access the mine. The mine is a constant 12°C (54°F), so regardless of the weather outside, it's best to dress appropriately with sneakers and pants. Children under 10 are not allowed on the tour, and it's not recommended for those with a fear of heights. They museum is a good alternative for those less inclined to go underground, highlighting the findings from below. The mines are about 6 kilometers (4 miles) by car outside Mons, or a 20-minute cycle. **Bus 134** (www.letec.be/#; 15 minutes; €3.50) also travels from Mons Station to SILEX's about once an hour.

LE GRAND HORNU

Rue Sainte-Louise 82 Boussu; tel. 065 65 21 21; www.grand-hornu.eu; 10am-6pm daily; adults €8, children €2

Located slightly outside Mons in the city of Hornu, a former coal-mining town, this site has been listed by UNESCO for its unique history as one of the earliest communities created by a company for its employees. In 1810, Honru was a worker town with more than 450 homes, each with hot water and a garden (luxuries at the time). The complex's impressive neoclassical exterior has been largely preserved, converted into a cultural center and museum of modern art. (Check the website for the latest exhibitions.) The Grand Hornu is about 13 kilometers (8 miles) outside Mons, a 20-minute drive. You can take **Bus 7** (Direction: Quiévrain; www.letec.be; 25 minutes; €3.50), which travels approximately once an hour from the Mons Train Station (Gare).

ENTERTAINMENT AND EVENTS

DOUDOU

www.doudou.mons.be; late May/early June (Trinity Sunday)

Although Belgium has a number of interesting festivals, the Doudou is one of the most notable festivals in the whole country. The festival begins at the Collegiate Church where the Shrine of Saint Waltrude is placed onto a golden carriage, specifically used for the festival. The organizers dress up in the medieval costumes of the canonesses, a group of noble women associated with Saint Waltrude, and other medieval costumes. During the festival, the Shrine of Saint Waltrude is carried around Mons in the golden carriage, and a re-enactment of Saint George and the dragon takes place. The festival lasts for eight days, culminating in returning the shrine back to St. Waldrude's Collegiate Chruch without

Van Gogh in Belgium

Maison Van Gogh

Although Van Gogh is most linked to the Netherlands, he spent time in what is now Belgium, in the Mons region as well as Brussels. After working in Paris, he attempted to enter theology school in Belgium and the Netherlands, which is how he ended up reading about the industrial are surrounding Mons, best known for being a working-class, coal mining region. It's thought that his painting *The Potato Eaters* is inspired by his time here.

From a Dutch aristocratic family himself, during his time here Van Gogh tried to reject his family's wealth. He moved to Petit-Wasmes, a small town outside Mons at the heart of Belgium's coal industry, to work as a Protestant missionary, a role that he struggled with. Instead, he was so struck

dropping it. After the shrine is returned, thousands of locals and tourists head to Mons to watch the re-enactment of the battle of Saint George and the dragon, which is always slayed. (For those with kids, there is also a children's version.) Visitors can watch the proceedings and perhaps help with ensuring that the shrine makes it back to its annual home without a hitch, despite the uphill path.

FOOD

CHEZ TONTON

Rue de la Clef 36; tel. 0485 68 20 66; www.cheztonton.co.uk; noon-2:30pm Tues.-Sat; €3

Chez Tonton is one of the best spots in Mons to get a fresh cone of *frites* (all fries freshly made on-site!) to enjoy outside in good weather. They also offer reasonable baguette sandwiches, burgers, and other fried favorites. It's a very casual place, beloved by Mons locals as the local *fritterie*.

WAFFLES & GO

Rue d'Havré 11; www.facebook.com/waffles.and.go.mons; 11:30am-10pm Mon.-Sat., noon-10pm Sun.; €5

Waffles & Go keeps things simple. They focus on creating delicious sweet waffles, including waffles on sticks, bubble waffles, and other sweets. There's nothing like having a warm waffle fresh off the grill! After all, you are in Belgium.

by the abject poverty and humbleness of the workers who welcomed him into their homes that he began learning to draw to capture the souls of the workers and the larger environment of the Borinage, the first steps toward becoming one of the world's most famous painters.

Visit some of the sites below to follow in Van Gogh's Belgian footsteps, integral to his time as an artist. Purchase a **Van Gogh Pass** (www.visitmons.be; €8) at the Mons Tourism Board office in Grand Place, which includes a bike rental along with entry to the Van Gogh sites in the region. It's possible to visit all of them within 3-4 hours by bike; the farthest point is 13 kilometers (8 miles; 42 minutes via bike) from Mons.

MAISON VAN GOGH

Rue Wilson 221, Colfontaine; tel. 065 88 74 88; https://cccolfontaine.com; 10am-4pm Sat.-Sun.

When Van Gogh first arrived in the area, he moved into this red house, now a small museum dedicated to his brief time in Belgium. It's a 20-minute (13-kilometer/8-mile) drive from Ypres via the N544.

VAN GOGH HOUSE

Rue du Pavillon 3, tel. 065 35 56 11; www.maisonvangogh.mons.be; 10am-4pm Tues.-Sun.

A year after his arrival in the area, Van Gogh lost his missionary position, and for a short time he resided with a local family, the Decrucqs. This is when the artist first began sketching. Now the Van Gogh House, it's a museum dedicated to Van Gogh's early work and life in the area.

CHARBONNAGE DE MARCASSE

Sentier de Saint-Ghislain 7, Colfontaine; tel. 0474 17 64 64; www.visitmons.be; open by appointment

During his time in the Mons area, it's said that Van Gogh descended into the local mines to understand the work. The one that he visited, the Charbonnage de Marcasse, is today a largely abandoned mining complex that has been overtaken by local historians and artists with plans to create a museum and retreats in its place. Not far from Van Gogh's first house in the region, it's a 20-minute (13-kilometer/8-mile) drive from Ypres on the N544.

MA BREIZH

Rue de la Clef 50; tel. 0499 13 89 44; 6pm-8pm Thurs.-Sat. (hours may expand post COVID-19); €8-13

For a delicious crepe, head to Ma Breizh, which is a popular Breton-style creperie that serves up delicious French-style crepes. Mons is just a border crossing away from France, and the savory crepes here make for a quick, inexpensive meal. The crepe with goat cheese and honey is particularly delicious!

CITIZEN FOX

Rue de la Coupe 7; tel. 065 33 81 01; www.facebook.com/CitizenFoxMons; noon-1am daily; €14

Citizen Fox takes direct inspiration from British-style pubs, even with an occasional Sunday roast. They serve creative burgers as well as salads with international flair, and the flexible hours make it a great spot for a late lunch or dinner with a pint of Belgian beer.

ACCOMMODATIONS

MARTIN'S DREAM HOTEL

Rue de la Grande Triperie 17; www.martinshotels.com/fr/hotel/martins-dream-hotel; €100

Housed in a former neo-Gothic chapel, Martin's Dream Hotel is a four-star hotel with a central location just two blocks from the heart of Mons, making it an ideal location for travelers. Amenities include a spa with hammam, fitness room, smartTV, and some rooms have views of the Belfry via the original stained-glass windows from the church.

GETTING THERE

Mons is a bit remote, close to the French border. Traveling by train is best only if you intend to stay strictly within the city center. To visit more of the surrounding region, a car is helpful given the limited bus schedules, especially on weekends.

Train

MONS/BERGEN STATION

Place Léopold, www.belgiantrain.be

From **Brussels,** there is a direct train to Mons that takes 55 minutes and costs €9.60 one-way. The train runs approximately every 30 minutes. From **Bruges,** you would need to transfer at Brussels in order to reach Mons with a total one-way journey of 2 hours at a cost of €17. The train station is located 850 meters (0.5 mi/10 minutes on foot) northwest of the city center.

Car

The 71-kilometer (44-mile) drive from **Brussels** via the **E19** takes about 1 hour without traffic. Mons is about 1 hour southeast of **Ypres,** 109 kilometers (68 miles) by car using the **E42** expressway.

Parking is available at a few locations close to the train station. Parking garages within the city center (Rue de la Halle 5) typically costs €1.20 per hour, but there is free parking available about 10 minutes on foot from the city center (Avenue du Pont Rouge 28). Street parking is limited. Narrow, hilly streets can make driving a bit tricky, so it's best to park outside the city center at a designated lot and then walk.

Dinant

Breathtakingly wedged into a river valley, Dinant is a tourist-friendly Wallonian town with great rock climbing, delicious beer, and fascinating history. Residents here extend typical Belgian hospitality to visitors, whether you're passing through the epic Bayard Rock (Rocher Bayard), a road wedged between a 35-meter (115-foot) ridge and a sharp cliff, or looking up at the dramatic Dinant Citadel, also built upon an impressive cliff. There's more than enough to do in this land of castles, Trappist beer, and outdoor sports. Dinant is also famous for being the birthplace of Antoine-Joseph "Adolphe" Sax, the creator of the saxophone. It's a great place to get away from the hustle and bustle of city tourism for a day or two.

Dinant spans a fairly large stretch of the Meuse River (about 4 kilometers/2 miles), so it's easy to get around by walking, but leaving the city center for farther destinations will take some time without a car. There is a narrow two-lane road for cars on both sides of river.

SIGHTS

Dinant Citadel

Place Reine Astrid 3; tel. 082 22 36 70; www.citadellededinant.be; 10am-6pm daily Apr.-Sept., 10am-5:30pm daily Oct.-Nov. 11, 10am-4:30pm Sat.-Thurs. Nov. 12-Mar., 10am-4:30pm Sat.-Sun. Jan.; adults €10, children €8

Dinant's showstopping attraction is certainly its Citadel, an impressive fortress looming over the city. Since 1051, a fortress has existed on this spot, specifically chosen for its proximity to the Meuse River, which provided a military advantage. However, the previous citadel (along with the city of Dinant) was destroyed during the Wars of Liège of 1466, a series of rebellions against the Burgundian rulers of the time. The Citadel has been rebuilt many times in its history as a means of preventing the other party from having the Citadel as a defensive point. The current citadel dates back to 1821 and was used as a barracks for Dutch soldiers. The year 1914 is dark spot in the Citadel's history, when the Citadel was taken by German troops and most of the city was burned to the ground.

A cable car, free with your ticket, travels to the top of the Citadel, but for the most part it isn't handicap-accessible. (You can also opt to climb the 408 16th-century stairs up from the city if you wish.) The citadel includes an impressive weapons museum as well as a re-enactment of World War I trench warfare. Perhaps most notably, the Citadel boasts impressive views over the valley and city. There's a **café** and **gift shop,** and also has guided **tours,** though the signage in the exhibitions is very informative on its own.

Grotte La Merveilleuse

Rue de Philippeville 142; tel. 082 22 22 10; www.valleedelameuse-tourisme.be; 11am-4pm Tues.-Sun. Apr.-Sept., noon-4pm Mon.-Fri., 11am-4pm Sat.-Sun. May-Aug.; 11am-3pm Sat.-Sun. Jan.-Mar.; adults €10, seniors €9 children €6,

One of Belgium's most impressive caves, Grotte La Merveilleuse and its underground river were discovered in 1904 by a railway worker. Of the more than 850 meters (2,800 feet) of caves that have been mapped so far, 650 meters (2,100 feet) are accessible, including the impressive "Great Room," a favorite of bats in the winter. With awesome stalactites and dramatically lit walkways, it's not hard not to understand why they call the cave "marvelous." The cave is not wheelchair accessible due to stairs.

Around Dinant

CASTLE DE FREŸR

Freyr 12 Le Nôtre; tel. 082 22 22 00; www.freyr.be; 11am-5pm daily July-Aug., 11am-5pm Sat.-Sun. Apr.-June and Sept.-Nov.; adults €8.50, seniors and students €7, children free

This beautiful Renaissance castle has been owned by the same aristocratic family for centuries, since it was given to them as a fief during feudal times. The castle you see today largely dates back to the early 17th century with an 18th-century interior, all beautifully maintained. Inside, you'll spot ceilings covered in Louis XV frescos, original furniture, and gifts from famous royals. The castle is perhaps best known for its gardens, designed in 1760. The property includes hedge mazes, views of the Meuse River, a functional Orangery with the oldest orange trees in Europe, and walled terraces.

The castle and its grounds make for a magnificent day out, a 7-minute (6-kilometer/4-mile) drive south of Dinant on the N96. It is possible to get there via **sightseeing cruise**

view of Dinant from its Citadel

Maredsous Abbey

Belgium's beer culture is renowned throughout the world, and the best of the best are Trappist beers, produced by Trappist monks living in monasteries that are an impressive testament to the importance of religion in Belgian culture. You'll find abbeys throughout Belgium, and one of the best-known in Wallonia, the southern part of Belgium, is Maredsous Abbey (Rue de Maredsous 11 Denée; https://tourisme-maredsous.be; 11am-6pm Mon.-Fri., 11am-7pm Sat.-Sun.), about 23 kilometers (14 miles) west of Dinant and 97 kilometers (60 miles) south of Brussels.

Maredsous Abbey beer and cheese

TASTING TRAPPIST BEER

The abbey is fairly new by Belgian standards, founded in 1872 by a monk. Its church, which is free to visit, is neo-Gothic and spacious, but the main attraction, of course, is the beer (as well as the cheese that is also produced by the monks on-site). Their Extra beer (4.9 percent ABV), straight from the tap, is why many make the trip, as it's not exported. At the abbey's **Saint-Joseph Visitor Center,** there's a terrace, shop, playground, and cafeteria, where you'll be able to order the house-made cheese. Take a **tour** of the grounds (2pm and 4pm Sat., Sun., and holidays; adults €7; children under 12 free), which includes a beer as well as a visit to the cheese museum (only included on the tour). Their **shop** is an eclectic place to pick up gifts including ceramic mugs made within the abbey.

GETTING THERE

From Dinant, the drive to Maredsous is fairly quick, at 24 minutes via N92 and N971, though the location makes it a bit less than ideal for indulging. It is possible to visit the abbey via public transit; **Bus 35** runs once every two hours (www.letec.be; 43 minutes; €3.50 one-way). The bus departs from the train station in Dinant. Visitors to the abbey will want to get off at Maredsous (Abbaye).

(Dinant Evasions; www.dinant-evasion.be/en/castle-of-freyr.html?IDC=172; €15/person). The cruise runs weekends and holidays at 2:30pm and daily in peak season (June-Sept.) from Avenue Winston Churchill, which sits south of the **Charles de Gaulle Bridge.** It's hard to miss the idling sightseeing ships.

ANNEVOIE CASTLE

Rue des jardins 37; tel. 082 67 97 97; www.annevoie.be; by appointment only; adults €9.50, students €5.50, children €4.50

North of Dinant on the Meuse River, Annevoie Castle is one of the most unmissable places in the region for its impressive gardens, oft called the grandest in Europe. The castle once belonged to the de Montpellier family, who gained their wealth via the engineering and casting trades. Development of the gardens began in 1758, a grand undertaking inspired by the family's European travels, with areas inspired by French, Italian, and English gardening traditions. There are waterfalls, a grotto, and a romantic "Drive of Desires" with a lush green tunnel. The grounds are beautiful and quiet, with a small **café** in the Orangery that provides snacks. The castle is not open to the public, but the grounds are extremely worthwhile.

Annevoie Castle is 13 kilometers (8 miles) north of Dinant on the N92, a 15-minute drive.

Birthplace of the Saxophone

The city pays homage to its famous son, Adolphe Sax (who, in addition to inventing the saxophone, invented the saxtuba, saxhorn, and saxotromba), with its impressive **Charles de Gaulle Bridge** (Pont Charles de Gaulle), which crosses the Meuse River. It's is lined on both sides with 28 saxophones, painted to represent different countries. Even if you're not a jazz lover, the bridge makes a great viewpoint for the Citadel.

You'll find other saxophones throughout Dinant, and true music lovers may be interested in the small museum dedicated to his life and work, **Maison Adolphe Sax** (Rue Sax 37; http://sax.dinant.be; 9am-7pm daily; free). There's a small bench with a statue of Sax in front.

★ SPORTS AND RECREATION

The lush rolling hills and forests around Dinant are a paradise for European travelers, who flock here for biking, climbing, hiking, kayaking, and mountain climbing. It's a great break from city-hopping in the Benelux region. You might need a car to reach trailheads here, or opt for an outdoor adventure outfitter to guide you and help with transportation. Independent climbers must be certified to climb in Belgium, but experienced guides can help you here, too. Dinant offers most of these activities, but many nearby towns in the Ardennes offer easy-to-follow biking and hiking trails.

Hiking

PARC DE FURFOOZ HIKE

Hiking Distance: *4 kilometers (2.5 miles)*

Hiking Time: *2 hours round-trip*

Trailhead: *Rue du Camp Romain 79*

Information and Maps: *www.parcdefurfooz.be*

Parc de Furfooz is a well-known trail that begins close to a reconstructed Roman bathhouse and leads hikers through caves that were inhabited in prehistoric times. This family-friendly walk is easy enough for beginners, and there are more difficult trails throughout the nearby forest, caves, meadows, and riverbanks. The trailhead is about 10 kilometers (6 miles) outside the city of Dinant, a 15-minute drive, and is also accessible by **Buses 20** and **67/1** (www.letec.be; €2.50 one-way), a 36-minute trip.

Cycling

MEUSE CYCLING PATH

Cycling Distance: *28 kilometers (17 miles) one-way*

Cycling Time: *2-3 hours one-way*

Trailhead: *Pont Charles de Gaulle in Dinant*

Information and Services: *www.routeyou.com/en-be/route/view/5779092/recreational-cycle-route/from-dinant-to-namur*

Ambitious bikers not afraid of some uphill peddling will enjoy the relatively difficult, although still leisurely, bike ride from Dinant to Namur. Namur is the capital of Wallonia, best known for its beautiful Citadel overlooking the Meuse River, located about 28 kilometers (17 miles) north of Dinant. Cyclists can opt to bring their bike on the train for the journey between Namur and Dinant (€4 supplement for bikes) if they don't want to cycle back. Trains depart about once every half hour and the train ride takes 30 minutes (€4.90 one-way). Though the maximum grade is 9.55 percent, most of the route is a fairly leisurely cruise along the Meuse River. You'll begin in Dinant close to the Citadel, cycling past the picturesque medieval villages of Bouvignes and passing the gardens of Annevoie Castle about halfway (12 kilometers/7 miles; 1.5 hours one-way) to Namur.

Rock-Climbing

DINANT ADVENTURE

Rue de la Carrière 1; www.dinant-evasion.be; adults €25-29

Adventurous travelers who enjoy a taste of adrenaline should try Dinant Adventure's

3-hour climbing course, which includes rope bridges more than 12 meters (39 feet) off the ground, a via ferrata (in which the climber is attached to a steel cable), and a zip line at the end, with a view of river. For those less keen on heights, there are variety of other packages, including one for kids, and an obstacle course that includes an underground tunnel and the longest rope bridge in Belgium.

Kayaking

KAYAKING RENTAL DINANT

Place Baudouin 1er 2, 5500 Anseremme; www.dinant-evasion.be; 8:30am-6pm daily; €25-28 including transport

Dinant Evasion offers a variety of kayaking trips, including a 2.5-hour kayaking trip past castles, forest, and beaches. They're based in Dinant, but their kayaking trips begin in Anseremme, a nearby village 3 kilometers (1.9 miles; 40-minute walk) down the river from the town center, also accessible by train or bus (transportation to the departure point costs extra).

FOOD

MICHEL DEFOSSEZ

Rue Grand 97; tel. 082 67 98 59; 7am-6pm daily; €5

For a casual lunch, Michel Defossez is a small local bakery that serves up delicious breads and pastries as well as quiche, sandwiches, and salads for a reasonable price. If the weather is good, this is a great place to pick up lunch to enjoy along the riverfront without breaking the budget.

LE CAFÉ ARDENNAIS

Avenue Franchet d'Esperey 4; tel. 082 22 33 50; www.lecafeardennais.be; 10am-11pm Sun.-Thurs., 10am-midnight Fri.-Sat.; €14

For Belgian as well as Italian favorites, opt for Le Café Ardennais, which uses regional ingredients to create delicious meals. Although the interior is not necessarily fancy, this is a great spot to try Belgian style-meatballs cooked in Leffe, a popular beer with origins in the Dinant region. They also offer a good selection of Belgian beers, including most of Leffe's offerings.

ACCOMMODATIONS

Dinant, despite its popularity with day trippers, has limited options for accommodations in the city center. If you will be traveling to Dinant by train during the summer (or a popular period) and intend to stay overnight, be sure to book accommodations ahead. If you are traveling by car, there are significantly more options at B&Bs and chateaus in the surrounding region of Dinant.

LA MERVEILLEUSE BY INFINITI RESORTS

Charreau Des Capucins 23; tel. 082 22 91 91; www.lamerveilleuse.be; €100

Named after the nearby caves discovered while building the railroad, La Merveilleuse has long been a staple of Dinant. The massive former orphanage, which was built in a neo-Gothic style, sits on top of a hill visible from across the river. The building is far from stuffy due to a recent renovation including a five-star spa (complete with a Finnish sauna and hammam), restaurant, and beer tastings of Leffe beer within a former chapel. The rooms are quite standard, but the view from the bar makes this hotel, one of the few options in Dinant, well worth the visit.

GETTING THERE

If you intend to explore the larger region of Wallonia, a car is the best way to reach Dinant, as it will offer far more flexibility than the train. Although Dinant easy to reach via train, not having a car will limit you to the city center and the bus schedule leaving Dinant to its surroundings.

Train

DINANT TRAIN STATION

www.belgiantrain.be

It's possible to reach Dinant by trains regularly departing **Brussels** for the south; there's usually one every 30 minutes or so. Dinant

Train Station is located at the foot of Charles De Gaulle Bridge just footsteps from the heart of Dinant. Traveling from Brussels usually requires a transfer in Namur and takes 1 hour 45 minutes (€13). From **Bruges,** Dinant is fairly far at over 3 hours by train with multiple changes (€21.30).

Car

Dinant is about 1 hour 15 minutes (103 kilometers/64 miles) south of **Brussels** by car, via the **E411.** From **Bruges,** the drive takes about 2.5 hours (206 kilometers/128 miles) without traffic via the **E40** and E411, and you're likely to hit traffic as you travel around the ring near Brussels.

There is a limited free **parking lot** across the street from Rue Alexandre Daoust 44, 1 kilometer (0.6 miles; 10 minutes) on foot from the city center and the citadel entrance. There is also free parking above the Citadel (Chemin de la Citadelle 15), but it requires taking the cable car during the Citadel's opening hours for access.

Background

The Landscape

GEOGRAPHY

The Netherlands

The Netherlands is 41,543 square kilometers (16,040 square miles), about half the size of New Jersey. It's located along the North Sea, with several islands belonging to the Netherlands located in the middle of the Wadden Sea, just off the eastern coast of the Dutch mainland.

The Wadden Sea, shared between the Netherlands, Germany, and Denmark, is part of the largest tidal flats system in the world. The Netherlands is mostly made of coastal lowlands; approximately half

the land in the Netherlands has been reclaimed from the sea using a sophisticated water management system considered one of the wonders of the modern world. Large-scale water management systems like the Afsluitdijk, a 32-kilometer (20-mile) dike and roadway, and the Deltaworks have protected the Netherlands from the threat of flooding. Heading south, the land turns into dunes and rolling hills. Though historically Holland was made up forests, most of the forests have now been logged.

The main rivers in the Netherlands are the Meuse/Maas, Rhine, Schelde, and IJssel. The Meuse and the Rhine are commonly referred to as "the Rivers," forming a distinct cultural and geographical boundary between the southern and northern parts of the country. The Rhine-Meuse-Scheldt delta is close to the Hague and Rotterdam; the 350-kilometer-long (217-mile-long) Schelde begins in Northern France and flows out just east of Antwerp. The IJssel is a Dutch distributary of the Rhine river that flows northward toward the IJsselmeer, a former bay of the North Sea that was dammed at the beginning of the 20th century.

THE DUTCH POLDER LANDSCAPE

The flat-as-a-pancake Dutch polder landscape is the source of many jokes: On a cycle, drive, or train ride through the Netherlands, you can see for miles on end. Polders are lowlands that are reclaimed from the sea using sluices, windmills, and pumping stations. A telltale sign of a polder are the long drainage channels and dikes that often circle the fields. The Dutch are true masters of water management, able to transform the sea into blooming fields of tulips.

Belgium

Belgium is smaller than the Netherlands at 30,689 square kilometers (11,849 square miles). It's mostly made up of flat plains, though forests remain in the hilly Ardennes to the south. The Meuse/Maas and Schelde, which flow into the Netherlands, are important rivers in Belgium as well.

WALLONIA'S "LITTLE" MOUNTAINS

Although the Ardennes are hardly the Alps, they are a major European mountain range, with more than 10,000 square kilometers (3,860 square miles) of verdant forests and rolling hills, part of the platform called the Middle Rhine Highlands. Their highest point is about 694 meters (2,277 feet), and there are some stunning rock features, such as the impressive 35-meter-high (115-foot-hight) Bayard Rock that welcomes visitors to Dinant. In between the summits are peat bogs, farmland, and a few natural hot springs.

CLIMATE

The climate in Belgium and the Netherlands is generally mild, with the North Sea preventing them from becoming too hot or cold. Average temperatures throughout the region typically range between 0-24°C (32-75°F). Early August is typically the warmest month, with highs of 24°C (75°F) and lows of 14°C (57°F).

Although they're certainly not the wettest countries in the world, both Belgium and the Netherlands are considered rainy, with 790 millimeters (31 inches) average annual rainfall in the Netherlands and 785 millimeters (31 inches) in Belgium. It's true that the likelihood of rain is fairly high; chances of rain average around 38 percent in Amsterdam during the winter, and bright blue skies in the region are fairly rare (the odds are best March-Oct.). The overcast and gray weather is a common complaint among residents.

ENVIRONMENTAL ISSUES

Climate change is strongly impacting the Netherlands, as half the country sits below sea

Previous: boat tour of Zaanse Schans.

Tulips

The tulip originated in Turkey and was first brought to the Netherlands in the late 16th century. The flowers took particularly well to the Dune and Bulb region around Lisse, not far from Amsterdam, where they still grow today.

TULIP MANIA

The tulip's intense, saturated color was virtually unknown in Europe when the flower arrived in the Low Countries, igniting a craze that was only intensified by variations in pattern and hue that began to pop up and were cultivated by botanists and collectors. Tulips with a striped pattern on their petals (actually caused by a virus) were especially coveted. As collectors sought out rare tulips, the sophistication of the Dutch economic system (at the time the most advanced in the world) created a sort of futures market for tulip bulbs; in the "Tulip Mania" that followed, some tulip bulbs were valued as much as monumental canal houses in Amsterdam.

TULIPS TODAY

Even after the price floor collapsed, tulips remained a favorite plant among the Dutch. The intense propagation of tulip varieties in the 17th century is part of why there are more than 3,000 species of tulip today, in all shapes and sizes, though the single tulip, with its uniform color and smooth six-petal shape, is still the most common in modern tulip fields. A tulip field in bloom is one of the most memorable sights you can see on a trip to the Netherlands; they're viewable throughout the country between April-May.

level and is at risk of flooding, in spite of the advanced Dutch water management system.

The Netherlands are one of Europe's densest countries, and as more land is converted into houses, businesses, and farms, there has been a loss of biodiversity and increased pollution in the waterways from agricultural run-off.

Belgium's history of coal mining is still causing issues with air pollution, as well as built-up waste, which can be seen in the heaps of coal outside Mons, so large that they might be mistaken for hills.

PLANTS

Trees

Forests in the Netherlands and Belgium are populated with European white birch, red European beech (copper beech), and downy birch. English and red oaks are quite common as well. Notably, the wild apple, sweet cherry, willow, chestnut, elm, alder, and hornbeam trees are specific to the Netherlands.

It's said that Holland comes from an old Dutch word for wood, "hout," but the plentiful forests are largely a thing of the past. There are some forests within major cities such as the Haagse Bos, but the forests of the Netherlands are largely concentrated in the east and southeast parts of the country. In Belgium, most of the forests are largely within Wallonia, but especially close to the Belgian-French border in the southwest.

Flowers

Wildflowers like daisies, buttercups, rhododendron, and purple heather are very common in the Netherlands, but what the country is really known for is bulb production. The Netherlands is the world's largest grower of flower bulbs; famous flowers include daffodils, hyacinths, and of course, the tulip. Daffodils are the first to bloom, generally in March-April, followed by the often-purple (sometimes white and pink) hyacinth. Last are the tulips, which generally bloom between mid-April and late May.

Though certainly not as well known for blooms as the Netherlands, flowers, especially azaleas and begonia, are one of Belgium's biggest agricultural products. The common red poppy (*Papaver rhoeas*) is the national flower, growing naturally throughout the country and blooming June-August. It became a symbol of Belgium after Canadian Lieutenant-Colonel John McCrae wrote the poem "In Flanders Fields," immortalizing the poppies that grew over gory World War I battlefields. Also notable is the bluebell (*Hyacinthoides non-scripta*), which is native to the region; thousands flock to Hallerbos, outside Brussels, to see bluebells in bloom.

ANIMALS

Mammals

Most mammals encountered by tourists in the Netherlands and Belgium will be domesticated, such as cats, dogs, mice, rats, goats, sheep, horses, and cows. The Dutch are well known for their specialized domesticated species, such as the Texel sheep and Friesian horses. Wildlife such as beavers live near swampy areas, and other mammal residents include rabbits, hedgehogs, shrews, bats, foxes, weasels, otters, deer, elk, brown bears, and bison; the farther you go from the region's dense urban areas, the more likely you are to see wildlife, especially in the southern part of Belgium.

In the Netherlands and Belgium, it's quite common to encounter mice in your accommodation, especially if you're staying in the historic buildings characteristic of the region's medieval cities. Your host or the hotel staff will be able to help solve the issue.

Sea Life

Along their shorelines with the North and Wadden Seas, the Netherlands and Belgium have a diverse population of sea life, ranging from common and gray seals to fish, porpoises (*Phocoena phocoena*), and sharks. You might even see a rare humpback whale migrating to or from colder waters! Across the region, mussels, oysters, and lobsters thrive; this fresh seafood bounty is enjoyed by Dutch and Belgians alike, especially the closer you get to the coast.

Birds

Both countries are known for their plentiful birdlife, especially the Netherlands. Common species include seagulls, pigeons, ducks, geese, crows, parakeets, coots, storks, herons, egrets, storks, and swans. Rarer are quails, partridges, ibises, grouses (including the black grouse), pheasants (including the ring-necked pheasant), grebes, cuckoos, woodpeckers, swifts, and birds of prey including owls, eagles, kestrels, falcons, kites, and the Egyptian vulture. Perhaps the most surprising bird sightings are the green, rose-ringed parakeets throughout city centers, escaped pets that have adapted to these urban environments. The marshy lands closer to the North Sea are home to migratory birds such as spoonbills, sandpipers, and pipers, especially in August.

Reptiles and Amphibians

There are only five varieties of snakes in the Netherlands and Belgium, and only one of them (the *Vipera berus,* or the European adder, identified by its red eyes and a zigzag pattern on its back) is poisonous. Close to the water, you might spot grass snakes (*Natrix natrix*) that thrive on eating amphibians. The smooth snake (*Coronella austriaca*) is an endangered species that looks like a cross between a grass snake and an adder and tends to shy away from humans.

Amphibians are more plentiful, including species such as newts, frogs, and salamanders, but increasing development of natural marshes for human use and habitation has resulted in a decrease in biodiversity.

Insects and Arachnids

The Netherlands are home to a large variety of spiders that come in all shapes and sizes. Although most are not poisonous, their size can be a shock. A few spider varieties such as the wolf spider, which can be up to 7 millimeters (0.3 inches) in length, can have painful bites. Mosquitos are a significant issue in the area due to the swampy environment. Crane flies, which look like giant mosquitos, luckily do not bite.

1

2

3

4

GODSHUIS ST·JOZEF 17DE EEUW

History

ANCIENT CIVILIZATIONS

Humanity has long lived in this region, especially in what is now Belgium, where Neanderthal fossils dating back to 100,000 BC have been found. These tribes were likely to be hunter-gatherers; farming and animal husbandry were introduced around 5,000 BC in the southern Netherlands and Belgium. One impressive feat from around this period (about 4,000 BC) is the massive stone graves known as dolmens mostly found in the eastern Netherlands, which predate the pyramids. Indo-European languages were introduced around 2,000 BC with the arrival of Germanic tribes. Around this period, peat bogs began to be excavated for bog iron, which left an indelible mark on the Dutch landscape.

EARLY HISTORY (ROMANESQUE)

Celtic tribes known as the Belgae, renowned for their bravery, arrived around 800 BC in parts of Belgium and the Netherlands. The Romans defeated the Belgae and took over in 57 BC, dividing the region into provinces. The oldest city in the Netherlands, Nijmegen, was established as a Roman military camp, while Tongeren was the capital of Civitas Tungrorum, the Romans' name for the region. In AD 69, a Germanic tribe known as the Batavi attempted to overthrow the Romans near Nijmegen. Although they were unsuccessful, the Batavian revolt has long been romanticized throughout Dutch history.

After the fall of the Roman Empire in 411, the Franks (and the subsequent Merovingian dynasty), led by Clovis I, conquered the region. Clovis I's conversion to Catholicism spreads Christianity throughout the region. The Carolingians succeeded the Merovingians, led by Charles the Great, or Charlemagne, who came to power in 768. Invasions by Hungarians and Vikings and civil war are constant threats to the empire over the next 200 years.

MIDDLE AGES

Many of the regional boundaries still seen in Belgium and the Netherlands today came from the borders of feudal domains established during the Middle Ages. Cities with access to the sea, including Bruges, Antwerp, and Amsterdam, grew rapidly as trade hubs, further enabled by the Hanseatic League. During this period, guilds enabled producers and craftsmen to gain more influence.

The region got caught up in the Hundred Years War (1337-1453) between England and France until Philip the Good (1396-1467), the Duke of Burgundy, rose to power. The Burgundians took control of territories that included the Netherlands and funded the work of great artists such as Jan van Eyck. Philip the Good's granddaughter Mary of Burgundy married one of the Hapsburgs, which resulted in the region falling under Hapsburg rule in the late 15th century. The throne ended up in the hands of Charles V, who united the lands of Spain, the New World, Germany, Belgium, and the Netherlands under one crown. In an attempt to quell rebellions by residents who disagreed with his attempts to fight the French, he allowed for autonomy within the 17 provinces of the Netherlands. He later left the crown of the Holy Roman Empire to his son Philip II (1537-98).

THE EIGHTY YEARS' WAR

Under Philip II's rule, the Spanish Inquisition persecuted Protestants, Jews, and many others. William of Orange-Nassau (William the Silent) banded together with other Protestant-friendly nobles who wished to see religious

1: rainy evening in Brussels **2:** tulips for sale in Amsterdam **3:** Jan van Eyck statue in Bruges **4:** historic building in Bruges

Historical Timeline

100,000 BC	First evidence of Neanderthal habitation of Belgium.
5,000 BC	Evidence of the introduction of farming and animal husbandry to the region.
4,000-3,000 BC	Building of dolmens (large stone graves) throughout the Netherlands.
800 BC-58 BC	Arrival of Celtic tribes known as the Belgae in what is now Belgium and the southern Netherlands.
57 BC-410	The Netherlands and Belgium are conquered and divided into Roman provinces; the oldest city in the Netherlands (Nijmegen) is established as a Roman military camp; Christianity introduced.
AD 69	Batavian revolt and attempted overthrow of the Romans.
AD 800	The Franks, led by Clovis I, conquer the region; increased spread of Catholicism; Charlemagne comes to power.
1150-1300	Dams built to prevent flooding and control the IJ river; Amsterdam founded in 1275.
1000-1432	Rule of German emperors via the Holy Roman Empire; continual feudal wars. Parts of the Netherlands are drained to allow for farming; guilds established; cities in Belgium begin to thrive, especially Bruges and Antwerp. Establishment of the Hanseatic League.
1433-1567	Most of the Netherlands and Belgium (17 provinces) united by the Duke of Burgundy in 1433; growth of Amsterdam as a major trading port.
1515	Charles V becomes to the Holy Roman Emperor; imposition of Spanish rule.
1566-1648	Revolt in the Netherlands and Belgium against Habsburg rule; large-scale suppression of Lutheranism and Calvinism.
1566	Beginning of the Eighty Years' War against the Spanish, led by William the Silent.
1581	Declaration of independence from Philip II and offer of assistance from the British; Dutch ships begin colonizing Asia.
1588	Establishment of the Dutch Republic.
1648	Peace of Westphalia marks the end of the Eighty Years' War, allowing the United Provinces (known as Holland) to become independent from Spain.
1602	Establishment of the Dutch East India Company (VOC); colonies in Indonesia, Brazil, New York, West Indies, and South Africa established.

tolerance enacted within the kingdom. In 1565, this attempt failed, and large-scale violence erupted in the region, resulting in the desecration of Catholic churches by Protestant mobs, known as the Iconoclastic Fury. In 1576, the Pacification of Ghent stopped the fighting, but true peace did not come to the region, as seven of the Dutch provinces opted to sign the Union of Utrecht, refusing to acknowledge Spanish rule. William became the governor of the United Provinces before he was assassinated in Delft in 1584. The rest of the Netherlands and Belgium remained under Spanish rule.

After the death of Philip II, Philip II's daughter Infanta Isabella took control of the Netherlands in 1609 and agreed to a truce, which allowed for temporary independence of the provinces. The next king unwisely chose to continue waging wars against the

1620	Pilgrims arrive in New World after departing Leiden and England.
1700	Austrian Habsburgs inherit Belgium from French rule.
1789-1790	Brabant rebels call for independence from Austrian rule; revolution crushed.
1794-1814	Belgium and the Netherlands annexed by France; Batavian Republic established.
1814-1815	Napoleon defeated at Waterloo; Congress of Vienna signed; the Netherlands becomes the Kingdom of the Netherlands.
1815-1840	Belgium rejoins the United Kingdom of the Netherlands; Dutch becomes the official language of the region.
1830	Dutch forces removed from Belgium during the Belgian Revolution; 1830 Belgian Congress allows Belgium to become an independent kingdom.
1831	Belgian king and Belgian constitution inaugurated.
1884	Establishment of the Congo Free State by Belgian King Leopold II; millions die of disease and exploitation.
1908	The Congo Free State is annexed by Belgium.
1914-1919	World War I breaks out in Europe; Belgium taken over by Germans while the Netherlands remains neutral.
1940-1944	Belgium and the Netherlands invaded and fall under Nazi control; the Holocaust and the Hunger Winter kill thousands.
1944-1945	The Netherlands and Belgium freed by Allied forces.
1946	International Court of Justice established in the Hague.
1948	Treaty of Brussels, predecessor to NATO, signed by Belgium, the Netherlands, Luxembourg, France, and the UK.
1949	Dutch East Indies (Indonesia) becomes independent from the Netherlands.
1957	Establishment of the European Economic Community, precursor to the EU.
1960	Congolese Independence from Belgium.
1975	Suriname gains independence from the Netherlands.
1993	Treaty of Maastricht creates the European Union.
2001	First same-sex marriage in the world happens in the Netherlands.

Protestants, which resulted in continuation of the what's now known as the Eighty Years' War until the Treaty of Munster, signed in 1648. At this point, the United Provinces of the Netherlands were acknowledged by the Spanish as an independent territory, a major turning point in Dutch history. The Dutch vied for power on the high seas and in commerce while establishing colonies, such as New Amsterdam and Java (Indonesia). The Dutch end up trading New Amsterdam (now New York) to the English for Surinam.

DECLINE OF THE HAPSBURGS

Following the Eighty Years' War, the Netherlands kicked French forces out of the region between 1701-1713, and control of what is now Belgium fell into the hands of the Austrian Hapsburg family. In 1713, war broke out after the accession of the daughter of Charles VI was rejected, which enabled the French to invade the Spanish Netherlands and the Netherlands in the mid-1700s. The Treaty of Aix-la-Chapelle resulted in the only female ruler of the Hapsburgs, Maria Theresa, taking control of the region. Under Maria Theresa, the Enlightenment prospered, despite the Brabant Revolution (1789-90), in which Belgian nobles protested the rule of a single monarch; attempts to form a United States of Belgium failed.

When the Hapsburgs fell, the French took over, renaming the region "the Batavian Republic." Trade prospered under Napoleon Bonaparte, though he proved to be unpopular among the locals. Other European powers, including England, Prussia, Austria, and Russia, banded together to defeat Napoleon definitively in 1815 in the Battle of Waterloo.

DUTCH AND BELGIAN INDEPENDENCE

In 1815, the Congress of Vienna redrew European boundaries to something much closer to what we know today, joining the Spanish Netherlands with the United Provinces to create the United Kingdom of the Netherlands. William I enacted a few regulations that deeply angered Belgians, including making Dutch the official language and secularizing Catholic schools. William I attempted to quell the uprisings, but on October 4, 1830, the Dutch retreated from Brussels and a provisional Belgian government declared independence as the Kingdom of Belgium. In 1831, the London Congress recognized Belgium's independence across Europe (except for the Netherlands). Since the Belgians did not have a king, the crown was offered to German Prince Leopold of Saxe-Coburg, who became King Leopold I in 1831. The Netherlands acknowledged Belgium's independence eight years older. In 1848, a new constitution in the Netherlands carved out a more definitive role for the Dutch monarchy.

Following Belgium's independence, Belgium invested heavily in industry and transportation, becoming a great European power. This was not enough for Leopold II, the son of Leopold I, who wished to carve out his own legacy. He hired administrator Henry Morton Stanley to establish a Belgian private venture in the Congo. In 1884, the Congo Free State was established under Leopold's private domain. Reports of massacres and abuse forced the Belgian government to take over the colony in 1908 in an attempt to allay concerns. Mining, diamonds, and gold in the Congo remained a huge source of wealth for the country under Belgian rule.

WORLD WARS

As World War I broke out throughout Europe, the Netherlands remained neutral, but Belgium was a major fighting ground. Belgium also attempted to stay neutral but was invaded by Germany on August 4, 1914. Germany's Schlieffen Plan intended to use Belgian territory to capture the French army along the border from the northeast. Belgium maintained control of a small area near the Yser River; Belgian resistance was key to helping the French to fight back against the Germans. Soldiers dug into Belgian farmlands for four years of trench warfare, in which Allied forces from Belgium, the UK, France, Canada, Australia, and New Zealand fought to take mere meters of enemy territory. Many Belgian cities, including Dinant, were destroyed, and the Ypres area saw some of the deadliest fighting. Allied victories in the Hundred Days Offensive forced Kaiser Wilhelm to abdicate, and a ceasefire occurred on November 11, 1918.

Between World War I and II, Brussels became fully bilingual, after Flemish speakers pushed for more influence. Albert I passed away in 1934, resulting in the coronation of Princess Astrid of Sweden, whose short yet popular reign was cut off by her death in 1935, succeeded by Leopold III.

In the onslaught of World War II, both

the Netherlands and Belgium were invaded by Nazi Germany; the Nazis destroyed Rotterdam to force a Dutch concession. Just 10 days of air blitzes forced Belgium to resign, and Leopold III opted to stay in the Royal Palace before being sent to Germany in 1944. Because Leopold met with Hitler at Berchtesgaden, he was exiled in the post-WWII era, eventually resulting in Prince Charles and then his son Baudouin taking charge. The Dutch royal family and the ruler at the time, Queen Wilhelmina, fled to the United Kingdom, the United States, and Canada, where she recorded messages for the Dutch who listened in secret.

In both countries, Jews, members of the LGBTQ community, Roma, and countless others were systematically murdered by the Nazis. Allied forces freed the Netherlands and Belgium in 1944 after the Battle of the Bulge in Belgium and the southern part of the Netherlands, just after a famine caused by blockades killed thousands. War trials actively punished those who openly collaborated with the Nazis in the Netherlands.

POST-WAR PERIOD AND CONTEMPORARY TIMES

The implementation of the Marshall Plan allowed both countries to rebuild and invest in new construction and transportation. The Netherlands received over $1 billion U.S., a huge sum at the time, while Belgium (and Luxembourg) received almost $800 million. In 1958, Brussels showcased its progress during the World's Fair Expo, for which the Atomium was built. Beginning in the 1950s, the Netherlands began on the Delta Works engineering projects to better protect the country from flooding.

The predecessor to NATO was formalized by the Treaty of Brussels, which cemented a defense union between Belgium, the Netherlands, Luxembourg, France, and the UK. The groundwork for the European Union began in 1951 with the European Coal and Steel Community (ECSC), founded to promote trade and fair competition in Europe. In 1957, the European Economic Community (EEC) was established to form a larger common market and customs union. The 1993 Treaty of Maastricht established the European Union, with Brussels hosting many of the institutions due to available land and an affordable cost of living. The euro was introduced in 1999 as a means of standardizing currencies within the European Union, adopted in 2002 by both Belgium and the Netherlands.

Dutch colonies declared independence throughout the 20th century, including Indonesia in 1949 and Suriname in 1975. Both independence events triggered large-scale migration from both countries. Congolese independence from Belgium occurred in 1960, followed by Rwanda and Burundi.

Starting from 1970 and up until 2011, Flanders has been pushing for more autonomy within Belgium, resulting in the formation of a federal Belgian state and the development of stronger regions to ensure better representation.

The Netherlands was the first country in the world to legalize same-sex marriage in 2001.

Government and Economy

ORGANIZATION

The Netherlands

The Netherlands is a parliamentary democracy, with a role of a king included within the Constitution. The government includes the king, prime minster, ministers, and parliament. The parliament is divided into a Senate (75 seats; determined indirectly by provincial councils and the electoral colleges of the Caribbean parts of the Netherlands) and House of Representatives (150 seats based on popular vote). There are also 12 semi-autonomous provinces in the Netherlands, including as Zuid Holland, which governs the province that includes the Hague and Rotterdam.

The prime minister is determined by the coalition in power, often the leader of the largest party in the coalition. This process is largely done independently of the royal family, although the ministers are appointed by the king. The king of the Netherlands at the time of writing is Willem-Alexander. At the time of writing, the acting prime minister was Mark Rutte, but there will likely be a new prime minister once a coalition is built following the 2021 elections.

Belgium

Belgium is federal constitutional monarchy with a parliamentary system. The ling as well as the prime minister are the heads of government. The Belgian system is notably complex; although there is a federal system, there are also regions and communities, such as native Dutch, French, and German speakers. Most of the Belgian system's issues stem from its attempts to account for regional and linguistic differences. Increasing the complication is the fact that citizens only vote for local parties, not at the national level. There is a parliament with a Senate (71 seats with 40 directly elected by popular vote) and Chamber of Representatives (150 seats; directly elected). At the time of writing, Alexander De Croo is serving as the prime minister of Belgium, appointed by the Belgian King Philippe.

POLITICAL PARTIES

The Netherlands

The largest parties in the Netherlands are:

- The VVD (People's Party for Freedom and Democracy), a conservative-liberal party best known for supporting business interests.
- The PVV (Party for Freedom), the most controversial party in the Netherlands due to its ring-wing platform, which supports banning immigration from Muslim countries and hijabs and "Nexit," or the Netherlands' exit from the European Union.
- The CDA (Christian Democratic Appeal), a Christian center party that believes that society, including churches and unions, should work together.
- The D66, which has strongly advocated for more direct democracy, including the direct election of the prime minister and the EU.
- The SP (Socialist Party), a left-wing social-democratic party.
- The GL (Groen Links), a left-leaning environmentalist party.
- TPvDA (Labour Party), a social-democratic party that advocates for investing in education, healthcare, and public safety.

Belgium

In Belgium, the major parties include the Flemish nationalist parties Nieuw-Vlaamse Alliantie (N-VA) and Vlaams Belang. "Tradition" is a large part of the Vlaams Belang party, which stands strongly against immigration, especially from Muslim countries. N-VA tends to be more fiscally

Royal Families 101

THE NETHERLANDS

The current Dutch royal family came into power in 1815 beginning with **William I,** who was descended from the House of Orange-Nassau, the reason for the popularity of the color orange throughout the Netherlands. Following the fall of Napoleon, he was proclaimed prince of the United Netherlands in 1814 before becoming king in 1815. The Netherlands also has a tradition of female monarchs, beginning with **Queen Emma** in 1858 and **Queen Wilhelmina** in 1880. The Dutch royal family is currently compromised of **King Willem-Alexander, Queen Máxima** (originally from Argentina), and their three daughters. The heir to the throne is **Princess Amalia.**

BELGIUM

The Belgian royal family is historically descended from German linage; however, the current Belgian king is a descent of many notable linages including the Orange-Nassau linage (William I), the wife of Emperor Napoleon I, the Hapsburgs, and the Dukes of Burgundy. All Belgian kings can be traced back to **Leopold I,** who ruled between 1831-1865. The current Belgian king, **King Philippe,** became king in 2013 after his father, **King Albert II,** abdicated the throne. The Belgian Queen, **Mathilde,** is the country's first Belgian-born queen. They have four children, the oldest of which, **Princess Elisabeth,** is destined to become the next queen of Belgium. Changes to Belgian succession laws allow for the eldest child to succeed a parent regardless of gender.

conservative, and advocates for any person living in Flanders to learn Dutch and for a safer society with less crime. PS (Parti Socialiste) is a social democratic French-speaking party active in Brussels and Wallonia, supported by the working class. They advocate for a more involved federal Belgian government. CD&V (Christian Democratic and Flemish) is a centrist Christian Democratic party that advocates for affordable healthcare, fiscal responsibility, a stronger Flemish identity, and a more efficient government.

ELECTIONS

The Netherlands

Elections in the Netherlands are held at multiple levels: national, provincial, municipality, and European Union, not to mention elections for the water boards, which are in charge of the waterways and dams. The national vote directly impacts representation in parliament's House of Representatives. A coalition government is formed if one party does not have a majority. The assignment of seats in the House of Representatives is equal to the percentage of the votes gotten by a party, with roughly 70,107 votes corresponding to one seat.

In the last national election in 2017, the VVD won the majority of seats (33) with PVV coming in second (20), although left-wing parties such as D66 and the GL had a strong showing. The CDA also gained 19 seats. The resulting coalition formed left the PVV out in the cold, leaving Mark Rutte, the head of the VVD, in power.

Belgium

Federal elections in Belgium generally occur generally every five years, to coincide with those of European Parliament. Belgian ballots vary quite a bit by region, causing intense polarization and making regional governments extremely important to daily life. The last election was in 2019, but a coalition wasn't formed until October 2020. The vast majority of the votes at the federal level went to Flemish nationalist parties such as the Nieuw-Vlaamse Alliantie (N-VA; 13%) and the VI.Belang (Vlaams Belang; 11.68%).

AGRICULTURE AND INDUSTRY

Agriculture in the Netherlands is largely focused on food production: Unbelievably, considering its small size, the country is the second-largest food exporter in the world, after the United States. Despite the relative lack of sun, greenhouses with a fraction of the usual agricultural footprint supply Europe with plants and flowers using innovative techniques. Dairy products, eggs, and meat are also mainstays of the Dutch economy. In Belgium, livestock (cattle, pig, and poultry) and crop production play a significant role in the economy, with sugar beets and potatoes being top exports.

The Netherlands is a world leader in information technology, finance, chemicals, logistics, water management and engineering, and energy. Belgium's major industries include raw materials, the service sector (related to the EU/Benelux organizations as well as tourism), manufacturing (metals, textiles, chemicals, food, diamonds, and lace), finance, and the production of motor vehicles.

DISTRIBUTION OF WEALTH

In both the Netherlands and Belgium, wealth above a certain level is highly taxed. The standard of living in both countries is fairly high, with a robust social safety net. Income inequality is relatively low in the Netherlands; it is slightly higher in Belgium, although it has one of the most egalitarian income distributions within the EU. That said, income inequality, especially in the Netherlands, is increasing, with higher costs of living in major cities and an exploding housing market where many young adults cannot afford to buy homes on their salaries. The top 20 percent of the population earns about four times as much as the bottom 20 percent. The average income in both countries is close to €30,000, with some regional differences: Flanders is more prosperous than Wallonia, for example.

TOURISM

Tourism made up about 4.4% of the Netherlands' GDP in 2018, with the majority of international tourists flocking to Amsterdam, Rotterdam, and Keukenhof to see the tulips. In Belgium, tourism made up 5.4% of Belgium's GDP in 2019; Bruges was visited by 8.3 million people in 2018 alone. Brussels, on the other hand, is primarily a destination for business travelers and the city is actively trying to bring more leisure travelers to Belgium's capital.

Overtourism is a significant issue in both Bruges and Amsterdam; in an attempt to control tourism in Amsterdam, the Netherlands is trying promote travel to other parts of the country, and to rehabilitate the city's image from a party hub to one that celebrates its rich history and culture. In particular, stricter rules have gone into place within Amsterdam's Red Light District as a means to make the neighborhood friendlier to residents, many of whom have left due to noise complaints and the public drinking. Amsterdam has also opted to ban Airbnb within the city center. In Amsterdam as well as Bruges, there have also been discussions of creating a day trip fee for those coming from docked cruise ships.

Of course, COVID-19 significantly impacted tourism in 2020 and 2021, reducing the number of visitors by 75 percent. But tourism bureaus hope to use this period to prepare for the next tourist rush. Many Dutch cities have opted to enact regulations to more strictly regulate the housing market, and Amsterdam may even ban non-Dutch residents from coffeeshops that sell marijuana. The city also opted to move its famous iAmsterdam sign to lesser-known spots in the city to promote other neighborhoods beyond the city center.

People and Culture

DEMOGRAPHY AND DIVERSITY

The Netherlands

The Netherlands has 17.4 million residents, and nearly 24 percent are immigrants or the children of immigrants. The vast majority come from other European Union member states, although there is a sizable Black and Asian population with roots in former Dutch colonies such as Indonesia, the former Netherlands Antilles, and Suriname. A labor program in the 1960s resulted in the sizable Moroccan and Turkish communities found in large cities such as Rotterdam and Amsterdam.

Belgium

Belgium has a population of 11.5 million residents, many of which are Europeans coming from other European countries such as Romania, France, the Netherlands, and Italy. Nearly a third of Belgian residents are immigrants or second-generation immigrants; about 15 percent of the population has a non-European background. Though the Belgium census does not collect data on ethnicity, there is a sizable Black community due to historic ties with the former Belgian colony of the Congo. Most of the immigrant populations are clustered in the Brussels region, although Ghent and Antwerp are also diverse.

RELIGION

Historically, the conversion of Clovis I to Catholicism popularized the religion throughout the Netherlands and Belgium until Lutheranism and Calvinism gained a following in the 16th century, but today the majority of people here are not affiliated with any religion. In the last 40 years, the Muslim population in the region has grown due to immigration from the Middle East.

LANGUAGE

Dutch is the primary language spoken in the Netherlands, though the Dutch have been rated as the highest level of non-native English proficiency in the world. In Belgium, three languages are spoken: Dutch, French, and German, though English is well spoken as well. Flanders is historically the Dutch-speaking region of Belgium, and although Flemish independence is often discussed, most Belgians living in Flanders are very proud to be Belgian. Wallonia is traditionally the French and German speaking region, with the German-speaking minority living in the southeast.

LITERATURE

Influential early medieval works from the Lowlands, written in Old Dutch, were often translations of sagas, religious works, compendia of nature, and overviews of history. Literature in the region has a legacy of tolerance and defying religious authority; one notable writer was Erasmus, a humanist born in Rotterdam in the 15th century, who challenged the authority of the Church at the time. One of the first printing houses in Europe, Plantin Moretus, was founded in Antwerp prior to the Eighty Years' War, and it's said pilgrims migrated to Holland in the hopes of finding friendly printers for their religious works.

Following the Eighty Years' War, enlightenment continued to prosper in Holland—notably, female intellectuals such as Anna Visscher and Maria Tesselschade would meet with male contemporaries such as Constantijn Huygens, a statesman, poet, and scientist from the Hague. Though the wars of the 20th century forced a pause in intellectual meetings, Anne Frank wrote her diaries during this period, along with many books about this difficult era in Belgium and the Netherlands. One of the Netherlands' best-known contemporary writers is Herman Koch, who writes dark novels, often about murder.

VISUAL ARTS

The earliest Dutch and Belgian paintings are known as the Early Netherlandish or Flemish Primitives, a movement comprised of artists who were born before 1500 who often depicted biblical scenes and portraits using rich oil paints. Famous painters of this period include Jan van Eyck, Rogier van der Weyden, and Hans Memling.

In the 16th century, the Italian Renaissance inspired Pieter Brueghel the Elder and Hieronymus Bosch, and following the Eighty Years' War, the Baroque period ushered in masters who defined the Dutch Golden Age of painting, such as Rembrandt, Frans Hals, Paulus Potter, Rubens, and Vermeer. Golden Age artists painted grand scenes, increasingly of everyday people, seascapes, landscapes, still lifes, and historical scenes.

Though the Low Countries are best known for their earlier artistic contributions within the earlier periods, Belgium and the Netherlands have also been at the forefront of quite a few artistic movements in the 19th and 20th centuries. When Impressionism thrived in France, the Hague school, which focused on landscapes and seascapes, thrived, and Vincent Van Gogh lived and painted in multiple cities around the region. In Belgium, symbolism, surrealism, and art nouveau flourished at the turn of the 20th century. Later, de Stijl (known as Neoplasticism) stood in contrast to the decadence of these earlier styles, trying to reduce art to its essential forms and colors. In the post war period, the CoBra (Copenhagen, Brussels, Amsterdam) school took root, encouraging a more free-form embrace of color and subject.

MUSIC

Carillons are one of Belgium and the Netherlands' best-known traditional instruments, and to this day the regions' churches and cathedrals are some of the best places to study and to hear these organ-like keyboards attached to bells. For something completely different, the Netherlands and Belgium shine particularly when it comes to electronic music; famous DJs such as Armin van Buuren and Tiësto hail from the Netherlands. Belgium is also particularly known for its heavy metal, home to groups like Valkyre, Skitsoy, and Channel Zero.

Essentials

Transportation

GETTING THERE

From North America

Schiphol Airport (AMS; Evert van de Beekstraat 202; www.schiphol.nl), outside of Amsterdam, and **Brussels Airport** (BRU; Leopoldlaan; www.brusselsairport.be) are the most convenient gateways to the region from North America. There are direct flights from the United States, Canada, and Mexico, especially from major hubs like New York, DC, San Francisco, Mexico City, and Toronto. **KLM Royal Dutch Airlines** (www.klm.com) dominates Schiphol

Coronavirus in the Netherlands and Belgium

At the time of writing in June 2021, both Belgium and the Netherlands have made significant progress against COVID-19, with more than 50% of the adult population receiving at least one dose of the coronavirus vaccine. This progress has resulted in the lifting of some of the previous restrictions such as on indoor dining and group sizes. As of late June, the Netherlands lifted face mask restrictions within indoor public spaces, but this requirement could be reinstated in the case of another wave. U.S. citizens are also now allowed into the Netherlands as tourists, and the EU will be opening in summer to fully vaccinated tourists, though still with testing and quarantine requirements in some cases. It's best to check with the embassy for the most up-to-date travel conditions.

Fully vaccinated people are expected to have more freedom, but admission into some major attractions and events where social distancing is not possible may require coronavirus tests or proof of being fully vaccinated.

Now more than ever, Moon encourages its readers to be courteous and ethical in their travel. We ask travelers to be respectful to residents, and mindful of the evolving situation in their chosen destination when planning their trip.

BEFORE YOU GO

- Check **local websites and resources** for information on restrictions and the overall health status of your destination and point of origin. If you're traveling to or from an area that is currently a COVID-19 hotspot, you may want to reconsider your trip.
- Get **vaccinated** if your health status allows, and if possible, take a **coronavirus test** with enough time to receive your results before your departure. Some destinations may require proof of vaccination or a negative COVID test result before arrival, along with other tests and potentially a self-quarantine period, once you've arrived. Check local requirements and factor these into your plans.
- If you plan to fly, check with your airline and the destination's health authority (RIVM, www.rivm.nl; FOD, www.info-coronavirus.be) for **updated travel requirements.** Some airlines may be taking more steps than others to help you travel safely, such as limited occupancy; check their websites for more information before buying your ticket, and consider a very early or very late flight, to limit exposure. Flights may be more infrequent, with increased cancellations.
- Check the website of any museums, restaurants, and other venues you wish to patronize to confirm that they're open, if their hours have been adjusted, and to learn about any specific visitation requirements, such as **mandatory reservations** or **limited occupancy.**
- Pack **hand sanitizer,** a **thermometer,** and **plenty of face masks.** Throughout your travels, consider packing **snacks** and **bottled water** to limit the number of stops along your route and anticipate closures.

Airport, but **Delta** (www.delta.com) and **United** (www.united.com) also fly there direct from North America. Travelers can also opt for other European transatlantic airlines like Lufthansa, Air France, SAS, Aer Lingus, and Turkish Airlines, which are more likely to have a connection via another European hub. For Brussels, KLM, United, Lufthansa, Aer Lingus, Turkish Airlines, Air France, and **Brussels Airlines** (www.brusselsairlines.com) are just of the few of the airlines operating flights to and from North America.

Previous: Amsterdam's modern bus terminal.

- **Assess the risk** of entering crowded spaces, joining tours, and taking public transit.
- Expect **general disruptions.** Events may be postponed or cancelled, and some tours and venues may require reservations, enforce limits on the number of guests, be operating during different hours than the ones listed, or be closed entirely.

RESOURCES

The **embassies** for your country in Belgium and the Netherlands are also good sources of information, especially for entry requirements. Most restaurants in the Netherlands and Belgium keep an active presence online. Beyond going in person, the best place to check a business's hours and any precautions they may have in place to combat COVID is their **Facebook or Instagram profiles.**

- For the Netherlands, **RIVM** (www.rivm.nl) is the main health authority.
- The **Dutch government** also keeps an active website (www.government.nl/topics/coronavirus-covid-19) on current regulations.
- For the most up-to-date information about the coronavirus in Belgium, go to their **coronavirus portal** (www.info-coronavirus.be).
- **iAmsterdam** (www.iamsterdam.com), the official website of the Amsterdam Tourism Board, keeps an impressive up-to-date list of activity recommendations, restaurants with outdoor dining, and information about openings and closings due to COVID.
- **TimeOut** is another good resource what's open and things to do in both Brussels (www.timeout.com/brussels) and Amsterdam (www.timeout.com/amsterdam).
- **Visit Brussels** (https://visit.brussels), the website of the Brussels Tourism Board, is up-to-date with tips on where to eat and drink, and what to do in Brussels.
- The most up-to-date website about Brussels specifically is **Everything Brussels** (www.everythingbrussels.be), run by a Brussels local, with information about the best places to go in both normal and COVID times.
- **Visit Bruges** (www.visitbruges.be) keeps a very active list of the best places to eat in Bruges and what to do during COVID.
- Both the **Flanders** (www.visitflanders.com) and **Wallonia** (https://walloniabelgiumtourism.co.uk) tourism boards also keep an updated list of regulations applicable to their regions.

From Europe and the United Kingdom

Travelers from the UK have many options for entering the region; the best option may be the high-speed train to Brussels, Antwerp, Rotterdam, or Amsterdam operated by **Eurostar** (www.eurostar.com), which get there from London in 4 hours, with minimal hassle and border security supposedly even after Brexit. UK travelers can also fly into Brussels Airport, Amsterdam Schiphol, or the **budget-friendly airports** of Eindhoven, Rotterdam-The Hague, or Brussels South Charleroi Airport; expect cheaper fares, but less convenience in getting to Amsterdam or Brussels. KLM, Air

Cruise Ship Stopovers in Amsterdam and Belgium

Amsterdam and Belgium are popular stopover points on European river cruises, many of which begin in Amsterdam. Popular companies within the region include:

- **Riviera Travel** (www.rivieratravel.co.uk)
- **Holland American Line** (www.hollandamerica.com)
- **Royal Carribean** (www.royalcaribbean.com)
- **Princess** (www.princess.com)
- **MSC Cruises** (www.msccruisesusa.com)
- **Norwegian Cruise Line** (www.ncl.com)
- **Viking River Cruises** (www.vikingrivercruises.co.uk)
- **Celebrity Cruises** (www.celebritycruises.com)
- **Scenic Luxury Cruises** (www.scenicusa.com)

Most river cruises allow for a few days in Amsterdam at the beginning or end of the trip. The cruises currently dock behind the Amsterdam Central Train Station, at the **Passenger Terminal Amsterdam** (www.ptamsterdam.com). This may change in the coming years, as Amsterdam further regulates the cruise industry to cut down on day tripping tourists and discourages cruise ships to dock in the city center. The new terminal is likely to be west of Amsterdam, near Zaandam in Zaanse Schans.

For Belgium, the main cruise port is **Zeebrugge,** which is located about 25 minutes away from Bruges. Many cruises from here depart to the Baltic States and Scandinavia.

France, British Airlines, and Lufthansa operate several flights a day between London and the Netherlands and Belgium. There are also daily flights to most major cities in the UK, such as Edinburgh, Belfast, Bristol, Birmingham, Liverpool, Leeds, and Glasgow. Another option is the daily overnight **ferry** between the Netherlands (Rotterdam/The Hague) and Hull or Harwich on east coast of the UK (www.poferries.com; www.stenaline.nl). Travelers to Belgium can also find an overnight ferry from Hull to Zeebrugge.

Visitors from the rest of Europe will find many flights to Schiphol and Brussels Airports, operated by KLM and Air France, as well as **budget airlines** like EastJet, TUI, Transavia, RyanAir, and WizzAir. **Buses** are also an option within the EU; in particular, **Flixbus** (https://global.flixbus.com) runs daily between Paris and Amste rdamor Brussels.

From Australia, New Zealand, and South Africa

Brussels Airport and Schiphol Airport are also the main entry point for Aussie, South African, and Kiwi travelers, though unfortunately the flights will usually be nowhere near as quick or direct. That said, KLM does operate regular direct flights to Amsterdam from Johannesburg as well as Cape Town. Aussie and Kiwi travelers will likely need need to **transfer in the Middle East** with an airline such as Emirates or Qatar Airlines, although KLM offers some flight options as well.

GETTING AROUND

Getting around the compact countries of the Netherlands and Belgium using public transportation is fairly straightforward. That said, to get to more rural areas, it's often best to rent a car.

Due to COVID-19, public transportation was reduced to account for fewer passengers over much of the time this book was written. During outbreaks, people on public transportation are expected to keep their distance and wear a face mask.

Train

The train networks in both the Netherlands and Belgium are extremely efficient and frequent, and usually tickets can be bought the same day. The Netherlands' railway network is mainly operated by state-owned **NS** (www.ns.nl), while the Belgian network is operated by **NMBS/SNCB** (www.belgiantrain.be; the different acronyms simply reflect the Dutch and French names of the company).

In terms of buying tickets, some travelers opt for a **Eurail pass** (www.eurail.com), which is valid throughout the entire Schengen zone, but it's not needed if you're only traveling in the Netherlands and Belgium. You'll save money by buying individual tickets. You can buy them in advance online, using either operator's mobile phone app, or simply when you arrive at the station.

There are elevators available between tracks and stations as well as ramps to stations, but passengers with disabilities may need to request assistance with wheelchairs or mobility scooters (www.belgiantrain.be/en/travel-info/prepare-for-your-journey/assistance-reduced-mobility, www.ns.nl/en/travel-information/traveling-with-a-functional-disability/traveling-with-a-wheelchair-scootmobile-or-special-bicycle.html); this service must be requested in advance.

Rental Car

The Dutch and Belgian train networks are so extensive and effective that rental cars are rarely needed, though they may be useful for travel to more rural regions, for example the World War I battlefields outside Ypres or for hiking around Dinant. It's fairly easy to navigate the countries' highway and road networks, which are well-signed and maintained, though traffic and parking do become a problem in denser urban areas, especially during rush hours. Highways and normal roads are generally toll-free, and there are convenient rest stops along most highways that make it easy to fill up your gas tank.

RENTING A CAR

International drivers' licenses are accepted at car rental facilities throughout the Netherlands and Belgium without hesitation as long as the license is printed in English, though drivers under 25 may have issues renting a car, and additional documents providing your identity might be necessary. Commercial rental companies like Enterprise, Budget, Avis, Sixt, and Alamo serve Brussels and Schiphol Airports. Many companies also have branches in major cities. It's important to check carefully whether you're renting a manual or automatic car; most cars available are manual, and there's often a higher rate for automatic cars.

RULES AND REGULATIONS

Cars drive on the right side of the road in both the Netherlands and Belgium. In both countries, seat belts are compulsory, there is no right on red at intersections, and vehicles coming from the right have priority. Small children must sit in a car seat and phones cannot be used unless in a hands-free mode. Your blood alcohol cannot exceed .05 percent will driving. An upside-down triangle (▼) on the pavement or at an intersection means that you are supposed to yield to traffic.

In the Netherlands, the speed limit on highways is 130 kph (80 mph), 100 kph (60 mph) on expressways, 50 kph (30 mph) on municipal roads, 30 kph (20 mph) on local access roads, and 15 kph (10 mph) in residential areas. Speed is enforced through cameras, and a mistake can be costly; for example, €108 for going 10 kph (6 mph) in a residential area.

Belgium is also quite big on catching speeders, with many cameras, and points where cars might need to randomly slow down after a period of driving at a higher speed. The maximum speed is 120 kph (85 mph) on freeways,

90 kph (55 mph) on outside built-up areas, 50 kph (30 mph) in urban areas, and 30 kph (20 mph) near schools.

DEALING WITH CYCLISTS AS A DRIVER

Drivers in the region need to be wary of cyclists while driving. Most Dutch and Belgian roads have a clearly marked bike lane, or signal that cars and bikes will be sharing a road. Drivers should ensure they don't cross into the bike lane, and carefully look to their right to make sure they're providing enough space for cyclists. At intersections with many cyclists, be sure to check carefully before crossing, as not all cyclists follow the rules or pay full attention to cars, especially in Amsterdam. In particular, do not open your car doors without looking behind you for cyclists, who might not have time to swerve out of the way.

Bus

Unlike the train systems, there is not a single company running the bus network in the Netherlands or Belgium. International buses such as Eurolines, Flixbus, and Megabus and regional buses connect major hubs, as well as local bus systems within cities. For regional buses, which often leave from the nearest major train station, it's best to book your ticket in advance, as it's not always possible to buy tickets in person for some of these routes.

Some local bus systems, including the system in Brussels, are moving to a cashless model. Belgian and Dutch public transportation websites are often intended for residents and hard for visitors to figure out, so it may be best to purchase your ticket at transit hubs before boarding your bus. On the other hand, the dedicated bus app for each region—**De Lijn** (www.delijn.be) for northern Belgium or **GVB** (https://en.gvb.nl) for Amsterdam—is very useful, especially to check the bus schedule.

Bike

Biking is an ideal means of transportation for those with more time who wish to take advantage of the Benelux region's small size. Both short- and long-distance cycling trips are fairly easy due to extensive Dutch and Belgian bike networks. They're especially easy on country roads where bikes have a separate bike path; in major cities, where bikes share the road with cars, biking may be more stressful. For beginner bikers, it may be best to take a guided biking tour to familiarize yourself with the rules of the road.

Lights on bikes are mandatory at night in both the Netherlands and Belgium. Bikers should always signal before turning, using their arm to denote the direction. Stoplights do apply to cyclists, and many busy roads with dedicated bike lanes might even have a special bike stoplight. A one-way road with a sign reading *"Uitgezonderd,"* with a bike symbol, means that bikes are excepted from the rule that traffic is one-way. Many pedestrian squares are bike-free, and bikers can get fined for biking through them. In most cases, cars are fairly aware of cyclists, but cyclists should stay as far to the right as possible where cyclists and cars share the road. Avoid using your phone while cycling and pull over if you need to check it. A great way to navigate without looking at your phone is to use headphones to listen to cycling directions.

Visas and Officialdom

PASSPORTS AND VISAS

United States, Canada, Australia, and New Zealand

At the time of writing, U.S. citizens, Canadians, Aussies, and Kiwis do not require a visa to enter the EU as long as they do not stay more than 90 days within a 180-day period. That said, after 2022, the European Travel Information and Authorization System (ETIAS; www.etiasvisa.com) goes into effect, which will require visitors to the EU/Schengen Zone to apply online to receive an electronic travel authorization.

EU/Schengen and the United Kingdom

Those with an EU passport can freely travel in the Netherlands and Belgium without a visa. It is still unclear how the United Kingdom's "Brexit" from the EU will affect the ability of British travels to enter the Netherlands and Belgium.

South Africa

South Africans must apply for a visa to enter the Netherlands or Belgium. The application for a short-stay visa in the Netherlands, which can be completed online, takes about 30 minutes. You will need to know your travel dates, accommodation, inviting party (if applicable), biometric data, and have your travel documents on hand. A company called **TLS** (https://be.tlscontact.com) handles the short-stay visa process for Belgium in South Africa. They have locations in both Cape Town and Johannesburg. The application is complete online before making an appointment to provide biometric data. If your goal is to visit multiple countries within the Schengen Zone, you need to apply for a multi-entry visa at the embassy where you will first enter the region.

CONSULATES AND EMBASSIES

With the UN's International Court of Justice headquartered in the Hague and Brussels being the European Union's administrative center, it's no surprise that consulates and embassies are well-represented in the Netherlands and Belgium.

Amsterdam

- **U.S. Consulate General Amsterdam** (Museumplein 19; tel. 31 20 575 5309; https://nl.usembassy.gov/embassy-consulate/amsterdam)

The Hague

- **Australian Embassy in the Netherlands** (Carnegielaan 4; tel. 31 070 310 8200; http://netherlands.embassy.gov.au)
- **Embassy of Canada to the Netherlands in the Hague** (Sophialaan 5-7; tel. 31 70 311 1600, www.canadainternational.gc.ca/netherlands-pays_bas)
- **New Zealand Embassy, The Hague, Netherlands** (Eisenhowerlaan 77N; tel. 31 70 346 9324; www.mfat.govt.nz/en/countries-and-regions/europe/netherlands/new-zealand-embassy)
- **South African Embassy in The Netherlands** (Wassenaarseweg 40; tel. 31 70 392 4501; www.zuidafrika.nl)
- **British Embassy The Hague** (Lange Voorhout 10; tel. 31 70 427 0427; www.gov.uk/government/world/organisations/british-embassy-the-hague)
- **U.S. Embassy The Hague** (John Adams Park 1; tel. 31 70 310 2209; https://nl.usembassy.gov)

Brussels

- **Australian Embassy - Brussels** (Avenue des Arts 55; tel. 32 2 286 05 00; http://belgium.embassy.gov.au/bslsfrench)
- **Embassy of Canada** to Belgium and Luxembourg (Avenue des Arts 58; tel. 32 2 741 06 11, www.canadainternational.gc.ca/belgium-belgique)
- **New Zealand Embassy, Brussels, Belgium** (Avenue des Nerviens 9; tel. 32 2 512 10 40; www.mfat.govt.nz/en/countries-and-regions/europe/belgium/new-zealand-embassy)
- **South Africa** (Rue Montoyer 19; tel. 32 2 285 44 00; www.southafrica.be)
- **British Embassy Brussels** (Avenue d'Auderghem 10; tel. 32 2 287 62 11; www.gov.uk/government/world/organisations/british-embassy-brussels)
- **U.S. Embassy in Belgium** (Boulevard du Régent 27; tel. 32 3 811 40 00; https://be.usembassy.gov)

CUSTOMS

Travelers to Belgium and the Netherlands must declare any cash over €10,000 as well as some cultural goods such as art and antiques, and cannot bring in or leave with animal or plant products. You can bring in up to one liter of spirits, two liters of wine, 16 liters of beer, 200 cigarettes, 250 grams of tobacco, and 50 cigars.

Recreation

BIKING

The Netherlands and Belgium are great for bikers, with a well-marked network of biking trails and many websites and maps to help you navigate them (for Flanders, https://cyclinginflanders.cc; for the Netherlands, www.hollandcyclingroutes.com). Most tourism boards have a map of nearby trails on their websites. Trails are traveled by casual bikers and commuters as well as long-distance bikers traveling between cities; you'll also find some mountain biking trails in southern Belgium. In both countries, a system called the *knooppunten* helps you navigate the biking routes, in which numbered points represent a junction that you need to head toward. Dedicated *knooppunten* apps help you follow the numbers in lieu of using a smart phone to navigate. Biking routes are also well-signed, directing you to nearby cities, major attractions, and tourist information. You can also look up directions using the Fietsnet website (www.fietsnet.be/routeplanner/default.aspx), which is better integrated with the biking network than Google Maps.

Larger cities like Amsterdam, Brussels, and Bruges are reasonably bike-friendly, but do require experience with urban biking, which is fast-paced enough that it may better to leave it to the professionals!

WATER SPORTS

In Belgian and Dutch canal cities such as Bruges, Utrecht, and Amsterdam, one of the best things to do is to take to the water in a boat or kayak. The Netherlands and Belgium also sit on the North Sea, and although Belgian and Dutch beaches aren't that sunny or warm, if you appreciate a good boardwalk, you'll enjoy walking along Scheveningen, also known for water sport activities like surfing, kitesurfing, and windsurfing.

SPECTATOR SPORTS

Soccer (football) is by far the biggest spectator sport in the region. If you're lucky enough to be in the Netherlands when the national football team is playing, be sure to pack something orange, as it will seem like everyone you meet is wearing it! Note that getting tickets for soccer games may be difficult upon short notice, but you may have just as much fun if you find a bar showing the game.

Festivals and Events

SPRING

DUTCH FLOWER PARADE

Netherlands Dune and Bulb Region; second or third Sat. in Apr.

In April, when the flower fields of Keukenhof bloom, a tulip-filled parade of floats made entirely of flowers traverses the Dune and Bulb region of the Netherlands, accompanied by live music.

KING'S DAY

Amsterdam, the Netherlands; Apr. 27

To celebrate the birthday of Dutch King Willem-Alexander, Dutchies deck themselves out in orange and roam the food and craft stands that have popped up all across the city. Concerts and parties are held in city parks as well as in bars and clubs.

PROCESSION OF THE HOLY BLOOD

Bruges, Belgium; May

This UNESCO-recognized parade accompanies the procession of the Relic of the Holy Blood around Bruges, which has taken place annually since the 14th century.

ROLLING KITCHENS

Amsterdam, the Netherlands; May

During the well-known Rolling Kitchens festival, hundreds of food trucks fill Westerpark, creating a convivial atmosphere.

CAT PARADE

Ypres, Belgium; second Sun. in May every three years

This quirky festival evolved from a macabre tradition, in which cats were thrown from the Cloth Hall Belfry for feline population control. Thankfully, this tradition ended in 1817, and now this festival celebrates our cat companions with a feline-themed parade.

SUMMER

DOUDOU

Mons, Belgium; late May/early June

Doudou is one of Belgium's most notable festivals. It's a religious event in which the

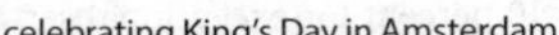

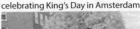

celebrating King's Day in Amsterdam

Shrine of St. Gertrude is carried around the town in a golden characters, and many in the procession and in attendance dress up in medieval costumes.

BRUSSELS FLOWER CARPET

Brussels, Belgium; every other Aug.

During this distinctive festival, a carpet-like tapestry of more than a million flowers is spread across Brussels's Grand Place, with concerts and entertainment staged throughout the city center.

FALL

OPEN MONUMENT DAY

Amsterdam, the Netherlands; Sept.

In the middle of September, more than 50 private buildings in Amsterdam open to the public, a great time to visit for history buffs.

WINTER

Christmas markets pop up all across the Netherlands and Belgium throughout December; the Christmas markets in Brussels, Bruges, Antwerp, and Ghent are particularly well known.

SINTERKLAAS

the Netherlands;

early Dec.

Rather than Christmas, the major winter holiday for the Flemish and Dutch is Sinterklaas, when Saint Nicholas is supposed to arrive in the region by boat from Spain. This is also a controversial holiday due to the presence of the controversial figure Zwarte Piet (Black Pete), whose costume typically includes blackface. A parade marks Saint Nicholas's arrival.

Food and Drink

EATING OUT

It's best to think of dining out in the Netherlands and Belgium on a spectrum, from casual to fine dining. At the most casual, you'll find carts where fried specialties like *frites* are served for customers who usually eat them in a nearby park or square. Above this, you'll find casual restaurants and bars that serve food and often drinks without much pretention. Fancier options include *rijsttafel* at one of Amsterdam's finest Indonesian spots or trying one of Belgium's many Michelin-starred restaurants.

Restaurants will generally be open between 11am-3pm for lunch, and 4pm-10pm for dinner, with peak hours between 6pm-8pm. Dinner is typically a lighter meal, with lunch traditionally being the main meal of the day, but with longer work days in busier, urban areas, many are finding it harder to find time for that bigger midday meal. Dining in the region is a leisurely activity, and how long diners linger at a table might come as a surprise to some tourists. Getting the attention of waiters can be a struggle, but the intention is not to be rude; they usually just want to leave your party to enjoy your meal in peace. Making eye contact or raising your hand slightly is typically enough to get the attention of a waiter.

It's not necessary to tip in Belgium or the Netherlands; 10 percent for exceptional service is appreciated.

Hours

Eating out is most often done during lunch and dinner, with brunch slowly catching on during weekends. Finding food prior to 8am is almost impossible without a hotel breakfast, and the running assumption is that people will have their breakfast at home or at their hotel. Most cafés for coffee open around 9am-10am at the earliest and may offer light pastries. Lunch begins around 11am and often is served until 3pm. Many restaurants in Belgium close after this time until dinner, but some may be open for *borrel* snacks in the Netherlands between 3pm-5pm. After 5pm-6pm, most restaurants will open for dinner and stay open until 9pm-10pm. Fried foods, especially fries, tend to dominate the late-night food options.

REGIONAL SPECIALTIES

Some well-known dishes and foods in the region include fresh fish and seafood, cheeses, *frites*, beer, chocolate, and, of course, waffles.

Belgium is the best place to seek out the best quality **chocolate** and **waffles.** Almost every Belgian city has at least a few great spots where these products are carefully made with care and integrity. In the Netherlands, you'll also find ***stroopwafels,*** soft waffles filled with caramel in between the layers.

Hearty **stews** can be found in both the Netherlands and Belgium; *paling in 't groen* is an eel stew made with herbs traditional to Antwerp while *waterzooi,* a stew made often with chicken or fish, traditionally comes from Ghent. Popular Belgian stews are often made with Trappist beers and include *hochepot (hutsepot),* which is made with oxtail, mutton, bacon, and vegetables.

Frites, or fries, are beloved in both Belgium and the Netherlands; which country makes the best ones is a longstanding argument. Traditionally served with mayo, there are countless *friteries* serving fries throughout the region; be sure to ask a local for the best pick. The same carts often serve other fried foods such as ***frikandel,*** a fried meat stick.

Seafood is particularly good in both countries; **mussels** are a well-known treat, found at sit-down restaurants all over Belgium, but especially close to the coast. A popular Belgian delicacy is the **shrimp croquette,** known as the *garnaalkroket* in Dutch. Even fishier, **herring** brined and eaten raw (or with onions) is a healthy snack that can be found at stands throughout both countries. You can also opt for a herring sandwich.

Bitterballen are fried beef balls traditionally served at Belgian and Dutch cafes during *borreltijd* (or the late afternoon) with drinks. Traditionally dipped in mustard, it's now possible to find vegan versions.

Cheeses are a major product of the Netherlands and Belgium, with most regions producing a local cheese. Dutch cheese are better known, especially Gouda, Beemster, and Edam. Lesser known are cheeses like graskaas, made with the first milk produced from spring, and other aged cheeses. Many of these cheese can be found at any cheese shop or supermarket in the region.

DIETARY RESTRICTIONS

Vegetarian visitors to the Netherlands and Belgium are having an easier time finding a tasty meal than in the past, with more and more Belgians and Dutch opting to reduce their meat intake. Most restaurants offer at least one vegetarian option, though meat or fish are integral to many traditional dishes. Vegans have more options than ever in Brussels, Bruges, Amsterdam, and other major cities in the region, but in smaller towns, finding food may be more difficult.

Those with deadly nut allergies will have a particularly difficult time in the Netherlands, where peanuts are a common ingredient in Indonesian fare, and many bars and cafés in both countries often serve nuts with drinks. Those with gluten allergies will also need to carefully screen restaurants to ensure zero contamination. In Amsterdam there's a dedicated website dedicated to celiac-friendly dining (www.glutenfreeamsterdam.com), but eating gluten-free will be much harder outside major cities. Restaurants are legally required to inform patrons of ingredients in case of food allergies, but functionally this policy can be very lax; many restaurants simply opt to inform patrons that it's not possible to accommodate allergies.

Accommodations

Accommodations in both the Netherlands are Belgium range from bed-and-breakfasts to Airbnbs, hostels for budget travelers, boutique hotels, and chains. Booking direct will often get you a reduced rate and potentially free breakfast.

If you're looking for something more atmospheric, many **B&Bs** and **boutique hotels** are housed in historic buildings, such as old canal houses or former churches. Bedandbreakfast.eu keeps a running list of bed-and-breakfasts within the region, but most owners prefer if you book direct by email or their website. When booking, note that historic buildings are unlikely to have an elevator and may have infamously narrow, winding stairs common in the region; inquire with the accommodation or carefully read reviews before booking if this will be an issue. Air-conditioning is also quite rare, except at at newly built or luxury hotels.

Another opportunity for an interesting stay in the Netherlands in particular are **canal boats** in Amsterdam, many of which have been converted into tourist accommodations.

Airbnb is becoming more regulated within the European Union, and it's possible these kind of rentals will become more restricted in the coming years. Today, many Airbnbs are also listed as bed-and-breakfasts or standalone apartments on other websites such as Booking.com.

Conduct and Customs

In the Netherlands, directness is valued: don't bother beating around the bush if you're looking for someone's help. Most people will respond in a straightforward manner, without necessarily bothering with niceties; this abruptness can be surprising for those who are used to a bit more conversation. It's typical for people to introduce themselves by their first name upon the first meeting. Formality has largely been done away with the Netherlands, even in work settings, with jeans being an evergreen staple of clothing. The concept of personal responsibility is key in Flemish and Dutch culture, where a client or customer is expected to have read the fine print. If something goes wrong, the first question is often whether you've followed the instructions to the T. If you haven't, expect to be told that nothing can be done!

Belgians can tend to come off a bit more polite, with formality being much more engrained in the languages; in conversations with strangers, formal tenses are often used. Though Belgians are known to be a bit hesitant to voice their true opinion until they get to know you well, Belgian culture is really quite gregarious, often considered warmer than the Dutch.

Health and Safety

EMERGENCY NUMBERS

In both countries, the emergency phone number is **112.** Operators speak English, Dutch, and French (in Belgium).

POLICE

Law enforcement in the Netherlands is provided by the National Police Corps (Korps Nationale Politie), which is broken down into regional units. The officers you're most likely to see on the streets are municipal enforcement officials (*handhavers*), who wear blue uniforms with a reflective black-and-white checkered strip across the chest. They are happy to help with directions as well as dealing with daily issues such as illegal car and bike parking and other offences. If you have been the victim of a crime in the Netherlands, report it to the police by calling 112; for a non-emergency police matter, make an appointment at the nearest police station.

In Belgium, police service is structured into federal and local forces. You'll see a municipal police presence on the ground in more crowded, touristy areas, to assist visitors with any questions they may have and to cut down on the petty crimes like pickpocketing that can occur in this part of town.

MEDICAL SERVICES

The standard of healthcare in both the Netherlands and Belgium is excellent, and there are few, if any, health issues specific to these countries for visitors to worry about. Medical treatment is not free for non-Dutch and Belgian visitors, so purchasing travel insurance may be advisable, but any fees occurred are generally reasonable. Hospitals and medical centers are generally as good as any in Western Europe. English-speaking doctors and medical staff are fairly common in both countries. For non-emergencies, rather than going to an emergency facility, ask your hotel or accommodation to call a doctor.

PHARMACIES

In the Netherlands, you'll find both drug stores (*drogist*) and pharmacies (*apotheek*); drug stores are generally open later and stock many essentials and conveniences, but don't usually staff pharmacists, while pharmacies are where you should go to have a prescription filled. Major drug store chains in the Netherlands include Etos and Kruidvat. In Belgium, pharmacies are widely available and called *apotheek* or *pharmacie*. They generally sell both prescription and over-the-counter medicines.

CRIME

The Netherlands and Belgium are safe destinations for travel, but crime can occur. The most common issue to affect tourists is pickpocketing and petty theft in crowded areas, such as Grand Place in Brussels, Dam Square in Amsterdam, and Bruges's Markt, and on public transportation. In order to avoid becoming a victim of pickpocketing, carry your camera or other valuables in a discreet case, pack an over-the-shoulder purse or bag that, unlike a backpack, is easy to keep a close eye on, and avoid carrying around large amounts of cash. As in any big city around the world, you should exercise common sense about which neighborhoods you're visiting and walking alone after dark.

Travel Tips

WHAT TO PACK

Bags and Luggage

Although a rolling suitcase is most practical for those traveling for a longer period, dragging one around on cobblestone streets isn't the most convenient, so you may want to opt to take a cab to your accommodation. For day trips, it might be worthwhile to bring a backpack to carry around with you that day. To minimize the risk of pickpocketing in crowded public places, bring a bag with a longer strap that can be tucked securely across your shoulder and under your arm, so you can keep an eye on it with minimal effort. A discreet camera bag is also ideal, as a larger tripod or flashy camera can attract the attention of petty thieves in some crowded squares.

Clothing

Both countries are quite rainy, so it's best to bring a waterproof (or water-resistant) jacket with you. Even in summer, Belgium and the Netherlands tend to be fairly chilly, especially in the evenings, so packing layers is advised; you'll want a thicker, semi-water-resistant coat for winter, as well as a hat to protect your ears against wind chill. For footwear, don't underestimate how much you'll be walking and opt for comfort; it's best to avoid heels, which can be problematic on cobblestone streets.

The dress, like the attitude in most of this region, is fairly informal. The style tends to classic and casual styles, rooted in clothing that's made well and fits well. "Dressing up" is usually reserved for an event like dinner at a high-end restaurant; jeans are extremely popular, often dressed up at for nicer occasions with a nice top or shirt. This also applies for houses of worship. That said, wearing sweatpants is still atypical. Travelers will find that both countries tend to prefer more somber colors (beyond a surprising love of animal print in the Netherlands!). Wearing more colorful styles will make you stand out.

Toiletries and Medication

Finding affordable, high-quality toiletries is fairly easy in Dutch and Belgian drugstores, pharmacies, and supermarkets. Getting specific medications, especially prescriptions, will be more difficult, so consider bringing your doctor's contact information or a copy of the prescription in case you need to refill the prescription, so a Dutch or Belgian pharmacist can find an equivalent.

Electronics

For your electronics, you'll need to bring a European converter for the Europlug, which has two round-pins and is rated for voltages up to 250 V and currents up to 2.5A. To save on space, you can purchase an adapter that allows multiple devices, including those that use a USB, to charge at once. If you plan to use your phone frequently to navigate or take photos, consider bringing a power bank.

LAUNDRY

If you need to do some laundry on your trip, laundromats are rarer than you might think outside major cities in the Netherlands and Belgium. They often have less-than-ideal hours, so if you have the opportunity to do laundry at your accommodation at a reasonable price, it might be worthwhile. Self-service laundromats often require cash. You can purchase laundry detergent at most supermarkets and late-night shops in the region.

MONEY

Currency

Both the Netherlands and Belgium use the euro. At the time of writing, $1 U.S. dollar was worth roughly €0.82. Banknotes begin at €5 euros and go up to €500, but many retailers do not accept bills larger than €100, so it's best to break your bills whenever possible and ensure that you have a change purse that

Budgeting

The following is a list of the average prices for a selection of common food and drink items.

- **Coffee:** €2-4
- **Beer:** €3-5
- **Cocktail:** €8-10
- **Sandwich:** €6-11
- **Lunch:** €8-15
- **Dinner:** 14-25
- **Hotel:** €100-150/night in peak season
- **Bike rental:** €10-15/day
- **Car rental:** €100/day
- **One-way train fare:** €10-20 Belgium: €8-10
- **Taxi:** €15-20 within city limits

can handle a larger number of coins. Coins come in €2 to €0.01 increments, though the €0.01 coin is not used in Netherlands, where prices will often be rounded up to the nearest 5 cent amount.

Debit and Credit Cards

The Netherlands is largely a cashless society, but foreign credit and debit cards don't always work as well, and in smaller towns and shops you might be asked to pay with cash. Belgium is a bit more flexible in terms of paying with cash or card payments, but outside of Bruges or Brussels, foreigners may have a harder time paying for items with non-European cards. It's best to carry some cash on you just in case your card doesn't work. Prior to leaving for your trip, it's best to ensure that you have at least one card that works with Mastercard or Visa, which are the most common payment systems available at shops as well as at ATMs. Discover, American Express, and other cards are rarer to be used beyond luxury stores that cater to tourists.

ATMs and Banks

In both countries, ATMs (or cash points) can be found throughout city centers. In the Netherlands, many branches of Albert Heijn (a popular grocery store) have an ATM available during their opening hours. It's typical to pay a small transaction fee for foreign cards. Exercise caution when using ATMs in the touristy areas of Amsterdam, Bruges, and Brussels, which are often the targets of scams.

COMMUNICATIONS

Cell Phones

The international dialing code for the Netherlands is +31; for Belgium, it's +32. You can look into a travel plan with your cell service provider that allows for international roaming and data, but often it's cheaper to buy a SIM upon your arrive in the EU. Just make sure your phone is compatible with GSM service and is unlocked. In Belgium and the Netherlands, 5G is now available, but the default is generally 4G. It's extremely rare to have limited phone service. WhatsApp, which operates on data rather than SMS, is the most popular app for messaging in the region.

Wi-Fi

Decent Wi-Fi is generally available and free in most public places in major cities in Belgium and the Netherlands, and even on some forms of public transportation. You might need to ask for a Wi-Fi code at restaurants or cafés.

Shipping and Postal Service

The Dutch Post (PostNL; www.postnl.nl) is privatized; travelers should look for book shops with the PostNL logo to send packages and postcards. Supermarkets such as Jumbo and Albert Heijn sell stamps and provide basic postal services, such as weighing letters, but you're better off going to Primera (www.primera.nl), a stationary store, which specializes in stamps, cards, and boxes. International stamps cost €1.50 per stamp; cards weighing over 20 grams may require more than one stamp. Mailboxes are well distributed across urban areas. Shipping packages can cost a pretty penny; sending a small package weighing less than 350 grams to the U.S. begins at around €11.

The Belgian Post (BPost; www.bpost.be) still has offices in major cities, where you can send postcards and buy stamps; you'll also find many postal points throughout city center, where you can send packages. Post offices are generally open 10am-6pm with a pause for lunch Mon.-Sat. Sending a postcard to the U.S. costs €1.77; shipping small packages starts at €8.70.

OPENING HOURS

In the Netherlands, businesses tend to have more fairly steady 9am-5pm business hours, though many businesses stay open late on Thursdays (until 7-8pm) and closures on Mondays are common. Churches are usually closed for visits on Sundays during services.

Restaurants and cafés generally do not open early in either country; finding coffee before 8am can be a struggle. Many restaurants often open around 11am for lunch. In between lunch and dinner, a pause in service is common, meaning that between 3pm-5pm only snacks (*borrel*) may be available. Restaurants that cater mostly to the dinner crowd open around 4pm and close around 10pm. Bars often close late, but the regulations on how late nightlife can be open depends on the city.

In Belgium, opening hours really depend on the establishment. Some businesses opt to open during standard business 9am-5pm hours during peak season and for a few hours in off-peak season. It's also common for Belgians to pause for an hour for lunch. It's safe to assume that most businesses are open 10am-noon and 2pm-5pm. Closures on Mondays and Tuesdays are common in Belgian cities, and travelers are likely to have issues finding activities and foods on these days. During off-season (January), many businesses are outright closed in Bruges for a vacation month. It's best to check an attraction's hours to ensure that you can visit.

Public Holidays

Both the Netherlands and Belgium have a few holidays that revolve around Easter, whose dates change each year, but fall sometime in March or April. In addition to the holidays listed below, hours in both countries might be limited on Sinterklaas (Dec. 5), Boxing Day (Dec. 26), and New Year's Eve (Dec. 31).

THE NETHERLANDS

- **January 1:** New Year's Day
- **March or April:** The Dutch traditionally get three days off around Easter, Good Friday, Easter Sunday, and Easter Monday
- **April 27:** King's Day
- **May 5:** Liberation Day
- **40 days after Easter:** Ascension Day
- **7 weeks after Easter:** Pentecost
- **December 25-26:** Christmas (the Dutch have two days of Christmas, Eerste Kerstdag and Tweede Kerstag, or First Christmas Day and Second Christmas Day)

BELGIUM

- **January 1:** New Year's Day
- **March or April:** Easter Monday
- **May 1:** Labor Day
- **39 days after Easter:** Ascension
- **Monday after Pentecost:** Pentecost Monday
- **July 21:** Belgium National Day
- **August 15:** Assumption Day
- **November 1:** All Saints' Day
- **November 11:** Armistice Day
- **December 25:** Christmas Day

WEIGHTS AND MEASURES

The Netherlands and Belgium use the **metric system. Celsius** is used to measure temperature, and both countries are on **Central European Time.**

TOURIST INFORMATION

Tourist offices are generally located in the center of every city center, just off major squares. They are generally well signed, and provide useful, free context and information in many languages, including English.

Free **maps** can be acquired at tourist information offices; if you're looking for something more specific, like a regional cycling map, try a local bookstore. Though maps generally provide good information for historic city centers, most will not be as helpful for less visited neighborhoods on the outskirts.

Traveler Advice

OPPORTUNITIES FOR STUDY AND EMPLOYMENT

Travelers interested in working in the Netherlands and Belgium will need to apply for a visa at their embassy. There is a strong demand for well-educated English-speaking professionals in both countries, but any employer must prove that they were unable to find a more qualified European candidate first, which can be a steep burden of proof. Young professionals might want to look into internships at international institutions and companies, such as with the UN in in the Hague; internships are a common way for young professionals to be offered a job within the Benelux region. Many international companies have offices in the Netherlands and Belgium, making it possible for employees to transfer to either country.

Students will find many study abroad opportunities at excellent Belgian and Dutch universities, with instruction often provided in in English. University of Amsterdam, TU Delft, Leiden University, Erasmus University, Utrecht University, KU Leuven, and Ghent University are the most famous universities in the region.

TRAVELING WITH CHILDREN

Both the Netherlands and Belgium are very child-friendly. Children are often welcome in spaces that might not be traditionally thought of as family-oriented, including cafés that serve alcohol. Children receive discounts, if not free admission, to most attractions, public transportation, and many events in both countries. Many attractions will offer a family pack that provides a good value. Though both countries are full of museums, parks, and attractions that cater specifically to kids, they're also likely to be entranced by the medieval cityscape and chocolate in Bruges, the fun atmosphere of Scheveningen Beach near the Hague, the bright colors of the Keukenhof Gardens, the windmills of Zaanse Schans, the cheese markets of Alkmaar, and the castles and canals of cities like Utrecht. Parents will find both countries particularly nice to travel in.

ACCESS FOR TRAVELERS WITH DISABILITIES

The cobblestone streets that lend charm to the Netherlands and Belgium can make life for those with wheelchairs and mobility issues particularly difficult. Accessibility in the region is unfortunately not standardized; every province has their own public transit system and many museums and hotels have their own rules, which makes it tedious to plan ahead. Older buildings are unlikely to be friendly to people with disabilities, and the toilet at some popular restaurants is in the basement, down a narrow staircase.

Many pedestrian crossings are made to be friendly to visually impaired people, and within stations, tracks are often fitted with tactile paving. Most train stations have a ramp to allow for wheelchair access. Smaller stations may not be accessible, though. There are a small number of wheelchair-accessible taxis in most cities, but these will need to be reserved in advance.

Despite all these difficulties, regional tourism boards in Belgium have taken special steps to provide information for travelers with disabilities.

- Brussels: https://handy.brussels/en
- Wallonia: https://walloniabelgiumtourism.co.uk/en-gb/3/i-am/travelling-with-reduced-mobility
- Flanders: www.visitflanders.com/en/accessibility

In the Netherlands, www.accessibletravelnl.com is a private website run by volunteers providing up-to-date information about accessible travel in the Netherlands.

Travelers with disabilities can request assistance with the Dutch (www.ns.nl/en/travel-information/traveling-with-a-disability/ns-travel-assistance.html) and Belgian (www.belgiantrain.be/en/travel-info/prepare-for-your-journey/assistance-reduced-mobility) train services, who will provide a staff member to help people who use wheelchairs or mobility scooters disembark from the trains. This service is free but needs to be reserved in advance. These services are also available at all major Belgian and Dutch airports.

WOMEN TRAVELING ALONE

The Netherlands and Belgium are good destinations for solo female travelers. Although incidents of sexual assault and harassment do certainly occur, as they do everywhere, both countries have a good infrastructure to allow for independent travel; Amsterdam in particular has a female-only hostel, and many hostels in the region will offer same-sex dorms. Street harassment is rare, and usually a polite *nee* ("no") works well enough to stop any unwanted attention. It's a good idea to ensure that your accommodation has good access to public transportation to minimize walking late at night.

Female solo travelers might also want to consider opting for group activities to feel more comfortable, but generally, people of both genders are very protective as well as friendly toward solo female travelers in both countries. It's not uncommon to be invited to sit with a larger group or couple if you are sitting alone for a longer period at a café or bar, especially later at night. Many bars in Holland have a codeword where women can seek help anonymously, using the term Angel Shot or Angela to get a quick escape if they do not feel safe.

SENIOR TRAVELERS

Both countries are quite friendly to senior travelers as a whole, though the many cobblestones and tiny staircases can be an issue. It's best to check if your hotel has an elevator before booking. When taking a train, you might want to consider booking first class, especially while traveling during rush hour, to ensure that you can sit down for longer journeys. For traveling in the larger region, renting a car might be easier, reducing the amount of walking required. Many seniors enjoy canal cruises through both Bruges and Amsterdam, a scenic and convenient way to travel the region.

Senior discounts aren't very common in the Netherlands, but in Belgium, seniors can enjoy discounts on items from train tickets to museum entry.

LGBTQ+ TRAVELERS

Both Belgium and the Netherlands are famously tolerant of the LGBTQ+ community, and same-sex couples should not have any concerns about showing public affection. The Netherlands in particular was the first country in the world to legalize same-sex marriage; the boisterous Amsterdam Pride (https://pride.amsterdam), which the entire city comes out to celebrate, is a good indication of how supportive they country is of LGBTQ+ rights. When isolated homophobic incidents occur, they are taken very seriously by the Dutch police. The Dutch police has a special division specializing in harassment and discrimination against the LGBTQ+ community called the Roze in Blauw. LGBTQ+ travelers in Amsterdam can ask for information at the **Pink Point** (Westermarkt 9; 10am-6pm Mon.-Sat., noon-6pm Sun.; tel. 020 428 10 70; www.pinkpoint.nl) staffed by the LGBTQ+ community, for the LGBTQ+ community.

TRAVELERS OF COLOR

The Netherlands' colonization of Indonesia and Suriname, and Belgium's in the Congo, has left a legacy of immigration from these former colonies. This, along with more recent immigration from North Africa, Turkey, and the Middle East, means that travelers of color might be surprised by the diversity within larger cities like Brussels, Amsterdam, the Hague, and Rotterdam. In Amsterdam, for example, recent demographic data showed the population was 49 percent Dutch and 50 percent foreign born.

More rural regions, however, are significantly less diverse, and even in the larger cites, travelers of color may feel out of place. Harmful stereotypes focusing on "exoticness" are still an issue in both countries. The Dutch have a term, *allochtoon,* that refers to Dutch people who have "recently" come from another country and almost exclusively is applied to POC, and there is a lot of emphasis on a person's "migration background." Instances of overt hostility and violence are rare, but microaggressions are common, and people of color have been shown to be more likely to be scrutinized by the police. There have been some improvements in recent years in acknowledging the experience of POC, from grappling with the exploitative history of colonialism to questioning traditions like Zwarte Piet (Black Pete), but more needs to be done. Dutch and Belgians are still quite quick to say that "they don't see color." That said, most of the Black travelers and expats from the U.S. to this region that I have spoken to have said that compared to the U.S., they feel safer overall, and have not felt physically threatened by racism. Websites like **Travel Noire** (http://tncityguides.com) often have articles on the experiences of Black travelers in Belgium and the Netherlands.

Islamophobia has unfortunately been on the rise for some years in both countries, and travelers of perceived Middle Eastern descent may run into issues. In particular, women who wear a hijab or religious hair coverings might be stared at or singled out for comments. Again, though, violence is rare.

Resources

Glossary

DUTCH

apotheek: pharmacy

bakfiets: a larger bike with a large bucket-like section in the front, which can be used to carry everything from young kids to groceries

bitterballen: fried Dutch balls made with beef that are dipped in mustard, often ordered with a beer

borrels: drinks, similar to happy hour, typically in the late afternoon

BTW: value-added tax (VAT)

chocolatier: a chocolate maker that specializes in artisanal chocolate

coffeeshop: an establishment in the Netherlands that sells marijuana, not coffee

Delftware: a specific kind of traditional pottery modeled on Chinese earthenware traditionally created in Delft, typically with blue and white colors

drop: a kind of licorice

frites: the Dutch word for fries (sometimes called *patat* in Northern Belgium). Frites in Belgium and the Netherlands are always served warm, often with a side of mayo or *fritessaus* ("frites sauce": a leaner version of mayo without eggs) from dedicated frites stands. (In French: *patate*)

garnaalkroketten: a fried croquette filled with shrimp, generally from the North Sea

gezellig/gezeligheid: cozy, comfortable, and intimate

gluhkriek: a fruit beer with spices that is meant to be warmed up in winter

glüwein: a mulled wine popular in winter that is warmed up with red wine (typically), cloves, cinnamon, oranges, and often anise

hagelslag: chocolate sprinkles enjoyed on toast with butter, a popular midday snack and breakfast favorite for children

hof: courtyard

hofje (NL)/godshuizen: a historic building with a courtyard inside that was used for housing the poor.

hutspot: a traditional and hearty Dutch dish made with potatoes, carrots, and onions invented during the Eighty Years' War

jenever: a Dutch and Belgian alcoholic drink made from juniper berries that predates gin, often drank in a tulip-shaped glass

kaaskoppen: a playful name for the Dutch rooted in their love of cheese—and their use of buckets used for cheese as hats notably in one battle in Alkmaar

knooppunten: junction points in the massive Dutch bike network with numbers that allow bikers to more easily follow bike routes without constantly checking a map

koffie verkeerd: literally translated as "wrong coffee"; a cup of coffee with foamed milk added to the top. A delicious Dutch take on the latte.

kopstoot: Meaning headbutt, this Dutch tradition at bars means that you order a jenever glass, often filled to the top, before sipping the top off the jenever before having the chaser of the beer once you're done with the jenever.

kruidenbitters: spiced liquor typically with the base of jenever, where anise and other traditional spices are added for flavor

markt: market

oliebol: a fried dough ball similar to a beignet,

traditionally consumed close to Christmas and New Year's Eve, often with raisins inside or powdered sugar on top

oranjebitter: an orange liquor traditionally made of oranges made in honor of the Dutch royal family, traditional drank during King's Day in the Netherlands

pepernoten: a seasonal miniature cookie traditionally eaten in winter, made with speculoos or a traditional seasoning similar to gingerbread

polder: a low-lying landscape that has generally been reclaimed from the sea using dykes

rendang: Indonesian-style beef slow-cooked in coconut milk and spices

rijsttafel: "rice table," or an Indonesian meal popularized by the Dutch during the colonization of Indonesia, made of elaborate miniature plates that allow the taster to sample many different dishes, both sweet and savory, along with a large amount of rice

Sinterklaas: A holiday in December celebrated in the Netherlands and Belgium focused on Sinterklaas, a Dutch saint based on to Saint Nicholas, with a controversial character (Zwarte Piet). The arrival of Sinterklaas is an important even in both countries. During Sinterklaas, children receive presents.

sluis: a lock (for a canal)

stamppot: a hearty Dutch dish made of mashed potatoes, often served with kale and sausage

straat: street

stroopwafel: a popular sweet made up of two thin waffles with a thin caramel layer in between

tempo doeloe: the old times

toko: the Indonesian word for shop or a shop that primarily sells Asian or Surinamese items or food items

tripel: "triple"; typically refers to a strong pale ale beer made with three times the amount of malt, resulting in a higher alcohol percentage (9 percent)

verse muntthee: fresh mint tea in Dutch, or tea made with freshly cut mint leaves dunked directly into the water. A favorite in winter.

V.O.C.: The abbreviation in Dutch for the Dutch East India Company, a company that was a major trade company during the 17th century that was partially funded by the Dutch government. The Dutch East India company was best known for spices and coffee, but also traded in enslaved people.

vrijmarkt: an open-air market where individuals can sell their goods without having to pay a fee, which takes place on King's Day in the Netherlands

witbier: a white beer or wheat beer (similar to the weißbier in Germany) with a hazy appearance and often with a light citrusy flavor. Hoegaarden Brewery is best known for this style globally.

Zinnekes: a word from Brussels dialect referring to Brussels locals

FRENCH

abbaye: abbey or a monastery where Christian monks and nuns lived and worked

art nouveau: An art and architectural moment with roots in Brussels from the turn of the 19th century, wherein artists created forms and artworks inspired by the curvatures of natural elements such as butterflies and flowers. Art nouveau is best known for its use of iron and glass.

beguinage: an architectural complex, often with a chapel and door to separate the complex from the street ,where religious women that belonged to commune-like groups similar to nuns worked and lived during medieval times.

bois: "woods"; this is common within park names in Belgium

Bruxellois: French term for Brussels residents

carbonnade: a word that refers to a cut of meat, often a shoulder of beef. Carbonnade à la Flamande is a popular slow-cooked beef stew, often made with the addition of beer and onions.

centrale: central

chemin: a route, path, or trajectory

croquettes: a fried and breaded snack often made with a vegetable or meat filling. Known as a *kroket* in Dutch.

fin-de-siècle: "end of the century"; often

refers to the end of the 19th century. Often referred to the Belle Epoque (the Beautiful Epoch) in France. This was a critical time for the design world due to innovations in symbolism, architecture, and philosophy.

framboise: "raspberry"; can also refer to a Belgian-style lambic beer made with raspberries, which is inspired by the tradition of using sour cherries in creating sour beers

frites: french fries

friterie: a shop that specializes in fried food items such as frites

galerie: "gallery"; refers to an enclosed shopping arcade, often dating back to the 19th century

gueze: a sour beer made of lambic beers aged 1-3 years, traditionally produced in Brussels and its surroundings

moules-frites: mussels with fries, a classic Belgian dish

midi: often means noon, but can also mean south directionally

musée: museum

nord: north

ouest: west

parc: park

rue: street

sentier: a smaller path or trail

Dutch Phrasebook

Dutch, or Nederlands, is a Germanic language closely related to English and German. There's a heavy overlap between Dutch and English words. Many American English words have Dutch origins, including *stoop* and *cookie*. However, this means that it's quite easy to mispronounce words without realizing it.

The Dutch language here includes both Dutch as spoken in the Netherlands and Dutch as spoken in Northern Belgium and some neighborhoods of Brussels (sometimes referred to as Flemish). To get a sense of the differences between Dutch spoken in the Netherlands versus Dutch spoken in Belgium, imagine the difference between American and British English. There are some significant differences, enough that native speakers of Dutch in the Netherlands often watch Flemish shows with subtitles. In addition, there are many different accents and dialects within this region, so pronunciation can vary widely between even cities, enough that two speakers of one dialect might not understand each other. Luckily, there's a standardized version of Dutch to help ensure that everyone can communicate with each other. In Belgium, Dutch tends to be more formal, while in the Netherlands, it's more common to speak more informally to strangers; however the entire guide assumes the formal (polite) tense in Dutch.

Some words and terms differ notably between the Netherlands and Belgium, but the basis for the language and its grammar is the same. Luckily, the Dutch and Belgians speak great English, so don't fret; a simple "Dankjewel" from visitors to the Netherlands and Dutch-speaking parts of Belgium is appreciated. As a note, this guide combines Dutch phrases across Belgium and the Netherlands, so if **NL** is indicated, it is more often used in the Netherlands rather than Belgium.

PRONUNCIATION

The hardest sounds in Dutch tend to be the vowels, some of which have no English equivalent, and the guttural "sch" and hard "g" sounds, both of which require a lot of phlegm. A Belgian once told me that the secret to making a convincing soft "g" (the Belgian and southern Dutch way of pronouncing the "g" sound) is to pretend that you are making a short cat hiss. Another tricky sound is the letter "w," which sounds closer to a "v." "R" is mostly similar to English, but it can sound more rolled in some dialects.

Dutch vowels can be very tricky, especially the "ui" and the "uu" sounds. These do not have an English equivalent, but if you place your tongue on the top of your palate while rounding your lips, you're a step closer to getting both the sounds right.

Vowels

a pronounced "a" as in "ah" or "father"
e pronounced "e" as in "egg"
ee pronounced "e" as in "Easter"
i pronounced "i" as in the i in "English"
o pronounced "aw" as in "Oh!"
u pronounced like the "u/ir" sound in "dirt"
ui pronounced "ow," with lips rounded and tongue touching the top of the palate
oo pronounced "oh" as in "moat"
uu pronounced "ew," with lips rounded and tongue touching the top of the palate
ei/ij pronounced "i" as in "eye"

Consonants

Most consonants are fairly similar to English, but the hard "g" and "sch" can take some practice to say. Syllables in Dutch generally work in a similar way to English, so even if you encounter a longer word that looks impossible, go through it syllable-by-syllable.

sch pronounced "s" with a guttural "ch" sound, almost like the "sk" in "skip"
ch/g a guttural sound similar to "ch" in Hebrew, or almost like coughing up phlegm. In Belgium, the "g" is much softer and is pronounced closer to an "h" (imagine a cat hissing; try to shorten this hissing sound until you make a short h-sound closer to a sharp exhale).
w pronounced v as in "Venus"
r pronounced as a short rolled r sound
j pronounced as the y sound
't a habit of old Dutch short for *het*

ESSENTIAL PHRASES

Hi Hoi
Hello Hallo
Good morning Goedemorgen
Good afternoon Goedenmiddag
Good evening Goedenavond
Good night Welterusten
Goodbye Tot ziens/Doei (NL)/Dag (BE)
Nice to meet you Aangenaam
Please Alstublieft
Excuse me Pardon
Thank you Dankjewel/Dank u wel/Bedankt
You're welcome Alstublieft
What's your name? Wat is uw naam?
My name is... Mijn naam is…
Where are you from? Waar komt u vandaan?
I am from... Ik kom uit…
Do you speak English? Spreekt u Engels?
I do not speak Dutch. Ik spreek geen Nederlands.
I do not understand. Ik begrijp het niet.
Yes Ja
No Nee
Where are the restrooms? Waar is het toilet?
Can you take my/our photo? Kan u een foto van mij/van ons maken?
Can you help me? Kan je me helpen?

TRANSPORTATION/ DIRECTIONS

Where is...? Waar is…?
How far is...? Hoe ver is…?
bus station het busstation
train station het treinstation
airport de luchthaven
Where is the ticket office? Waar is het loket?
Is there a bus to...? Is er een bus naar…?
Does this bus go to...? Gaat deze bus naar…?
What time does the bus/train leave? Wanneer vertrekt de bus/trein?
What time does the bus/train arrive? Wanneer komt de bus/trein aan?
I would like to look at the train/bus timetable. Ik wil het schema zien.
I would like to purchase a ticket to... Ik wil een enkele naar…

SHOPPING

money geld

cash contant geld
credit card kredietkaart
How much does it cost? Hoeveel kost dit?
I'm just looking. Ik kijk rond/Ik kijk gewoon.
It's too expensive. Het is te duur.

RESTAURANTS

Can I make a reservation for one/two? Kan ik een/twee reserveren?
The menu, please. Het menu/de menukaart alstublieft.
Do you have a menu in English? Heeft u een menu in het Engels?
I'm a vegetarian/vegan. Ik ben vegetarisch/veganistisch.
I would like... Ik wil graag...
The bill, please. De rekening alstublieft.
breakfast ontbijt
lunch lunch
dinner diner
snack borrel/snack
water water
coffee koffie
tea thee
beer bier
wine wijn
gluten-free glutenvrij

HEALTH

drugstore/pharmacy drogisterij/apotheek
medicine medicijn
hospital ziekenhuis
It hurts here. Het doet hier pijn.
I have a fever. Ik heb koorts.
I feel nauseated. Ik voel me misselijk.
I am allergic. Ik ben allergisch.
I need a doctor. Ik heb een dokter nodig.
I am diabetic. Ik ben diabetisch.
I am pregnant. Ik ben zwanger.
blood type bloedtype

NUMBERS

0 nul
1 een
2 twee
3 drie
4 vier
5 vijf
6 zes
7 zeven
8 acht
9 negen
10 tien
11 elf
12 twaalf
13 dertien
14 veertien
15 vijftien
16 zestien
17 zeventien
18 achttien
19 negentien
20 twintig
21 eenentwintig
30 dertig
40 veertig
50 vijftig
60 zestig
70 zeventig
80 tachtig
90 negentig
100 honderd
200 tweehonderd
500 vijfhonderd
1,000 duizend
10,000 tienduizend
1,000,000 een miljoen

TIME

In Dutch, to say "It's 3:30," you say, "It's half four" (*half vier*), short for halfway to 4. This can create confusion for some English speakers who might assume that the speaker means 4:30pm. Similarly, if someone tells that you that it's a quarter past three (*kwart over drie*), it means that the time is 3:15pm, while a quarter before four (*kwart voor vier*) means that it's 3:45pm. With Dutch time, you often are adding and subtracting time. For instance, *vijf over half vier* (five over half four) would mean that it's five minutes past 3:30pm, or 3:35pm (or 25 minutes to go until 4pm). Be careful to verify times before agreeing to appointments!

It's typical to use the 24-hour system with written Dutch (6pm is equivalent to 18:00), but in spoken conversation, the speaker usually will just say six, often clarifying the time of the day (six in the evening).

What time is it? Hoe laat is het?
It's 1am/3pm. Het is één uur/drie uur.
morning ochtend
afternoon middag
evening avond
night nacht
yesterday gisteren
today vandaag
tomorrow morgen
now nu

DAYS AND MONTHS

week week
month maand
year jaar
Monday maandag
Tuesday dinsdag
Wednesday woensdag
Thursday donderdag
Friday vrijdag
Saturday zaterdag
Sunday zondag
January januari
February februari
March maart
April april
May mei
June juni
July juli
August augustus
September september
October oktober
November november
December december

French Phrasebook

French is primarily used in Belgium, especially Brussels and Wallonia, along with several other languages—most websites will have information in three or four languages. If you can remember some of your high school French, it might be useful: French as spoken in Belgium is very close to standard French, with the exception of counting higher numbers and a handful of terms. Even if your French is not particularly good, a polite *Bonjour* and *Merci* are always appreciated by native French speakers. Many Belgian native French speakers are bilingual in English at a minimum, if not knowledgeable in more languages, so many people will switch to English at the first sign of struggling, though this is less common farther south in Wallonia. There is also a generational difference, with younger Belgians tending to be more comfortable with English.

PRONUNCIATION

French words are not pronounced the same way as they would be in English, and there are more sounds in French than there are letters in the Roman alphabet. But there is a consistency within the language, and once you learn the ways in which individual letters should be said and how they can be combined to make new sounds, you won't encounter too many surprises. In general, you pronounce all of a word's syllables as they appear (this is not a cast-iron rule as it is in Spanish, say, but much more the case than it is in English). Below is a general guide to how different letters are pronounced.

Vowels

a tends to be pronounced fairly short and sharp, somewhere between how it appears in "cat" and "bar." The sharpness is emphasized when it has a grave accent (à). It is also frequently seen with a circumflex (â), but this doesn't make much of a difference to how it is pronounced.

au pronounced like the "o" sound in the British word "no." This is the same sound as you'd have with bureau in English or eau (*water*) in French.

e usually pronounced short and sharp, like in "bet." It can also appear at the end of a word, often signifying the word is feminine. In this case, the "e" is left silent, but the final consonant becomes harder. When "e" appears with an acute accent (é), it means it should be pronounced more like in "way." This is the case if it appears at the end of a word as well, when it can indicate the past participle or adjective form of the verb. A grave accent or circumflex (è or ê) emphasizes the shortness, again like bet.

i generally pronounced like "ee", as in "keep"

o pronounced either as a close "o" sound as in "no," or as an open sound as in "rot." The former often appears with a circumflex (ô), the latter in syllables that end with a consonant, and always if the syllable ends in a double consonant.

oi pronounced usually like a shortened version of the "aw" sound in the English word "squawk"

ou pronounced like the "oo" noise in the middle of the English word "food"

u pronounced closest to the end of the English word "do"; there is not a true equivalent sound in English. You need to purse your lips tightly to pronounce it.

Consonants

c pronounced "s" before "e," "I," or "y," pronounced "k" before "a," "o," or "u"

ç always pronounced "s" no matter what comes after it

ch "sh," as in shut

g before "e," "I," or "y," is pronounced soft, like the "g" in the word "message," or sometimes harder, as in "gurgle"

h not pronounced in French and is mostly treated as though it doesn't exist. *L'hôtel* (the hotel), for example, would be pronounced *l'ôtel.*

j pronounced like the "g" in the English word "message" wherever it appears

ll mostly pronounced as an "ee" sound, though there are a couple of dozen words where this isn't the case and it's pronounced "l"—of these ville or village, meaning town or village are the ones you're most likely to encounter. It can also be pronounced like the "y" in "why," if preceded by two or more vowels.

qu mostly pronounced as a "k" sound, and only occasionally as a "kw" sound as it is in English, usually on Latinate words

r a particularly tricky one to get perfect, not having an easy equivalent in English—it's probably most like the "ch" at the end of "loch" being mostly pronounced in the throat. It also has the ghost of a hard "r" in it, however. At the same time, don't sweat it too much: Pronouncing it the English way, most people will get what you mean.

s mostly pronounced in the same way as it is in English. However, when it appears at the end of a word making it plural, it's not pronounced, unless the word following begins in a vowel.

th pronounced like a hard "t."

w not a common letter in French apart from in imported words, with "le site Web," or the neologism "wifi" being among the most likely ones you'll encounter. In those cases, it's pronounced just like it is in English. Otherwise, the "w" sound is made at the beginning of words with an "ou," as in "oui," meaning "yes."

Tips

As much as reading how to speak the language can help, there's no substitute for time spent listening to it. Before you travel to Belgium, it can be worth watching a few Belgian or French films with subtitles, just to train your ear to the different sounds. If you're feeling particularly virtuous, try watching the French films with French subtitles, helping you to divide the sounds into different words. This is especially useful if you already know the film well in English.

A final piece of advice: Don't be afraid to really go for it! You know that exaggerated

French accent you might put on when doing an impression of a French person speaking English? Use that when you speak French. It won't sound half as silly to the locals as you trying to pronounce their language in your own accent. Of course, make sure you are actually speaking French when you do this: saying "Pleaze caan ah 'ave ze bill," is not going to help anyone's comprehension. At least in Belgium, it's better to speak in English and stick to a polite *Merci* if that's all you remember! If that's not working, pointing along with a *S'il vous plait* should suffice, and a translation app on your phone will save you a lot of frustration.

Note: All the phrases here are formulated in the formal or polite tense.

ESSENTIAL PHRASES

Hi Salut
Hello/Good morning Bonjour
Good evening Bonsoir
Good night Bonne nuit
Goodbye Au revoir
Nice to meet you. Enchanté(e).
Please S'il vous plaît
Excuse me Excusez-moi
Thank you (very much) Merci (beaucoup)
You're welcome De rien
What's your name? Comment vous-appelez vous?
My name is... Je m'appelle...
Where are you from? D'où venez-vous?
I am from... Je suis de...
Do you speak English? Parlez-vous anglais?
I do not speak French. Je ne parle pas français.
I do not understand. Je ne comprends pas.
Yes Oui
No Non
Where are the restrooms? Où sont les toilettes?
Can you take my/our photo? Pouvez-vous prendre ma/notre photo?
Can you help me? Pouvez-vous m'aider?

TRANSPORTATION/ DIRECTIONS

Where is...? Où est...?
How far is...? À quelle distance est...?
bus station la gare de bus
train station la gare
airport l'aéroport
Where is the ticket office? Où est la billetterie?
Is there a bus to...? Est-ce qu'il y a un bus pour...?
Does this bus go to...? Est-ce que ce bus va à ...?
What time does the bus/train leave/ arrive? A quelle heure s'en va/arrive le bus/train?
I would like to look at the timetable. J'aimerais voir le calendrier / Je voudrais voir le calendrier .
I would like to purchase a ticket to... J'aimerais acheter un billet pour...

SHOPPING

money l'argent
credit card la carte de crédit
How much does it cost? Combien ça coute? / Combien cela coute-t-il?
I'm just looking. Je ne fais que regarder. / Je regarde seulement.
It's too expensive. C'est trop cher.

RESTAURANTS

Can I make a reservation for one/ two? Puis-je faire une réservation pour un(e)/deux?
The menu, please. Le menu, s'il vous plaît.
Do you have a menu in English? Avez-vous un menu en anglais?
I'm a vegetarian/vegan. Je suis végétarien/vegan.
I would like... Je voudrais...
The bill, please. L'addition, s'il vous plaît.
breakfast le petit déjeuner
lunch le dîner
dinner le souper
water l'eau
coffee le café
tea le thé

beer la bière
wine le vin
gluten-free sans gluten

HEALTH

drugstore/pharmacy pharmacie
medicine médicament
hospital l'hôpital
It hurts here. J'ai mal ici.
I have a fever. J'ai de la fièvre.
I feel nauseated. Je me sens nauséeux.
I am allergic. Je suis allergique.
I need a doctor. J'ai besoin de voir un médecin.
I am diabetic. Je suis diabétique.
I am pregnant. Je suis enceinte.
blood type group sanguin

NUMBERS

0 zéro
1 un
2 deux
3 trois
4 quatre
5 cinq
6 six
7 sept
8 huit
9 neuf
10 dix
11 onze
12 douze
13 treize
14 quatorze
15 quinze
16 seize
17 dix-sept
18 dix-huit
19 dix-neuf
20 vingt
21 vingt et un
30 trente
40 quarante
50 cinquante
60 soixante
70 septante
80 quatre-vingt
90 nonante
100 cent
200 deux cents
500 cinq cents
1,000 mille
10,000 dix mille
1,000,000 un million

TIME

What time is it? Quelle heure est-il?
It's 1am/3pm. Il est une heure du matin/Il est 15 heures.
morning matin
afternoon après-midi
evening soir
night nuit
yesterday hier
today aujourd'hui
tomorrow demain
now maintenant

DAYS AND MONTHS

week semaine
month mois
year an
Monday lundi
Tuesday mardi
Wednesday mercredi
Thursday jeudi
Friday vendredi
Saturday samedi
Sunday dimanche
January janvier
February février
March mars
April avril
May mai
June juin
July juillet
August août
September septembre
October octobre
November novembre
December décembre

Suggested Reading

FICTION

The Coffee Trader by David Liss (2004). A historical fiction novel set in 17th-century Amsterdam about a Jewish trader who gets involved in the developing market of a new commodity: coffee.

The Fault in Our Stars by John Green (2014). In this extremely successful young adult novel, a cancer patient travels to Amsterdam to meet her favorite author.

King Ottokar's Seuptre by Hergé (1939). Filled with classic Belgian humor, this comic features the iconic Tintin, a Belgian reporter and adventurer, who gets embroiled in a plot to steal a scepter from a king.

The Lady and the Unicorn by Tracy Chevalier (2004). This historical fiction novel dives deep into Brussels's 15th-century weaving industry, telling the story of the creation of one of the best-known medieval tapestries.

The Miniaturist by Jessie Burton (2014). A fictional story of a young woman who discovers a magical dollhouse in 17th-century Amsterdam.

The Sorrow of Belgium by Hugo Claus (1983). A novel set in the 1930s focusing on the experience of a Flemish child during World War II.

Tulip Fever by Deborah Moggach (1999). This romance novel is set in the middle of 17th-century "tulip mania," when the inhabitants of Amsterdam went to crazy lengths and expense to obtain rare tulip varietals.

NONFICTION

Amsterdam Slavery Heritage Guide by Dienke Hondius, Nancy Jouwe, Dineke Stam, Annemarie de Wildt, and Jennifer Tosch (2014). A guide to historical buildings in Amsterdam exploring Black history, both in plain sight and beyond the facades. Part of The Vrije Universiteit Amsterdam's Mapping Slavery Project.

Amsterdam: A History of the World's Most Liberal City by Russell Shorto (2013). This not-so-brief history covers Amsterdam from its humble roots to thriving city, through the lens of the liberalism that has categorized it since the 16th century.

Anne Frank: The Diary of a Young Girl by Anne Frank (1947). This heart-wrenching diary of a Jewish teen living in hiding during the Nazi occupation of Amsterdam has touched millions around the world.

The Guns of August by Barbara W. Tuchman (1962). A Pulitzer-Prize winning account documenting the beginning of World War I.

In Flanders Fields: The 1917 Campaign by Leon Wolff (1958). A comprehensive guide to the causes of World War I and the battles that took place in Flanders in 1917.

King Leopold's Ghost: A Story of Greed, Terror, and Heroism in Colonial Africa by Adam Hochschild (1998). A condemning and fascinating history book outlining the life and toxic colonial legacy of King Leopold II in Belgium.

Murder in Amsterdam: The Death of Theo van Gogh and the Limits of Tolerance by Ian Buruma (2006). An investigative book exploring the pivotal 2004 murder of Theo van Gogh, a controversial filmmaker.

Stealing the Mystic Lamb: The True Story of the World's Most Coveted Masterpiece by Noah Chaney (2010). This astounding nonfiction book tells the story of the world's most stolen artwork, the Ghent Altarpiece.

Why the Dutch are Different: A Journey into the Hidden Heart of the Netherlands by Ben Coates (2015). An entertaining book that explores Dutch culture via its history and its people's common behaviors.

The Wisdom of the Beguines: The Forgotten Story of a Medieval Women's Movement by Laura Swan (2014). An interesting account of the women, unusually independent for the time, who took part in the medieval Beguine religious movement.

Internet Resources and Apps

BLOGS

The Netherlands

https://ben-coates.com
A personal blog with in-depth entries exploring Dutch culture and society by Brit-Dutch author Ben Coates.

https://denhaag.com
The official website for the Hague Tourism Board with tips, information, and ideas for exploring the Hague.

www.holland.com
The official Dutch tourism board's website with tips, advice, and access to tickets.

www.iamsterdam.com
The official Amsterdam website for tourists, with a link to the iAmsterdam card and tips for exploring Amsterdam.

www.invadingholland.com
An amusing blog featuring comics about Dutch culture and life created by a longtime Brit living in the Netherlands.

https://en.rotterdam.info
The official website for exploring Rotterdam from Rotterdam Tourist Information with blogs and trip recommendations.

www.wanderlustingk.com
A popular Dutch travel blog with itineraries and practical advice for exploring the Netherlands.

www.yourlittleblackbook.me
A popular Dutch blog translated into English that features popular restaurants and hotspots in the Netherlands and beyond.

Belgium

https://fullsuitcase.com
A family-friendly travel blog created by a longtime Belgian resident, with practical advice and itineraries.

https://paulinaontheroad.com/category/europe/belgium
A travel blog created by a Luxembourg native with travel advice especially for Wallonian cities.

https://visit.brussels
The official website for the Brussels Tourism board with tips, itineraries, and advice.

www.visitflanders.com
The official website for the Flanders Tourism Board.

https://walloniabelgiumtourism.co.uk
The official website for the Wallonian Tourism Board, with interesting ideas and tips for traveling in Wallonia.

https://wonderfulwanderings.com
The first major travel blog in Belgium created by a Belgian, with many entries exploring Belgian food and destinations.

APPS

Contactless payment options like **Google** and **Apple Pay** are increasingly accepted throughout Belgium and the Netherlands. **Google Maps** and Google Translate are also very reliable.

Citymapper
Quickly check public transit schedules and maps.

MAPS.me
Offline maps for exploring on foot.

HappyCow
An app for finding vegan and vegetarian friendly restaurants.

HoogNood
Find toilets near you quickly!

NS (Train Schedules + Tickets)
The official Dutch train app.

SNCB
The official Belgian train app.

Untappd
A great app for finding great bars and cafés with craft beers.

NEWS

The Netherlands

www.dutchnews.nl
An online newspaper that reports on news stories relevant to foreigners in the Netherlands, as well as politics and major events.

https://nltimes.nl
Online Dutch newspaper that regularly translates important news stories into English for a local expat audience.

Belgium

www.brusselstimes.com
A Belgian newspaper that covers European and Belgian news for an international audience.

www.vrt.be/vrtnws
The national Belgian public-service broadcasting service, with limited news stories in English.

TRANSPORTATION

www.belgiantrain.be
The official website for trains within Belgium, and also for international trains originating in Belgium.

www.blue-bike.be
The official website for the main Belgian bike-sharing program.

www.delijn.be
The official website for public transportation in Flanders.

www.gvb.nl
The official website for public transportation in Amsterdam.

www.htm.nl
The official website for public transportation in the Hague and Delft region.

www.letec.be
The official website for public transportation in Wallonia.

https://ns.nl
The official website for trains within the Netherlands.

https://nsinternational.com
The official Dutch website for international trains to and from the Netherlands.

www.ret.nl
The official website for public transportation in Rotterdam.

www.stib-mivb.be
The official website for public transportation in the Brussels.

Index

C

H

IJ

K

L

M

N

INDEX

V

WYZ

List of Maps

Photo Credits

Title page: Canal Spiegel in Bruges © Olgacov | Dreamstime.com
All interior photos © Karen Turner, except: page 5 © Ekaterinabelova | Dreamstime.com; page 6 (top left) © Alexis Bélec | Dreamstime.com; page 7 (bottom right) © Mistervlad | Dreamstime.com; page 9 (top) © Rostislav Glinsky | Dreamstime.com, (bottom right) © Avii | Dreamstime.com; pages 12-13 (top) © Nanookofthenorth | Dreamstime.com, (bottom) © Madrabothair | Dreamstime.com; page 15 (bottom) © Izabog | Dreamstime.com; page 16 © Pawel Szczepanski| Dreamstime.com; page 17 (top) © Dechev | Dreamstime.com, (bottom) © Cebas1 | Dreamstime.com; page 18 © Oleg Bashkirov | Dreamstime.com; page 20 © OlenaZ | Dreamstime.com; page 21 © Jelena Maximova | Dreamstime.com; page 26 © Ivo De | Dreamstime.com; page 27 © Alexander Tolstykh | Dreamstime.com; page 27 © (left) © Dudlajzov | Dreamstime.com, (right) Emicristea | Dreamstime.com; page 34 © Olrat | Dreamstime.com; page 36 © © Tagor784 | Dreamstime.com; page 37 © (left) Ahavelaar | Dreamstime.com; page 74 © (top right) Pavel Kavalenkau | Dreamstime.com; page 116 © (bottom right) Ahavelaar | Dreamstime.com; page 129 © (top) Nikolai Sorokin | Dreamstime.com; page 131 © Dudlajzov | Dreamstime.com; page 132 © (right) Rob3rt82 | Dreamstime.com; page 137 © (bottom) Dudlajzov | Dreamstime.com; page 145 © (bottom) TasFoto | Dreamstime.com; page 148 © Chon Kit Leong | Dreamstime.com; page 152 © (top left) Mistervlad | Dreamstime.com; page 160 © (middle right) Madrabothair | Dreamstime.com; page 171 © (top right) Dudlajzov | Dreamstime.com; page 173 © Jan Kranendonk | Dreamstime.com; page 178 © (top right) Rawf88 | Dreamstime.com, (bottom) Donald Böing | Dreamstime.com; page 185 © (left) Lyngbyvej | Dreamstime.com; page 210 © (middle right) Amedididda | Dreamstime.com; page 241 © (top left) Milosk50 | Dreamstime.com, (bottom) Bonandbon Dw | Dreamstime.com; page 300 © Emicristea | Dreamstime.com; Page 301 © (left) Havana1234 | Dreamstime.com; page 307 © (bottom) Kristof Lauwers | Dreamstime.com; page 311 © (bottom) Jonkio4 | Dreamstime.com; page 316 © (bottom right) Sapientisat | Dreamstime.com; page 326 © Nancy Pauwels | Dreamstime.com; page 336 © Serghei Starus | Dreamstime.com; page 340 © (top left) Joyfull | Dreamstime, (top right) LE; page 351 © LE

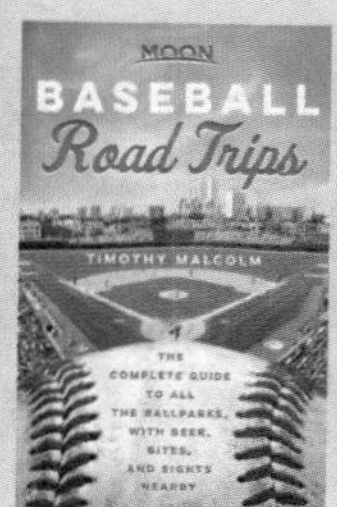

Great Road Trips in the U.S. & Canada

Trips to Remember

ISLAND ESCAPES WITH TIMELESS VILLAGES, SCENIC HIKES, AND LOCAL FLAVORS

Epic Treks

Beachy Getaways

MOON.COM
@MOONGUIDES

MAP SYMBOLS

Expressway	City/Town	Information Center	Park
Primary Road	State Capital	Parking Area	Golf Course
Secondary Road	National Capital	Church	Unique Feature
Unpaved Road	Highlight	Winery/Vineyard	Waterfall
Trail	Point of Interest	Trailhead	Camping
Ferry	Accommodation	Train Station	Mountain
Railroad	Restaurant/Bar	Airport	Ski Area
Pedestrian Walkway	Other Location	Airfield	Glacier
Stairs			

CONVERSION TABLES

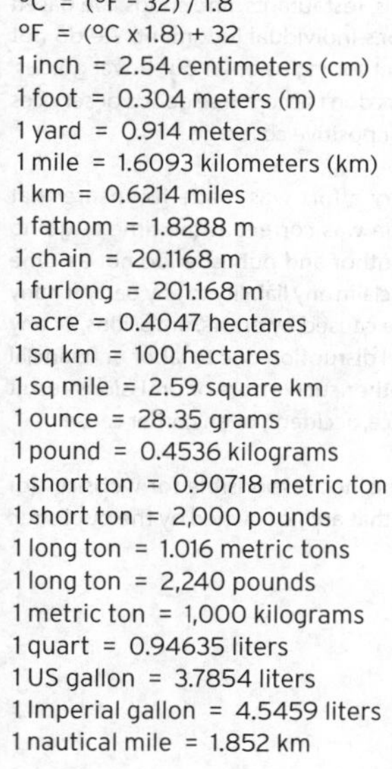

°C = (°F - 32) / 1.8
°F = (°C x 1.8) + 32
1 inch = 2.54 centimeters (cm)
1 foot = 0.304 meters (m)
1 yard = 0.914 meters
1 mile = 1.6093 kilometers (km)
1 km = 0.6214 miles
1 fathom = 1.8288 m
1 chain = 20.1168 m
1 furlong = 201.168 m
1 acre = 0.4047 hectares
1 sq km = 100 hectares
1 sq mile = 2.59 square km
1 ounce = 28.35 grams
1 pound = 0.4536 kilograms
1 short ton = 0.90718 metric ton
1 short ton = 2,000 pounds
1 long ton = 1.016 metric tons
1 long ton = 2,240 pounds
1 metric ton = 1,000 kilograms
1 quart = 0.94635 liters
1 US gallon = 3.7854 liters
1 Imperial gallon = 4.5459 liters
1 nautical mile = 1.852 km

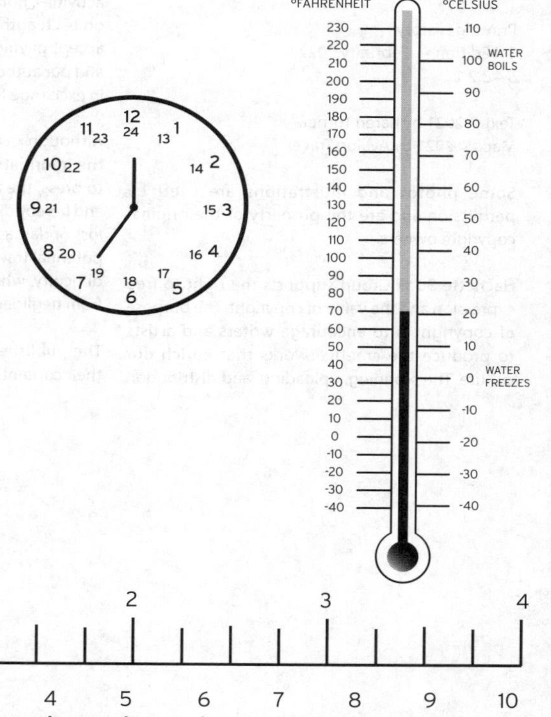

INCH 0 1 2 3 4

CM 0 1 2 3 4 5 6 7 8 9 10

MOON AMSTERDAM, BRUSSELS & BRUGES

Avalon Travel
Hachette Book Group
1700 Fourth Street
Berkeley, CA 94710, USA
www.moon.com

Editor: Megan Anderluh
Managing Editor: Hannah Brezack
Graphics and Production Coordinator: Lucie Ericksen
Cover Design: Faceout Studio, Charles Brock
Interior Design: Domini Dragoone
Moon Logo: Tim McGrath
Map Editor: Albert Angulo
Cartographers: Karin Dahl, Albert Angulo
Proofreader: Nikki Ioakimedes

ISBN-13: 978-1-64049-426-8

Printing History
1st Edition — February 2022
5 4 3 2 1

Front cover photo: Bloemgracht Canal, Amsterdam © Oliver Strewe/GettyImages
Back cover photo: Keukenhof Park, Netherlands © TasFoto | Dreamstime.com

Printed in Malaysia for Imago